No Fear

Also by Diana West

From St. Martin's Press:

*The Death of the Grown-Up:
How America's Arrested Development
is Bringing Down Western Civilization*

*American Betrayal: The Secret Assault
on Our Nation's Character*

Diana West

No Fear

Selected Columns (1999-2013) from America's
Most Politically Incorrect Journalist

Bravura Books
Washington, D.C.

Published by Bravura Books
Washington, D.C., 2013

NO FEAR. Copyright © 2013 by Diana West.

These columns were first published by The Washington Times, United Media, or Universal Uclick.

Cover photo by Stephen Crowley

West, Diana
  No Fear

ISBN-13: 9781484180228
ISBN-10: 1484180224

First edition: July 2013

Contents

Preface 9
9/11 11
Afghanistan and the Doomed
   "Democracy" Project 26
Benghazi 74
Clintonism 132
Counterjihad 155
Culture Clash 194
Denial 213
Eurabia 275
The Forbidden Columns 295
Who Blacklisted Whom? 327
Immigration, Amnesty & the Border 347
Media In the Tank 362
Intelligence? Secrets? 385
Iraq and the Doomed
   "Democracy" Project 409
The Murdoch Problem 473
Obama 483
Peering into the Cultural Abyss 513
Scales of Injustice 565
Shutting Up About Islam 594
Turning Points on the
   Road to Jihad 647
What is Terrorism, Anyway? 693
What We Learned from 9/11 704

Preface

My first column ran in the Washington Times in early 1999. It was about Elia Kazan, his Special Oscar, and the geysers of raging bile it set off among Hollywood's aged Stalinist remnant (see *Elia Kazan's Last Oscar,* page 341). I didn't realize it at the time, but I was looking at yet another demonstration of the inversion of morality powered by the hiding or denial of the facts.

Then again, maybe I was looking at the denial of the facts powered by the inversion of morality. In many ways, I would spend the next 14 years, weekly column by weekly column, trying to figure out which.

This mission became peculiarly complicated after 9/11, when digging into the facts of the matter – Islam's age-old jihad against the West – became a risky business. Or, rather, risky *for* business. Frankness about Islam – about the institution of jihad, both hot and cold, about the warping, stunting impact of "dhimmitude" in the West, about the sharia (Islamic law) itself – seemed to be the last thing practiced or wanted in the public square.

Thanks entirely to supportive editors – in particular, Helle Dale, who first offered me the opportunity to write a column, and the late Tony Blankley at The Washington Times, Peter Copeland and Jay Ambrose at Scripps-Howard, the late Sidney Goldberg and Saul Ferrer at United Media, and Gail Borelli and Clint Hooker at Universal Uclick – I was able to follow my curiosity and concerns wherever they took the column.

To say the column traveled far and wide is certainly true, ranging from multi-layered Islam itself to countries such as Iraq and Afghanistan, which, like Nicaragua in the 1980s or Vietnam in the 1960s, had previously been off America's charts. But the place I always found myself returning to for deeper analysis was the Western mind. What came to fascinate me was not Islam itself (in truth, I can scarcely abide another factoid about it) but rather Islam's impact on us.

From the transformations wrought by varying stages of submission to Islam we can trace military disasters in Iraq and Afghanistan, which even includes the Islamization of our military; the acceptance of speech codes in Western countries in compliance with sharia; and some large part of the erosion of liberty itself that is covered in the chapters of this book.

There is also the influence of money – Islamic oil money, to be precise – which plays a prominent role not only in this same disintegration, but in the corruption of our politics, our media, and in particular Rupert Murdoch's media empire, a subject I also have tried to track and understand.

I won't go so far as to promise a first draft of history in the pages that follow. I do hope, though, that this collection stands as a useful and informative diary.

DW

Washington, D.C.

July 2013

9/11

When our dead will finally rest in hallowed ground

9/14/01

As brave men burrow through the rubble of our shattered peace, searching in vain for the living, recovering only the dead, there is something else that eludes them, something that may be lost to us all, thankfully, for a long, long time: The "other" side of the story.

Once upon a time before September 11, the world was filled with double-sided uncertainties, open-ended philosophical questions that resisted any grasp of good and evil. A spectrum of elegant grey, it was said, was far superior to simplistic notions of black and white. Who were we to say, it was said, what was right and what was wrong? Indeed, how could one way of life be "better" than another?

No more. As rights and freedoms more basic than anything delineated by the Constitution have come under violent assault--beginning with the right to live through rush hour--what was once the almost delicious torture of "moral equivalence" has become a distasteful luxury of a privileged past. In this desperate new era, a throbbing, black-hearted evil has materialized in the form of the Islamic terror networks and the nations that harbor, assist and even recruit them. Only through their annihilation may a life-affirming, law-abiding, and freedom-loving good ever rise from the colossal national debris that surrounds us.

Personally, I have never used terminology like this before. Then again, nothing like this has ever happened before. The ground has shifted and the lines have been drawn. As the New York Times reported, a senior White House official said that the message that went out this week to foreign nations was, "You're either with us or against us."

The fact is, when an honest-to-goodness battle is joined, there can be no more middle ground. We simply have to know where our friends are--as well as our enemies. Not that their whereabouts are secret. Long before the smoke had thinned to reveal the scope of the carnage in the United States, there was revelry in the Middle East, from Beirut to East Jerusalem, from Cairo to Baghdad. No matter how much lip service (or how many pints of blood) Yassir Arafat offers America, those peace-processing Palestinians of his were elated by the destruction of American life and property, taking their uncontainable jubilation to the streets.

(The world saw some of this grisly carnival on television, but not all. According to the Jerusalem Post, the Associated Press reportedly held back film of uniformed Palestinian Authority policemen cavorting with civilians in the West Bank town of Nablus due to pressure from a PA cabinet secretary, Abdel Ahmed Rahman, who is said to have told AP producers that if their pictures were broadcast, "they would not be able to guarantee their safety.")

Meanwhile, across the divide, the state of Israel, better understanding our woe than any nation, dropped its flags to half-staff and declared a day of mourning--a respectful pause before the inevitable next engagement. Ra'anan Gissin, a senior aide to Prime Minister Ariel Sharon, put the struggle ahead in appropriately vigorous terms as being one "between civilizations, between the good and bad, between the civilized and the uncivilized."

"The civilized and the uncivilized." "You're either with us or against us." This is all about as black and white as it gets. Indeed, the only place left where things fuzz up is here at home. The sickening fact is, not only did Tuesday's terrorists turn our own planes into smart bombs and our skies into killing fields, they appear to have learned how to do it in American flight schools. Indeed, the ease with which these agents of terror, at least one of whom was familiar to authorities for an earlier act of terrorism, were able to enter and operate in this country is--or, rather, should be--shocking.

Meanwhile, Osama bin Laden, suspect No. 1, turns out to be, if not exactly as American as apple pie, certainly not without American links. These include what are reported to be "close family ties" to Boston, "associates" who were Boston cabbies, and a brother who actually endowed a scholarship fund at Harvard. One has to wonder about the chances of survival for a civilization that plays host to such deadly forces of chaos.

Of course, that could change. If Americans are able to reclaim their confidence in the goodness of Western culture, to rediscover that life, law and liberty make civilization worth defending, they will also come to realize that terror, primitivism and destruction must be rooted out and destroyed at any cost. It is then that our dead will finally rest in hallowed ground.

Prejudice or prudence?

9/21/01

For some odd reason, one of the countless factoids scrolling across the bottom of the television screen last week entered my memory bank and stayed. As the story of what happened on September 11 pieced itself together from a mass of presidential statements, black-box updates and dragnet bulletins, along came an offbeat bit of news about Osama bin Laden's brother having endowed a scholarship at Harvard. Certainly, this info-scrap bears no weight on what President Bush inspirationally called "this crusade, this war on terrorism." (His spokesman has since expressed regret for riling Arab and Muslim quarters with the word "crusade." More on that later.) But the symbolism of Brother bin Laden and Harvard turns out to have a heft of its own.

Remember when Yale couldn't bring itself to spend a $20 million gift from the Bass family to set up a humanities program in Western civilization? Not long before Lee Bass took his money back from Yale, Sheik Bakr Mohammed bin Laden was handing over an undisclosed sum to Harvard to fund Islamic legal studies at Harvard Law School and Islamic art and architecture studies at the Harvard School of Design. Without belaboring the point, it seems reasonable to say that in multicultural academe, where the creed is "diversity" or bust, Islamic studies will trump Western civ every time -- and maybe even after September 11.

But what does the predictable political correctness of the Ivy League have to do with the surprise attack of militant Islam against the United States? Simply this: There may be an enlightening glimmer to be found in the comparison between Harvard's swift embrace of bin-Laden-funded Islamic studies and the Western civilization obstacle course encountered at Yale. Maybe the fashionable pursuit of diversity to the point of cultural abnegation explains something about the ease with which the terrorists were able to launch their attacks on America from America.

Assuredly, it's a testament to the seemingly boundless tolerance of the American people that so many men of militant Islam were able to live, train, and travel to their deadly mission without seeming to have furrowed a single brow in suspicion. In the end, of course, this is nothing to be proud of. Take the case of the security checker who, with a cheery "have a nice flight," sent five Arabic men in khaki pants and tennis shirts through the gate at Logan Airport onto United Airlines Flight 175. Understandably, as the New York Post reports, she is now and forever a haunted woman, particularly by one hijacker she recalls as having acted "odd" -- neither speaking nor making eye contact. Why, she must wonder, did she not pause to check him out? Was she fighting an internal battle against the targeted prejudice of "profiling"? Americans must now begin to ask themselves where the onus of prejudice ends and the liberating effects of prudence begin.

For now, though, there is still a weird reluctance to accept crucial facts about our adversaries, beginning with their ethnic and religious identities. While we all have a responsibility to ensure the safety of guiltless citizens of Islamic faith and Arab ancestry, it's beginning to feel as though Americans have entered into a state of perpetual denial. We are now living under an unendurable threat of murder and mayhem from Islamics, however extreme, of Arab ancestry. But there is no official attempt to come to grips with this.

At the highest levels, Washington tells us our war is with generic "terrorism" and generic "terrorists," or, alternately, with one particular terrorist named Osama bin Laden. At the local level, a New York tip sheet for helping children through the trauma of the attack warns parents to "Be careful not to stereotype or demean the people or countries thought to be homes of the terrorists. Children can easily generalize negative statements and develop prejudice."

Kiddies aside, is it "stereotyping" to identify the hateful scourge of radical Islam as our enemy or our attackers? Is it "demeaning" to want to defeat that scourge wherever it exists? Are there no "negative statements" that may be fairly "generalized," if only for safety's sake? Meanwhile, it seems a tad self-defeating to launch a campaign against a terror network that includes large swaths of humanity without a few good stereotypes.

That's foolish political correctness, one of whose worst aspects is its distortion of the truth for political ends. This notion came to mind on hearing White House spokesman Ari Fleischer hedge on the president's apt choice of the word "crusade" to describe the struggle ahead. It may seem like a small thing to cling to, but the fact is, this fight is a crusade -- or it should be. And winning it will depend as much on facing the truth as facing the enemy.

Drawing a line in stone

9/28/01

Part of the horror of Sept. 11 was watching the unthinkable become reality -- an event that required an act of will to impose mental order on the senselessness of it all. As weeks pass, we may yet have to steel ourselves against another kind of blow to the collective brain: this one, only theoretical to date, but no less surreal for being self-inflicted. What Americans may have to come to grips with is the logic-defying notion of fighting terrorism with -- not against -- what might well be called terrorist-friendly nations.

Granted, the Bush alliance is still on the drawing board. But early reports from the diplomatic front reveal an ongoing effort to found an international coalition on a dangerous lie: that the global terror network now threatening Western civilization has no identity, that the explosive forces of militant Islam have neither religion, nor ethnicity, nor sense of nationhood. Led by Secretary of State Colin Powell, the diplomatic wing of the Bush administration seems to be negotiating the booby-trapped world stage by carefully sidestepping this crucial issue.

It identifies the enemy as generic "terrorists" who commit generic "terrorism." By opening the doors of alliance to an array of Arab nations whose embrace of such "terrorists" ranges from tight, to secret, to (at best) arm's-length, the United States could very well create a broad-based coalition -- but one marked by a grievous moral vacuum that would surely undermine any American-led war effort to save the civilized world from the forces of violence, fear and instability.

Judging by bulletins from the Middle East, such a vacuum is already being filled by an Arab effort to base any cooperation with the United States on two points: a strategic isolation of Israel, and an untenable philosophical distinction between the terrorism inflicted on Americans two weeks or so ago and the terrorism inflicted on Israelis on a daily basis. Aside from its moral debasement, this concept defies logic. There is no separating Osama bin Laden's al Qaeda organization from, say, Hamas or Islamic Jihad (al Jihad); nor is there any meaningful distinction to be made among their various fronts against the West, democracy and the modern age -- in short, civilization -- whether they lie in New York City or Tel Aviv. (One possible difference among them might be that Osama bin Laden appears to consider Israel small potatoes next to the Great Satan.)

Already, Yemen, Syria and Lebanon have rejected the parallels between bombing the World Trade Center and bombing the Israeli pizza parlor. (Or disco. Or school bus.) While such "news" isn't likely to put any pacemakers on the fritz, it must be said that such twisted logic packs a certain wallop. Lebanon, for example, "is all for a war to crush terrorism," Reuters reports, "so long as the battle starts with Washington's Mideast ally, Israel, and excludes groups who fight it." Then there's Iran. Even as it is wooed by the European Union, Iran declares, according to AFP, that the "'war against terrorism' ... must start by curbing the Jewish state" -- which, of course, Iran refuses even to recognize.

But perhaps no one puts it quite like Amr Moussa, Secretary-General of the 22-nation Arab League. Calling any strikes against any Arab states (including Iraq) "unacceptable," he has let it be known that "if Israel takes part in the alliance, say good-bye to this alliance." IF Israel takes part in the alliance? The very concept clouds the moral purpose of the West's mission, not to mention its chances of surviving militant Islam's assault.

And what of Arab "moderates"? The Associated Press reports on the evident discomfort in Saudi Arabia and other Persian Gulf states over any war effort that could include the terrorist networks Hamas, Islamic Jihad or Hizbullah., while Egyptian President Hosni Mubarak and Jordan's King Abdullah II say they would just as soon see the fight against terrorism take place in the United Nations -- not in the countries that harbor them. Editorializing on President Bush's declaration that "either you are with us, or you are with the terrorists," the Egyptian Gazette, an English-language government daily, recently chose to echo some of Mubarak's concerns (on the whole, not surprising in a government daily). The editorial's title says it all: "Foe or friend policy: A divisive formula." Someone should mention to Cairo that such "divisiveness" -- drawing a straight line between sponsoring terrorism and defending civilization -- is precisely the point of Bush's strategy.

Meanwhile, moderates and extremists alike recoil from connecting an Islamic or Arabic identity to terrorism, insisting, as King Abdullah and Mubarak have jointly put it, "terrorism has no religion or homeland." This statement is false. Its religion is militant Islam and its homeland is any nation that doesn't seek to eradicate it.

Can't keep a good man down

11/26/01

When President Bush said this month that "out of evil can come great good," he put words to something Americans have come to understand since Sept. 11, watching and assisting the effort to rescue and restore, honor and avenge, assist, heal and donate to a wounded nation. If there has been an "awakening to service," as Bush takes pride in noting, there has also been an awakening of another kind: a realization that much of the good Americans are seeing in their country has been there all along.

One way this aspect becomes obvious, and painfully so, is to read through (or try to) the sketches of the dead that appear in The New York Times, day after day after day, as the newspaper fulfills an honorable mission to remember each of the nearly 5,000 human beings who died in the attack on the World Trade Center.

Reading these short pieces -- "glimpses," the newspaper calls them -- is not just a sobering exercise. It is an agonizing, angering and humbling one. In these very personal remembrances, we learn of the families, even the pets, left behind. We read about the teams these people used to coach, and the reunions they once organized. We become privy to the wedding invitations they didn't get the chance to send and the summer barbecues that will never be the same. We find out about the 9 a.m. meeting at Windows on the World, and the brand-new office on the 92nd floor -- all the particulars of chance and design that placed so many people at the center of the world on the morning of Sept. 11.

Amid all those who perished simply because they went to work, there also appear sketches of the 343 New York City firemen, the 37 Port Authority policemen and the 23 New York City policemen who perished trying to rescue them. These are the gallant ones, almost all of them men, who lived to serve and died doing so. And through these glimpses, we see into a world few outsiders are privy to: a place in the culture where it is not unusual for men to marry their high school sweethearts, follow their firemen-fathers into the force and, in general, live lives that, in certain basic ways, seem unchanged by the cultural revolutions of recent decades.

You might say, to paraphrase the president, out of evil can come an appreciation for great good. As further testament to these lost lives, such appreciation just might become an ennobling experience for us all. Acknowledging the selfless heroism of the men who kept climbing into the fire has already stirred a renewed respect, not to mention gratitude, for the old-fashioned virtues associated with what was once, a very long time ago, esteemed as "manliness." Courage. Duty. Endurance. Brotherhood. All the things that the corrosive elites -- the media, academia and the entertainment world -- have long undermined and vilified, if not eradicated, in society at large.

Writing in the left-wing weekly The Nation, Katha Pollitt correctly observes that the terrorism attacks and their aftermath "have definitely rehabilitated such traditional masculine values as physical courage, upper-body strength, toughness, resolve." But wrinkle your nose when you read her words for the proper inflection. Pollitt, who earlier in the season lamented her 14-year-old's sudden desire for a flag, is appalled by this revival and does what she can to pervert it. "The WTC attack is men vs. men -- firefighters and fanatics," she writes in one of the uglier bits of analysis to congeal in this crisis, adding: "(It would seem positively ungrateful to ask why, in a city half black and brown, the 'heroes' were still mostly white, and, for that matter, still mostly male.)" She continues: "You can see the gender skew everywhere, in the absence of female bylines in the Op-Eds about the war, in the booing of Hillary Clinton during the Concert for New York at Madison Square Garden, in the slavish eagerness of the media to promote the callow and inadequate Dubya as a strong leader whose 'cockiness' -- interesting word -- and swagger are just what Americans need in the hour of crisis."

Men vs. men, black, brown and white, "gender skews" and swagger: Talk about fanatics. It must be an unnerving experience to see life through such a cracked prism. Well worth remembering, though, is that, even through the black smoke and flame of the imploding towers, the heroes of Sept. 11 could still see a better world, one we would all do well to envision as we rebuild our lives from the ruins.

Don't blame the heroes

5/21/04

When an NYFD chief reminded the 9/11 Commission this week that it was never in "anyone's consciousness" that the Twin Towers would fall, he underscored the terrible truth, often forgotten, that we now live in the Age of the Unthinkable. Seared into our consciousness is that the Twin Towers could and did fall — as could the Empire State Building, the U.S. Capitol and the Superdome. Our children know, as we never before imagined, that passenger planes may become guided missiles, and skyscrapers may turn into scorched rubble. Islamic jihad has indeed expanded our consciousness.

But if we look back on the blinkered bliss that ended with the catastrophic triumph of a despicable Islamic conspiracy, we also see the shining wellspring of courage and sacrifice the day revealed. It is painful to behold, but it has steadied and strengthened a reeling nation. What could be worse, two and a half years later, than to watch it sullied by a poisonous government commission?

There is a strange pathology in the 9/11 Commission that goes beyond the Bush-bashing grandstanding of the old days (remember Richard Clarke?), back when the president of the USAG (United States of Abu Ghraib) was taking it on the chin for not having enacted serious measures, pre-9/11, to stop Islamic terrorists — such as putting women's underwear on the heads of racially profiled Muslim men at airport check-ins, I suppose.

In the commission's findings, there now emerges a weird sense that what happened on 9/11 — when out of the most heavenly azure sky, Al Qaeda simultaneously launched four air attacks on American cities — was something the Big Apple should have planned and drilled for to the point of preventing all casualties. Indeed, according to commission thinking, it is almost as if New York's response to the Al Qaeda attacks created all of the mayhem in the first place.

Built into this twisted point of view is the equally bizarre notion that, given enough taxpayer-funded analysis, the federal commission will discover just what caused 3,000 Americans to lose their lives on 9/11 — and, in so doing, presumably make New York City safe for terrorism. Forget about a surprise attack launched in broad daylight by soldiers of an extremist Muslim army hidden from detection by our own politically correct blinders. Were New York's Finest at fault? Were New York's

Bravest sloughing off? Could Mayor Giuliani have done more?

The most egregious example of commission scapegoating concerns the stalwart service on 9/11 of Deputy Assistant Chief Joseph W. Pfeifer. Chief Pfeifer arrived at the north tower six minutes after seeing the first jet strike, helping to bring order to the fearful chaos in the lobby and direct rescue units to the upper floors. He also sent his only brother, Fire Lt. Kevin Pfeifer, up the stairs. "We spent a couple of seconds looking at each other," Chief Pfeifer told The New York Times. "He didn't say anything. It was just a look." Lt. Pfeifer was among the 343 members of the NYFD who died in the inferno.

Now, two and half years later, Chief Pfeifer is being raked over 9/11's coals for a command decision he made to switch radio channels from a stronger signal the chief says wasn't working that morning, to a weaker, functioning alternate, thereby losing the ability to communicate with all units, and thereby failing to learn immediately when the south tower collapsed. The commission finding is that an unnamed chief — Chief Pfeifer — was mistaken: The better, stronger radio channel was indeed working. The chief robustly disagrees. He also points out that even with the weaker radio signal, he was able to direct the evacuation of the north tower for a hellish hour-plus until it, too, collapsed, saving the lives of countless civilians and firemen.

Why should this man be called on to sweat over and defend his undeniably valiant service on 9/11? Is Chief Pfeifer — a dutiful, courageous fireman who, following his best instincts, helped saved thousands of Americans on 9/11 — to blame for even one death? Two deaths? One hundred deaths? The implications of the commission's findings — that America's heroes share blame for the carnage — are outrageous.

When commissioner Bob Kerrey asked WTC director Alan Reiss whether he was "angry" (is this "Oprah"?) the FBI didn't reveal more about Al Qaeda before 9/11, Reiss, according to the New York Post, "shot back" he was angry at "19 people in an airplane," not the FBI.

Nineteen men in an airplane is right. Of course, if the "chatter" before 9/11 had been listened to, these men would have been racially profiled right off their flights. That's the only logical conclusion of any serious inquiry into how 9/11 might have been prevented — one the 9/11 Commission will never get to.

Thank you, America, for the golden age of Islam

9/9/11

It is something to have gone 10 years without an Islamic attack of similarly gigantic proportions to those of Sept. 11, 2001, but it is not enough. That's because the decade we look back on is marked by a specifically Islamic brand of security from jihad. It was a security bought by the Bush and Obama administrations' policies of appeasement based in apology for, and irrational denial of, Islam's war doctrine, its anti-liberty laws and its non-Western customs. As a result of this policy of appeasement -- submission -- we now stand poised on the brink of a golden age.

Tragically for freedom of speech, conscience and equality before the law, however, it is an Islamic golden age. It's not just the post-9/11 rush into Western society of Islamic tenets and traditions on everything from law to finance to diet that has heralded this golden age, although that's part of it. More important is the fact that our central institutions have actively primed themselves for it, having absorbed and implemented the central codes of Islam in the years since the 9/11 attacks, exactly as the jihadists hoped and schemed.

Take the U.S. military, symbol plus enforcer of American security.

In Afghanistan, our forces are now "trained on the sanctity of the holy book (the Quran) and go to significant steps to protect it," as the official International Security Assistance Force (ISAF) website reported last year.

Are they similarly trained to take "significant steps" to "protect" other books? Hardly. It's reckless and irresponsible to demand that troops make the protection of any book a priority in a war zone. But it's not merely the case that U.S. troops have become protectors of the Quran in the decade following 9/11. "Never talk badly about the Qu'ran or its contents," ISAF ordered troops earlier this year. Did the Pentagon restrict language about "Mein Kampf" or the "Communist Manifesto"? They, too, were blueprints for world conquest that the United States opposed. Of course not. But the Quran is different. It is protected by Islamic law, and that's enough for the Pentagon. Not incidentally, ISAF further cautioned troops to direct suspects to remove any Qurans from the vicinity before troops conduct a search -- no doubt for the unstated fear that infidel troops might defile the protected book.

None may "touch the Qu'ran except in the state of ritual purity," the Islamic law book Reliance of the Traveller declares. And "ritual purity," naturally, is a state a non-Muslim can never, ever achieve under Islam.

Since when did Uncle Sam incorporate Islamic law into military protocols?

Since 9/11.

Now take the State Department, symbol and nerve center of U.S. action on the world stage.

In July, Secretary of State Hillary Clinton announced a collaborative effort between the United States and the OIC, newly repackaged as Organization of the Islamic Cooperation. (It used to be "C" for Conference.) The get-together planned for Washington, D.C., is supposed to implement a non-binding resolution against religious "stereotyping" (read: Islamic "stereotyping") that passed last March at the U.N. Human Rights Council. Such "stereotyping," of course, includes everything from honest assessments of the links between Islamic doctrine and Islamic terrorism to political cartoons. This makes this U.S.-led international effort nothing short of a sinister attempt to snuff free speech about Islam. And that sure sounds like a U.S.-co-chaired assault on the First Amendment. Not only is this treachery on the part of the U.S. government, it also happens to be part and parcel of the OIC's official 10-year-plan.

Since when did Uncle Sam get in the business of doing the bidding of the OIC?

Since 9/11. This is just a snapshot of what the rush toward Islamization as a goal of national policy looks like, 10 years since the Twin Towers collapsed in a colossal cloud of dust and fire. The air has cleared, but the appeasement and the Islamization go on. Thus, a golden age begins, but unless we throw off this mental yoke of submission, it cannot be our own.

Muslim bullies shroud the true face of 9/11

9/16/11

Having passed the 10th anniversary of 9/11, I can now say with certainty that something major was missing from all of the ceremonies, the symbolism and the media coverage. It was something that not only captures the meaning of the attacks themselves, but better defines our response to them than any other single thing. It is the face of the age itself, and it is not Osama bin Laden's.

I refer to the most familiar of the 12 Danish Muhammad cartoons, the one by Kurt Westergaard. I always think of this world-famous drawing as "Bomb-head Muhammad," for the lit bomb that serves as Muhammad's turban. (This is no fantastical image, as we learned last month when Afghan President Hamid Karzai prevailed upon local imams to implore their flocks to stop putting bombs in their turbans after three separate assassinations via turban bombs took place.)

I say "world-famous drawing," but have you ever actually seen this cartoon printed in a newspaper, or shown on a news broadcast? No. With exceptions to be counted on one hand, this ultra-potent image has never received mainstream media display, despite its almost continual newsworthiness.

Yes, the media have covered the most violent eruptions of jihad that Muslims still wage against Denmark for having a free press with the temerity to function in dereliction of Islamic law. These have ranged from Islamic rioting that killed more than 100 people, to Islamic attacks on Danish interests, to Islamic boycotts of Danish products, to Islamic plots against the Danish newspaper Jyllands-Posten, to this week's Islamic security threat against Westergaard that sent him home early from a trip to Norway.

But Western media have almost never dared flout Islamic law (Shariah) to show what "the fuss" was all about. They have almost never published the Westergaard Muhammad, which not only depicts Muhammad, Islam's prophet (verboten) but also illustrates the violence of Islamic jihad -- an implicit criticism of Islam, also verboten.

Instead, the free press of the West has accepted and enforced Islamic limits on expression by voluntarily censoring this skillfully executed, pointed political cartoon. Even when on Jan. 1, 2010, Westergaard was almost assassinated inside his home in Denmark, along with his 5-year-old granddaughter, by an ax-wielding Muslim, Western media again bowed to Shariah by omitting the "offending" cartoon from coverage of the attack. It is that censorship, that bow to Shariah, that defines the post-9/11 age. It also makes the Westergaard Muhammad its poster child.

Little did Westergaard imagine in 2005 that he was drawing an image for all time when he sat down to contribute a sketch to an artists' page full of Muhammads for Jyllands-Posten -- an exercise editor Flemming Rose specifically devised to demonstrate that Denmark wasn't under Islamic law, which prohibits such drawings.

But more than any shot of Osama bin Laden, the Westergaard Muhammad symbolizes our age. Bin Laden was a mass murderer, an external threat to ward off, hunt down and kill like an uncommon criminal. But the Westergaard Muhammad turned out to be one Westerner's mirror on the 9/11 attacks, and the wider West flinched at the reflection. From government to the academy, from media to the military, we couldn't -- and can't -- look at it in public. To this day, we refuse to face the history of jihad to extend Islam's law that the 9/11 attacks exemplify and that this cartoon so sharply symbolizes. Instead, we avert our eyes from the face of jihad and accept Islam's law.

This tells us that 9/11 wasn't a crisis about security. Rather, it was a crisis about our own insecurity -- our inability to stand up and defend the liberties that made us who we are -- or, rather, who we were, or at least tried to be. Even worse, it exposed our inability as a society to emulate, let alone celebrate, those who would fight for those liberties with just their pens and brushes, their cameras and voices.

For the decade after 9/11, we chose the dhimmitude that the taboo on the Westergaard Muhammad symbolizes. It may seem like a lot to put on a quickly sketched newspaper drawing, but not until we assert our right to publish the Westergaard Muhammad will the West ever be free again.

Even after deadly attack, U.S. kowtows to Islam

9/14/12

Two historic attacks on U.S. territory marked the 11th anniversary of the 9/11 attacks, and what happened? The Obama administration surrendered our constitutional principles.

The first was a "blasphemy" riot that breached the walls of the U.S. Embassy in Cairo, whereupon thugs burned the American flag and hoisted in its place the traditional black flag of Islam that flies over al-Qaida and other jihad movements.

The second was a military-style assault against the U.S. Consulate in Benghazi, Libya, believed to have been mounted by a militia known as Ansar al-Sharia ("Partisans of Islamic Law"), which formed in the U.S.-supported anti-Gadhafi revolution. Christopher Stevens, U.S. ambassador to Libya and former point man to the al-Qaida-linked revolutionaries, and three staff members were killed. Five more Americans were wounded, and the American outpost burned under another black flag of jihad.

An obscure, made-in-the-USA movie critical of Muhammad has been blamed for "causing" these attacks. In fact, it is people in Egypt and Libya who committed these two unprovoked acts of war to mark the 9/11 anniversary. The official response?

The first response actually preceded the mayhem in Cairo when the U.S. Embassy, having suspended regular business in anticipation of the planned movie protest, posted on its website on Sept. 11: "The Embassy of the United States in Cairo condemns the continuing efforts by misguided individuals to hurt the religious feelings of Muslims -- as we condemn efforts to offend believers of all religions." (As Middle East and Islamic expert Raymond Ibrahim pointed out, the embassy expressed no such solicitude for the "feelings" of a Christian on trial in Egypt for "insulting" Islam, "even as a throng of Muslims besieged the courthouse, interrupting the hearing and calling for the man's death.")

Noting the 9/11 anniversary, the embassy statement continued: "We firmly reject the actions by those who abuse the universal right of free speech to hurt the religious beliefs of others."

Here we see Uncle Sam conceding the First Amendment to safeguard the "feelings" of Muslims, and accepting the basis of Islamic laws against criticizing Islam.

In response, GOP presidential nominee Mitt Romney issued an initial statement expressing outrage over the violence and the Cairo embassy statement, which the embassy Twitter feed would underscore in both English and Arabic messages. (Both the statement and subsequent tweets have since been removed.) In the meantime, the White House disowned the embassy statement as unauthorized.

But Secretary of State Hillary Clinton echoed the embassy message to "deplore" free speech. Clinton said: "Some have sought to justify this vicious behavior as a response to inflammatory material posted on the Internet. The United States deplores any intentional effort to denigrate the religious beliefs of others. Our commitment to religious tolerance goes back to the very beginning of our nation. But let me be clear: There is never any justification for violent acts of this kind."

Actually, the nation's founding commitment is to religious "liberty." It's important to realize that Clinton supports an anti-liberty, U.N. anti-blasphemy resolution designed to curb criticism of Islam, advocating the circumvention of the First Amendment through what she calls "plain old-fashioned peer pressure and shaming." Assaults on sovereign territory, it would seem, simply go too far.

Then came details of the assault in Libya. Addressing Libya only, President Obama also inserted the government into free speech, while criticizing the violence (and taking no media questions). "While the United States rejects efforts to denigrate the religious beliefs of others," he said, "we must all unequivocally oppose the kind of senseless violence that took the lives of these public servants."

Afghan President Hamid Karzai weighed in, denouncing the "heinous act" -- the Muhammad movie! -- and calling for "efforts to prevent" its release and other restrictions on the lawful activities of its producer and pastor Terry Jones, who endorsed the movie. Karzai ignored both attacks on the United States.

Similarly, Mohamed Morsi, the Muslim Brotherhood president of Egypt (who denies al-Qaida attacked the U.S. on 9/11), directed the Egyptian Embassy in Washington to "take legal action" against the movie's producers. Morsi doesn't seem to understand First Amendment protections; of course, neither does the Obama administration. (Maybe they will discuss a "solution" to free speech when Obama hosts Morsi at the White House this month.)

Egyptian Prime Minister Hisham Qandil asked for similar action "within the framework of international charters that criminalize acts that stir strife on the basis of race, color or religion." This is a direct appeal to hold Americans accountable to the U.N. blasphemy resolution that Hillary Clinton, along with the Islamic bloc, has championed, despite its repressive controls on free speech.

The administration response gets worse. Joint Chiefs Chairman Gen. Martin Dempsey telephoned Jones to implore him to withdraw his endorsement of the Muhammad movie to "prevent" violence in Afghanistan. Apparently, Dempsey and the administration he serves believe a movie blurb is a self-firing assault weapon, and Islamic law nullifies the First Amendment.

In a Wednesday press conference, Mitt Romney stated: "America will not tolerate attacks against our citizens and against our embassies. We'll defend also our constitutional rights of speech and assembly and religion .... We stand for the principles our Constitution protects. We encourage other nations to understand and respect the principles of our Constitution, because we recognize that these principles are the ultimate source of freedom for individuals around the world."

At least one American leader is willing to defend our country and Constitution.

Afghanistan and the Doomed 'Democracy' Project

Win the 'trust' of people who hate us? What?

2/20/09

The buzzword on Afghanistan is "trust."

Having routed the Taliban, liberated millions, midwived a (Sharia-supreme) constitution, assisted in elections, propped up a government and routed the Taliban some more, all the United States needs now to win victory in Afghanistan is to win the "trust" of the Afghan people.

So, cockamamiely, wrote Adm. Mike Mullen, chairman of the Joint Chiefs, in a column appearing in the Washington Post just days before President Obama ordered 17,000 new troops to Afghanistan, nearly doubling the American presence there.

The president's top military adviser explained the policy this way: "We have learned, after seven years of war, that trust is the coin of the realm — that building it takes time, losing it take mere seconds, and maintaining it may be our most important and most difficult objective."

Sorry, admiral, but if that is what we have "learned" in a war that has claimed more than 600 American lives, wounded and maimed thousands more, and cost billions of pre-bailout dollars, we are practically done for.

Why? The short answer is that in making a primary objective out of winning the "trust" of the Afghan people, the chairman of the Joint Chiefs has, by definition, abandoned all rational war policy. Indeed, he has placed the marker for American success not on the ability of U.S. forces to execute their missions, but on the emotional reaction of the average, illiterate, infidel-hostile, modernity-challenged Afghan to those missions.

"Lose the (Afghan) people's trust," Mullen writes, "and we lose the war." I wish I could say I've never heard such fatuous counsel, but the entire so-called war on terror, from start to non-finish, reverberates with this same sort of line. It tends to turn profound Islamic differences from the West into profound Western failings toward Islam. Rather than walk our nation up to the cultural chasm between Islam and the West and show us what it looks like, our leaders have, in effect, made that chasm into their own personal responsibility, something to fill in, paper over and, above all, never, ever mention.

Thus, Mullen blames the Afghan failure to hail the United States as the conquering hero on a purely American failure to maintain Afghan "trust" — an unfair rap, frankly, on dedicated troops stretched thin by far too many years of deployment. Indeed, Mullen broaches the "trust" topic with a distasteful allusion to Pleminius, a Roman tyrant, who became notorious for his and his soldier's raping, pillaging and plundering of the Locrians, who expected and ultimately received restitution from Rome.

"We are not Romans, of course," Mullen writes.

Gee, thanks a lot.

He continues: "Our brigade combat teams are not the legions of old. But we in the U.S. military are likewise held to a high standard. Like the Romans, we are expected to do the right thing, and when we don't, to make it right again."

And what exactly has the United States done that isn't right?

"It doesn't matter how hard we try to avoid hurting the innocent, and we do try very hard," Mullen writes. "It doesn't matter how proportional the force we deploy, how precisely we strike. It doesn't even matter if the enemy hides behind civilians. What matters are the death and destruction that result and the expectation that we could have avoided it. In the end, all that matters is that, despite our best efforts, sometimes we take the very lives we are trying to protect."

He adds: "You cannot defeat an insurgency this way."

Oh yeah? Betcha could if the "civilians" he's talking about loathed the "insurgents" he's talking about more than the "us" he's talking about. But that never happens in "insurgencies," and Afghanistan is no different. Not even when the new U.N. survey on civilian deaths in Afghanistan reveals that the Taliban and other insurgents are responsible for most such civilians deaths, as The New York Times reports, "primarily through suicide bombers and roadside bombs, many aimed at killing as many civilians as possible."

But all nonrational — or, more accurately, non-Western — Afghan reactions to America's best efforts and great sacrifices against the jihadists in Afghanistan are, in Mullen's telling, America's responsibility, if not fault. Mullen goes on to accept, with resignation — practically with equanimity — the thoroughly bizarre idea that "each civilian casualty for which we are even remotely responsible sets back our efforts to gain the confidence of the Afghan people months, if not years." The implication is, of course, that we must fight on, and now with twice as many troops, to win that Afghan "confidence."

Frankly, this is cracked. Don't we ever lose patience with Afghanistan? Don't we ever realize that not only is there no "trust" or "confidence" for us to "win" there, but there isn't anything else, either? Because there isn't, and that's the lesson I draw from seven years of war in Afghanistan, not to mention six years of war in Iraq.

This has been a far costlier lesson than we yet realize. That's because in our woefully misguided efforts to establish chimerical Western outposts in these spheres of Sharia on the other side of the world, we seem to have lost sight of the desperate need to fight incursions of Sharia at home in the West.

I am not suggesting that the U.S. remove itself from a "war footing" because we are still in a war, however ill-defined, that is by no means over. But the lessons of six and seven years of fighting should teach us that Afghanistan and Iraq are not defensible fronts in this battle against expansionist, jihadist Islam. The lessons of six and seven years of war should teach us that these countries constitute a pit in which our resources sink and disappear without even the possibility of resurrecting them as a bulwark against jihad in the future.

In other words, it is not regional "trust" that we lack; it is our own common sense and survival instinct to realize that we must redraw the battle line around the West itself to stave off the depredations of Islamization — the endgoal after all, of all jihadists, violent and not.

What about "Al Qaeda" — I use quotation marks here because there are many jihadist groups but we persist in branding them all "Al Qaeda" — in Iraq, Afghanistan and Pakistan? What about Pakistani nukes? I can hear the questions now, and they are good questions. The answer is that there remain potential military targets throughout this violent and chaotic region. That doesn't change.

But remember, it's not as if "Al Qaeda" is neatly confined to our current battlegrounds. What about Al Qaeda in Iran? (What about Iran?) In Yemen? In Gaza? In Madrid? In London? Perhaps in Washington, D.C.? The infiltration of jihadists is as advanced as it is complex, and defeating it requires more than massive deployments of troops abroad. For starters, it requires total reconfigurations of two national policies: our energy policy to decouple us from Islamic oil; and our immigration policy, including travel restrictions, in order to stop any further demographic incursions of Sharia and jihad into the West.

Sadly — tragically — such required reconfigurations won't happen in the Obama years. But it is vital, it is urgent, that we plan now for what comes after.

What do you mean 'if we ever want to leave' Afghanistan?

4/3/09

Beware, America. You are about to be duped by an alliance of Obama-niks and Bush-ites who, together, are laying the groundwork for nation-building in Afghanistan — nation-building in Iraq having worked out so well (insert acid shot of sarcasm here). Only they are not going to call it "nation-building." Worse, they are forging ahead without heeding the remedial lesson of Iraq: No matter how many American dollars spent, no matter how many American lives lost, it's not possible to transform an Islamic republic that enshrines Islamic law (Sharia) into an ally against Islamic jihad, even if Islamic jihad is euphemized as "extremism," "man-caused disasters" or "overseas contingency operations."

That's because Islamic jihad is ultimately waged to extend Sharia. See the disconnect? Good. That's more than our experts can do, which is why it now looks as if we're going to give this flawed strategy another multi-trillion dollar try in Afghanistan. This is what I heard at what you might call a "war is the answer" teach-in, Washington-style, at the Mayflower Hotel this week. There, a conference sponsored by the newly formed neoconservative think tank, the Foreign Policy Initiative, brought an audience of media and policy types up to war-in-Afghanistan speed. And, as usual in Washington, they did it without ever once mentioning "Islam" (until I asked a quick question at the end).

This was neither a secret session of the so-called "neocon cabal" — although some charter members were present — nor an Obama White House war room presentation. Still, I caught the faintest whiff of backroom smoke in talk of just how "clever," as Carnegie's Ashley Tellis put it, the Obama team was for packaging a nation-building agenda in the terminology of fighting Al Qaeda, a far narrower and presumably more popular objective. Robert Kagan noted that President Obama may not be talking about democratization, but his goals are similar. Hence, the warm enthusiasm for the Obama Afghan policy from such Iraq War proponents as Kagan, his brother and Iraq "surge" co-author Frederick Kagan, the Weekly Standard's William Kristol, and by John Nagl, a co-author of the U.S. Army's counterinsurgency manual and fellow of the Center for a New American Security, a left-leaning think tank associated with Obama defense policy circles.

And what are Obama's goals? Below the headline news of targeting Al Qaeda, and expanding Afghan police and army (but not enough, speakers agreed), the president spoke last week of advancing "security, opportunity and justice, not just in Kabul but from the bottom up in the provinces." That's a lot of security, opportunity and justice to advance even for Kabul, where the supreme court there recently upheld Pervez Kambakhsh's 20-year prison term for "blasphemy," and Afghan President Hamid Karzai recently signed a Sharia-influenced law that legalizes Shiite marital rape, among other anti-women measures, to curry favor with Shiite clerics. (One opponent said the law was "worse than during the Taliban.")

President Obama also discussed the importance of "not (turning) a blind eye to the corruption that causes Afghans to lose faith in their own leaders." The fact that Afghan corruption — an endemic, culture-based, veritable Afghan national pastime — is now considered a U.S. problem is testament to the utopian lure of nation-building. Question is, will the American people support this wild mongoose chase after six extremely mixed — no, failed — years of nation-building in Iraq? There, despite post-surge security gains, the nation we have built remains "fragile" and "uneven," according to the most recent Pentagon report, even as the United States prepares its exit. Had the State Department not granted Iraq a waiver, it would also be designated a Country of Particular Concern (CPC), the worst rating for religious freedom violations. Meanwhile, U.S.-liberated Iraq remains an enthusiastic participant in the Arab boycott of Israel, and an OPEC member that never even let a U.S. humvee fill up for free.

And Iraq consistently votes with the Organization of the Islamic Conference (OIC) against the United States at the United Nations. Never mind — what's a few trillion dollars among non-allies?

Onto Afghanistan, where we are told U.S. national security depends on denying sanctuary to Al Qaeda and related jihadists. Meanwhile, the world is riddled with jihadism in the form of active agents, sleeper cells, propagandists and sympathizers from the Bekaa Valley to Belgium, from Iran to London, from Saudi Arabia to South Florida. Nearly eight years after 9/11, the United States still has unsecured borders, but it is Afghanistan where we must establish security and clean government — for our own good.

Why? Frederick Kagan said "we have to establish the legitimacy of the Afghan government (because) that's how you end an insurgency." John Nagl was more emphatic still, stating, "If we ever want to leave, we have to build an Afghan government that can accomplish those goals (of good government) on its own."

If we ever want to leave?

During a coffee break, I asked military historian Frederick Kagan whether there was any successful historical model for this strategy. Ticking off a few non-matches including the Boer War in South Africa, Malaya, and civil war in El Salvador, he, a little sheepishly, offered Iraq.

Iraq? Heaven help the United States.

Let Afghanistan go

4/24/09

Saw an unforgettably stark photo of Taliban fighters in Afghanistan's Wardak province, the same province Joint Chiefs Chairman Adm. Mike Mullen visited this week: Eight robed, turbaned fighters, a sandy ridge, a cloudy sky. All that was missing was the incoming American drone strike to turn the men into dust.

Question: Should the United States call in that strike? How great a security threat to the United States do these eight barbarians pose? How many dollars, how much blood is it worth to our nation to pulverize them into that lunar-like landscape?

I recently read a military e-mail from Afghanistan that marveled over a similar scene: "As far as BDA (battle damage assessment) goes, check this one out. 2 GBU 36's (bomblets) dropped the other day on estimated 6 guys!!!! That is half a million dollars on 6 guys!!!!" The e-mailer guessed that all the sniper ammunition the jihadists have used in the whole war hasn't cost close to that.

The point is, the United States is getting a lot of bang for a lot of buck but not much else. Don't get me wrong: If killing small bands of Taliban is in the best interest of the United States, I'm for it. But I do not believe it is — and certainly not as part of the grand strategy conceived first by the Bush administration and now expanded by the Obama administration to turn Afghanistan into a state capable of warding off what is daintily known as "extremism," but is, in fact, bona-fide jihad to advance Sharia (Islamic law). Anybody remember Sisyphus? Well, trying to transform Afghanistan into an anti-jihad, anti-Sharia player — let alone functional nation — is like trying to roll Sisyphus' rock up the hill.

This is not to suggest that there is no war or enemies to fight, which is what both the Left and the Paleo-Right will say; there most certainly are. But sinking all possible men, materiel and bureaucracy into Afghanistan, as the Obama people and most conservatives favor, to try to bring a corrupt Islamic culture into working modernity while simultaneously fighting Taliban and wading deep into treacherous Pakistani wars is no way to victory — at least not to U.S. victory. On the contrary, it is the best way to bleed and further degrade U.S. military capabilities. Indeed, if I were a jihad chieftain, I couldn't imagine a better strategy than to entrap tens of thousands of America's very best young men in an open-ended war of mortal hide-and-seek in the North West Frontier.

I decided to ask someone with real military experience how we could fend off jihad without further digging ourselves into Central Asia. I called up retired Maj. Gen. Paul Vallely, one of the few top military leaders who talks on the record, to ask for his strategy recommendation for Afghanistan.

"Basically, let it go," he said.

Let Afghanistan go — music to my ears, particularly given the source is no Hate-America-First professor or Moveon-dot-org-nik, but a lifelong patriotic conservative warrior. "There's nothing to win there," he explained, engaging in an all-too-exotic display of common sense. "What do you get for it? What's the return? Well, the return's all negative for the United States."

The general continued: "This doesn't mean giving up battle. What it means is you transition to a more realistic, affordable strategy that keeps them (the jihadist enemy) from spreading."

Such a strategy, Vallely explained, relies on "the maximum use of unconventional forces," such as Navy SEALS and other special forces, who can be deployed as needed from what are known in military parlance as "lily pads" — outposts or jumping-off points in friendly countries (Israel, Northern Kurdistan, India, Philippines, Italy, Djibouti ...) and from U.S. aircraft carrier strike groups. Such strike groups generally include eight to 10 vessels "with more fire power," the general noted, "than most nations." These lily pads become "bases we can launch from any time we want to," eliminating the need for massive land bases such as Bagram Air Base in Afghanistan, by now a small city of 20,000 American personnel who continuously need to be supplied and secured at enormous expense.

"There's no permanent force," the general said. "That's the beauty of it." We watch, we wait and when U.S. interests are threatened, "we basically use our strike forces to take them out, target by target." This would work whether the threat came from Al Qaeda, Pakistani nukes or anything else.

He continued: "This idea that we're going to go in and bring democracy to these tribal cultures isn't going to work. If we have a problem with terrorist countries, like Iran, it's a lot cheaper to go in and hit them and get back out."

In other words, don't give up the battle; just give up the nation-building. "It's up to somebody else to build nations," the general said. "Not us."

He went on: That old myth that (Colin) Powell had — if you break it you own it — that's a myth. You break it, you decide whether you own it. You don't have to go in and own it."

And especially not when it is Islamic land that doesn't belong in the West.

When does someone apologize to our military?

5/22/09

Afghanistan has been dubbed "Obama's War" but maybe it should be called "the war on civilian casualties."

You may have thought the United States was at war in Afghanistan to "defeat" the Taliban and win one for our loyal ally in counter-jihad, the Afghan people. But even that pipedream is beside the point. The latest concern-turned-obsession of the United States is eliminating as many as possible, if not all, "civilian casualties." If we can only do that, according to brain-trust, top-brass, fairy-tale thinking, we will surely win the hearts and minds of the Afghan people. If we can't, Afghan hearts and minds will go to those globally recognized humanitarians, the Taliban.

Indeed, there is something wrong with this picture. That is, if the Afghan people were really with us, they would be, well, really with us — not constantly on or past the brink of "alienation." But who wants to admit this? It would necessarily mark the end of the Bush and now Obama Islamic nation-building fantasy that began seven years ago with the U.S. invasion of Afghanistan in Operation Infinite Justice. Come to think of it, we hurriedly changed that operation name also for — guess what? — fear of alienating Muslims. Tacitly accepting the Islamic position that only Allah dispenses "infinite justice," the U.S. government launched Operation Enduring Freedom and "won" its first battle against Muslim alienation. Chalk one up for dhimmitude.

Now, a new battle against such alienation rages in Afghanistan. "Mullen: Civilian Deaths Hurt US in Afghanistan" reports the Associated Press; "U.S. Envoy Vows to Help Cut Afghan Civilian Deaths," reports the New York Times. The premise of these stories is that it is our own shortcomings, our own failures — not inculcated Islamic attitudes in the population at large — that are responsible for Afghan resentment over our nation's continued efforts to defeat the Taliban. "We cannot succeed in Afghanistan or anywhere else, but let's talk specifically about Afghanistan, by killing Afghan civilians," Joint Chiefs Chairman Adm. Mike Mullen said recently, practically as if killing Afghan civilians were U.S. policy. He added: "We can't keep going through incidents like this and expect the strategy to work."

By "incidents like this," Mullen was referring to a battle early this month in Afghanistan's Farah province where, according to Afghan government claims, 140-plus civilians were killed during a U.S. aerial bombardment. Even as the U.S. military was still investigating the incident, U.S. ambassador to Afghanistan Lt. Gen. Karl W. Eikenberry hightailed it to an Afghan mosque with Afghan president Hamid Karzai to present both U.S. condolences and mea culpas.

According to the New York Times, Karzai, who is seeking re-election, promised to rebuild the villagers' houses, to arrange for some of the survivors to go on the haj pilgrimage to Mecca, and to build schools, clinics and roads in the province. This sounds like your tax dollars at work.

"It is clear to me that if we don't get this right, we do run the risk of alienating the Afghan people and creating what David Kilcullen has called the accidental guerilla," Eikenberry later told the New York Times, referring to the Australian former aide to Gen. David Petraeus, who once infamously claimed that if he were a Muslim, he would be a jihadist out of a shared "sense of adventure." (This, truth be told, alienated me.)

As Eikenberry sees it, it's all our fault. Except that it's not. On Wednesday, Centcom issued interim findings indicating that 60 to 65 Taliban were killed in the engagements in question along with 20 to 30 civilians — a far cry from 140-plus. Which makes me wonder: Could the ambassador have apologized to imposters in that audience of "survivors"? Perish the alienating thought.

Worth mentioning are some details about the battle itself. According to Centcom, after Taliban fighters beheaded three civilians in an Afghan town, Afghan police and army forces were ambushed en route by 200 to 300 waiting Taliban forces. Two policemen were killed. "Outgunned and outmanned," Centcom reports, "the provincial governor requested help from a coalition quick-reaction force."

At this point, Taliban launched another attack on Afghan and U.S. forces, and "a U.S. Navy corpsman was shot in the shoulder attempting to rescue a wounded Afghan soldier. The coalition force used F-18 close-air support to suppress enemy fire from nearby buildings and allow for the rescue of the wounded Afghan first sergeant, who was trapped by heavy Taliban machine-gun and rocket-propelled-grenade fire." Coordinated by a ground commander, "a B-1 bomber crew fired on enemy firing and gathering positions in buildings and a tree grove. Afghan and U.S. forces remained in the area and observed the villagers returning after the fighting had ceased…"

"We strongly condemn the Taliban for their brutality in deliberately targeting and using human shields," a U.S. military spokesman said. Which is precisely what Mullen and Eikenberry should have said, praising our forces for a job well done. If that "alienates" Afghans, good riddance. But meanwhile, an apology is owed here — to the U.S. military.

Will our new Afghan policy be 'fatal hesitation'?

8/6/09

I saw some fresh figures on 2009 civilian casualties in Afghanistan this week from the U.N. Assistance Mission in Afghanistan (UNAMA). They are, I'm betting, on the generous side both when it comes to counting casualties as "civilian," and counting "civilian casualties" as American-caused.

The underreported news is, air strikes in Afghanistan, widely depicted as indiscriminate American causes of Afghan outrage, account for only 20 percent of the total. Suicide attacks and roadside bombs, attributable to jihadists, killed 39 percent. Assassinations — another Taliban specialty — claimed 11 percent, while "other," divided between pro- and anti- government forces, was responsible for 29 percent. In its own reckoning, UNAMA states that "59 percent of civilians were killed by AGEs (Anti-Government Elements) and 30.5 percent were killed by PGF (Pro-Government Forces)."

This is an important finding. Civilian casualties have been widely, if not exclusively, portrayed by U.S. military leadership as the stumbling block to our winning "hearts and minds" — a.k.a. "trust" — in Afghanistan. Winning "hearts and minds," in turn, is widely portrayed by U.S. military leadership as the key to victory.

A question for our brass: If the Taliban is responsible for disproportionately more casualties than the United States — and purposely so where ours are inadvertent — shouldn't, by our brass' own reckoning, all those Afghan hearts and minds already belong to us? Could there be something else - such as the Islamic religion - causing Afghans to reject our infidel "hearts and minds" pathetically pressed on them, along with grotesque sums of money, like hopeless valentines?

These are questions the brass can't answer, can't even think about, because the answers would upend America's entire Afghan strategy. We are in a war on civilian casualties in Afghanistan to win Afghan hearts and minds. Period. And woe to statistics, let alone basic and intractable religious differences, that undermine this illusory strategy.

But there is something else Americans should become aware of regarding the military's obsession with further decreasing casualties as a means to victory. Our troops, the brass says, are the ones who are ultimately going to have to find what Gen. Stanley A. McChrystal, our new commander in Afghanistan, earnestly calls the "balance."

I watched McChrystal discuss his mission to further decrease civilian casualties in an online BBC video this week. "It's a balance for the young soldier on the ground who is in combat," he explained. "One of the assets that he has that might save his life might be air power or indirect fire from artillery or mortars and we don't want to take away that protection for him."

No, we don't, General. So why are we even talking about it? The lightly hinted implication — that our troops may be called on to think twice about saving their own lives — is chilling. He went on:

"What we want to do is build into our systems, and more importantly, build into the minds of all of our soldiers that everything that they do is important in this fight, and we're here to protect the Afghan people. And we're here to protect them from everything that can hurt them, both enemy activity but also inadvertent activity by Afghan forces or ours. So we're trying to build into the culture of our force tremendous sensitivity that everything they may do must be balanced against the possibility of hurting anyone."

Tremendous sensitivity is right. "The Afghan people are the reason we're here," McChrystal explained, weirdly disconnecting the American war machine from national interests. And to gain their "support," it seems the United States will do anything, even build potentially fatal hesitation into "the culture of our force," instilling possibly dangerous second thoughts into split-second decision-making. This way, these best and brightest of ours tell us, we will placate the trumped-up boogey-man of "civilian casualties," which is the sure-fire way, they promise, to win Afghan "hearts and minds."

"Victory in this conflict is about winning the hearts and minds of the Afghan people and engendering their trust," Brig. Gen. Steven Kwast, commander of 5,000 airmen at Bagram Field, told the Air Force Times last week. "When the Afghan people trust us and believe us ... we will win this overnight."

Just don't anyone hold his breath.

Only a fool calls it surrender

9/4/09

Finally, some debate over U.S. war policy in Afghanistan. Or at least debate over George F. Will's call to pull the plug on U.S. war policy in Afghanistan, headlined "Time to Get Out of Afghanistan."

The negative response from conservatives was revealing. It showed that after eight years of America's post-9/11 war efforts, which started out as President Bush's vaguely named "war on terror" and never crystallized into a cogent strategy against the jihad driving the "terror," ambiguity and confusion still cloud the prevailing thinking, from the conventional wisdom to war strategy.

Most conservative rebuttals ignored Will's reckoning of just how grossly ill-suited Afghanistan is to the hallucinogenic U.S. policy of constructing a modern society out of dust as our military worms affection from a hostile population. Instead, they focused on the concept of leaving Afghanistan — a move I, too, have advocated since April in my column and at my blog as a necessary precondition to better repulsing global jihad. Such an effort is, or should be, a multi-level campaign to reverse jihad's ultimate goal, which is to extend Islamic law by both violent and other means. In this larger context, Afghanistan is not only just one front, it is also a front too far.

Most of my conservative colleagues, however, see withdrawal from Afghanistan as surrender.

This assumption, based in the fallacy that U.S. forces are simply fighting an army called "the Taliban," rather than struggling with a culture called Islam shared by enemy and civilian alike, makes sense only if withdrawing from Afghanistan means ending our efforts against global jihad. The point of withdrawal is not to stop destroying America's active enemies in Afghanistan or elsewhere; this can continue from worldwide bases, or "lily pads," as necessary, as Maj. Gen. Paul Vallely (USA ret.) argues. The point of withdrawal is to stop trying to create an American ally out of Sharia-supreme Afghanistan, something we attempted at great expense in Sharia-supreme Iraq, and failed.

Of course, what animates and drives most conservatives today is their vision of Iraq as a "success," and their desire to repeat that "success" in Afghanistan. What has become increasingly clear to me, however, is that an infidel nation cannot fight for the soul of an Islamic nation. This, in effect, is what our "nation-building" troops have been ordered to do both in Iraq and Afghanistan. Let me rephrase: An infidel nation can indeed fight for the soul of an Islamic nation. It just can't win it.

It also turns out there is nothing there for infidels to win. After six U.S.-intensive years, Iraq remains just another OPEC-participating, Israel-boycotting, Hezbollah-sympathetic, Sharia-supreme, anti-U.S. entity with new and improved ties to Iran. Why? Our belief systems, Islam's and the West's, are so diametrically opposed that our interests cannot intersect. Left and Right in this country, however, scrub this truth and its centuries of confirming history from all policy — an antiseptic way to view conflict in the world that will always miss the cure by ignoring the germs.

On this count, Will's column is no different, never once contemplating Islam. Which is why his conclusion may be a little fuzzy. Describing his "offshore" alternatives to basing a massive army inside Afghanistan, Will identifies the key mission as "concentrating on the porous 1,500-mile border with Pakistan, a nation that actually matters."

I'm not sure what Will means by calling Pakistan "a nation that actually matters." Certainly, Pakistan's nuclear arsenal "matters" because it could hurt us, and thus our national security demands an execution-ready plan to neutralize it. But Pakistan, a jihad-based culture, doesn't "matter" in terms of fitting into an anti-jihad alliance — the ultimate goal, whether admitted or not, of efforts to work together. It can't. Quick facts: Pakistan's army's motto is "Faith, piety and holy war in the path of Allah." Seventy-eight percent of its people, the latest Pew Poll tells us, support the death penalty for leaving Islam. Not exactly our ideal match.

But we keep such politically incorrect facts out of focus. Then we struggle to see why things go wrong. More clarity is required. More debate is essential. Eight years after 9/11, this means finally reckoning with Islam — discussing jihad, analyzing Sharia, understanding dhimmitude — as a strategic factor in U.S. policy.

New strategy in Afghanistan: Protect everyone but Americans

9/11/09

Well, it happened. Or, rather it happened and was reported, which is something else again. I will wager it has already happened, unnoticed, unrecorded, totally ignored.

But on this occasion, there was someone to witness it, write it down and publish it. I refer to death by rules of engagement. Specifically, the deaths of four U.S. Marines seemingly by the new rules of engagement (ROE) in Afghanistan. They took place on Tuesday in an ambush against Afghan forces and their U.S. trainers around the village of Ganjgal. There, journalist Jonathan S. Landay of McClatchey Newspapers lived through the deadly firefight to write the following:

"U.S. commanders, citing new rules to avoid civilian casualties, rejected repeated calls to unleash artillery rounds at attackers dug into the slopes and tree lines — despite being told repeatedly that they weren't near the village."

What Landay describes sounds like a disastrous manifestation of what Afghanistan commander Gen. Stanley A. McChrystal talked about all summer — what I've called our war on civilian casualties. It is being waged, the hallucinatory thinking goes, to win Afghan "hearts and minds" and thus the "counterinsurgency" against the Taliban.

McChrystal and this strategy currently enjoy the support of both the Obama Left and the surger-cons on the Right, who, under the auspices of a new conservative think tank, the Foreign Policy Initiative, recently wrote an open letter to President Obama specifically applauding the president for choosing the McChrystal team, and expressing confidence

Afghanistan and the Doomed 'Democracy' Project

in its new strategy.

This infidel pursuit of Islamic "hearts and minds" is a wild yak chase that begins with ever-stricter rules of engagement (ROE). According to this extremely fuzzy thinking (don't be fooled by the buzz cuts), protecting the Afghan people from "everything that can hurt them" (McChrystal's words) not only will make the people like us, they will, in effect, then do our infidel bidding — i.e., sprout distinctly non-Islamic attitudes about everything from liberty to thwarting jihad, to good government (or just government). But this is cracked. Worse, it excessively endangers our troops.

McChrystal explained how to the BBC: "It's a balance for the young soldier on the ground who is in combat. One of the assets that he has that might save his life might be air power or indirect fire from artillery or mortars and we don't want to take away that protection for him."

No, we don't, general. So why, I wondered last month, were we even talking about it?

The implication — that our troops might be called on to think twice about saving their own lives — was chilling.

It still is. And especially when what may have happened this week is less soldier-on-the-ground hesitation than commander-at-the-base implacability. Read Landay's account again:

"U.S. commanders, citing new rules to avoid civilian casualties, rejected repeated calls to unleash artillery rounds at attackers dug into the slopes and tree lines — despite being told repeatedly that they weren't near the village." In other words, McChrystal's soldiers on the ground wanted protection to save their lives — and didn't get it.

If true, this is a national disgrace. A NATO-led investigation is under way into the incident, which on its face appears to be a natural result of the "hearts and minds" policy endorsed by Left and Right alike. As McChrystal put it last month: "We're here to protect the Afghan people. And we're here to protect them from everything that can hurt them, both enemy activity but also inadvertent activity by Afghan forces or ours. So we're trying to build into the culture of our force tremendous sensitivity that everything they may do must be balanced against the possibility of hurting anyone."

Anyone except our own.

We've come a long way — too long — from George S. Patton's attributed words as spoken by George C. Scott in the movie "Patton": "I want you to remember that no bastard ever won a war by dying for his country. He won it by making the other poor, dumb bastard die for his country."

Today, our leading generals have something else in mind — as when McChrystal says: "The Afghan people are the reason we're here."

Well, according to McClatchey's report this week, there is the haunting suspicion that the Afghan people, villagers and even security personnel, were behind the Ganjgal ambush in the first place.

So what kind of reason is that?

Ready, aim, fire McChrystal

9/25/09

There are many reasons to fire Gen. Stanley A. McChrystal, and all of them are contained within his 66-page "assessment" of the war in Afghanistan.

The document is fascinating, just as the work of zealots is always fascinating. As a high priest of the politically correct orthodoxy, McChrystal has laid out a strategy to combat Taliban jihad in the Islamic Republic of Afghanistan without once mentioning Islam, and forget about jihad (fireable offense No. 1).

The resulting black hole leads the commander to conclude, for example, that the reason the 99 percent-plus Muslim people of Afghanistan are "reluctant to align with us" is due to the "perception" — eight years and untold billions in largesse after we entered the country — "that our resolve is uncertain." Nothing so simple as what a member of the Afghan parliament recently told the Economist: "The Taliban tell them the Koran says they have to fight the Crusaders and they believe them."

No, it's all our fault. Seizing on the Left's favorite villain, the general blames us — our troops — for the Afghan people not liking us. And that, according to the report, is why we're losing this war (fireable offense No. 2).

To win what McChrystal describes not as a battle in the war on global jihad (fireable offense No. 3), but rather as "the struggle to gain the support of the (Afghan) people," (fireable offense No. 4), he writes that we must "connect with the people" — the same "people," he acknowledges, who "can often change sides and provide tacit or real support to the insurgents" (fireable offense No. 5).

Turning battle-hardened Marines into Miss Congenialities who "must be seen as guests of the Afghan people" doesn't mean our men have to wear swimsuits, but they do have to take off their armor (fireable offense No. 6). "Pre-occupied with protection of our own forces," McChrystal writes, "we have operated in a manner that distances us — physically and psychologically — from the people we seek to protect."

McChrystal is "pre-occupied" with what he calls "population protection" in a manner that "distances" him — psychologically and emotionally — from the men and women under his command (fireable offense No. 7).

That a general could write so disparagingly of the means to preserve his soldiers at least to fight another day is despicable. But this is what zealots do. They serve theories, not men; they see visions, not reality. And that theory, that vision is akin to the familiar Marxist notion, likely imbibed during PC school days, that denies that identity, religion and culture matter. In the resulting tunnel vision, the so-called hearts-and-minds strategy looks like a winner.

This is the underlying basis of the counterinsurgency warfare now in vogue. "Hearts and minds" is not only the flawed rationale behind "nation-building," it also inspires the restrictive rules of engagement finally causing unease at home. This strategy — now framed as "the battle for the support of the (Afghan) people" — must be junked as a fraud if our military is ever to be used effectively and appropriately.

Remember, Iraq was a "hearts and minds" war, too. Early on, Gen. David Petraeus ordered signs posted in every barracks asking: "What Have You Done to Win Iraqi Hearts and Minds Today?" Many years, billions and casualties later, behold OPEC-participating, Israel-boycotting, Hezbollah-supporting Iraq. Does it count as a "hearts and minds" victory? The "ungrateful volcano," as Churchill called it, never let us fill up a humvee for free, and even after everything we've put into the country doesn't grant us staging rights for an attack on Iran (or anywhere else).

The zealots call that success, and want to repeat it in Afghanistan. But any more such "success" will break us completely.

Still, the war goes on, and far from Afghanistan. Jihadists learned from the Taliban rout not to rely on one safe haven, "creating many safe havens, one to replace the other," as Jamestown Foundation analyst Murad Batal Al-shishani puts it. Besides the Af-Pak region, he writes, varying jihadist presences exist in regions including Yemen, Somalia, Central Asia, Lebanon and, yes, even Iraq. Plus, I would add, the leading cities of Europe and the United States.

For this global war, we not only need a new general, we need a completely fresh re-assessment.

Stop nation-building, just save our way of life

10/23/09

When it comes to Afghanistan, what separates President Barack Obama and Gen. Stanley McChrystal?

Not much. Neither wants to destroy the Taliban — just tamp it down to the point where an as-yet non-existent Afghan state can function. Which is why — prediction time — McChrystal won't quit when Obama gives him fewer forces than McChrystal is asking for.

McChrystal's assessment frankly states that what the general calls his "new strategy" — an intensification of "population protection" at the expense of "force protection" — is his top priority, not increased troop levels. But this strategy is ignored in the debate, and certainly by most conservatives, who only emphasize the need to "give the general the forces he needs to win." What it is that McChrystal actually wants to win — namely, the support of the Afghan people — is rarely mentioned.

And how to win that Afghan support? The man has a plan. It amounts to a taxpayer-funded, military-implemented bribery scheme. As the New York Times' Dexter Filkins recently put it: "McChrystal's plan is a blueprint for an extensive American commitment to build a modern state in Afghanistan, where one has never existed. ... Even under the best of circumstances, this effort would most likely last many more years, cost hundreds of billions of dollars and entail the deaths of many more American women and men. And that's if it succeeds. "

In other words, the Afghan "surge" under consideration is for "nation-building," not war-making.

But guess what? The United States of America already tried building a modern state in Afghanistan — or, at least, building a state of modernity in Afghanistan — and it just didn't stick. And this was no fly-by-night operation. University of Indiana professor Nick Cullather describes the 30-plus years of sustained U.S. development in Afghanistan as "an 'integrated' development scheme, with education, industry, agriculture, medicine, and marketing under a single controlling authority" — a massive dam project known as the Helmand Valley Authority. As historian Arnold Toynbee observed in 1960: "The domain of the Helmand Valley Authority has become a piece of America inserted into the Afghan landscape." And from the project's beginning in 1946 — designed by Morrison Knudson, builder of Hoover Dam, the Golden Gate Bridge and Cape Canaveral — to 1979 when it ended, there was no Taliban "insurgency" complicating the social work of nation-building.

But this crucial episode of U.S.-Afghan history has been erased from national consciousness, pricked only by the odd remember-when news story. Of course, these historic U.S. efforts in Helmand Province — the Taliban-spawning, opium region into which 4,000 U.S. Marines "surged" this summer — have themselves been erased from Afghanistan, which may explain the amnesia.

Still, for nation-building utopians such as Gen. McChrystal, those from Left to Right who see different peoples and cultures as interchangeable markers on a game board, reality never tempers the fanaticism. A blind faith empowers believers both to see their utopian visions and to block out the reasons they can never materialize — in this case, the specifically Islamic reasons (Sharia) Afghanistan can neither serve nor fulfill Western ends.

A similar blindness afflicted the Soviets in the USSR's war on Afghan "insurgents." Christopher Andrew, citing KGB archives smuggled out of the USSR by Vasili Mitrokhin in "The World Was Going Our Way," writes: "Islam became the unifying bond of opposition to the (Afghan Communist Party) and its Soviet backers. Afghan resistance to the regime was thus transformed into a jihad in defense of Islam whose significance was grossly underestimated by the KGB. None of the reports noted by Mitrokhin even mention the threat of jihad…" — a point I have made about the McChrystal assessment, among all too many other U.S. policy documents.

Once again, here lies the fatal flaw in our strategy. Like the doomed Soviets, the United States and its Western allies ignore the threat of jihad, a threat now on a global level unimagined in 1979 when Soviet tanks rolled into Kabul. "We miniaturize the challenge," writes Andrew C. McCarthy at National Review Online. "Thus, the war is said only to be in Afghanistan. The 'challenge' is framed as isolating a relative handful (of extremists) rather than confronting the fact that tens of millions of Muslims despise the West." And even worse, the fact that tens of millions of Muslims work to assuage their feelings by following and imposing Islamic law across the West.

In other word, nation-building in the Islamic world is a distraction from nation-saving in the Western one.

Insane ROEs end with our troops RIP

12-11-09

Gen. Stanley McChrystal's long-awaited testimony before Congress on the Afghanistan "surge" was, according to one account, "uneventful." The general himself, another story noted, was "a study in circumspection." And questioning from lawmakers was, said a third, "gentle."

That's a nice word for it. "Ineffectual" is more like it. Throw in "callous," too, given House members' obligations to constituents in the war zone, operating under what are surely the most restrictive rules of engagement (ROE) in U.S. history.

But not a single lawmaker appears to have ventured one question about these dangerously disarming ROEs, which, in Gen. McChrystal's controversial view, are key to the success of his "counterinsurgency" strategy. What kind of a commander puts his forces' lives at increased risk for a historically unsuccessful theory that depends not on winning battles against enemies, but on winning the "trust," or, as we used to say (and as Gen. David Petraeus put it in Iraq), the "hearts and minds" of a primitive people immersed in the anti-Western traditions of Islam?

That would have made a nice ice-breaker of a question for any lawmaker troubled by the Petraeus-McChrystal policy of elevating Afghan "population protection" over U.S. "force protection" to win "the support" of this 99 percent Islamic country, and the rules that American forces must follow to do so. If, that is, there were any lawmakers so troubled.

Things really tightened up back in July, when Gen. McChrystal essentially grounded air support for troops except in dire circumstances. This, in the words of British defense intelligence analyst John McCreary, is "like fighting with a hand behind your back." And with deadly results, such as the September firefight in Ganjgal where three Marines and a Navy Corpsman were killed when, according to McClatchy newspapers' Jonathan S. Landay, repeated requests for support were nixed due to "new rules to avoid civilian casualties."

As the Washington Times recently reported, the McChrystal counterinsurgency rules now include: No night searches. Villagers must be warned prior to searches. Afghan National Army or Afghan Police must accompany U.S. units on searches. Searches must account, according to International Security Assistance Force (ISAF) headquarters, "for the unique cultural sensitivities toward local women." ("Islamic repressiveness" is more accurate, but that's another story.)

U.S. soldiers may not fire on the enemy unless the enemy is preparing to fire first. U.S. forces may not engage the enemy if civilians are present. U.S. forces may fire at an enemy caught in the act of placing an IED, but not walking away from an IED area. And on it goes.

Here's another ROE that Gen. McChrystal should have been asked to justify to all Americans who hope to see their loved ones return home in one piece. The London Times recently reported that Marines, about to embark on a dangerous supply mission, were shown a PowerPoint presentation that first illustrated locations of IEDs along the way and then warned the Marines "not to fire indiscriminately even if they were fired on."

Even if they were fired on? Could they fire at all — even "discriminately"? How long does Gen. McChrystal think troops can hold their fire and maintain healthy morale? And how about a progress report on the investigation into that deadly disaster at Ganjgal? Congress wasn't interested in any of these questions.

The Times story went on to note: "The briefing ended with a projected screen of McChrystal's quote: "It's not how many you kill, it's how many you convince."

Another question: How many you convince of what, general? Of the depravity of child marriage? Of the injustice of Sharia laws that subjugate women and non-Muslims? Of the inhumanity of jihad?

Of course not. In an oblique reference that likely took in Islam, Gen. McChrystal told Congress: "I think it's very important that from an overall point of view, we understand how Afghan culture must define itself, and we be limited in our desire to change the fundamentals of it.

Fine. I don't want to change Afghan culture, either. But acknowledging its roots in an ideology that is anti-Western is crucial to devising strategy for the region. That's obvious. But not to any of our leaders.Final question: Are such leaders, civilian and military, doing their duty when they send the nation to war with a strategy that totally ignores jihad, the war doctrine of the enemy?

I repeat, you cannot win Afghan hearts

1/15/10

This wasn't supposed to happen there. According to a "counterinsurgency" plan (COIN), anti-US, anti-infidel violence just wasn't supposed to erupt in Garmsir, Afghanistan, of all places. But it did. And at least eight Afghans died in this Helmand Province district in rioting this week inspired by rumors that U.S. troops had roughed up a Koran.

Somewhere between "one thousand" (UPI) and "several thousand" (The New York Times) Afghans converged on the central bazaar in response to these rumors. "The Taliban were provoking the people," an Afghan police official told the Times. "The Taliban were telling the people, 'This is jihad; you should sacrifice yourselves.'"

Jihad? What's jihad? Among see-no-Islam Western policymakers, Islamic war doctrine is a cipher, a taboo, so policy is made in ignorance. But thousands of uneducated Afghans knew exactly what the Taliban meant. And what's more, they acted on it.

It was "like watching the movie 'Blackhawk Down,'" a Marine master sergeant told UPI, except "I was in it. My gunner kept yelling he had definite targets, people shooting at us but he couldn't fire back because there were unarmed people around them."

Ah, the Obama-McChrystal rules of non-engagement, a pillar of the see-no-Islam COIN strategy designed to eliminate civilian casualties from war — maybe all casualties, and maybe all war, if McChrystal's latest interview is any guide. "It's not about destroying the enemy's cities," he told the German magazine Der Spiegel. "It's not even about destroying their army, their fighters.... "It's really about convincing the people that they want (the counterinsurgency) to stop and they ultimately will."

Or so thinks the man drawing on the limited power of infidel persuasion in an Islamic land. All that his soldiers must do, U.S. Army Gen. Stanley A. McChrystal says, is "interact" across the language, cultural and religious barriers with "the people" to "build that relationship" — assisted by mega-sweeteners such as massive public works programs — and "the people" in effect, will jilt the "insurgency." (Then what — onto Yemen?) But don't shoot, please, because, as the general puts it, "you can't bring a civilian who has been killed back to life."

You can't bring a soldier who has been killed back to life, either, but this general, who values Afghan "population protection" over U.S. "force protection," didn't mention that.

Fortunately, no Americans were killed during the Garmsir rioting, and fortunately (for their legal health) they didn't shoot, either. Reports indicate only rioters and Afghan intelligence officers exchanged fire, with Americans targeting only a sniper aiming into their base. Of course, every window of the master sergeant's mine-resistant vehicle was "spider-webbed from bullets."

Just last week, NBC Nightly News dubbed Garmsir "a model of counterinsurgency success." In November, the Marine Corps Web site said it was beginning to be "a model of economic progress." In September, a Marine battalion commander took a visiting British general to the central bazaar for ice cream. And why not? Garmsir, first in U.S. hands, then British, and now U.S. hands again, was more than a Taliban battleground. It was a proving ground for the infidel-Islamic "interaction" strategy of giving away stuff.

British gifts to Garmsir include new roads, wells, ditches, pumps and a 70-ton bridge (built in body armor and helmets) across the main canal. If I'm not mistaken, this same bridge gave rioters easy access to the central bazaar — the same bazaar where last year, the New York Times Magazine reports, McChrystal asked every Afghan he met: "What do you need?"

His subordinates followed up — "unfailingly polite, even deferential" — at a district council meeting where the agenda "was to decide on a list of development projects, which the Americans would pay for."

First choice (since they already had a bridge)?

Repairs to the irrigation system "built by American aid workers in the 1950s (that) were badly in need of repair." Yes, as readers of this column know, we are on our second prolonged stint of nation-building in Afghanistan, and no, the first one didn't work, either.

They still like our stuff. But somehow it doesn't fortify local yokels — even U.S.-secured ones — against a call to "jihad" over a simplistic lie about Koran abuse.

Why? You won't get an answer from on high where Islam is verboten in formulating policy.

Outpost decision an insane strategy

2/12/10

Sorry, but this Washington Post headline — "U.S. commanders in Afghanistan face tougher discipline for battlefield failures" — misses the point.

The story concerns "failures" all right, but the three recently investigated incidents in question are not "battlefield" failures. No, these failures, whose names are Wanat, Ganjgal and Kamdesh, have their provenance in the climate-controlled conference rooms of the White House and the Pentagon. These are failures of U.S. military policy, and it is the top leadership of the current and last administrations, those who have formulated, approved and executed the policy, who are responsible for them — not the mid-level officers, the squadron leader or battalion commander, who, according to the Post story on the unreleased investigations, will be taking the official fall.

I refer, of course, to the policy of "counterinsurgency" warfare, particularly as promoted by Gen. Stanley McChrystal, the supreme infidel commander now waging a popularity contest against the Koranically correct Taliban for the affections of the Islamic peoples of Afghanistan. The prize, booby at best, is supposed to enable the United States, at Treasury-breaking and military-wrecking cost, to tame wild Afghanistan into a non-dysfunctional, jihad-free society. Our main weapons: "population-protection," cash and massive public works projects. (Sending troops so equipped into valleys of death like Wanat, Gankgal and Kamdesh is pure "counterinsurgency" negligence, I mean, doctrine.) The Taliban's main weapons: the Koran, jihad and Sharia. After eight-plus years, the Islamic peoples of Afghanistan still can't decide between us. Still, we keep trying, pursuing the unicorn of hearts and minds across Afghanistan even as the reality of Islamic law spreads unchecked across the West.

One place we tried too long is the Nuristan province village of Kamdesh. There, in August 2006, a foothold later known as Combat Outpost Keating was established on indefensibly low ground ringed by mountains as a Provincial Reconstruction Team. Whose criminally stupid idea was it to put an outpost there and leave it there? I doubt investigators asked.

The mission was "nation-building at a local level," as Salon's Matthew Cole reported in 2007. Under continual attack, however, the troops had switched from dispensing goodies to "simply securing the base" — and for three, pointless years until Oct. 3, 2009. On that day, the battle of Kamdesh left eight Americans dead over a piece of real estate that — and this is key — the United States had already planned to abandon. Whose negligence delayed the evacuation? I don't think investigators asked that, either.

Fact is, Keating and some other outposts were scheduled to close in July 2009 — not, alas, in recognition of the futility of "counterinsurgency," but of fighting it undermanned in remote areas. As Maj. Gen. Curtis Scaparrotti explained McChrystal's outpost-closing order to the Washington Post, "This is all about freeing up some forces so I can get them out more among the people."

But not so fast. Seems that also in July, the Post notes, Afghan President Hamid Karzai asked "senior U.S. officials" to send U.S. troops to secure Barge Matal, a remote Nuristan village, before the Aug. 20 elections. What should have taken a week stretched into months, with "ripple effects throughout eastern Afghanistan, forcing frustrated U.S. military officials to postpone plans made months earlier to abandon other remote bases."

NBC's Richard Engels reports: "Four American soldiers were killed from July through September while securing Barge Matal. But this was only the beginning. Five more American troops were killed on Sept. 8 in nearby Ganjgal, in part because resources they required (air and drone support) were diverted to help the soldiers in Barge Matal. If air assets are sent to one area, they must be pulled from another. The knock-on effect of Barge Matal" — where, Engels writes in a bitter coda, ballot boxes were stuffed, literally, with 10 times more ballots than the number of citizens in the town — "appears to have also indirectly contributed to the deaths of the eight American soldiers at COP Keating."

Barge Matal aside, almost seven weeks passed between the election and the attack on Keating. Why wasn't Keating at least closed in the interim? Where does McChrystal's buck stop?

Then again, maybe nothing short of disaster was ever going to shut down Keating. Roughly 10 days before the Oct. 3 attack, the Washington Post reports, Col. Randy George, who oversees U.S. forces in eastern Afghanistan, told commanders at Keating and Lowell, another remote outpost, to prepare their bases ... for the coming winter.

I wonder if investigators asked why.

You don't 'win hearts and minds' by losing your own

4/9/10

A reader e-mailed me to comment on a column by David Ignatius, who recently accompanied the chairman of the Joint Chiefs of Staff, Adm. Mike Mullen, to a shura, or local council meeting, in Marja, Afghanistan.

Ignatius wrote: "Given the weakness of the central government in Kabul, U.S. commanders are working to align American power with the most basic political structures, the tribal shuras. 'Culturally, this country works,' says Rear Adm. Gregory Smith, the chief military spokesman (in Afghanistan). 'People sitting down together can solve almost anything.'"

Slap a happy-face sticker on the man's briefing book to commemorate the dopiest spin ever on the primitivism, violence and misogyny of Afghan culture. My reader, naturally, had a different take from the admiral's: "So that's why we're there, bleeding and dying and spending, to facilitate Sharia law. Great, just great."

I can relate. Of course, there's nothing new here, given that the U.S.-drafted Afghan constitution (like Iraq's) has recognized Sharia law as supreme since ratification in 2004. What seems different now, or maybe just more noticeable, is an unseemly American pandering before such law — Sharia law, tribal law, any law but our own — increasingly manifested by official U.S. military policy.

I don't know how else to describe Mullen's decision to plop down, cross-legged, on a rug in a tent in Marja, where, dhimmi-like, he proceeded to take orders for public works projects from a line of Afghan "elders." As Reuters puts it, "From the litany of requests ... from asphalt for roads to fertilizer for fields — one might think he was a visiting aid worker, not the chairman of the U.S. Joint Chiefs of Staff.

'We want educational centres ... There is no good hospital ... We want all these roads to be paved,' a man with a long black beard told Mullen."

And what did the highest military officer in the USA, as Time magazine reported, tell the turbaned locals? "Inshallah, we will provide the services as soon as possible."

Inshallah — Allah willing? This is what happens when cultural sensitivity replaces cultural identity, when the effort to win Islamic "hearts and minds" — or, updated, "the sentiments and perceptions of local communities," as Col. Christopher Kolenda wrote in Joint Forces Quarterly — ends with us losing our own. Under no other circumstances could U.S. policy continue to "bleed, die and spend" to shore up Sharia-based governments anywhere and at any level.

I recently re-read a paper by a highly decorated special forces officer, Maj. Jim Gant, that is credited with helping to promote the tribal-council option in Afghanistan. Praised by Defense Secretary Robert Gates and Gens. David Petraeus and Stanley McChrystal on down, the paper is called "One Tribe at a Time," and it describes how Gant and his team in 2003 formed an arbitrary alliance with one tribe, fighting its enemies over grudges, admiring its culture (even rationalizing its misogyny), and developing a bad case of hero worship for its old chieftain whom Gant dubbed "Sitting Bull" (for that perfect touch of cultural self-loathing).

Gant tells a story about the tribal concept of revenge in action. "When at one point, members of Hezb-e-Islami (HIG) accused (Sitting Bull) of letting Christianity be spread in his village, we both knew and understood this was a lie. However, it was the issue of his tribe's honor that caused our combined reaction of violence towards HIG."

In other words, this undoubtedly brave officer took U.S. forces to war for worse than nothing: to avenge the "honor" of an Islamic tribe besmirched by Taliban allegations of Christianity contamination. What Gant describes is the perfect PC battle of a post-modern crusade that can only end in a triumph for nihilism.

Gant's big idea is to insert small teams like his own into other tribes. "They must be able to 'go native,'" Gant writes, and "steadily integrate themselves into tribal life and customs." As my reader might say: Great, just great.

Whether Gant's plan for special forces is fully implemented, one thing is as clear as a Joint Chief on a rug: You don't have to be fighting for Sitting Bull to see the horizon through the other's eyes. But that's not how you win hearts and minds; it's how you lose your own.

McChrystal's fate should be a COIN quip, not etched in stone

6/25/10

So Gen. Stanley McChrystal lost his job. Does it matter? Aside from the fact that with Wednesday's announcement the nation's capital could finally exhale for the first time since news broke about the profanity-laced Rolling Stone profile in which the now-former Afghanistan commander made disparaging comments about members of President Obama's Afghanistan team (including Obama himself), absolutely nothing of consequence resulted from the whole breathless melodrama.

Why not? Half the world by now has read the magazine article describing senior staff behavior more Animal House than conduct becoming the average adult, let alone officers and gentlemen. But despite the scandalous headlines, what we mainly gleaned was: most of the f-words salting the copy came from the reporter; the general's actual antics weren't so much disparaging as childishly indiscreet ("'Oh, not another e-mail from Holbrooke,' he groans ..."); and crude ("McChrystal gives him the middle finger"); and his top aides sounded like a bunch of dorks ("Make sure you don't get any of that on your leg," an aide jokes, referring to the Holbrooke e-mail). Even McChrystal's most egregious "insubordination," as media ecstatically called it, came down to second-hand descriptions of the general's distress over the time it took for Obama to approve McChrystal's "surge" of 30,000 troops (not 40,000 as requested), and Obama's apparent unfamiliarity with The Stanley McChrystal Story ("He (Obama) clearly didn't know anything about him, who he was" said an aide describing Obama's and McChrystal's first face-to-face meeting. "The Boss was pretty disappointed").

More significant is the fact that the article revealed no policy difference where it counts between McChrystal, a self-declared Obama voter and zealous adherent of counterinsurgency doctrine (COIN) -- the nation-building, hearts-and-minds strategy Obama inherited from George W. Bush and, after review, approved and intensified — and Obama himself. In other words, this was all so trivial. No life-and-death issues here; no philosophical divide. It was just a collision between vanity and coarse indiscretion. And with or without McChrystal, with or without his mouthy staff, the COIN nightmare continues.

And why is it a "nightmare"? Like the frustrating dream in which cries of "Look out!" are stifled, like the cult whose high priests make reality a taboo, COIN doctrine overrides all comprehension of the Islamic crucible of laws and practices in which the peoples of Afghanistan and the greater umma (Islamic community) are forged.

Instead, COIN-deployed troops are ordered to execute fantasies of cultural relativism that make lefty sense in a PC classroom, but are nothing short of appalling on the front line. And McChrystal admitted as much in the infamous article. After spending 20 tense minutes in front of a white board diagramming COIN concepts for soldiers at an outpost where COIN's restrictive rules of engagement (ROEs) had recently led to the death of a corporal, Rolling Stone reported, McChrystal sensed the men's frustration: "'This is the philosophical part that works with think tanks,' McChrystal tries to joke. 'But it doesn't get the same reception from infantry companies.'"

That's because COIN doesn't work, and the men on the ground know it. Founded on a deadly pretense — namely, that fundamental cultural differences don't exist between Islam and the West — COIN proposes that elevating generic "population protection" over generic "force protection" will someday, some way, convince that generic protected population (in this case, grossly primitive, Islamically oriented, female-oppressing, girl-molesting tribal peoples) to fall in with the American Way — or at least to support the U.S.-propped Karzai government. It is this COIN theory that is directly responsible for the unconscionably restrictive ROEs that have been attracting media attention, a postmodern form of human sacrifice staged to appease the endlessly demanding requirements of political correctness regarding Islam. There is no separating the two. If we have COIN, we have these same heinous ROEs.

It is this COIN travesty that should have made Washington hyperventilate, not tidbits of glossy-mag gossip. And it is for ramping up this COIN travesty that McChrystal should have been fired, as I first wrote back in September 2009.

But no. And there is no sign of the COIN nightmare ending anytime soon. Alas, the new commander in Afghanistan, Gen. David Petraeus, is the man who literally wrote the COIN book.

Petraeus continues COIN nightmare

7/2/10

Anyone who believes that Gen. David H. Petraeus plans to overhaul the rules of engagement (ROEs) in Afghanistan due to the critical mass of ROE-caused casualties finally catching American's attention just wasn't listening to the general at his Senate confirmation hearing this week. But judging by both senatorial deference on the topic (Petraeus was confirmed 99-0) and a practically MIA media, that describes a lot of people.

Here's the first ROE question, submitted to the general prior to the hearing: "If confirmed, what general changes, if any, would you make to the current ROEs?" In response, Petraeus wrote: "One of my highest priorities, should I be confirmed as Commander of USFOR-A, will be to assess the effect of our ROE on the safety of our forces and the successful conduct of our mission."

"Assess," he said, not "change." But that was just the beginning. Yes, he declared there was a "moral imperative" to ensure that his "troopers" had the "enablers" (back-up firepower) they needed when they "got into a tough spot." More to the main point — that restrictive ROEs are in fact the lynchpin of the disastrous counterinsurgency doctrine (COIN) that Petraeus, like Gen. Stanley A. McChrystal, stands for — were Petraeus' unequivocal statements indicating that the ROE issue was "more about executing than redesign," that his overall policy review would "see if there are tweaks needed."

Tweaks?

Or, as he stated in response to one senator's question, "It's really about the implementation of the rules of engagement and the tactical directive, both of which I think are fundamentally sound."

Fundamentally sound?

"I don't see any reason to change them in significant ways," he continued. "Rather, what we do need to do is make sure that the intent behind those, the intent being to reduce the loss of innocent civilian life in the course of military operations to an absolute minimum — that's an imperative for any (counterinsurgency). We must achieve that. I have pledged to continue to do that, to continue the great work that General McChrystal did in that regard."

There's your headline: Petraeus Pledges to Continue McChrystal's "Great Work." COINdinistas rule.

Most Americans don't know what the ascendance of counterinsurgency doctrine in the US military means. Judging by the failure of the senators to raise the topic with the most famous contemporary COIN author seated before them, neither do our elected representatives. Some senators were obviously distressed by restrictive battle rules, but they didn't seem to regard them as a crucial means to COIN's fantasy-end: winning so-called hearts and minds.

The whole nation-building endeavor, too, is just another COIN fantasy effort designed to make them like us. "Soldiers and Marines are expected to be nation-builders as well as warriors," Petraeus himself co-wrote in the foreword of the 2007 COIN manual (with Gen. F. James Amos, recently tapped to serve as the new Marine Commandant). "They must be prepared to help re-establish institutions and local security forces and assist in rebuilding infrastructure and basic services. They must be able to facilitate establishing local

governance and the rule of law. The list of such tasks is long ..."

You can say that again. Better, though, for our elected representatives to have read just that statement back to Gen. Petraeus and to have asked for a reaction, a reckoning, his defense of a theory that, I would argue (and frequently do), has for years misused and abused the U.S. military through its willful ignorance of the Islam-West culture clash that forever dooms all of our do-gooding. The Great Society, it's worth recalling, didn't work here on our own people. It's no more plausible, even at ROE-controlled gunpoint, on an alien society.

History confirms this. The United States engaged in intensive Afghan nation-building between 1946 and 1979 — specifically, in Helmand Province, now, ironically, a Taliban stronghold. In other words, the program was not, as Gen. Petraeus told the Senate this week, "hugely successful." For details, read Indiana University History professor Nick Cullather's 2002 paper, "From New Deal to New Frontier in Afghanistan," which is available online. It catalogues decades of failure apparent as far back as 1949. "If illusions doomed the project they also created and sustained it," Cullather wrote, summing up American denial on Afghanistan.

And for the ages.

Is a Petraeus victory in Afghanistan another Iraq?

7/9/10

I've sworn off predictions, having guessed wrong that a deeply apologetic Gen. Stanley McChrystal would keep his Afghanistan command. But what about GOP chairman Michael Steele? So far, at least as I write, he is weathering his own Afghan storm after dubbing the protracted counterinsurgency, President Obama's war — as though the Obama policy were not in fact an extension and intensification of the Bush administration plan — and then noting that history tells us war in Afghanistan is unwinnable.

But not always, as I learned after consulting Andrew Bostom's invaluable compendium, "The Legacy of Jihad." Turns out Islamized Turkic nomads came out on top, conquering the Hindu Kingdom of Kabul in the late 9th century, ending Hindu rule in Afghanistan with a victory that was, as a 13th-century-Indian-chronicler put it, "the result of treachery and deception, such as no one had ever committed."

That's one way to win. I have long argued that counterinsurgency's PC battle for hearts and minds (which Steele appears to be rejecting without articulating why) is, alas, not another. And what could we possibly get from a hearts-and- minds victory in Afghanistan — another Iraq?

I'm afraid the answer is "bingo." Judging by the 99-0 Senate vote that confirmed Petraeus as Afghanistan commander last week, another Iraq is precisely what America wants, as though Iraq were an American "victory" worth the cost, human and monetary, of repeating.

It all depends on what the meaning of "win" is, a definition that includes pretty much anything in Iraq, even the shocking possibility, as noted by Iraq commander Gen. Ray Odierno, that United Nations forces might be needed to secure Iraq's oil-rich northern provinces after U.S. forces depart in 2011.

Funny, I thought the United States fought a war about securing Iraq, or something. And funny, northern Iraq happens to be the neighborhood in which Petraeus, as commander of the 101st Airborne, first made his personal counterinsurgency mark back in 2003, 2004. A revealing Senate question for Petraeus last week might have been to ask him to assess how his policy of winning Iraqi hearts and minds (as exemplified by the posters he ordered up in 2003 in barracks asking "WHAT HAVE YOU DONE TO WIN IRAQI HEARTS AND MINDS TODAY?") has fared after all these years. Further, could there be anything about Islamic culture — the institution of jihad, the animus toward infidels — that is derailing his best-laid counterinsurgency plans in Iraq and Afghanistan?

But there was only silence on the part of lawmakers, the kind of lazy deference to military brass that inspired the British weekly New Statesman to publish an eye-catching cover story this week called "The Cult of the Generals." The piece argues that U.S. civilian leadership has abdicated its policy-making responsibilities to weirdly deified four-star generals (read: Petraeus). In a sense, Steele tripped this peculiar power circuit in his own bumbling way. There's an argument to be made that as chairman of the apparently pro-COIN GOP, that's not his job. But that doesn't absolve the rest of us, and particularly not our elected leaders, from joining the debate over COIN strategy, with its grossly unrealistic goals and unconscionable methods, and its failure to enhance American national security. After all, even an "Iraq" in Afghanistan would do nothing to neutralize Iranian and Pakistani nukes, the signal threat to U.S. interests in the region (so long as we control our points of entry against immigration and travel from the region, at least for the duration). The war doesn't make sense.

Maybe that's the case because we are so vague about what constitutes American interests—even threats thereto. In his Fourth of July letter to forces in Afghanistan, Petraeus described the enemy as being "those who embrace indiscriminate violence and transnational extremists." Sorry, but that's loosey-goosey enough to include certain pitbull owners and Greenpeace activists.

"Together with our Afghan partners, we must secure and serve the people of Afghanistan," Petraeus continued, sounding that disconcerting (especially on Independence Day) non-American refrain of what you might call the "transnational extremists" of the COIN world. "We must never forget that decisive terrain in Afghanistan is the human terrain."

Haven't we been down this road before?

Why does a pentagon shape the Oval Office?

10/4/10

Bob Woodward's latest publishing event, "Obama's Wars," includes maybe the most significant scoop of his career: Directing not only Obama's wars, but also America's, is a veritable military junta.

I exaggerate—some. Frankly, I don't know how else to assess the information in Washington Post excerpts of Woodward's coverage of the deliberations leading up to President Obama's decision last year to send 30,000 additional troops to Afghanistan. The stories—anonymously sourced as usual and, as such, questionable even as they undoubtedly influence subsequent coverage—describe a president frustrated, ill-served and finally overwhelmed by military muscle concentrated in the hands of Defense Secretary Gates, Joint Chiefs Chairman Mullen and then-CENTCOM chief Petraeus (all longtime regulars, if not favorites, of this column). Headline No. 1 says it all:

"Military thwarted president seeking choice in Afghanistan." If the military "thwarts" a president, the president isn't in charge, which is not a good thing unless military dictatorships are your bag.

As Woodward frames the behind-the-scenes struggle, Obama "was looking for choices that would limit U.S. involvement and provide a way out."

Meanwhile, "his top three military advisers were unrelenting advocates for 40,000 more troops and an expanded mission that seemed to have no clear end."

But the problem wasn't that the military men pushed their pet strategy, it was that they failed to present the president with alternatives as asked, bidden and ordered.

For example, Woodward writes: "When Mullen learned of the hybrid option" — Vice President Biden's plan to eschew nation-building and focus on Taliban-hunting and training Afghans — "he (Mullen) didn't want to take it to Obama. 'We're not providing that,'" he told Joint Chiefs Vice Chairman Gen. James E. Cartright.

"We're" not? Who do "we" think "we" are?

Obama heard about the option anyway and "instructed Gates and Mullen to present it." Woodward continues: "Mullen had other ideas" — namely, a war game exercise "to support his case against the option." What comes next describes something rotten in the chain of command. According to Woodward's reporting, the Joint Chiefs Chairman went on to rig the wheel, in effect, against the hybrid option by failing to take it completely through war game exercises — a halfway effort attended by Mullen and, not incidentally, Petraeus. At a meeting with Obama a few weeks later, Woodward writes, "Petraeus cited the war game as evidence that the hybrid option would not work. ... 'OK,' Obama said. 'If you tell me that we can't do that, and you war-gamed it, I'll accept that.'" Then: "No one contradicted the claim."

If this is true, it's outrageous. After all, Gen. Stanley McChrystal was fired for trash talk about the civilian leadership. What Woodward describes is trash treatment of the civilian leadership, which is worse.

But it's hard to imagine Obama firing anyone over this case. What also comes across in Woodward's account is a weak-in-the-war-making-department president who recoils from the potential consequences of overruling the military: namely, the resignations of people blocking the very policy changes he set out to enact. Why he flinches, I don't know.

According to Woodward, Obama said he wanted to devise a way out of, not deeper into Afghanistan; he even wanted to move away from the insupportable nation-building that lies at the theoretical root of the perfect "counterinsurgency." (I agree with both goals while realizing the meeting of the minds likely ends right there.) Neither goal is central to the "surge" as finally ordered. Obama's "decision" to send 30,000, not 40,000 troops, is marginal, while his 2011 "withdrawal" has been publicly discounted from the beginning.

So, Obama's war is, in fact, an expanded mission that has no clear end, something that seems to suit his leading general fine. "I don't think you win this war," Petraeus is quoted as saying privately. "I think you keep fighting. It's a little bit like Iraq, actually ... Yes, there have been enormous progress in Iraq. But there are still horrific attacks in Iraq and you have to stay vigilant. You have to stay after it. This is the kind of fight we're in for the rest of our lives and probably our kids' lives."

Call it a 100-year-war. By that point, if we get there, the Oval Office will have long become a pentagon.

Let's COIN another strategy: Pull out our troops now

4/15/11

Reading about another catastrophically maimed casualty of the counterinsurgency strategy (COIN) in Afghanistan, I was struck by a biographical note. This young American, now a triple amputee after stepping on an IED while on foot patrol, an integral feature of COIN's hearts-and-minds efforts, was only 11 years old when the war in Afghanistan began.
Come October, this war will have lasted a decade. Last month, the Iraq War passed the eight-year mark. During the Vietnam War, the question was whether there was any "light at the end of the tunnel." In these wars, we have to wonder whether there is any tunnel. If so, no one seems to be in any hurry to get out.

Why? Why is it that we have come to accept war without end — not to mention, I would (and do) argue, war without benefit? And why does it actually seem as though our leaders want it this way?

There are reasons and they are shocking.

Watching Defense Secretary Gates in Iraq recently where he practically begged to leave U.S. forces in place after the scheduled pullout in December 2011, Jed Babbin, I think, nailed it. Writing in the American Spectator, Babbin guessed that President Obama just doesn't want Iraq to fall apart, at least not on the eve of the 2012 election. Ditto Afghanistan. And falling apart — I would call it reverting to type — is the inevitable result of U.S. withdrawal. "Who lost Iraq and Afghanistan?" is not a question Obama wants to get into during the election. Thus, Obama will slog on with COIN, maintaining his weirdly logical wartime alliance with the neoconservative, democracy-project Right. On Obama's part, this is a political calculation, pure and simple. On the Right, something else is going on.

The fact is, so long as we are still in Iraq, still in Afghanistan, the policy born of neoconservatism's lights, embraced by nation-building Bushies, promulgated and entrenched by Gen. David Petraeus, still has a theoretical chance of working. A constant refrain from these camps is that prematurely withdrawing from either country would jeopardize what Petraeus has dubbed for more than four years "fragile and reversible" security gains. To them, staying forever is leaving too soon. It isn't so much that in withdrawal lies defeat; it's that in withdrawal lies confirmation of the defeat of their prized COIN strategy. In the strategy's defeat lies the abyss.

And so they must keep reality at bay. And they do that by keeping Iraq and Afghanistan a work in progress. As such, it is up to our troops to try harder to win "hearts and minds," walk more IED-strewn patrols, distribute more cash to make "them" like us, adopt more Shariah practices in dealing with Islam (as literally suggested by ISAF). In this way, the COINdinistas are hamster-footing it to keep the ride from stopping at any cost.

That's their prerogative, but only until someone finds the courage to fire them. That won't happen until people connect the human toll of these wars — ROE-related combat deaths, IED casualties, frequent unfriendly fire murders — with dead-end COIN strategy. It's no secret. In a recent report on new military medical statistics that reveal a horrific spike in multiple amputations and genital injuries due to IEDs in Afghanistan, the Los Angeles Times noted: "Troops are increasingly vulnerable to injuries from such makeshift bombs as they mount foot patrols in an effort to win support from Afghan villagers, a key strategy in the counterinsurgency campaign."

Either our representatives are as deeply vested in "success" as the military brass is, or they're too timid to demand answers. Just look what happened when Rep. Walter Jones, R-NC, expressed his frustration about war unending to Gen. Petraeus last month. "You know, 15, 16, 17 years, for G0d sakes, how much more can we take, how much more can we give treasure and blood?" asked Jones. Petraeus won the day by announcing, to great but irrelevant effect, that his own son had completed his first Afghanistan tour in November.

"I don't think you win this war," Petraeus is quoted as saying in Bob Woodward's last book "Obama's War." "I think you keep fighting. ... This is the kind of fight we're in for the rest of our lives and probably our kids' lives."

This "kind of fight" — COIN — needs to stop, if only for the 11-year-olds.

Why did generals listen to Greg Mortenson?

4/22/11

To say that the memoir "Three Cups of Tea" is the basis of the bitter pill that is American counterinsurgency (COIN) strategy in Afghanistan is a falsehood and gross exaggeration—like much of the book itself, as it turns out. But it is a fact that the 2006 mega-seller, "required" reading for the U.S. military in Afghanistan (not to mention a large chunk of the nation's schoolchildren and college students), has washed that strategy down, swirled it around and given its key tenets a weird charisma in the person of author Greg Mortenson. What—since "60 Minutes" unmasked Mortenson and his book as a colossal fraud—now?

I don't mean what about the Montana Attorney General's office inquiry into Mortenson's Central Asian Institute (CAI), the tax-exempt charity he founded 15 years ago to build schools in AfPak, and which, according to Gordon Wiltsie, a former CAI board member who served as board treasurer, "Greg regards ... as his personal ATM."

Or the thumping, 75-page smackdown "Three Cups of Deceit" (wherein Wiltsie's statement appears) that author-turned-whistleblower Jon Krakauer posted online to elaborate on the fabrications and Mortenson's shocking financial practices.

Or the fact that Viking, publisher of the 5 million copies of "Three Cups of Tea" in print, announced that charges against its golden goose are being "reviewed."

Or even all the schoolchildren across the country who in 2009 donated $1.7 million to Mortenson's program Pennies for Peace (P4P). That same year, Krakauer writes, CAI's outlay for the things P4P is supposed to pay for—teachers salaries, school supplies, etc.—came to $612,000. "By comparison," he writes, "CAI spent more than $1 million to promote (Mortenson's books) and another $1.4 million to fly Mortenson around in chartered jets. Donors unknowingly picked up the tab."

In a much larger sense, so did we all. That's because Mortenson is not just another flim-flam artist who turned a good yarn into fool's gold (and no book royalties for CAI, by the way, Krakauer reports). He's also a Gandhi-like guru to the Pentagon who preaches to top brass that "extremism" can be defeated by "education." Mortenson's Big Idea is teaching hearts and minds, and it slides neatly into any Pentagon PowerPoint on "population-centric COIN."

Mortenson's unusual life as counselor to generals started back in September 2007, when then-Lt. Col. Christopher D. Kolenda "reached out" to him. Kolenda's wife had sent "Three Cups" to Kolenda in

Afghanistan where, as the New York Times put it, "Kolenda knew well the instructions about building relationships with elders that were in the Army and Marine Corps' new counterinsurgency manual, which had been released in late 2006. But 'Three Cups of Tea' brought the lessons to life."

By the end of 2008, the Wall Street Journal reported, Mortenson was in the Pentagon for a private meeting with Joint Chiefs Chairman Adm. Mike Mullen. By the summer of 2009, Mortenson had met with Mullen several times, Mortenson wrote on his blog, "to consult on new approaches to strategic policy in Afghanistan." And "in the frantic last hours of Gen. Stanley A. McChrystal's command in Afghanistan" last year, the Times reported somewhat breathlessly, Mortenson was among those the general "reached out" to via email en route from Kabul to Washington. This, the Times wrote, showed the extent to which military leaders "have increasingly turned to Mortenson ... to help translate the theory of counterinsurgency into tribal realities on the ground."

But what happens now that a bunch of those theory-translating realities turn out to be fake?

Ladies and gentlemen, we've been had. But not by Mortenson. The military culture that grabbed Mortenson's "Three Cups" and didn't let go was already lost, already in thrall to the Leftist theories and see-no-Islam strategies that have turned U.S. foreign policy into the Great Society with guns. Independently, Mortenson dressed it all up with a heady mix of popular appeal and ever-so-high purpose. Education, not terrorism; ploughshares, not swords; love, not war. Clear, hold and build, build, build!

From COIN to "Three Cups," it's a perfectly irresistible way to avoid the facts and features of jihad culture where such institutional naivete leads to stratospheric waste, fraud and mounting casualties.

Anything to keep the teacups from getting chipped.

Idiotic politeness doctrine is killing soldiers

7/22/11

This week, the madness of the counterinsurgency doctrine (COIN), which drives the war in Afghanistan, reached new heights — or depths — as revealed by two news stories.

In Great Britain, a former Royal Marine told the Sun newspaper after the inquest into the 2010 death of Sgt. Peter Rayner that soldiers were prevented from opening fire at Taliban fighters in the act of laying IEDs (crude, handmade bombs), so as not to disturb the local population.

So as not to disturb?

In Iowa, a community mourns the death of National Guard

Afghanistan and the Doomed 'Democracy' Project

soldier Terry L. Pasker, who, along with contractor Paul Protzenko, was killed last week in yet another attack by an Afghan army soldier. DesMoinesRegister.com reports: "The U.S. military considered the area so safe that soldiers didn't wear body armor, so as not to offend the friendly locals."

So as not to offend?

Fear of offending has long been a salient feature of our culture. It's become an expression of a self-deprecating, if not self-loathing, society where the "dead white males" who brought us "Hamlet," the Constitution and the light bulb have become embarrassments for non-Western religion, the very lack of which is deemed offensive.

Since 9/11, however, this psychosis has had a new application — the ultimate point of my book "The Death of the Grown-Up" (St. Martin's Press, 2007). In today's war zone, fear of giving offense is fatal, as noted above. But it also applies as the foundational precept of "dhimmitude," the twisted state of non-Muslims in thrall to Islam, a condition long observed and documented by the visionary historian Bat Ye'or.

The fear of giving Muslims offense is the most profound acquiescence to Islamic cultural pressures because it is driven, at base, by a conviction that self-preservation as a non-Muslim is itself offensive in a Muslim society. The fact is, Muslim societies across time and continents have forced non-Muslims to pay a tax, the jizya, to remain non-Muslims and have inflicted all manner of humiliations, physical and mental, upon them as a matter of Islamic law, or Shariah, for doing so. Where Islamic law is not officially in effect, Bat Ye'or explains, the de facto state of dhimmitude may still arise and flourish in the habitual appeasement of Islamic sensibilities to forestall the occasional violent eruption or attempt — the odd 9/11, 7/7 or thwarted Times Square bombing. The net effect of all this appeasement, this dhimmitude, is the creeping — galloping — incursions of Islamic law into non-Islamic institutions and societies.

In Afghanistan, the same triggers are in place. We have an infidel army walking on eggs to placate, cajole and bribe an Islamic society into supporting what are, any way you cut them, infidel values and interests against those of the indigenous Islamic jihadist groups. To this end, Western military authorities now specifically ordain that the Quran must be revered (or else violence might ensue). They, in effect, require that Islamic customs on polygamy, on the sexual abuse of children, be tolerated (or else violence might ensue). The Danish cartoons, the Rev. Terry Jones, freedom of speech must be denounced by the highest Western military officials (or else violence might ensue). These capitulations on bedrock Western traditions of speech, conscience and human rights could occur only under a debased leadership, military and civilian.

When the fear of giving offense to the local Islamic community (by shooting Taliban or wearing body armor) trumps self-preservation (by shooting Taliban or wearing body armor), we know the military's dhimmitude is complete.

What I am describing, of course, is the execution of COIN doctrine to win Afghan "trust," also known as "hearts and minds." As Brig. Gen. Steven Kwast put it in 2009: "Victory in this conflict is about winning the hearts and minds of the Afghan people and engendering their trust. When the Afghan people trust us and believe us when we tell them what we're going to do, we will win this overnight."

Tell it to the Easter Bunny. Meanwhile, our troops pay the price and our military is dhimmified. Taking off troops' body armor so as not to offend friendly Afghans?

Are they kidding?

How many limbs must be lost in Afghanistan?

9/23/11

Only the U.S. military could build a defensive wall of words — "dismounted complex blast injury" (DCBI) -- around the bare fact that single, double, triple, even quadruple amputations are up sharply among U.S. forces on foot patrol in Afghanistan. So are associated pelvic, abdominal and genital injuries, according to a newly released report.

Even the antiseptic language of the report is excruciating, as when it calls for "further refinement" of "aggressive pain management at the POI (point of injury)," or highlights the need to train more military urologists in "phallic reconstruction surgery."

It isn't management but prevention that is called for.

These grievous injuries have increased because more U.S. forces are on foot patrol in Afghanistan. More Americans are on foot patrol in Afghanistan because counterinsurgency strategy puts them there. Every story I've seen on the new amputation report makes this connection. The Associated Press account is typical: "The counterinsurgency tactic that is sending U.S. soldiers out on foot patrols among the Afghan people, rather than riding in armored vehicles, has contributed to a dramatic increase in arm and leg amputations, genital injuries and the loss of multiple limbs following blast injuries."

But what exactly this counterinsurgency (COIN) tactic is designed to accomplish remains off the radar. The fact is, Uncle Sam is asking young Americans to risk limbs, urinary function and testicles to win something not only intangible but also fantastical. They walk the bomb-packed byways of Afghanistan to win — to "earn" — "the trust of the Afghan people." This is the mythological, see-no-Islam quest that drives U.S.

COIN strategy.

Once we finally admit that the unicorn hunters are wrong, once we stop trying to remake Afghanistan in something akin to our own image, once we start preventing Islam from remaking the West into a Shariah-compliant zone (with counterterrorism strikes, not foot patrols, as needed), these shattering body blasts to young Americans on the other side of the world will cease.

Meanwhile, "the trust of the Afghan people" is the holy grail of the Washington establishment, and, even after retiring from the military, Gen. David Petraeus, now director of the CIA, remains chief myth-maker. "Earn the people's trust," Petraeus wrote in a signal "Counterinsurgency Guidance" issued Aug. 1, 2010. From his list of how-tos—which range from dispense payola ("COIN-contracting"), to "help them develop checks and balances to prevent abuses" (good luck with that), to "drink lots of tea"—one order stands out, particularly in light of this week's report on amputations resulting from foot patrols.

Petraeus wrote: "Walk. Stop by, don't drive by. Patrol on foot whenever possible and engage the population."

One year later, the Army is reckoning with the carnage and after-care requirements that are consequences of this key tactic of COIN strategy. It is high time for the rest of us to reckon with them, too. Is COIN working? Is the burden of suffering that the nation is placing on the military worth the return? Frankly, when it comes to winning "the trust of the Afghan people," is there any return?

These questions didn't come up in the new report, naturally. Which isn't to say the report was devoid of political consciousness. By way of background, the report defines "dismounted complex blast injury" as a new pattern of injury. The definition is: "An injury caused by an explosion occurring to a Service Member while dismounted in a combat theater that results in amputation of at least one lower extremity at the knee or above, with either amputation or severe injury to the opposite lower limb, combined with pelvic, abdominal or urogenital injury. This definition is not meant to define a subset of injuries for policy-making decisions."

Oh, yeah?

No rapport with Afghan leaders? Good.

9/27/10

Your tax dollars at work:

"In a mock Afghan village on the Quantico Marine base," the Washington Post reports, "Sloan Mann, a military contractor, guided several Marines into a sweltering concrete room. They came to meet a fake mullah, played by an Afghan American actor. Mann, a former Army infantry officer, watched as the Marines practiced the seemingly straightforward tactic of chatting up Afghan village leaders."

The article goes on to describe Sgt. Walton Cabrera, 25, who "sat before the mullah but couldn't ease into a groove. 'So ... how's everything in the village so far?' he asked. 'Has the population changed?'

"Armed with a pen and report card, Mann, 36, handed up harsh feedback. 'No rapport,' he wrote.'"

No rapport? But that's a good thing. America will truly be in trouble when our best young people actually relate to the dominant members of Afghanistan's violent, misogynistic, pederasty-prone, polygamous, tribal, Islamically supremacist and corrupt culture. But Mann, currently delivering on a tidy $1.5 million annual contract with the Pentagon, has a job to do. He pulled several Marines aside near the mock Afghan bazaar to give them expert instruction: "You guys don't like building rapport? Chill. Have a conversation. Hang out with them."

So it goes, up and down the military food chain, all eyes on The Relationship between Americans and Afghans, which, given the constant and remedial attention, would appear to be sparkless — again, civilizationally speaking, a good thing.

Last July, with the initial deployment of Marines to Helmand Province, it was Brig. Gen Lawrence D. Nicholson telling his men: "You're going to drink lots of tea. You're going to eat lots of goat. Get to know the people. That's the reason why we're here."

Last month, it was Gen. David Petraeus' new counterinsurgency guidelines, which open with "The decisive terrain is the human terrain" Later: "Take off your sunglasses.

... Earn the people's trust, talk to them, ask them questions, and learn about their lives."

Now, it's come to this: A military contractor is hired to help Marines pull themselves out of the Lonely Hearts (and Minds) Club that is, in the words of the Post reporter, making their "encounters with the 'mullah' (feel) like bad first dates."

But, honestly, what would count as ice-breakers with a Pashtun tribal elder? In all likelihood he has several wives, some of whom are no more than children (in homage to Muhammad's child bride Aisha). He may well be a "bacha baz," which is the term for an older man who has a sexual relationship with a boy. (As research recently highlighted by Joel Brinkley shows, this is common practice in Kandahar and other southern Afghan towns.)

How's — the wives? What's a night out in Kandahar like with — the boys? And by the way, wherever do you shop for all of those American flags to light up for Islam?

Clearly, it's all too easy to get off on the wrong foot, and Sgt. Cabrera just never clicked with his "mullah." By the newspaper's account, he earned "zero out of five points for his 'build rapport' and five out of 10 for having 'effectively weaved questions into a conversation.'" Cabrera explained he had been "worrying too much about avoiding insult to the mullah" — always a conversation-chiller.

By session's end, Mann delivered his final assessment to Marine commanders. "Three things," he told them. "One, lack of preparation. Two, it was a full-on interrogation. Three, lack of rapport."

And yes, that contract was for $1.5 million.

But maybe it's worth the price to know Marines aren't simpatico with mullahs. You already knew that? Well, let's hope it sticks. The Petraeus guidelines are also big on pushing Afghan empathy, specifically encouraging troops to "view our actions through the eyes of the Afghans." That's perfectly fine for the Afghans, but when an American commander exhorts his troops to "consult with elders before pursuing new initiatives and operations," we can only hope he doesn't mean consulting them before pursuing polygamy, pederasty or wife-beating.

The truth is, for our civilization's sake, we can't afford for our people to hit it off.

For sale: Afghanistan's government

10/29/10

Last Sunday, the New York Times described a crude scene that smacked of not exactly petty graft. There was Afghanistan's presidential plane on the Tehran airport tarmac, waiting for one last passenger before wheels up to Kabul. The missing passenger was Iran's ambassador to Afghanistan. The ambassador, Feda Hussein Maliki, climbed aboard and took his tardy seat next to Umar Daudzai, Afghanistan President Hamid Karzai's chief of staff and closest adviser. Maliki then presented Daudzai with a plastic bag bulging with about $1 million in packets of euros. From Iran with love.

This, the Times reported, was "part of a secret, steady stream of Iranian cash intended to buy the loyalty of Mr. Daudzai and promote Iran's interest in the presidential palace" in Kabul.

Bad enough, but it gets worse.

On Tuesday, the New York Times revealed that it wasn't just the infamously anti-American Afghan chief of staff trucking home with mullah moolah as originally reported. Karzai himself was in on this fix. Answering a question at a press conference on Monday about whether his chief of staff had indeed received Iranian cash, Karzai replied, matter-of-fact, the practice was government-wide, "transparent" even: "They do give us bags of money—yes, yes, it is done. We are grateful to the

Iranians for this."

Welcome to transparency, Afghanistan-style: payola in plain sight. And why not? In that wonderful bazaar that is Afghanistan, as Karzai put it, "Patriotism has a price."

But what price suckerhood? I regret to say this is the only spoil left in Afghanistan for the United States. Iran, a global sponsor of jihadist terror long before al-Qaida attacked the United States on 9/11, has simultaneously spent most of the past decade buying, cajoling, pressing, weaseling and forcing its influence into the highest circles of our so-called Iraqi and Afghan "allies" even as it fights American troops on those very same Iraqi and Afghan battlefields. This most recent spate of news stories about our Afghan "ally" is just the bag of cash that broke the sucker's back—or should have. The question is, how do we ask the American military to fight and possibly die for the Islamic Republic of Afghanistan when that same Islamic Republic of Afghanistan's government is unabashedly in Iran's pocket even as Iran is simultaneously training Taliban fighters to bring it down? Also this week, the Washington Examiner reported Iran is training Taliban fighters on the use of surface-to-air missiles. Aside from NATO forces fighting alongside the United States in Afghanistan, is there an ally left in Afghanistan?

What we are witnessing in Afghanistan is the bifurcated template Iran perfected in Iraq, which infiltrated governing circles even as it fought Americans risking their lives and limbs on the battlefield for that same Iraqi government.

But Zombie Nation—at least when it comes to the two wars American soldiers remained ensnared in—doesn't ponder this, let alone question it. As far as our leadership goes, it's all so much more to manage, to set into context, to rationalize and move on. But isn't war more important than spin? Not so long as "spin" keeps the war in a blur.

Case in point: "We do not question Iran's right to provide financial assistance to Afghanistan, nor do we question Afghanistan's right to accept that assistance," said State Department spokesman Philip Crowley.

That's one way to avoid unpleasant answers.

Crowley continued: "What we think is important is Afghans having the ability to shape their own future without negative influences from its neighbors. We'll let the Government of Afghanistan speak to how they spend the financial assistance received from other countries, but we remain skeptical of Iran's motives given its history of playing a destabilizing role with its neighbors. We hope that Iran will take responsibility to play a constructive role in the future of Afghanistan."

So, we don't question Iranian financial assistance (bags o' cash) or Afghanistan's acceptance of Iranian financial assistance (bags o' cash) but we "remain skeptical" of Iran's "destabilizing role" even as we "hope" Iran will play a "constructive role." Diplomatic niceties aside, there are limitations to such doubletalk. It's no match for the double game Iran is playing, one in which Uncle Sucker will be lucky to come home with just a booby prize.

We need to leave Afghanistan — now

4/8/11

Two more American soldiers were killed this week by a "lone" Afghan "ally." These latest murders took place inside a compound in the northern Afghan province of Faryab where the soldiers were providing security for a meeting between U.S. trainers and Afghan border police.

I can't find more details, not even the soldiers' names, but let's use our imagination. Two presumably young soldiers arrived safely with their team at the Afghan border police compound near the Afghan border with Turkmenistan. They probably thought the first hard part of the day was over, that they were behind a secure perimeter and could have a smoke or a chew or a stick of gum and wait until they had to mount up and face the booby-traps and sniper harassment that would follow them home. It was at this point that their killer, an Afghan police officer, moved in on them. Maybe he was even assigned to "partner" with them. He greeted them, offered something to eat, might even have told them a joke, who knows? While they were eating, smoking, laughing, somehow off guard, he shot them dead.

Did he shout "Allahu Akbar," or keep it under his breath, or wait until he had gotten clean away for a big loud, "Allah be praised, I got me two infidels"?

This "incident" brings the total of U.S. troops murdered by our Afghan allies since December by my unofficial and possibly incomplete count to 17. If I add two Italian troops killed in January by an Afghan soldier firing an M-16 at close range while the Italians were cleaning their guns, and three German troops killed in February by an Afghan soldier firing a submachine gun at close range while the Germans were working on a vehicle, the total is 22 NATO soldiers killed by Afghan security forces in four months. That means every month, five Westerners have been sacrificed specifically for being "infidels" ordered by their dhimmi leaders to curry favor (win "hearts and minds") in the umma through an unprecedented campaign of payola and public works. This is an outrage, a national scandal. Every elected representative of these fallen soldiers and their bereaved families is AWOL, and isn't that a crime?

Apparently not. To our unflustered leaders, the sacrifices are lamentable but acceptable — just part of the human price of the privilege of spending $350 million a day to be in Afghanistan in the first place. The main problem is our leaders treat these "incidents" as unfortunate by-products of a chosen nation-building strategy that must be pursued forever; not manifestations of a disastrous counter-insurgency (COIN) strategy that must be junked ASAP. Which reminds of what an ex-Green Beret friend with multiple stints in Afghanistan recently told me was his "winning strategy." He wrote: "Oh, by 'winning' I mean leaving Afghanistan as soon as possible, burning in place or blowing up all our materiel we can't carry with us quickly." Amen, brother.

But about these COIN-killed Western troops: They attract little attention beside local coverage. If you look around online, you can find videos of the flag-draped processionals, the young people dressed for mourning in a high school gym. This is not an adequate memorial to these irresponsibly lost lives.

If Congress were worth the bother, it would demand change on behalf of these and all of our fallen young Americans from a military in denial, a government in thrall to a policy with more in common with the utterly failed ideas of the Great Society than with national security strategy. I am talking about COIN theory, which holds that if you sink enough money, enough public works projects, enough nation-building, then somehow, some way, these alien cultures bridged by Islamic law and custom will adopt essentially un-Islamic law and custom and — presto — become an ally in the war on terror.

Sounds funny now, but isn't that what was supposed to happen? The truth is, no one in power, military and civilian, knows what their point and purpose is anymore. This perpetual madness must stop.

Where's the outrage over murders in Afghanistan?

1/20/12

Is there a single public official who is examining — who cares about — the murder spree by Afghan security forces against Western troops and security contractors in Afghanistan? I can list well over 40 such murders in the past two years. These incidents even have their own phrase in military jargon — "green-on-blue" shootings — but the color we should all be seeing is red. Does Obama see red? Pelosi? Romney? Newt? Anyone?

In the last several months, there have been six separate attacks on Western forces by uniformed Afghan army members. The toll includes three Australian soldiers killed (as they ended a regular, weekly parade) and 10 wounded; six French troops killed and 16 wounded; and one American killed and seven wounded. The American fatality, 20-year-old

Afghanistan and the Doomed 'Democracy' Project

Army Pfc. Dustin Paul Napier of Kentucky, was shot in the head earlier this month by an Afghan service member during a game of volleyball on base.

The International Security Assistance Force (ISAF) didn't offer that painfully vivid detail about the volleyball game; the media did. Official details on these shootings are scarce, and, according to ISAF's "new policy" reported this week by USA Today, will become nonexistent now that ISAF plans to withhold information on such Afghan shootings of Western forces. (Outrageous!) Meanwhile, follow-up investigations are practically unheard of. Only a Freedom of Information Act request by the Air Force Times pried from the Pentagon's clutches the September 2011 report on the murder of nine Americans at Kabul Airport in April 2011 by an Afghan air force officer.

The military's findings? The killer, Ahmed Gul, 46, "acted alone." Reading through the Air Force report, I get the impression that collaboration with "the Taliban" is the only hypothesis the investigators consider worth exploring. It is as though the military believes infiltration by hostile forces is the only conceivable threat posed to U.S. and other allied personnel on their bases in Afghanistan. Having failed to dig up concrete evidence of a more or less conventional enemy conspiracy, military investigators close their eyes to anything else—such as good, ol'-fashioned Islamic jihad. As Muslims, Afghans and Taliban alike are subject to its call. Fact. Sorry about that, but I didn't write the Quran.

The report states: "The information collected regarding SUBJECT (shooter) and his background does not support his involvement in insurgent activity. (Air Force) analysts, in concert with other analysts and agencies, have reviewed multiple intelligence documents, investigative reports, and Open Source reporting to determine SUBJECT's motive for the attacks. This analysis is not stating that there are no insurgent connections to SUBJECT, but that none have been established thus far during this investigation. Additionally, there are multiple reports that indicated SUBJECT may have had mental issues that were possibly compounded by alleged financial problems."

I may not have read every word of the 436-page report this statement sums up, but I've already picked up a few clues to support the hypothesis that Gul was simply on a jihad.

Gul was said to have returned from Pakistan in 2008 because he "wanted to kill Americans."

Gul frequented a mosque known for being anti-American and pro-Pakistan. (Reminds me of Shafiullah, the volleyball jihadist.)

Gul stayed up all night before his rampage, praying and cleaning his gun. (Reminds me of Maj. Hassan, the Fort Hood jihadist.)

During the melee, Gul shouted to Afghan security forces from a window: "Good Muslims—please stay away! Muslims don't come close or you will be killed!" (Reminds me of the Mumbai jihadists.)

In a hallway outside the carnage, Gul dipped his finger in blood and wrote on the wall in the Afghan tongue of Dari: "Allah is one," and "Allah in your name."

One witness apparently heard the gunshots as Gul committed suicide, then a voice moaning, "Allah, Allah," then silence.

Silence is right. According to our Inspector Clouseaus with wings, money problems and other stress must have been the murder motive. Some 1,500 Afghans turned out to pay respects to Gul at his funeral. No doubt they all shared similar financial setbacks.

Shame. Jihad is the secret these investigators are keeping, but only from themselves. It drives the murder spree against infidel troops. It also is part of the culture that renders U.S. utopian plans to train an Afghan army and police force dead on arrival. Not saying so doesn't make it go away. It just wastes the lives of our people. Does anyone care?

Nonchalance about U.S. Marines' safety is appalling

3/9/12

This week, a bombshell wrapped in an SOS landed on the desk of the inspector general at the Pentagon.

The SOS was a legal complaint from attorney Mark L. Waple. It called for an investigation into whether the Marine Corps was attempting to drive Waple's client, Marine Corps Maj. Fred C. Galvin, from the service through what is known as a "board of inquiry" in retribution for Galvin's legally protected communications with Congress regarding an incident last year in Afghanistan. Such a reprisal, Waple charges, would violate the Military Whistleblower Protection Act.

Even as I was preparing to file this column, the board of inquiry concluded there was no cause to force Galvin, whose 24-year career includes a Bronze Star and five combat tours in Iraq and Afghanistan, from the Marine Corps.

But that still leaves the bombshell.

I'm referring to the letters, sworn statements, reports, even a certified polygraph test result, that sit inside the complaint still at the Pentagon. The documents attest to the incident Galvin witnessed and communicated to members of Congress, among them Republican Reps. Walter Jones of North Carolina and Allen West of Florida.

Here's the short version: One day last June in Sangin, where Galvin was serving as operations officer of the 3rd Reconnaissance Battalion, a request for supporting fire came in from Marines in B Company.

Afghanistan and the Doomed 'Democracy' Project

On patrol in enemy-controlled territory, a group of these Marines had become "enveloped" in a complex ambush by 30 to 40 enemy soldiers. Soon the enemy was firing from an array of positions — rocket-propelled grenades, machine guns, AK-47s — some as close as 34 meters from the Marines, a distance not much longer than a basketball court. The company commander requested supporting fire.

Fifty minutes passed before the battalion commander, Lt. Col. Travis Homiak, complied with the request. Were civilians in the area? No. Further discussion turned on whether to use small, precision munitions, such as a Hellfire laser-guided missile with a 10-pound shape charge — Galvin's strong recommendation — or to use something much larger, which, in Homiak's stated opinion, would drive away enemy forces. With Marines well within "danger close" proximity to enemy forces, Galvin, a former Marine instructor in fire support for raids and reconnaissance, was concerned that the probability of injury or even fratricide from a large bomb was too high.

Even so, the battalion commander chose to drop a whopping 500-pound bomb on the enemy position near the Marines. Probably the only reason I am not now describing a scene of carnage is that, unbeknownst to either Galvin or Homiak, there was a canal that shielded the Marines from the worst effects of the colossal explosion. Meanwhile, the enemy had fled to another position to continue fighting.

Another request for fire support came in. Galvin again recommended precision munitions, given the proximity of Marines to the enemy, and Homiak again went for the biggest available bomb — this time, 200-pound warheads. Finally, although the firefight would continue for a total of four hours, Homiak denied any further fire support. Thankfully, all the Marines came home.

I have to interrupt the narrative here to flag Homiak as a counterinsurgency (COIN) enthusiast, a true believer in fighting to win Afghan hearts and minds through what, in a Department of Defense news report, Homiak discusses as "the concept of restraint" and "being nice to people."

But maybe not so nice to Marines. In conversation with Galvin the following day, Homiak justified what a layman might see, first, as a reckless use of munitions too close to Marines under fire, and, second, as a reckless denial of munitions to Marines under fire. According to the documents filed with the Pentagon inspector general, which include the corroborating results of a polygraph test Galvin took, Homiak told Galvin he "was willing to sacrifice the lives of these Marines for the greater good."

Homiak even repeated this appalling statement, a point additionally supported by Galvin's polygraph results.

Homiak went on to say that if Galvin "had 'a crisis of conscience' with supporting or executing Homiak's philosophy ... Homiak had to know."

Willing to sacrifice Marines for the greater good?

Did I mention that Galvin, unable to accept Homiak's COIN-baked philosophy, requested to be relieved of duty? That Homiak subsequently gave Galvin two adverse fitness reports? That Galvin has seemingly exhausted all avenues in his quest for an investigation into this incident? Galvin triumphed in the board of inquiry examination into his fitness to remain a Marine, but a thorough, deliberate investigation, certainly by Congress, into this incident and the COIN mindset it exemplifies is urgently required.

Because the bombshell is still ticking.

We'll hear an Afghan 'thanks!' when Hell freezes over

3/16/12

I am looking at a heartwarming 1945 photograph of a Canadian-liberated town in the Netherlands, all joyous spontaneity and relief as townspeople (two wearing wooden shoes) celebrate their liberation from Nazi Germany. Nearly 70 years later, this snapshot in time is relevant to events currently swirling around a tragic, aberrational incident in which a U.S. Army staff sergeant apparently walked off base and killed 16 Afghan civilians.

Nazi liberation was a costly liberation. Allied air raids on German-occupied Rotterdam alone killed 884 citizens and wounded 631. Such losses were negligible next to the millions of civilian casualties during World War II caused by Axis and Allies alike.

How, I have long wondered, might Presidents Bush and Obama and all of our top military commanders explain the welcome that Allied forces received across Europe in 1945 despite the massive suffering the Allies, too, inflicted on unarmed citizens? The answer is that the liberated peoples rejected the Nazis and their ideology. So why doesn't the same logic work on 'liberated' Afghans? Maybe they don't reject either the Taliban or their ideology. Maybe there's just way too much overlap on both counts.

Nah, say our counterinsurgency (COIN) strategists. *The problem is too many civilian casualties.* So goes the COIN mantra of at least the past three years in Afghanistan, since Gen. Stanley McChrystal came on the scene openly promoting 'population protection' over 'force protection.' Indeed, more than anything else, the war in Afghanistan may be seen as a war on civilian casualties in which the ultimate prize is the 'trust' of the Afghan people. Or, as current military commander Gen. John R. Allen likes to

Afghanistan and the Doomed 'Democracy' Project

say, 'the noble Afghan people.'

A week ago, the website of international forces in Afghanistan (ISAF) ran a report on the third Civilian Casualty Conference, where new figures on civilian casualties were unveiled. 'In the last four months, insurgents have caused 93 percent, or 958 civilian casualties,' Lt. Gen. Adrian Bradshaw, ISAF deputy commander, reported, explaining that the majority are inflicted by roadside bombs (IEDs). 'In the same period of time, 7 percent, or 72 civilian casualties, regrettably were caused by ISAF forces,' he said.

The report went on to quote Bradshaw as saying 'that 72 casualties are too many and that ISAF is committed to bring that number down to zero.' Ninety-three percent of the civilian casualties are caused by Taliban and other jihadist forces, and 7 percent are caused by pro-government forces. If COIN theory were correct, numbers like these should produce scenes of relief and joy as seen in my 1945 photo from Holland.

But COIN theory is, to say the least, not correct. It runs on a rigid adherence to an ideology and not on an appraisal of the facts. In the service of this ideology, the alleged actions of a staff sergeant have been greatly exaggerated in their overall relevance to this war waged by nations to serve as a crutch for COIN. Tragic as they are, the apparent murders of 16 Afghans—a figure that wouldn't move the needle a notch in the Taliban tally of death—now become another excuse to explain why COIN isn't working, why the Afghan people—sorry, 'the noble Afghan people'—aren't being won over, hearts and minds.

So wed to COIN are our leaders, military and civilian, that they eschew logic, preferring to enter into the Islamic maelstrom of aggrievement and apology, promising to do better. Good 'dhimmi' that we are (no one said even a cross word about six American murders by Afghan forces last month), we have just about promised to take this soldier, brain injury or not, too many COIN combat tours or not, and string him up to sate the bloodlust of the noble Afghan people—anything to quell Islamic rage. Naturally, we will continue to send our men on ever more IED death marches (foot patrols), happily. We do it all for the noble people of Afghanistan. Do they like us yet? No? We'll do *more*.

They call this strategy COIN and wear uniforms, but really it's psychosis and these strategists should be wearing hospital robes.

Meanwhile, if Afghans were 'with us,' if they were actually against the true butchers, the Taliban, if they were concerned about which side had innocent blood on its hands and which side did everything humanly possible to prevent such violence, even at the expense of its own people, Afghan hearts and minds would have been 'won' long ago.

But that will never be. In fact, guess what happens if ISAF reaches its goal of zero civilian casualties? Nothing.

Benghazi

Three Men and a Couch

9/12/12

From a joint statement by Sens. Graham, Lieberman and McCain on the burning of the US consulate in Benghazi and murders of the US ambassador and three staffers.

> "Yesterday's attack is a tragic and terrible reminder that – despite the **hopes** of the Arab Spring – the forces of violent extremism in the Middle East are far from defeated, and that the revolutions inspired by millions of people who **dream** of freedom and democracy can still be hijacked by small groups of violent extremists who are eager to kill to advance their evil ideology."

The main "hope" on the part of Tweedles Dum, Dum and Dee is that there in fact exist "millions of people" who dream of freedom -- not "huriyya" -- and democracy -- not sharia -- in the Middle East.

Alas, there is no evidence of the senators' dream-millions of Muslims with a deep and abiding connection to the values and principles the senators espouse. That's because such Judeo-Christian-derived values and principles are at odds with the Islamic culture that has, quite naturally, set the perspectives and formed the core of the societies across this region. (Except, of course, for the Jewish state of Israel.) The senators could examine 14 centuries of violent jihad that brutally converted northern Africa, large sections of Europe and the Near East into Islamic servitude to understand why the basis of such values and principles disappeared. They could, more conveniently. simply review recent Pew polling that reveals the results of the centuries of relentless Islamization: large majorities in Islamic countries actually like Islamic law ("strict sharia") and hope for the return of the caliphate. But the

Three Amigos prefer to dream on.

> "Despite this horrific attack, **we cannot give in** to the temptation to believe that our support for the democratic aspirations of people in Libya, Egypt, and elsewhere in the broader Middle East is **naive or mistaken**.
>
> **We cannot resign ourselves** to the false belief that the **Arab Spring is doomed** to be defined not by the desire for democracy and freedom that has inspired millions of people to peaceful action, but by the dark fanaticism of terrorists."

Notice it's all about them. Evidence of their error in supporting al Qaeda-Muslim-Brother-generic-jihad revolutions across the Arab world is penetrating the collective dome, but they are trying to resist with all of their might. What we are looking at is textbook, Psych 101 *denial*.

The pivot:

> "To follow this misguided path" -- [following evidence is "misguided"!] --"would not only be a victory for the extremists and their associates, but a betrayal of everything for which Chris Stevens and his colleagues stood and gave their lives."

I.e., if we face facts, the terrorists win.

> **In short, it would be a betrayal of our own best ideals** as Americans and our own enduring interest in using our great influence to support the overwhelming majority of people in the Middle East who want to be free from the kinds of murderers and terrorists who killed our people yesterday in Benghazi."

Translation: The facts aren't fitting our ideology, folks, so the facts must go. But fear not. Our ideology remains unscathed.

Even after deadly attack, U.S. kowtows to Islam

9/14/12

Two historic attacks on U.S. territory marked the 11th anniversary of the 9/11 attacks, and what happened? The Obama administration surrendered our constitutional principles.

The first was a "blasphemy" riot that breached the walls of the U.S. Embassy in Cairo, whereupon thugs burned the American flag and hoisted in its place the traditional black flag of Islam that flies over al-Qaida and other jihad movements.

The second was a military-style assault against the U.S. Consulate in Benghazi, Libya, believed to have been mounted by a militia known as Ansar al-Sharia ("Partisans of Islamic Law"), which formed in the U.S.-supported anti-Gadhafi revolution. Christopher Stevens, U.S. ambassador to Libya and former point man to the al-Qaida-linked revolutionaries, and three staff members were killed. Five more Americans were wounded, and the American outpost burned under another black flag of jihad.

An obscure, made-in-the-USA movie critical of Muhammad has been blamed for "causing" these attacks. In fact, it is people in Egypt and Libya who committed these two unprovoked acts of war to mark the 9/11 anniversary. The official response?

The first response actually preceded the mayhem in Cairo when the U.S. Embassy, having suspended regular business in anticipation of the planned movie protest, posted on its website on Sept. 11: "The Embassy of the United States in Cairo condemns the continuing efforts by misguided individuals to hurt the religious feelings of Muslims -- as we condemn efforts to offend believers of all religions." (As Middle East and Islamic expert Raymond Ibrahim pointed out, the embassy expressed no such solicitude for the "feelings" of a Christian on trial in Egypt for "insulting" Islam, "even as a throng of Muslims besieged the courthouse, interrupting the hearing and calling for the man's death.")

Noting the 9/11 anniversary, the embassy statement continued: "We firmly reject the actions by those who abuse the universal right of free speech to hurt the religious beliefs of others."

Here we see Uncle Sam conceding the First Amendment to safeguard the "feelings" of Muslims, and accepting the basis of Islamic laws against criticizing Islam.

In response, GOP presidential nominee Mitt Romney issued an initial statement expressing outrage over the violence and the Cairo embassy statement, which the embassy Twitter feed would underscore in both English and Arabic messages. (Both the statement and subsequent tweets have since been removed.) In the meantime, the White House disowned the embassy statement as unauthorized.

But Secretary of State Hillary Clinton echoed the embassy message to "deplore" free speech. Clinton said: "Some have sought to justify this vicious behavior as a response to inflammatory material posted on the Internet. The United States deplores any intentional effort to denigrate the religious beliefs of others. Our commitment to religious tolerance goes back to the very beginning of our nation. But let me be clear: There is never any justification for violent acts of this kind."

Actually, the nation's founding commitment is to religious "liberty." It's important to realize that Clinton supports an anti-liberty, U.N. anti-blasphemy resolution designed to curb criticism of Islam, advocating the circumvention of the First Amendment through what she calls "plain old-fashioned peer pressure and shaming." Assaults on sovereign territory, it would seem, simply go too far.

Then came details of the assault in Libya. Addressing Libya only, President Obama also inserted the government into free speech, while criticizing the violence (and taking no media questions). "While the United States rejects efforts to denigrate the religious beliefs of others," he said, "we must all unequivocally oppose the kind of senseless violence that took the lives of these public servants."

Afghan President Hamid Karzai weighed in, denouncing the "heinous act" -- the Muhammad movie! -- and calling for "efforts to prevent" its release and other restrictions on the lawful activities of its producer and pastor Terry Jones, who endorsed the movie. Karzai ignored both attacks on the United States.

Similarly, Mohamed Morsi, the Muslim Brotherhood president of Egypt (who denies that al-Qaida attacked the U.S. on 9/11, by the way), directed the Egyptian Embassy in Washington to "take legal action" against the movie's producers. Morsi doesn't seem to understand First Amendment protections; of course, neither does the Obama administration. (Maybe they will discuss a "solution" to free speech when Obama hosts Morsi at the White House this month.)

Egyptian Prime Minister Hisham Qandil asked for similar action "within the framework of international charters that criminalize acts that stir strife on the basis of race, color or religion." This is a direct appeal to hold Americans accountable to the U.N. blasphemy resolution that Hillary Clinton, along with the Islamic bloc, has championed, despite its repressive controls on free speech.

The administration response gets worse. Joint Chiefs Chairman Gen. Martin Dempsey telephoned Jones to implore him to withdraw his endorsement of the Muhammad movie to "prevent" violence in Afghanistan. Apparently, Dempsey and the administration he serves believe a movie blurb is a self-firing assault weapon, and Islamic law nullifies the First Amendment.

In a Wednesday press conference, Mitt Romney stated: "America will not tolerate attacks against our citizens and against our embassies. We'll defend also our constitutional rights of speech and assembly and religion .... We stand for the principles our Constitution protects. We encourage other nations to understand and respect the principles of our Constitution, because we recognize that these principles are the ultimate source of freedom for individuals around the world."

At least one American leader is willing to defend our country and Constitution.

Slain American's mother: Just tell me what happened

10/11/12

Pat Smith's son Sean was killed during the 9/11/12 assault on the American consulate in Benghazi that left three other Americans dead, including Ambassador Christopher Stevens. In her initial grief, Mrs. Smith describes being embraced by the Obama administration and being told by "all of them" that her son's death was caused by the video.

They promised her facts about his death; that's all she wanted. Biden, she says, was "a treasure." Panetta took her face in his hands and promised her the truth. She cried on President Obama's shoulder and "then he kind of looked off into the distance."

She has heard nothing. She sees bloody handprints in pictures of the sacked US building and wonders if they are her son's. They are still studying it, they tell her, "and the things they are telling me are outright lies."

Administration welcomed wolves into the sheepfold

10/12/12

Imagine, pre-9/11/12, that you were responsible for arranging the defense of the U.S. Consulate in Benghazi, Libya. Would you have considered American interests and personnel best protected by bringing in a local security outfit called the February 17 Martyrs Brigade?

The question has yet to come up in House hearings, but I think it holds the key to the Obama administration's betrayal of the American people in "Benghazi-gate." To an American with common sense not subverted by advanced degrees, the thought of putting Islamic "martyrs" in charge of American "infidels" in Benghazi -- which, fun fact, literally means "city of holy warriors" -- would trigger the inevitable "heck, no." And that's without even knowing what is significant about Feb. 17.

But I'm talking about Washington, D.C. Here, placing the lives of Americans in the hands of a thug-army linked to multiple atrocities and drawn from jihad-epicentral eastern Libya disturbs no collective brain wave. No matter that Benghazi and nearby Derna sent more men, per capita, to Iraq to kill Americans than anywhere else in the world. As far as the Obama administration is concerned, putting local boys in barracks inside the consulate compound was a great idea. Why not? President Obama's ambassador, the late Christopher Stevens, was, as they say, "reaching out" across the jihad spectrum on official business.

Meanwhile, Ansar al Sharia ("Supporters of Islamic Law"), the al-Qaida-linked militia believed to have led the consulate assault in September, is a spinoff of the February 17 Martyrs Brigade, but that didn't scratch the lacquered political surface, either. And even as reports remind us of ties among February 17 Martyrs Brigade leadership, the Muslim Brotherhood and the web of jihad-poison spun by Qatar's Yusuf al-Qaradawi and Libya's Ali al-Salabi -- the latter having been tapped by the Qatari dictatorship to distribute $2 billion to Libyan "rebels" -- the focal point remains elsewhere.

Partly, that's because the breathtaking lies the Obama administration has told us post-9/11/12 distract our attention from the disastrous policy previously in place. Plus, there remains a lingering confusion over good guys and bad guys. After all, Uncle Sam isn't supposed to support bad guys. The Obama administration, however, threw in Uncle Sam's lot with bad guys -- the "rebels," the "martyrs," the Muslim Brothers, the whole jihad-happy crew in Libya and the wider Middle East. Uncle Sam, more or less, crossed to the "Other Side." It is this alliance or support for "martyrs" and their sympathizers in Libya, Tunisia, Egypt and Syria that is the betrayal from which Benghazi-gate rises, particularly as our veterans cemeteries and hospitals are filled with casualties caused by such "martyrs."

Whether, as The Daily Beast reported, the February 17 Martyrs Brigade may have been ordered by a pro-al-Qaida Libyan politician to "stand down" for the attack remains to be verified. Meanwhile, the State Department reminds us not to forget the service of two brigade members who were beaten and two who were shot defending the compound. "But there were some bad apples in there as well," one intelligence source told The Daily Beast.

How could there not be? And here is where the significance of Feb. 17 comes in.

John Rosenthal, an independent journalist based in Europe, wrote early on that the Libyan rebellion wasn't led only by al-Qaida commanders. This anti-Gadhafi movement was symbolically also an Islamic jihad on Western liberty itself. We know this because, as Rosenthal reported, the "Day of Rage" called for Feb. 17, 2011, to kick off the Libyan civil war was the fifth anniversary of another assault on the West, also in Benghazi.

Following Friday prayers on Feb. 17, 2006, thousands of Benghazians attacked the Italian Consulate to punish the temerity of an Italian minister, Roberto Calderoli, who several days earlier had publicly defended free speech in the West. The world was then experiencing another cycle of Islamic violence, this one orchestrated to punish a tiny Danish newspaper for publishing a sheet of Muhammad cartoons and, in turn, Denmark itself for refusing to punish the journalist-transgressors of Islamic law, which outlaws any critiques and all depictions of Muhammad.

Calderoli didn't merely defend free speech. During his TV interview, he dramatically unbuttoned his shirt to reveal a T-shirt featuring a cartoon of Muhammad. Referring to Islamic rioters worldwide, he added: "When they recognize our rights, I'll take off this shirt." He was forced to resign from his post the next day, a sacrifice on the altar of Shariah (Islamic law) by Prime Minister Silvio Berlusconi. It wasn't enough.

"We feared for our lives," the wife of the Italian consul later told the Italian newspaper Corriere della Sera, describing the attack in which the consulate was set on fire. All personnel were safely evacuated. Libyan police used tear gas to try to disperse the rioters, later opening fire and killing 11 attackers.

These are the "martyrs" who serve as role models for the security team that was defending the U.S. Consulate. Symbolically, they figure into the wider war in Libya, which is often called the February 17 Revolution. With this in mind, it becomes clear that the Islamic war on free speech, the basis of our liberty, was an inspiration of "regime change" in Libya. And we supported it.

That's the real scandal.

About the gate to the compound in Benghazi

10/15/12

Just read the State Department blow-by-blow briefing, or "tick-tock," on events in Benghazi given reporters on background on October 9. As senior official #2 summed up the attack in his concluding remarks:

> The lethality and the number of armed people is unprecedented. There had been no attacks like that anywhere in Libya – Tripoli, Benghazi, or elsewhere – in the time that we had been there. And so it is unprecedented. In fact, it would be very, very hard to find a precedent for an attack like that in recent diplomatic history.

Aside from harrowing descriptions of terror and entrapment, loss and courage, what stands out is the depiction of a quiet night suddenly broken by massive armed attack. No Youtube protest Gone Wrong, in other words as the Obama White House has continually insisted, lying in such a way as to advance the world Islamic movement against free speech about Islam, whose leaders seek laws against "religious blasphemy." (Working with the Islamic bloc in the so-called Istanbul Process, the Obama administration has pledged America's support for

UN Resolution 16/18 against such "blasphemy," while SecState Hillary Clinton has called for "some old fashioned techniues of peer pressure and shaming" to enforce it at home. This, of course, blatantly defies the First Amendment.)

Senior official #1:

> Okay. The Ambassador has arrived in Benghazi on the 10th of September. He does meetings both on the compound and off the compound on that day, spends the night.

Whom did the Ambassador meet with? Given Stevens' penchant for "outreach" across the jihad spectrum -- the Obama administration's policy throughout the Arab ("Spring") World -- this is a highly relevant question.

> The next day is 9/11. He has all his – because it is 9/11, out of prudence, he has all his meetings on the compound. He receives a succession of visitors during the day.
>
> About 7:30 in the evening, he has his last meeting. It is with a Turkish diplomat. And at – when the meeting is over, at 8:30 – he has all these meetings, by the way, in what I call Building C – when the meeting is over, he escorts the Turkish diplomat to the main gate. There is an agent there with them. They say goodbye. They're out in a street in front of the compound. **Everything is calm at 8:30 p.m. There's nothing unusual. There has been nothing unusual during the day at all outside.**

So who created the Youtube Lie which every top Obama administration official including the president parroted for days, weeks?

> After he sees the Turkish diplomat off, the Ambassador returns to Building C, where the information management officer – his name is Sean Smith, and who is one of the victims – the information management officer – I'll just call him Sean from now on, on this call – and four other – four Diplomatic Security agents are all at Building C. One Diplomatic Security agent is in the TOC, the Tactical Operations Center. All of these agents have their side arms.
>
> A few minutes later – we're talking about 9 o'clock at night – the Ambassador retires to his room, the others are still at Building C, and the one agent in the TOC. **At 9:40 p.m., the agent in the TOC and the agents in Building C hear loud noises coming from the front gate. They also hear gunfire and an explosion. The agent in the TOC looks at his cameras – these are cameras that have pictures of the perimeter – and the camera on the**

main gate reveals a large number of people – a large number of men, armed men, flowing into the compound. One special agent immediately goes to get the Ambassador in his bedroom and gets Sean, and the three of them enter the safe haven inside the building.

I wonder how armed men just "flowed" into the compound? Members of the February 17th Martyrs Brigade -- now sanitized as the "Feb. 17 Brigade" -- occupied the small barracks by the compound gate. Did the attackers break down the gate undetected? Did the "explosion" the US official heard open the gate? Could the attackers have been allowed in? Just wondering. "Bad apples," we have been told, belonged to this local militia hired to protect the compound. (And here's why -- Uncle Sam joined the jihad in Libya, but his fellow jihadis don't like him anyway.) Does video exist of the gate?

The Jihad and Christopher Stevens, part 1

10/18/12

In analyzing the Benghazi scandal, it is crucial to highlight not only the dangers of relying on jihadist armed gangs for American security in Benghazi, but also the betrayal of American principle undertaken by the Obama administration in setting such a policy in place. The fact is, relying on "local militias" was not some stop-gap practice; it was official US *policy*. This begins to tell us why "Benghazi-gate" is so much more than an inquiry into a calamitous security break-down, and the ghastly chain of lies the administration told thereafter.

On March 28, 2012, Regional Security Officer Eric Nordstrom sent a cable from Libya requesting more security. His request was denied. This cable, however, is evidence of more than State's negligence in failing to address a dangerous security situation that would be exploited by al Qaeda affiliates on September 11, 2012. In the cable, Nordstrom makes note of the fact that "rebuilding and expanding post's PSA Local Guard Force" was one of his "core objectives." Further: "As recommended by the Department, post is developing plans to transition our security staffing ... to [a model] that incorporates more locally-based and non-emergency assets."

Naturally. these "plans" weren't working. Hence, Nordstrom's request for more American security. And hence the denial from State for reasons, Nordstrom recently told Congress, that came down to the fact "there was going to be too much political cost." But what politics drove such a recommendation? Here is where the entire Libyan debacle, the debacle of "Arab Spring" -- Arab Jihad -- comes into play. It is time to reckon with the fact that despite the grand talk of democracy and human rights, President Obama ordered Uncle Sam to join that jihad in 2011, precipitously pulling support from a long-standing ally in Egypt and a post-9/11 ally in Libya to empower the vanguards of liberty-supressing Islam, extending the reach and dominion of a hostile, totalitarian system.

Obama was hardly alone, drawing support from left-wing Democrats, the UN crowd, media, the GOP establishment, George W. Bush, "neocons," all of whom boosted this same "Arab Spring," often for different reasons. One of the great champions of what we should start thinking of as the jihad outreach such a policy necessarily entails was the late Ambassador Christopher Stevens, and long before he arrived in Benghazi during "Arab Spring."

Thanks to Wikileaks, we have a series of US Libyan embassy cables, starting in December 2007, which document what became rather an abiding interest in two repatriated ex-Guatanamo detainees, Ben Qumu Abu Sufian Ahmed Hamouda and Muhammad Abdallah Mansur al-Rimi -- ben Qumu in particular.

For the next six months or so, cables, some by Stevens, some by other personnel, track embassy access to these detainees, their condition, and their welfare in their Libyan detention. One cable (not by Stevens) details an extended family visit to Qumu. His relatives, the cable reports, "were able to bring some food, clothes, personal hygiene items and reading materials to him. Tarnish [a security officer] described [Qumu's] physical condition and spirits as `very good' and indicated that security officials at the facility ... had allowed the family to stay with him for a few extra hours in light of the impending New Year's holiday."

Why the solicitude for a high-ranking al Qaeda member with connections to a terror financier? Ben Qumu, a native of Derna in eastern Libya, rose in the al Qaeda ranks after training at an al-Qaeda camp in Afghanistan in the 1990s, reportedly serving under bin Laden in Sudan after which he fought with the Talban. He was captured in 2002 along the Af-Pak border and sent to Gitmo before being repatriated to Libyan custody in 2007. He would be released in a Libyan government reconciliation program in 2010.

Another cable, this one by Stevens on June 6, 12, 2008, assesses the attitudes of ben Qumu and al-Rimi toward their new prison, Abu Salim, compared to their old facility, known as ESO. They both "expressed a desire to return from Abu Salim prison to the ESO facility," Stevens wrote.

Why did Stevens care? Why was the US Embassy so concerned? Something else I wonder is who among the diplomats who served with Stevens has made the connection between Stevens' interest in ben Qumu in 2008 and news reports identifying ben Qumu as the leader of the terrorist attack in which Stevens and three other Americans were murdered.

This US government report on al Qaeda infiltration of Libyan militias further identifies Qumu as a leader of Ansar al Sharia, the group believed to have led the consulate assault.

It's a stunning, sickening circle, but it is also the noxious metaphor for the deadly course of Uncle Sam's outreach to jihad.

To be cont'd.

The Jihad and Christopher Stevens, part 2

10/18/12

To attempt to understand Christopher Stevens' long-standing interest in ben Qumu, the al Qaeda terrorist suspected of leading the Benghazi attack on September 11, 2012 in which Stevens and three other Americans were murdered, we must seek context in more of Stevens' cables. (Thanks be to Wikileaks.)

On February 15, 2008, Stevens wrote a lengthy cable titled EXTREMISM IN EASTERN LIBYA. On one level it confirms that Stevens was NOT some liberal naif when he docked in Benghazi in April 2011 to serve as point man to the so-called "rebels"-- that cutesy bluff of a name which disguises a movement better described by Clare M. Lopez as "individuals and groups that were, at a minimum, allied ideologically with Al Qaeda." No real stretch to simplify and call Stevens the Obama administration's point man to al Qaeda.

This early 2008 cable recounts the analysis of a US-Libyan dual national who regularly visited eastern Libya concerning the "social, political and economic factors that have contributed to and faciliated participation by a disproportionately large number of eastern Libya's native sons in `martyrdom acts' and other insurgency operations in eastern Libya."

Notice what's missing from the list -- Islam. It's not completely missing, of course. Stevens makes note of mosques and "radical" imams who use "phraseology urging worshippers to support jihad in Iraq and elsewhere through direct participation and financial contributions." Islam itself, however, never is discussed as the doctrinal motivation for jihad "martyrdom." The following line sums up how it is that the centrality of jihad in Islam is circumvented: "Citing conversations with relatives, [redacted] said the unemployed, disenfranchised young men of eastern Libya had `nothing to lose' and are therefore `willing for sacrifice themselves' for something greater than themselves by **engaging in extremism in the name of religion."**

The cable also opens a window onto the ordinariness of this hate-filled pathology among the people of the region. Stevens' source describes a large dinner he attended in Derna -- hometown of ben Qumu and hotbed, bar none, of jihad-in-Iraq recruitment -- hosted by a family friend. "Conversation among the mostly middle-aged male group of guests focused on news that two young men from Derna had recently killed themseles in suicide operations in Iraq. **Dinner guests offered a mix of `condolences and congratulations.'** " The source "said he was struck by the level [of] sentiment against Coalition forces in Iraq, and by the **obvious pride** the dinner guests took in the fact that two of their native sons had `struck a blow' against `occupying Crusader forces in Iraq.' He emphasized that the dinner was one of the relatively few occasions in Libya in which he felt uncomfortable by dint of having US citizenship."

Stevens later being point man to the "rebels" would mean being point man also to these dinner guests, still swelled with pride over maiming and killing American troops in Iraq. Such is the poisonous essence of "Arab Spring."

The flow of eastern Libyan "pride" doesn't stop. The cable notes: "During [source's] last visit to the east in December [2007], relatives and friends cited media reports to the effect that Libyans, most of them from Derna and points east, comprised the second largest cohort of foreign fighters identified in documents seized during last September's Objective Massey operation on the Syria-Iraq border. [Redacted] noted that a majority of those in Derna who raised the issue appeared to take pride in the fact that their small cty city had contributed disproportionately to the jihad against coalition forces in Iraq."

The cable continues, adding more fascinating if also sickening detail. Among other "martyrdom" factors, Stevens discusses "the influence of Libyan fighters who had fought in Afghanistan and now recruited young eastern Libyans for operations in Iraq, the influence of Arabic-language satellite televison broadcasts" -- al-Jazeera, the Qatari dictatorship's greatest weapon -- and the difficulties GOL (Government of Libya) had controlling the mosques in this region.

> Part of the difficulty for GOL authorities in controlling eastern mosques is that the most zealous imams tend to preach in small suburban and rural mosques. He [source] mentioned the almost **festive atmosphere** of one trip, when relatives gathered to travel to a remote rural mosque to hear a `controversial' imam's sermon.

In his final "comment" section, Stevens writes: "The most troubling and **difficult** aspect of [redacted's] account is the pride that many eastern

Libyans ... appear to take in the role their native sons have played in the insurgency in Iraq."

"Troubling," yes (putting it way mildly). But what did Stevens mean by "difficult"?

Two months later on April 10, 2008, Stevens wrote another cable detailing the Libyan government's rebuff over an idea proposing "US-Libyan cooperation on counter-ideological or `soft power' efforts to blunt the appeal of the extremist message in eastern Libya, arguing such efforts would be counterproductive."

On June 12, 2008, Stevens wrote a cable noted in Part 1 about the incarceration conditions of two ex-Gitmo detainees, including that of al Qaeda's ben Qumu, a son of Derna currently leading Ansar al Sharia.

The previous week, on June 2, 2008, Stevens wrote a cable that seems particularly significant. It stands out first for its florid title: DIE HARD IN DERNA.

From the "Summary":

> Frustration at the inability of eastern Libyans to effectively challenge Qadhafi's regime, together with a concerted ideological campaign by returned Libyan fighters from earlier conflicts, have played important roles in Derna's development as a wellspring of Libyan foreign fighters in Iraq. ... One Libyan interlocutor likened young men in Derna to Bruce Willis' character in the action picture "Die Hard", who stubbornly refused to die quietly. For them, resistance against coalition forces in Iraq is an important act of 'jihad' and a last act of defiance

Resistance, huh? Didn't Stevens forget his quotation marks? Or is that how US diplomats think of acts of war against American troops who, if memory serves, were at that moment still attempting to stamp out al Qaeda in Iraq, prevent sectarian civil war from breaking out and "nation-build," all at the same time.

Also worth noting here is that this "frustration" about eastern Libyans' inability to challenge Qaddafi regime is not mentioned in the February 2008 cable. In the earlier cable, unemployment, disenfranchisement, etc., are the main political factors cited (as opposed to mosque/jihadist/"pride" factors) for inciting the high flow of eastern Libyan "martyrs" to Iraq. Another factor was opposition to "U.S. military presence in Iraq or any other Muslim country." There is nothing stipulating that frustration over Qaddafi's regime per se was inspiring jihad to Iraq.

Stevens goes on to discuss a trip made to Benghazi in early May 2008 during which his party made a side trip to Derna to visit the "old fort." Just a fun little tourist excursion into the heart of jihad, it seems.

> While asking directions to the city's old fort, P/E Chief met local resident [Redacted] who happened to hail from the same tribe as P/E Chief's driver/guide. In typical fashion, [Redacted] promptly dropped what he was doing and spent and spent the next several hours accompanying us around Derna, a town of some 50,000 people.

That famous Derna hospitality. Or is it possible, given that the driver was tribal-kin with the source, this was a pre-planned meeting?

> P/E/ Chief visited the Baab al-Shiha neighborhood, the site of the town's old fort (now all but gone) and the district from which a large number of the Libyan foreign fighters identified in documents captured during September's Objective Massey operation in Iraq had hailed.

Tourism or intelligence gathering? It would be interesting to ask the P/E Chief. Stevens goes on to describe the many mosques tucked away in the 'hood and also a palpable unfriendliness of the people. Then on to lunch in Derna, described in a section titled:

PERCEIVED U.S. SUPPORT FOR QADHAFI FUELS DESIRE TO FIGHT IN IRAQ.

> Over lunch at a popular restaurant just off the waterfront, [Redacted] and his business partner (who declined to give his name) discussed at length the local political-economic, cultural and religious scene, noting that it was "well-known" that a large number of suicide bombers (invariably described as "martyrs") and foreign fighters in Iraq hailed from Derna, a fact in which the town "takes great pride". [Redacted] stressed the importance of the link between the domestic political situation in Libya and the flow of foreign fighters in Iraq.

I don't know how any American just sits there listening to a discussion of the "great pride" Derna men take in blowing up American men, who if they aren't dead now are fated to live out their lives without limbs, genitals or pieces of their brains. Meanwhile, is it just me, or has a strong line of disinformation just entered the cable? Suddenly and explicitly, it's not Islamic culture, it's not the "pride" of Benghazi, it's not the call of jihad against the wider West, it's not young Muslim men brainwashed by al Jazeera and incited to jihad by their imams, it's US support of Qaddafi that is responsible for the flow of men to fight the US in Iraq.

But.

> There was a strong perception, [source] said, that the U.S. had decided in the wake of Qadhafi's decision to abandon WMD aspirations and renounce terrorism to support the regime to secure counter-terrorism cooperation and ensure continued oil and natural gas production.

The source's perception was correct.

> Many easterners feared the U.S. would not allow Qadhafi's regime to fall and therefore viewed direct confrontation with the GOL in the near-term as a fool's errand.

Wasn't that a very good thing? Stevens continues his account:

> At the same time, sending young Libyans to fight in Iraq was "an embarrassment" to Qadhafi. **Fighting against U.S. and coalition forces in Iraq represented a way for frustrated young radicals to strike a blow against both Qadhafi and against his perceived American backers.**

The wheels turn ...if we could just get rid of Qadhafi....then the fine young men of Derna would ... what?

I wonder: Could Derna 2008 be the real birthplace of "Arab Spring"?

To be continued.

Clinton sidesteps blame even as she accepts it

10/19/12

Honestly, did the buck really stop with Secretary of State Hillary Clinton on Benghazi-gate, or did the buck just stop?

Here's what Clinton said: "I take responsibility. I'm in charge of the State Department's 60,000-plus people all over the world, 275 posts. The president and the vice president wouldn't be knowledgeable about specific decisions that are made by security professionals. They're the ones who weigh all of the threats and the risks and the needs and make a considered decision."

Stop. Clinton's taken responsibility, she's in charge -- and then she declares that "security professionals" make the decisions? Not only is this a non sequitur, it's nonsense. One thing Americans learned from recent House hearings about the Sept. 11 orchestrated terrorist attack on the U.S. Consulate in Libya -- which killed four Americans and which President Barack Obama insisted for two weeks was sparked by a YouTube video -- is that the security professional in question, Eric Nordstrom, asked Clinton's State Department for more security and was denied.

Clinton went on to say an internal investigation was under way. And who is leading the investigation? Former Ambassador Thomas Pickering, a noted career diplomat. Part of what he's noted for, however, is sitting on boards of two pro-Tehran groups, the American Iranian Council and the National Iranian American Council, and for meeting with Hamas and promoting negotiations with the Taliban. Perhaps not the most "responsible" choice.

Then again, is "responsibility" Clinton's goal? "What I want to avoid is some kind of political 'gotcha' or blame game," she said. Translation: Taking "responsibility" -- an empty phrase without resigning -- avoids the "blame game" and eliminates the need to air the facts. She continued: "I know that we're very close to an election. I want to just take a step back here and say from my own experience, we are at our best as Americans when we pull together." Translation: I know we're very close to an election, so, as good Americans, shut up already about Benghazi.

The secretary of state took to the airwaves, where CBS brought up U.N. Ambassador Susan Rice's five appearances on Sunday talk shows on Sept. 16 to beat the drum that the Benghazi assault began as a "spontaneous protest" over a YouTube video that "spun from there into something much, much more violent." It is now part of the established record that there was no protest outside the consulate in Benghazi, and the U.S. government knew it from the start.

CBS News correspondent Margaret Brennan asked Clinton if she approved the message Rice delivered that day.

"I think she very clearly said, 'Here's what we know now, but this is going to change,'" Clinton said, which is not at all what Rice said. "This is what we have at present, but it will evolve -- and the intelligence community has said the same thing." Is that taking responsibility? CBS reported: "Clinton said she did not speak to Rice prior to her Sunday talk show appearances, but added that 'everyone had the same information.'"

Not everyone. The State Department knew right away that 9/11/12 was a quiet day and night in Benghazi until the attack began at 9:40 p.m. But there was another point to make. The secretary of state said: "I have to say I know there's been a lot of attention paid to who said what, but I think what happened is more important."

What was that again? "I have to say I know there's been a lot of attention paid to who said what" -- who said what lies, to be specific -- "but I think what happened is more important." No doubt Bill's hat is off to the little woman -- unless he is the phrase crafter himself!

Clinton also cautioned against making premature assumptions about the security situation at Benghazi as the investigation continues. "I don't want us to reach any conclusions about what we did or didn't do without the full context."

Wait, I thought she already took "responsibility"!

"I understand why people want to ask questions, but I just caution that we need to look at everything, and everything needs to be explained at the same time," Clinton said.

Translation: after the election.

Meanwhile, Clinton said: "I'm not going to get into the blame game."

Such a declaration is always a preface to getting into the blame game. She continued: "I think intelligence is very hard to do, and what we're going to find out as we do this accountability review and we get what will be the best possible chronology, that will be attached to what we knew when, which takes time. I understand the, you know, the anxiety and the desire to try to get answers. Nobody wants to get answers more than I do."

What was that again? "I think intelligence is very hard to do ..."

Intelligence. It's their fault. And we thought Hillary went noble on us.

Meet Wissam bin Hamid, Uncle Sam's jihadist security officer

10/24/12

About that Libya Shield Brigade which 1) fought under the black flag of al Qaeda during the February 17 Revolution, and 2) escorted the eight US Marines who arrived from Tripoli to aid the Benghazi consulate under attack on the night of 9/11/12.

Two Libya Shield Brigade leaders met with US diplomat(s) on September 9, according to a US embassy cable drafted by David C. McFarland, signed by Christopher Stevens and dispatched on September 11. (It was posted online by the House Oversight Committee.) This cable was first discussed in the Daily Beast on October 8 in a story recounting the fact that generic militia leaders had threatened to pull security from US interests in Benghazi, but it contains some interesting details not previously noted.

Here is the cable's Item 4 in toto:

> Militia commanders discuss Muslim Brotherhood, Jibril, their political aspirations, the economy, and security: In a September 9 meeting, local area militia commanders **Wissam bin Ahmed (Commander, Libya Shield 1)** and Muhammad al-Gharabi (Commander, Rafa' al-Sahti Brigade, Libya Shield 2) discussed the **very fluid relationships and blurry lines they say define**

membership in Benghazi-based brigades under the February 17, Libya Shield, and SSC umbrellas. They themselves were members of multiple brigades, they said. They debated -- hotly and without resolution -- about which brigades supported or opposed specific causes. They claimed to exercise "control" over Libyan Armed Forces Chief of Staff Yusef Mangoush who "depends" on them to secure eastern Libya. In times of crisis, Magoush has no other choice than to turn to their brigades for help, they said, as he did recently with unrest in Kufra. As part of this arrangement, Mangoush often provides the brigades direct stocks of weapons and ammunition, they said. **Al-Gharabi and bin-Ahmed support the Libyan Muslim Brotherhood's Justice and Construction Party backed candidate Minister of Electricity Awad Al Barasi for Prime Minister** and they said that. if elected, Al Barasi would appoint Fawzi Bukatif, Commander of the February 17 Brigade, as Minister of Defense. Bukatif's appointment would open the MOD and other security ministries and offices to plum-appointments for his most favored brigade commanders -- giving February 17 and Libya Shield tacit control of the armed forces. **They criticized the USG for "supporting" National Forces Alliance (NFA) leader and Prime Mininster Candidate Mahmoud Jibril. If Jibril wom, they said, they would not continue to guarantee security in Benghazi, a crtical function they asserted they were currently providing.** Growing problem with security would discourage foreign investment and led [sic] to persistent stagnation in eastern Libya, but the US could play a role by "pressuring" American business to invest in Benghazi.

We know from John Rosenthal's original story that Libya Shield fought under black flag of al Qaeda. Its leader Wissam bin Ahmed -- I've seen Libya Shield's commander spelled "bin Hamid"; seems to be the same guy UPDATE: An authoritative source confirms that Libya Shield commander "bin Hamid" and "bin Ahmed" are one and the same -- it bears repeating, is a supporter of rule by sharia.

Rosenthal writes:

> Moreover, according to Arabic-language Islamist websites, already in October 2011 – just days after the killing of Moammar al-Gadhafi – **Libya Shield commander Wisam bin Hamid issued a declaration stating that "The Islamic shariah is a red line, we will not cede one rule of it, and Islam is the only law-giver and not [merely] the foundation [of the law]."**
>
> Arabic sources report that bin Hamid commanded the rebel forces that besieged Gadhafi's hometown of Sirte and ultimately

captured and killed him. Per a glowing biography of bin Hamid that appeared on the jihadist forum al-Fetn.com, **he is a veteran of jihad in both Iraq and Afghanistan.**

The jihadist inclinations of bin Hamid and his Libya Shield forces are not unknown to the U.S. government. Indeed, a recent study prepared by the research division of the Library of Congress links the Libya Shield Brigade to al-Qaida and even cites speculation that **bin Hamid may be the leader of the al-Qaida network in Libya.**

This man is not only meeting with American diplomats, he is providing security for them and threatening to withdraw security at the same time. Ansar al Sharia (Supporters of Sharia) may have spearheaded the 9/11 assault on the consulate, but bin Hamid's philosophy earns him at least honorary membership. A sharia supporter, a Muslim Brotherhood supporter, seemingly a veteran of Iraq and Afghanistan -- on the OTHER side, it must be stressed -- and, according to US government research, possibly a leader of the AQ network in Libya, bin Hamid is quite a piece of work.

Why, oh why, is guarding American interests? Why was he even meeting with American diplomats? What were we doing in Benghazi? This is the result of the poisonous policy of "Arab Spring." Uncle Sam joined the jihad, and it exploded is his face.

It should be noted that news accounts make clear that the second-wave-attack on the secret annex did not occur until after Libya Shield, escorting the 8 Marines, arrived on the scene.

Ex-SEAL's father: We need to find out who gave the order not to save Benghazi

10/25/12

Charles Woods, father of fallen ex-SEAL Tyrone Woods, called in to the Lars Larsen radio show yesterday to express his thoughts about the news that Benghazi was known to be a terrorist attack right away, was observed via Drone cameras in real time, and that relief forces remained undeployed from nearby countries.

Tyrone and ex-SEAL Glen Doherty were both killed by a mortar fired at the safe house annex late in the firefight, after Wissam bin Hamid's Libya Shield Brigade had escorted eight Marines from Tripoli to the safe house.

Charles Woods says: "Someone had to say `don't go rescue them.'

We need to find out who gave that order and why."

Woods says he's not angry at anybody but believes "something doesn't smell right." He recounted his experience at Andrews Air Force Base on the day that the bodies of the four Americans killed in Benghazi returned home. In a building near the hangar, the four grieving families were arranged in what he described as "pods" and the dignataries on hand visited each pod separately. The president "kind of mumbled," Woods said, "totally insincere," His face was looking at Woods, he said, but his eyes were looking over Woods' shoulder -- "like he couldn't look me in the eye." Woods added: "It was like shaking hands with a dead fish."

Pat Smith, Sean Smith's mother, has also described the coldness of the commander in chief on this occasion.

Woods also met with Hillary Clinton. He described Clinton as coming over to him, they embraced, shook hands -- "she did not appear to be one bit sincere at all" -- and then: **"She said ... we're going to have that person arrested and prosecuted, that did the video," Woods said.**

The video lie -- and to the face of a grieving father. Who created it? Why? This was already Sepetmber 14. On that same day CIA Director Petraeus, briefing the House Intelligence Committee, also passed along this same lie, blaming the the video for a protest that never happened. Two days later, UN Ambassador Susan Rice hit the talk shows with the same lie. On September 25, it was in the president's message to the world at the UN.

The President, the SecState, the CIA Director, the UN Ambassador have much explaining to do to the American people. None of them defend the First Amendment, but they'll say absolutely anything for their own ends.

Obama in cahoots with known terrorists

10/26/12

A couple of weeks ago, I wrote a column addressing the national scandal that investigation into the security failures and lies surrounding Benghazi-gate must also expose. This even larger scandal concerns the fact that throughout the revolutionary cycle known as Arab Spring, the Obama administration threw in Uncle Sam's lot with the bad guys -- the "rebels," the "martyrs," the Muslim Brothers, the whole jihad-happy and Shariah-ruling crew in Libya and the wider Middle East. In so doing, Uncle Sam, more or less, crossed to the "other side."

We are continuing this same treacherous policy in Syria, something I hope Mitt Romney (as president, I also hope) comes to understand quickly. In Libya, Obama's Arab Spring policy -- supported by U.N.-

niks, Republicans and media alike -- meant making common cause with al-Qaida forces and other jihadists, including Libyan veterans of Afghanistan and Iraq who fought and killed Americans. It was if the whole world had gone mad.

Take the Libya Shield Brigade, an eastern Libyan militia aligned with the Libyan government. Libya Shield members met the eight U.S. Marines who arrived in Benghazi from Tripoli in the wee hours of Sept. 12, 2012. Libya Shield escorted our Marines to the secret annex -- relying on GPS coordinates the Marines brought with them -- where the survivors of the consulate attack had successfully taken cover. This annex did not come under mortar attack until soon after Libya Shield and the Marines arrived. Coincidence? It was in this barrage, by the way, that ex-SEALs Tyrone Woods and Glen Doherty were killed.

John Rosenthal has reported at WND.com that the Libya Shield Brigade fought in the anti-Gadhafi revolution -- which Uncle Sam, of course, supported -- under the black flag of al-Qaida. Rosenthal further notes that in October 2011, Libya Shield's leader, Wissam Bin Hamid, issued a statement to Arabic jihadist websites stating: "The Islamic Shariah is a red line, we will not cede one rule of it, and Islam is the only law-giver and not (merely) the foundation (of the law)."

Bin Hamid, not at all incidentally, is also described on an online jihadist forum as a veteran of jihad in both Iraq and Afghanistan. This is what I mean by Libyan "allies" who have fought and killed Americans from the Other Side. Now, they're escorting Marines to secret American annexes, and doing so as a matter of Obama administration policy.

This is a crucial piece of the Benghazi story. The U.S. wasn't relying on Libya Shield and, as I've written before, the February 17 Martyrs Brigade in some ad hoc security arrangement. This is all part of continuing Arab Spring policy.

A U.S. embassy cable made public by congressional investigators makes this patently clear. While requesting more security on March 28, 2012, Eric Nordstrom, then U.S. regional security officer in Libya, notes that "rebuilding and expanding" the "local" guard force is one of his "core objectives." This objective directly relates to what he describes as the State Department's recommendation for "developing plans to transition our security staffing ... to (a model) that incorporates more locally based and nonemergency assets."

Naturally, these "plans" weren't working. Hence, Nordstrom's request for more American security. And hence the denial from State for reasons, Nordstrom told Congress this month, that came down to the fact "there was going to be too much political cost." It is these "politics" -- this Obama policy of outreach to jihadists -- that must be exposed and stopped.

The final diplomatic cable to go out under the late Ambassador

Christopher Stevens' name is dated Sept. 11, 2012. It recounts events of the previous week in Benghazi, including a Sept. 9 meeting between an unnamed U.S. diplomat and, whaddya know, Wissam Bin Hamid, commander of Libya Shield. A second Libya Shield commander, Muhammad al-Gharabi, was also present. During a fractious-sounding meeting, the Libyans declared their support for the Muslim Brotherhood candidate then running to become Libyan prime minister, and threatened to withdraw security from the U.S. in Benghazi if another candidate won in upcoming elections.

It makes for surreal reading. Here we see a Muslim Brotherhood supporter, jihadist veteran of Iraq and Afghanistan, and fighter for Shariah under the al-Qaida flag threatening American officials, and it's just another bulleted point in a routine cable home to the State Department. Little wonder, of course, that two days later, Bin Hamid's militia and others like it in eastern Libya were unable to forestall disaster. What a dastardly joke: They were all too likely involved in it.

It gets worse. As Rosenthal notes in his WND.com article, "The jihadist inclinations of Bin Hamid and his Libya Shield forces are not unknown to the U.S. government. Indeed, a recent study prepared by the research division of the Library of Congress links the Libya Shield Brigade to al-Qaida and even cites speculation that Bin Hamid may be the leader of the al-Qaida network in Libya."

We must find out how we got to this perilous place and why. But first we have another question to answer: Do we really want four more years of the same?

The Jihad and Christopher Stevens, part 3

10/27/12

In the last installment, I examined cables written by Christopher Stevens in 2008 (and available courtesy Wikileaks) that seem to capture a significant trend in his thinking, and, perhaps the thinking of others in the US government, which may have helped drive the evolution of the disastrous US "Arab Spring" policy that put Uncle Sam in alliance with al Qaeda, Muslim Brotherhood and other groups driving the spread of sharia (Islamic law).

This trend appears as Stevens learned how to explain -- how to rationalize, really -- the jihad corridor that eastern Libyans in particular followed to fight Americans in Iraq. While the Washington Post today quite narrowly (ignorantly) tells readers that Derna sent more jihadists to Iraq "during the U.S. occupation [sic] than any other place in Libya," the larger truth is that eastern Libya, led by Derna and Benghazi, sent more jihadists to kill and maim Americans -- whose Iraq "occupation," by the way, included fighting AQ, preventing Sunni-Shiite civil war and "nation-building" all at the same time -- per capita than any place *in the world*. And, as discussed in Part 2, the citizenry is extremely proud of this ultimate anti-American fact.

The explanation, to Stevens, had little to do with an Islamic culture well-primed to heed the age-old Islamic call to jihad. Citing the poverty, boredom and Al Jazeera (as though poverty, boredom and Al Jazeera would inexorably lead all people everywhere to strap bombs to their bodies and kill Americans while yelling Allahu Akbar), Stevens passed along the rationale of a source who described the men of the region as engaging in "extremism in the name of religion" -- never, ever mind the "extremism" of the "religion" itself as reinforced by the pride the local culture took according to these same cables, in such "extremism."

This pride, however, still bothered Stevens, who wrote: "The most troubling and **difficult** aspect of [redacted's] account is the pride that many eastern Libyans ... appear to take in the role their native sons have played in the insurgency in Iraq."

What did Stevens mean by "difficult"? What obstace to what path did he have in mind? He wrote this, by the way, in February 15, 2008. By June 2, 2008, Stevens seemed have found his way around this difficulty: The anti-Western, jihadist activity of eastern Libya, he concluded in the June 2, 2008 cable, was largely due to local frustration with Qaddafi's regime. This was the message, loud and clear, pressed upon him by a source he had met accidentally ("accidentally"?) over lunch at the Derna waterfront in May 2008. In sum, Qaddafi was the problem. Eliminate Qaddafi, and the anti-American animus would be eliminated, too. (This is discussed in Pt. 2.)

Of course, that was also the goal of violently anti-American Al Qaeda and its affiliates in the Mahgreb. This shared AQ goal would become US policy in 2011, and Stevens would become a major broker of this policy on the ground in Libya.

This didn't seem possible in June 2008, a time when, also according to the June 2 cable, eastern Libyans "feared the US would not allow Qaddafi's regime to fall and therefore viewed direct confrontation with the GOL (Government of Libya) in the near-term as a fool's errand."

Wasn't that further reason to uphold our agreement to support Qaddafi? Apparently not to people like Christopher Stevens, who have a different outook than the average American. (Remember Stevens' and the US embassy's solicitousness of ex-Gitmo al Qaeda detainees repatriated to Libya, including Bin Qumu, now leader of Ansar al-Sharia (described in Part 1.)

The June 2, 2008 cable continues:

> Rejecting the idea that Derna was uniformly extremist, [Redacted] and his business partner described the town as being divided between religiously conservative and secular residents. ... Elaborating, [he] attributed more extreme iterations of Islam to "unnatural foreign influences" on religious practices in Derna. ...

Really? The cables next elaborates on this notion of foreign or prodigal Libyans returning home with an unnatural, rather than purely Islamic message. For good measure, it throws in "a dearth of social outlets" and a weak educational system as conditions that further "enabled conservative clerics" -- always as if people are unable to swing a few more "social outlets" and improve education somewhat instead of sending their sons to "martyr" themselves in jihad.

Stevens continued:

> A heavy influx of Arabic-language satellite television ... also fostered a hard view of the world. ... Not everyone liked the "bearded ones" (a reference to conservative imams) or their message, [Redacted] said, but **the duty of a Muslim in general -- and a son of Derna in particular -- was to resist occupation of Muslim lands through jihad.** "It's jihad -- it's our duty, and you're talking about people who don't have much else to be proud of." Derna's residents might take issue with attempts to ban smoking or restrict social activities, but **there was consensus on "basic issues" like jihad.**

This is a striking comment, and in keeping with other cable reports attesting to both the normalcy and acceptance of jihad among the population at large. Interestingly enough, it is only the manners and mores of sharia -- smoking bans, restricted social activities -- that are at all controversial in this culture. Jihad, then, becomes a defining attribute, and, a deal-breaker for making common cause, *or so an average American might think*. But in the next sentence Stevens seems to fall back to invoking the political propaganda of Al Jazeera as a driver of general violence. It's not that Al Jazeera *doesn't* play a role in inciting jihad and anti-Americanism; obviously, it does. But the role it plays it reinforced or, better, enabled by Islam itself. Stevens then goes on to apply what might be described as a Western gloss:

> Depictions on al-Jazeera of events in Iraq and Palestine [sic] fueled the widely held view in Derna that resistance [sic] to coalition forces was "correct and necessary." Referring to actor Bruce Willis' character in the action picture "Die Hard," who stubbornly refused to die quietly, he said many young men in Derna viewed

resistance against Qadhafi's regime and against coalition forces in Iraq as an important last act of defiance.

Thus, the evolution of US foreign service thinking: When Islam has nothing much to do with anything, it's Die Hard time in Derna. So, take away Qaddafi, you take away "resistance," right?

Q: When did removing Qaddafi become US policy in Libya? Most of us only heard about it last year. Libyans, meanwhile, seem to have been suspicious for some time. In a cable dated August 29, 2008 preparing for SecState Rice's visit to Libya, Stevens noted: "Conservative regime elements are still wary that our ultimate goal is regime change."

Was it?

Eighth question: "Jay, there are some emails that have emerged ..."

10/28/12

Yesterday, Reuters, Fox, CNN, CBS and other media reported that on 9/11/12 emails went to top Obama administration officials alerting them that the Benghazi consulate was under terrorist attack. The first arrived at 4:05 pm ET on 9/11/12 -- 10:05 pm Benghazi time, about 25 minutes into the attack. At 6:07 pm ET, another email reported that Ansar Al-Sharia had claimed responsibility for the attack.

At some point after that, the White House cook-up-a-protest-that-didn't-happen and blame-the-video lie began.

Yesterday, also, White House spokesman Jay Carney -- he who repeatedly perepetrated the above lie in the weeks after the terrorist attack in Benghazi -- went before the press, the Fourth Estate, our eyes and ears. The skeptics. The questioners of authority.

And?

The Benghazi emails didnt come up until Question #8.

For scene-setting purposes, it's worth nothing Question #7 was: "Based on some of those stats that you just shared, would you say that it's your campaign that has the momentum?" Question #9 was: "One light question to end -- how much sleep did you guys get last night?"

Words fail.

Here, for the people, is #8:

Q   Jay, there are some emails that have emerged, which suggest that the White House and other areas of the government were told within hours of the Benghazi attack that an extremist group had claimed responsibility. How is that compatible with the idea that it was a spontaneous attack?

MR. CARNEY: There were emails about all sorts of information that was becoming available in the aftermath of the attack. The email you're referring to was an open-source, unclassified email referring to an assertion made on a social media site that everyone in this room had access to and knew about instantaneously.

There was a variety of information coming in. The whole point of an intelligence community and what they do is to assess strands of information and make judgments about what happened and who was responsible. And I would refer you to what we've already said about, and what the DNI has already said about, the initial assessments of the intelligence community, and the fact that throughout this process, I and others made very clear that our preliminary assessments were preliminary, that an investigation was underway, and that as more facts became available, we would make the American people aware of them.

Again, this was an open-source, unclassified email about a posting on a Facebook site. I would also note I think that within a few hours, that organization itself claimed that it had not been responsible. Neither should be taken as fact -- that's why there's an investigation underway.

Q   Thanks.

Thanks?

Will Benghazi lies determine the election? Not if the media have their way

11/1/12

Washington, DC -- Two weeks ago, I reported here that the Obama administration had dug itself into a minefield of lies about the Benghazi terrorist attack that the president would have to cross to get to Election Day. Whether he will do so unscathed remains unclear, but if Barack Obama is re-elected president on November 6, it will be for one reason only. It will be because the US media threw themselves on every Benghazi bombshell that threatened the president, shutting down democracy in the process.

Not all of the media, of course. Fox News, WND.com, Daily Beast, Reuters, CNN, CBS and others have reported most of the key facts now available. These include, first, the revelation that intelligence immediately indicated the US consulate in Benghazi was destroyed in a planned terrorist attack, not as the result of a "spontaneous" protest triggered by a Youtube video. The latter scenario, however, is the demonstrable lie the Obama administration, including President Obama, repeatedly told for weeks. Later, the State Department established the fact that no "protest" at all occurred before the attack. The Obama administration explanation for these and other discrepancies? "Bad intelligence" or "fog of war." The major media largely agree, no questions asked. Literally.

This past week, a new set of factors emerged darkly underscoring the appearance of a White House cover-up. These include the publication of the email bulletins that alerted the highest administration officials that the US consulate in Benghazi was under terrorist attack. These emails began arriving in Washington within the first hour of what would stretch into an eight-hour battle. We also learned that the Americans under rocket and mortar fire in Libya repeatedly called for military support; that military support was within two hours' flying time; and that no help was ever deployed. Four Americans, including the US Ambassador, were killed in the attack that left many others wounded.

Did President Obama order the US military *not* to come to the aid of Americans under attack on 11 September 2012? This is the terrible question that inevitably forms on grasping the newly established sequence of events -- only not if you're a member of the US media elite. Take Brian Williams, the $13-million-per-year anchorman of NBC Nightly News. On Friday, October 26, after news of the email alerts and reports of unheeded distress calls had broken, Williams' single Benghazi question to the president was the following: "The question becomes: Have you been happy with the intelligence, especially in our post 9-11 world? ... Were you happy with what you were able to learn as this [Benghazi] unfolded?

Obama sat for another interview that same day, this time with a reporter in the hotly contested state of Colorado. This far more professional (if less highly paid) local reporter asked Obama whether Americans in Benghazi were denied military relief during the attack – and he asked the question twice. Perhaps flustered, Obama finally replied that he made his priorities clear "the minute I found out what was happening." He continued: "Number one, make sure that we are securing our personnel and doing whatever we need to."

If Obama issued ever such a directive, we know it wasn't carried out. This would be a scandal, a failure in the chain of command that led to many casualties. If, however, Obama didn't issue this order and is lying, the situation is even worse. Either way, it's a tremendous news story – only not in the estimation of the editors of the Washington Post, the New York Times or the Wall Street Journal. These and other leading newspapers failed to report anything at all about Benghazi in the following days. As for the Sunday political affairs TV shows, every one of these well-known hosts (Fox News' Chris Wallace excepted) failed to bring up Benghazi. And in most cases (CBS's Bob Schieffier excepted), they shushed up the guests who did. "On the issue of trust, what is going on with regard to Libya?" one Republican guest asked, bringing up Obama's Friday comments in Colorado. "Well, let's get to Libya a little bit later," said David Gregory, host of NBC's "Meet the Press." Later never came.

The national press has continued to punt their opportunities to extract information from the president. "Why," MSNBC co-host Mika Brzezinski asked Barack Obama, "has it been so easy for critics to say the administration does not have its story straight on Benghazi?" Maybe because the administration hasn't told a straight story, a fact which fails to pique the curiosity of the White House press corps. After the story about the email alerts broke, White House spokesman Jay Carney held a briefing. How, Carney was asked in Question #8, were the emails alerts "compatible" with the idea that a "spontaneous" attack had taken place? (Question #7: "Would you say that it's your campaign that has the momentum?") Carney dismissed the email evidence as being part of "a variety of information" that was coming in. That settled it, judging by Question #9: "How much did you guys sleep last night?"

After Charles Woods, father of slain ex-Navy SEAL Tyrone Woods, decided to speak out recently, Benghazi-gate took a dramatic turn. Woods recounts how on the day his sons' remains returned home, Secretary of State Hillary Clinton promised him, in effect, that revenge would soon be taken against the producer of the Youtube video. She said the moviemaker would be arrested and prosecuted, thus simultaneously obscuring the terrorism that killed Woods' son while eviscerating the First Amendment guarantees of freedom of speech. To date, Woods' story has appeared only in conservative media. Producer Nakoula Basseley Nakoula, meanwhile, has indeed been arrested and remains in jail on "parole violations." And no one in the mainstream media except Britain's Daily Mail has touched Woods' account of Vice President Biden's crude attempt at extending condolences: "Did your son always have balls the size of cue balls?"

Benghazi-gate, of course, is about much more than demented insensitivity. "You don't just passively allow Americans to remain under attack for eight hours at a time when you have forces within range and do nothing," Robert C. McFarlane, former National Security Advisor under Ronald Reagan, told Fox News. "To have known what he [Obama] had available, to have known that Americans were under fire, and to have done nothing, is dereliction of duty that I have never seen in a Commander in Chief from a president of any party."

If anything, the media's dereliction of duty is even worse.

Pickering's Red Flags

11/2/12

As we arrive at Election Day, some of the most crucial questions left unanswered about Benghazi are, in fact, the simplest. They are not "fog of war" questions. They are not questions rendered unanswerable by "conflicting intelligence." They are questions that probe clear actions taking place not on the roof of a safe house under mortar fire, but inside the fortress-like, orderly and well-lit White House.

Who turned down requests for military relief for Americans under rocket and mortar fire? Who decided to suppress the fact that no protest preceded this attack on the U.S. consulate in Libya that claimed four American lives? Who ordered senior Obama administration officials to lie to the American people for two weeks by blaming a YouTube video for a "spontaneous" outbreak of violence that was, in fact, a coordinated terrorist assault?

President Obama declared he made his priorities about Benghazi clear "the minute I found out what was happening." He said: "Number one, make sure that we are securing our personnel and doing whatever we need to." If he issued an unexecuted order to this effect, there was a grievous breakdown in the chain of command that must be exposed. If, on the other hand, Barack Obama is lying, that must be exposed, too. It's not a hard fact to find out.

But is Thomas Pickering, Obama's choice to lead the Benghazi investigation, the proper person to search for it? On first glance, Pickering, a retired top diplomat and State Department official, sets off conflict-of-interest alarms for heading an investigation that must focus closely on the State Department. On closer inspection, however, so many red flags pop up around Pickering that his selection becomes another Benghazi-gate scandal in itself.

Pickering is one of those Washington insiders whose public record is less a matter of what he's done than what he's been: U.S. ambassador to Russia, Israel, El Salvador, Jordan, India, Nigeria and the United Nations. What such postings may obscure, however, is that the man is a foreign policy establishment leftist. It's not just that Pickering serves as chairman of the board of trustees of the International Crisis Group, a George Soros group that, for example, advocated engagement with the Shariah-supremacist Muslim Brotherhood in Egypt. Pickering has personally explored opening relations with Hamas; pushed peace talks with the Taliban; argued for getting rid of, or removing to the U.S., all tactical nuclear weapons in Europe (and moving Russia's to east of the Urals); and promoted bilateral talks with Iran without preconditions. And speaking of Iran, Pickering sits on the boards of two pro-Tehran groups, the American Iranian Council and the National Iranian American Council. The Iranian connections are additionally disturbing since one Benghazi scenario to be explored is whether Iran was involved, possibly in retribution for U.S. support of anti-Assad forces (including jihadists) in Syria.

Pickering's politics place him squarely inside the Obama foreign policy mainstream, but that's not the proper point from which to investigate an Obama foreign policy fiasco. Indeed, Pickering has expressed support for Obama's Libya policy, "where," as he put it in March, "we play a major role behind the scenes and ... incorporate many other people in the activities we did in Libya." Explaining the Libyan "experimentation" in "consultative leadership" that minimizes the U.S. military role, Pickering sounds as if he also endorsed the disastrous policy of relying on local jihadist militias for U.S. security.

On a panel titled "The Muslim Experience in America" at Washington's National Cathedral, Pickering recently advocated "dialogue with the Iranians ... informed by an effort to develop religious understanding and perhaps harmony," while also bridging the "gulf" with Islam in America more generally. He also made an ominous call for "strong efforts ... to deal with opinion leaders who harbor (anti-Islam) prejudices, who espouse them and spread them." Then he took a question on how returning Iraq and Afghanistan veterans might "complicate efforts to promote the acceptance of Muslims in America." His answer, in a nutshell, was that it wouldn't. He noted that soldiers "understand that as loyal Americans that kind of prejudice is not to be expressed."

This drew a fervent rebuttal from co-panelist James J. Zogby of the Arab American Institute, who argued that "the racism [of soldiers] was really intense"; further, that it resulted from manuals and classes now expunged from Pentagon and Justice training. ("The FBI training program is shameful," he added, referring to Islamic educational materials and trainers "purged" earlier this year.)

"There's a direct correlation between the president of the United States and Islamophobia," Zogby said, adding: "This hatred toward Muslims is largely concentrated with middle-class, middle-aged white people. And men. And it overlaps almost identically with the Tea Party."

Racism, hatred and the Tea Party: Zogby put this whole concoction down not to jihad, not to the Islamic movement to spread Shariah (Islamic law), but solely to economic hard times. "And in the midst of all of that," he continued, "this group of white, middle-aged, middle-class men looked around and saw a young African-American, educated at Harvard, with the middle name Hussein, get elected president of the United States. It fueled this phenomenon. It opened the door for the wedge issue to operate."

Noting polls reflecting persistent doubts about the president's birth certificate and other documents, Zogby concluded: "So there's an overlay between the racism and the Islamophobia, and I think that we have to understand it and address it. And realize that there is this dangerous cancer that has affected the electorate. And is being used as a wedge issue."

Pickering's response? "Let me just go further. Jim, I agree with what you say about both domestic politics and the wedge issue. And the effect on the attitude toward the president. I'm deeply concerned. I don't agree with you that the veterans are a problem. I agree with you we had a huge problem with the armed forces, and you're right: It is the enemy."

Those "racist" armed forces are "the enemy"? That's a U.S. diplomat talking? Perhaps this most undiplomatic expression of institutional animus toward the military represents the mindset that helped lead us to Benghazi.

Could someone who agrees that jihad is a poisonous figment of envious Tea Partiers and not an age-old institution of Islam possibly find out what's at the bottom of Benghazi? Of course not. And who doesn't think that's why Barack Obama picked him?

Petraeus of Benghazi

11/3/12

First, the WSJ, now the NYT: CIA Director David Petraeus is feeling a little heat from the spotlight regarding Benghazi. It's an extremely soft-focus spot, however, one that obscures the most important question regarding Petraeus' role in Obama administration mendacity in characterizing what was a planned terrorist attack as a violent melee growing from a "spontaneous" protest over a Youtube video.

That most important question is, Why, three days after this terrorist attack that killed four Americans in Benghazi, did Petraeus go before the House Intelligence Committee and brief lawmakers that a Youtube video was to blame for a "spontaneous" protest -- wholly fictitious -- that "went on," as ranking Democrat Dutch Ruppersberger told ABC on September 14 following the Petraeus briefing, "for two to three hours"?

Ruppersberger:

> "In the Benghazi area, in the beginning we feel that it was spontaneous – the protest- because it went on for two or three hours, **which is very relevant because if it was something that was planned, then they could have come and attacked right away,**" Ruppersberger, D-Md., said following the hour-long briefing by Petraeus. "At this point it looks as if there was a spontaneous situation that occurred and that as a result of that, the extreme groups that were probably connected to al Qaeda took advantage of that situation and then the attack started."

It *was* something that was planned; they *did* attack right away. There was *no protest at all*. But that's not what Petraeus appears to have told the Intell Comittee members. Why?

Meanwhile, ABC also reported in that same September 14 story:

> Members of the Senate Armed Services Committee were also briefed today by Defense Secretary Leon Panetta and Vice Chair of the Joint Chiefs Admiral James Winnefeld. **But senators emerging from that private briefing reported that they believed the attack in Libya was premeditated.**

Call it "A Tale of Two Briefings."

In yesterday's Journal story and today's Times story, it's important to note that there is no examination of the administration's repeated lie that Benghazi was the result of a non-existent protest over a Youtube video "gone wrong" -- a lie which Petraeus was a leading purveyor of. The Times' Scott Shane gingerly raises and then abandons the subject this way: "Some news reports faulted his secret testimony to Congress days after the attack for supposedly supporting the view that it was not a planned strike but a spontaneous response to an offensive anti-Muslim video." The Wall Street Journal doesn't mention it at all.

Who concocted this lie, why and when? Who pulled the plug on it following Obama's September 25 UN address in which he cited the video six times (and declared: "The future must not belong to those who slander the prophet of Islam")? That's a timeline that needs to be established as much as any other. I suppose these latest MSM stories represent some modicum of progress: Remember those trial-turned-lead balloons that went up recently to exonerate the CIA (Petraeus), including the notion that the Benghazi terrorists might have watched the Cairo protests on TV and *then* planned the attack (Ignatius); or that the CIA's bureaucratic layers prevented the truth that there was no "spontaneous" protest from getting to the top (Boot). But I don't think we should be grateful, and certainly not satisfied. The MSM is still covering-up more than covering Benghazi, despite the Page One placement.

It somehow seems a propos to interject here a 1901 statement of Lenin's which I came across yesterday in an exhibition at the National Gallery called "Shock of the News." Lenin said: "A newspaper is not only a collective propagandist and an agitator, it is also a collective organizer."

That said, the Wall Street Collective Organizer report does offer a little insight into how Petraeus is regarded on the inside:

> Mr. Petraeus didn't attend funerals held later for the two CIA contractors, irking some administration officials and CIA veterans.

Also:

> In the aftermath of the assault, questions have been raised within the administration and on Capitol Hill about Mr. Petraeus's role in responding to the attack. On Oct. 10, lawmakers grilled senior State Department officials about the attack. At one point, lawmakers and officials alluded for the first time to the existence of the CIA facility. That set off alarms at the agency and at the State Department because that information was classified.

> Some senior administration officials say they were surprised Mr. Petraeus went to that night's private Washington screening of the movie "Argo," about a covert CIA operation in 1979 in Tehran.

That would have been on October 10. I noted that premiere here, as covered by the Washington Examiner, because it broke the Examiner's recent months of silence on Huma Abedin by noting her presence at the screening -- along with that of Petraeus. (Further establishing CIA party-presence, General Counsel Stephen Preston was also at the screening.) Such fun. Affleck, it turns out, is a huge fan of Petraeus, whom he calls "one of the most remarkable living Americans." He likes Huma Abedin, too.

> Affleck explained why he invited his "good friend" Abedin, who in turn brought along her husband. "The reason why she is here, is she was instrumental in helping us shoot at the State Department," Affleck said. "As you noticed, we shot at the real State Department ... our production designers were allowed to go inside and look at the seventh floor and recreate it."

Wonder if Abedin would extend the same hospitality to a movie called "Benghazi"? And would David Petraeus be able to make it to the DC premiere?

Another (Benghazi) thing:
Vote for Romney for love of country

11/5/12

On September 17, Reuters ran a story headlined: "Intel agencies warned U.S. Embassy in Egypt of possible violence."

That's nice. So why didn't "intel agencies" warn the US Embassy in Libya of possible violence, too? Presumably because the "intel agences" -- Petraeus' CIA, no doubt -- were focused on a "video threat" in Egypt, not in Libya, and on September 10 they cabled the embassy in Egypt accordingly. Egypt was indeed jump-starting another Islamic rage cycle from a Youtube video clip, "Innocence of Muslims," whose producer, incredibly, remains in jail on "parole violations." But, conveniently forgotten amid the many administration statements that there was no forwarning of an attack in Libya, AQ leader Ayman al-Zawaheri uploaded a video of his own on September 9 and 10 calling for Libyans to attack the US to avenge the US killing of a senior AQ leader from Libya, Yahya al-Libi. This video apparently went ignored by these same "intel agencies."

Why did a clip from a Mohammed movie focus the attention of US intelligence agencies while a genuine terror kingpin's direct incitement to jihad against Americans went ignored?

Gosh, I missed the answer to that question in the "CIA timeline."

Could this blinkered concentration of US intel agencies on the Youtube Mohammed movie clip have had something to do with an unfolding strategy inside the Obama White House to use the video to advance the so-called Istambul Process as led by Hillary Clinton and the Islamic bloc to implement anti-blasphemy laws designed to prohibit criticism of Islam? Fourteen days after Benghazi, President Obama would lend support to this same movement against the First Amendment in his UN address in which cited the Mohammed video six times, declaring: "The future must not belong to those who slander the prophet of Islam." For that statement alone, Obama should not be re-elected because it proves he is unwilling to defend the US Constitution.

Meanwhile, speaking of the CIA timeline, Fox News Bret Baier today seizes on a clash of timelines underscored by the CBS release -- *unconscionably* only two days before the election -- of a statement by Obama to "60 Minutes" showing the president was disavowing Benghazi as terrorist attack on September 12, despite Obama's claiming during the second debate that he had called Benghazi an "acts of terror" on September 12 in the Rose Garden (prior to the "60 Minutes" interview).

The words passed his lips in the Rose Garden but not to characterize Benghazi; more to the point, Obama spent the next two weeks blaming "Innocence of Muslims" for a non-existent, but what the President insisted was a "natural" protest that became violent.

Baier writes:

> Of all the details of the specific times the CIA contractors respond to the fight, I found this one most interesting:
>
> "1:15 a.m.: CIA reinforcements arrive on a 45-minute flight from Tripoli in a plane they've hastily chartered. The Tripoli team includes four GRS security officers, a CIA case officer and two U.S. military personnel who are on loan to the agency. They don't leave Benghazi airport until 4:30. The delay is caused by negotiations with Libyan authorities over permission to leave the airport, obtaining vehicles, and the need to frame a clear mission plan. The first idea is to go to a Benghazi hospital to recover Stevens, who they correctly suspect is already dead. **But the hospital is surrounded by the Al Qaeda-linked Ansar al-Shariah militia that mounted the consulate attack.**"

Baier:

> So the U.S. Ambassador to Libya is at the Benghazi hospital and suspected dead. The CIA contractors know that, but they can't get there because **the hospital is surrounded by the Al Qaeda-linked group Ansar al Shariah, the "militia that mounted the consulate attack."**
>
> This goes up the chain communication at 1:15 a.m. on Sept. 12. The White House, the Situation Room, and all of those paying attention to intel channels know that the guys on the ground have determined the group that's behind this. It's the Al Qaeda-linked militia that are still fighting and have the hospital surrounded.
>
> About 12 hours later -- before heading to Las Vegas for a campaign event -- Obama sits down for that "60 Minutes" interview with Steve Kroft.
>
> And Sunday night, 54 days after the attack and almost two weeks after putting out the first additional clip that appeared to back up the president after the second debate, CBS without fanfare posted the rest of the Benghazi question online -- the question before the question.
>
> Remember this is from a president who has been saying he was calling Benghazi a terrorist attack from the very first moment in the Rose Garden. Also, remember what he said in the debate and

notice the new part -- highlighted in bold.

> KROFT: Mr. President, this morning you went out of your way to avoid the use of the word terrorism in connection with the Libya Attack, do you believe that this was a terrorism attack?
>
> OBAMA: Well it's too early to tell exactly how this came about, what group was involved, but obviously it was an attack on Americans. And we are going to be working with the Libyan government to make sure that we bring these folks to justice, one way or the other.

Update: I just watched this clip, rather than merely reading the above transcript. More accurately, the transcript should read:

> KROFT: Mr. President, this morning you went out of your way to avoid the use of the word terrorism in connection with the Libya Attack.
>
> OBAMA: Right.
>
> KROFT: Do you believe that this was a terrorism attack?
>
> OBAMA: Well it's too early to tell exactly how this came about, what group was involved, but obviously it was an attack on Americans. And we are going to be working with the Libyan government to make sure that we bring these folks to justice, one way or the other.

No, it *was not* too early to tell -- unless the President of the United States wanted to tell the American people something other than the truth. Obama and Hillary and Petraeus and Rice and the rest would lie and continue to lie to us on this count, with Obama stretching it out for two weeks to that UN address on September 25. Even now, they all continue to stonewall. Are such duplicitous and scheming public servants to be empowered for four more years? For many reasons, I hope for every Americans' sake the answer is a resounding landslide of a "NO." But I'll take a squeaker.

Why did Petraeus lie again?

11/17/12

As CIA Director, David Petraeus testified before the House Intel Committee in a closed hearing on Benghazi on September 14.

(Mistake #1: These hearings should have been open.)

A recap from a post of October 20 titled "What Did the CIA Know and When Did It Stop Knowing It":

> On September 14, ABC established that a bifurcated narrative was emerging from different wings of the administration. On the one hand, CIA Director David Petraeus was putting out the (non-existent) protest story; on the other hand, the Pentagon was already talking terrorist attack.
>
> (Worth tucking away as background from an earlier Ignatius column is that the CIA Director "is also said to have pushed hard in Libya, rushing case officers there to work with the opposition" -- a.k.a. al Qaeda.)

ABC reported:

> The attack that killed four Americans in the Libyan consulate began as a spontaneous protest against the film "The Innocence of Muslims," but Islamic militants who may have links to Al Qaeda used the opportunity to launch an attack, CIA Director David Petraeus told the House Intelligence Committee today according to one lawmaker who attended a closed-door briefing.
>
> Rep. Dutch Ruppersberger, the top Democrat on the House Intel committee, said Petraeus laid out "a chronological order exactly what we felt happened, how it happened, and where we're going in the future."
>
> **"In the Benghazi area, in the beginning we feel that it was spontaneous – the protest- because it went on for two or three hours, which is very relevant because if it was something that was planned, then they could have come and attacked right away," Ruppersberger, D-Md., said following the hour-long briefing by Petraeus.** "At this point it looks as if there was a spontaneous situation that occurred and that as a result of that, **the extreme groups that were probably connected to al Qaeda took advantage of that situation** and then the attack started."

This is damningly concrete information to hang onto like an anchor now that Petraeus and his Democratic allies are trying to slip away on an oily re-interpretation of the September briefing.

Based on Ruppersberger's on-the-record impressions of the closed-door Petraeus briefing on September 14 we know:

1) In a one-hour-briefing, Petraeus laid out for members in chronological order the what-happened, how-it-happened and where-we're-going story.

2) The first thing that happened in this Petraeus chronology was a "spontaneous" protest in Benghazi that lasted "two to three hours."

3) The spontaneity of the protest was "very relevant" to the Petraeus presentation because it was evidence that the attack that followed the protest was also unplanned.

4) With the spontaneous protest raging, extremist groups "probably connected" to al Qaeda "took advantage of the situation, " as Ruppersberger put it, "and then the attack started."

We, the People now know without a doubt that no protest, "spontaneous" or other, took place outside the US compound in Benghazi on 9/11/12. On the contrary, the compound had come under a planned al-Qaeda-linked attack.Within one to two to twelve to 24 hours of the start of the Ansar al Sharia-led assault, the White House, the State Department, the Pentagon, the intelligence agencies knew this, too.

Nonetheless, on September 12, President Obama in his Rose Garden statement "went out of [his] way to avoid the use of the word `terrorism' in connection with the Libya attack," as CBS' Steve Kroft put it (and Obama agreed). On September 14, Petraeus went before the House Intel Committee and identified the "spontaneous protest" as the trigger for the terrorist violence that killed four Americans in Benghazi; also, on September 14, SecState Hillary Clinton went to the father of slain ex-SEAL Tyrone Woods and furthered the administration's Big Lie that the video was responsible, promising arrest and prosecution of the video-maker. (He is now serving one year in prison on "unrelated" charges.) Two days later on September 16, UN Ambassador Susan Rice put out the same story on five Sunday talk shows; On September 25, President Obama, after having given various interviews blaming the video for the Benghazi violence, cited the video six times before declaring: "The future must not belong to those who slander the prophet of Islam." Obama lied. Petraeus lied. Clinton lied. Rice lied. Obama lied.

Why? Why did the O administration claim a "spontaneous protest" over the Mohammed video triggered a similarly spontaneous attack on the US compound in Benghazi -- and hang onto that lie until President Obama addressed the UN on September 25?

There are domestic and international reasons -- all of them bad -- which Congress must explore to expose this festering scandal. These include probable Obama concerns that an admission of the facts would have adversely affected his re-election campaign, and, in the international arena, his administration's policy to prohibit criticism of Islam in accordance with the aims of the OIC, the Islamic bloc, through UN Resolution 16/18. Then there is the whole "Arab Spring" policy which should come under scrutiny for aligning the US with al Qaeda and other jihadist organizations in Libya and elsewhere in the Middle East.

Meanwhile, the facts of the matter become only more obscured.

On November 16, Petraeus went before the House Intel committee, again in a closed hearing.

(Mistake #2: These hearings should have been open.)

News reports based on members' statements following the November 16 briefing indicate Petraeus is no longer pushing the administration's Big Lie of 14 days in September; namely, that a (non-existent) protest over a video in Benghazi spontaneously combusted into an al-Qaeda-linked terrorist attack. However, Petraeus insisted that his briefings in September and November are entirely consistent, as if he had never, ever identified a "spontaneous" protest lasting "two to three hours," as Rep. Rupperberger declared on September 14 immediately after Petraeus' briefing, as the trigger for the "probably" al-Qaeda-linked attack.

So far, the only thing between this latest Petraeus lie and its total acceptance is Rep. Peter King (R-NY). As a member of the House Intel committee, King heard both Petraeus testimonies, and came out last week to note the discrepancies, although all too politely and with misplaced protestations of his respect for Petraeus. King's statements have been boiled down to King saying "I had a very different recollection of what he told us on September 14."

King's complete comments to Fox News' Megyn Kelly were more emphatic.

King:

> Gen. Petraeus said that when he came to the committee back on Friday September 14 he had then told us that he thought it was a terrorist attack and the CIA had believed that. He said there were different streams coming in but they definitely believed it was a terrorist attack.
>
> Again, I have a great regard for Gen. Petraeus, I emphasized that today.
>
> But I told him I had a very different recollection of what he told us on September 14. **He barely mentioned terrorism at that time, he deemphasized it. He emphasized the video, he emphasized spontaneous demonstration, and as far as the terrorist question, he really minimized it totally.**

In September, Petraeus blamed a spontaneous protest for an unplanned terrorist attack. In November, Petraeus attributed the violence that left four Americans dead in Benghazi to a planned terrorist attack.

There's a big difference between the two. It matters because it leaves the crucial question unanswered: Why did the Obama administration lie to the American people about 9/11/12 in Benghazi? Why are they still lying?

Petraeus betrayed his country before he betrayed his wife

11/15/12

Was David Petraeus as great a general as the write-ups of his downfall routinely claim? This is a provocative question that I will begin to answer with another question: Did America prevail in the Iraq War? I suspect few would say "yes" and believe it, which is no reflection on the valor and sacrifice of the American and allied troops who fought there. On the contrary, it was the vaunted strategy of the two-step Petraeus "surge" that was the blueprint of failure.

While U.S. troops carried out Part One successfully by fighting to establish basic security, the "trust" and "political reconciliation" that such security was supposed to trigger within Iraqi society never materialized in Part Two. Meanwhile, the "Sunni awakening" lasted only as long as the U.S. payroll for Sunni fighters did.

Today, Iraq is more an ally of Iran than the United States (while dollars keep flowing to Baghdad). This failure is one of imagination as much as strategy. But having blocked rational analysis of Islam from entering into military plans for the Islamic world, the Bush administration effectively blinded itself and undermined its own warmaking capacity. In this knowledge vacuum, David Petraeus' see-no-Islam counterinsurgency (COIN) doctrine would fill but not satisfy the void.

The basis of COIN is "population protection" -- Iraqi populations, Afghan populations -- over "force protection." Or, as lead author David Petraeus wrote in the 2007 Counterinsurgency Field Manual: "Ultimate success in COIN is gained by protecting the populace, not the COIN force." ("COIN force" families must have loved that.) Further, the Petraeus COIN manual tells us: "The more successful the counterinsurgency is, the less force can be used and the more risk can be accepted." "Less force" and "more risk" translate into highly restrictive rules of engagement.

More risk accepted by whom? By U.S. forces. Thus we see how, at least in the eyes of senior commanders, we get the few, the proud, the sacrificial lambs. And sacrificed to what? A theory.

The Petraeus COIN manual continues: "Soldiers and Marines may also have to accept more risk to maintain involvement with the people." As Petraeus wrote in a COIN "guidance" to troops in 2010 upon assuming command in Afghanistan: "The people are the center of gravity. Only by providing them security and earning their trust and confidence can the Afghan government and ISAF (International Security Assistance Force) prevail." That was a theory, too. Now, after two long COIN wars, we know it was wrong.

COIN doctrine approaches war from an ivory tower, a place where such theories thrive untested and without hurting anyone. On the battlefields of Iraq and Afghanistan, however, the results have been catastrophic. Tens of thousands of young Americans answered their country's call and were told to accept more "risk" and less "protection." Many lost lives, limbs and pieces of their brains as a result of serving under a military command structure and government in thrall to a leftist ideology that argues, in defiance of human history, that cultures, beliefs and peoples are all the same, or want to be.

Attributing such losses to Petraeus' see-no-Islam COIN is no exaggeration. In his 2010 COIN guidance, Petraeus told troops: "Walk. Stop by, don't drive by. Patrol on foot whenever possible and engage the population." As the Los Angeles Times reported last year, "The counterinsurgency tactic that is sending U.S. soldiers out on foot patrols among the Afghan people, rather than riding in armored vehicles, has contributed to a dramatic increase in arm and leg amputations, genital injuries and the loss of multiple limbs following blast injuries."

Indeed, the military has had to devise a new category of injury -- "dismounted complex blast injury" -- while military medicine has had to pioneer, for example, new modes of "aggressive pain management at the POI (point of injury)" and "phallic reconstruction surgery."

But not even such COIN sacrifices have won the "trust" of the Islamic world. On the contrary, we have seen spiraling rates of murder by our Muslim "partners" -- camouflaged by the phrase "green on blue" killings. COIN commanders, ever mindful of winning (appeasing) "hearts and minds," blame not the Islamic imperatives of jihad but rather summer heat, Ramadan fasting and the "cultural insensitivity" of the murder victims themselves. Such is the shameful paralysis induced by COIN, whose manual teaches: "Arguably, the decisive battle is for the people's minds. ... While security is essential to setting the stage for overall progress, lasting victory comes from a vibrant economy, political participation and restored hope."

Notice the assumption that something called "overall progress" will just naturally follow "security." Another theory. It didn't happen in Iraq. It hasn't happened in Afghanistan. Since nothing succeeds like failure, the doctrine's leading general was rewarded with the directorship of the CIA.

There is more at work here than a foundationally flawed strategy. In its drive to win Islamic hearts and minds, COIN doctrine has become an engine of Islamization inside the U.S. military. To win a Muslim population's "trust," U.S. troops are taught deference to Islam -- to revere the Quran; not to spit toward Mecca (thousands of miles away); and to condone such un- or anti-Western practices as religious supremacism, misogyny, polygamy, pederasty and cruelty to dogs. Our military has even permitted Islamic law to trump the First Amendment to further COIN goals, as when ISAF commander Petraeus publicly condemned an American citizen for exercising his lawful right to freedom of speech to burn a Quran.

This explains why the reports that CIA director David Petraeus went before the House Intelligence Committee in September and blamed a YouTube Muhammad video for the deadly attack on the U.S. consulate in Benghazi, Libya, sounded so familiar. Whatever his motivation, it was all too easy for Petraeus to make free speech the scapegoat for Islamic violence. But so it goes in COIN-world, where jihad and Shariah (Islamic law) are off the table and the First Amendment is always to blame.

If there is a lesson here, it is simple: A leader who will betray the First Amendment will betray anything.

King on Petraeus

11/20/12

Below is a CNN transcript of Rep. Peter King's appearance before the press after David Petraeus appeared before the House Intelligence Committee on November 16. King is clearly struggling with what he has heard from Petraeus: a version of Petraeus' September 14 briefing at odds with what King and, more important, the record as set at the time by the ranking Democrat Dutch Ruppersberger, recall. In a nutshell, on September 14, Petraeus emphasized a "spontaneous," video-driven protest that became violent as "extreme" groups opportunistically attacked the US compound (with RPGs and mortars).

Petraeus spun this false narrative to the intell committee at a time when the US government already knew no protest whatsoever had taken place in Benghazi; rather, that the ambassador and three other Americans had been killed in a planned assault by al-Qaeda linked groups on the anniversary of 9/11. Petraeus' testimony, in other words, was a lie and an outrage -- but no one seems to care. Meanwhile, it is a crime to lie to Congress, oath or no oath.

On November 16, King made it clear that Petraeus had actually made things worse by changing his story; in this most recent testimony, the former CIA director maintained he attributed the Benghazi attack to a coordinated terrorist assault all along. Will any other members weigh in? Anyone?

The transcript:

...Let's listen to Congressman King.

REP. PETER KING (R), NEW YORK: The original talking points prepared by the CIA were different from the ones that were finally put out. As far as General Petraeus, his testimony today was that from the start he had told us that this was a terrorist attack, terrorists involved from the start. I told him, my questions had a very different recollection of that.

The clear impression we were given was that the overwhelming amount of evidence is that it was -- rose out of a spontaneous demonstration and it was not a terrorist attack and I pointed out the following week when Matt Olsen said it was a terrorist attack and it made headlines because until then, the administration was saying it was not terrorists.

Again, it was very cordial, as you will. General Petraeus is an outstanding patriot. We shook hands before and afterwards. We all thanked him for his service. I think he has a different impression of the impressions he left on September 14th.

(CROSSTALK)

DANA BASH, CNN SENIOR CONGRESSIONAL CORRESPONDENT: Mr. Chairman, can you tell us whether or not his affair or security surrounding his affair came up at all?

KING: Only in -- one question he was asked at the start, did that have any impact on his testimony, he said no.

(CROSSTALK)

UNIDENTIFIED REPORTER: How are the talking points different?

KING: The original talking points were much more specific about our prior involvement. And yet final ones, he said indications of extremists. Said indicate even though it was clearly evidence to the CIA that there was al Qaeda involvement.

UNIDENTIFIED REPORTER: Did you get any idea why it was changed?

KING: They just said it goes through a long process, interagency process, and when they come back that had been taken out.

UNIDENTIFIED REPORTER: Did he seem concern that things have been changed? Was that surprising to him?

KING: He said at the time they didn't realize the full significance of that and that an unclassified statement this was acceptable Again it's still very vague.

UNIDENTIFIED REPORTER: Was Petraeus under oath?

KING: No. There's no given. No.

UNIDENTIFIED REPORTER: Mr. King, are you -- did he allay any of your concerns? Are you satisfied with the presentation he made today?

KING: I'm satisfied with the ultimate conclusion he reached. I told him I honestly disagree with his recollection of what he told us on September 14th.

(CROSSTALK)

UNIDENTIFIED REPORTER: What did he say about the affair with Paula Broadwell?

KING: No -- there's no comment to that at all.

UNIDENTIFIED REPORTER: Did that make it -- did that make it hard, though, to get past that because of those salacious details have dominated the news? Did that make it hard to get to the brass tacks and (INAUDIBLE)?

KING: No. No. There was -- made clear at the start that would not be a focus of the questioning. And I would say 10 seconds into it, that was -- that was off to the side.

(CROSSTALK)

BASH: Is there a reason why you all wanted to hear from him is because since he briefed you the first time, he went to Libya? So he obviously had a bit of a trip report.

KING: Yes.

BASH: Is there anything you can tell us that he clearly learned from actually being on the ground?

KING: Yes, that would be classified. Other than the fact that they now clearly believe there was -- did not arise out of a demonstration. It was not spontaneous and it was clear terrorist involvement.

BASH: He said that straight up?

KING: Yes.

UNIDENTIFIED REPORTER: Mr. Chairman, (INAUDIBLE) right away.

KING: You know, this is ongoing. I mean this is -- it still can be --

obviously, you know, the secretary of state, the secretary of defense, and also people at the White House, to see if anyone at the White House changed their talking points.

UNIDENTIFIED REPORTER: Do you think you get to hear from him again on this and then also in the Broadwell situation?

KING: Well, you know -- we'll have to see. One day at a time.

(CROSSTALK)

UNIDENTIFIED REPORTER: Are you saying he still couldn't provide any explanation at all as to why they came to that conclusion?

KING: He was saying --

UNIDENTIFIED REPORTER: -- today that there's explanation?

KING: He was saying there are many strings of intelligence but he also stated that he thought all along he made it clear that there was significant terrorist involvement. And that is not my recollection of what he told us on September 14th.

UNIDENTIFIED REPORTER: How did he seem? Did he seem tired or worn down from this -- sort of what's been plaguing him?

KING: No. He was a strong soldier. Absolutely. He was very professional, very knowledgeable. Very strong. And again, spoke to him at the beginning of the hearing, end of the hearing. And he was a solid guy. I consider him a friend, which made the questioning tough to be honest with you.

(CROSSTALK)

UNIDENTIFIED REPORTER: How long did the testimony last?

UNIDENTIFIED REPORTER: Why is that?

KING: What's that?

BASH: You said you consider him a friend, it made the questioning tough. Meaning --

(CROSSTALK)

KING: We can ask the questions. Sometimes in a hearing, the adrenaline is pumping, and you're going back and forth. Now you realize there's a tragedy here and you realized that he's going through an awful lot. On the other hand we have an obligation to find out what we could. So that's always --

UNIDENTIFIED REPORTER: Did he give an indication --

KING: It's a lot easier when you dislike the guy when you ask them questions. I think you guys ask tough questions.

(LAUGHTER)

UNIDENTIFIED REPORTER: Did he give any indication of how he felt about Ambassador Rice's testimony after watching tonight?

KING: He didn't watch the testimony.

UNIDENTIFIED REPORTER: Did he speak with her beforehand?

KING: No.

UNIDENTIFIED REPORTER: But you were saying that the points that the CIA gave the White House included al Qaeda involvement and afterwards that was taken out?

KING: But the CIA -- I don't know if it was with him -- said that the report -- the talking points were drafted were specific about al Qaeda affiliations or al Qaeda terrorist activities. They didn't have it in front of them. They said that was -- after it went through the process, whatever that process is, which they seemed unclear about, that was taken out.

(CROSSTALK)

UNIDENTIFIED REPORTER: Sir, how long did the hearing last?

KING: An hour and -- he spoke for about -- he had an opening statement about 20 minutes. And so an hour and 10 minutes of questions.

BASH: Was he asked about the statement that Paula Broadwell made at a speech? You know, about the CIA?

KING: No.

BASH: OK.

UNIDENTIFIED REPORTER: Are you saying the DNI took it out or the administration took it out?

KING: No, that's the DNI. Well, again, it was not -- I guess it's how you define the administration because it also went to the Department of Justice, State Department, and I believe the National Security Council.

UNIDENTIFIED REPORTER: Did he talk about the films, the videos and how -- what he interprets?

KING: Yes.

UNIDENTIFIED REPORTER: And what did he say about those?

KING: Well, I can't get into that. There was nothing -- nothing controversial.

UNIDENTIFIED REPORTER: But did you guys watch any films today like --

KING: No. No. We saw them yesterday.

UNIDENTIFIED REPORTER: Yesterday? Senate Intelligence? KING: We saw them yesterday.

UNIDENTIFIED REPORTER: You saw them.

UNIDENTIFIED REPORTER: Did he say why it was taken out of the talking points that it was al Qaeda --

KING: He didn't know.

UNIDENTIFIED REPORTER: He didn't know?

KING: They were not involved.

UNIDENTIFIED REPORTER: How could he not know?

KING: It was done -- process was completed and they said OK, go with those talking points.

(CROSSTALK)

KING: I got the impression about seven or eight -- seven, eight, nine different agencies.

UNIDENTIFIED REPORTER: Did he give you the impression he was upset that it was taken out?

KING: No.

UNIDENTIFIED REPORTER: Did he say the CIA said OK to the revised reports?

KING: No, they -- well, in that interim process they OK'd it to go. They didn't see -- yes, they said OK for it to go.

(CROSSTALK)

UNIDENTIFIED REPORTER: Yes. Who did he say -- who did he say --

KING: I don't know.

UNIDENTIFIED REPORTER: Who did he say he thinks committed the attack then?

KING: I would just leave it at al Qaeda affiliates.

BASH: (INAUDIBLE) awkward to have him in the room within a week after he resigned, under the circumstances in which he did?

KING: There was a certain amount of -- sure. Obviously all of us in the room, certainly myself, and all of us have a great regard for him. I've known him for nine years now. So it's -- I actually urged him to run for president a few years ago. So -- and I went to dinner with him. I consider him -- I know him fairly well.

BASH: Was there any discussion --

(CROSSTALK)

KING: Every time you see a human tragedy to a good person, it's tough to go through.

UNIDENTIFIED REPORTER: Was there any discussion of the national security implications of his resignation?

KING: No. The resignation -- he just addressed in the beginning that he regretted what happened and that was basically it.

(CROSSTALK)

UNIDENTIFIED REPORTER: Sir, were there any talk of --

UNIDENTIFIED REPORTER: Were all members of the committee --

UNIDENTIFIED REPORTER: The night of the attack about whether it was --

(CROSSTALK)

KING: As far as I know they were all there.

UNIDENTIFIED REPORTER: Was he involved in the actual decision-making the night of the attack?

KING: I don't want to get into that, but he was -- he was definitely fully aware of what was going on, yes.

UNIDENTIFIED REPORTER: Did he ask for military backup?

KING: I am never going to get into that. I can't get into any of that.

UNIDENTIFIED REPORTER: Did he stick to the story that the first attack was -- the first attack was spontaneous, but the second seemed to be more organized, the mortar attack, the second attack may have --

KING: I can tell you the spontaneous aspect is definitely minimized right now. It just is. It was primarily a terrorist attack.

UNIDENTIFIED REPORTER: How about how -- I want to be careful about this. Did he address how he interpreted the anti-Muslim film and how that sort of got to be part of this discussion even though he downplayed it?

KING: It was based on reports that we're getting at the time.

UNIDENTIFIED REPORTER: But OK. But -- so that was part of what was going into this intelligence product that they were creating?

KING: Right.

UNIDENTIFIED REPORTER: And they got other information later that said this wasn't? KING: Well -- yes, but also -- they also at the time, prior to September 14th, had clear information that this was strong involvement with al Qaeda affiliates. And that was not made part of their presentation at the time.

BASH: Our understanding of the incident is that the former director was going to explain that he saw kind of two streams of intelligence, one suggesting maybe Ansar al-Sharia was involved and the other, which at the time was more robust, that it was the protest resulting from the anti-Muslim video? Is that the way he described it to you?

KING: He did but he said today that -- at the time he was also emphasizing the involvement of Ansar al-Sharia and my recollection was that he was actually minimizing the role of Ansar al-Sharia. That's it. OK?

(CROSSTALK)

UNIDENTIFIED REPORTER: Is the hearing over?

KING: Yes.

Petraeus scandal diverts focus from Benghazi cover-up

11/22/12

I think I know what David Petraeus is thankful for this week.
    Even though it appears the former CIA director lied to the House Intelligence Committee on Sept. 14, and may have lied again to the same committee on Nov. 16, he is starting to slip out of the inner ring of Benghazi cover-up suspects. We are losing sight of his official role in the deception as the media lens ossifies over a tawdry love triangle. For this, he must be thankful. Maybe to ensure the good fortune continues, Petraeus has hired Bob Barnett, the $975-per-hour Washington superlawyer to officials with issues and/or big book deals, to manage what reports call Petraeus' "transition to civilian life."

Here, for the record, is what the media and politicians are letting slip away with him.

After Petraeus appeared before the House Intelligence Committee on

Sept. 14 to brief members behind closed doors on the Benghazi attack of Sept. 11, the ranking Democrat on the committee, Maryland Rep. Dutch Ruppersberger, gave ABC an account of the briefing.

"In the Benghazi area," Ruppersberger said, "in the beginning we feel that it was spontaneous -- the protest -- because it went on for two or three hours, which is very relevant, because if it was something that was planned, they could have come and attacked right away. At this point, it looks as if there was a spontaneous situation that occurred and that as a result of that, the extreme groups that were probably connected to al-Qaida took advantage of that situation and then the attack started."

Spontaneous protest, unplanned attack: That was Petraeus' testimony as CIA director three days after U.S. Ambassador Christopher Stevens and three other Americans were killed in Benghazi, Libya.

Within 24 hours of the attack, however, the White House and top officials at the State Department, the Pentagon and the intelligence agencies knew that no protest, spontaneous or other, had taken place. They knew the U.S. had been hit on the 9/11 anniversary by a planned attack by al-Qaida affiliates. Ruppersberger's account, then, indicates Petraeus deceived the committee. When committed knowingly, as former federal prosecutor Andrew C. McCarthy recently pointed out, such deception is a felony.

This same phony story -- that "extreme groups" took advantage of a "spontaneous" protest over a YouTube video to mount an "unplanned" attack on the U.S. consulate in Benghazi -- would be repeated by the Obama White House for two weeks, climaxing in the president's U.N. address on Sept. 25. There, President Obama cited the video six times and declared to the world body, dominated by the Organization of Islamic Cooperation (an Islamic bloc of 56 nations plus the Palestinian Authority): "The future must not belong to those who slander the prophet of Islam."

Blaming the YouTube video for the violence was, in effect, blaming free speech, which is also OIC policy. Additionally, it denied the reality of the planned jihad attack, which, by extension, denied that al-Qaida-style jihad terrorism still exists at the vanguard of expansionist Islam.

To date, the media haven't asked President Obama and his top officials, why? Why the administration-wide cover-up? Why didn't military help get to Battleground Benghazi? Without coming clean, President Obama has been re-elected, Secretary of State Hillary Clinton mentioned as a 2016 presidential candidate, and U.N. Ambassador Susan Rice floated as the next secretary of state.

And Petraeus? On Nov. 12, Fox News reported that "congressional leaders," believing Petraeus lied to them in September, had "already considered charging Petraeus with perjury, but said they planned to withhold judgment until he testified this week." (Under oath or not, it is a crime to lie to federal officials.) We have heard no such tough talk since.

Except, that is, from the OIC. While the administration has publicly dropped the video (although its producer is serving one year in jail for "parole violations"), the OIC nations continue to cite it in escalating calls for laws criminalizing "defamation" of Islam. And Uncle Sam continues to lend a sympathetic ear. Just this week, Anne Casper, U.S. consul general in Jiddah, Saudi Arabia, spoke at an OIC symposium on "Defamation of Islam."

Connected? You bet. I submit that the September cycle of Islamic rage, ostensibly over a YouTube video, was another assault in the OIC war on free speech about Islam, which the U.S. has officially joined by co-sponsoring with the OIC the so-called Istanbul Process. Unexpectedly, an al-Qaida terror attack in Benghazi on 9/11/12 threatened to get in the way. That same al-Qaida attack almost blew the lid off the Obama campaign mantra that since Osama bin Laden is dead, so is al-Qaida, and the even greater fakery that Obama's Arab Spring policy is a success.

And what about reports that Benghazi was a secret U.S. gunrunning hub for "rebels" in Syria? These are the scandals that probing Benghazi would uncover, but in Washington, all we hear about are sweet nothings.

On Nov. 16, Republican Rep. Peter King of New York went before the media to discuss the second Petraeus briefing. Amid elaborate testimonials for the retired general, King revealed Petraeus had not been straight with the committee.

"As far as General Petraeus," King said, "his testimony today was that from the start he had told us that this was a terrorist attack, terrorists involved from the start." King stated that he had "a very different recollection of that. The clear impression we were given (on Sept. 14) was that (the violence) rose out of a spontaneous demonstration and it was not a terrorist attack." King's recollection matches the Ruppersberger account of the first Petraeus briefing.

King underscored the notion that Petraeus has since changed his story. In last week's briefing, King conveyed that Petraeus said he had "all along made it clear that there was significant terrorist involvement. And that is not my recollection of what he told us on September 14."

An unidentified reporter asked: "Was he involved in the actual decision-making the night of the attack?"

King: "I don't want to get into that, but he was -- he was definitely fully aware of what was going on, yes."

Unidentified reporter: "Did he ask for military backup?"

King: "I am never going to get into that. I can't get into any of that." Never? Can't?

Getting into every aspect of Benghazi-gate is the responsibility of Congress. The American people are owed the truth.

Benghazi probe must not get sidetracked

11/30/12

It is neither "racist" nor "sexist" to question U.N. Ambassador Susan Rice's role in the Benghazi scandal. It is, however, almost entirely beside the point.

Rice wasn't making life-and-death decisions on Sept. 11, 2012, when the U.S. compound in the Libyan city of Benghazi came under attack; President Obama was. Rice, therefore, is unable to answer the all-important question about what order President Obama issued upon hearing that U.S. diplomats in Benghazi were under fire. She can't look America in the eye and answer whether the U.S. military was ordered not to rescue Americans fighting for their lives.

Nor is Rice likely to be the Obama administration official who first concocted the false narrative blaming a YouTube video for a (nonexistent) protest in Benghazi, which, the false narrative continues, "spontaneously" erupted into "unplanned" violence -- the whopper President Obama told for two full weeks.

Another key piece of the puzzle Rice is unlikely to possess is why Secretary of State Hillary Clinton, three days after the Benghazi attack, was out there flogging that same concocted story, as when Clinton tried to console the father of slain ex-SEAL Tyrone Wood by promising him the video's producer would be arrested and prosecuted. Further, it is unlikely Susan Rice can explain why CIA Director David Petraeus went before the House Intelligence Committee, also on Sept. 14, in a closed session and similarly lied, deceiving members into believing that an "unplanned" attack left four Americans, including an American ambassador, dead.

These are just some of the red flags over Benghazi that can never be checked if GOP Sens. John McCain of Arizona, Lindsey Graham of South Carolina and Kelly Ayotte of New Hampshire continue to monopolize the issue and focus solely on Rice and those not-all-that-interesting talking points. It's almost as if they wish to tighten the lens over Benghazi so closely that we never notice that what's really needed is a review of the administration's Arab Spring policies. It is these policies, which, thanks in large part to Hillary Clinton, Susan Rice and White House adviser Samantha Power, actually put Uncle Sam on the path to jihad in Libya by supporting al-Qaida and other jihad terrorists in their bid for power. Maybe that's because the GOP largely supported these same disastrous policies, too.

Here are some of the Benghazi questions that still demand answers:

Who came up with the administration plan to discard early intelligence confirming the U.S. had sustained an al-Qaida-linked terrorist attack in Benghazi on the anniversary of 9/11, and to seize on a lie blaming a YouTube video for the attack? Who got everyone -- White House, State, CIA (but not, it seems, Defense) -- on board? After the president addressed the United Nations on Sept. 25 (citing the video six times), the false video narrative peters out. Who called the whole thing off?

Speaking of the president's U.N. address -- notorious for declaring, "The future must not belong to those who slander the prophet of Islam" -- who wrote it? Its underlying message that "slander" (read: free speech) of Islam causes violence dovetails neatly with the Istanbul Process, an Obama administration initiative to prohibit and even criminalize speech critical of Islam. The initiative is spearheaded by Hillary Clinton in conjunction with the Organization of Islamic Cooperation (OIC), an Islamic bloc of 56 nations, plus the Palestinian Authority.

President Obama stated to an outside-the-Washington-Beltway reporter that "the minute" he found out what was happening in Benghazi, he sprang into action. "Number one," the president said, "make sure that we are securing our personnel and doing whatever we need to do."

Did Obama, in fact, issue such an order? If so, it appears to have been ignored. Shouldn't someone be fired for insubordination? If no U.S. military assets were available -- a big "if" for the sake of argument -- why weren't NATO allies such as Turkey or Britain called on to help? What exactly was the president doing during the eight-hour span of the terror attack?

On Sept. 9 and again on Sept. 10, a YouTube video featuring al-Qaida leader Ayman al-Zawahiri was posted online. In it, Zawahiri exhorted Libyans to attack Americans in revenge for the killing of al-Qaida senior leader Abu Yahya al-Libi. The CIA and other intelligence agencies appear to have ignored this video entirely. Why?

Why was the United States in Benghazi relying on Libyan jihadists for security? This is where we might pick up on the Arab Spring trail the Obama administration followed to this whole disaster. For example, the small CIA contingent that flew in to Benghazi in the wee hours of Sept. 12 was "aided" (delayed) on arrival by Libya Shield. Not only did this militia fight in the Libyan revolution under the black flag of al-Qaida, but U.S. government analysts believe its leader, Wissam bin Hamid, a jihadist veteran of Iraq and Afghanistan, may be the leader of al-Qaida in Libya.

What was the Benghazi mission (it did not function as a consulate) doing there in the first place? Troubling reports indicate the U.S. presence in Benghazi may have been part of a secret CIA operation to run weapons to Syria's anti-Assad rebel forces, which, as was the case with Libya's anti-Gadhafi forces, include a heavy contingent of jihadist actors seeking to spread Shariah (Islamic law). Was the late Ambassador Christopher Stevens, previously point man to jihadists in Libya, party to this unauthorized operation?

Notice I haven't even mentioned Petraeus' affair with his biographer, Paula Broadwell. While not altogether unimportant, it is a distraction from weightier matters. For example: How can David Petraeus lie to Congress -- a felony -- and get away with it?

Ask President Obama.

Benghazi hearings provide few answers

1/25/13

One day, I hope, Hillary Clinton's Benghazi hearings will stand as testament to the smoke-and-mirrors dangerousness of U.S. foreign policy, circa 2013 -- both as executed by the executive branch of government and as weakly grasped by the legislative branch.

Did we learn who in the Obama administration concocted and/or coordinated the story about a totally imaginary video protest that was supposed to have led to the attacks in Benghazi, Libya, on 9/11/12? No.

Did we learn why the maker of the so-called anti-Islamic YouTube video clip is the only person in the world in jail for the attacks (for "parole violations")? No.

Did we learn whether it was coincidental that the video-protest lie ended after President Obama blamed the video (six times) in a Sept. 25 address before the United Nations in which he declared, "The future must not belong to those who slander the prophet of Islam"? No.

Did we learn anything about the decision-making process that prevented U.S. military relief from being ordered to Benghazi during the seven-hour attack? No.

Did we even learn about the official madness that permitted the U.S. government to hire jihadist militias -- the February 17 Martyrs Brigade and Libya Shield -- to secure U.S. lives and interests in the first place?

No, but we did learn that Secretary of State Clinton is now concerned about the "spreading jihadist threat." This was unexpected news -- not the existence of the threat, or the fact it's spreading, but rather that Mrs. Clinton was using the word "jihadist." What was that about?

The Obama administration has worked relentlessly to eradicate "jihad" -- the word, anyway -- by replacing it with the content-free and thus blinding term "violent extremism." Besides, al-Qaida is dead along with Osama bin Laden, or so the Obama campaign has always told us (hence, one motive for White House lies to the American people that a video -- free speech -- caused the attacks in Benghazi, not terrorists). Did this lurch in lingo indicate a lurch in policy?

No question on that from the good people of Congress.

And why was Mrs. Clinton warning against allowing Mali, hot spot du jour, to become safe haven for AQIM (al-Qaida in the Maghreb)? It has become such a haven mainly due to Obama-Clinton policies that toppled "war on terror" ally Moammar Gadhafi in Libya. ("We came, we saw, he died," as Clinton unforgettably gloated.) Clinton may be talking up "global jihad" this week, but it's worth remembering that Gadhafi already was its opponent on the northern African front -- at least until he was killed by U.S.-backed, al Qaida-linked Libyan "rebels."

How does she square all of that? No questions. Such curiosity, a call for accountability, might expose the Arab Spring, which all too many Democrats and Republicans supported, thus enabling regimes or democracies guided by Islamic law to take power across the Middle East. As far as American liberty goes, what's the difference between governments guided by Islamic law and global jihadists guided by the same Islamic law? Answer: not much. If Congress were to consider such a concept -- that Islamic law is dangerous, whether advanced by terrorists or governments -- the potential for clarity and creation of a policy in the American interest would become simply too dangerous to contemplate. Dangerous, that is, for the status quo. Maybe that's why lawmakers, with rare but welcome exceptions, stuck to the unrevealing nuts and bolts of "security."

Still, if they were so worried about security at the Benghazi compound, couldn't someone have asked Clinton why the suspected head of al-Qaida in Libya, Wissam bin Hamid, leader of Libya Shield, a militia that fought Gadhafi under al-Qaida's black flag, was one of the U.S. compound's security providers?

At least one congressman, Republican Rep. Tom Marino of Pennsylvania, did go to the trouble of displaying pictures of black al-Qaida flags recently waving over Libya and the wider Islamic world. He also asked Clinton whether she was aware of the Library of Congress report "Al-Qaida in Libya" (which happens to include the dossier on Wissam bin Hamid and a reported tie to AQIM).

Clinton's response was to note the many reports out there -- also the many flags. "The United States has to be as effective in partnering with the non-jihadists, whether they fly a black flag or any other color flag, to be successful."

Madame Secretary, what "non-jihadists" would ever fly the black al-Qaida flag?

We'll never know her answer. Of course, Clinton might well have replied -- as she did when Republican Sen. Ron Johnson asked why the administration said a video-driven protest, not terrorism, caused the Benghazi attacks -- "What difference, at this point, does it make?" It was pure Clinton, Hill or Bill. The ends always justify the means.

We still don't even know what reason the late Ambassador Chris Stevens had to be in the lightly protected compound in Benghazi on the

Sept. 11 anniversary.

Republican Sen. Rand Paul of Kentucky, however, did open an important, possibly related line of questioning. He asked: "Is the U.S. involved with any procuring of weapons, transfer of weapons, buying, selling, anyhow transferring weapons to Turkey out of Libya?"

"To Turkey?" Clinton said, after a pause. "I will have to take that question for the record. Nobody has ever raised that with me." Paul continued, noting news reports regarding ships leaving Libya with arms bound for Turkey and eventually the "rebels" in Syria. If this is true, we're looking at the "gun-walking" scandal known as Fast and Furious on an exponential scale.

Paul then asked whether the CIA annex in Benghazi was "involved with procuring, buying, selling, obtaining weapons, and were any of these weapons being transferred to other countries, any countries, Turkey included?"

"Well, senator, you'll have to direct that question to the agency that ran the annex," Clinton said. "I will see what information is available."

"You're saying you don't know?" asked Paul.

"I do not know," Clinton said. "I don't have any information on that."

That's funny. House Speaker John Boehner does. Following Clinton's testimony, Boehner told radio host Laura Ingraham that he was familiar with "the chatter about this (arms story) and the fact that these arms were moving toward Turkey." He continued: "But most of what I know about this came from a classified source and I really can't elaborate on it."

Is it possible that Speaker Boehner received a classified briefing that the secretary of state did not? Or did Clinton just tell a lie?

The Senate should invite her back and find out.

Tell me again why the U.S. used jihadists to guard Benghazi

5/10/13

"I want to ask a couple of questions about the February 17 Martyrs Brigade," said Rep. Blake Farenthold.

The Texas Republican was addressing the three State Department "whistleblowers" who testified before the House Oversight and Government Reform Committee about the attack in Benghazi that killed four Americans, including Ambassador Christopher Stevens. The three witnesses were Mark Thompson, acting deputy assistant Secretary of State for counterterrorism; Greg Hicks, former deputy chief of mission in

Libya; and Eric Nordstrom, former regional security officer in Libya.

When Farenthold introduced this crucial subject into the hearings, he also opened a window into Benghazi that shone light not only on disastrous Western support for "Arab Spring," but also on the core crisis in U.S. foreign policy.

Farenthold: "Mr. Nordstrom, can you tell me the role of February 17 Martyrs Brigade in protecting the consulate in Benghazi?"

Nordstrom: "Certainly. That was the unit, for lack of a better term, that was provided to us by the Libyan government."

This already was news to me: The Libyan government provided known jihadists to guard U.S. interests?

On second thought, there is nothing fantastic about this when -- or, rather, if -- we consider that the U.S. government supported an army of known jihadists in its revolution against Libya's anti-jihadist former leader Moammar Gadhafi. I say "if" because I don't expect even the members of the committee to see "Arab Spring" this way. Uncle Sam's open support for jihad is an epic scandal that is never even acknowledged.

Farenthold: "Were you aware of any ties by that militia to Islamic extremists?"

Nordstrom: "Absolutely. Yeah, we had that discussion on a number of occasions, the last of which was when there was a Facebook posting of a threat that named Ambassador Stevens and Sen. (John) McCain, who was coming out for the elections. That was in the July (2012) time frame. I met with some of my agents and also some (CIA) annex personnel and we discussed that."

More news: Nordstrom seems to be saying that the February 17 Martyrs Brigade actually threatened both the U.S. ambassador and a U.S. senator -- and still served as U.S. security guards. This is shocking to read in black and white, although, again, when it becomes clear that Uncle Sam supported the same, exact jihad in Libya that al-Qaida supported, it makes -- if not sense exactly, then certainly a pattern.

Farenthold: "Mr. Hicks, you were in Libya on the night of the attack. Do you believe the February 17 militia played a role in those attacks, was complacent in those attacks?"

Hicks: "Certainly, elements of that militia were complicit in the attacks. The attackers had to make a long approach march through multiple checkpoints that were manned by February 17 militia."

More news: Most media accounts identified al-Qaida-linked Ansar al-Sharia ("Supporters of Sharia") as the militia manning the checkpoints around the compound that horrible night. Of course, Libya militias seem to be loose organizations with overlapping membership. More important, though, as John Rosenthal, author of "The Jihadist Plot: The Untold Story of Al-Qaeda and the Libyan Rebellion," puts it, virtually all of them "sympathize" with Ansar al-Sharia. "In fact," Rosenthal said in a recent interview with me, "in the literal sense of the term, virtually all of the Eastern Libyan militias are 'Ansar al-Sharia' -- that is to say 'supporters of the sharia.'"

February 17 Martyrs Brigade is no different. Its Facebook page has displayed a photo featuring the black flag of al-Qaida, and more important, the brigade demonstrated for sharia in Benghazi last summer.

In March 2013, Rosenthal reported at Newsmax.com that the brigade's Facebook page also featured "a graphic celebrating Jabhat al-Nusra," the U.S.-designated terrorist offshoot of al-Qaida in Iraq fighting Syria's Bashar Assad.

"In defiance of the U.S. designation," Rosenthal wrote, "the Arabic on the graphic declares, 'We are all Jabhat al-Nusra.'"

"We" were also U.S. security guards.

Farenthold: "I'm stunned that the State Department was relying on a militia with extremist ties to protect American diplomats. That doesn't make any sense. How does that happen?"

For me, Nordstrom's reply was the most candid moment in the hearings. Out came the man's evident frustration at serving a country gone mad in crippling alliances with jihadist enemies everywhere.

Nordstrom: "You mean like in Afghanistan, where Afghanis that are working with our military ... turn on them and shoot them? Or in Yemen, where our embassy was attacked in 2008 by attackers wearing police uniforms? Or in Saudi Arabia, in Jeddah, we had an attack in 2004. The Saudi National Guard that was protecting our facility reportedly ran from the scene and then it took 90 minutes before we could get help."

It felt as if Nordstrom could have continued, but the congressman, perhaps mindful of the clock, jumped back in.

Farenthold: "There's pretty high unemployment in the United States. I would imagine there's some Americans that'd be willing to take jobs overseas."

Nordstrom: "We couldn't agree with you more. But unfortunately, as I said earlier ... that was the 'best' bad plan. That was the unit that the Libyan government had initially designated for VIP protection. It was very difficult to extract ourselves from that."

If Americans ever learn how and why this is so, why our government is making common cause with jihadist groups everywhere, they will realize that Uncle Sam has himself joined the jihad. Let's hope we learn before it's too late.

Clintonism

If Only ...

2/12/01

"They were two political partners who had barely spoken for a year, but a few days after Al Gore conceded the 2000 election, he and Bill Clinton were finally talking face to face." So begins a juicy little chronicle by the Washington Post's John F. Harris about a private "showdown session" called by Gore to hash out why he, Gore, having presided over eight years of peace and prosperity under him, the Big He, did not win the White House.
There are no direct quotations from the two men in this newspaper account.

Indeed, the writer relied entirely on unnamed sources "close" to them both. What pops out, though, is a vivid, almost 3-D picture of two disgruntled rivals who blame each other for losing the presidency - in, as Harris writes, "uncommonly blunt language." While there are no reports that paperweights or staplers were put to the test of the laws of gravity during the exchange, you might say that the recriminations flew.

"You and your stupid sex scandals," said Al - or words to that effect.

"You and your not remembering, 'It's the economy, stupid,' Stupid!" said Bill - or words to that effect. While this confrontation might not make it as Greek tragedy, it packs a wallop despite the more burlesque trappings of the scene - from the humidor that had to be on the desk, to the ghost-of-"is-is"- past that had to be haunting the room. In other words, even though this face-off between Bill and Al is less "Henry IV" than "Bubba Meets Gore-zilla," it offers some keenly telling insights.

It all goes back to Bill Clinton's historic impeachment - and Al Gore's historic defense of the impeached president. Remember that hang-tough Democratic pep rally on Impeachment Day? Administration luminaries along with the Democratic Party leadership (all of whom had been lied to by Clinton) gathered on the White House lawn to listen to Gore praise Clinton as "one of our greatest presidents." That December day in 1998 - not the last Democratic Convention, not Election Day, and not the night of his concession speech - was the turning point in Gore's political life.

Imagine that instead of having agreed to save Clinton's political life, Gore had quietly signaled his disappointment. Imagine that his disappointment had emboldened and ultimately inspired party elders to go, as senior Republicans once did, to the disgraced president and press for his resignation. These are big "ifs," sure. But it's by no means an exercise in science fiction to consider the possibility that Gore might have been able to run for president in 2000 as the bona fide incumbent who, Excelsior-style, had himself restored "honor and integrity" to the Oval Office while presiding over a high-flying Dow. Almost certainly he would have won.

Instead, a Republican president is preparing to see a Reaganesque tax cut through a Republican Congress, Gore is teaching a journalism class - initially off the record (go figure) - and Clinton is feeling the blistering heat of a spate of post-presidential scandals that have rankled his most devoted supporters. Little wonder the word is that Team Clinton and Team Gore have become "estranged." While none of this is a bad thing for those who support the Republican Party, it seems as if the nation as a whole remains distracted by the real-life morality play - still unresolved - that was the Clinton-Gore years.

The fact is, justice was never served, not really. Successfully escaping indictment is no badge of honor to make a country proud. Returning $28,000 in White House knickknacks doesn't instantly placate concerns over what appears to have been a post-presidential bout of kleptomania. Copping a last-minute plea with the independent counsel doesn't atone for the serial indignities Bill Clinton inflicted on the body politic.

The failure to reach what might be described as a catharsis concerning the Clintons has left a strange, restless energy in their wake. It probably explains the seemingly pent-up furor that the Clintons' most loyal allies have unleashed upon the practically hapless couple during these past weeks of Bookgate, Pardongate, Sofagate and Officegate. While the good ol' vast-right-wing-conspiracy dutifully saddled up for one more round-up on the Clinton front (or two, or three - but who's counting?), the anything-goes-left went ballistic for the first time, as if shaking down pals for a few pricey place-settings is a more serious threat to the nation' s founding principles than perjury and obstruction of justice. That's a skewed perspective for you - and it's what you get when you decide to wait too long, as Al Gore did, to get a few things off your chest.

Who's sorry now?

3/2/01

Pity the Democrats. They seem to have run out of the kind of double-edged adjectives that cut Bill Clinton down to size and pump themselves up to a righteous, if temporary, stature. The subject—what else?--is the presidential pardons that have all but put on a lock on the news since Mr. Clinton (thankfully) became our former president on January 20. The adjectives range from "indefensible" and "squalid," choice terms now branded across once-Clintonite editorial pages, to "disgraceful," a word that summed up the situation for Jimmy Carter. Barney Frank picked "outrageous," as did Hamilton Jordan, while Bill Daley, the man who directed Al Gore's presidential campaign both before and after Election Day, couldn't decide between "terrible," "devastating" or "rather" —rather?--"appalling." Ed Koch settled for nothing less than "Snake oil pitchman."

All this and more, according to reports, have left Mr. Clinton "perplexed." And why shouldn't he be? These are the same folks who hung tough with him through scandals far seamier than this current batch. Having gotten their last cuff link emblazoned with the presidential seal from the man, these stalwart supporters have finally turned into vociferous opponents. No wonder Mr. Clinton is in a "funk." Lead-off apologist Paul Begala (a man who offers, straight-faced, a pardon-mess explanation to the effect that Mr. Clinton is just "a big-hearted guy") described the former president's current state of mind to the New York Times: "More than anything, I've found him to be puzzled. It's like: 'How can anyone think that way?' "

How, indeed. This sort of reaction verges on what's known as being in denial. The paper also reports, rather coyly, that "people who have spoken to [Mr. Clinton] say he believes that Republicans would have found a way to demonize him out of office without" —this is the coy part—" what even his friends acknowledge is the assistance he has provided them." In other words, damned if he did provide "Republicans" with "assistance" by issuing pardons to a fugitive billionaire who trafficked with terrorist nations, a Cali-connected drug king-pin, and assorted fraudsters and scam artists who tried to fill his brother (brothers?)-in-law's pockets—and dammed if he didn't. This notion definitely comes under the heading of being in denial.

But Mr. Clinton is not alone. Where conservatives see just one more assault by the Clintons on the presidency, his erstwhile allies feign an almost maidenly shock at discovering a pay-per-pardon scheme run by the Clinton family out of the Oval Office. Look how the New York Times described the scandal's impact: The nation, the paper opined, "seldom finds itself in the state of stunned bipartisan unanimity produced by President Clinton's pardons." "Bipartisan unanimity," sure—but "stunned"?

It is in such protestations of shock that Mr. Clinton finds company in denial. No one who faces up to the facts every day could be stunned by anything Bill or Hillary Clinton might do. Of course, for liberals to place Pardongate in context—to see it as a seamless extension of the serial lawlessness of the Clinton years—they would have to do something truly great: Admit that they were wrong. No matter how many big words they'll throw around these days, they don't seem up to the task.

"The idea that somehow there was a bunch of criminality that went on for eight years and this just proves it, that is, utter, complete nonsense," said the Wall Street Journal's Al Hunt. In an essay headlined, "Unpardonable"—one of those righteous word choices—Salon.com editor Joan Walsh writes that conservatives "insist that Clinton's demoralized backers really only have themselves to blame since they looked away from eight years of scandals from Whitewater to Travelgate to the Lewinsky mess. I don't buy that." Too bad she chooses not to explain why. The New Republic, meanwhile, looks at the paralysis Pardongate has inflicted on national affairs and writes that because Bill Clinton is now being punished "politically," "the system is working."

But the system is not working, not unless the mechanisms that prevent such grotesque dishonesties are in good order. This hasn't been the case since, oh, say, some time around 1993. The fact is, with the indispensable collaboration of American liberals, Bill Clinton was able to throw monkey- wrench after monkey-wrench into the works until the system broke down around him—not to mention the rest of us. Why? Even Ms. Walsh goes so far as to admit that "maybe" after impeachment, "the normal rules just didn't apply to him."

Too many Americans thought that was just hunky dory. And no matter how many bad names people call Mr. Clinton now, that fact, more than anything Bill Clinton ever did, is the real problem.

The last classic Clinton cover-up

4/20/01

You've heard of Monica's old dress; the missing billing records; "is is;" and all those other clues to classic Clinton cover-ups. But have you heard of Kennewick Man?

Perhaps the last—and positively the most literal—victim targeted for cover-up by the Clinton White House, the ancient skeleton known as Kennewick Man was ordered by former Interior Secretary Bruce Babbitt to be turned over last fall to a coalition of American Indian tribes for burial—and quick, before scientists managed to learn anything about him. Why? The answer to that very simple question takes us into one of those murky battle zones of the so-called culture wars where the irrational forces of political correctness have made destabilizing inroads into the vital preserve of free inquiry.

Kennewick Man is one of the oldest remains ever found in North America. Accidentally discovered in the summer of 1996 by boat-race spectators along Oregon's Columbia River, he presented scientists with a thrilling find: the well-preserved remains of a battle-scarred man thought to have been in his forties, who, perhaps until an arrowhead in his hip brought him down roughly ninety centuries ago, stood about 5 feet 10 inches tall. Even more intriguing was his surprisingly long face and large, protruding nose—facial features that resemble those of no known American Indian tribe.

Could he have had Caucasoid origins? While scientists have remarked on Kennewick Man's similarities to Polynesian, northern Japanese and southern Asian populations, the initial speculation in the local press suggested he may have been an "early white settler," likely spurring the forces of political correction into instant action. After all, there's no room in "Native America"—that peaceable, environmentally friendly myth of pre-Columbian perfection—for "natives" of the "wrong" color.

Indeed, American Indians could hardly claim their uniquely privileged "native" status if it were discovered that they were comparative newcomers to the continent. Clearly, Kennewick Man had to buried—both figuratively and literally.

The Clinton administration seems to have agreed. First, the Army Corps of Engineers, which administers the land on which the skeleton was found, announced it would turn the remains over to Indian tribes for burial. This prompted eight prominent anthropologists, including two from the Smithsonian, to file suit to study the skeleton, a move which has put the big funeral on indefinite hold.

But there's more. In 1998, in an act of near-Talibanesque obliteration, the Corps, acting in concert with what a spokesman called "participation and interest at the Executive level," dropped 500 tons of rock and dirt on top of the very spot along the riverbank where Kennewick Man had been found, effectively sealing the site against further study. The Corps likes to say it simply stabilized the site for scientists—like a cement pair of shoes cures corns—and, as Mark Lasswell reported in the Wall Street Journal, ensured, on behalf of Indian interests, "the protection of any additional skeletal material or cultural artifacts from further revelation." Too bad the Corps wasn't operating in Egypt when Howard Carter and the Earl of Carnarvon discovered the tomb of Tutankhamen— incidentally, about 7,000 years younger than Kennewick Man—to "protect" his remains and artifacts from similar "revelation."

But not even a 500-ton cover-up rids us of the question, Who was Kennewick Man and where did he come from? Last September, four years after his discovery, most of which time he has remained locked away by the government in an Oregon museum, Mr. Babbitt arrived at the answer: Based on oral tribal histories--9,000-year-old oral histories?--Mr. Babbitt concluded that Kennewick Man was of either Yakama, Umatilla, Nez Pierce, Colville or Wanapum tribe origin and should therefore, without further ado (or testing), go to his rest with his Yakama, Umatilla, Nez Pierce, Colville or Wanapum people.

But not so fast. The scientists who filed suit for the right to study the skeleton have not yet had their day in court. The Associated Press reported that their lawyers filed documents in federal court in Portland last week contending that the Clinton administration improperly tried to prevent their research "to avoid a debate over North America's first inhabitants," all the while maintaining what they called "inexcusable" contacts with the five Indian tribes that included "coaching the [Indian] coalition on how to plead its case." The Interior Department, which maintains it has done no wrong, has until May 17 to file a response, and the case is expected to go to trial in June.

This is a landmark case, with profound implications. Should Kennewick Man be forever lost to research for, in essence, fear of what he might teach us about our past, freedom of inquiry will have lost another battle to the forces of political correction — a reason to fear for the future of knowledge itself.

'Honest Bill' Clinton and other Ratheresian Logic

5/18/01

Bill O'Reilly, of the Fox News Channel and a JWR columnist, had a question this week for Dan Rather of CBS that sparked one of the more phantasmagorical exchanges this side of Wonderland. "I want to ask you flat out, "said Mr. O'Reilly. "Do you think Bill Clinton's an honest man?"

"Yes, I think he's an honest man, "replied Mr. Rather, according to the transcript posted by the Media Research Center at mediaresearch.org.

Mr. O'Reilly, incredulous: "Do you really?"

"I do, "the CBS Evening News anchorman said.

"Even though he lied to Jim Lehrer's face about the Lewinsky case?" asked Mr. O'Reilly, seizing on the one Clintonian whopper that, anchor to anchor, should have gotten Mr. Rather's nanny.

"Who among us has not lied about something? "said Mr. Rather, deflecting the question with a little fortune-cookie-style mysticism.

"Well, I didn't lie to anybody's face on national television. I don't think you have, have you?" responded Mr. O'Reilly.

"I don't think I ever have. I hope I never have..." He *hopes* he never has?

"Then how you can say he's an honest guy then?"

"Well, because I think he is."

There's Ratheresian Logic for you: Dan Rather thinks Bill Clinton is honest, therefore he is. No matter how many acts of dishonesty this former president committed, Mr. Rather chooses to call him "honest." As the CBS Evening News anchorman went on to say, "I think at core he's an honest person. I think you can be an honest person and lie about any number of things."

It's difficult to know what is more impressive: Mr. Rather's deceitful illogic, or the blithely prosaic reading he gives his deceitful and illogical mouthful. At the risk of sounding pedantic, it seems worth noting that it's just not possible for an "honest" person to "lie about any number of things," at least not so long as Webster's has any say in the matter. After all, an honest reputation depends upon acts of honesty — or should if there is any hope of preserving the vital link between word and deed that makes communication possible.

This sort of disconnect, of course, is by no means unique to the mental processes of multi-million-dollar network anchormen. The Democratic frenzy over President Bush's judicial nominees, for example, is scrambling such words as "centrist" and "extreme" beyond recognition, rendering reasoned debate practically impossible. The ongoing toll of so-called political correctness on the language may be continually catalogued. Now, recent developments suggest that a new problem has arisen in bringing words and deeds into line in our schools' efforts to save lives.

It all started with "zero tolerance," a perfectly sane law enacted in 1994 against guns on campus. With every deplorable school shooting that has occurred since, this policy has variously expanded, with many districts across the country now adopting "zero tolerance" rules against any violence and all threats of violence. This has led to some ludicrous results, capped perhaps by the Louisiana boy who was suspended for two days after warning his classmates ahead of him in the cafeteria line that they better not eat all the potatoes or else: "I'm gonna get you!"

In the New Jersey suburb of Manalapan, according to the New York Times, the policy has become practically draconian as suspension now triggers an entry in a police file. The Manalapan crime blotter now includes the 10-year-old girl who said "I could kill her!" after her teacher refused to let her go to the bathroom and she wet her pants (3-day suspension); the 10-year-old boy who muttered, "I oughtta murder his face "when someone left his desk a mess (3-day suspension); and the 12-year-old shoved during a touch football game who was suspended for yelling, "I'll kill you!"

Interestingly enough, the student who did the shoving wasn't disciplined. The question is, when does "kill "mean "kill"? In a society of causal profanity and untamed coarseness, hardly ever. Granted: Mr. "I oughtta murder his face" oughtta stay after school and write "I will not direct such boorish exclamations at my schoolfellows "about 300 times. But there seems to be a fundamental misreading of the language leading these children to accrue actual police records. Wouldn't a few demerits do in most of these cases—or would that be too injurious to their self-esteem? The fact is, the message we are sending has become garbled, one terrible consequence of the general degradation of the language.

Of course, that doesn't mean that zero tolerance is always a bad thing—especially when it comes to Dan Rather and "honest" Bill.

Is graciousness the culprit?

6/1/01

This week's Associated Press headline may not say it all, but it comes close: "White House Vandalism Still Debated."

All those saying "aye"—the Bush administration—have finally come forward in the person of White House spokesman Ari Fleischer to offer a public accounting of the crude mess—the sabotaged phones, damaged computers, graffiti-covered walls, overturned desks and pornographic pictures—members of the outgoing Clinton administration left behind for members of the incoming Bush administration to dig their way out of. Only now, four and a half months after the fact, the Great Clintonista Trashing of the White House has emerged as a topic of "debate," a matter of one man's—or, rather, one administration's—opinion. Or even worse, as Democrats now clamor, it has suddenly been framed as an unfair, unfounded, outright lie.

How did this happen? It all started back in January, after the first juicy rush of vandalism reports from anonymous Bush sources dried up as word came from on high that it was "time to move on"—and stop rubbernecking at the carnage of the Clinton years. Not only were all those post-Clinton post-mortems sucking up political oxygen, they appeared to strike the new president as a matter of what used to known as—and this will sound quaint—"bad form." As the White House edged itself away from the vandalism story, Mr. Fleischer told the Washington Post, "All the White House stories were aimed at moving forward. It was all in the context of drawing reporters back from the story because that's what the president wanted."

The president, naturally, got what he wanted. The White House may never have gone so far as to deny that any vandalism had taken place, but the story shut down at the source. Given that the White House decided not to document the damage—fear of "bad form" strikes again?--subsequent inquiries by the General Accounting Office (GAO), Congress's investigative arm, and the General Service Administration (GSA), which manages federal property, were inconclusive. As the Washington Post reported, the GSA "issued a letter saying it found no damage to White House real estate but said it was not addressing possible damage to furnishings or equipment. The GAO said it could reach no additional conclusions because of ' the lack of records ... reported by the White House."

Far from inspiring President Bush's Democratic opponents to give a cheer—pip, pip, Old Bean—for his innate sense of discretion and good cheer, the "lack of records" has convinced them to claim that no vandalism ever took place. As Joe Lockhart, one of Bill Clinton's press secretaries put it, "If there was anything there, they should have put it out at the time. Now, they're expecting us to just take their word for it."

(Spoken like a true Clintonista.) Rep. Anthony Weiner, New York Democrat, has gone farther still, demanding that the Bush administration apologize for having "deliberately misled the American people and smeared the names of public servants who were guilty of nothing." And the outrage only grows—as do the numbers of supposed victims. Jake Siewart, another Clinton press secretary, recently told the Kansas City Star, whose misinterpretation of the GSA's initial inquiry seems to have kick started this whole phase of the vandalism story, "The White House has been smearing a whole class of people without providing any evidence."

It is, of course, the White House that is now being smeared. "The White House's continuing campaign of disinformation and possible violation of federal law for noncompliance with a GAO investigation calls its credibility—and its list of damaged property—into question," Mr. Weiner's spokeswoman Serena Torrey none-too-serenely told the Washington Post.

All of which has left Ari Fleischer bemoaning the administration's strange predicament. "The White House bent over backward to make this issue go away, to be gracious to the previous administration" Mr. Fleischer told the AP. "We tried to be gracious, but the last administration would not take graciousness," he said to the Washington Post.

Is graciousness really the culprit here? Certainly, it would have been possible for the Bush administration to be gracious—and carry a big video camera. The problem seems to be one of maturity, which may come as a surprise given the relief of having a "grown-up" administration in place. But, as President Bush has said, there is today a profound need to restore a concrete sense of accountability in our government, and in our country. In averting its eyes from the calumnies of the Clinton era, both great and, in this case, puny, the Bush administration no doubt believed it was acting wisely—not to mention downright nobly

In the end, though, there is something a little naive about believing that any administration could begin anew without facing up to the facts about the old.

Lost files, lost presidency

12/13/01

Good news, sort of, for Bill Clinton and Madeline Albright. Having persisted in telling tales at cross-purposes to explain why the Clinton administration didn't do too much about Osama bin Laden and the Al Qaeda network for all those Clinton years, these two erstwhile officeholders may now read from the same page—literally—and discover in the January issue of Vanity Fair what went wrong on their watch.

With the publication of "The Osama Files" by David Rose, the former president and former secretary of state get a second chance to see the letters and secret memoranda that they, along with their top aides at the White House and the State Department, once ignored or failed to act upon. The rest of us, meanwhile, get a first look at a paper trail documenting the futile efforts by Sudan, of all places, to alert the United States to the workings, the identities and the movements of the Al Qaeda network, including Osama bin Laden.

Sudan, of course, is no land of milk and honey. Indeed, it is a pit of violence, persecution, and even slavery of Christians and animists. But, amazingly, there is a "but"—beginning in 1996, Sudan made a series of diplomatic overtures to the Clinton administration.

Hoping to see its terrorism sanctions lifted, Sudan initiated a campaign to establish anti-terrorism credentials based on its apparently extensive files on the Al Qaeda network. In the leisure of political retirement, Clinton and Albright may now reconsider the wisdom of having rejected Sudanese President Omar al-Bashir's written offer to open his country to American investigators in 1997.

They may now look back on the repeated efforts Sudan made to share its dossiers on known terrorists with the United States and reflect on whether it was really such a brilliant idea, for example, for the State Department to have nixed even a meeting between the FBI and Sudanese intelligence in 1998. As Janet McElligott, a lobbyist who served in the first Bush administration, said at the time when urging the Clinton administration to examine Sudan's info-trove, "You do realize bin Laden lived there [Sudan] and they have files on his main people?"

The Vanity Fair article—a dramatic expansion of a piece David Rose wrote for a British newspaper in late September—reports that Sudan began trying to open the books on bin Laden in February 1996, well before the terrorist attacks that would make the Saudi-born terrorist infamous. That means that for more than four years the Clinton administration refused even to consider intelligence that might have prevented the bombing of the Khobar Towers (June 1996), the destruction of the American embassies in Kenya and Tanzania (August 1998), the attack on the USS Cole (October 2000), and, of course, Sept. 11.

No wonder Mansoor Ijaz, a wealthy Pakistani-American Muslim and Clinton supporter who participated in a series of failed back-channel efforts to persuade Clinton officials to study Sudan's files, wrote last week in the Los Angeles Times that this blindfolded American approach "represents one of the most serious foreign policy failures in American history." But why was such potentially vital information not only ignored, but never even evaluated?

"The simple answer is that the Clinton administration had accused Sudan of sponsoring terrorism, and refused to believe that anything it did to prove its bona fides could be genuine," Vanity Fair reports. No doubt this is true. But there could be more to this scandalous foul-up than the politicization of intelligence.

Just ask what mattered more to Clintonites in June of 1996: the news on June 25 that a truck bomb had exploded at Khobar Towers in Dharan, Saudi Arabia, or the Supreme Court's decision of the day before to hear Jones v. Clinton after the 1996 re-election campaign? Or compare another strange confluence of events. What more likely pre-occupied Bill Clinton and his advisers in August of 1998: the embassy bombings in Africa on Aug. 7, or Clinton's appearance before a grand jury in connection with the Lewinsky matter 10 days later?

Given the permanent reconfiguration of the Clinton White House into a scandal-busting spin machine, the answers to such questions are obvious, if distasteful. They may help explain, for example, why Sudan's offer to extradite two suspected bombers (and Al Qaeda members), made in the days between the 1998 embassy bombing and Clinton's grand jury appearance, was met with silence—except, of course, for the sound of American bombs falling on what was reportedly a medicine factory in Khartoum. Scandal-riddled, the Clinton administration simply failed to function. That, surely, is the biggest scandal of all.

Legacy of lasciviousness

6/25/04

This being National Bill Clinton Awareness Week, I have some questions for the former president. I would like to know more about the "sofa" he says he slept on after informing his wife, the future junior senator from New York, that Monica Lewinsky was not a figment of the imagination of the vast right-wing conspiracy. Is it still in the White House? Shouldn't this historic piece of furniture go to the Clinton Legacy Wing of the Smithsonian Institution?

After all, that sofa is posterity's direct link to what Bill Clinton singularly calls "the worst day" of his administration. Worse than the day of Mogadishu, or impeachment, or any Al Qaeda attack that occurred on his watch, that "worst" day must have been pretty bad. At least for him. For the rest of us, this revelation recalls the essence of the Clinton presidency: the narcissism of it all. It was all about him, and it still is.

Clinton can laugh about it now — and he does, which is extremely weird to behold. And he insists, as he did to the BBC's Jonathan Dimbleby during his spout-blowing interview, that none of the scandal-related turmoil had any impact on his presidential duties, including his recent, hindsighted campaign against Al Qaeda. And if you believe that, I think I can find a sofa to sell you.

Clinton credits his ability to live "parallel lives" with his success in eliminating Osama bin Laden — sorry, I mean his success, period. And then he adds this: "Frankly — perhaps I shouldn't acknowledge this — but it was a relief to have to have to go to work and concentrate on something else. Otherwise, I would have nothing to think about all day long but what a bad fella I'd been." Shucks, maybe it was a good thing Osama bin Laden and the attack on the USS Cole came along to help the poor guy through some tough times.

Such as that "worst day." Most people would find a measure of relief in coming clean. But "clean" complicated things for Bill Clinton. Besides the betrayal of his wife and daughter, there were all those cabinet secretaries, for instance, who publicly lied at Clinton's behest. Remember that 1998 day when a slew of cabinet officers, led by Secretary of State Madeleine Albright, stood in the rain outside the White House to vouch for Bill Clinton's honesty? In lieu of the honorable exit (resignation), Siberia-on-the-sofa becomes an increasingly apt metaphor for the Clinton years.

But there's more to the Clinton legacy than a couch. Toughing it out for all the wrong reasons — because, as Clinton now explains his gross behavior, "he could" — is the Clinton endowment to American politics. The distinction between "could" and "should" has been obscured, if not almost lost.

The political unraveling of Jack Ryan, a once-promising GOP candidate for the U.S. Senate from Illinois, offers an example of this dubious legacy. When Ryan's child custody court records — which contain his former wife's ultra-sordid allegations that Ryan tried to compel her to participate at "explicit sex clubs" in New Orleans, New

York and Paris — were unsealed this week, the candidate found himself trying to throw a political blanket over unsavory, now-exposed appetites he had hoped would remain hidden.

Should they have remained private? Yes, but so should have Ryan. And would have, I think, had he described to his GOP boosters the exact nature of the skeletons that his ex-wife, fairly or not, had hung in his closet. Ryan says he didn't break the law, his marriage vows or the Ten Commandments. This appears to be true, but his private life as a husband has nonetheless sorely undermined his public character as a potential Republican senator.

He disagrees. "I think if that's the worst people can say about me ... I think it speaks very well about my character," he says. I'm not sure Ryan should be touting "character" now that his GOP boosters in Illinois — which include former governors and state officials — have been stung. It may not be the Clinton cabinet in the rain exactly, but it's little wonder some of his supporters are feeling all wet.

Bill Clinton — publicly disgraced by the tatty climax to a seemingly endless string of notorious "bimbo eruptions" and assorted abuses of power and position — taught us that if you could stay in the ring, you should. Ryan, tarred by his ex-wife's charges, has learned not to consider whether he should stay in the ring (or whether he should have ventured forth in the first place), only whether he'll be able to remain. Voters deserve better, or should. If only they could find it in themselves to demand it.

Don't close the book on the Clintons

12/10/07

A few weeks ago, I went rummaging through my attic looking for a box of books. Not just any box of books: my Clinton books. Or, should I say, given the range and number of tomes, my Clinton library.

I'd tucked it all away sometime after 9/11 when a burgeoning collection on Islam needed shelf space. Being able to reach for "What the Koran Really Says" by Ibn Warraq, say, and not chapter and verse on Clinton corruption, was suddenly an obvious priority. We were at war, yes, but there was some consolation in the fact that our long national nightmare — the Clintons — was over. At least it was safe to pack away the books. Temporarily.

We are still at war, but, like a recurring dream, the Clintons — or, as Mark Levin pointedly prefers, "the Clinton crime family" — is back, the missus now leading in their well-worn slot at the focal point of national politics. But there is something missing this time around. Something colossal.

That something is their past — the Clinton past of political malfeasance and corruption. I'm not just talking about Bill's impeachment, although that's part of it, what with Hillary's never-revised contention that "a vast right-wing conspiracy" was behind all her husband's political travails. But I refer also to the commonplace lies and routine treachery the American people were confronted with, subjected to and degraded by over two Clinton terms. In other words, the Clinton past is our past as well — the history of every American who lived through those years. And it has gone missing. To behold this presidential election cycle, it seems as if the entire nation has metaphorically put their Clinton libraries in their attics.

The resulting gap in national discourse keeps presenting itself to me, particularly when called on to discuss Mrs. Clinton just as though she were an ordinary presidential candidate — someone with a modest Senate record and a keen interest in political affairs, weighing in on the events of the day.

She's not. There's not only all that shameful Clinton "baggage," but all those questions about what's inside that baggage, questions she has never, ever acknowledged, let alone answered. It's as though Hillary Clinton believes she has no past to reckon with; no broken trust to mend; no reason to acknowledge that, to name one example, amassing hundreds of FBI files of Reagan and Bush (I) officials for political use in the White House is a Bad Thing, even if neither she nor anyone else in the White House was actually indicted for it. And it's as though everyone else agrees.

That's why the spectacle of Hillary's political progress toward the White House looks nothing less than surreal. And hence my compulsion to seek out that big box of books upstairs, to regain the physical evidence of the complex weave of money-grubbing and power-playing that made the Clintons and their White House years unique.

I found the box, finally (after whacking my head on an attic beam), filled with "Sellout" by David Schippers, "The Breach" by Peter Baker, "Friends in High Places" by Webb Hubbell, "State of a Union" by Jerry Oppenheimer, "Hell to Pay" by Barbara Olson, and on and on.

Frankly, it all adds up to a giant cascade of yuck, which both Clintons have always ducked by, well, ducking...evading questions..."moving on." National Review's Jay Nordlinger recently recalled attending a 2000 press conference of then Senate-candidate Hillary Clinton and asking: "Do you stand by your assertion that the charges against your husband stemmed from 'a vast right-wing conspiracy'?" Her reply: "I'm not going back, I'm going forward."

But what if it turns out she can't really leave the past behind? This question I have after picking up the 1998 book "Year of the Rat: How Bill Clinton Compromised U.S. Security for Chinese Cash" by

Edward Timperlake and William C. Triplett II. It's a detailed account of presidential perfidy in, essentially, making available White House access, policy secrets, supercomputers and military technology (including advanced rocket-guidance technology) to China even as a rogue's gallery of Chinese communist agents, spies, arms dealers, pimps and gangsters were pumping massive infusions of cash in Clinton campaign coffers.

For starters, shouldn't Hillary Clinton at least have to explain how, as president, she would ensure that these compromises to national security that happened on her husband's watch wouldn't happen on hers?

I'd say yes, of course, and much more. In other words, this is no time to close the book.

Rubber stamp for Hillary

1/9/09

If I were Gov. Bill Richardson, still smarting somewhere in New Mexico over his lost Cabinet post in the incoming Obama administration, I would be plenty sore about Sen. Hillary Clinton. According to all rosy media predictions, Clinton is destined to sail through Senate confirmation hearings and become secretary of state next week, a veritable regatta's worth of clapping senators trailing in her wake. Richardson, meanwhile, is out on his ear.

Why? As the story goes, Richardson wasn't forthcoming enough about a federal probe into whether officials in his New Mexico administration tipped a state project to a firm run by a major financial contributor to Richardson's PAC.

Clinton, meanwhile, wasn't forthcoming — period — about legislation she helped pass that made tax-exempt bonds available to a businessman who, practically simultaneously, donated $100,000 to hubby Bill's foundation. The main difference is Richardson's troubles are being sorted out in a federal investigation; Clinton's appeared in a news story. And even though The New York Times saw fit to flick at a so-called pay-for-play scandal with its headline "A Donor's Gift Soon Followed Clinton's Help," the story just doesn't seem to stick.

So, what else is new with the Clintons?

Actually, there is something — the long-awaited list of nations, organizations and people who have ponied up nearly $500 million for the Bill fund, known officially, since our Bill now is all growed up, as The William J. Clinton Foundation.

It was from this donor list — released in the media black hole just before Christmas — that the Times, sorting through the Soros, the Bings and the Waltons, the Nigerians, the Ukrainians and the Canadians, made the Bill-donation Hill-legislation connection.

But such a story is nothing next to what else the list reveals: deep and disturbing and disqualifying conflicts of interest for Mrs. Clinton due to her husband's monetary ties to some of the worst despots in the world. And why has Bill made his post-presidential life one long fundraiser?

According to the foundation's Web site, the purpose is to fund such efforts as "combating climate change," "transforming ideas into action" and other global, if not cosmic, missions. Too bad for Hillary that Bill didn't just sign up as a roving ambassador for UNICEF.

One major conflict the Clinton foundation creates for Hillary regards Saudi Arabia, listed among the Clinton foundation's largest donors. "The Kingdom of Saudi Arabia" dropped somewhere between $10 million and $25 million into the foundation's kitty, while the pro-Saudi advocacy group Friends of Saudi Arabia threw in another $1 to $5 million. (I won't even mention the assortment of Saudi nationals showering the foundation with moolah.)

How does Madame Secretary Clinton talk tough, clean and independent to "the Kingdom" with all that Saudi cash in her husband's foundational pockets? Whether she could in fact rise above the money flowing into the Clinton foundation coffers, she could not rise above it in appearance. And it is appearance here that counts for the good offices of the USA. The problem is hardly limited to Saudi money. Many millions of dollars have come sloshing into the Clinton foundation from Oman, Kuwait, Qatar and other Persian Gulf nations, including as much as $5 million from the Zayed family of the U.A.E. The Zayeds, as Jacob Laksin pointed out, have made headlines for past philanthropic acts related to a family think tank for anti-Semites, Holocaust deniers and jihadists.

Money pouring in from the Dubai Foundation — between $1 and $5 million — is at least as disquieting.

Remember the furor when, in 2005, the Bush administration wanted to transfer security and management of U.S. ports to Dubai Ports? That's a business owned by the Dubai Foundation, essentially a business owned by Dubai's ruler, Sheikh Mohammed bin Rashid Al Maktoum.

Bill Clinton still has non-foundation business dealings with Mohammed, along with supermarket magnate Ron Burkle, as the Wall Street Journal noted. This doesn't look good for Hillary — or for our country.

Naturally, there's more. For digging up somewhere between $1 and $5 million for Bill's foundation, Issam M. Fares presents another unfortunate association for the wife who wants to be secretary of state. Fares, a former Lebanese Deputy prime minister, is hot for Hezbollah and tight with Syria. The fact that he has ties to Republicans, donating $100,000 to George W. Bush's 2000 inauguration and paying $100,000 apiece for speeches by George Bush (the father) and James Baker doesn't help Mrs. C. Again, whether these are ties that would actually bind her, they would certainly trip her up in question marks.

I could go on. For instance, there's Clinton foundation donor Alibaba.com, a Chinese Internet company that the Los Angeles Times described as being "accused of collaborating with China's censorship of the Web." How's that for complicating a secretary of state's Chinese portfolio?

And then there's the Alavi Foundation. Writing at Forbes.com, Rachel Ehrenfeld this week reported that this group, which supports Iranian causes, gave the Clinton foundation between $25,000 and $50,000 on Dec. 19, 2008 — the very day the Alavi Foundation's president, Farshid Jahedi, was indicted on federal charges related to a probe of the foundation's relationship with Iran's Bank Melli. (The donation, according to Ehrenfeld's report, also came two days after the U.S. Treasury Department designated Alavi's partner, the New York-based ASSA Corp., as a terrorist entity.)

Both the Alavi Foundation and Bank Melli, Ehrenfeld reported, have been "recognized as procurement fronts for Iran's nuclear program," with Bank Melli being designated in 2007 as a terrorist entity.

The point is not to argue that Hillary Clinton is indeed beholden to those among her husband's donors who run the gamut from unseemly to indicted. The point is that as secretary of state, she would appear to be, and that appearance would lower her standing — and our country's — throughout the world. This is an extremely urgent and grave matter coming before the U.S. Senate next week.

Unfortunately — tragically — for the United States, the Senate is all too likely to approach it with a rubber stamp.

Rubber-stamp approval slips over Hil's chasms of conflicts

1/16/09

That was some confirmation hearing for madame secretary of State this week. One for the annals. Not so much for what Hillary Clinton said (boilerplate stuff) but for what the Senate Foreign Relations Committee did. The senators showed up to examine, at least, the many red flags popping up between Bill Clinton's ongoing global charitable foundation and Hillary Clinton's upcoming global diplomatic portfolio, but they stayed on to gawk and burble. On Thursday, the committee voted 16-to-1 to give the lady a big, fat stamp of approval.

But sometimes inexplicably: "The (William J.) Clinton Foundation exists as a temptation for any foreign entity or government that believes it could curry favor through a donation," cautioned Sen. Richard Lugar of Indiana. "It also sets up potential perception problems with any action taken by the secretary of state in relation to foreign givers or their countries...." Therefore, he concluded, in a sharp reversal of his own logic, "I believe that every member of this committee will seek ways to support Senator Clinton's work as secretary of state." Huh?

And sometimes with hearts and flowers: "I truly appreciate all that you are poised to do and what you have done in the past," Sen. Lisa Murkowski of Alaska told Mrs. Clinton.

Or with an awkward turn of phrase: "Despite the news accounts that say that I'm the one that's going to ask you the hard questions about potential conflicts of interest, I have no questions about your integrity," said Sen. Jim DeMint of South Carolina. And none about the Clinton foundation. Weirdly, DeMint then appealed to Mrs. Clinton "to do whatever is necessary to silence any critics before you take office."

Whatever is necessary? That'll give a turn to old Clinton hands who still can't shake the image of Webb Hubbell rolling "over one more time," or of Kathleen Willey's poor cat. "Enough said," said DeMint. Maybe too much.

"I'm just a junior senator from Tennessee, but it seems to me that everything has a season and this is your season," Sen. Bob Corker of Tennessee told Mrs. C., splashing the Senate hearing room with chicken soup for the soul. "It just seems to me there's no reason whatsoever to have continual press comments and other kinds of things that might take away from, I think, what might be extraordinary efforts on your part."

Such was the loyal Republican "opposition."

"I believe that the better your diplomacy, the better your ability to defend yourself," Sen. Johnny Isakson of Georgia, another Republican, explained to Mrs. Clinton. "A strong military is a great foundation for good diplomacy. And then if you add the development, which I think is "soft power" or "smart power," you have a great trilogy. Do you agree with that?"

Penetrating question.

"Senator Isakson, I couldn't say it any better," said Mrs. Clinton. "I certainly do agree."

All of which goes to show this confirmation hearing wasn't exactly a trial by fire — unless, of course, "fire" means the kind of "fire" Mrs. Clinton said targeted her 1996 airport arrival into Bosnia — i.e., nonexistent fire.

But, as Corker put it, there's no reason for "continual press comments." Why bring up the millions of dollars bubbling out of the Middle East and into the Clinton foundation from Saudi Arabia, Qatar, Oman, Dubai and the United Arab Emirates? No Arab sheikh will give any of that moolah a thought when Secretary of State Clinton comes to call, right?

And just forget about the millions passing into the foundation coffers from, say, Lebanese-Canadian businessman Victor Dahdaleh, now facing a U.S. federal investigation into charges that he helped defraud a Bahrain-government controlled metals company — Bahrain being home of the U.S. Navy's Fifth Fleet. And never mind the donations of Gilbert Chagoury, a Lebanese-Nigerian businessman closely tied to former Nigerian dictator Sani Abacha. Chagoury, as the Wall Street Journal reported, has donated millions to the Clinton foundation. He also donated to Bill Clinton's 1996 re-election campaign — later helping to arrange a hefty speaking fee for the former president — while members of his family donated thousands of dollars to Hillary Clinton's presidential campaign. Just because this Clintonian sugar daddy has large oil interests in Nigeria, not to mention close ties to Lebanonese religious factions, let there be no "continual press comments" about these and other conflicts of interest. As DeMint put it, "Enough said."

But Senate gag aside, these colossal conflicts of interest Mrs. Clinton carries with her to the State Department won't go away.

Kudos to Sen. David Vitter, Republican of Louisiana, who voted against Mrs. Clinton's nomination due to conflicts posed by her husband's globe-spanning charities. And at least he asked whether and how donations to the Clinton Global Initiative, a breakaway arm of the Clinton foundation not covered by the agreement worked out between the Obama team and the Clinton foundation, will be monitored. In his final allotted moments, he even mentioned extremely troubling donations to the Clinton foundation from Iran-linked terror-tainted interests. But to no avail.

The situation was "unprecedented," said Lugar at hearing's end, adding: "I am hopeful that, as we go through the history of this, that people will not say, well, Senator Lugar, Senator Kerry and others were pressing it. They saw the problems. And we'll get full credit, but that will not be helpful to our foreign policy, to you, to your husband, to the foundation."

Full credit, senator? Full blame, I'd say.

Wake up, GOP, and quit ostracizing Todd Akin

8/24/12

Prediction: If the GOP establishment doesn't follow Republican Rep. Todd Akin's example with a big, fat apology — to Akin — the whole party goes down in flames come November.

I don't mean every Republican will lose, but there is great political peril in not sealing the hole in Republican armor that has opened in Missouri and instead permitting it to remain a Democratic pressure point. Further, "for the good of the country" (the mantra accompanying the partywide chorus of pleas to Akin to drop out of his U.S. Senate race), Republicans must resume funding Akin's viable campaign ASAP, after cutting it off in a mad fit of political pique. Finally, every one of them — the party standard-bearer, party bosses, congressional delegations, allied pundits — should come together for a group-smack on the head, as in, "What were we thinking?"

I can't recall anything in public life more widely craven and uncalled for than the open panic and bullying set off across the Republican Party by the first replay of Akin's perplexingly ignorant interview comments on rape and pregnancy. The veteran conservative lawmaker, former engineer, former businessman and grandfather of eight recanted these remarks. He apologized for them.

But as the left began to bay for blood over a Republican and, by preposterous extension, Republican Party it hopes to smear as "anti-woman," Republicans across the board, incredibly, joined in. Rather than jouncing Democrats back into some semblance of decent behavior with a firm, partywide reality check — comparing a dumb comment about rape from one among their ranks with, say, accusations of actual rape against Democrats' two-term hero Bill Clinton — Republicans obligingly cut off their own noses and handed them to their political opponents.

The headline in The New York Times this week said it all: "GOP Is Pressing Candidate to Quit Over Rape Remark." Funny how we never, ever saw anything similar in the 1990s, when bombshells about Bill Clinton's serial sexual harassment and assault of women were a common occurrence. Something like: "Dems Pressing President to Quit Over Rape."

Didn't happen. In fact, far from "pressuring" the former president into a quiet post-presidency retirement, the Democrats are spotlighting the overexposed sexual reprobate with a center-stage role at their upcoming convention. There, Clinton will officially renominate Barack Obama for president.

What else can we expect from the party that still lionizes Ted Kennedy, the late Massachusetts politician who notoriously left a young female campaign worker to drown in a sinking car rather than get help? Just as serial sexual improprieties perpetrated by Bill Clinton don't count in Democrat-land as "anti-woman," neither does Kennedy's unconscionable behavior at Chappaquiddick. Both men not only remained in office, they remain the Democrats' ideal.

A muddled, recanted remark about reproductive biology, however, puts a Republican one or two steps away from Hitler. He must be shunned by "decent" society, his whole career destroyed, the primary votes he won nullified, to expiate his "sin."

Worst of all is the Republican Party's unified acquiescence to this illogical, unjust and amoral equivalence. In fact, without the GOP's lockstep, take-me-to-your-leader obedience to the Democrats' rigged rules, the pitch of this controversy would have died down already. Without the Republicans' vigorous enforcement of the left's double standards, Akin would probably still be facing favorable odds of winning the Missouri Senate seat.

But no. Which is what deeply concerns me. Indulging ginned-up, hack hysterics is not the behavior of a leader or a winner. Worse, accommodating unjust attacks on a solid citizen in the name of practicality or the "greater good" is a very dangerous precedent, as totalitarian history tells us. That's why the GOP needs to rethink Missouri and make amends with Akin before "moving on." Otherwise, I fear that in its vital quest to prevent Barack Obama from winning a second term, it won't be moving anywhere.

Hillary Clinton doesn't deserve Americans' admiration

1/4/13

Americans, Gallup tells us, admire Hillary Clinton more than any other woman in the world — again. This latest accolade marks the 17th time Gallup has found Clinton to be the Most Admired Woman (MAW?) since she became first lady nearly 20 years ago. Only Eleanor Roosevelt (13 MAWs) comes close. Only Mother Teresa (1995 and 1996) and Laura Bush (2001) have interrupted Clinton's winning streak, and even then, Clinton came in second.
And therein lies America's cosmic flaw. A country that could time and again embrace Hillary Clinton as its MAW has lost its mind or its memory or both.

Does the phrase "congenital liar" tinkle any bells? I know such non-admirable sentiments are thought to be in the worst of taste, if not also banishable offenses. Still, as conjured by the late New York Times columnist William Safire in 1996, the phrase described the then-first lady for her shameless prevarications. These included what sure looked like bribery ("cattle futures"), defrauding taxpayers ("Whitewater"), obstructing justice — or, rather, "finding" her Rose Law Firm billing records (under subpoena for two years) just days after the statute of limitations ran out — among other corrupt behaviors that must have slightly suppressed Hillary-admiration that same year. The phrase remains apt.

"I remember landing under sniper fire," Clinton declared on the presidential campaign trail in 2008, describing a 1996 trip to Bosnia. "There was supposed to be some kind of a greeting ceremony at the airport, but instead we just ran with our heads down (chuckles) to get into the vehicles to get to our base." It was a vivid but debunkable whopper, as CBS footage of the event proved. In reality, Clinton, accompanied by daughter Chelsea, made her ceremonial way into Bosnia through a warm throng marked by smiling faces and a kiss from a local girl—not bullets. Admirable?

On a more nationally significant level, Clinton recently supported President Obama's Big Lie that a movie trailer of "Innocence of Muslims" on YouTube "resulted" (her word) in the September attack on the U.S. compound in Benghazi, Libya—a concerted falsehood for which neither Clinton nor Obama nor former CIA Director David Petraeus has yet answered. Even several days after intelligence agencies determined that a planned assault, not a video-driven protest, had taken place, Clinton went so far as to promise a grieving Charles Woods, father of slain former SEAL Tyrone Woods, that "we" were going to have the video maker "arrested and prosecuted."

Why was Clinton still perpetuating the false narrative that the exercise of free speech under the First Amendment, not Islamic jihad, had resulted in the attack? Was that admirable? Clinton has lately let it be known that she will voluntarily testify about Benghazi following her hospitalization for a blood clot, but I seriously doubt whether mere House members will risk asking this crucial question of the Most Admired Woman in America, especially now that she has risen from her sickbed. If they don't, they're not admirable, either.

Meanwhile, the video maker, Nakoula Basseley Nakoula, was indeed arrested and swiftly prosecuted, and is now serving one year in jail for "parole violations." His incarceration, however, is better understood as punishment for violating the Islamic ban on free speech about Islam. To be sure, one year is nothing compared to the death penalty an Egyptian court recently slapped on Nakoula and other Americans associated with the movie in absentia—and without a peep of protest from the Obama administration, including Clinton.

The fact is, Hillary Clinton has worked assiduously with the Islamic bloc nations, known as the Organization of Islamic Cooperation (OIC), to promote Islamically correct speech codes through the so-called Istanbul Process. The goal of this process—and the goal of transnational Islam—is to implement Shariah speech codes via U.N. Human Rights Council Resolution 16/18, which seeks to criminalize "defamation"—free speech—about Islam. In leading this drive against free speech, Hillary Clinton is actually leading a drive against the First Amendment.

Most Americans don't know about the Istanbul Process, let alone how Islamic speech codes are unconstitutional, but it is this policy against free speech that may stand as Clinton's enduring legacy as secretary of state. It is of a piece with having presided over, first, the shredding of U.S. alliances with Egypt's Hosni Mubarak and Libya's Moammar Gadhafi and then supporting jihadist factions and organizations, such as the Muslim Brotherhood, now implementing Islamic law across the Middle East. This, of course, is President Obama's policy, but Hillary Clinton has been an active team player.

Another aspect of this same foreign policy Clinton has spearheaded is the launch of the Global Counterterrorism Forum. The forum's roster of 29 nations plus the European Union is stunning for its exclusion of Israel, a leading counterterrorism force as much as it is a leading terrorism victim. But not so, according to Islamic definitions. Knowingly or not, as a leader of this forum, one-third of whose members come from the Islamic bloc, Clinton has accepted the Arab League and OIC definitions of terrorism, which both deny the existence of Israeli victims (sometimes U.S. soldiers) and legitimize the terrorism of Hamas, a wing of the Muslim Brotherhood, and Hezbollah.

How could this be? What influences have led Clinton to formulate or follow such policies? We don't know, although it is hard not to wonder about the input of top Clinton aide Huma Abedin, a young woman with well-established familial and personal ties to Muslim Brotherhood figures and front groups (including a "charity" linked to al-Qaida and a group banned in Israel for ties to Hamas). Indeed, what may be most astounding and mysterious about Clinton's whole public tenure is how Abedin ever received the security clearance necessary to work so closely with the secretary of state.

Even broaching such a simple if burning national security question, as Rep. Michele Bachmann and others discovered last summer, is also a banishable offense. After all, Hillary Clinton is our MAW!

That's life. But it isn't admirable.

Counterjihad

Hating the indoctrination of hate

3/8/02

We've heard about Pakistan's Islamic religious schools, or madrassas, where hundreds of thousands of Pakistani boys and young men have been indoctrinated in the hate-based teachings of radical Islam. A goodly chunk of the $600 million in economic aid the Bush administration has designated for Pakistan this year is for re-establishing that nation's school system, which both governments now recognize as having long been a state-sponsored, terrorist training ground.

But a radicalizing Islamic school system turns out not to be exclusive to any one country. The Wall Street Journal reports that the Netherlands is investigating 10 of the country's 32 state-sponsored Islamic elementary schools after a Dutch intelligence study found that many of these schools are funded "by what it called an intolerant Islamist foundation in Saudi Arabia and a society it said is controlled by Libyan intelligence." The intelligence report also says, "a number of the schools are run by boards with contacts to militant Islamic organizations such as Hamas."

The government insists it's not attacking Islamic education, but rather seeking to guarantee that Islamic schools, like other government-sponsored schools, "work toward the integration of minorities into Dutch society." (With a population of 16 million, the Netherlands is home to some 800,000 Muslims.) This rationale may say more about the politeness of the Dutch than the blamelessness of Islamic education, because the more we learn about Islamic schools, abroad and at home, the more at odds their all-too-often intolerant curricula seem to be with the tolerant societies in which they exist.

The Washington Post, for example, recently reported on a couple of Washington-area Islamic schools, including the Al-Qalam All-Girls School, where maps of the Middle East simply omit the state of Israel, and the Islamic Saudi Academy, where several students told a reporter "they are taught that it is better to shun and even to dislike Christians, Jews and Shiite Muslims." Some teachers "focus more on hatred," one teenager said. "They teach students that whatever is kuffar," or non-Muslim, "it is okay for you" to hurt or steal from such a person. A school text teaches that a sign of the Day of Judgment is "that Muslims will fight and kill Jews, who will hide behind trees that say: 'Oh, Muslim, Oh servant of God, here is a Jew hiding behind me. Come here and kill him.'"

The Journal story about the Netherlands doesn't include so many gory details, just mentioning a Dutch grade school that showed its pupils "a Hamas videotape that referred to Jews in derogatory language." Gory enough. In the Netherlands — the country, after all, of Anne Frank — the government determined that such heinous indoctrination is not adequate preparation for life in the Dutch mainstream. Being a Western country — that is, boundlessly tolerant and absolutely open — this determination has provoked some controversy, with certain groups demanding that Catholic, Protestant and Jewish schools come under similar scrutiny. Such groups, of course, are the same ones that would demand strip searches for Granny to avoid "profiling" potential hijackers, and, as such, form a predictable part of the liberal landscape.

What is pleasingly unpredictable is that the Dutch government embarked on such an investigation in the first place. In a country known for the vigor and bloom of both its tulips and its moral relativism (think euthanasia and legalized drugs), it is astonishing indeed that tolerance and openness — which, as critic Roger Kimball has noted, when "absolutized" lead to moral paralysis — have finally hit the wall. Is it a passive virtue to tolerate aggressive intolerance? The Netherlands says no.

"I believe it is bad to prepare children for a society in which you have to hate people, in which you instigate hate," said Dutch Deputy Education Minister Karen Adelmund, describing those aspects of the Islamic curricula now under investigation. "That is, by the way, in complete violation of our constitution ... I hate that kind of education."

Hating the indoctrination of hate: What a good way to love your fellow man.

What President Bush should say to us, part 1

8/21/06

My fellow Americans.

I come to you now, gravely aware that what I am about to say will radically change the course of what we have, for nearly five long years now, called the war on terror.

For almost as long as I have held this office, I have been leading this war. On my watch, the United States sent troops into Afghanistan to destroy the Taliban and drive al Qaeda from the safe haven it used to plan attacks on our country. On my watch, we sent troops into Iraq to topple Saddam Hussein and break this link in the terrorism food chain. On my watch, the United States spearheaded an ambitious drive to bring democracy to regions of the Middle and Near East as part of an effort to touch brutalized peoples with the salve of freedom and see them recover their free will, forever strengthened by what we in America prize as G-d-given rights to life, liberty and the pursuit of happiness.

I made this democratization process the centerpiece of my second term, the core of my political strategy against global terrorism, because history has taught us that democracies don't make war, or support terrorist attacks, on one another. I didn't, as one predecessor of mine famously put it, simply want "to make the world safe for democracy." I wanted to make the world — that part of the world from which terrorism mainly springs — democratic and therefore safe.

Over the past few years, then, the United States has supported fledgling democracies in Afghanistan, Iraq, and the Palestinian Authority. We have proudly assisted in making free and fair elections possible in these places, and with excellent results — at least with regard to the freeness and the fairness of the elections. But the fact is, when these peoples have spoken, what we have heard, or should have been hearing, in the expression of their collective will is that the mechanics of democracy alone (one citizen, one vote) do not automatically manufacture democrats — if by democrats we mean citizens who believe first and foremost in the kind of liberty that guarantees freedom of conscience and equality before the law.

On the contrary, each of these new democracies has produced constitutions that enshrine Islamic law. Because Islamic law, known as "Shariah," does not permit equality between the sexes or among religions, it is anything but what we in American consider "democratic."

Indeed, Shariah law endows Muslims, and Muslim men in particular, with a superior position in society. It also outlaws words and deeds that oppose this, frankly, repressive power structure for being "un-Islamic." From this same Islamic legal tradition comes the mandate for jihad (holy war, usually against non-Muslims) and dhimmitude, the official state of inferiority of non-Muslims under Islam.

With their devotion to Islamic tradition, then, these new democracies have, in effect, peacefully voted themselves into the same doctrinal camp as the many terror groups that violently strike at the non-Muslim world in the name of jihad for the sake of a caliphate — a Muslim world government ruled according to Shariah.

So be it. What I mean by that is, it is neither in the national interest nor in the national will for the United States of America to attempt to reshape such a culture to conform to our notions of liberty and justice for all. It is neither in the national interest nor in the national will to attempt to reform the belief system that animates this culture to conform to our notions of freedom of worship.

It is, however, in our national interest, and must become a part of our national will, to ensure that Islamic law does not come to our own shores, whether by means of violent jihad terrorism as practiced by the likes of al Qaeda or Hezbollah, or through peaceful patterns of migration, such as those that have already Islamized large parts of Europe.

The shift I am describing-from a pro-democracy offensive to an anti-Shariah defensive — means a national course correction. Rather than continuing to emphasize the democratization of the Muslim Middle East as our key tool in the war on terror, I will henceforth emphasize the prevention of Shariah from reaching the West as our key tool in the war on terror.

This will entail the immediate adoption of the following steps.

To be continued ...

What President Bush should say to us, part 2

8/28/06

Last week, in one of our most-accessed — and forwarded — stories of late, our columnist had the President delivering the first half of a speech announcing his re-direction in the "war on terror". Here's the remainder

At home, the line of defense is clear. It is our border. My new strategy calls on us to think of our border as more than just a line on a map. We need to see the border as a cultural line also, a defining line of freedom against proponents of sharia, which, I cannot emphasize enough, poses a direct threat to our founding principles of liberty and equality. It is that simple. There is a crucial military component to the anti-sharia defensive, which I will outline momentarily. But without taking civil precautions at the border, even a decisive military victory abroad could be nullified by non-violent means at home.

How? Through largely unregulated immigration of peoples from "sharia states" — those regions whose governing traditions derive, wholly or in some important part, from the edicts of Islam. If such an influx continues, Islamic law will be accommodated, adopted and even legislated, at least in some jurisdictions, according to majority will. We know this to be true because such a "sharia shift" is already transforming what sociologists call post-Christian Europe into an increasingly Islamic sphere. If we do not want to see such changes here, we must act. Accordingly, I am asking Congress to amend our laws to bar further Islamic immigration, beginning with immigration from sharia states.

This, the most crucial domestic component of my anti-sharia program, will undoubtedly be regarded as the most controversial because it necessitates making a definitive judgment against the laws promulgated by Islam, a religion.

This may appear to go against our cherished tradition of religious tolerance, not to mention good manners. But if the laws promulgated by Islam directly threaten freedom of conscience, freedom of expression and religion, women's rights and key concepts of equality — and they do — it is a sign of intellectual rigor mortis not to say so. And I do say so, but, again, not to launch a transformative military or cultural offensive against Islam, but to initiate the mobilization of a defensive movement to prevent the Islamization of American law and liberty.

And what about Iraq? Thanks to American-led coalition troops, a Ba'athist dictatorship has been dismantled, and Iraq is a parliamentary democracy under a new constitution. It is a matter of increasing significance, however, that this new constitution, ratified by the people of Iraq, enshrines Islamic law above all. This means that when the new Iraq joined the ranks of democratic nations, it simultaneously joined the ranks of sharia states. This may help explain widespread Iraqi sympathy for Hezbollah, for example, the Iranian-supported Shi'ite terrorist group that not only attacks American and Israeli interests, but also seeks the expansion of sharia. It also begs the question about long-term American support: How, in the war on terrorism, can we uphold a partner that feels solidarity with terrorists?

We cannot — certainly not as a realistic war strategy to safeguard the liberty of the Free World. Once, I saw the war that began on Sept. 11, 2001, as dividing the world between those countries that were with us, and those that were against us. I have now come to define the crisis, both cultural and military, as occurring between the Free World and the Sharia World. The centrality of sharia in Islam is not something Americans can or should try to change. But it is not something we can ignore, either.

With this centrality in mind, our goals in the Middle East should change from, in effect, promoting sharia-democracy to preventing the export of sharia and terrorism to advance sharia. Accordingly, I have directed our military to formulate a plan to redeploy American troops from Iraq's cities, where they have been operating at great risk to attain stability for the Iraqi government, to bases in the north. From there, they may assist as needed in our mission to neutralize the terrorism- and sharia-exporting capabilities of freedom's enemies in the region.

These would include nuke-seeking Iran and Syria, without whose support Hezbollah would not exist, and Saudi Arabia, from whose coffers comes global jihad.

What we call the war on terror now moves into a more focused phase, which better defines our mission and makes it more attainable. The road ahead is long and difficult, but our next steps are clear.

G-d bless the United States.

Ports and pitchforks

3/6/06

One of the weirder sideshows to open alongside a main event — the proposed operational transfer of six major American ports to a firm owned by the United Arab Emirates — is the growing chorus of road-company Zolas, "J'accusing" everybody opposed to the sale of "xenophobia," "isolationist mass hysteria," "bigotry," "nativism," "panic," and "prejudice" against innocent Araby.

Such accusations are supposed to make you hang your head in shame. They make me shake mine in consternation — wondering how in tarnation a hefty chunk of the American elite has the chutzpah to castigate the American people (64 percent of whom, says a Rasmussen Poll, think the deal is a Bad Thing) for "xenophobia" and "prejudice" on behalf of a culture that is the embodiment of xenophobia and prejudice. The words precisely describe the official state of normal in the Arab-Islamic world since at least 1948, when the modern state of Israel was founded.

Nonetheless, we're the "pitchfork-wielding xenophobes" en route to the "Dark Ages," says The New York Times' Thomas Friedman. I'd say we're heading in the other direction, trying to escape the Dark Ages — as represented by the spreading influence of sharia (Islamic law), which, in terms of the sharia-compliant port deal, would make deep inroads into global financial markets. I would add, as Rachel Ehrenfeld and Alyssa A. Lappen have suggested in The Washington Times, "It's time for the United States to limit financial transactions that involve American companies" — and the U.S. government — "to governance by secular laws."

Tut tut. Isn't that "Islamophobia"? — a subject National Review's

Larry Kudlow denounces in his defense of the deal. "There is no room for prejudice and bigotry here," he writes. Here? What about there, in the UAE (a huge Hamas supporter, by the way)? As the Jerusalem Post reports, the UAE-owned firm Dubai Ports World "participates in the Arab boycott of Israel." And why not? The UAE doesn't even recognize Israel — although it did recognize the Taliban, which is about as prejudiced and bigoted as it gets. As a UAE customs employee told the paper, "If a product contained even some components that were made in Israel ... it would be a problem."

And we're the xenophobic pitchfork-wielding ones? No doubt my old pal David Brooks would think so. In a New York Times column unforgettably called, "Kicking Arabs in the Teeth," Brooks seethes about the "collective mania," the "xenophobic tsunami" that threatens to wash out the ports deal. "The oil-rich nations of the Middle East," he writes, "have plenty of places to invest their money and don't need to do favors for nations that kick them in the teeth." Favors? What are we — the United Supplicants of America? But I digress. Besides, he adds, "the United Arab Emirates is a modernizing, globalizing place."

This week, the UAE modernized and globalized by seizing 100 sixth-grade social studies textbooks at a private American school in Abu Dhabi. Why? Because, as the Khaleej Times Online put it, the books "promoted Israel as one of the few democracies in North Africa and the Middle East, and some Arab countries as sponsors of terrorism."

Horrors. Or perhaps I should say: xenophobes and nativists. In a pro-book-banning editorial called "What about damage that's already done?" the UAE newspaper said the books gave off the "smell of racism," adding: "The ministry might have withdrawn copies of the textbook ... but will it be possible to withdraw the information already fed into the minds of students?" Nobody will know for sure until the kids pick up their first pitchforks.

Of course, everybody gets carried away sometimes. After the Columbia shuttle disaster in 2003, according to the Middle East Media Research Institute (MEMRI), a UAE columnist named Hamed Salamin was moved to write that the death of Israeli astronaut Ilan Ramon was "enough to arouse joy in every heart that beats Arabism and Islam."

Then there's Ali Al-Hamadi, the founder of something in the UAE called "The Creative Thinking Center." According to a MEMRI translation, Al-Hamadi waxed rhapsodic in 2005 about mothers of Palestinian suicide bombers who, he maintained during an Iqra TV interview, actually listen in on their offspring's detonation via cell phone ("then she utters cries of joy ..."). Maybe it's nativist or tsunamist to mention this, but I found a Creative Thinking Center client list online that includes — can you guess? — our pals at the Dubai Ports.

If that's modern and global, I'm sharpening my pitchfork.

America's eyes should look to Europe

3/19/07

Without attracting much attention, representatives of the Belgian political party Vlaams Belang recently visited Washington, D.C. Frank Vanhecke and Filip Dewinter hoped to meet members of Congress; but Congress was in recess. They hoped to engender some understanding of their program to reverse the Islamization of Belgium; but the media were strip-mining the tinsel life and tawdry times of Anna Nicole Smith.

Maybe they should have known that Tabloid America doesn't care about the likely transformation of Europe into an Islamic continent, let alone the fate of a French- and Dutch-speaking country of 10 million people. And while Literary America does write books about the transformation — "While Europe Slept" by Bruce Bawer, "The War for the West" by Tony Blankley, and "America Alone" by Mark Steyn come to mind — Political America has yet to acknowledge or even notice this colossal, epoch-defining shift now taking place.

Why don't our leaders face it? This may be one of those questions our children will ask some day. But if such natural curiosity isn't expressed until the next generation, the civilizational struggle for Europe will certainly have been lost. Better to question our politicians now. Better to examine the issue today.

Europe, as we may readily observe, is very far along in an accommodation with its still-increasing Muslim immigrant population that is resulting not in the Europeanizing of Islam, but rather the Islamizing of Europe. As Bernard Lewis declared in 2004, Europe will have an Islamic majority by the end of the 21st century at the latest. As Vlaams Belang's Dewinter recently put it, "We are becoming foreigners in our own land."

Such tragic pronouncements turn conversation with Vlaams Belang into a kind of political free verse — sadly evocative but rooted in a desperate reality that should shake American complacency. That is, "foreigners in our land" is poetry; Mohammed as the most popular boy's name in Brussels for six years running is implacable fact. The idea that "We are living on a dying continent but we are not dead yet," as Dewinter has explained, is metaphorical. His citation from Libyan dictator Muammar Qaddafi that "Allah is mobilizing Muslim Turkey to add ... 50 million more Muslims" to the European Union augurs world-class revolution.

Is such a revolution desirable? After writing nearly incessantly about Islamization since Sept. 11, I won't surprise anyone by saying no — not if freedom of conscience, religious equality or women's rights are your bag (not to mention the glorious representational artworks Europe's museums are stuffed with). Besides, the strategic implications for the United States are, in a word, bleak.

In multicultural totalitarian Belgium, however, you make such judgments at your own risk. Vlaams Belang, a conservative, free-market party that stands for Flemish secession from the French-speaking part of Belgium and opposes continued immigration, now stands trial in a Belgian court for a comment — a comment! — Dewinter made in 2005 to a New York publication, The Jewish Week. When asked why Belgian Jews should vote for a party that espouses "xenophobia," Dewinter replied: "Xenophobia is not the word I would use. If (it) absolutely must be a 'phobia,' let it be 'Islamophobia.' Yes, we're afraid of Islam. The Islamization of Europe is a frightening thing."

If convicted of the "crime" of "Islamophobia" ("1984," anyone?), the party would lose its state funding. In a country that effectively prohibits private political fund-raising, Vlaams Belang — the largest party in Belgium — would ultimately cease to exist. And so, too, would free speech in the center of Europe.

Before I met Vlaams Belang's Frank Vanhecke and Filip Dewinter in Washington, I believed Europe's rush to Islamize itself was a stampede, its transformation all but inevitable. Now, I think these men have at least earned Europe the benefit of the doubt. Studying their various statements and interviews, I found no evidence to support the crude slanders to which they are continually subjected in the media for being a right-wing party opposed to the massive Islamic immigration now transforming traditional European culture. Indeed, their statements on Israel are more supportive than any European party I know of.

As Vanhecke put it in a recent speech, "They call us 'intolerant' because we oppose intolerance. They call us 'fascists' because we oppose Islamo-fascism. They call us 'the children of holocaust perpetrators,' because we oppose Islamists who are preparing a new holocaust against the Jews.' "

America must start paying attention to Europe. And to Vlaams Belang.

The Islamicizing of Oklahoma

10/26/07

I could start today's column this way: Something downright incendiary is happening in Oklahoma. First one, then 17 and now 24 state lawmakers have declined a copy of the Koran offered to all 149 members of the legislature by an official Muslim advisory group to Oklahoma's governor. State Rep. Rex Duncan, Republican, explained his rejection of the Koran this way: "Most Oklahomans do not endorse the idea of killing innocent women and children in the name of ideology."

That's one way. Or I could start it this way:

Something downright incendiary is happening in Oklahoma. Gov. Brad Henry's Muslim advisory council is offering personalized Korans to lawmakers to mark the state's centennial, with each copy to be embossed with the Oklahoma state seal and the recipient lawmaker's name. The all-Muslim group — plain-vanilla-named the American Ethnic Advisory Council — asked lawmakers to notify it if they didn't want a Koran, which the group described as "the record of the exact words revealed by G-d through the Angel Gabriel to the Prophet Muhammad." So far, 24 have declined.

Of course, it's the rejection of the Korans that's making headlines, not their state-sealed if privately funded distribution. No one asks what the Koran has to do with Oklahoma's centennial, for Pete's sake; or why a government organization is proselytizing about "the exact words" of Allah; or how those words in that book sound to non-Muslims leery of Islam's age-old message to convert, submit or die. In our weird world, it's not the Islamic message that's branded hateful or even insensitive; it's the person who rejects it. This is the technique that usually shuts people up.

Maybe not this time. The reaction in the local media to this perfect PC storm has so far been somewhat subdued. I haven't heard calls for anyone's head — figuratively speaking, of course — although there is a steady cluck-clucking over the legislators' unenlightened "bad manners" and statehouse talk of "finding homes" for the rejected Korans. (Oh, brother.) Meanwhile, local Muslim advocates display utter bewilderment that anyone could construe Islam as anything but "very peaceful, very inclusive." To enlighten them, someone might bring up the key Koranic concept of jihad, or maybe ask a Muslim "apostate" in fear of his safety for leaving Islam, or a persecuted Christian or Jew in fear of his safety living under Islam, to explain.

Or, to keep things local, someone might ask Allison Moore, an Oklahoma Muslim quoted in recent stories, for elaboration. Why? Ms. Moore works on a newsletter published by the Tulsa Islamic Center. I downloaded the October issue and read an article that compares consorting with lax Muslims, ex-Muslims and non-Muslims — "people of religious innovation and misguidance, those who abandon the sunnah of the Messenger of Allah (pbuh) and advocate other beliefs" — to nothing short of "doom itself" and "taking poison."

The article continues: "A man with any intellect should not sit in their assemblies nor mix with them. The result of doing so will either be the death of his heart, or, at the very best, its falling seriously ill." This is... how shall I put it?... not very inclusive. Obviously, while the media remain stuck on spin — un-inclusive Christian yahoos reject kindly

Muslim gift — there's more to the story. For instance, what's up with the governor's council? According to the 2004 executive order creating it, the group is supposed to include "Ethnic Americans" from Oklahoma's "Middle East/Near East community."

Besides Arab-American Muslims, this should include Israeli-American Jews or Lebanese-American Christians, no? No. Euphemistically "Ethnic," the group is solidly Muslim. Bumping around on the Internet, I found uncomfortably few degrees of separation between one of the council members, Malaka Elyazgi, and a Hamas kingpin. (Her husband, Mohamed Elyazgi, was a business partner of Mufid Abdulqader, a defendant in the Holy Land Foundation trial and half-brother to the political chief of Hamas.) And what's the council all about? Judging by its push for, say, preliminary school recognition of Muslim holidays, or Muslim displays at the Oklahoma History Center, I'd say it's about advancing Islam in Oklahoma. Last I looked, this isn't the role of state organizations. (Imagine the furor over an all-Christian council promoting Christianity from a state office.) And this is particularly so in a state that still counts as part of the Judeo-Christian tradition, which includes freedom of conscience — forbidden under Islamic law.

Ultimately, such freedom of conscience is exactly what Mr. Duncan and colleagues are exercising in declining a Koran. And that's something worth hanging tough for.

Apologists throwing a 'Fitna' over upcoming film

3/28/08

Any day now, a short film connecting the Koran to Islamic violence is expected to be released.

The film is by Geert Wilders, a Dutch member of parliament who wants to reverse the Islamization of Europe and believes the Koran should be banned along with Hitler's "Mein Kampf" for inciting hatred and violence. The film is called "Fitna," Arabic for upheaval. And just the thought of "Fitna" has Europe in an upheaval, anticipating Islamic outrage expected to range from diplomatic huff, to economic boycott, to rioting, even bloodshed over this still unseen, 10-minute film.

Similar mass psychosis has erupted before — Satanic Verses Rage, Koran Rage, Cartoon Rage, Pope Rage, even Teddy Bear Rage. But never has an Islamic "rage" begun to build without actual cause. For the first time, we are seeing rage preparations and precautions before "offense" has been given or taken.

In other words, Pre-Emptive Rage is something new. It works like this: Because Wilders' film is expected to criticize Islam, Muslims who brook no religious criticism are expected to freak out. Therefore — just as if this were the most normal, everyday, ordinary state of affairs — Muslims and Europeans are making their respective arrangements.

In Afghanistan, Muslims have been igniting Dutch and Danish flags (did I mention Danish Cartoon Rage is back?), threatening to eject Dutch and Danish troops, and practicing their "Death to America" chants. Iranian officials have promised diplomatic rupture and worse if the film comes out. Meanwhile, the Dutch have embarked on a veritable world tour of pre-emptive appeasement. The MEMRI Blog reported that the Dutch government sent a letter disavowing Wilders to Egyptian Sheikh Muhammad Sayyed Tantawi, Sunni Islam's foremost figure (who has variously called for "jihad" against U.S. forces in Iraq and sanctioned suicide bombings against Israeli women and children). The Sheikh's response? He "demanded that the Netherlands government take more action against Wilders, and added that protection given to those harming Islam will negatively affect Egyptian-Dutch relations."

Pre-emptive "Fitna" rage has made European elites hopping mad — only not at the rioters and blackmailers (the healthy, normal reaction), but at Geert Wilders. Here, multiculti Europeans and perpetually aggrieved Muslims are finding common ground.

Thus, as reported by Dutch blogger Klein Verzet, the Grand Mufti of Syria, Ahmad Badr Al-Din Hassoun, admonished the European Parliament about film-related "riots, bloodshed and violence" for which "Wilders will be responsible." And thus Dutch prime minister Jan Peter Balkenende said exactly the same thing (in between begging Wilders not to release his film). The online Dutch site NIS News Bulletin reported Balkenende has "stressed repeatedly and with irritation that Wilders and no one else was responsible for any violence that might break out after his film's release."

And when Sheikh Tantawi indicates that providing "protection" for Mr. Wilders is a bad idea, it not only sounds like a mafia don calling for a hit, it also echoes the dean of Dutch journalists, Henk Hofland. As Thomas Landen of The Brussels Journal reported, Hofland urged the Dutch government to withdraw state protection from Wilders, who lives under constant threat of assassination. "Let him feel what it is like for those whose lives he endangers," said Hofland, adding that any murders committed in retaliation for Wilders' opinions on Islam would be the responsibility of Wilders, not the murderers.

Such thinking reveals a disconnect from both reality and morality. Killers, not a movie, kill people, and killers are duly responsible. But there's more to consider: The unified effort of Muslims and Europeans to censor a critique of Islam for being a critique of Islam — something not tolerated under Islam.

From EU to NATO officials, from the head of France to (sadly) the head of Denmark, the official European response to "Fitna" is less in line with Western traditions of free speech than with the censorship of Islamic law. Indeed, Dutch officials couldn't find a Dutch law under which to ban "Fitna," and they tried. The pressure to silence "Fitna," however, reveals the extent to which Islamic law has already eroded core conceptions of Western liberty.

Wilders refuses to submit. "I'm not bound to any Afghan or Sufi or Pakistani law," he told The Spectator. "I am bound to the Dutch law and I'm sure that my movie will be within all the boundaries of the Dutch law."

But who besides courageous Wilders will act to uphold Dutch law against Islamic-style censorship?

Jihadism 101: Congresswoman aces it, DC flunks

4/25/08

Reading U.S. Rep. Sue Myrick's "Wake Up America" agenda — a 10-point plan targeting potential jihadist infiltration into this country's military, security, educational and financial institutions — triggers mixed emotions.

First, relief. Finally, there is an elected official who understands the urgency of these festering national security threats. Virtually every other elected U.S. official, up to and including the president (and presidential candidates) has shockingly ignored these same threats.

Which leads to a flash of panic: How could our leaders have allowed so many years go by without taking action? Then comes, for me at least, a sense of resolve to help Myrick accomplish her goals by trying to boost a much-needed national conversation about the jihadist threat at home.

The North Carolina Republican's plan warms up with two calls for investigations into those U.S. chaplains, in both the US military and the prison system, who were approved by Abdurahman Alamoudi, the convicted terrorist and Muslim Brotherhood (MB) member now serving 23 years in prison.

(Normal person's reaction: What do you mean an MB member later convicted of terrorism chose our Muslim military and prison chaplains? Tell me more. Government reaction: Zzzzz.)

In the early 1990s, back when he was something of a Washington power broker, Alamoudi helped set up the Pentagon's Muslim chaplain corps in conjunction with the Institute of Islamic and Arabic Sciences in America, a Saudi-funded operation that specializes in what you might call Jihadism 101. (Way to be awake, Pentagon.)

Alamoudi went to prison back in 2004, but no one since, in the military or the prisons, seems to have taken a second look at what his prodigies might be preaching (terrorism? treason? whatever?). Myrick plans to check into it herself.

Next, she plans to ask the Government Accounting Office (GAO) to examine the process by which the FBI and Defense Department select Arabic translators. Of particular concern to Myrick — but not, incredibly, to the FBI or the Defense Department — is these two agencies' mind-boggling practice of advertising for recruits in what can only be described as pro-terrorism publications.

(Normal person's reaction: What do you mean the government is trolling pro-terrorism sites for Arabic translators? Government reaction: Did someone say something?)

Next on the congresswoman's to-do list is a call for an Internal Revenue Service investigation into the nonprofit status of the Hamas-linked Council on American-Islamic Relations (CAIR). Such status restricts "lobbying on behalf of a foreign government," but, as Myrick notes, plenty of foreign funds have found their way into CAIR's coffers to beg the question.

Another Myrick plan is to introduce a bill to make preaching, publishing, distributing or financing calls for the death of Americans or American troops an act of sedition or solicitation of treason. She also wants to ask the GAO to assess total sovereign wealth fund investment in the United States. Such massive funds, owned and controlled by governments, first came to many Americans' attention with the recent purchase by the United Arab Emirates of a large stake in Citigroup; in recent years, however, there has been a spike in such foreign government investment in the United States. This raises concerns (that is, it should raise concerns) about the political goals of such funds — for example, the spread of Islamic law through "Sharia-compliant banking." Thankfully, Myrick is concerned.

The last few points on the Myrick agenda focus on the appalling lack of reciprocity and common sense in our nation's dealings with Saudi Arabia. Regarding the student visa program that is supposed to bring 21,000 Saudi students to this country, Myrick would attach the condition that the Saudis rewrite their textbooks to omit incitement against non-Muslims; regarding religious visas for imams, she would require of Islamic countries reciprocal visa arrangements for non-Muslim clergy; and regarding U.S. training of Saudi security forces, she would insist that the Saudis prosecute known Al Qaeda financiers and stop releasing repatriated Guantanamo Bay terrorists in exchange for their pledges not to attack ... Saudi Arabia. She will also be introducing a bill to block the sale of state-of-the-art offensive munitions to Saudi Arabia, especially

Joint Direct Attack Munitions or JDAMs.

Ambitious? You bet. Myrick deserves an "A" for effort for filling the leadership vacuum left by Republicans and Democrats alike regarding these and other home-front threats. Whether she can accomplish her goals, she will certainly help educate Americans on gravely important issues most of our politicians are too timid to talk about.

Academic dares to question the 'religion of peace'

6/16/08

On Sept. 11, 2001, Andrew Bostom, an academic research physician at Rhode Island Hospital, did what many outraged and shocked Americans did. On his way home from work, he stopped at a bookstore and bought a book about Islam.

As he recalls, it was something by Karen Armstrong, who, he didn't know at the time, is famous — infamous — for being a serial apologist for Islam. Reading parts of the book aloud that same night to his wife, also an academic, as they went about accounting for friends and family in their native New York City, he found the book "treacley" and superficial, lacking not only the scholarly heft he was used to in scientific research, but also a connection to unfolding events. Even a more extensive survey of readily available works on Islam yielded similar platitudes rooted less in Islamic theology and history than in the contemporary political dictates of multiculturalism. The scientist in him wanted to know more.

Thus marked the unexpected beginning of a rigorous and illuminating academic odyssey deep into the study of Islam — "this depressing obsession of mine," as Bostom calls it. It has also acquainted the medical researcher with a global fraternity of Islamic scholars, which includes the two he calls his mentors: the Egyptian-born historian of dhimmitude, Bat Ye'or, and the Pakistani-born scholar of Islam and the West, Ibn Warraq.

So far, his studies have resulted in two meticulously researched and trail-blazing tomes of his own: "The Legacy of Jihad," published in 2005, and "The Legacy of Islamic Antisemitism," which has just come out, garnering enthusiastic advance comment from academics ("a ground breaking event" said Steven T. Katz, director of the Elie Wiesel Center for Judaic Studies, Boston University), historians ("It is magnificent," said Martin Gilbert, official biographer of Winston Churchill), and experts ("One of the most important books of our time," said Ayaan Hirsi Ali, author, "Infidel"). The obvious question is: How does a medical researcher studying homocysteine's effect on cardiovascular disease in patients suffering from chronic kidney problems shift his focus to the study of jihad and anti-Semitism in Islam?

Answer: He doesn't. That is, while embarked on his Islamic studies, Bostom — a lifelong Democrat, by the way — has remained the Principle Investigator in a $40 million, decade-long National Institutes of Health renal study involving more than 4,000 patients in the United States, Canada and Brazil. Not only that (and this is something that has impressed me, both as what you might call a confrere in Islamic inquiry and also as a friend), he has applied essentially the same scientific principles he uses in medical research to the study of Islam.

"We are used to analyzing things very critically and taking almost everything with a grain of salt," Bostom explained recently, discussing his work as a medical researcher at Rhode Island Hospital, the major teaching hospital affiliated with Brown University. Such analysis includes, for example, monthly gatherings known as morbidity and mortality reviews where errors and oversights in medical treatment are critically examined. "We are trained to think the stakes are never higher because we are dealing with life and death. If you get something wrong, you kill people."

Bringing such skepticism and urgency to the study of Islam (where, he maintains, "getting something wrong" can kill even more people), Bostom soon found himself butting up against consensus teachings contradicted by the voluminous evidence he was gathering. Take anti-Semitism in Islam, the subject of his new book. The view that Islamic anti-Semitism is a relatively recent import into Islam from Christian Europe and Nazi Germany is declared as settled fact by historians such as Bernard Lewis and popular authors such as Lawrence Wright ("The Looming Tower"). Bostom's conclusions, based on an array of religious texts and commentaries, historical analyses and eyewitness accounts, which he presents in "The Legacy of Islamic Antisemitism," suggest otherwise.

Both the anti-Semitism book and the jihad book before it are constructed similarly. They open with long introductory essays by Bostom, comparable, he says, to scientific grant proposals. In these essays, he presents his hypothesis based on his interpretation of the evidence and data reproduced in the rest of the book. In both books, such "raw material" includes key works from both Muslim and non-Muslim sources that have never before been translated into English. Such materials serve "as a reality check," Bostom says, "for people to read for themselves" in order to test his hypothesis.

After all, in history, as in science, the truth lies in the evidence.

We have a lot to learn from 'over there'

6/27/08

As a dutiful American columnist, I should probably be pondering the half-baked presumption behind Barack Obama's bizarre "presidential" seal. Or shaking my head at John McCain's hair-trigger panic over an aide's answer to a question about terrorism's political impact. Or clucking over the irresponsibly childish $300 billion goodie bag — I mean, mortgage bailout bill — that just passed in the U.S. Senate. But I can't stop thinking about Europe.

No surprise there. I just returned from a swift-moving, fact-finding journey through six European countries. And that tally doesn't even include two side-trips: one to Luxemburg just to buy cheaper diesel fuel (no kidding); and one to the German town of Monschau in the northern Ardennes where my G.I. father, still wearing the summer-weight uniform that perfectly suited Normandy in June of 1944, contracted pneumonia in December of the same year, and was thus taken off the front line for medical treatment just days before the Germans launched their final offensive later known as the Battle of the Bulge. In all, 19,000 Americans were killed.

Sacred soil, you might say. But not necessarily regarded as such in the same way by its native populations. Nearby Belgium and Holland, for example, didn't field armies after they were swiftly occupied by Nazi Germany. That means, as a very perceptive Flemish lady pointed out to me, for many Europeans on this Western front the war was more a civilian matter of personal survival than the military exercise in national sacrifice that the United States and Great Britain in particular underwent.

All these decades later, such basic experiential differences still play out in ways both obvious and subtle in the American and European disconnect on sundry issues and attitudes — the fissures Americans airily dismiss as anti-Americanism, or perhaps see as doctrinal differences (eroding but historical) over socialism and capitalism. Such differences have helped turn Europe into the European Union, a nation-destroying behemoth both driven and empowered by the infantilizing machinery of the welfare state. Indeed, so shockingly totalitarian is the orientation of the EU, it strikes me that President Bush's misguided effort to democratize the Islamic Middle East might well have been better aimed at liberating the hostage peoples of the Brussels-dominated supra-state.

That said, it's crucial to recognize the precious common ground between the United States and Europe. While on a different plane from those fallow battlefields of the Ardennes, it is also sacred soil. I refer to our shared cultural and historical progressions as civilizations whose ideals are founded on liberty. Such liberty is once again under threat and from an ideological enemy — the ideology of Islam, which, as spread by a massive influx of Islamic immigration over the past several decades, promises, as historians and writers from Bat Ye'or to Mark Steyn have copiously explained, to transform all of Europe into an Islamic continent.

And what do our presidential candidates think of the strategic ramifications of an Islamic Europe? Who knows? The likely but not inevitable civilizational shift is so far off the U.S. radar screen (with our government keeping it there, what with its recommended lexicon discouraging all terror-related references to Islam) it is invisible. American tourists — those flush enough to pay their way with Euros, that is (and I didn't see many) — can still visit the old Europe of gingerbread towns and Gothic cathedrals without noticing much more than a few hijabbed women, signs of Islamization that usually fail to register more than a multicultural nod.

Of course, even many (most?) residents are blind to the staggering changes in progress. This is something I discovered, to take one example, in conversation with a conservative British MEP (Member of European Parliament), who, after nine years of representing a sector of southern England in Brussels, both doubts the existence of "no-go zones" in Britain — despite the writings on the subject by the Bishop of Rochester — and has never visited the Brussels neighborhood of Molenbeek. A stone's throw from the ritzy EU environs in which we sat, this Islamic enclave more closely resembles a bustling outpost of the umma than the so-called capital of Europe.

"You ought to get out more," I suggested.

As should we all — which is why I embarked on this expedition in the first place. In the following weeks, I hope to turn the mountain of raw material I brought home with me into a series of reports from Over There, augmented by interview transcripts and photos that I plan to post at my Web site (dianawest.net).

We have a lot to learn from Europe.

Geert Wilders: Prisoner of Islam

7/3/08

THE HAGUE, The Netherlands — Having run the polite-but-grim gauntlet of Dutch government security to gain access to Geert Wilders, I finally understood what the 24-hour security requirements of the man's continued existence really mean: To make the survival of Western-style liberty in the Netherlands his political cause, this Dutch parliamentarian has to live under high-tech lock and key.

This stunning paradox, with no end in sight, illustrates how far political freedom in the West has already eroded. Think of it: For writing about the repressive ideology of Islam, for arguing against the inequities of Sharia (Islamic law), for making a video ("Fitna") to warn about Islamic jihad, Wilders lives in his own non-Islamic country under a specifically Islamic death threat.

If it is politically incorrect to notice this, it is also indisputably true. True, too, is that, sans state security, this death threat could conceivably be carried out anytime, anywhere — from the picturesque streets outside the Dutch parliament, to the house Wilders hasn't slept in since 2004. That, of course, was when, on an Amsterdam street, a Muslim assassin plunged a knife into Theo van Gogh's corpse, thus attaching the Islamic manifesto threatening both Wilders and his then-parliamentary colleague, Ayaan Hirsi Ali, with death.

Not long ago, political debate in the Netherlands met with, well, more political debate. Now, however, with a growing Muslim minority — and it's politically incorrect to notice this, too — political debate sometimes meets with Islam-inspired political assassination. At least it has, traumatically, twice in recent years: once, with the 2002 murder of the anti-Islamic-immigration politician Pim Fortuyn by an animal rights activist who claimed Fortuyn was scapegoating Muslims; and the following year with the ritualistic Islamic murder of Van Gogh, director of "Submission," a short video made with Hirsi Ali about Islamic mistreatment of women. In all, such Islam-inspired violence has been enough to chill Islam-inspired debate.

And that's just the situation at home. This week, even as Amsterdam's chief public prosecutor, Leo de Wit, announced that no charges would be brought against Wilders for "discrimination" or "incitement to hatred" related to Wilders' writings or video ("We find Mr. Wilders' remarks were limited to Islam as a religious movement," De Wit said), Jordan announced it is bringing a "Fitna"-related criminal case against the Dutch parliamentarian.

In other words, Jordan will indict a Dutch politician according to Jordanian (read: Islam-inspired) law. "Jordanian authorities are not aiming to arrest" the Dutch leader of the Freedom Party, Radio Netherlands Online reports. "They say the decision to prosecute was taken in order to send a signal to the Netherlands."

A "signal"? How about a gag? Of course, like other Western peoples, the Dutch seem content to censor themselves, happily mouthing multicultural platitudes that effectively rationalize their own culture's Islamization. Not Wilders.

I recently asked the 44-year-old Dutchman what was stronger in his country: Islam or multiculturalism.

"Unfortunately, they are both strong," he replied, seated in his lightly furnished but heavily guarded office. "But cultural relativism is the biggest problem." He went on to explain: "Multicultural society would not be that bad — I don't really believe in it — but it would not be that bad if, at least, we would be strong enough to say that our culture is better and dominant. But when you combine multicultural society with a dominant sense of cultural relativism, you are heading in the wrong direction. You are committing suicide when it comes to your own culture."

He continued: "I am not advocating a monocultural society. I just want what the Germans call leitkultur (leading culture). I want our own culture to be dominant — not the only one, but to be dominant. I have a big problem with the cultural relativists who say every culture is equal. I don't believe every culture is equal."

Hoping to preserve the primacy of Western culture in this Dutch corner of the West, Wilders advocates a halt to Islamic immigration. "I'm not saying that every Muslim in the Netherlands is a criminal or a terrorist," he explains. "We know the majority is not. Still," he continues, "there is good reason to stop the immigration, because the more we have an influx of Muslims in the Netherlands, the strength of the (Islamic) culture will grow, and the change of our societies will increase." He sees his efforts as "a fight against an ideology that I believe at the end of the day will kill our freedom, kill our societies and change everything we stand for."

He's right — and, yes, it's politically incorrect to say that, too. Everything the West stands for, starting with freedom of speech, is already changing as our institutions, up to and including, for example, the U.S. Department of Homeland Security, increasingly proscribe critical references, or indeed, any references to Islam. While it's clear that the European manifestation of Islamic ideology has already killed Wilders' personal freedom in the Netherlands, the general impact on freedom throughout the West has yet to be fully appreciated.

"I have a mission," Wilders said. "I believe very strongly in what I say, and my party fortunately shares this view. And nobody in the Netherlands is doing (what I do). And somebody should. And I pay a high price for it."

What is the expression — freedom isn't free? This is literally and acutely the case when it comes to this heroic and dedicated Dutchman.

A Swiss 'extremist' against Islamic law

7/18/08

THE SWISS ALPS, SWITZERLAND — "Explain the minaret ban," I asked.

I was sitting in the side room of a house, overlooking a flat plot somewhat larger than the trampoline outside. Beyond that trampoline, still visible in the evening light, rose the Swiss Alps. Across the table, Oskar Freysinger sat poised to address my query over some cups of espresso, speaking as a local leader of the Swiss People's Party.

Or perhaps I should say — a local leader of the "extremist," "bigoted" and "xenophobic" Swiss People's Party. That's how this largest political party in tiny Switzerland is routinely discussed, or, rather, dismissed by elites, glitterati and other social deadweights.

Why? Because the Swiss People's Party is, with noticeable success, fighting to bring massive immigration, including Islamic immigration, under control in Switzerland before this rigidly neutral, quite independent, non-European Union country loses its uniquely Swiss character. (Hardly unimaginable given that 21.1 percent of Swiss residents are foreign.) This makes men like Freysinger a dire threat to the multicultural world order. Hence the very nasty, but meaningless names.

Now engaged in probably its greatest battle yet, the Swiss People's Party has just amassed more than the requisite 100,000 signatures on a petition to trigger a national referendum, in this controversial case, on whether Switzerland should ban minarets, the towers that often soar high enough over mosques to transform the skyline of any cathedral town in Europe. Out of 90 mosques in Switzerland, only two have minarets. Three more are now in political limbo.

"We have long reflected on this," said Freysinger, 48, a strongly built man whose intelligent face, long, dark pony tail and summer sandals confound the Tyrolean-capped, alpine stereotype. A high school teacher of German literature, he is bilingual in German and French, and plenty serviceable in both Italian and English, the latter being our interview lingo.

Discussing the "long progression" of Islam — now 4.3 percent of Switzerland's mainly Christian population of 7.5 million — into Swiss life, he explains that what concerns him is "not the (Islamic) religion, but the law," meaning Islamic law, or Sharia. And while there is religious freedom in Switzerland for new mosques, this same freedom does not extend to minarets, which he sees as political more than religious symbols. "Minarets are not necessary for the practice" of Islam, he explains.

Indeed, historically, the minaret has often served as a sign of Islamic political power. In our own era, it may be seen to symbolize the introduction of Islamic law into formerly non-Islamic societies.

"In that case," Freysinger continued, "we said: 'OK. We'll attack the symbol. It's always about symbols because symbols have a big truth behind them. And so we attack this symbol of conquering Islam and we say: You are welcome in our country, but there is one law, and one constitution for every person in this country. And there is no special law for an Islamic girl, or an Islamic man. There is no Sharia. Nothing."

Given the premodern inequities of Sharia, the notion of one enlightened law and constitution for all should be a simple, desirable state of Western affairs. But no. As the West tilts Islamic to accommodate aspects of Sharia ranging from diet to sexual segregation to polygamous marriage to Sharia banking to censorship regarding Islam itself, Freysinger's point of view becomes, to appeasers, an increasingly controversial and dangerous one, reliably eliciting catcalls and worse from world media and political establishments. In their postmodern parlance, to be opposed to the totalitarian tenets of Sharia is be an "extremist." My only question is, How do you say, Ich bin ein extremist?

One litmus test I applied to the many politicians on the European Right I've recently interviewed concerned their views on Israel. As supposed "extremists," "fascists," even "neo-Nazis," what would they say?

I asked Freysinger where Israel fits into his worldview. "Our party has always defended Israel because we are well aware that if Israel disappears, we lose a vanguard," he replied. "They are fighting now our fight in fact; and as long as the Muslims are concentrated on Israel, it is not so hard for us. But as soon as Israel will have disappeared, well, they will come to get the other part."

I think by "the other part" he meant the rest of the West. In this outlook, Freysinger is by no means alone on the European Right: members of other such parties — for example, Belgium's Vlaams Belang, the Danish People's Party and Holland's Freedom Party — explained to me how they find in Israel's struggle against both Islamization and jihad common cause.

"The right-wing parties should join their forces to fight Islamization," Freysinger said.

Good idea.

We are losing Europe to Islam

9/22/08

With Wall Street convulsing, and the White House race intensifying, the question "Who lost Europe" is on no one's lips, let alone minds. Indeed, the question begs another: "Is Europe lost?"

The answer to the second question is, "No, not yet." And losing Europe, I would add, is by no means inevitable. But that doesn't mean the continent isn't currently hell-bent to accommodate the dictates of Islamic law, bit by increasingly larger bit. Such a course of accommodation, barring reversal, will only hasten Bernard Lewis' famous prediction that Europe will be Islamic by century's end.

And what do I mean by "accommodation"? Well, to take one tiny example, one snowflake in a blizzard of such examples, there are schools in Belgium that not only serve halal food to Muslim and non-Muslim alike (old news), but, according to a recent French magazine report, no longer teach authors deemed offensive to Muslims, including Voltaire and Diderot; the same is increasingly true of Darwin. (Don't even ask about the Holocaust.)

For a more substantial, indeed, keystone example of accommodation, we can look to England, where, it pains me to write, Sharia courts are now officially part of the British legal system. According to press reports this week, the British government has quietly, cravenly elevated five Sharia courts to the level of tribunal hearings, thus making their rulings legally binding.

It may be difficult to quantify the impact of a Voltaire vacuum on the continent, but we can instantly see the inequities of British Sharia (I can't believe I'm writing that phrase). Among the first official verdicts were those upholding the Islamic belief in male supremacy. These included an inheritance decision in which male heirs received twice as much as female; and several cases of domestic violence in which husbands were acquitted and wives' charges were dropped.

In a decidedly minuscule minority, I say we ignore the spread of Islamic law across Europe, from the schoolroom to the courtroom, at our peril, particularly given that in so doing, we also ignore the vital political parties that have arisen in reaction to this threat to Western civilization. Why at our peril? Because the same type of liberty-shrinking, Sharia-driven accommodation is happening here.

Of the parties dedicated to resisting Islamization that I examined in Europe last summer, the most promising range from the sizeable Vlaams Belang in Belgium to the tiny Sweden Democrats, and include the Lega Nord in Italy, the Party for Freedom of Geert Wilders in Holland, the Danish People's Party, the Swiss People's Party and the Austrian Freedom Party. Such parties are unknown here, or ignored. Worse, they are shunned. Why? I believe it's because their respective political opponents — the leftist media and governing establishments that are increasingly dependent on Islamic support, by the way — have successfully slandered these parties as "extremists," "racists," "fascists" and "Nazis."

Is advocating freedom of speech "extreme" or "fascist"? Is opposing Islam's law, which knows no race, "racist"? Is supporting Israel (which these parties do far more than other European parties) "Nazi"? The outrageously empty epithets of the Islamo-socialist left seem calculated to stop thought cold and trigger a massive rejection reflex. In this way, resistance becomes anathema, and Islamic law, unchecked, spreads across Europe.

Does that sound "Islamophobic"? You bet. How can anyone who

values freedom of conscience, equality before the law and other such Western jewels not have a healthy fear of Islamic law, which values none of these things? Incredibly, this is an emotion that is supposed to be suppressed — and, in Europe, on pain of prosecution. Indeed, because Filip Dewinter admitted to such "Islamophobia" in an interview, his party, the Vlaams Belang, has been taken to court in Belgium on charges of racism, and, if convicted, will be effectively shut down through defunding by the government.

That hasn't stopped Dewinter, who, in accepting an award at a memorial event dedicated to Oriana Fallaci in Florence, last week, said: "Islamophobia is not merely a phenomenon of unparalleled fear, but it is the duty of every one who wants to safeguard Europe's future. Europe means Rome, Greece, Enlightenment and Judeo-Christian roots. Europe is a continent of castles and cathedrals, not of mosques and minarets."

Of course, even as Dewinter admits to fearing the Islamization of Europe, he and his colleagues act with exceptional political — and physical — bravery in rallying voters against it. This coming weekend, he joins several other politicians on the Sharia-fighting right in Europe — among them two other men I interviewed, Mario Borghezio of Lega Nord, which is part of Italy's ruling coalition, and Heinz-Christian Strache of Austria's Freedom Party, which is expected to become part of Austria's ruling coalition after elections this month — in Cologne, Germany. In that ancient cathedral city, where the city council recently approved the construction of a long-controversial mega-mosque, these men will address a rally against European Islamization. (Contrary to initial reports, Jean-Marie Le Pen will not be at the demonstration.) The Sharia-fighters expect 1,500 demonstrators. Police expect 40,000 counter-demonstrators.

These are frightening odds — a metaphor, perhaps, for Europe's chances of staving off Islamic law. Who lost Europe? If it does happen, we certainly won't be able to say we weren't warned.

Dutchman flies Islamization into world spotlight

2/27/09

What a difference a year makes.

I say this on realizing that just over one year ago, Dutch parliamentarian Geert Wilders — who has been on a multi-stop media and speaking tour of New York, Boston and Washington, D.C. — that includes a screening of his film "Fitna," hosted by Sen. Jon Kyl, R-Ariz., in the U.S. Capitol — was little known outside the Netherlands.

Indeed, most of what people seemed to know about him — and I refer to those of us irresistibly riveted on Islamization as the great, ignored, existential peril — was that Wilders, along with then-fellow Dutch parliamentarian Ayaan Hirsi Ali, had lived under threat of assassination since 2004. That was when a five-page Islamic manifesto calling for Wilders' and Hirsi Ali's murder was found impaled with a knife to the stabbed and bullet-riddled corpse of Theo van Gogh, a critic of Islam and great-great-nephew of Vincent van Gogh. Theo, as some will recall, was assassinated, ritualistically, his head nearly severed from his body, on the streets of Amsterdam on the morning of Nov. 2, 2004, by Dutch-Moroccan dual-national Mohammed Bouyeri. Linked to the jihadist Hofstad group, Bouyeri is serving a life sentence without the possibility of parole.

Bouyeri's motive? Criticism of Islam. Van Gogh and Hirsi Ali had together made a very short film titled "Submission" to call attention to the plight of women abused according to Islamic law; Wilders was an outspoken critic of Islamic law in the Netherlands. Bouyeri sought retribution, taking Van Gogh's life and consigning both Hirsi Ali and Wilders to the wary existence of perpetual prey, both of them requiring armed guards to help ensure their continued survival in their own country and beyond.

Hirsi Ali would eventually leave Dutch parliament and the Netherlands, finding renown in a peripatetic if guarded exile as the author of a bestselling memoir, "Infidel," and as a couture-sheathed subject for Vogue magazine. Wilders remained in Dutch politics, his stance against Islamization reported to the wider world in shorthand briefs about the so-called Dutch firebrand with the platinum-blond hair who opposed Islamic law, and wanted to halt Islamic immigration into the Netherlands.

Then, last year, in late January, FoxNews reporter Greg Palkot conducted what was likely the first televised U.S. interview with Wilders. The "Dutch firebrand" had begun making international headlines for his upcoming documentary critique of the Bible — I mean, the Talmud. Or was it the Bhagavad Gita? No, the 17-minute film was called "Fitna," and it was about the Koran. No matter how short, no matter how small, such critiques of Islam draw notice because Islam brooks no criticism, and responds variously, as we have seen with Salman Rushdie's Satanic Verses, the Danish Mohammed cartoons, the Pope's Regensburg address and other uniquely Islamic flashpoints, with boycotts, lawsuits, threats, riots, arson, attacks — even murder.

As noted on my blog at the time (dianawest.net), Wilders appeared in that first U.S. interview as "serious, certainly forthright and articulately nonapologetic in his defense of Dutch culture and identity (and, by extension, Western culture and identity) against the Islamization process well under way in his country and the wider West." I would see these same qualities firsthand when I interviewed him last summer in The Hague.

Fox's Palkot, on the other hand, was obviously rattled by Wilders' message, and came across, I wrote, "as what you might call the Nolo Contendere Westerner whose idea of coexistence is based on self-censorship." Palkot practically begged "Wilders to soften, i.e., censor, his views so as not to inflame the Islamic world, including those 'moderates' whose so-called moderation morphs into radicalism at the first barb of criticism." Wilders explained he couldn't do that "because such self-censorship would concede victory to those who would impose Islamic law on him and his country."

In many ways, nothing has changed since January 2008. Wilders' anti-Islamization message remains much the same, and it still rattles most media. But where last year, for example, a well-known anchorman told me he had never heard of Wilders, not even at the height of the "Fitna" controversy last March, his show recently interviewed the Dutch MP. On watching other interviews with Wilders this week, one with Fox's Glenn Beck and one with Fox's Bill O'Reilly, it seems safe to say, particularly on considering his progress up and down the Bos-Wash corridor, there's noticeably more room now for Wilders to air his anti-Islamization ideas. It was rather amazing, after all, to hear O'Reilly recap Wilders's argument without even the smallest smirk: "You don't want to deport anybody, but you want to halt immigration (from Islamic countries)." I don't think Americans have ever heard such ideas spoken on prime-time television.

It's not that these ideas are not "out there"; they are. But "out there" in books, columns or blogs is not the same thing as breaking news, and that is what these ideas become when an international political celebrity promotes them. This is precisely what Wilders has become, and it is exactly what Wilders is doing.

Paradoxically, Wilders' international profile and media allure result from concerted efforts to corral him and censor his message, efforts that recently culminated in a Dutch appeals-court order to prosecute him for "hate speech"; in Jordanian efforts to extradite the Dutch MP and try him for "blasphemy"; and in the shameful British decision to bar Wilders from entering the United Kingdom (where he'd been invited by Lord Malcolm Pearson to speak and show "Fitna" at the House of Lords) as a threat to "community (read: Muslim) harmony."

Non-paradoxically, it is also the result of extended video interviews with Wilders conducted over the last several months by such bloggers as author Robert Spencer, Atlas Shrugs and Tom Trento, all of which are easily accessed on the Internet.

The point is, the conversation about Islam's impact on the West —

on freedom of speech and conscience, on women's rights, on religious equality and other key issues — has long been "out there." Lately, thanks to a series of nefarious governments' missteps and the boldness of a Dutch political "firebrand," this conversation has suddenly been picked up for the first time and broadcast in new, very public arenas.

The question is, will we be able to keep it going after the Dutchman flies home?

Losing our way to victory

10/2/09

Today's column is for all hawkish Americans currently wrestling with looming doubts about the pointlessness of the U.S. mission in Afghanistan and clubbing those doubts down with the much-mentioned perils of leaving Afghanistan to "the terrorists." In short, it's about how to "lose" Afghanistan and win the war.

And what war would that be? Since 9/11, the answer to this question has eluded our leaders, civilian and military, but it remains the missing link to a cogent U.S. foreign policy.

It is not, as our presidents vaguely invoke, a war against "terrorism," "radicalism" or "extremism"; and it is not, as the current hearts-and-minds-obsessed Afghanistan commander calls it, "a struggle to gain the support of the (Afghan) people." It is something more specific than presidents describe, and it is something larger than the outlines of Iraq or Afghanistan. The war that has fallen to our generation is to halt the spread of Islamic law (Sharia) in the West, whether driven by the explosive belts of violent jihad, the morality-laundering of petro-dollars or decisive demographic shifts.

This mission demands a new line of battle around the West itself, one supported by a multilevel strategy in which the purpose of military action is not to nation-build in the Islamic world, but to nation-save in the Western one. Secure the borders, for starters, something "war president" George W. Bush should have done but never did. Eliminate the nuclear capabilities of jihadist nations such as Iran, another thing George W. Bush should have done but never did — Pakistan's, too. Destroy jihadist actors, camps and havens wherever and whenever needed (the strategy in place and never executed by Bill Clinton in the run-up to 9/11). But not by basing, supplying and supporting a military colossus in Islamic, landlocked Central Asia. It is time, as Maj. Gen. Paul Vallely (USA ret.) first told me last April, to "let Afghanistan go." It is not in our interests to civilize it.

But we would "lose face" in leaving Afghanistan, supporters say. News flash: We lose face every day in Afghanistan executing a costly, impotent policy based on massive state bribery, the public devaluation of American life ("population protection" trumps "force protection"), and deference to Islamic custom, as when women Marines are ordered to wind head scarves under their helmets for missions. And the point of this mass American supplication? To win a local popularity contest in which the only competition is the Taliban. Earth to military geniuses: The people are already with you, or they're against you.

In other words, it's time to toss the policy of standing up Sharia states such as Iraq and Afghanistan onto that ash heap of history. It's time to shore up liberty in the West, which, while we are stretched and distracted by Eastern adventures, is currently contracting in its accommodations of Sharia, a legal system best described as sacralized totalitarianism.

Such a war — to block Sharia in the West — requires more than military solutions. For starters, it requires an unflinching assessment of Sharia's incompatibility with the U.S. Constitution, and legal bars to Sharia-compliant petro-dollars now flowing into banking and business centers, into universities and media. It absolutely requires weaning ourselves from Islamic oil — what a concept — and drilling far and widely for our own.

Halting the spread of Islamic law in the democratic West requires halting Islamic immigration, something I've written before. But there's another aspect to consider. On examining a photo of armed Taliban on an Afghan hill, it occurred to me that these men and others like them can't hurt us from their hilltops. That is, what happens in Afghanistan stays in Afghanistan — or Pakistan or Saudi Arabia — if we (duh) impose wartime restrictions on travel from and to Sharia states.

But that cramps our freedom, critics will say. Well, so does standing in line to de-clothe and show our toothpaste because Hani Hanjour might be on the plane. Funny kind of "freedom" we're now used to. And funny kind of war we now fight to protect it — a war for Sharia states abroad while a growing state of Sharia shrinks freedom at home.

The faster we extricate our military from the Islamic world, the faster we can figure out how to fight the real war, the Sharia war on the West.

Rally behind Denmark

10/30/09

Pakistani jihad death squads were much in the news this week. In Peshawar, Pakistan, they bombed a marketplace, claiming more than 100 lives, and in Chicago, they were thwarted, according to an FBI affidavit, from carrying out a planned attack on a newspaper in Denmark to kill two Danish journalists, cartoonist Kurt Westergaard and cultural editor, Flemming Rose.

It's important to link these events to put them into proper perspective. According to the FBI, the Danish operation — busted in Chicago with arrests of David Coleman Headley (aka Daood Gilani) and Tahawwur Hussain Rana, both of Pakistani origin with American and Canadian citizenship, respectively — was planned in conjunction with Pakistani jihadists. One is identified as Individual A, a member of Lashkar-e-Taiba (LeT), the jihadist group behind the 2008 Mumbai massacre, among other atrocities. The other is identified as Ilyas Kashmiri, operations chief of Harakat-ul-Jihad Islami (HUJI). Bill Roggio of the Long War Journal writes that Kashmiri is "considered by U.S. intelligence to be one of Al Qaeda's most dangerous commanders." Roggio further notes that LeT and HUJI, along with several other Pakistan jihadist groups, including Laskhar-e-Jhangvi, Jaish-e-Mohammed, have merged with Al Qaeda in Pakistan and operate under the name Brigade 313.

While the triggermen behind the Peshawar carnage have not been identified yet, it is highly likely, to say the least, that they come from this same jihad network. So, let's probe a little. Let's think beyond the scenes of the Pakistani market-turned-charnel-house to save the newspaper office in Denmark from a similar fate. Let's think beyond the "terror" to the point of the terror — a place we as politically correct multiculturalists are never supposed to go: The point of Islamic terror is to assert Islamic law. Period.

In the Pakistani case, the terror further enmeshes the United States in misbegotten efforts to "stabilize" the jihadist-riddled government, but that serves Islamic law as well. Such terror further asserts the power of those who bring Islamic law to a nation that already embraces its brand of "justice" as the findings of an August Pew poll confirm yet again. An overwhelming 78 percent of Pakistanis believe those who leave Islam should be killed, 80 percent favor whippings and cutting off hands for crimes like theft and robbery, and 83 percent favor stoning adulterers.

And how many billions did the Obama administration just shovel down that hole? As a condition of such aid, Pakistan should be required to dismantle its nukes and trust key components to us for safekeeping while the threat of seizure by "extremists" endures. Isn't that what a bona fide ally would do?

In the Danish case, the Islamic terror is designed to punish and make examples of the two men chiefly responsible for the revolt that began four years ago against the emergence of Islamic law in Denmark. Flemming Rose, having discovered that a Danish publisher couldn't find an artist willing to violate Islamic prohibitions on imagery of Mohammed to illustrate a Danish children's book, commissioned 12 cartoons of Mohammed in 2005 to reassert Denmark's freedom of the press, which in this case also meant freedom from Islamic law. Kurt Westergaard's cartoon — ask your local newspaper to run it, as the Chicago Sun-Times did this week, to assert America's freedom of the press — has become the symbol of this victorious affirmation of free speech for which Denmark remains under continued threat of Islamic attack, as this Pakistani plot dramatically shows.

So, what to do about which assault? In Pakistan, Secretary of State Hillary Clinton told government officials: "I want you to know that this fight is not Pakistan's alone. This is our struggle as well." To Denmark, the U.S. government said nothing.

This is exactly backward. Pakistan's struggle, feckless and conflicted as it is has been and will continue to be (Roggio also reports, for example, that Ilyas Kashmiri is a "longtime asset of Pakistan's military and intelligence services") is not America's fight. Rather, this fight is among factions of Islam, and far from being a player in this treacherous game, the United States is a dupe. If Pakistan's nuclear arsenal poses a dire threat to the West (like Iran's), the correct military solution is its destruction, not nation-building around it. Clinton's statement of solidarity should have been directed to Denmark, a tiny Western nation valiantly asserting the core principles of liberty, and subsequently threatened for doing so with catastrophic attack, meted out according to Islamic law. It is Denmark's struggle that is our own, or should be.

Will we ever learn?

Anti-Islamization proponents should take cues from Europe

3/5/10

When the Netherlands' Party for Freedom leader Geert Wilders recently addressed voters in Almere, a Dutch city of 200,000 where his party handily won elections this week, he told them what to expect as his once-tiny, anti-Islamization party started flexing its new political muscle. Aside from lower taxes and other political staples, his plans for this city not far from Amsterdam include a ban on Muslim headscarves.

Wilders' ban would apply to "headscarves in municipal bodies and all other institutions (that) receive even one penny of subsidy from the municipality." He continued: "And for all clarity: This (ban) is not meant for crosses or yarmulkes because those are symbols of religions that belong to our own culture and are not — as is the case with headscarves — a sign of an oppressive totalitarian ideology."

Here, Wilders is distinguishing between the religions of Christianity and Judaism, and the religio-political ideology of Islam, noting not only the near-indigenous nature of the former, but also the encroaching totalitarianism of the latter. This is the crucial cultural argument to make if a cultural Reconquista of Europe from Islamization is to be successful.

Certainly, we have seen glimmers. Last year, Filip Dewinter of the Vlaams Belang party of Belgium led a winning campaign to ban the hijab - what he calls "the propaganda weapon of choice for the establishment of Islamic society in Europe" — in the Flemish schools of his country, making the same vital judgment call that Wilders did. "(He) who defends the headscarf out of reasons of tolerance and pluralism has little or no understanding of Islam," Dewinter said. "The hidden agenda behind the veil leads to segregation," a veritable apartheid-regime, he explained, with which Islam seeks to control and dominate the West. Equating the Muslim head scarf with the Christian cross or the Jewish yamulke is "therefore incorrect," Dewinter continued, identifying the headscarf as "the flag of a political ideology" in which it is not the individual religious experience that is central, but rather "the realization of a theocratic society based on sharia, or Islamic law."

Maybe that's a lot for Americans to take in, but they haven't lived through the Islamization Decades that their European cousins have. As Europe's neighborhoods, banlieues and cities have repeatedly seen, headscarf-friendly zones yield to other Muslim demands, from single-sex recreation and medicine, to a refusal to tolerate certain Western texts or foods, to the institution of Islamic banking, to the acceptance of jihadist treason in the mosques, to the entrenchment of Islamic marriage (forced and polygamous), to the ultimate recognition of Islamic courtrooms run according to sharia.

But take the French approach. After determining that the Muslim headscarf inserted religion into state-run secular schools, the French government in 2003 banned the headscarf in the public schools along with the Star of David, the yamulke, "large" crucifixes and the turban of the Sikhs. This decision made it appear as though the hijab hadn't been singled out as a symbol of a specifically Muslim way of life that seeks to extend sharia. Thus, in the name of tolerance, all religious symbols were deemed provocative. In the name of inclusion, all were banned. This is precisely how the traditional (pre-Islamic) society dismantles itself, symbol by symbol, law by law.

And this is precisely why acknowledging and affirming the differences — "discriminating" — between Western religions and Islamic religio-political ideology is so important. Alas, it is also unthinkable for the average post-modern, multicultural Westerner. Rather than reject the symbols of imperial Islam, he capitulates, further stripping his civilization of its own identity, further enabling the Islamization process.

Now, the French government seeks to ban the full veil, or burka, in public buildings, a measure, as a recent Harris Poll tells us, that garners support from a whopping 70 percent of French respondents. Large majorities also support a ban in Italy (65 percent), Spain (63 percent), and the United Kingdom (57 percent). (A burka ban draws 33 percent support in the United States.)

Notably, that support plummets when other religious symbols are included in the burka ban. French support drops to 22 percent. Italian (10 percent), Spanish (9 percent) and British (4 percent) support follows. (American support drops to about 1 percent.)

Defiance of the multicultural orthodoxy is more popular in Europe than anyone imagined.

The Left and Islam: A love story

6/4/10

At some future date, when what Andrew C. McCarthy calls "the freedom culture" is again secure (we hope), the jihad-opposition will see itself divided into two camps in histories written about our current time: those who ineffectually supported efforts to stop "terrorism" and other supposedly generic outbreaks of violence in such lands as Iraq and Afghanistan; and those, far fewer in number (at least in that difficult decade following 9/11), who recognized terrorism as but one aspect of the civilizational assault emanating from expansionist Islam.

If the freedom culture wins, it will be because the latter group grew in influence. And if the latter group grows in influence, it will be due to such books as McCarthy's excellent, ground-breaking new work, "The Grand Jihad: How Islam and the Left Sabotage America."

Islam and the Left? Since this notion will raise some eyebrows, I asked Andrew himself to elaborate on this and some other related questions.

Q: Why are Islam and the Left, as you demonstrate in "The Grand Jihad," not such strange bedfellows?

A: "For all their disagreements on matters like women's rights, gay rights and abortion, Islam and the Left are in harmony on big-picture matters: They are authoritarian, totalitarian in the sense of wanting to control all aspects of human existence, virulently anti-capitalist, and regard the individual as existing merely to serve the collective. Consequently, they have the same obstacle in common: our freedom culture - i.e., Western liberalism, U.S. constitutional republicanism, and their foundation, individual liberty. Historically, Islam and the Left ally when there is a common enemy. But I'd stress that what I am talking about here is an alliance, not a merger. I am not claiming, as someone ridiculously suggested to me the day the book came out, that Barack

Obama wants to impose Sharia."

That appropriately noted, the book does highlight the closely interweaving principles of Islam and the Left, the ummah (Islamic community) and ACORN, both of which "bore from within," in Saul Alinsky's phrase, to hollow out what we might think of as "the Unum" — as in E Pluribus Unum. Linking these points, having documented President Obama's career as a community organizer, his embrace of ACORN, his radical associations, Andrew writes in "The Grand Jihad":

"The common denominator (throughout Obama's career) is a purpose to break down the Unum at its foundations, what he (Obama) called the 'grass roots.' For America he plans an atom bomb. Or to be more precise, an atoms bomb: countless communities in cities and towns across the land, organized along Saul Alinsky's brand of Marxism, into socialist enclaves. It fits hand and glove with Yusuf Qaradawi's voluntary (Islamic) apartheid, the enclave strategy of the Muslim Brotherhood. Each atom smothers the individual freedom and enterprise that have defined the American character, replacing it with welfare states that prize dysfunction and reward the rabble-rousers."

But we ignore the assault through "willful blindness," to borrow the title of Andrew McCarthy's first book about his role as a federal prosecutor in convicting the "blind sheik" and his accomplices for bombing the World Trade Center in 1993. Instead, he observes in the book, our policy-makers obsess over "one tactic, terrorism" while ignoring terrorism's goal: Islamization through the implementation of Sharia (Islamic law). I asked him to explain.

He replied: "From the beginning of my involvement in counterterrorism in the early nineties, I've been struck by the government's portrayal of terrorists as beasts who kill for no better reason than to kill - as if the fact that they are brutal means that they are insane. Government does this as part of its narrative that terrorists couldn't possibly be accurately representing a well-grounded interpretation of Islam, and therefore must be 'perverting' or 'hijacking' Islam, or must be traitors against the 'true Islam.'

"There is a logic to terrorism. It is jihad, the purpose of which is to implement, spread, defend or vindicate Sharia, the Muslim legal code. Sharia is deemed in Islamist ideology to be the necessary precondition to Islamicizing a society. Once you realize that, you quickly realize that the same Sharia-driven campaign can be waged, and is being waged, by non-violent means, and that the violent and non-violent methods are inextricably linked."

Read "The Grand Jihad" and so realize. And quickly!

We need to stand up and say 'no' to Shariah

11/12/10

When Barack Obama spoke in Mumbai about "the different meanings" of jihad, he set up us up again for the Big Lie: "I think," the 44th president said, sounding much like the 43rd president, "all of us recognize that this great religion in the hands of a few extremists has been distorted to justify violence toward innocent people that is never justified."

All — all — of the sacred books and schools of Islam say differently. Every, single one. The fact is - not the fantasy — there is no distortion of Islamic texts required to justify the violence of jihad from Mumbai to Tel Aviv to New York City to Bali to Madrid and beyond. But we, dhimmi-citizens of an Islamizing world, are not supposed to notice the links between the violence and the faith, the faith and the law, the law and the violence — and certainly not say so out loud. Most people don't. Increasingly, this state of denial is enforced by actual states of denial - the most recent example being Austria, which, in a trial on Nov. 23, will attempt to use "hate speech" laws to send Elisabeth Sabaditsch-Wolff to prison for as long as three years for statements about Islam very similar to those I've just written.

The Viennese mother and housewife originally approached the subject of Islam from her unique background that includes a childhood stint in Iran during the Islamic Revolution in 1979 when her diplomat-father was stationed there; and her own work experience with Austrian embassies in both Kuwait at the time of the Iraqi invasion in 1990, and Libya, on 9/11 ("The Jews did it!" Elisabeth's Libyan landlord shouted at her that same day).

She studied the Islamic texts and commentaries, the apologetics and the critiques. Empowered by her natural right to free speech, she decided to educate others in her native Austria about the Koran, about Islamic law (Shariah), in seminars she offered under the auspices of the pro-Western-civilization think tank Wiener Akademikerbund (Association of Vienna Academics). Contracted by the anti-Islamization Freedom Party (FPO) in 2008, Sabaditsch-Wolff has been educating Austrians about Islam ever since.

"The groups were very small at first, sometimes as few as five or six people" she recently told me. "Later on, the numbers rose to 35." Last fall, one attendee in particular seemed "overly enthusiastic about the topic," Elisabeth recalls. She turned out to be a journalist who would brand the seminar a "hate school" in a sensational story for NEWS, a left-wing publication.

"It causes a huge uproar among the establishment," Elisabeth says, although now that her trial approaches Austrian media are silent.

"Bishops, rabbis, politicians, all of whom had never attended any of my seminars and knew nothing of the content, were asked to weigh in and condemn me. The bishop said, 'One must never speak about any religion the way Ms. Sabaditsch-Wolff did about Islam.' This was especially painful for me."

Elisabeth's husband, a military surgeon, is very supportive of her. "My mother had to come to terms with her daughter being maligned in the media," she says. "My sister has cocooned herself and believes the NEWS story rather than confronting reality. My father, who has attended all of my seminars, knows the truth and supports me 100 percent."

Of course, when she enters that Vienna courtroom, she will face the state alone. "The thought that the state—a state that I love very much and that I represented proudly all my life—is prosecuting me for thoughts is a painful one. It is hard to understand that I should have to stand trial for thoughts that are not only based on experience but are the product of careful study of the texts that make up Islam." But Elisabeth Sabaditsch-Wolff is also standing trial for her courage, which threatens all states of denial. "It is interesting to note that once the topic is raised, most friends out themselves as feeling the exact same way I do, however, there is fear. They do not want to become active out of fear for losing their jobs (which is a very real possibility) or getting hurt by some Muslim wacko. My response is always, 'Fear is the wrong feeling here. We need to stand up and say, No to Shariah, gender apartheid, theocracy, parallel legal systems.' "By the way," she adds. "I am being charged for saying all of this!"

Book explains clearly why the U.S. shouldn't kowtow to Islam

5/24/12

Every time I see Dutch Party for Freedom leader Geert Wilders interact with America, I am struck anew by how deeply he confounds us. We aren't used to hearing the truth, particularly about Islam, expressed by a politician—of all people! -- who not only says what he's found to be true, but also acts on it.

For this same reason, however, by Islamic decree (Fatwa), Wilders has been "marked for death," which is the title of his terrific new book. "Marked for Death: Islam's War Against the West and Me" (Regnery Publishing, $27.95) informs and inspires in an elegantly concise but also comprehensive volume. Including an excellent foreword by Mark Steyn, "Marked for Death" is the best single book on Islam and its impact on the West—a book every American should read.

After all, Wilders, a Dutchman with great affection and admiration for the USA (especially the First Amendment and Ronald Reagan), has written this book for *us*. Many chapters open with an epigraph on liberty by an American president, almost as if Wilders wants to explain his devotion to liberty in our own terms, while gently reminding us to be true to our best ideals.

More instructively, Wilders, for eight years a political prisoner of Islam requiring round-the-clock security to avoid assassination, quotes from the anti-Islamic writings of our presidents John Quincy Adams and Teddy Roosevelt. Both men warned against the dangers that Islam poses to liberty and Christianity. These writings will jolt the postmodern reader, alerting us that we are reading something society outlaws as *taboo*: criticism of Islam.

In 1916, Roosevelt observed: "Wherever the Mohammedans have had a complete sway, wherever the Christians have been unable to resist them by the sword, Christianity has ultimately disappeared" (ditto Judaism, Buddhism, Zoroastrianism ...). Roosevelt rejected as "naive" the notion that "all religions are the same." Some religions, he explained, "give a higher value to each human life, and some religions and belief systems give a lower value." Our "social values," including equality before the law, exist "only because the Christians of Europe (did) what the Christians of Asia and Africa had failed to do — that is, to beat back the Moslem invader."

John Quincy Adams wrote that Muhammad "poisoned the sources of human felicity at the fountain, by degrading the condition of the female sex, and the allowance of polygamy; and he declared undistinguishing and exterminating war as part of his religion, against all the rest of mankind. THE ESSENCE OF HIS DOCTRINE WAS VIOLENCE AND LUST; TO EXALT THE BRUTAL OVER THE SPIRITUAL PART OF HUMAN NATURE."

The capital letters are Adams', by the way, and the source Wilders draws from is "The American Annual Register of 1827-28-29," where Adams published unsigned essays in 1830 (listed in Lynn H. Parsons' annotated bibliography of Adams' works) in between his tenure as president and his return to Congress.

In our day, it's not hard to imagine that both Adams and Roosevelt would also be "marked for death" for criticizing Islam. They, too, would experience daily life as a Kafkaesque exercise in staying alive inside a state security bubble. So would others Wilders brings to our attention, including Winston Churchill, Aldous Huxley, Andre Malraux and Alexis de Tocqueville, all of whom freely discussed Islam's strangling effect on individual liberty, the jewel in the crown of Western civilization.

Today, however, with liberty shrinking in direct proportion to Islam's rising influence in the West, Wilders' voice is one of few to make itself heard. Why? Wilders points to the entrenchment of cultural relativism, an ideology that rises from the ashes of Judeo-Christian-humanism to promote, as interchangeable, all other cultures, religions, creeds, over our own.

This self-crushing ideology, as Wilders lucidly explains, permits business as usual to include, for example, regarding the 57-nation Organization of Islamic Cooperation (OIC), the largest bloc in the United Nations, as a normal diplomatic partner. But the OIC promotes Shariah (Islamic law), a supremacist, misogynist and totalitarian system. As opposed to other U.N. member states, the OIC adheres to a discriminatory, Shariah-rights document known as the Cairo Declaration. This Islamic rights document negates the United Nations' 1948 declaration on *universal* human rights. Until OIC member states revoke the Cairo Declaration, Wilders writes, Western nations should demand they be barred from the U.N.; conversely, the West should stop funding the U.N. until it ejects Shariah-supremacist members.

A never-never plan? Only until we enact it. Back in 2007, Wilders introduced a measure in the Dutch parliament to cut aid to OIC states adhering to the Cairo Declaration and minimize bilateral relations.

As noted above: Wilders says what he believes and acts on it. How confounding. Read his book and learn how we can do it, too.

House Republicans question influence of Muslim Brotherhood

7/20/12

Be alarmed: The U.S. government continues to be "advised by organizations and individuals that the U.S. government itself has identified in federal courts as fronts for the international Muslim Brotherhood."

So wrote Rep. Michele Bachmann, R-Minn., in a lengthy, heavily footnoted answer to a query last week from Rep. Keith Ellison, D-Minn. He was seeking more information about the reasons Bachmann plus four other House Republicans — Louis Gohmert (Texas), Trent Franks (Ariz.), Lynn Westmoreland (Ga.) and Thomas Rooney (Fla.) -- requested Inspector General investigations into "potential Muslim Brotherhood infiltration" of the government.

Yes, that would be the same Muslim Brotherhood whose leaders are sweeping to power in the Middle East — most recently in Egypt. There, the new president, Mohamed Morsi, fired up voters this spring by declaring: "The Koran is our constitution. The Prophet Muhammad is our leader. Jihad is our path. And death for the sake of Allah is our most lofty aspiration." That, by the way, is the Muslim Brotherhood's motto.

Brotherhood-linked groups in the U.S. still take a low-key approach, at least publicly. Thanks to the FBI discovery of a key Muslim Brotherhood document, we know what they're up to, even who some of them are. The document, entered into evidence during the landmark Holy Land Foundation terrorism finance trial, presents the Brotherhood plan for "civilization-jihad" against the U.S. It describes the group's "grand jihad" to destroy "the Western civilization from within ... so that it is eliminated and (Islam) is made victorious over all religions." Further, it declares Brotherhood support for "the global Islamic state wherever it is." It also lists 29 of "our organization and the organizations of our friends" — i.e., front groups. Among them are such well-known Islamic organizations as the Islamic Society of North America (ISNA) and the Council on American Islamic Relations (CAIR), both of which remain unindicted co-conspirators.

What is beyond shocking — beyond reason — is that such anti-American Brotherhood-linked groups and individuals have variously engaged, particularly since 9/11, with the U.S. government. Is it a coincidence that U.S. policy has since become receptive to, if not openly supportive of the Muslim Brotherhood? This is the serious question these House Republicans want answered.

"Influence" can be an intangible thing, but sometimes there are signs. For example, someone, something, somehow managed to convince Director of National Intelligence James Clapper to testify before the House Intelligence Committee in 2011 that the Muslim Brotherhood was a "largely secular organization" without "an overarching agenda."

This is a laughable statement — unless spoken in earnest by the DNI. Then the question becomes: Is it possible that in Clapper's chain of information there is, in fact, disinformation? Other questions Bachmann and her colleagues have concern the Homeland Security Department, where, for example, Mohamed Magid, head of ISNA, the largest Brotherhood front group, according to the U.S. government itself, also serves as a member of Homeland Security's Countering Violent Extremism Working Group.

Are there national security implications in the influence of Brotherhood front groups on Justice Department and FBI policies on terrorism? Bachmann & Co. want to find out. How about the ongoing relationship between domestic Brotherhood front groups and the Organization of Islamic Cooperation (OIC)? As Bachmann notes, this foreign bloc of 57 Muslim nations "claims jurisdiction over Muslims in non-Muslim lands, defines human rights as shariah, and advocates that Muslims not assimilate into the cultures of non-Muslims." What of Secretary of State Hillary Clinton's decision to team up with the OIC to pass a U.N. resolution to restrict free speech deemed to be "defamation" of Islam? Such an effort flouts the First Amendment and also reverses U.S. policy. Could malign influence be a factor?

These five Republicans have also expressed concern over media reports that Clinton's longtime top aide Huma Abedin has family relations (late father, mother, brother) with ties to Muslim Brotherhood groups. Her mother, for example, reportedly belongs to the Muslim Sisterhood, a group the new first lady of Egypt also reportedly belongs to. Are such reports true? Do they have security implications? These are questions Americans have a right to know.

"For us to raise issues about a highly based U.S. government official with known immediate family connections to foreign extremist organizations is not a question of singling out Ms. Abedin," Bachmann writes. "In fact, these questions are raised by the U.S. government of anyone seeking a security clearance."

I'm guessing the bit about Abedin is the only piece of this complex story most readers have heard of. It has come to dominate and distort the response to a rational and patriotic effort to bring more transparency to government decision-making in order to ensure that it remains Muslim Brotherhood-free.

Why would anyone want to stay in the dark about that?

Culture Clash

Taliban Idyll

12/24/01

Awhile back, when the kids were toddlers, I had a conversation with another writer and his wife, then expecting their first child. Upon discovering my deep, dark secret -- that my husband and I denied the lifeblood of Barney, "Sesame Street" and "Rugrats" to our wee ones and had no intention of hooking them up to the IV of popular culture any time soon -- they were shocked. Upon learning we privately hoped our children might develop imaginations unaided by googly dinosaurs, hyperactive alphabet letters or sassy cartoon characters, they began to see this for the truly countercultural act it was. "Now, that's subversive," he said (I think) admiringly.

I liked the notion, never having thought of it quite that way. Such "deprivations" had simply struck us as an obvious course of child rearing. Why institutionalize something we didn't particularly like for tots who hadn't even begun asking (or screaming) for it?

My friend and I talked over the more fanciful extensions of this singular world view, even imagining a colony for people who shared a desire to escape the crushing ubiquity of pop culture, from Barney to Brittany, and seek their own way -- as stimulating or mundane as that might be. In this land, MTV wouldn't set behavioral norms; girls would be free from the tyranny of designer labels; boys could play without Pokemon (or Nintendo; or fill-in-the-fad); and citizens wouldn't be required to prove their cultural fealty by rending all their garments for the late George Harrison.

Colony citizenship would begin with the act of pulling the cable (or junking the dish) and an effort to abstain, with exceptions, from mass entertainments created after, say, 1960. This self-selecting group would come together regardless of race, color and creed; indeed, I have found that a vague yearning for something like this exists across political lines.

Take Disney. I find Disney animation, particularly since the "Little Mermaid," unappealing on an aesthetic level. I don't like the garish palette or the airbrushed look of the characters. (Beyond aesthetics, I once returned some slippers because the plastic Little Mermaids on them had plastic little cleavages--which seemed all wrong for a youngster's real feet.) But left-leaning friends fault Disney for its portrayal (or nonportrayal) of minorities and women. They don't even like Snow White. But there is common ground -- as long as you don't dig too deep. Barbie is another image that iconoclasts on the left and right can disavow together -- libs for its objectification of women, and cons for its sexualization of children. The same may be said for the latest in soft-pornish pop stars.

The culture-colony idea went no further than that conversation, forgotten until recently. One night this fall, CNN was broadcasting the docu-shocker "Inside the Taliban." The bestial stadium executions; the despair of the ghostly women; the misery of brutalized children: These horrific images were unforgettable. So was the truly weird sight of utility poles decked with snarled wreaths of unraveled cassette and videotapes. In order to achieve Islamist perfection, the narrator said, the Taliban banned entertainment --music, movies, books and more -- on pain of something awful. The tangles of tape were reminders that rock 'n' roll was out. Western-style cine-flesh and -violence were anathema. My husband and I exchanged glances: Could we be looking at our retro-topia? A Taliban idyll was not exactly what we'd had in mind.

Experts point to Islam's dysfunctional relationship with "modernity" -- as vividly illustrated by those cassette-tape crucifications. This, of course, is the kind of thing that gives dysfunctional relationships with modernity a bad name. It's one thing not to let your daughter out of the house wearing Christine Aguillera's latest threads (emphasis on threads); it's quite another not to let her out of the house. The fact is, this form of Islam rejects more than contemporary culture; it also rejects both the past and future of anything alien, obliterating the offending symbols -- quite literally as in the case of the 1,500-year-old Buddhas of Bamiyan. That means that not only is 21st-century-Marilyn Manson verboten, so is sixth-century Buddhism, along with Renaissance art, the Bill of Rights, Chanel suits and Fred Astaire. Such a monolith nullifies all individuality -- in taste and expression, not to mention politics and religion.

By contrast, retro-topia, while rejecting what could be described as modernity, seeks a place apart from a different sort of monolith -- the all-absorbing entertainment world that squelches individualism and originality. The idea is probably rooted in an appreciation of the cultural past (another contrast with history-eradicating Islamic conquest) and the realization that our own pop culture has marginalized, if not completely obliterated, that past. Of course, given that great void, it's little wonder retro-topia is an idea whose time has gone.

Disconnected dialogue

1/29/02

On a personal level, there was something strangely comforting in watching a dozen or so well educated, philosophically astute Christian clergymen and religious scholars struggling to grasp the very elusive ins and outs of Islam as presented by several Muslim leaders during a Christian-Muslim "dialogue" sponsored by the National Clergy Council (and broadcast on C-Span 2) this week. That is, it looks as if it's not just the average layman -- or lay-columnist, as the case may be -- who's still having trouble getting a good look behind the veil. There are still too many questions hanging in the way of most of us looking on from the Judeo-Christian perspective.

For instance: How does a Muslim choose between the verses of the Koran that espouse tolerance and those that espouse a fairly excruciating death to all infidels? The answer -- Muslims must "debate" their varying interpretations -- offers an inkling as to how Islam may be "hijacked" by militants, but not much explicit instruction. Other topics floated during this unusual forum included the plight of non-Muslim minorities in Muslim countries, and the troubling (to Westerners) primacy of Sharia, or rule by Islamic law (which may call for the amputation of a hand for theft, or death by stoning for nonmarital sex), in Islamic societies.

I say "floated" because such topics were never actually pinned to earth. Give the three Muslim leaders credit -- Imam Aly Abuzaakouk of the American Muslim Council, Imam Yayha Hendi of Georgetown University and Souheil Ghannouchi of the Muslim American Society -- for taking their places on a dais that at times must have felt more like a hot seat. Still, they let some of the most compelling lines of questioning go unanswered. James Beverly, author of "Understanding Islam," (Meridian Books, 1995) twice asked the imams to say whether, ideally, they would like to see Islamic law in force in America and Canada, but to no avail. The Rev. Aham Nnorom injected a shocking jolt of reality to the largely theoretical discussion by introducing evidence of Muslim massacres of Christians in his native Nigeria. His presentation heightened a mood of drama that hung undispelled over the gathering. But while the Muslim leaders never directly addressed such subjects, the salient disagreement between East and West was made perfectly clear.

At issue was, and remains, the antithetical ways the largely Christian West and the largely Muslim East regard religious liberty. Whether the point of discussion was the supposed Western "misunderstandings" or "mistranslations" of those verses of the Quran that go on about dismembering a hapless infidel's limbs (or merely slicing off his fingertips), or a dispute over the specific rights granted under Islamic law, freedom of worship was most often the underlying theme.

On this subject, the exchange was revealing. Elaborating on comments made by his Christian co-panelists, David Aikman of the Ethics and Public Policy Center asked his Muslim counterparts to "speak out forcefully and resolutely for the whole principle of living with freedom of conscience -- not just here in the United States where it already obtains, but in the Muslim world itself." He went on to say, "Let us see this principle of separation of state power from religious practice experienced in all of the Muslim world," adding that if such a thing came to pass, "the great conflicts between civilizations would evaporate almost overnight."

Sounds pretty good, right? But not necessarily to these Muslim leaders. While acknowledging the religious liberty they enjoy in this country -- "we have much more freedom in the United States than in 95 percent of the Muslim world," said Ghannouchi -- they appeared to regard the introduction of such liberty into the Muslim world as an imposition of the West. "No authority on earth should interfere with the choice of the individual to follow their faith," began Imam Abazaakouk, wending his way to a thought-twisting "but" that went like this: "Neither you nor I have the right to tell any Muslim community, if they want to apply Islamic law on themselves, to say, 'No,'" he said.

"Because Islam is a way of life. And when it is a way of life, if we believe in democracy ... (and) if the majority decides to have the Sharia ... that is their right. Not our right to tell them, 'No.' It is as if somebody from the outside world telling us we have no right to apply the Constitution here."

Is it? There's a novel thought: that the abolition of our liberty-protecting Constitution would equate with the abolition of Islam's liberty-repressing Sharia. New questions arise: Does the freedom of the Western world, expansive as it is, also include the freedom to be oppressed? Conversely, is there a place for liberty under Islamic law? It may be that what we face is less a clash of civilizations than a fundamental disconnection.

When understanding the East means losing the West

1-21-03

Breaking news from Saudi Arabia: "U.S. women interact with local populace." According to the Arab News, actual "female" Americans of the Saudi-American Exchange Program met with a bona fide Saudi "female date farmer." The reason? "To promote understanding and encourage dialogue between the two sides," Arab News reports.

It was a success, naturally. Understanding was busting out all over Ye Olde Saudi Date Ranch, while dialogue also occurred -- at least with the state-controlled press. "The portrayal in the Western media and culture is that Muslim women, especially in Saudi Arabia, are oppressed and subservient," said one American participant. "Many Americans believed that women here were forced to wear the traditional abaya and veil. However, I have come to learn that the women here wear the veil by choice." While a Saudi censor couldn't have said it better, this quotation is attributed to Lorna Hadley, a student at Yale University School of Public Health.

And, judging by the comments of fellow student Amelia Shaw, a fine choice wearing the veil is: "I thought women, by wearing the veil, would be silenced, and that symbolized not being allowed any verbal expression. However, when I did wear it, I felt free from being looked at as a sexual object." What a relief. Thanks to Saudi-American exchange, it now becomes clear that, all this time, while Western women were junking their corsets, bobbing their hair, lifting their hemlines, donning slacks, burning bras and discovering the easy cling of stretch denim, they really should have been shopping for the perfect abaya. And why not? As Maryvonne Van Der Bauwede, a "jewelry designer from France," told the Arab News, "It's very comfortable and beautifies the eyes."

Me, I'll take Maybelline. Not that it matters. In fact, maybe we should leave the exchange students to their continuing adventures -- "The Preppy Handbook" meets "Let's Go Mecca and Medina" -- and consider the more serious import of this kind of cross-cultural "understanding."

It's one thing to learn about Muslim dress -- which, despite all the "understanding" this program has managed to promote, is about as voluntary a choice for your average Saudi gal as her religion. It's quite another when presumably liberty-loving American women become apologists for a sartorial brand of servitude that, of course, is just one oppressive fact of life for women living under Islamic Sharia law as legal, professional and social nonentities. And another thing: A woman may not look like a "sex object" when she dresses up like a haystack, but she still looks like an object, period -- one wholly devoid of a recognizable human shape.

Or maybe that's my Western bias showing. It slips through now and again, particularly as cross-cultural "understanding" catches on to a potentially dangerous point. I refer not just to the fashion non-sense of grad students on a junket. While it's easy to poke fun at such exploitable naivete, the impulse to understand is no laughing matter when it requires drastic compromises on principles of life and liberty.

When cultures really clash, outreach becomes less a tool of coexistence than of transformation. Such attempts, in other words, may end up undermining the basic precepts of the Free World. This becomes more obviously apparent in the alarming effort in the West to understand, perhaps even accommodate, what may be best described as a cult of death found in regions to the East.

Maybe it's just a feeling that comes from observing the shocked-no-more responses to the latest suicide-bombing in Israel, or from reading the smooth reportage of a New York Times article on Sri Lanka's "masters" of suicide bombing and their territory ("a place steeped in the notion of self-sacrifice"), but it does seem that suicide bombers aren't quite the pariahs they once were. British enthusiasm over a recent conference on Palestinian Authority reform only intensifies the queasiness.

Among other things, the PA agreed to a "cease-fire" against "pre-1967" Israel. This means that citizens of post-1967 Israel -- namely, the West Bank, Gaza Strip and eastern Jerusalem -- remain what Palestinians consider fair game. Of course, the cease-fire expires after Israeli elections this month, and then it's back to suicide-bombings as usual throughout Israel -- post-1967, pre-1967, A.D., B.C., whatever. In Great Britain today, this counts as progress.

Is it? Jan. 7 was "Palestinian Martyrs' Day," an occasion marked by PA memorials to Palestinians killed in the intifada, including those praised by one government speaker as "the most noble among us" -- the shahidim, or suicide bombers. According to The Media Line (www.themedialine.org), festivities included a government TV special "featuring pictures of dead babies with uncovered faces" and exhortations to Palestinians "to follow in (the suicide bombers') path." Such a death cult seems largely incomprehensible to Westerners. The only way to understand it is to renounce all respect for human life, a measure that still remains beyond our understanding -- one hopes.

Fellowships and flagellation

5-02-03

Flash: This just in from Harvard. The Committee on College Life has renewed its official recognition of the Harvard Radcliffe Christian Fellowship. Big deal? You bet. It turns out that while anyone may join this small campus Christian group, it continues to draw its leadership from among candidates who actually believe in the Holy Spirit and the resurrection of Jesus Christ.

This, according to the editors of the Harvard Crimson, violates Harvard's anti-discrimination policy. As a recent editorial in the college paper put it, Harvard is "in error for not demanding that the club remove its discriminatory policy from its constitution. All students should be free to participate in College activities without being discriminated against because of belief."

Zounds. Given that a Christian Fellowship is one big college activity singularly dependent on belief, it would seem that Muffy and Jason and Savonarola have gone a little too far this time. According to this next generation of sensitivity trainers and diversity consultants any student who wants to lead the Christian Fellowship "should not be excluded because of a reluctance to accept certain tenets." Indeed, Harvard should have "forced" Fellowship members to drop these "certain tenets" -- you know, Christ, the Holy Spirit -- from their leadership requirements "or lose College recognition."

The good news is this didn't happen. That doesn't mean, of course, that the controversy and confusion over enforcing "non-discrimination" and regimenting "diversity" are over. While there is in the Crimson editorial a sloppy disregard for the rights of a campus Christian group, this arrogance may be due less to overt religious hostility than to a fundamentally flawed, if politically correct, school of thought. It teaches our children both to embrace "diversity," since we are all different, and to deny difference, since we are all the same. Understandably, this leads to much muddle. Even as the Crimson editorial demands the exclusion of a Christian group in the name of inclusion and diversity, it reflects the utopian, indeed, totalitarian urge to suppress difference and distinction that is at the root of multiculturalism.

The kids may have learned their lessons well, but that's not to say the rest of us are well served by this scholarship saturating the education system, kindergarten through college. Having had the occasion to walk through several schools, both public and private, in and around Washington, D.C., lately, I can attest that they teach off the same page, and in big letters. What with all the global curricula, "diversity" fairs and feasts, giant international flag displays, and murals of handholding nationals in native costumes, the lesson of the day is that it's a Benetton world, where cultural differences come down to a changing palette of flag colors and quaint costumes.

But what do such lessons teach us about the real world? Freedom in Iraq was just days old when The New York Times published a challenging report from Karbala. It began: "Long forbidden, long hidden, the whips of mortification were flagellating today as Iraq's Shiite Muslim majority celebrated its newfound political freedom -- and potential political power. 'For 25 years they were hidden in our houses,' said a man from the Shiite south as a group of young men lashed their backs in rhythm with whips made from chains. 'The father taught his son.'"

That was, of course, whips that were hidden for 25 years. Not copies of the Universal Declaration of Human Rights, the Magna Carta or the Declaration of Independence. And not Baedeker's Paris or Mickey Mouse ears, either. Whips. Chains. The father taught his son. Necks liberated from the jackboot of Saddam Hussein, backs are now free for self-mutilation. This is not the response Americans expected.

Question: What is the multiculturally sensitive response to the freedom to flagellate? "For this we liberated Iraq?" Hardly. "This is not your father's liberation." Nah. "Different strokes ... ?" Please. Silence? Perhaps.

The terrible fact is that we have no words for culture clash. That is, we're not just missing the words to describe or assess one barbaric custom. We don't even have the words for the culture chasm that exists between the Universal Declaration of Human Rights and the Universal Islamic Declaration of Human Rights, which, based on Sharia (Islamic law), infringes on the human rights of non-Muslims and all women. We speak of Islamic reform, and of something as fanciful as "Islamic democracy," but we fail to bring up the stumbling blocks to such reform and democracy -- the deleterious Islamic institutions of jihad (violent religious conquest) and dhimmitude (the inequality of non-Muslims under Muslim rule).

We talk and teach about diversity. And we talk and teach about difference. But for all the talk and teaching, we don't know the meaning of the words.

Facing reality at the DMV

5-30-03

The Associated Press reports that experts in Islamic law are being summoned to testify at the trial of Sultanna Freeman, a 35-year-old Muslim woman whose religious rights, she claims, have been violated by the state of Florida. How? Sunshine State officials say Freeman must allow the Department of Motor Vehicles to photograph her whole face

-- not just a veil-shrouded slit around her eyes -- if she wants a state driver's license. She maintains that submitting to the DMV mugshot-maker would be "disobeying my L-rd" because she would briefly -- just the pop of a flash bulb -- have to drop the hijab (a head- and face-masking veil).

Let's hope the experts have easy access to the copy of the Koran that has been entered into trial evidence, because finding a chapter on "my L-rd" and "my driver's license" is going to take some doing. Meanwhile, the state plods on, dusting off arguments grounded so deeply in common sense they haven't before seen the light of day.

"It's the primary method of identification in Florida and the nation," explained state Assistant Attorney General Jason Vail to the Associated Press, rather patiently referring to the snapshots that appear on driver's licenses. "I don't think there can be any doubt there is a public safety interest."

While there may indeed be a case against DMVs everywhere for foisting consistently gruesome I.D. photos of the public on the public (mental cruelty? identity theft?), turning a full-face snapshot into a full-frontal clash between East and West takes multiculturalism to a new extreme. My hunch is Freeman's case won't fly -- and it certainly shouldn't drive.

Which, of course, is an option for Freeman, one already, if non-freely, exercised by her Muslim sisters in Saudi Arabia, where the hijab is mandatory and female drivers are against the law. Sultanna, however, being a good American, prefers to litigate. "This is about religious liberty," said her lawyer Howard Marks, an attorney with the American Civil Liberties Union of Florida, opening proceedings in Freeman's nonjury lawsuit against the state. "This is about whether this country is going to have religious diversity. Allowing the state to chip away at religious liberties is not a path we want to go down."

Please.

The nuts and bolts of this case have nothing to do with Freeman's right to worship, freely or diversely, and everything to do with her responsibility to drive lawfully. On the highway, she is a driver first, not a Muslim. As such, she is subject to the same rules and regulations that govern every other driver -- Catholic, Jew or Jesse James. As a licensing body, the state is hardly chipping away at religious liberties; on the contrary, Freeman's religion-based plaint may be seen as an attempt to chip away at the legal tradition of conducting state affairs without regard to religion.

So what to do? Both sides have Islamic experts on the case. Maybe one of them will pull a fatwa out of a hijab and rule that Muslim women may remain in good religious standing, with or without the veil.

Oddly enough, just such a fatwa, sort of, came down this week from Sheik Yusuf Al-Qaradawi, world renowned Islamic "moderate," scholar, and Al Jazeera tele-imam. (The late Daniel Pearl flagged Mr. Qaradawi early on as a centrist; just this past spring the Christian Science Monitor identified him as a "moderate Egyptian cleric," and, more significant, Noah Feldman, the chief U.S. adviser on the Iraqi constitution, has labeled him an "Islamic democrat.") Such positive PR stems from the cleric's condemnation of the Sept. 11 attacks; nothing subsequently -- not his sanctions of suicide "operations"; his pronouncement that shaking hands with Israeli government official Shimon Peres requires washing hands seven times (once with dirt); or his rulings against the war in Iraq -- has altered this reputation.

Qaradawi's latest religious ruling, reported by the Jerusalem Post, not only permits women to venture out alone in public without wearing a hijab, but also to do so without their husband's permission. This sounds downright liberating, not just for Freeman, but for all Muslim women (not to mention the Florida DMV). But there's a catch: The free dress fatwa is restricted to the Muslim woman who is about to blow herself up "for the cause of Allah" in a suicide bombing -- an act of mass murder Sheik Qaradawi calls "one of the most praised acts of worship."

Suffice it to say that if this is the face of moderation unveiled, Sultanna Freeman will just have to do without a driver's license.

Has the Vatican changed its mind about Islam?

11-10-03

You just might think you've struck a nerve when a guy who goes to work every day at the U.S. Conference of Catholic Bishops to promote interfaith dialogue — someone who keeps people talking — hangs up on you. You've certainly struck out, anyway.

But "dialogue" with John Borelli, the bishops' staff man on Catholic-Muslim relations, didn't hold much promise after he said he wouldn't comment on an extraordinary article about the desperate plight of Christians in Islamic societies that appeared in La Civilta Cattolica, a Jesuit magazine thought of as the semi-official voice of the Vatican.

"I won't comment on an article that I have not read in its entirety," Mr. Borelli said, noting that the English translation of the Italian article, "Christians in Islamic Countries" by Giuseppe De Rosa S.I., available at www.chiesa.espressonline.it/english under the headline "The Church and Islam. 'La Civilta Cattolica' Breaks the Ceasefire," is incomplete. (It is a 3,083-word excerpt.) "I don't know what the point of the article is."

Here's the point: For the first time in almost 30 years, a source close to the heart of the Catholic Church (articles in La Civilta Cattolica are approved by the secretary of state of the Vatican) has published what Vatican-watcher Sandro Magister calls "a strikingly severe" account of the Christian condition under Islamic rule. The article may represent a shift, if not a break, in the long-standing Vatican policy of silence on the persecution of Christians in Muslim countries.

The article highlights the "seemingly rather curious fact" that wherever Islam has imposed itself by conquest — in what is now Egypt, Libya, Tunisia, Algeria, Morocco, Lebanon, Syria, Jordan, Turkey, and in the regions of historic Mesopotamia and Palestine — "Christianity, which had been extraordinarily vigorous and rooted for centuries, practically disappeared." And, the article further notes, "for almost a thousand years, Europe was under constant threat from Islam, which twice put its survival in serious danger."

The explanation? As if taking a page from the historian Bat Ye'or, the article cites the Islamic precepts of jihad (holy war) and dhimmitude (inferior status of non-Muslims). It also stipulates that there are two meanings of jihad — the spiritual war, or struggle, to be faithful to the teachings of the Koran, and the literal war that is waged to spread Islam. Both meanings, it says, are "equally essential and must not be dissociated, as if one could exist without the other." The article continues: "Obedience to the precept of 'holy war' explains why the history of Islam is one of unending warfare for the conquest of infidel lands." This same "obedience" has led to recent anti-Christian violence in Algeria, Pakistan, Nigeria, Java, East Timor, the Moluccas and, most dramatically, Sudan. Little wonder, as the article also reports, that between roughly one-quarter and one-third of the estimated Christian population of the Middle East has emigrated over the past decade to the free world.

Such tidings could bring a pause in the "dialogue," but they provide plenty to talk about. "I personally welcome the greater straightforwardness evident in these statements," said Richard John Neuhaus, a Catholic priest and editor of First Things magazine. "Of course, we are committed to (interfaith) dialogue, but we ask our Muslim interlocutors to take seriously some of the difficulties posed by Islam." As examples, he listed Islam's failure to allow religious freedom, its persecution of Christian minorities and its hateful attitude toward Jews. Dialogue, Neuhaus said, "cannot be purchased at the price of telling the truth."

But what is true now was true in the past: What accounts for the new frankness? The American Enterprise Institute's Michael Novak wonders whether the Vatican has been encouraged to speak out both by the failure of the so-called "Arab street" to revolt against U.S.-led wars in Afghanistan and Iraq, and by the large numbers of Muslims Mr. Novak believes are seeking human rights in Iran and elsewhere. "My own hypothesis," he said, "is that change in the Arab world has allowed the

Vatican to be more candid."

Others are not so sanguine. Nina Shea, director of the Center for Religious Freedom at Freedom House, suggests that the new frankness in Rome may be linked to the increasingly dire plight of Christians at the hands of Muslims in Sudan, Nigeria and other parts of Africa. The situation in Europe, where immigration policies have created large, unassimilated Muslim communities within traditionally Christian, secular societies, could also be influencing Vatican thinking. "Before the 1990s," Ms. Shea said, "the biggest persecutors of Christians were communist countries." With the fall of the Soviet Union, radical Islam took communism's place. "We're still very naive," she said. "We need to educate people."

Newsweek's blunder illuminates extremists' major shortcoming

5/20/05

So, Newsweek had "little idea how explosive" its Quran-down-the-toilet story would be, theorizes Paul Marshall in National Review Online.

OK, I buy that — although Newsweek is hardly exceptional in its failure to understand Islam 101. Still, the anonymously sourced, now retracted story — evidence of "media mistrust of the military," writes the Wall Street Journal — didn't become "explosive" until after Imran Khan, a Pakistani anti-U.S. opposition leader (and divorced son-in-law of the late financier Sir Jimmy Goldsmith) held a press conference to light the fuse.

And then what happened? White House spokesman Scott McLellan put it this way: "The report had real consequences. People have lost their lives. Our image abroad has been damaged." Regarding the spate of killing and mayhem across the Muslim world, the New York Post's John Podhoretz wrote that people "are dead for no reason other than some 'good and credible' source had an axe to grind with one of his bosses 15,000 miles away in the United States."

The "report" did this? Our "image" has been damaged — only now? For no "other" reason? Something's missing. That is, Quran-gate offers more than just another example of Washington politicking or good, old-fashioned media bias. Neither drove rioters to murder last week on the Arab-Muslim "street" any more than they drove Mohammed Atta to mass-murder a few years ago in the friendly skies. It was jihad then, and jihad now, the rigid ideology that infuses medieval bloodlust with an unlikely longevity in a post-Enlightenment, technological age.

Which is why the Newsweek story is not about Us. Rather, it underscores something about Them that is much more significant.

Us and Them: the words are "divisive," the concept politically incorrect. But what Michael Isikoff and Newsweek have done with their admittedly flimsy instance of reporting is focus our eyes on the chasm that lies between the Muslim world in which a book — one book — is sacred and life is cheap, and the Western world where speech is free and life is precious.

At least life is supposed to be precious here, just as speech is supposed to be free. The other revelation this story brought to light is the cringe-making extent to which we are willing to censor ourselves when it comes to Islam and the Quran — or, as our Secretary of State has kowtowingly taken to calling it, "the Holy Quran," an adjectival distinction I've never heard officially appended to the Bible.

National Review Online's Marshall suggested Newsweek probably didn't know desecrating a Quran is a capital offense in "Saudi Arabia, Iran, Afghanistan, and elsewhere" — with enlightened Pakistan meting out only life imprisonment. But whether American news editors are up on their Islamic law is, for once, not the issue. The draconian repression of Islamic dictatorships is nothing for us to emulate or pander to, in our policy or our coverage. Frankly, if we tolerate artwork such as "Piss Christ" and "Dung Virgin," we should be able to shrug off Commode Quran.

Whether the toilet caper actually happened — in seeking to secure American lives, after all, not score an NEA grant — is also beside the point; the "damage," the pundits keep saying, is done. As a Pakistani journalist told The New York Times, the Newsweek item confirmed suspicions of "a straight disrespect for the sensitivities of Muslims."

Please. We see the "sensitivities" of some Muslims blowing up other Muslims on a daily basis in Iraq. We saw the sensitivities of Albanian Muslims on a rampage in March 2004, when they destroyed more than 30 Orthodox churches and monasteries in Kosovo. We saw the sensitivities of Taliban Muslims in 2001 when they dynamited the Buddhas of Bamiyan in Afghanistan. We saw the sensitivities of Palestinian Muslims when in 2000 they violently obliterated Joseph's Tomb in Nablus. In 2002, Nigerian Muslims took their sensitivities to the streets after This Day newspaper reported on beauty pageant contestants so lovely the prophet Mohammed would "probably have chosen a wife from one of them." Before you could say, "The Quran is in the toilet," more than 200 people lost their lives in riots that also left 11,000 people homeless. Also in 2002, armed Palestinian guerrillas and their sensitivities occupied the Church of the Nativity in Bethlehem. As the Jerusalem Post reported, "Catholic priests later said that some Bibles were torn up for toilet paper."

I don't recall riots breaking out in St. Peter's Square. Which is why the West still stands on one side of the chasm, and Islam stands on the other. From this vantage point, we can give Newsweek a pass — but not such violently uncivilized behavior.

Sharia and liberty don't mix

3/27/06

Q: What's worse than Afghanistan's barbaric prosecution of Abdul Rahman for the Islamic crime of converting to Christianity?
A: The muffled U.S. reaction.

The president is "troubled, deeply troubled," a response that doesn't exactly ring the red phone, and the State Department really isn't — troubled, deeply or otherwise. On the contrary, responding to this Afghan assault on freedom of conscience (indirectly enabled by the best intentions of the U.S. military), Foggy Bottom actually tried to look on the bright side: "Previously, under the Taliban, anybody considered an apostate was subject to torture and death," spokesman Sean McCormack said. "Right now," he continued, "you have a legal proceeding that's underway in Afghanistan." Which means, I guess, thanks to Uncle Sam, nobody has to submit to "torture and death" anymore without first getting his day in court.

Welcome to U.S.-liberated Afghanistan, a place where, as far as freedom of conscience goes, the Sharia-based constitution is well worth the paper it's written on (nothing), and process trumps principle every time. "It's a constitutional matter," McCormack explained, "so it's a legal matter. So what that tells you is that there are two sides to this."

Two sides — meaning that Rahman may or may not be guilty as charged? It's hard to believe that any American, even a State Department spokesman, could buy into a "proceeding" that makes religion a matter of state control. On the other hand — and this is where things get truly shameful — no representative of the Bush administration has denounced, critiqued or even questioned U.S.-liberated Afghanistan's right to try, let alone take the life of, any person for leaving Islam.

Instead, we talk about Afghanistan's "judicial case" — as if it had one — and the need for "transparency" — as if it's not clear that Afghanistan is merely enforcing Sharia (Islamic law). We also tend to "hope very much," as Under Secretary of State Nicholas Burns put it, "that ... freedom of religion will be upheld in Afghan court." But how can freedom of religion be upheld in Afghan court when freedom of religion isn't written into Afghanistan's constitution?

Yes, the constitution's preamble talks up the United Nation's Universal Declaration of Human Rights, whose Article 18 guarantees freedom of conscience; and yes, Article 2 in the Afghan constitution guarantees limited freedom for non-Muslim-born Afghans (although anyone promoting a religion other than Islam is thrown out of the country, said the Rev. Giuseppe Moretti, Afghanistan's lone Catholic priest). But here's the salient point: According to Article 3, "no law can be contrary to the beliefs and provisions of the sacred religion of Islam."

Because Islam's "beliefs and provisions" prohibit Muslims from leaving Islam on pain of death, and because the Afghanistan constitution is bound to follow Islamic law, converts from Islam have no freedom and no protection under the U.S.-supported Karzai government.

Similar provisions entrenching Sharia are included in both the Iraqi and the Palestinian Authority constitutions, two other U.S.-assisted exercises in nation-building — or, rather, Islamic-nation-building. Maybe now, thanks to Abdul Rahman, more Americans will see that the seeds of Islamic theocracy are planted when a nation's founding document is rooted in Sharia, thus outlawing what we think of as "universal" human rights. It could be that, having signed off on such Islamic-nation-building — inspired by a heady mix of optimism, confusion or naivet_ — the United States isn't working itself into a liberty-affirming lather over Rahman from a sense of strategic resignation, or even embarrassment over the results.

But that shouldn't condemn us to indefinite and deferential silence about the chasm that opens up when basic Islamic law overrules fundamental Western liberties. Rather than sinking into a "deeply troubled" and non-communicative funk, rather than pretending the Afghan constitution doesn't contain a blueprint for a Sharia state, the president and his people should explain the fundamental conflict between emerging Islamic democracies and the Western world — a conflict that looms larger than any military front in the so-called "war on terror": Sharia and liberty don't mix.

Rahman may avoid prosecution by being declared mentally incompetent. That might defuse the immediate crisis, but not the long-term conflict — and it certainly wouldn't guarantee Rahman's safety. (It's grisly to imagine him in an Afghan mental hospital for Christian converts and other state-diagnosed lunatics.) Nor would it guarantee ours. Sugarcoating Sharia and underplaying liberty doesn't win any wars. It just wins more Sharia and less liberty.

Their freedom is not our freedom

2/4/11

Americans must learn two concepts to better understand the political earthquake the United States is now pushing as President Obama gives his nod to "the Arab street," predominantly organized, it seems, by the Muslim Brotherhood, to force out an ally, Hosni Mubarak.

Many on the right have seen in the anti-Mubarak movement vindication of George W. Bush's Big Idea -- that ballot-box democracy would transform the umma into Jeffersonian, or, at least, pro-Western and anti-jihad republics. That this hasn't happened anywhere (and in spades) doesn't dampen their enthusiasm. In fact, citing Bush to bolster pro-"opposition" commentary is in vogue. Writing in the Washington Post, Elliott Abrams quotes Bush, circa 2003, as saying: "Are the peoples of the Middle East somehow beyond the reach of liberty? ... Are they alone never to know freedom ...?" Jay Nordlinger at National Review quotes Bush, circa 2008, as saying: "The truth is that freedom is a universal right -- the Almighty's gift to every man, woman, and child on the face of the earth."

Such is "universalist" gospel. Universalists believe all peoples prefer freedom to its absence, which is probably true. But they also believe all peoples define "freedom" in the same way. Is that true?

The answer -- and first concept -- is no. The entry on freedom, or hurriyya, in the "Encyclopedia of Islam" describes a state of divine enthrallment that bears no resemblance to any Western understanding of freedom as predicated on the workings of the individual conscience. According to the encyclopedia, Islamic freedom is "the recognition of the essential relationship between God the master and His human slaves who are completely dependent on Him." Ibn Arabi, a Sufi scholar of note, is cited for having defined freedom as "being perfect slavery" to Allah. To put it another way, Islamic-style "freedom" is freedom from unbelief.

Suddenly, something seems very lost in Bush-speak translation. It has been from the start, which helps explain what's gone wrong in U.S. wars in the umma. Bringing Western-style "freedom" to the Islamic world may have resembled an idealistic extension of the civil rights crusade in the eyes of President Bush and his followers, but it was actually one big cultural misunderstanding.

At this point, I can imagine being quizzed on whether the Islamic definition of freedom applies outside of a strictly Islamic religious milieu. But judging by the most solid indicators we have -- polling data on Egyptian attitudes from Pew (2010) and University of Maryland/ WorldOpinion.Org (2007) -- I would have to say that Egypt is a strictly Islamic religious milieu. These findings reveal a population steeped in the teachings and attitudes of Sharia (Islamic law). For example, Pew tells us 84 percent of Egyptians favor the death penalty for leaving Islam; 95 percent say it's good for Islam to play a big role in politics. The Maryland/WorldOpinon poll shows that 74 percent of Egyptians favor "strict Sharia," and that 67 percent favor a "caliphate" uniting all of Islam. In free elections, such potential pluralities might well rate as "democratic" in terms of majority rule. But would the West consider them to be "democratic" in terms of individual rights?

Writing in the Washington Examiner, Byron York considered some of these same Egyptian data and found an apparent contradiction between the huge popularity of the death penalty for leaving Islam ("apostasy") on the one hand, and "freedom of religion" (90 percent) on the other. This would be a contradiction in the Western context. But we are not looking at a Western context. Which brings me to Concept Two.

Islam does not recognize as valid any religion but Islam. That means that what we in the West hear as "freedom of religion" becomes, in the Islamic context, freedom of Islam. Indeed, as Stephen Coughlin, the brilliant analyst of Sharia, has pointed out to me, citing both the Koran and quoting the classic Sunni law book "Reliance of the Traveler," Judaism and Christianity "were abrogated by the universal message of Islam." That means overruled. Further, it is "unbelief (kufr)" -- grounds for the capital crime of apostasy -- "to hold that the remnant cults now bearing the names of formerly valid religions, such as "Christianity" or "Judaism," are acceptable to Allah Most High."

Suddenly, a post-Mubarak Egypt run by the Muslim Brothers is not so difficult to imagine.

Did Nora Ephron liberate women or debase them?

6/29/12

With so many assaults on the boundaries of governance and sovereignty in the news lately, reflecting on the career of writer and Hollywood director Nora Ephron, who died this week at 71, may seem off-topic. But upon reading through many glowing Ephron appreciations, I realize that in her work lies another broken boundary. It is a cultural one, and every bit as significant as lines on the map or in the Constitution.

In a scene from her most famous movie, "When Harry Met Sally" (1989), Ephron brought to mainstream, predominantly female audiences the spectacle of a professional actress (Meg Ryan), not a porn prop, performing an extended impression of an orgasm in a crowded delicatessen. It was supposed to be the ultimate put-down of her crass male companion (Billy Crystal). Was this merely a smart update of the onscreen battle of the sexes once famously waged by Katharine Hepburn and Spencer Tracy? Or had we become party to something darker? Either way, America laughed, and Ephron is today eulogized for this unforgettable display.

It was a first, all right, but maybe not so funny, since it was also a milestone in the pornification of the American middle class. This has been a long process in which increasingly voyeuristic audiences watch as increasingly untrammeled moviemakers rob human sexuality of intimacy and consequence. "When Harry Met Sally" took us over the top, cauterizing audiences to a new convention of shamelessness — the ideal of Betty Friedan feminism.

And then what happened? Ever since, as a Salon.com critic approvingly wrote, "rom-coms have gotten increasingly raunchy and foulmouthed, often desperately so. But whatever supposed new twists writers dream up — make the lovers casual-sex partners or bisexual polyamorists or ex-lovers of each other's parents — they're just spraying Cool Whip on a cake that Ephron baked."

This must make Ephron the mother of the transgressive "gross-out" comedy, even if she is more politely celebrated as the queen of romantic comedy. To be sure, two subsequent Ephron "rom-coms," "Sleepless in Seattle" (1993) and "You've Got Mail" (1998), were more conventional entertainments. But the lines had blurred.

Such was the crowning achievement of a wonderfully successful career cocooned amid the entertainment Left. There was the short marriage to Watergate-famous Carl Bernstein and the early movie "Silkwood" (1983), directed by Mike Nichols and starring Meryl Streep battling an Evil Corporation. Ephron's divorce from Bernstein was novelized in the best-selling "Heartburn" (1983), which in 1986 became another Streep and Nichols collaboration that also starred Jack Nicholson. Even after Ephron's segue into comedy, the odd political barb poked through. In "Julie & Julia" (2009), Ephron's final movie with Streep as Julia Child, Julia's discordant character of a father is a rich, Republican McCarthyite. The character of Julie, meanwhile, is admonished by her Democrat boss that a Republican would have fired her.

Such is the lingo of the entertainment Left, for whom invoking McCarthyism, mean-spirited Republicans and other stock villains is like breathing. "I forget how white they are, and mean-spirited, and thin-lipped," Ephron wrote of Republicans in 2008 at Huffington Post. In a 2010 list of things she would not miss (dry skin, bad dinners), Ephron included: "polls showing that 32 percent of Americans believe in creationism" and Clarence Thomas.

Clarence Thomas? In 1996, Ephron warned Wellesley graduates: "Understand: Every attack on Hillary Clinton for not knowing her place is an attack on you. Underneath almost all those attacks are the words: Get back, get back to where you (women) once belonged ... Any move to limit abortion rights is an attack on you — whether or not you believe in abortion. The fact that Clarence Thomas is sitting on the Supreme Court today is an attack on you."

The world that crowned Ephron with laurels was a dark, dark place—if only these college-educated young women could see it: "What I'm saying is, don't delude yourself that the powerful cultural values that wrecked the lives of so many of my classmates have vanished from the earth. Don't let the *New York Times* article about the brilliant success of Wellesley graduates in the business world fool you—there's still a glass ceiling. Don't let the number of women in the workforce trick you—there are still lots of magazines devoted almost exclusively to making perfect casseroles."

Aha! In Ephron World, there was no place for the nonfeminist female. Rom-coms were fine, so long as the female lead was sufficently "liberated" from Republicans, Clarence Thomas and abortion hang-ups. In fact, maybe such re-education was what was really behind Meg Ryan's big moment in the deli, in front of all those people.

And America laughed.

Denial

Good, bad or ... diplomacy

10/01/01

Thanks to British Foreign Secretary Jack Straw, we now see how it's really done: how a wily mastery of diplomacy can coalesce any coalition, poof, before you can say "Death to America."

Hang on a second. You mean that's not what happened following Straw's "historic" visit to Tehran this week? Not exactly. As Straw put it, according to the London Telegraph, "The phrase that I think would be more appropriate [than coalition-building] is that of an international consensus."

"Consensus" may be a couple notches down from "coalition," but it's a start. What sort of consensus did Straw build, and, equally important, how did he build it?

One day after conferring with Secretary of State Colin Powell, Straw jetted to Tehran, marking the first time a British Foreign Secretary had traveled to the radically anti-Western country since the 1979 Islamic Revolution. Carrying what the State Department characterized as "no particular message" from the United States (which, of course, severed diplomatic relations with Iran following the fall of the Shah and the seizure of the American Embassy in Tehran), Straw was clearly out to gauge the chances of Iran joining the international coalition to be led by the United States against state-sponsored terrorism.

Problem is, Iran itself is a state sponsor of terrorism — often against the United States. Remember the 1983 suicide bombing of the U.S. Marines barracks in Beirut that killed 241 young men? That was the work of Hezbollah, the Iranian-backed militia. Among other massacres, Iran is implicated in the 1996 bombing in Saudi Arabia that killed 19 airmen, and is a suspect, along with Osama bin Laden's al Qaeda, in the 1998 bombings of the U.S. embassies in Kenya and Tanzania. It may even have had a bloody hand in the attack on America of Sept. 11. This sort of thing might present a stumbling block to the average Joe, but not to the professionals in the British Foreign Office.

Straw determined that the best way to defuse the pesky terror issue was, to coin a phrase, to feel the terrorists' pain. On the day before his arrival, he contributed an inflammatory op-ed piece to the Iranian press in which he came perilously close to rationalizing terrorism by linking it to the plight of "Palestine."

That old canard requires a willful misreading of the facts, from Ehud Barak's shockingly numerous concessions to Yassir Arafat (rejected), to Osama bin Laden's infamous hatred not for Israel, but for the United States and its interests in the Middle East. Perhaps worse, it reveals a fundamental misunderstanding of the global and cultural scope of the mission before us.

Too bad not every Iranian could concentrate on his article; the chanting outside the British embassy of "Death to Britain," "Death to America," was too loud. And who could possibly hear that Straw was actually offering Iran a significant role in shaping Afghanistan's post-Taliban government? The important thing, of course, is that Iran's leaders heard him out. This seems to have been rather thrilling to the Foreign

Secretary, who declared Britain and Iran to be in "absolute agreement." About what, however, wasn't clear. "What I've started today is a high-level dialogue with the Iranians of a kind that we've not enjoyed for years," Straw said before departing for Tel Aviv, where he would face understandably livid Israelis. "I want to see that continued."

What continued? Iran waited until Straw was out of town before Ayatollah Ali Khamenei gave an answer. Amid cries of "Death to America" — kind of brings on nostalgia for the hostage crisis — and "Death to Israel," the Ayatollah announced that Iran would provide zero help to America and its allies, whoever they might be. "We do not trust America. We do not think America has the competence and sincerity to lead an international move against terrorism, as the world's most dangerous terrorists are sitting next to it," he said, referring to, of all countries, Israel. He went on to say that America was "over-expectant" in regard to assembling a coalition, and, in general, engaging in "disgusting" behavior. Which seemed to remind the Ayatollah that, as he put it, "Israeli leaders are all terrorists ... America ... blood ... Zionist regime ..." The coalition needs this guy like it needs Osama bin Laden.

Believe it or not, the State Department isn't so sure. "We would still be interested in what Iran is prepared to do against terrorism," spokesman Richard Boucher said after the Ayatollah's outburst. Didn't Iran make itself clear? Even its "moderate" president, Mohammad Khatami, came out to dismiss President Bush as "arrogant" for attempting to "distinguish between good and bad." Meanwhile, thank heavens for Bush's "arrogance" — a "vice" diplomats don't seem to have.

How the West has won

10/8/01

The most successful movement ever to have swept the West may be the drive to eradicate discrimination. Racism, of course, is out. Sexism is out also. While "ageism" has never really caught on as anathema, practitioners of what is known as "lookism" (and even "species-ism") can no longer gaze upon Venus de Milo (or chicken cordon bleu) without a guilty pang or two. In the increasingly expansive name of tolerance and equality, Western civilization has managed to call the very concept of superiority into doubt.

But what happens when the West goes further still and calls the superiority of tolerance and equality into doubt? That, in effect, is what happened last week after the Italian Prime Minister Silvio Berlusconi ignited a diplomatic firestorm while in Berlin to meet with Chancellor Gerhard Schroeder and the Russian President Vladimir V. Putin.

Whatever the three leaders had to say about global terrorism was lost in the glare of Berlusconi's bombshell. It wasn't just that he predicted the West is "bound to occidentalize and conquer new people" as it had already "done with the Communist world and part of the Islamic world." The Italian leader also declared, "We should be confident of the superiority of our civilization, which consists of a value system that has given people widespread prosperity in those countries that embrace it, and guarantees respect for human rights and religion. This respect," he added, "certainly does not exist in Islamic countries."

Tsk, tsk. By letting such unvarnished truths pass his lips — thus replacing them with his foot — Berlusconi set off a chain reaction of outrage and eyeball-rolling disbelief across Europe and the Middle East. "I can hardly believe that the Italian prime minister made such statements," huffed Guy Verhofstadt, the Belgian premier and current European Union president. Amr Moussa, secretary general of the Arab League, condemned the prime minister's remarks as nothing less than "racist" — odd, considering the multi-racial appeal of Islam — and added that Berlusconi had "crossed the limits of reason and decency." From a seat beside Moussa at a Cairo news conference, Louis Michel, leader of the (to date) spectacularly unsuccessful European Union bid to win Arab support for the anti-terrorism coalition, characterized Berlusconi's statement as "totally contradicting the values in which we believe."

Which ones: widespread prosperity, respect for human rights, or respect for religion? However, shall we say, impolitic Berlusconi's remarks may have been, any rational comparison between representative democracy and Muslim theocracy is bound to favor representative democracy every time—unless, that is, one-party rule, draconian penal codes and intolerance of dissent is your idea of heaven on earth. And that's not even taking into account more "extreme" Islamic states such as Afghanistan, where women have no rights, property, education, or even medical treatment, and adultery, for example, is a capital offense (by stoning).

It looks as if something besides an unwelcome intrusion of reality motivates Berlusconi's critics, something perhaps related to the decades during which Western Civilization has come under attack in its own universities. There, the West has been demoted to just another exploitative power scheme, not better and often worse than other exploitative power schemes.

Ten years ago, as dean of Yale College, history professor Donald Kagan addressed this often one-sided struggle. Western Civilization's "flaws are real enough," he said, "but they are common to almost all civilizations known on any continent at any time in human history. What is remarkable about the Western heritage ... is the important ways in which it has departed from the common experience." Enumerating the West's varied attributes, perhaps chief among them the assertion of the claims of the individual against those of the state, Kagan went on to note that, "at its core is a tolerance and respect for diversity unknown in most cultures. One of its most telling characteristics is its encouragement of criticism of itself and its ways. Only in the West can one imagine a movement to neglect the culture of one's heritage in favor of some other."

Kagan, of course, was reflecting on the toll of what became known as the "culture wars." At the time, this was largely an academic exercise. Now, as a real war on the West breaks out, the stakes are suddenly not only higher, but the outcome—the future—seems to depend as much on the West's faith in itself as its firepower.

Western self-loathing numbs us to violence

5/1/02

Two things that happened last September are key to what happens from here on out—and both incidents occurred after Sept. 11.

First: On Sept. 23, 2001, Hamas supporters at a Palestinian university marked the anniversary of the year-old return to war against Israel with an exhibition celebrating terrorism. Highlights included an installation re-creating the lunch-time attack on a Jerusalem pizza parlor, killing 15, which came complete with body-part props, fake pizza slices and a black-masked "bomber" who obliged passing spectators by setting off play-explosions. Another tableau featured a mannequin dressed in the garb of an ultra-Orthodox Jew standing behind a large rock—a large TALKING rock—that said, "O believer, there is a Jewish man behind me. Come and kill him."

In other words, this was a real West-Bank crowd-pleaser. But while the show may have gone over in Nablus like Monet at the Met, it repelled the West—at least the small segment that actually got wind of it. Despite relatively scant coverage, the genuine revulsion generated by this exhibition indicates that two weeks into the new age of terror, a celebration of civilian carnage, whether in New York or Jerusalem, was still shocking in the extreme and utterly incomprehensible.

Second: A few days later, Italian Prime Minister Silvio Berlusconi remarked that the West—at that point still definable by its unmitigated outrage over terrorist attacks great and small—should take heart from a demonstrable superiority to Islamic society.

"We should be confident of the superiority of our civilization," Berlusconi said, because "it consists of a value system that has given people widespread prosperity in those countries that embrace it, and guarantees respect for human rights and religion." Such respect, he continued, "certainly does not exist in Islamic countries."

Judging by the widespread outrage Berlusconi sparked—outrage emanating from the highest government levels in Europe and burning beyond the West—he, too, had defined an outer limit of acceptable behavior. The Italian leader may have been addressing himself to the new world of Islamist terror, but he was also speaking in the old era of multiculturalism, where openly boosting representative democracy over repressive theocracy and dictatorships was also shocking in the extreme and utterly incomprehensible.

And now? To be sure, there have been no more Berlusconi-style bloopers. The assault on the West by radical Islam is more or less depicted as a security issue, not the "clash of civilizations" that it is. The open glorification of terrorism throughout the Islamic world, however, has only grown more brazen. While Westerners still wouldn't line up alongside Palestinians to see the exploding pizza-parlor exhibit, it's fair to say that many in the West, Europe especially, have become strangely numb to terrorism, particularly as practiced against Israel, and have even embarked upon a barbarous process of rationalization that seemed unimaginable just seven months ago. Back then, a chamber of horrors like the Hamas terror show would still end a debate, not—now that the shock is over—open one.

What accounts for the change? The answer may lie closer to the spontaneous chorus of enlightened disgust that greeted Berlusconi's affirmation of Western civilization than to a newfound affinity for terrorism itself. Writing in The Times of London, Mick Hume makes a point along these lines by describing the "anti-Israel turn in Western opinion" as a "symptom of the West's loss of conviction in itself." This is a profoundly important observation. As Hume—a self-described Palestinian sympathizer, by the way—goes on to explain, "In the eyes of many today, Israel's crime is to be the most forceful expression of Western values. The Israeli state is seen as a beachhead of Western civilization in a hostile world.

"That used to be its greatest asset," he continues. "Today, however, Western civilization has fallen into disrepute even within its own heartlands, and Israel's image has suffered accordingly."

For decades now, the relativist school of thought known as multiculturalism has been pushing Western civilization into disrepute. Maybe it has finally fallen. Something has shifted, certainly, reshaping the global topography to the point where most of what counts as the free world now gravitates toward the repressive forces of terror that surround a vibrant democratic society engaging, however fiercely, in self-defense.

That just might make this, then, the penultimate triumph of multiculturalism. In other words, don't count on the battle ending at Israel's borders, wherever they ultimately lie. "A global consensus against Israel has taken shape among all those who hate the values of Western society," Hume writes.

What we didn't fully realize in September was how much of Western society that also includes. Which doesn't, needless to say, bode too well for the rest of us.

Boykin and the war for Muslim outreach

10-24-03

Confused over the Lt. Gen. William Boykin furor? There may come a time when the future's historians explain the controversy this way:

"The 'war on terror,' later rechristened—sorry, renamed—the 'war for Muslim outreach,' began on Sept. 16, 2001, the day President George W. Bush carelessly spoke of a 'crusade.' His remark was heard neither as an echo of Dwight D. Eisenhower's World War II book 'Crusade in Europe,' nor as a sober pledge to avenge thousands of American dead still smoldering at Ground Zero—victims, as Muslims on the outer reaches would reveal, of a joint CIA-Mossad plot. Instead, the word 'crusade' was perceived as a calculated insult to all of Islam still stewing over Holy Land incursions by Really Old Europe a millennium earlier.

"Early victories in the war for Muslim outreach were small but significant, such as forcing a new name onto 'Operation Infinite Justice,' the distinctly dis-Iamic moniker for the war in Afghanistan. This was necessary, of course, since it is Allah who dispenses infinite justice, not the United States military. It wasn't long before 'Islam is love' was the word from the president, and post-Sept. 16 outreach included annual Ramadan suppers at the White House.

"But there were setbacks, too, including the rapid disintegration of the democratic Baathist republic of Iraq, the elevation of Daniel Pipes to the U.S. Peace Council, and the stubborn refusal of the United States to 'seek a new paradigm,' as Syafii Maarif, head of the second-largest Muslim group in Indonesia, advised President Bush during a presidential visit in Oct. 2003.

"'We told him U.S. foreign policy should seek a new paradigm if the U.S. wants to be respected by the world community and be safe,' Maarif explained at the time, exuding only the faintest whiff of blackmail. 'New paradigm,' of course, was a fancy phrase for ditching Israel and bailing on Iraq. Which would come later. Muslim outreach was still a work in progress in the fall of 2003, when The Washington Post reported, 'The administration's close ties to Israel are a perennial complaint of these (Muslim) critics, and the invasion of Iraq inflamed opposition overseas.'

"Luckily, the president had already green-lighted a commission on public diplomacy to investigate Muslim discontent. 'Hostility toward America has reached shocking levels' in the Muslim world, the commission concluded, adding sagely: 'Surveys show that specific policies' (read: specific policies on Islamic terrorism, Israel and Iraq) 'profoundly affect attitudes towards the United States.' In other words, the United States could have its Muslim outreach or it could have its 'specific policies,' but it couldn't have both.

"Then along came Gen. Boykin. In every war, there are generals who want to fight an earlier war. This was true of Gen. Boykin. He wanted to fight the war of Sept. 11, the attack that is now, of course, but a tiny footnote to Sept. 16th, Death to Crusades Day, the first new national holiday since Martin Luther King Day.

"Gen. Boykin saw in the emergence of Muslim terror networks a resumption of the old wars of Islamic expansion against the Judeo-Christian West. And he saw fit to explain his vision in stark religious terms when he spoke in American Christian churches. Islamic terrorists hate the United States, he said in June 2003, 'because we're a Christian nation, because our foundation and our roots are Judeo-Christian. And the enemy is a guy named Satan.' When such statements became public through the now-defunct Los Angeles Times, all hell, pardon the expression, broke loose, spreading a plague of damning liberal editorials, columns and statements.

"'General Boykin, the New York Times editorialized in calling for his head, 'should not be ... providing ammunition for those who portray the war against terror as a war against Islam.' (Note the implicit denial of the specifically Islamic character of the terrorism aimed at the non-Islamic West—a semantic victory dating back to early outreach.) Fareed Zakaria, a Washington columnist of the day, suggested Gen. Boykin be fired simply to assuage Arab/Islamic suspicions of the United States. Others compared the American officer's biblical perspective with that of holy war-mongering Osama bin Laden.

"But it was the president himself who may have tipped the balance when he rejected even the basis of the three-star general's worldview—that the war on terrorism had its undeniable religious dimension in being a response to Islamic jihad on the West, a civilization with Judeo-Christian roots.

"Some say that was the point at which outreach trumped terrorism as the war's priority. Once Gen. Boykin was history it was just a matter of time before Hamas had its AWACS, and jailed Shiite cleric Moqtada Sadr was installed as supreme ayatollah of the United Nations Mandate of Iraq. Soon, the war's ultimate objective—high U.S. poll numbers throughout Muslim culture—was ours."

Burnt offerings on the altar of multiculturalism

7/15/05

Only one faith on Earth may be more messianic than Islam: multiculturalism. Without it — without its fanatics who believe all civilizations are the same — the engine that projects Islam into the unprotected heart of Western civilization would stall and fail.

It's as simple as that. To live among the believers — the multiculturalists — is to watch the assault, the jihad, take place unrepulsed by our suicidal societies. These societies are not doomed to submit; rather, they are eager to do so in the name of a masochistic brand of tolerance that, short of drastic measures, is surely terminal.

I'm not talking about our soldiers, policemen, rescue workers and, now, even train conductors, who bravely and steadfastly risk their lives for civilization abroad and at home. Instead, I'm thinking about who we are as a society at this somewhat advanced stage of war. It is a strange, tentative civilization we have become, with leaders who strut their promises of "no surrender" even as they flinch at identifying the foe. Four years past 9/11, we continue to shadow-box "terror," even as we go on about "an ideology of hate."

It's a script that smacks of sci-fi fantasy more than realpolitik. But our grim reality is no summer blockbuster, and there's no special-effects-enhanced plot twist that is going to thwart "terror" or "hate" in the London Underground anymore than it did on the roof of the World

Trade Center. Or in the Bali nightclub. Or on the first day of school in Beslan. Or in any disco, city bus or shopping mall in Israel.

Body bags, burn masks and prosthetics are no better protections than make-believe. But these are our weapons, according to the powers that be. These, and an array of high-tech scopes and scanners designed to identify retinas and fingerprints, to detect explosives and metals — ultimately, I presume, as we whisk through the automatic supermarket door. How strange, though, that even as we devise new ways to see inside ourselves to our most elemental components, we also prevent ourselves from looking full-face at the danger to our way of life posed by Islam.

Notice I didn't say "Islamists." Or "Islamofascists." Or "fundamentalist extremists." I've tried out such terms in the past, but I've come to find them artificial and confusing, and maybe purposefully so, because in their imprecision I think they allow us all to give a wide berth to a great problem: the gross incompatibility of Islam — the religious force that shrinks freedom even as it "moderately" enables or "extremistly" advances jihad — with the West. Am I right? Who's to say? The very topic of Islamization — for that is what is at hand, and very soon in Europe — is verboten. A leaked British report prepared for Prime Minister Tony Blair last year warned even against "expressions of concern about Islamic fundamentalism" (another one of those amorphous terms) because "many perfectly moderate Muslims follow strict adherence to traditional Islamic teachings and are likely to perceive such expressions as a negative comment on their own approach to their faith." Much better to watch subterranean tunnels fill with charred body parts in silence. As the London Times' Simon Jenkins wrote, "The sane response to urban terrorism is to regard it as an avoidable accident."

In not discussing the roots of terror in Islam itself, in not learning about them, the multicultural clergy that shepherds our elites prevents us from having to do anything about them. This is key, because any serious action — stopping immigration from jihad-sponsoring nations, shutting down mosques that preach violence and expelling their imams, just for starters — means to renounce the multicultural creed. In the West, that's the greatest apostasy.

And while the penalty is not death — as it is for leaving Islam under Islamic law — the existential crisis is to be avoided at all costs. Including extinction.

This is the lesson of the atrocities in London. It's unlikely that the 21st century will remember that this new Western crossroads for global jihad was once the home of Churchill, Piccadilly and Sherlock Holmes. Then again, who will notice? The BBC has retroactively purged its online bombing coverage of the word "terrorist"; the spokesman for the London police commissioner has declared that "Islam and terrorism simply don't go together"; and within sight of a forensics team sifting through rubble, an Anglican priest urged his flock, as The Guardian reported, to "rejoice in the capital's rich diversity of cultures, traditions, ethnic groups and faiths." Just don't, he said, "name them as Muslims."

Their faith renewed, Londoners soldier on.

Reality and Islam

7/22/05

By refusing to confront the truth we are not only deluding, but hurting, ourselves.

On Monday, I outlined the problem of the age: the incompatibility of Islam with a multicultural West that hides away inconvenient history and disturbing doctrine under layers of political correctness. Without stripping them off to examine the problem, all we get is a lot of wishful thinking.

Historian Niall Ferguson, writing in the Telegraph on the intensifying "Muslim colonization" of Europe, has decided that such "demographic shifts" are not "invariably a bad thing." After all, seven centuries of jihad-imposed dhimmitude for infidels in Muslim Spain gave us the Alhambra, or something. It's that pesky "ideology" of conquest that follows all the shifting that's the problem — something he thinks European Muslims ought to take "a much closer look at." Really stern stuff.

Over at the Boston Globe, a lefty editorial mantra turns culture clash into harmonic convergence: "European Muslims and non-Muslims must learn to live together. Each will have to practice the tolerance that [Theo van Gogh] assassin Bouyeri proudly scorned." They must, must they? As sharia law becomes a democratic option, who will enforce such tolerance?

As conservatives, JWR columnist Charles Krauthammer and blogger-cum-radio host Hugh Hewitt still fight the good fight, but, in these multicultural days, that means sorting through "extremism" and finding nothing too terribly Islamic about it. Mr. Hewitt writes that my arguments of last week were wrong, citing "functioning democracies in Turkey and other predominantly Islamic countries" as evidence of Islamo-Western compatibility. He throws in the loyal host ("millions of loyal British and American citizens") for good measure. Problem is, the extent to which Turkey — where, just incidentally, "Mein Kampf" was a top 10 bestseller this spring — has ever functioned as a democracy is directly related to the efforts of a strong man, Ataturk, to constrain Islam's grip on the country's institutions, replacing religion with a doctrine of Turkish racial and civilizational supremacy. And while it tugs on the heartstrings, the loyalty of individual Muslims fails to neutralize or reform the institutions of jihad and dhimmitude that rise from Islamic teachings. That I even raised the issue, Mr. Hewitt writes, "underscores the almost desperate need for Muslim leaders in the West again and again, to denounce, without argument or sidebar mentions of Israel, etc., the use of terrorism as a weapon." Almost desperate is right.

Having determined that "99 percent" of European Muslims are "peace-loving and not engaged in terror," Charles Krauthammer sounds a similar alarm. "They must actively denounce not just ... the terrorist attacks, but their source: the Islamist ideology and its practitioners. Where are the fatwas against Osama bin Laden? Where are the denunciations of the very idea of suicide bombing? Europeans must demand this of all their Muslim leaders."

Why Europeans? Why not the Krauthammer 99 percent, or the Hewitt millions? This is where it gets tricky, where those cultural ties to terrorism's tactics and/or goals seem to be all too binding. It is true that in March, something called the Spanish Muslim Council issued a fatwa against Osama bin Laden, calling him an apostate for his atrocities. Judea Pearl, father of slain journalist Daniel Pearl, mentions this in his Boston Globe piece about a clerically star-studded conference on Islam in Jordan this month. Mr. Pearl notes that the fatwa led many to believe it would be followed by others, "and," he writes, "that using the Islamic instruments of fatwa, apostasy and fasad (corruption), Muslims would be able to disassociate themselves from those who hijacked their religion."

He continues: "Unfortunately, the realization of these expectations will need to wait for a brave new leadership to emerge. The final communiqué of the Amman conference, issued July 6, states explicitly: 'It is not possible to declare as apostates any group of Muslims who believes in Allah the Mighty and Sublime and His Messenger (may Peace and Blessings be upon him) and the pillars of faith, and respects the pillars of Islam and does not deny any necessary article of religion.'"

Mr. Pearl spells out the chilling ramifications: "In other words, belief in basic tenets of faith provides an immutable protection from charges of apostasy." Even what Mr. Pearl calls "anti-Islamic behavior," including "the advocacy of mass murder in the name of religion, cannot remove that protection," he writes. "Bin Laden, Abu Musab al-Zarqawi and the murderers of Daniel Pearl and Nick Berg will remain bona fide members of the Muslim faith, as long as they do not explicitly renounce it."

Which leaves conservative Muslims, liberal Muslims and everybody else between a rock and hard place. Isn't it time to crack things open?

Life in post-identity America

7/29/05

Will the American identity — the save-the-world American, the quiet American, the ugly American, the generous American, the can-do American — disappear during the long war on Islamic terror? In the following three quotations of the week — random, but not unconnected — you can see it slipping away, the victim of a debilitating cultural amnesia. Which may be pretty tough stuff for the middle of the summer, but that's the way 2005 goes.

The first quotation is a headline: "Poll Shows Americans, for First Time, Divided on Use of A-Bombs in 1945." According to this Associated Press poll, commissioned to mark the 60th anniversary of the atomic bombings of Hiroshima and Nagasaki, a "historical switch" has taken place. The strong majorities that always supported the use of "the bomb" to end World War II in the Pacific have, for the first time, dwindled to an almost even split, with 48 percent of Americans "strongly" or "somewhat" approving, and 47 percent "strongly" or "somewhat" disapproving.

Whether this shift is inspired by plain ignorance or a civilizational death wish, it hardly reflects a robust culture bent on military triumph, let alone survival. In their disapproval of the Truman decision that spared a million American casualties (the projected cost of an invasion of mainland Japan), 47 percent of Americans reveal a lack of will, even in historical terms, not only to prize American lives, but also to support the hard decisions to save them. If not defeatism exactly, such national torpor, stemming from an unrequited empathy with the enemy, tends to make any victory ambiguous. Remember Iraq, where, upon liberation, the American flag draping Saddam's toppled statue had to be whisked away in deference to similar, politically correct tendencies. And that was just the beginning.

We muddle through, but the terrible tendencies remain — as revealed in a stunning installment of In the Red Zone, a blog from Iraq by journalist Steven Vincent. Mr. Vincent reports from Basra, where he says crooks and corruption are the problem, not terrorism. There, a Gary Cooper-esque U.S. Air Force captain is in charge of awarding contracting jobs of up to $1 million. Mr. Vincent's Iraqi friend Layla has her doubts about the bidders: How does the captain know, she asks, that he isn't funneling money to extremists or religious parties that have put a woman's name on their letterhead to win a bid?

And here goes quotation No. 2: "I certainly hope none of these contracts are going to the wrong people," he replies, continuing: "But should we really get involved in choosing one political group over another? ... I mean, I've always believed that we shouldn't project

American values onto other cultures — that we should let them be. Who is to say we are right and they are wrong?"

Et tu, Captain America? It's one thing to get this mindless mantra from a Montgomery County public school teacher with rings on his toes and multiculturalism on his agenda. Maybe projecting American values onto certain cultures is a stupid idea, but clearly that's their loss. Meanwhile, there we are, doling out the dollars. Just listen to Layla: "These religious parties are wrong! Look at them, their corruption ... the way they treat women! How can you say you cannot judge them? Why shouldn't you apply your own cultural values?"

Why, indeed. Do "American values" still exist? Or have they been re-educated out of existence? Maybe their absence is what explains the insipid mania for Democracy, The Process, across the Middle East, regardless of whether terrorists run for office or sharia is the law of the land. Such non-judgmentalism is everywhere, even informing Security, The Process, at home.

Or, rather, especially informing Security, The Process, at home. Consider quotation No. 3, from a New York Times editorial on commuter safety measures, which — post 9/11, 3/11, 7/7 and 7/21 — are a brave new way of life. The topic is pretending to search for bombs, which is what we do in post-identity America. "The police officers must be careful not to give the impression that every rider who looks Arab or South Asian is automatically a subject of suspicion. ... Those who are selected simply because they are carrying packages should be chosen in a way that does not raise fears of racial profiling — by, for example, searching every fifth or 12th person, with the exact sequence chosen at random."

Anything to avoid "fears of racial profiling" — even death by murder-bomber. As the captain said, who's to say? In the Exact Sequence Chosen at Random We Trust. If we deny their identity long enough, our own will cease to matter.

A full nelson for Europe

10/7/05

What does the prospect of Turkey joining the European Union (EU) have to do with plans to erect a statue to Nelson Mandela in London's Trafalgar Square? In multiculti patois, both are "inclusive" acts. This means that they introduce non-Western elements (in Turkey's case, 70-plus million Muslims, in Mandela's case, South Africa's anti-apartheid hero) into historically Western milieus, such as Europe generally, or London specifically. The result is what is currently known as "diversity." Contrary to definition, however, diversity of the multicultural kind actually means that every place becomes like any other. Or, rather, every

Western place becomes like any other Western place.

For example, when more than a third of London schoolchildren speak one of 300 languages other than English at home, and 43 percent of New York City schoolchildren speak one of 170 languages other than English at home, both cities have achieved an indistinguishable "diversity." No longer singularly British or singularly American, they are interchangeably global. Grouping Nelson Mandela with Horatio, Lord Nelson and several other British military heroes in Trafalgar Square would have a similar, if symbolic, effect. No longer would Trafalgar Square conjure up the quintessence of British civilization. It would be, as London Mayor Ken Livingstone puts it, a "world square." Meanwhile, the rest of the "world" (the non-Western nations about which the West is so assiduously "inclusive") remains strikingly non-diverse — ethnically, religiously and culturally. So when Mr. Livingstone declares that a Mandela statue in Trafalgar Square "would signify the peaceful transition" from British empire as symbolized by Lord Nelson "to a multiracial and multicultural world," what he's really talking about is the British transition to a multiracial and multicultural London.

For confirmation of this cosmo-reality, no statue is necessary, but Mr. Mandela's likeness is probably on its way. Opposition is weak, bickering only over where (not whether) the statue should stand and other aesthetic concerns. It seems as if there are no British cultural or historical imperatives at issue here, because there are no British cultural or historical imperatives, period.

This new Battle of Trafalgar is a fitting backdrop for what appears to be the inevitable inclusion of Turkey into the EU, a political move with more than political consequences. If approved, Turkey, second in EU population only to Germany, would bring its tens of millions of Muslims into largely post-Christian, secular European society; with them comes a weighty Islamic influence on European affairs that would boost the transition, as Mr. Livingstone might say, of Europe to a multicultural, multiracial and — more pertinent — Islamized continent of Eurabia.

Not that this salient point is ever raised. "Europe can either decide to become a global actor or it can fence itself off as a Christian club," Turkish Prime Minister Recep Tayyip Erdogan said, flipping the issue on its head before the EU voted to open membership talks with Turkey. In light of the EU's deliberate omission of "God" or "Christianity" in its 439-page constitution, this was a fairly obnoxious comment. Besides, Turkey has long "fenced itself off" into such Islamic "clubs" as the Organization of the Islamic Conference, and the Cairo Declaration of Human Rights in Islam. The latter is an Islamic version of the United Nations' Universal Declaration of Human Rights; it elevates sharia (Islamic law) over universal human rights, and declares the Muslim community's role is to "guide" humanity. Which is more than just clubby.

But there was another implication to the Turkish leader's words: that Western identity is merely a tribal expression of petty insularity. Free will, free conscience — the evolution of individual liberty — is the gift of Judeo-Christian civilization, and it is one that Islam has never accepted. Tragically, it is one that Westerners may be throwing away. Britain's foreign minister, Jack Straw, was equally dismissive of Europe's "so-called Christian heritage," while Britain's Lord Patten, a former EU official, pegged opposition to Turkish membership to "relics of Christianity, "a rather nasty way to belittle natural concern over a proposed event one European minister has compared to the fall of the Berlin Wall.

"To define Europe today as though it were an introverted, cohesive, medieval Christian community is, I think, terrible," said Lord Patten. Maybe he means that to define Europe as European is terrible. Better to rework it as one, big "world square," an "inclusive" place of "diversity," where no one can tell Nelson from Nelson.

Jihadism and denial

11/4/05

"We in America know the benevolence that is at the heart of Islam," declared Condoleezza Rice, addressing assembled Muslim dignitaries at the annual Ramadan dinner at the State Department — and provoking a second, consecutive examination in this column of the rhetoric of the most important US official next to the president.

The secretary of state's annual Ramadan dinner at the State Department is not to be confused with the president's annual Ramadan dinner at the White House, although it's easy to get mixed up. The legacy of September 11 has left us with: an open-ended war abroad; the introduction of homeland hyper-insecurity; and the open-ended introduction of Ramadan celebrations all over official Washington. Which is worth a question or two on its own, beginning with: "Why"? Why has it become the post-September 11 function of the U.S. government to celebrate Ramadan? The buzzword of "Muslim outreach" comes to mind, but, as the Judeo-Christian culture hit by Islamikazes on September 11, haven't we got it exactly backward? That is, wouldn't Muslims better outreach themselves if the Saudi Embassy, for example, celebrated Christmas and Hanukah?

But I digress. Getting back to Miss Rice's shindig, Ramadan wouldn't be Ramadan without Nihad Awad, the executive director of the notorious Council on American-Islamic Relations (CAIR). His invitation alone deserves separate mention — and maybe an investigation into whether security concerns arose over bringing into the State Department someone from a Hamas-linked group boasting five current or former officials arrested, convicted or deported on terrorism-related charges. Oh well. In the holiday spirit, let's just recall, as bestselling author Robert Spencer did at www.jihadwatch.com, the words of CAIR's former board chairman, Omar Ahmad: "Islam isn't in American to be equal to any other faiths, but to be dominant." By Washington's Ramadan measure, Mr. Ahmad's wish is America's command. After all, George W. Bush and Condoleezza Rice aren't breaking the fast with Jews on Yom Kippur, supping with Hindus on Diwali, or cavorting with Druids on the Winter Solstice. And they certainly aren't feting official Christendom on Christmas Day — and no, the children's Easter Egg roll doesn't compare.

But I digress again. "We in America know the benevolence that is at the heart of Islam," Miss Rice said. Really? Is that what history tells us? Is that what current events tell us? Miss Rice's speechifying, which included a personal riff on Ramadan as being a time "characterized by sacrifice and abiding faith, by prayer and self-reflection and by compassion and profound joy," makes a wicked contrast to real-live Ramadan headlines. Not the big ones about Scooter and Judy and Matt and Peter; or bird flu; or Charles and Camilla, or even the substantial ones about the new Supreme Court nominee, Samuel Alito.

I'm thinking of the Muslim suicide bombing in Tel Aviv that killed five, and the Hitlerian promise of Iran's Shiite president that "the stain of disgrace" — Israel — will be "purged from the center of the Islamic world." I'm thinking of the week of Muslim rioting in Paris, and the news that a July 7 London suicide bomber was buried in Pakistan (his exploded remains, anyway) at the shrine of an Islamic saint. In New Delhi, Muslims are suspected of killing 60, while actor Omar Sharif has received Internet death threats, thought to come from Muslims in Italy, for playing St. Peter. And I can't stop thinking about the three Christian girls who were beheaded in Indonesia en route to their Christian high school. The killers carried off one of the severed heads to a new church, where they left it.

I could go on about the magazine editor in Afghanistan just sentenced to two years in jail for "blasphemy" — that is, criticizing Sharia law. Then there's Jyllands-Posten, the newspaper in Denmark that has received bomb threats, become a potential terror target on an Al Qaeda Internet list and drawn official diplomatic protests from 11 Muslim ambassadors for having published 12 cartoons of Mohammed. Depictions of the Islamic prophet may be a no-no under Islamic law, but redoubtable Denmark and its free (non-apologizing) newspaper are not under Islamic law.

Condoleezza Rice isn't either. But her soft-soap routine comes across as supplication, not statecraft. The United States should never kowtow to the Islamic diplomatic community by pretending that no doctrinal or institutional links exist between the teachings of Islam and the terrorism that has benighted our days. She and they must face facts. An informative place to start would be to challenge these same Ramadan diplomats to denounce, not newspapers that publish funny faces of Mohammed, but anyone who chops a schoolgirl's head off.

Where there's smoke ...

11/11/05

At least the once-Western world is consistent: Like the terrorism that has engraved the blood-drenched anniversaries of 9/11, 3/11, and 7/7 into collective memory, and has transformed Amman, Amsterdam, Baghdad, Bali, Beslan, Davao, Hadera, Haifa, Jakarta, Jerusalem, Nairobi, New Dehli, Sharm al-Sheik, Tel Aviv and Tunisia into hallowed outposts of mass murder, the rioting that has convulsed France has nothing to do with Islam. At least, that's the agreed-upon narrative. It's Our Story, the subtext, the thread to which we cling. The problem driving "youths" to incinerate lines of parked buses or immolate the occasional grand-mere on crutches is French racism, institutional neglect, failure to integrate. It's also snobbery, and don't forget George W. Bush. But not Islam. Not anything to do with Islam and its non-assimilable legions in the heart of Europe.

That's the word from intelligentsia all over. Even before the riot's last fires have been kindled, let alone cooled, The Washington Post editorial page, for example, said — no, it insisted: "Islamic ideology and leaders have played no part in the disturbances and many of those who are participating are not Muslim." Writing in The New York Times, Olivier Roy ruled Islam out with equally categorical and doctrinal confidence.

How do they know? Yes, the thugs we see depicted through the smoke of burning civilization aren't dressed for the part by Central Casting — either in the beards and robes of the mosque, or the mask and scimitar of the jihad. They look like urban punks, "scum," as French Interior Minister Nicolas Sarkozy called them before diving under the covers with the rest of the Gallic government. They are, we hear tell, unemployed toughs and secular criminals, devoted not to Allah so much as to what you might call, loosely and very grimly, French "culture" — French pop culture, that is.

Writing in the Weekly Standard, Olivier Guitta offers a shocking look at one expression of that culture — rap music as we in the United States have never quite heard it, even at its "cop-killing" worst. As Mr. Guitta explains, some of the most successful bands in France are made up "mostly of French citizens of Arab or African descent" — like our pals in the French projects, or "cites." But where so-called gangsta rap, American style, glorifies senseless violence and sexual bestiality, Muslim rap, French style, fuses that same violence and sexuality to attack the State.

Mr. Guitta has translated some choice examples. There is the rap band Sniper (nice), which, not incidentally, was unsuccessfully sued in 2004 by Mr. Sarkozy for violence and incitement in the song "La France." Sniper sings: "We're all hot for a mission to exterminate the government and the fascists. ... France is a b—and we've been betrayed ... We f— — France, we don't care about the Republic and freedom of speech. We should change the laws so we can see Arabs and Blacks in power in the Elysee Palace. Things have to explode." Well, of course, things did. But not, our elites instruct us, because of Islamic attitudes toward a non-Islamic country, but because of establishment attitudes toward a downtrodden minority. Integration, we hear, or the lack thereof, is the problem, so integration is also the answer. But how will France — or "FranSSe," as rapper Mr. R has titled this song — integrate this? "France is a b— —, don't forget to f—her to exhaustion. You have to treat her like a whore, man! ... France is one of the b— — — who gave birth to you ... I am not at home and I don't give a d— —, and besides the state can go f— itself. I pee on Napoleon and General de Gaulle ... F— — — cops, sons of whores ...." It goes on, lashing out in a similarly poisonous vein. Not that this stopped Fnac, the largest chain of French music stores, from praising the popular Mr. R as "a revelation."

And so he and his rap brethren are. But a revelation of what — urban blight or ghetto jihad? Or some new, cultural permutation of both? The vicious contempt, the exhortation to humiliation, the vindictive rape imagery: These are the motifs, at least, of brutal conquest, patterns and expressions familiar to students of jihad for having repeated themselves over the centuries as non-Muslim lands — Dar al Harb (Land of War) — were conquered and subjugated as Dar al Islam (Land of Islam). Is that what's going on in France? Without doubt, such music prefigures a state of war, although no one but the rioters seems to have been listening. Too bad no one is listening still.

Submission is all in your dhimmitude

2/13/06

We need to learn a new word: dhimmitude.
I've written about dhimmitude periodically, lo, these many years since Sept. 11, but it takes time to sink in. Dhimmitude is the coinage of a brilliant historian, Bat Ye'or, whose pioneering studies of the dhimmi, populations of Jews and Christians vanquished by Islamic

jihad, have led her to conclude that a common culture has existed through the centuries among the varied dhimmi populations. From Egypt and Palestine to Iraq and Syria, from Morocco and Algeria to Spain, Sicily and Greece, from Armenia and the Balkans to the Caucasus: Wherever Islam conquered, surrendering dhimmi, known to Muslims as "people of the book (the Bible)," were tolerated, allowed to practice their religion, but at a dehumanizing cost.

There were literal taxes (jizya) to be paid; these bought the dhimmi the right to remain non-Muslim, the price not of religious freedom, but of religious identity. Freedom was lost, sorely circumscribed by a body of Islamic law (sharia) designed to subjugate, denigrate and humiliate the dhimmi. The resulting culture of self-abnegation, self-censorship and fear shared by far-flung dhimmi is the basis of dhimmitude. The extremely distressing, but highly significant fact is, dhimmitude doesn't only exist in lands where Islamic law rules.

This is the lesson of Cartoon Rage 2006, a cultural nuke set off by an Islamic chain reaction to those 12 cartoons of Mohammed appearing in a Danish newspaper. We have watched the Muslim meltdown with shocked attention, but there is little recognition that its poisonous fallout is fear. Fear in the State Department, which, like Islam, called the cartoons unacceptable. Fear in Whitehall (where British government offices reside), which did the same. Fear in the Vatican, which did the same. And fear in the media, which have failed, with few, few exceptions, to reprint or show the images. With only a small roll of brave journals, mainly in Europe, to salute, we have seen the proud Western tradition of a free press bow its head and submit to an Islamic law against depictions of Mohammed. That's dhimmitude.

Not that we admit it: We dress up our capitulation in fancy talk of "tolerance," "responsibility" and "sensitivity." We even congratulate ourselves for having the "editorial judgment" to make "pluralism" possible. "Readers were well-served ... without publishing the cartoons," said a Wall Street Journal spokesman. "CNN has chosen to not show the cartoons in respect for Islam," reported the cable network. On behalf of the BBC, which did show some of the cartoons on the air, a news editor subsequently apologized, adding: "We've taken a decision not to go further ... in order not to gratuitously offend the significant number" of Muslim viewers worldwide. Left unmentioned is the understanding (editorial judgment?) that "gratuitous offense" leads to gratuitous violence. Hence, fear — not the inspiration of tolerance but of capitulation — and a condition of dhimmitude.

How far does it go? Worth noting, for example, is that on the BBC Web site, a religion page about Islam presents the angels and revelations of Islamic belief as historical fact, rather than spiritual conjecture (as is the case with its Christianity Web page); plus, it follows every mention of Mohammed with "(pbuh)," which means "peace be upon him" — "as if," writes Will Wyatt, former BBC chief executive, in a letter to the Times of London, "the corporation itself were Muslim."

Is it? Are we? These questions may not seem so outlandish if we assess the extent to which encroaching sharia has already changed the Western way. Calling these cartoons "unacceptable," and censoring ourselves "in respect" to Islam brings the West into compliance with a central statute of sharia. As Jyllands Posten's Flemming Rose has noted, that's not respect, that's submission. And if that's not dhimmitude, what is?

The publication of the Mohammed cartoons solicited by Denmark's Jyllands Posten was an act of anti-dhimmitude. Since no Danish artist would dare illustrate a PC children's book about Mohammed for fear of Islamic law (and Islamic violence), the newspaper boldly set out to reassert the rule of (non-Islamic) Danish law. It's as simple as that. And as vital. The cartoons ran to establish — or re-establish — Denmark as bastion of Western-style liberty. But in trying to set up a force field against encroaching sharia, Jyllands Posten and the Danes have showed us that no single bastion of Western liberty can stand alone.

So, how do you say solidarity in Danish? If we don't find out now, our future is more dhimmitude.

Pollyanna Rice on the Potomac

8/14/06

I'm all for looking on the bright side, but this is ridiculous. Commenting on the largest demonstration in favor of Hezbollah's war on Israel — a demonstration that took place in American-liberated Baghdad — Condoleezza Rice had this to say to NBC's Tim Russert: "That people would go out and demonstrate and say what they feel is one sign that perhaps Iraq is one place in the Middle East where people are exercising their right to free speech." Come again? Hundreds of thousands of Iraqi Shi'ites, calling "Death to Israel" and "Death to America," voice their support for a terrorist organization that hides behind human shields in Lebanon as it rains rockets down on cities in Israel, and the secretary of state praises freedom of speech in Iraq? It's enough to make a happy face weep. But Miss Rice beams on, diplomatically speaking, Pollyanna on the Potomac.

A more realistic approach would wipe the smile off anyone's assessment. But our foreign policy is increasingly driven by a sanguine un-reality. Oh, for an administration official who could respond to this intractable situation with an unabashedly unpleasant analysis.

"Yes, Tim," my dream secretary of state would say. "What you see in these pro-Hezbollah protests is the unfettered expression of the people of the Republic of Iraq. I wish I could say this was limited to a vocal minority, but we're seeing this same sentiment expressed across sectarian lines, in the now-free press, even in back channel communications. Why, Iraq's parliament came together unanimously — a democratic first — to condemn Israel, never mentioning Hezbollah. And why should it? Iraqi officials have refused to condemn the Iranian proxy as a terrorist group."

That might leave the host speechless — but just momentarily before he'd ask: "So what are we doing there?"

"Well, Tim, "she would respond, "the president is currently working on a major address — the most important address of his second term, I would imagine — to prepare the American people for entry into what we like to think of as the post-PC world. What I mean by that is, American efforts to extend the pacifying, enriching and ennobling benefits of democratic liberty to the Muslim Middle East have bumped up against our own erroneous teachings of political correctness.

"For generations now, Americans have been taught that all peoples are the same, all cultures are the same, all religions are the same — hard-wired to live by the same self-evident truths. Our experience in Iraq, our experience with Islam, if you will, tells us, in fact, that we are not all the same. We do not all want the same things out of governments, our cultures or our religions. This is something our experience in Iraq has finally taught us. There are vast differences between Islam and the West, differences that are not the mission of the United States military, or in the interest of the United States to bridge."

My dream secretary would continue: "Whether posterity judges us kindly and calls ours a noble experiment in Iraq, Tim, the bottom line here and now is that we're not getting results. I mean, how do you expect to fight a war on terror for, or alongside, terrorist sympathizers? It can't be done. And the war on terror is the president's primary concern. As a result, you will see the mission of American troops changing as they leave the streets of Iraq's cities to be redeployed to strongholds in Kurdistan — and beyond."

"Where?"

"Let's just say we'll be talking much more about Iran and Syria in the coming weeks, and their roles in sponsoring terrorism and nuclear blackmail." Poof.

Alas, Coleridge-like, I find my vision of chat-show Xanadu has gone black. On the real-life program, Miss Rice went on to offer a typically reality-challenged solution for Lebanon: Her idea — the U.S. idea — is "to flow the authority of the Lebanese government and Lebanese forces with the help of international forces" into Hezbollah-controlled areas. Just keep smiling, and never mind that all too much of the Lebanese government, the Lebanese forces, not to mention the Lebanese people are rootin'-tootin' Hezbollah boosters.

But wait, what's that voice in my head? "Given the Free World's stake in the destruction of Hezbollah's terrorist forces," my dream secretary is saying, "the president will be calling on our friends in the international community to offer Israel our shared gratitude and unified support for taking on this common enemy."

Poof again.

Will 'Khaled' Centanni and 'Ya'aqob' Wiig, as apostates, be marked for death?

9/6/06

This is one case where silence isn't golden and ignorance isn't bliss. They are dangerous and dumb

It's not easy to be shocked by jihad these days, five years and numberless atrocities after the Twin Towers imploded on almost 3,000 fellow citizens. That said, I admit my own jihad-fatigue was broken — shattered, really — by the "conversion" to Islam of Fox journalists Steve Centanni and Olaf Wiig videotaped during their two-week ordeal as captives of Palestinians in Gaza.

Why? Andrew G. Bostom, writing at Frontpage mag. tells us forced conversions to Islam "have been the norm, across three continents — Asia, Africa and Europe — for over 13 centuries," and cites contemporary examples in the jihad campaigns of Sudan and Indonesia. Even so, religious coercion, let alone "jihad campaigns," still seems appallingly new to us — if by "us" I can still make myself understood to mean, generally, Western peoples in modern times. Indeed, I can't think of another hostage to jihad forced into Islam — not even Daniel Pearl or Nicolas Berg, and not the U.S. Embassy hostages in Tehran a quarter century ago.

Is this incident a tip-off to a new level of unabashed religious abuse of traditionally (once upon a time) inviolate Westerners? In the "conversion" video, we see such abuse as the American and the New Zealander sit, costumed in Arabic robes, "forced to convert to Islam at gunpoint," as Centanni later revealed. Holding up a symbolic first finger, they read their lines in both Arabic and English, proclaiming their "new" faith, declaring their "new" names — Khaled and Ya'aqob — and calling on President Bush and Prime Minister Blair to do likewise. I didn't see the videotape on television (more on that below), but rather on Internet, where, like high-tech specters, "Khaled" and "Ya'aqob" will haunt their freed selves into cyber-eternity.

Or will they? Whether this "conversion" is legit probably depends on the eye or, rather, the religion of the beholder. The Koran says "there is no compulsion in religion" — as did, absurdly, the video — but, as Robert Spencer writes at Frontpage mag., traditional Islamic teachings about Muhammad, which reveal that the Islamic prophet's invitation to Islam was accompanied by "an inescapable threat" of subjugation and war, have left Islam with a different interpretation of "compulsion" from the West. That is, given accounts of Muhammad's own example, Islam doesn't really see forcible conversion in commonly understood terms of "compulsion."

So, what if Centanni and Wiig "revert" to their non-Muslim identities? Would such "apostasy" sentence them to death? (Leaving Islam is a capital crime under Islamic law.) Shocking thought. Of course, there's something even more shocking to the story than the religious charade itself.

No, it isn't the bizarre disclaimer Centanni felt compelled to append to his account of the shotgun-conversion — "Don't get me wrong here. I have the highest respect for Islam, and I learned a lot of good things about it." While it's more than strange to hear a person who has been forced to choose between death and Islam flack for Islam as he resumes his life, there's something else. And it isn't praise for the "beautiful and kind-hearted" Palestinian people Centanni slathered around the microphone at his Gaza City press conference before, as Bostom noted, high-tailing it to safety in infidel-Israel.

The most shocking thing about the Centanni-Wiig "conversion" is the silence that has followed. First, there is silence from Islam. Shouldn't Muslim religious leaders, and particularly "beautiful and kind-hearted" Palestinian Muslim religious leaders, vehemently condemn the forced conversions? As Bostom put it, "Will such Muslim authorities at least recognize the acute predicament of Centanni and Wiig by issuing a fatwa stating that their 'conversion,' being under duress, was not bona fide, condemning in advance any Muslim who might now attack these journalists for 'apostasy' from Islam?"

Yes, of course, they should — at least according to any Western understanding of compulsion and morality — but don't hold your breath. Meanwhile, holding their breath is exactly what Western media are doing when it comes to covering (not covering) the story. Even Fox's Greta van Susteren, a tabloidesque host who never met a bodily fluid she couldn't elaborate on, went delicate on us the other night, failing, in a one-hour "exclusive" interview with the two men, to ask a single question about their religious ordeal — presumably at their request.

Why? Who or what is served by shutting up? Only forces of coercion — a word which, after all, implies the nullification of individual will. Which means this is one case where silence isn't golden and ignorance isn't bliss. They are dangerous and dumb.

Guilt for the ages

1/15/07

It only took PBS one hour to uncover the causes of anti-Semitism, now in an alarming heyday. In "Antisemitism in the 21st Century: The Resurgence," narrated by Judy Woodruff, PBS offered the answer: The reason for Jew-hatred, now widely promulgated among Muslim populations, is, well... Jews! Israel! Even Christianity!

Oh, brother. This wreck of a thesis emerged early in the documentary as fact and fiction collided, mangling cause and effect. According to the show, Jews basically caused anti-Semitism in the Arab-Muslim region around them by first building the tiny modern state of Israel (500 times smaller than that Arab Muslim region), and then actually trying to defend it against a host of Muslim armies and terror groups. As PBS tells it, it isn't the genocidal proclivities of surrounding Muslim nations that have caused war unending on the Jewish state; it's the continued existence of the Jewish state that has caused the genocidal proclivities. The show practically begs a viewer to ask, Well, what else could you expect?

But there's more to this lefty apology for the luridly vicious anti-Semitism expressed on a daily basis in the Islamic world in sermons, schoolbooks, television shows and newspapers, some of which is helpfully shown in the documentary. We are told that anti-Semitism is something new to Islam. According to the practically oracular authority of Princeton's Bernard Lewis, never in 1200 years did Muslims even think of anti-Semitism, let alone act on it — not until European Christian empire-builders introduced the pathology to the region in the 19th century, what with tales of Christ-killers and, later, the forged "Protocols of the Elders of Zion."

It wasn't that those first 1200 years of Islam and Shariah were exactly paradise for Jews, Lewis said, but Jews were "tolerated" so long as they accepted their "inferiority." This was a pretty breezy way to dismiss centuries of violence, oppression, fear and degradation inflicted, according to Islamic law, on "dhimmi" Jews (and on "dhimmi" Christians for that matter), as copiously documented by historian Bat Yeor. But Lewis stuck to this story: "Antisemitism was introduced into the Middle East by Christians."

Even oracles get it wrong sometimes, I guess, because Lewis's explanation doesn't square with a long and vivid historical record, and that includes the Koran. The notion that Christians introduced Muslims to anti-Semitism may well be the conventional wisdom — indeed, it may even be that nonagenarian Lewis is the source of that conventional wisdom — but just as surely as anti-Semitism historically existed in Christianity, it also historically existed in Islam. And I can actually footnote that statement because, quite by chance, the same week the documentary aired, I happened to read the first chapter of a forthcoming book called "The Legacy of Islamic Antisemitism" by Andrew G. Bostom, author of "The Legacy of Jihad."

Bostom examines the origins of anti-Semitism in the Koran (such as in 2:61, which decrees an eternal curse of humiliation and wretchedness on Jews, repeated in 3:112), in the canonical commentaries on the Koran, and in the historical record. And it all begins practically 1,000 years before, say, Queen Victoria made herself an empress. The question is, does anti-Semitism's origin in Islam, whether Christian or Islamic, become a chicken-egg question for scholars, or does it actually matter?

It matters a great deal, and here's why. The conventional wisdom, as expressed on PBS, does two things. It blames Christianity and the West for introducing anti-Semitism to a practically Edenic Islamic world, and it minimizes Islam's non-original sin of partaking of it. Indeed, this same conventional wisdom suggests that anti-Semitism is the natural, if unfortunate, response of "unempowered" Muslims to contemporary political events beyond their control — namely, the essentially Christian/Western-sponsored establishment of the modern state of Israel.

If we bothered — if we dared — to examine anti-Semitism in its historical Islamic context (just as we have examined anti-Semitism in its historical Christian context), we would better understand Islam's hysterical rejection of Israel, which, in Islamic terms, is a state of "dhimmi" inferiors restored to equality, if not economic and military superiority, its very existence a violation of traditional Islamic code.

Failing to do this, the West overlooks and effectively absolves Islam of its animus against Jews, and, by modern extension, Israel. The West also consigns itself, and, weirdly enough, Israel also, to the role of guilty parties who must continually try to appease an aggrieved Islam.

Twisted? You bet. But there's no hope of unraveling things without first setting a grievous historical record straight.

Denial is an ugly thing, but it's urgent that we confront it

2/2/07

I've finally discovered what they call "linkage" between the war in Iraq and the Israeli-Palestinian conflict. But, instead of seeing any connection between what goes on inside Iraq and that fraudulent "peace process" by which the one party wanting "peace" (Israel) is gradually destroyed by the other party using "process" (the Palestinians) I see linkage in the overall American approach to the two war zones. Our strategy is identical. In both cases, it is based on a complete and willful suspension of disbelief. It ignores all evidence to ward off reality.

Take a recent report from Fox News explaining why the Bush administration this week postponed the release of a dossier linking Iran to murder and mayhem in Iraq.

"U.S. military officials say the decision to go public with the findings has been put on hold for several reasons, including concerns over the reaction from Iran's President Mahmoud Ahmadinejad — as well as inevitable follow-up questions that would be raised over what the U.S. should do about it."

There's so much wrong with this picture it's hard to know where to start. Surely it is Mr. Ahmadinejad who should be concerned about the reaction from the world's sole superpower to findings of Iranian complicity in American combat deaths, and not vice versa. Incredibly, the administration doesn't appear to think so. This is deeply upsetting.

Equally upsetting is the news report's implied suggestion that "follow-up questions" about Iranian aggression are, in effect, more difficult to face than the aggression itself. It's as if the logical conclusion to such findings — in all likelihood, the obvious inference that Iran is already waging war against us — is to be avoided more than the war itself. Better to take the Iranian facts on the ground — the bombings and kidnappings, the backstabbing and subversion, and the American casualties — and just bury them. Otherwise, reality would ruin everything.

This same ostrich-like viewpoint drives administration policy on the Palestinian Authority, which hinges on the contrafactual belief that PA President Mahmoud Abbas is a "moderate." Indeed, the ostrich outlook helps explain President Bush's see-no-, speak-no-, hear-no-evil order this week to bestow an additional $86 million on Abbas. It's not just, for example, as Palestinian Media Watch has noted, that the PA municipality of Yaabid has recently named a school and its main street (newly paved by American taxpayer dollars) in honor of Saddam Hussein. Or that a city block in Jenin was named after a suicide-bomber who killed four Americans in Fallujah. Or that American funds built the PA's Salaf Khalef Sports Center, named for the head of the Black September terror group that was behind the murder of two American diplomats in Sudan and 11 Israeli athletes in Munich.

Bush's order came shortly after Abbas himself, in a speech marking the 42nd anniversary of co-founding the Fatah Party with terror kingpin Yasser Arafat, exhorted Palestinians to put "our internal fighting aside and raise our rifles only against Israeli occupation." In other words, not only was the "moderate" calling for violence against Israel — a call quickly answered this week when the Fatah-linked Al Aqsa Martyr Brigades, acting with Islamic Jihad, sent a killer to self-detonate in an

Israeli bakery — e was also calling for reconciliation with forces of Hamas, the jihadist terror group. As if to underscore his message, Abbas went on to praise assassinated Hamas guru, Ahmed Yassin. He also invoked rankly anti-Semitic verses from the Koran (5:64) to claim that Jews are corrupting the world.

As Andrew C. McCarthy has written at National Review Online, such actions and behaviors merit "not one thin dime" from the U.S. Regarding this most recent outrage, it is true, as Worldnetdaily.com noted, that most media didn't report the full extent of Abbas' remarks. Indeed, the Associated Press' shamelessly sanitized account — "Abbas calls for respect at Fatah rally" — was mainstream typical. But if I, sitting deskside, could get the real skinny, certainly the U.S. government, with all of its resources, could do the same. In other words, being uninformed is no excuse. The terrible conclusion to draw is that the president, along with too many other political leaders, simply prefers to be uninformed.

Their world looks rosier that way. Which isn't at all to say it's a pretty sight. In fact, it's hideous in its own way, something I'd prefer not to look at. Denial is an ugly thing. But it's urgent that we confront it.

America must not ignore a dangerous percentage

5/25/07

Funny how small 26 percent sounds when it describes, for example, the number of American voters who support the Senate's mass-amnesty, goody-bag bill for illegal aliens. In this case, the one in four people polled by Rasmussen this week who hope the legislation passes comes off as a minority voice, especially when compared to the whopping 72 percent of voters who favor border enforcement and the reduction of illegal immigration.

But 26 percent looms large when it describes the number of American Muslims, ages 18-29, who support suicide bombings "in defense of Islam" — one of the sensational, if sensationally underreported, findings of a recent Pew poll. According to Pew, the total Muslim population in America is 2.35 million, 30 percent of whom are between 18 and 29. By my figuring, the suicide-bomb-approving cohort works out to 183,000 people. The poll also tells us that 69 percent of younger American Muslims say suicide bombings are never justified. While representing a majority almost as great as the percentage of American voters who favor border enforcement, 69 percent in this particular case is wholly inadequate; indeed, a strikingly poor showing.

Why?

In the case of the immigration bill, the poll reflects public opinion pertaining to a political process, a no-holds-barred, expletive-laced, free-for-all that, loathsome as it may sometimes seem, remains democratically rooted in a nonviolent contest of ideas, politics and flim-flam. In such a context, one-quarter of anything pales next to three-quarters of anything.

In the case of suicide bombing, however, the context changes. According to Pew's data, one-quarter of younger American Muslims approve of the presence of skin-ripping, skull-crushing, organ-piercing violence in civilian life as a religious imperative — "in defense of Islam." (The Pew pollsters declined to define "defense of Islam," but having lived through Pope Rage, Cartoon Rage, Koran Rage, Satanic Verses Rage, etc., I think it's safe to say this is a rather broad category.)

Such approval for religious violence is not just another unfettered political opinion finding expression in a poll-taker's tally. On the contrary, the fact that a significant young chunk of American Islam believes such violence has a place in society indicates something closer to the end of unfettered political opinion. It may signal the beginning of physical coercion as a factor in the American political process. Which helps explain why the 69 percent figure is no consolation prize; only unanimity is acceptable here.

It's not that a physical fear factor pertaining to mainly Islamic terrorism hasn't long existed — just take a look at the dispiriting security perimeter erected around the Capitol, for instance. But this Pew poll may mark the first official acknowledgement that such violence and, equally important, the threat of such violence, actually find approval within the American polity.

Something new and barbarous under the sun, right? This is why it's all the more disturbing to review the happy headline-spin the story received. The blogger Ace of Spades provided an early roundup of the Orwellian tags, which included: "Poll: Most Muslims seek to adopt American lifestyle" (USA Today); "Muslims assimilate better in U.S. than Europe, poll finds" (*The International Herald Tribune*); "Poll: U.S. Muslims Feel Post-9/11 Backlash Despite Moderate Outlook" (Voice of America). My personal fave: "Upbeat portrait of U.S. Muslims" (Sacramento Bee). The accompanying stories were no less giddy.

But why the journalistic rush to depict the shocking story as so much happy talk? Therein lies a tale, one of fanatical religious fervor — on the part of the mainstream media (MSM). Like other politically correct elites, the MSM follow their own version of the "true faith": multiculturalism.

Multiculturalism preaches that all civilizations are the same, all religions are the same, all peoples are the same. The Pew results, meanwhile, tell them something else again: Some people — some young American Muslim people — approve of suicide bombing in defense of Islam. Does this finding perhaps introduce a qualitative difference among civilizations, religions and peoples? That is, is there something more desirable about societies that don't inspire and glorify suicide bombings — something worth preserving? Conversely, is there something about Islam our own society requires protection against? This is very tricky territory for the MSM. The logical answers are multiculturally blasphemous.

The MSM response: Better to say nothing at all. Or better yet, just smile. Big grin. Happy story. It's one measly quarter, after all. Just one in four. And isn't that something to be upbeat about?

Making jihad go away

7/6/07

Q: Who is winning the really important war of ideas — the one between the West and itself?

A: Not the side that understands jihad as a foundational Islamic institution.

This is nothing new. From 9/11 forward, the yeoman effort of elites has been to wrench "Islam" away from all acts of jihad. But now, particularly after the London and Glasgow attacks, their efforts have achieved a deeper level of denial and worse, broader consensus.

The new British prime minister, Gordon Brown, has directed ministers to omit "Muslim" when discussing (Muslim) terrorism. And forget the generic "war on terror;" even that pathetic phrase is off-limits. (This has absolutely nothing to do with Brown's unctuously stated goal to make Britain "the gateway for Islamic finance.") The new Home Secretary, Jacqui Smith, refers to British Muslims as "communities" — maybe a prelude to not mentioning them at all. Both have done the "perversion of a great faith" dance to enlightened applause, taking cues from the unpublished "EU Lexicon," which reportedly nixes such "offensive" phrases as "Islamic terrorism." British literary lions couldn't agree more. Philosopher John Gray and historian Eric Hobsbawm recently said on British television that even the word "Islamist" was "unfair" because "it implied a strong link to Islam."

Never mind that the link is doctrinally accurate. Better to accommodate mortal threat without identifying its Islamic roots. Instead of defending their nations — for starters, stopping Islamic immigration and with it, the progression of Islamic law into Western societies — our elites have decided to pretend Islam isn't there at all.

In the media, the effort is misleading to the point of farce. Joel Mowbray, writing at the Power Line blog, noted that The New York Times has identified Britain's Muslim terrorists as "South Asian people" — which, considering Britain's largest South Asian population is

Hindu, is beyond absurd. "Diverse group allegedly in British plot," the Associated Press reported, missing that unifying Islamic thread. "All eight detainees have ties to health service," wrote the Toronto Star, "but genesis of terror scheme still eludes investigators."

If they read Robert Spencer's jihadwatch.org, the essential daily compendium of jihad and dhimmi news, they might get a clue. But, very ominously, Spencer's Web site is being blocked by assorted organizations which, according to his readers, continue to provide access to assorted pro-jihad sites. Spencer reports he's "never received word of so many organizations banning this site all at once." These include the City of Chicago, Bank of America, Fidelity Investments, GE IT, JPMorgan Chase, Defense Finance and Accounting Services and now, a federal employee in Dallas informs him, the federal government.

Reason given? Some Internet providers deem the factually-based, meticulous analysis on display at jihadwatch.org to be "hate speech." This should send Orwellian shivers up society's spine, but, alarmingly, such reactions to jihad analysis are increasingly the norm.

Case in point: Objecting to a recent column characterizing his views as being non-comprehending or indifferent to jihad, Lt. Col. David Kilcullen, senior counterinsurgency adviser to our forces in Iraq, wondered in an e-mail whether I "may not like Muslims, and that's your choice." It was a long e-mail — one of several — but even these few words convey the increasingly prevalent viewpoint that discounts the doctrinal centrality of Islam to jihad violence convulsing the world from Iraq to London. In the mental no-jihad zone (and, in Lt. Col. Kilcullen's case, despite what he calls his "significant personal body count of terrorists and insurgents killed or captured"), only personal animus can explain alarm over the Islamic institution of jihad (let alone dhimmitude). "Alternatively," he wrote, "you may think Islam contains illiberal and dangerous tendencies."

I may think? I do think — "tendencies" such as jihad and dhimmitude. "Again," he said, "you're entitled to that view...."

"That view" is increasingly absent at the top, where Islam itself is politically and strategically beside the point. Consider current military thought, as expressed by Lt. Col. Kilcullen: Typical terrorists, he wrote, are "driven by fundamentally non-religious motivational factors." I wonder which non-religious motivational factors inspired Glasgow's terror-docs to scream "Allah, Allah" while ramming a flaming car into the airport.

Of course, it gets worse. Debate now divides the Pentagon over a new lexicon for Centcom. At stake is the Islamic term "jihad" itself, which could become officially verboten within the ranks of the fighting force that is actually supposed to defeat it.

This might leave us speechless, but it better not shut us up.

Paying Islam for our Western guilt

12/29/07

Christmas came early to the Palestinian Authority when the "international community" decided not only to meet PA President Mahmoud Abbas' request for $5.6 billion in aid, but to throw in almost $2 billion more. Why? Did the PA end its terrorist ways? Stop state-sanctioned incitement against Israel and the West? Change Fatah's charter (forget about Hamas) calling for Israel's destruction?

Alas, no, no and no. We are heaping riches on the PA for other reasons, one of which I discuss below.

But first, a digression: Christmas, obviously, doesn't come to the PA, even if Western billions do. Despite a tiny (and decreasing) number of Christians, the PA is a land of Islam — Dar al-Islam. That makes Israel, the object of the PA's destructive animus, Dar al-Harb, land of war, right?

Right. But not according to the PC script of the "international community." We never, ever discuss the Islamic context of "Arab-Israeli" conflicts. But how else can we hope to understand them? Jihad ideology inspires the Arab struggle against Israel. It also explains it. As the only non-Muslim country amid Middle Eastern Dar-al Islam, as the only "dhimmi" nation to reclaim its land once conquered by Islam, Israel's very existence is a religious offense to the "umma," or Islamic community. In this same context, what we call "foreign aid" to the PA may be understood as a form of "jizya," the protection money paid to Muslims by non-Muslims.

But the non-Muslim world prefers not to think like that. We avert our collective eye from the goals of jihad, from the history and teachings of Islam. Instead, we see ourselves as villains — Israel for its existence, and Israel's supporters for, well, their support for Israel's existence.

In so doing, we create a sinkhole of Western guilt and responsibility for suffering Muslims, in this case in the PA. They suffer not as a consequence of their religio-political bloodlust to destroy the Jews in Israel (the nearest infidels), but because there are Jews in Israel. In other words, it's everyone else's fault but their own. Islam — particularly, jihadist ideology — is not to blame. Throw more money down the hole.

Of course, this works only until we stop misreading such ideology. And how long will that take? Probably forever — so long as we continue leaning on the same authorities who got us into this mental mess in the first place.

As it happens, I began the calendar year thinking about this subject — exonerating Islam — while discussing a PBS documentary on anti-Semitism in the Islamic world. The show's conclusion: What isn't Israel's fault is that of the West.

Well, you can't expect much more from (lefty) PBS. What was

startling about the message, however, was one of the messenger's: none other than the eminent historian Bernard Lewis. He declared that anti-Semitism didn't even exist in the Middle East until European Christian colonizers brought it. You don't need to be a scholar of Lewis' stature to know that European colonization of the Middle East didn't begin until some 1,100 years after Islamic anti-Semitism got going in the Koran, the canonical commentaries on the Koran, and in a long and painful (for Christians also) historical record.

Because Lewis is probably the most influential voice on Islam in our time — particularly for the U.S. foreign policy establishment — his pronouncements are more than significant. Right or, in this case, wrong, they become the conventional wisdom, or reinforce it.

This comes to mind because Lewis has done it again — holding Europe responsible for unpalatable traditions of Islam. Writing at The American Thinker blog, Andrew Bostom, author of "The Legacy of Jihad" (Prometheus, 2005) and, forthcoming, "The Legacy of Islamic Anti-Semitism," quotes a recent speech in which Lewis said: "The authoritarianism present in the Middle East region is not part of the Arab and Muslim traditions, but it has been imported from Europe." Bostom goes on to cite copious chapter and verse — including earlier writings by Lewis himself — demonstrating that "the Arab and Muslim tradition" needed no lessons from Europe on authoritarianism.

Why is Lewis making statements contradicted by the historical record? If European Christendom truly is the source of Islamic evil — e.g., anti-Semitism and authoritarianism — Islam is let off the hook, and blame falls on the West. Whether that is Lewis' point, it is certainly Lewis' effect.

And it is certainly the conventional wisdom. Not very wise, though, when it helps feed the kind of guilt assuaged only by giving billions of dollars to murderers and thieves.

Middle East 'bright side' blinding us to costly U.S. reality

3/14/08

As a reasonably optimistic person, I try to look on the bright side whenever possible — unless bright-side facts are completely blotted out by bleak ones.

Example: In a recent e-mail blast, former Republican senator Rick Santorum urged readers to be heartened by Middle East developments that may have been obscured by bad news elsewhere.

There was even good news, he wrote, coming out of Iran. To wit:

"A new poll in Iran suggests that Iranians want more democracy and less theocracy, including the power to elect their Supreme Leader," Santorum wrote, referring to recent findings from the polling group Terror Free Tomorrow. "Three-quarters also wished for normal relations and trade with the U.S."

Gee, that sounds swell — so long as you don't read the rest of the poll results. These include the finding that roughly six in 10 Iranians support Iran's military and financial assistance for Hezbollah, Shiite militias in Iraq and assorted Palestinian terror groups. The good news (I guess) that Iranians want to elect their Supreme Leader directly is overridden by the bad news that they will probably elect someone who supports global jihad. This makes it tough to buy into Santorum's happy-dappy assessment.

Similarly, consider the reaction to Iranian President Mahmoud Ahmadinejad's recent trip to Iraq. Conservatives seem to agree — I say "seem" because few pundits have actually ventured an opinion on this momentous visit (in itself more than passing strange) — that it was a "debacle" for Iran, as the headline of Amir Taheri's New York Post piece called it.

Huh? In last week's column, I called the visit a Mesopotamian slap across the American face — a symbolic outrage, at least, to the U.S. troops who continue to be killed and maimed by Iran in Iraq.

But no. According to my fellow conservatives, the visit was a Good Thing. Far from catching Iraq two-timing with a barbaric rival of the United States, it rather demonstrated, as Taheri put it in his oft-cited column, "the limits" of Iran's influence in Iraq.

This argument rests on two main points. First, there was the absence of Iraqi crowds cheering for Ahmadinejad, and the presence of protestors in Iraqi cities — largely, but not exclusively, in Sunni enclaves, which are unsurprisingly hostile to the Iranian Shiite president. (No protest was very large — infinitesimal next to the 100,000-plus Iraqis who in 2006 demonstrated in support of Iranian proxy Hezbollah.) The other main point concerns Ahmadinejad's failure to arrange face-time with the Grand Ayatollah Al Sistani, the leading Shiite in Iraq.

The first point might be more telling if Iraq were not, as we all surely know by now, a democracy. It was Iraq's democratically elected leaders — including the Kurdish president and Shiite prime minister — who welcomed the genocidal terror master with fanfare, regardless of whether some Iraqis took to the streets (or not). For years now, these same elected leaders have been effectively intertwining Iraq's economy with Iran's to the point where Radio Free Liberty analyst Kathleen Ridolfo recently noted that "observers say Iraq is becoming economically, if not politically, subordinate to Iran." Little wonder, then, that the Iraqi government put out the red carpet for the Thug of Tehran.

This bilateral relationship — the energy accords, export market (Iraq is Iran's largest), oil trade, cooperation in education, customs, insurance, transportation, industrial projects, tourism, Iran's billion-dollar loan (interest free), and, to cap it off, the joint statement condemning Israel for taking action in Gaza to stop Hamas rockets — presents a conflict as the U.S. combats the very terrorism Iran exports. For example, last year, the U.S. Treasury blacklisted Iran's Bank Melli for its involvement in terrorism and the pursuit of nuclear weaponry. Last year, Ridolfo reported, Bank Melli opened a branch in Baghdad. (No word on whether Ahmadinejad opened an account during his visit.)

As for Point No. 2, who can claim to know the inside skinny on the Sistani meeting? One possibility, reported by Stratfor.com, was that domestic Iranian opposition — not Sistanian opposition — might have been a factor. Perhaps more to the point is the fact that Sistani, who retains Iranian citizenship, has met with every other Iranian government officials to visit Iraq before Ahmadinejad. And that includes Iranian Foreign Minister Manouchehr Mottaki, national security official Ali Larijani and, shortly before Ahmadinejad arrived, Tehran Mayor Mohammed-Baqer Qalibaf. Sounds to me as if Iran is too close to Iraq for U.S. comfort.

I try to look on the bright side — really. Just not when the brightness is blinding.

It's Islamic jihad, not extremism, Uncle Sam

5/9/08

A few years ago, Harvard psychiatric instructor Kenneth Levin wrote "The Oslo Syndrome: Delusions of a People Under Siege." In this illuminating book, Levin examines the Israeli experience of concessionary negotiations with a "peace partner" openly dedicated to Israel's destruction. He also examines the historical Jewish Diaspora experience in which Jewish populations typically identified with their tormentors and even echoed their anti-Semitism.

Such interactions are driven by a permanent condition of siege mentality, Levin explains, and clearly manifest two kinds of delusional thinking.

First, there is the fantasy about the intentions of the aggressor (Arab Muslim or European Christian); then, there is the fantasy about changing the aggressor's intentions. Such thinking, Levin says, is common to victims of chronic abuse, particularly children. They fool themselves into thinking that they, the victims, control the abuser by linking the abuse they suffer to their own behavior.

In other words, they believe they cause their own abuse. This mind game, Levin says, actually gives victims a sense of control over situations beyond their control (an abusive parent, for instance). This allows them to avoid feelings of helplessness and despair.

And so the besieged victim pretends: Daddy doesn't really want to hurt me; if I'm a better girl, he'll stop. Israel pretends: Muslims don't really want to destroy our state, and so we'll give them land for peace. Jews in pre-Nazi Europe pretended: The anti-Semites are really right; we deserve a pogrom. Intriguingly, Levin writes:

"But the book's themes have a still broader relevance. Even ostensibly powerful and secure populations, under conditions that entail ongoing threat and vulnerability, can manifest similar trends."

I got a new one for the doctor: a trend of delusion so enormous as to beg for immediate hospitalization and a transfer of power of attorney. Problem is, the patient here is the United States government (USG), which now says: If we just stop talking about jihad, Muslims will neither become jihadis nor sympathize with them.

Such is the message of a crazy new government guide called "Words that Work and Words that Don't" urging federal agencies, including the Department of Homeland Security, to eliminate all references to Islam when discussing, well, Islamic terrorism.

Not only does that mean no more talk of "Islam," it also means no more talk of "jihad." ("Extremism" is the new "jihad.") And forget about the "caliphate." (Try "global totalitarian state.") Even such politically correct terms as "Islamist" and "Islamofascist," which take the traditional teachings of Islam off the hook, are now verboten. And so, more curiously, is the term "Muslim moderate." Says the government: "The term 'moderate' has become offensive to many Muslims, who believe that it refers to individuals whom the USG prefers to deal with, and who are only marginally religious."

So "moderates" don't want to look like patsies next to "jihadists," and the USG doesn't want to be insensitive to their needs. Sounds like a rest cure for Uncle Sam is long overdue.

Of course, the no-Islam (no-"moderate") lexicon itself — which reads like disinformation designed to confuse the American public — is just scratching the delusional surface. Animating the directive, written with considerable input from unidentified American Muslim "experts," is the delusional belief that what we say (or don't say) has transformative power over Muslim attitudes and behaviors regarding Islamic terrorism, the Islamic caliphate, the advance of Islamic law (Sharia) and the so-called war on (Islamic) terror — rebranded here, no kidding, as "A Global Struggle for Security and Progress." ("Liberty," Uncle Sam tells us, was "rejected" as "a buzzword for American hegemony.")

The basic idea is to shut the United States up. Or, more diplomatically: "The terminology ... should avoid helping the terrorists by inflating the religious bases and glamorous appeal of their ideology." (Glamorous?) For example, "When we respond loudly (to Osama bin Laden and other jihadists), we raise their prestige in the Muslim world."

"We" raise their prestige? Come on. If a human being thinks turning passenger jets into WMDs is an abomination, nothing anyone says can raise the perpetrators' "prestige." Could our government rationally think otherwise?

Alas, reason escapes the Oslo Syndrome sufferer.

This may explain why Uncle Sam is now actually assuming responsibility for jihad itself: "Our terminology must be properly calibrated to diminish the recruitment efforts of extremists (read: jihadists) who argue the West is at war with Islam."

News flash for Uncle Sam: Islam, in myriad forms, is at war with the West. And even if we never say the words, we can still darn well lose.

Pundits, get out of the Iran's 'green' zone

6/26/09

Aside from a mass deployment of force against unarmed protestors (which, unfortunately, is not unlikely) what is the worst possible outcome in Iran?

Answer: That it becomes unavoidably clear the post-election conflict isn't a struggle between tyranny and freedom — the epic narrative we've been hearing in absolute, non-contestable terms. The worst thing that could happen next, at least for the absolute, non-contestable punditocracy, is that it becomes clear we're looking at an intra-Islamic power struggle that has nothing to do with liberty and justice for anybody.

If this happens, the next question becomes: At what point do said pundits change the color of their Twitter avatars (Joe Scarborough) and their blog backgrounds (Andrew Sullivan) back from Islam green? And will they ever apologize for the fuss?

Dream on. There's something about commenting on the Middle East — really, commenting on Islam — that causes pundits never to say they're sorry. Even if Iran's protests reflect a theocratic power struggle between rival mullahs — namely, between Akbar Hashemi Rafsanjani, who backs Mir Hossein Mousavi, and Ali Khamenei, who backs Mahmoud Ahmadinejad, it will just be time to move on.

Such a revelation — that this may be a battle between theocratic, anti-American, anti-Israel, pro-jihad, Khomeinist factions — should be enough to chill the enthusiasm of any pro-democracy booster. But would the Wall Street Journal's Bret Stephens, for example, so far the swooniest of all commentators, (harkening to the "sweet" sound of "Allahu Akbar" as "the rallying cry of the protesters"), continue to push the opposition propaganda that "there are two interpretations of Islam: the aggressive Islam of Ahmadinejad, or the mercy Islam of Mousavi"? Probably.

And if a Stalinist-style power struggle by way of Mecca were unmasked, would Pulitzer Prize winner Charles Krauthammer withdraw his sweeping claims that on Tehran's streets "all hangs in the balance"? I doubt it. After all, he's still cooing over "Iraq establishing the institutions of a young democracy" even as Prime Minister Nouri al-Maliki is now declaring a "great victory" over the "foreign presence" now leaving Iraq — meaning all U.S. troops who have fought and died for that lousy country.

And how about this: If the Iranian opposition movement turns out not to be expressing, as Krauthammer recently wrote, its "anti-regime fervor" but rather fervor for its own regime, will we even get the news? Unlikely. "Our fundamental values demand that America stand with demonstrators opposing a regime that is the antithesis of all we believe," Krauthammer wrote. If the demonstrators' regime is also "the antithesis of all we believe" — no worries; it's all good.

Amazingly, the thought that there might not be a pro-West horse to ride here doesn't enter the collective media mind, from Left to Right. Such unbraked credulity reflects the media failure to deal competently with any non-Western aspect of Islamic society. They instantly project their Western selves onto everything every time.

It would seem advisable to feel one's way into this story, particularly after picking up on the mullah-versus-mullah action, along with a few choice highlights of "opposition" candidate Mousavi's resume. Mousavi (who defended the seizure of American hostages taken from the U.S. embassy there in 1979) served as the Ayatollah Khomeini's prime minister (and is believed to have had a connection to the 1983 attack on the Marine Corps barracks in Beirut), reportedly initiated contact with Pakistan's A.Q. Khan to launch Iran's nuclear program, and, as John Bolton recently pointed out, "is fully committed to Iranian terrorism." (So much for the Wall Street Journal's uncontested mention of Mousavi's "mercy Islam.") In a recent Al Jazeera interview, Mousavi revealed his opinion of Ahmadinejad's genocidal intention to "wipe Israel off the map." Mousavi said: "From the beginning, I objected to that phrase."

The phrase?

But there's more. In a seminal but barely reported speech on June 20, Mousavi explained his movement. It has nothing to do with freedom, with modernity or, as Iran-watcher Michael Ledeen has written, a call "in effect for the end of the Islamic Republic as we know it." Indeed, Mousavi's vision as laid out in this speech has everything to do with returning Iran to the past — 1979, to be precise.

In a paean to the 1979 Islamic Revolution — "an illumination, never experienced before" — that empowered the noxious Ayatollah Khomeini,

Mousavi explains his intent to revive "the Islamic revolution as it was" and "the Islamic Republic as it should be." Noting that this "noble message ... excited the younger generation, a generation that had not seen those times, and felt a distance between ... this great inheritance," he speaks of the "rights of the people" to fair election results, and pledges his loyalty to this cause. And finally this:

"We are not up against our sacred regime and its legal structures; this structure guards our Independence, Freedom and Islamic Republic. We are up against the deviations and deceptions and we want to reform them; a reformation that returns us to the pure principles of the Islamic Revolution."

Returning the "sacred regime" to the "pure principles of the Islamic Revolution" isn't the kind of "reform" most pundits have in mind. Which should be enough to turn their faces green — jihad green — but it won't.

U.S. military ignoring glaring Islamic threats

11/13/09

Stephen Coughlin is an attorney and intelligence officer who was once the Pentagon's sole specialist on Islamic law. He lectured on jihad doctrine — what the Koran and key Islamic texts actually say about waging war — to military leaders who had been (and continue to be) strategizing, planning and fighting the so-called war on terror without any knowledge of the jihad doctrine behind the terror.

Hesham Islam, an Islamic aide to then-Deputy Secretary of Defense Gordon England, rejected what Coughlin's brief said about Islamic jihad, even though the brief, which I've had the opportunity to attend, relies solely on authoritative Islamic sources. Under Islam's tutelage, England and the rest of the Pentagon brass preferred outreach — you know, Muslim outreach — even to unindicted Muslim co-conspirators in government terrorism cases. Long story short: Muslim outreach was "in," and Coughlin and his famous brief on jihad doctrine (later transformed into a masters thesis published by National Defense Intelligence University as "To Our Great Detriment: Ignoring What Extremists Say About Jihad") were "out."

That was January 2008. Fast forward to November 2009.

The Washington Post this week published a story about Maj. Nidal Malik Hasan headlined: "Fort Hood suspect warned of threat within the ranks." The story opens by explaining that Hasan, using a PowerPoint presentation, "warned a roomful of senior Army physicians a year and a half ago that to avoid 'adverse events'" — meaning such events as the

2003 jihad attack on Army personnel in Kuwait by Sgt. Hasan Akbar, killing two and wounding 14 — "the military should allow Muslim soldiers to be released as conscientious objectors instead of fighting in wars against other Muslims."

Good idea. More sensational was the fact that the senior Army psychiatrists who witnessed the 50-slide PowerPoint presentation, based not on medical research as scheduled, but rather on classical jihad doctrine from the Koran and Hadiths, did nothing that rid the armed forces of this jihad threat in uniform. Hasan's presentation, called "The Koranic World View As It Relates to Muslims in the U.S. Military" and viewable online at the Washington Post, describes, in Hasan's words, "what the Koran inculcates in the minds of Muslims and the potential implications this may have for the U.S. military." This series of Islamic lessons culminates in the message: "Fighting to establish an Islamic State to please Allah, even by force, is condoned by Islam."

And what did the Army's senior shrinks do about this? As NPR reports, they essentially went into denial, discussing, but not addressing, the threat they believed Hasan posed to others, including the U.S. military, as recently as last spring.

This dereliction of every kind of duty is staggering, and I wish I could convene a court martial myself. But here's the thing. Using standard, non-"extremist" Islamic texts, Hasan warned of the Muslim threat to the U.S. military from within. Using standard, non-"extremist" Islamic texts, Coughlin warned of the Muslim threat to the U.S. military from without. The Koranic intersection of these warnings is significant. So is the fact that both were shut down for similarly PC reasons: the institutional aversion to facing facts about Islam and jihad, either as they pertain to what the military knows as the "enemy threat doctrine," or, in Hasan's case, as they pertain to the enemy threat within — Hasan himself, for instance.

Now that Hasan has fulfilled his own jihad prophesy, is anyone taking Islam and jihad more seriously? Not so long as our PC senior military leadership remains in place to fret, as Army Chief of Staff Gen. George Casey frets, about the fate of "diversity" post-Fort Hood. "Our diversity, not only in our Army, but in our country, is a strength," Casey told NBC's "Meet the Press." "And as horrific as this tragedy was, if our diversity becomes a casualty, I think that's worse."

Only a zealot could say such a thing, a zealot whose duty is to prioritize "diversity" over the lives of his troops. And only a "diversity"-zealot could be blinded to the Fort Hood-underscored fact that the teachings of Islam are irreconcilable with the goals of the U.S. military, and that anyone who takes those teachings seriously shouldn't be serving in the U.S. military.

The zealotry lives on, even as Fort Hood buries its dead.

Yet another way political correctness will kill us

1/8/10

It's more than strange when a former CIA director and the head of an Islamic advocacy group arrive at the same place on profiling terrorists — or, rather, not profiling terrorists. I refer to ex-spy chief James Woolsey and executive director of the Council on American Islamic Relations (CAIR) Nihad Awad, whose post-Abdulmutallab (the so-called "underwear bomber") statements are startlingly similar.

First, Awad's statement. It is pointed as befits a media-trusted quote-meister — a gig unchanged, shockingly, by Awad's past links to Hamas and other jihadist groups, and CAIR's status as an unindicted co-conspirator in the Holy Land Foundation terror financing trial and Muslim Brotherhood affiliate. "First look at behavior, not at faith or skin color," Awad told the New York Times. "Then spend what it takes to obtain more bomb-sniffing dogs, to install more sophisticated bomb-detection equipment and to train security personnel in identifying the behavior of real terror suspects."

Operative message: Ignore Islam. Watch for suspicious behavior and beef up the security gauntlet. That's a sure-fire way to deny the existence of jihad and never end it, choosing instead to submit indefinitely to its untenable siege, equal parts frightening, humiliating and inconvenient. But — and this is where things get really disturbing — Woolsey's idea of deterrent strategy is no different.

"I don't think we should focus just on people from the Middle East," he told National Review Online, euphemistically dismissing the heart of the Islamic world. "But generally speaking, we are talking about males in their late teens to 40 or so. I don't see any reason why one shouldn't put young men under particularly rigorous scrutiny and double-check all of them."

All of them? To Woolsey, this counts as being tough-minded. "You really have to be an extremist with respect to political correctness to think you can't treat young men differently from grandmothers."

He added: "My family, we're all WASPS. All three of my sons say we should be scrutinizing people like them: guys in their 20s and 30s. They say they'd be glad to go through three checks at the airport."

Is he kidding? Nope. He wants us to believe that generic "young men," not agents of Islamic jihad, are the problem. "Behavioral distinctions are also something to focus on," he continued. "People who are acting funny, people who don't have baggage, people who pay in cash. Those things have nothing to do with race, ethnicity, or religion and seem entirely appropriate as reasons for double-checking or having them go through special scanning machines."

Woolsey's message is the same as CAIR's: Ignore Islam. Look at behavior, and beef up the security gauntlet. Oh, and watch those young WASP men. And thank goodness, his message implies, "acting funny" has nothing to do with "race, ethnicity or religion." Because who in his politically correct mind wants to examine whether race, ethnicity or religion (emphasis on religion) factors into our airports' having become Dar al-harb — Islamic war zones? The results would undoubtedly be what is known as "insensitive." While not "racist" (Islam is not a race), they would certainly be prejudiced against a religion. Praise the multiculturalism and pass through the whole body scanner. It's better to be dead than politically incorrect.

This isn't to say that security personnel shouldn't watch young men or zero in on "behavioral distinctions" to prevent imminent attacks. And people from outside the Middle East may indeed be killers. I've never forgotten an old story of a young Irish girlfriend of a Libyan terrorist who unwittingly boarded a plane with a bomb in her carry-on luggage that exploded in flight. Nearly 300 people died.

But denying the threat within Islamic ideology blinds us to the threat that Islam poses to the West. This denial prevents us from erecting immigrational, legislative, financial and other defenses against further incursions of jihad and reversing the spread of Islamic law (Sharia).

It's one thing to get the Islam run-around from a CAIR official. Indeed, the effort to decouple discussion of Islam from terrorism is official policy at the Organization of the Islamic Conference (OIC), the 57-member Islamic body that counts heads of state and foreign ministers as working members. But it's another thing to get the same see-no-Islam message from a former U.S. intelligence chief like Woolsey. That's when you know you're losing.

Useless Fort Hood leaves Americans unprotected

1/25/10

"Do you believe in 'radical Islam'?" the famous Dutch parliamentarian Geert Wilders once asked me.

The occasion was a banquet last summer at the Reagan Library outside of Los Angeles where later that evening Wilders would receive a Hero of Conscience award from the American Freedom Alliance. I would have the honor of introducing him. "What did you say?" I could barely hear him over the speaker at the podium elaborating on the perils of, yes, "radical Islam."

"'Radical Islam,'" he repeated. "Do you think there is 'radical Islam,' or only 'Islam'"? Me, I'm an "only Islam" kind of gal, as I told him. Who am I to argue with Muslims ranging from terror-cleric Abu Qatada to Turkish Prime Minister Tayyip Erdogan? Erdogan is particularly interesting as a democratically elected Islamic leader who eschews all word-modifiers of Islam including "moderate," the adjective the media often applies to his AKP political party. "These descriptions are very ugly," Erdogan said in 2007. "It is offensive and an insult to our religion. There is no moderate or immoderate Islam. Islam is Islam, and that's it." Erdogan has also bluntly rejected descriptions of Turkey itself as an example of "moderate Islam," saying last April: "It is unacceptable for us to agree with such a definition. Turkey has never been a country to represent such a concept. Moreover, Islam cannot be classified as moderate or not."

I mention this now because after the fireworks over Scott Brown's U.S. Senate victory in Massachusetts have died down, we will have to return to the same, old, equal parts humdrum and deadly wrangle over how to think, talk about and grapple with Islam in what remains a post-9/11 world.

Two related events took place just as the Massachusetts miracle sucked the oxygen from non-election news excepting Haiti coverage. First, the Pentagon report on the Fort Hood massacre came out. It is 86 pages long and doesn't mention the words "Muslim," "Islam," "jihad," "Sharia" (Islamic law), "Koran" — despite the fact that we know, among other things, that the killer, who initiated his massacre with a cry of "Allahu Akbar," was a Muslim inspired by Islam to perform an act of jihad as sanctioned by Sharia derived from the Koran.

These facts, however, rate official silence. So what else is new? From the Bush years to the present, see-no-Islam denial has turned U.S. government attempts to assess and discuss national security issues into Kabuki gibberish, a perpetual exercise in make-believe that the core doctrines and traditional institutions of Islam — not "radical Islam," not "Islamism," not other aliases — pose no threat to the core doctrines and traditional institutions of the non-Islamic Free World. Naturally, mum's the Pentagon word over jihad at Fort Hood. Or, rather, "self-radicalization" is the word. It is mentioned more than a dozen times in the report.

I can't imagine a greater dereliction of duty than this failure of U.S. government leaders to recognize, articulate and defend against what in military parlance is known as the "enemy threat doctrine." But this dereliction, this failure will trigger no investigations or court proceedings on how and why our leaders consistently mask, soft-soap and otherwise fail to assess and repel the existential threat posed by the imposition or accommodation of these same Islamic doctrines.

Talk about irony: Within days of the report's release, one of the few politicians in the world who understands, articulates and fights the imposition and accommodation of these same Islamic doctrines went on trial in the Netherlands for doing exactly that.

I refer again to Geert Wilders, now enmeshed in a Kafkaesque court trial in which the Dutch government is subverting its own democratic institutions — namely, freedom of speech and the will of the people — in an effort to shut down Wilders and his political opposition to the Islamization of the Netherlands. The government's case rests on Wilders' increasingly successful efforts to win support for his anti-Islamization program from the Dutch people through speeches, writings and the short film "Fitna" (easily viewable online) — a body of work that only a tyrannical, Islamically correct government could designate as "evidence" of a crime.

How Dutch government officials must envy America's Sharia-compliant public servants who willingly generate see-no-Islam blather such as the Fort Hood report.

They can have it.

'Is there anyone left with America's interests at heart?'

5/7/10

There were some big losers in the national guessing game over the identity of the failed Times Square bomber this week. New York Mayor Michael Bloomberg took the booby prize for picking "someone who doesn't like the healthcare bill or something."

That was before Pakistani-born, 2009-naturalized Faisal Shahzad was apprehended Sunday night trying to flee to Dubai. Even after that point, Democratic strategist Bob Beckel was holding out for "a right-wing militia man," while an array of MSM commentators, tracked by Newsbusters.com, seized on jihad-alternate theories as the trigger. One favorite: Foreclosure Rage. It seems, as the AP noted, Shahzad ran out on his home mortgage when he abandoned "the path to respectability." Of course, that was when he also chose the path to jihad, not that the media would go there. Instead, the early narrative dwelled on the "suburban" family man who had lost his home — a two-story, grayish brown colonial, we gratuitously learned. "One would have to imagine that that brought a lot of pressure and a lot of heartache on that family," said CNN's Jim Acosta.

One sure would, but only if "one" had remained blind to advancing global Islamization, eight-plus years and 15,247 acts of Islamic terrorism (as tallied by thereligionofpeace.com) since 9/11, and therefore to the possibility that Shahzad, who received five months of weapons training in Pakistan before assembling his car bomb, might be part of it. But no. Indeed, "there was a part of me that was hoping (the Times Square bomber) was not going to be anybody with ties to any kind of Islamic country," said MSNBC host Contessa Brewer. Of course, she inadvertently revealed there was a part of her that strongly suspected otherwise.

But that tiny voice of reason, Brewer and her peers seem to believe, is from the dark side. Brewer explains: "There are a lot of people who want to use terrorist intent" — jihad! — "to justify writing off people who believe in a certain way" — people who believe in jihad! — "or come from certain countries" — that is, countries that practice Sharia and promote jihad! — "or whose skin color is a certain way." This last bit, a non-applicable race card, works like a last-ditch sympathy-trigger. "I mean," she said, "they use it for justification for really outdated bigotry."

Welcome to your world, where self-defense is bigotry, and thus worse than death by fireball, axe or vaporizing over the Atlantic.

This is as ridiculous as it is obscene. There is no "bigotry" in understanding jihad as the engine of Islamic supremacism driven by the imperative to spread Islamic law (Sharia). Our leading lights shrink from this basic truth lest its clean logic wither the fuzzy, cultural-relativism-based universalism that orders our society.

If our leaders faced facts, you see, they might also have to act. They might have to consider such measures as halting Islamic immigration to stop the demographic spread of Sharia. Even a wartime immigration moratorium would help. Come to think of it, a simple ban on return travel from especially fertile jihad regions such as Pakistan — a ban on return travel from the Northwest frontier alone — would do wonders to shore up our vulnerabilities.

In Pakistan, after all, 79 percent of the people, according to a 2007 survey by WorldPublicOpinion.org, favor the "strict application of Sharia." Notorious jihadists have traveled to Pakistan for terrorism training, including lucky-for-us failures Shahzad, subway bomber Najibullah Zazi (also two high school classmates), and David Coleman Headley, implicated in an assassination plot against cartoonist Kurt Westergaard also targeting Jyllands Posten newspaper. Jihadists who trained in Pakistan have also killed and maimed scores of innocents in Mumbai and in the London Underground.

Our leaders haven't noticed. They stay riveted on their own navels, devising higher-tech ways to stare into the navels of rest of us. Post-Shahzad, AFP reports, New York City officials plan to expand a "controversial security blanket of cameras, sensors and analytical software" into midtown Manhattan. The New York Times notes cutting-edge research in pixel conversion that promises to enhance the readability of security cameras. Meanwhile, the advice of a terrorism expert such as Richard A. Clarke is summed up in the following Times subhead: "Don't Panic, Get Used to It."

Is there anyone left with America's interests at heart?

No matter their U.S. name, they're the Muslim Brotherhood

2/11/11

Guess who said the following:
"The earliest defenders of Islam would defend their more numerous and better-equipped oppressors because the early Muslims loved death — dying for the sake of almighty Allah — more than the oppressors of Muslims loved life. This must be the case when we are fighting life's other battles."

I know I haven't asked a fair question. As Andrew McCarthy put it recently, "that leitmotif — We love death more than you love life — has been a staple of every jihadist from bin Laden through Maj. Nidal Hasan, the Fort Hood killer."

He isn't kidding. In 2008, as McCarthy notes, the "Supreme Guide" of the Muslim Brotherhood, Muhammad Mahdi Akef, while praising Osama bin Laden, urged teaching young people "the principles of jihad so as to create mujahidin who love to die as much as others love to live." In 2004, the 3/11 bombers in Madrid left behind a tape saying, "We choose death, while you choose life." MEMRI's Steven Stalinsky has noted the origins of this necro-parable in the Battle of Qadisiyya, 636, when the Muslim commander called for the conversion to Islam of his Persian enemies "for if you don't, you should know that I have come to you with an army of men that love death, as you love life."

Just to be sporting, here's more of the same mystery quotation: "What are our oppressors going to do with a people like us? We are prepared to give our lives for the cause of Islam."

Chilling, but not helpful, right? Similar death-cult code could come from any jihadist, from Mohammed Atta, in his night-before-9/11 instructions, to Anwar al-Awlaki, in his e-mails "ministering" to the underpants bomber, Umar F. Abdulmutallab.

But could it also come from a former Bush administration appointee? A board director of the American Conservative Union (ACU), sponsor of the C-PAC convention in Washington, D.C., where the newest batch of 2012 presidential hopefuls have been speech-o-flexing before 10,000 grassroots activists?

The surprise answer is yes. The former Bush official and ACU board member who I am quoting above is Suhail Khan, a protégé, you might say, of the weirdly influential, not-very-conservative activist Grover Norquist. Khan's shocking quotation—shocking, that is, for a classic conservative, but not for a classical jihadist—comes from a 1999 speech Khan gave at another convention, that of the Islamic Society of North America (ISNA).

As Suhail Khan has said himself, his father, Mahboob Khan, helped found and was very active in ISNA. He said so in that same 1999 speech, further pledging as his "life's work, inspired by my dear father's shining legacy ... to work for the umma," which means transnational Islam. According to a key internal document of the Muslim Brotherhood, ISNA is a Muslim Brotherhood front, probably the largest one in America. Which means that no matter what CNN's Anderson Cooper ignorantly accepted from Khan as fact recently, Khan's father, Mahboob Khan, was part of the Muslim Brotherhood (MB or Ikhwan) in America.

That's right, America. The Brotherhood isn't merely an Egyptian movement committed to Islamic world government (caliphate) and Shariah (Islamic law); the Brothers are here. According to evidence introduced by the U.S. government in the 2008 Holy Land Foundation trial, MB claims 29 front and "friendly" organizations that include virtually every big Muslim organization such as ISNA and CAIR. Due to the mass suicidal reflex known as "Muslim Outreach,' representatives from these fronts are routinely invited into practically every American institution to pronounce on all things Islamic. What we're talking about is an influence operation to rival, or perhaps surpass, that of the communist Kremlin.

Are the ACU and C-PAC easier marks? I have read through and watched what is by now a compendium of literature on the subject, the lion's share on the subject by Frank Gaffney, a former Reagan Pentagon official who started tracking this phenomenon in 1999. I believe all the signs of an MB influence operation are there—troubling signs that spell an ultimate transformation of C-PAC conservatism. Conservative leaders, the 10,000 activists and all those presidential hopefuls must ask themselves: At what point does MB influence become a liability for conservatives? After it's completely successful?

Let's talk about a caliphate

2/24/11

I almost forgot how the Pundit Right smacked down Glenn Beck over his wholly rational concern that out of Tahrir Square a new caliphate might arise in the Islamic world until I read William Kristol's op-ed this week.

Earlier this month, Weekly Standard editor and Fox analyst Kristol had led off the anti-Beck attack with a heated column accusing Beck of "hysteria" for his "rants about the caliphate taking over the Middle East" and connections to the American Left. Kristol was seconded by National Review editor Rich Lowry. The New York Times' David Brooks entered the debate lambasting Beck for his "delusional ravings about the caliphate coming back" while "the conservative establishment" saw Mubarak's fall as "a fulfillment of Ronald Reagan's democracy dream." (Count me out.)

For the next week or so, taunting "delusional" Beck became a regular feature on cable TV. The Pundit Left congratulated the responsible Right for "addressing" the Beck "problem." And maybe a solution was near. "I've heard, from more than a couple of conservative sources, that prominent Republicans have approached Rupert Murdoch and Roger Ailes about the potential embarrassment that the paranoid-messianic rodeo clown may bring upon their brand," Time's Joe Klein blogged. "I wouldn't be surprised if we saw a mirror-Olbermann situation soon."

Somehow it all slipped my mind.

And then I read Kristol's Wednesday lament in the Washington Post over what he sees as President Obama's dithering over what he also sees as "Arab spring." This is a jarringly dainty euphemism for a blur of regional events that now includes: the triumphal return to Egypt of the poisonous Yusef al Qaradawi, the Muslim Brotherhood's favorite cleric who just drew 2 million Egyptians back to Tahrir Square where he prayed for the Muslim conquest of Jerusalem; panicky EU promises of billions of dollars in aid (protection money?) to its "Southern neighborhood"; emergency preparations for as many as 300,000 Islamic "migrants" washing up on just Italy's shores any day. By the way, one disastrous effect of mass Islamic immigration (hijra) to Europe to date may be gleaned from the current political climate in which a new edition of Jean Raspail's 1973 novel "Camp of the Saints," the prophetic account of France's inability to survive massive Third World immigration, is expected to land the 85-year-old author and his publisher in French court on "hate speech" charges.

But I digress, sort of. What is noteworthy about the beef against Beck is the rock-hard certitude with which his critics, Right and Left, dismiss the caliphate concept as though it were a mythological beast, not a historical system of Islamic governance still revered and yearned for by most Muslims. Speaking of Tahrir Square, a 2007 University of Maryland/WorldOpinon poll indicated that 74 percent of Egyptians favor "strict Shariah," while 67 percent favor a "caliphate" uniting all of Islam.

But woe to anyone who takes notice. Harvard historian Niall Ferguson, for example, was recently accused on a noted blog of "(slinging) caliphate tripe" when Ferguson pointed out that the Muslim Brotherhood "remains by far the best organized opposition force in the country, and wholly committed to the restoration of the caliphate and the strict application of Shariah." "Hilariously stupid" was the not-so-hilariously stupid comment.

But even if "Arab spring" should fail, Kristol writes, "there would be still be a case, for reasons of honor and duty ... to stand with the opponents of tyranny." Doing so, he continues, would not only "vindicate American principles and mean a gain for American interests but because we claim those American principles to be universal principles."

Here is what is "delusional": the belief that American principles — freedom of religion, freedom of speech, equality before the law — have a natural place as "universal principles" in a culture grounded in Shariah principles. This is the pure fantasy that has driven our foreign policy through a decade of "nation-building" wars. Meanwhile, the only way I know how to get to anything you might call "universal principles" into the Islamic world is through the establishment of ... a caliphate.

How will Congress react to latest Afghan shooting?

4/29/11

Even before the carnage inside Kabul airport was sorted and identified, before the squads of sober officers were deployed to inform stateside next of kin, and before the caskets were filled, closed, and draped with flags for the final flight home, this much we knew: Another Afghan Muslim "partner" in uniform — a veteran Air Force pilot — had opened fire on NATO trainers in a meeting, killing eight U.S. military personnel and an American contractor.

Question: Will our U.S. representatives — and those of the deceased — pay attention to this latest Afghan attack on Americans? If so, will they a) yawn; b) cluck; c) raise hell; d) none of the above?

The fact is, these murders are not "just one of those things" — the unfortunate outcome of a "disagreement," or even "financial pressures" as mentioned, straight-faced, in early reports. These ritualistic murders of Westerners, like similar assaults before them, are the most shocking manifestations of our foundationally flawed policy of nation building in the Islamic world. They are some of the flesh-and-blood sacrifices to the make-believe "Democracy Project," whose postmodern-day missionaries believe must be advanced on the backs of the U.S. military according to the quasi-holy doctrine of counterinsurgency (COIN).

It's way past time to call it off. The simplest reason is because it's crazy, and probably literally so in a certifiable sense. We, the people, have empowered elected officials to order our military forces to risk their lives not for our country but for a theory. A theory based on the absurd premise that the Western way is also the "universal" way. A theory whose practitioners must suppress logic, historical knowledge, moral principle and, most basic of all, survival instinct. And that's crazy.

Consider this evidence from the Clarksville (Tenn.) Leaf Chronicle. Last week, the newspaper sent a reporter to witness a bizarre event that tragically defines our age: a Fort Campbell send-off for troops en route to Afghanistan to "partner" with Afghan "allies," one of whom had just killed five U.S. troops, also from Fort Campbell (a separate killing spree). The story's headline is "NCOs offer stern message for war-bound soldiers." That message is, "Don't trust anyone but you still have to partner up."

The crazy thing is, "trust" is the essence of "partnering up," particularly when live ammunition is involved. Which is why this order, this policy, is irrational. Pvt. Buddy McLain knew as much. In late 2010, the 24-year-old expressed misgivings about arming Afghan trainees to his wife; one week later, he and five other U.S. troops (also from Fort Campbell) were dead, murdered by one such "partner" after drinking tea with him. End of story? Nope. Where our leaders are concerned, it was just another chapter.

The Leaf Chronicle reporter tries to explain the inexplicable: "Those twin messages can seem confusing to a 19-year-old soldier, which is why the senior noncommissioned officers will have to train the junior NCOs to deliver both messages effectively and maintain the balance the mission requires."

In other words, the U.S. military will have to make schizophrenia the new normal. And that's really crazy. Ex-Marine John Bernard of the blog Let Them Fight pointed out to me that nowhere else in society does "doing your job require this dual mentality." Bernard, whose son Lance Cpl. Joshua Bernard was killed in action in Afghanistan in 2010, further noted that such fractured orders are "an indication of just how convoluted ... the entire mission is." After all, he added, Afghan army and police "are from that segment of society that we had already deemed to be the good guys and should have an expectation of peaceful coexistence. We don't." Our soldiers "should not be dealing with this level of uncertainty at this state in the operation, period." If the strategy were correct to begin with, he explained, we would have already defeated the enemy.

What, if anything, will Congress do about this scandal? So far, we see nothing but almost heel-clicking adulation, inexhaustible patience and an open purse for the generals, the policymakers and their crazy strategy. But how many more U.S. troops will die in an airport office or at a tea table "mentoring" a never-never Afghan security force that our exit supposedly depends on before lawmakers notice the whole big, beautiful theory just isn't working? Is it really too much for them to hold a hearing to try to find out why not, who's responsible, and what we should do instead?

'Senseless' seems easier than saying 'jihad'

5/26/11

The Army honored a fallen hero of the Ft. Hood Jihad Massacre with a medal this week. Not, of course, that the Army describes the November 2009 attack in such meaningful terms. Army psychiatrist Maj. Nidal Hasan may have shouted "Allahu Akbar" (Arabic for "Allah is great") as he killed 14 and wounded more than two dozen; may have been in contact with jihad cleric Anwar al-Awlaki and frequented jihadist websites; may have had business cards proclaiming himself a "SoA" (Soldier of Allah); and may have created and presented an Islamically correct PowerPoint brief outlining reasons for jihad by Muslims within the U.S. Armed Forces, but no matter. His actions remain a total mystery to the U.S. Army.

To wit: "Although we may never know why it happened, we do know that heroic actions took place that day," Brig. Gen. Joseph DiSalvo said in presenting the Secretary of the Army Award for Valor to Joleen Cahill, widow of Michael Grant Cahill. Cahill is recognized as the first person to have tried to stop Hasan and the only civilian to have been killed by Hasan that day. "He will forever be a source of inspiration."

Alas, I have my doubts about the deputy commanding general of Ft. Hood. Despite overwhelming evidence that Hasan committed an act of jihad, DiSalvo—like the Army, like the U.S. government—looks the other way. "We may never know why" the Hasan attack happened, DiSalvo said without, apparently, turning red or rolling his eyes.

It's hard to overstate the impact of these words. In honoring the very last thing Cahill did on this Earth, the general pointedly chose to omit its significance. Like a potent spell, his words made all the context of the 62-year-old Cahill's valorous act—charging Hasan with a chair as Hasan fired on the crowd—disappear. Of course, the general's omission takes nothing away from Cahill's courage. It does, however, wrongly release the rest of us from our debt to Cahill. In treating Hasan's rampage as no more purposeful than a flood or a cougar attack, the general has also reduced Cahill's ultimate sacrifice to its most personal level; exemplary, admirable, but of no consequence beyond the scene, outside the circle. This is morally wrong. It was the general's duty to place Cahill's death in perspective, to impress upon both his loved ones and his fellow citizens that he died not only to stop a bloodletting but also in defense of liberty, then and now under jihadist attack.

In other words, the general flinched. No surprise there. Ft. Hood may have been a war zone that day but, with few exceptions (Texas Republicans Rep. John Carter and Sens. Kay Bailey Hutchinson and John Cornyn are pressing to see Purple Hearts awarded), neither our military nor our government has the courage to admit it.

There is a ripple effect. This Memorial Day, by U.S. government reckoning, by U.S. military non-fiat, the Ft. Hood fallen do not rate remembrance as war dead. As a result, there have been no Purple Hearts awarded to military dead and wounded (as there were to casualties of the 9/11 attacks), no combat death benefits awarded to their survivors, no recognition of Hasan's jihad. Indeed, as the general says, we may never even know why they died.

This is just the way our leadership wants it—"senseless," as President Obama put it, describing another 2009 jihadist attack the U.S. government refuses to recognize as an act of war, this one in Little Rock in which Pvt. William Long was killed and Pvt. Quinton Ezeagwula was severely wounded outside a military recruiting station. The trial, which begins in July, is currently subject to a tug-of-war, almost literally, between the lawyers and defendant Abdulhakim Mujahid Muhammad. Prosecutor Larry Jegley is determined to prosecute Muhammad as "nothing but a street thug" accused of "just a drive-by shooting," defense attorneys want Muhammad to plead insanity, while Muhammad, a Muslim convert who may have studied with a jihadist imam in Yemen where he drew the attention of the FBI, is pleading, strenuously, to be tried as a sane, confessed jihadist. Like the US military, like the White House, the court seems to be pushing jihad, kicking and screaming in this case, down the memory hole.

Which makes you wonder: By next Memorial Day, who will remember?

Islamic threat as bright as the sun

6/10/11

My best guess is the sun is hot. I feel its heat. I see by its light. I understand its role in the growth of crops and other living things. If I were to come across scholarly data attesting to its high temperatures, I would probably look at the fiery pictures (if there were any) and turn to something else.

On one level, I approach a new study on violence and Islam in the Middle East Quarterly in much the same way. That is, I've lived through 9/11 and the 17,298 Islamic terror attacks since (as tabulated by the website thereligionofpeace.com). I've seen pictures of Muslims rampaging around the world over a cartoon. I also understand Islam's animating role in the terror and subversion designed to extend Islamic law (Shariah) to a point where an Islamic government, or caliphate, rules the world.

But there is something transfixing about the new study, "Shari'a and Violence in American Mosques." The authors have amassed a solid bank of peer-reviewed data attesting to the presence and promotion of literature advocating violence in the majority of 100 randomly selected American mosques. And yes: that's majority of "American" mosques. Not Saudi mosques. Not Pakistani. Not Iranian. Not Turkish. Not even British mosques.

American mosques.

There goes that post-9/11 myth—the one that tells us that American Islam is a happily assimilating creed, wholly different from the aggressive Islam transforming Europe. The new data collected by Israeli scholar Mordechai Kedar and attorney David Yerushalmi of the Center for Security Policy (and one of my 18 co-authors on the book "Shariah: The Threat to America") indicate that most American mosques are sanctioning, if not also promoting, the study of material of similar peril.

For me, the six tables of data boil down to two simple and stunning facts. More than 80 percent of the mosques in the study feature Islamic literature that advocates violence. (The authors divide the "violence-positive material" into two categories: 30 percent "moderate" violence, and 51 percent "severe" violence.) Further, 85 percent of the imams recommend this literature—both lay-written and authoritative Islamic texts (not including the Quran or Sunnah, writings said to be words and deeds of Mohammed). It is a slim 19 percent of the mosques that don't feature such violent materials, and an even slimmer 15 percent of the imams who don't recommend it. I guess it is in these small fractions where we might find the real "tiny band of extremists"—perhaps among the followers of the four imams in the 100 mosques who, the authors point out in a footnote, "instructed against the study of violence-positive material."

The authors follow a line of inquiry into whether signs of adherence to Shariah (Islamic law) within the mosque—for example, sex-segregated prayer, regimented prayer lines, bearded imams—indicate the presence of inflammatory material. Take sex-segregated prayer. They found that 95 percent of the mosques where men and women pray separately contain violent literature. At the same time, however, so do 74 percent of the mosques where men and women pray together. Similarly, 94 percent of the imams presiding over sex-segregated congregations recommend the study of violence-positive material; but so do 80 percent of the imams leading co-ed services. So, yes, Shariah-adherence is a sure-fire indicator, but it's not the only indicator.

No wonder the authors consider the conclusions to be drawn from their survey as "dismal at best." But what will those conclusions be? What should they be? I conclude, just for starters, that there is an urgent need to halt Islamic immigration to ensure that the demographic for more such mosques doesn't grow. But having dug up the hard data on the textual embrace of Islam-inspired violence within organized Islam in America, the authors almost seem content to throw it all away: "This survey suggests that, first and foremost, Muslim community leaders must take a more active role in educating their own faith community about the dangers associated with providing a safe haven for violent literature and its promotion."

The data may be new, but this is the same old mistake we've made since 9/11: outsourcing our response to the ideological threat posed by Islam to "Muslim community leaders" — and usually linked to the Muslim Brotherhood. This isn't an internal Islamic problem. These alarming data on the promotion of violence within Islam in American mosques are for the wider, still non-Islamic society to address, and before it's too late.

Destruction of Copts is Islamically correct

10-14-11

I am looking at a reproduction of an old engraving of Jerusalem's Church of the Holy Sepulcher. It is in Bat Ye'or's book "The Dhimmi," which collects primary documents from history to chronicle the impact of Islamic law on non-Muslims through the centuries.

What is notable about the image, which is based on an 1856 photograph, is that the church, said to be at the site of Jesus Christ's crucifixion and burial, has no cross and no belfry. Stripped of its Christian symbols, the church stood in compliance with the Islamic law and traditions of the Ottoman (Turkish) Empire, which ruled Jerusalem at the time.

I went back to the book to find this image for a reason. It had to do with last weekend's massacre of two dozen Coptic Christians in Cairo by Egyptian military and street mobs, which also left hundreds wounded. The unarmed Copts were protesting the destruction of yet another church in Egypt, St. George's, which on Sept. 30 was set upon by thousands of Muslim men following Friday prayers. Why? The trigger was repair work on the building – work that the local council and governor had approved.

Does that explanation make any sense? Not to anyone ignorant of Islamic law. Unfortunately, that criterion includes virtually all media reporting the story.

Raymond Ibrahim, an Islam specialist, Arabic speaker and author of "The Al Qaeda Reader" (Broadway, 2007), catalogs the key sequence of events that turned a church renovation project into terror and flames. With repair work in progress, he writes online at Hudson New York, "It was not long before local Muslims began complaining, making various demands, including that the church be devoid of crosses and bells – even though the permit approved them – citing that 'the cross irritates Muslims and their children.'"

Those details drove me to re-examine the de-Christianized 19th-century image of the Church of the Holy Sepulcher – no cross, no bells. It becomes a revealing illustration of Islamic history repeating itself in this "Shariah Autumn," the deadly but natural harvest of the grotesquely branded "Arab Spring."

Given our see-no-Shariah media (and government), we have no context in which to place such events. That context is Shariah society, advanced (but by no means initiated) by "Arab Spring," where non-Muslims – "dhimmi" – occupy a place defined for them by Islamic law and tradition. Theologian, author and Anglican pastor Mark Durie elaborates at markdurie.com: "Dhimmi are permitted to live in an Islamic state under terms of surrender as laid out in the 'dhimma' pact." Such terms, Durie writes, "are a well-established part of Islamic law and can be found laid out in countless legal text books." When non-Muslims violate these terms, they become subject to attack.

To place the dhimmi pact in comparable Western terms is to say the West has its Magna Carta, Islam has its Pact of Umar. Among other things, this seminal pact governing Muslim and non-Muslims relations stipulates, Durie notes, the condition that Christians "will neither erect in our areas a monastery, church or sanctuary for a monk, nor restore any place of worship that needs restoration."

Thus, this anti-Coptic violence, which for the moment has caught world attention, is Islamically correct. This is the piece of the puzzle Westerners fail to grasp. But Durie takes us through the theological steps: "For some pious Muslims in Egypt today, the act of repairing a church is a flagrant provocation, a breach of the peace, which amounts to a deliberate revocation of one's right to exist in the land." As such, it "becomes a legitimate topic for sermons in the mosque (where) the faithful are urged ... to uphold the honor of Islam." In Islamic terms, then, the destruction of the church is no injustice, as Durie writes. It is "even a duty to destroy the church and even the lives of Christians who have the temerity to repair their churches." That's because dhimmi who take to the streets to protest the Islamically just destruction of the church "are also rebels who have forfeited their rights (under the pact) to 'safety and protection.'" As violators of the "dhimmi" pact, they become fair game.

It's quite simple, but the theology eludes us. Why? I think the answer is that to expose the facts about Shariah in the Western milieu is to invite their criticism. Such criticism is forbidden under Shariah. So, we remain silent – which is what good "dhimmi" do.

Iraq hawks leave a door dpen that should be slammed shut

12/16/11

I wish I could find the perfect label for the depths of denial and the heights of delusion manifested in Frederick and Kimberly Kagan's latest declarations on Iraq, published this week in The Washington Post as "opinion."

"Fantasy," is more like it. The premise of these two military advisers closely associated with the "surge" strategy in Iraq is that Western-style nation-building there failed not because the policy was an exercise in hothouse academic utopianism (leftist cant) that withered in the real-world conditions of the Islamic Republic of Iraq, but because the exercise didn't go on long enough.

Even as our troops withdraw after eight fruitless years, the husband-wife team still sees "American core interests" in Iraq, including "ensuring that Iraq contributes to the security of the Middle East, rather than undermining it through state collapse, civil war or the establishment of a sectarian dictatorship."

Is that all? Ensuring that Iraq doesn't collapse, enter civil war or establish a sectarian dictatorship requires an indefinite occupation on a colossal scale (why?) or the total transformation of Iraqi Man (read: Muslim Man), which is the Frankensteinian basis of "winning hearts and minds," the cornerstone of counterinsurgency theory (COIN).

In another epoch, armies of Christian missionaries might have been the force of choice to rework Islamic culture to such an end; then again, Western nations haven't fared so well in such endeavors. (Remember the Crusades.) COIN-inspired nation-building is the contemporary, secular alternative. Its adherents burn with a blind zeal that admits no cultural difference between the West and Islam, that sees most arrogantly a universal appeal in their own Judeo-Christian-derived values.

The only stumbling block between COIN values and Islamic acceptance, as COIN elites see it, is PR. The sales pitch. Take off those protective, ballistic glasses, soldier. Eat parasite-ridden goat and wreck your digestive system maybe forever, grunt. Smile. Get to know the people. Walk those roads (bang) and see that those wells and bridges are built, those mosques mended, those tribal conflicts settled, and don't call in fire support when a "kinetic" incident occurs or the "population" will think you don't trust them. And whatever you do, don't forget the payola.

But remaking human beings, "re-educating" people to conform to ideological goals, doesn't ever work out well, whether the policy is enacted through bribery by nation-builders with guns bearing gifts, or through force by commissars destroying civilization with gulags.

No doubt the Kagans would disagree with my premise. They see no gulf so existential between the West and the Islamic world. In their eyes, it's an easy-peasy fix when it comes to Iraq, requiring just two conditions. "First," they write, "Iraq must be able to control, police and defend its territory, airspace and waters. Second, Iraq must preserve and solidify the multiethnic and cross-sectarian political accommodation that was established in 2008 and 2009 but that has been eroding since the formation of the current government."

Again, is that all? Not only are these beyond Iraqi competence and scope, they aren't American interests. They are Iraqi interests, if Iraqis care. They are also international interests that global interventionists arbitrarily obsess about, whether in Iraq, Libya or any other hot spot du jour. It is not in America's interest whether Iraq preserves and solidifies multiethnic and cross-sectarian blah blah blah. It is, however, in the interest of the unreconstructed Iraq Hawks, the COINdinistas, and their political allies because these are the theoretical justifications for their failed missions. In many ways, Obama's reluctant troop withdrawal, which, last time I looked, fulfilled George W. Bush's agreement with Iraq, is the best thing that has happened to them. It keeps the fantasy of "if only" alive.

"Neither condition is likely to be met in the coming years," the Kagans write. Thanks to Obama, they hereby absolve themselves of any and all responsibility for the impossibility of these conditions—the conditions of COIN nation-building—ever being met. They are free. Or so they seem to think.

But maybe there's a chance to take another whack at things. Noting violations of international agreements by Iraq's Prime Minister Nouri al-Maliki, the Kagans write: "Responsible nations should insist that Iraq demonstrate its commitment to those obligations. The president should tell Maliki in no uncertain terms that Washington will hold him to account in the international arena if Iraq does not."

Excuse me, isn't that where we came in?

GOP candidates walk a tightrope on Iraq

1/6/12

On Dec. 31, 2011, Iraq's Nouri al-Maliki declared a national holiday to celebrate the withdrawal of U.S. forces from Iraq. Funny way to say "thank you" for all the blood and treasure, no?

Not that Maliki was saying thank you. He wasn't even saying good riddance. He was saying, in effect, it was all a dream. Or, in the Associated Press' words: "The prime minister sought to credit Iraqis with the overthrow of Saddam Hussein and made no mention of the role played by U.S. forces that invaded Iraq in March 2003."

No mention, huh? I guess it was just a trillion-dollar mirage, a figment, a never-never fantasy best dropped from speeches, polite conversation, maybe history books. Then again, silence suits the American political classes fine. Amazingly, following the U.S. withdrawal, the questions, "What was that all about?" or, "What went wrong in Iraq?" or even, "Did something go wrong in Iraq?" (never mind, "What is going wrong in Afghanistan?") don't rise even to the level of conversation-enders. They don't rise, period, not even among GOP presidential candidates, beyond the odd sound bite.

Famously, of course, Ron Paul calls for withdrawal of U.S. troops everywhere, a rollback of the international security force the U.S. military has become, certainly since entering World War II. While Paul's constitutional position is strong, his misunderstanding of Islam undermines his rationale for me; indeed, it transforms his policy into submission. The aftermath of withdrawal under a Paul presidency could be as dangerous as it would be under more Obama.

I support withdrawal from guaranteed recidivist hellholes such as Iraq and Afghanistan as a means to shore up the wall against the spread of Shariah (Islamic law) in the West rather than, in effect, continuing to fight/accommodate Shariah culture in the Islamic world. This is a no-win struggle in which only a see-no-Shariah utopian could still engage. It is this Islam-blind engagement that is the simple but devastating flaw of the Bush-Obama counterinsurgencies (COIN). But it continues to get a national pass.

Indeed, most GOP candidates tend to promise more of the same Bush-Obama COIN. (Jon Huntsman is the other main GOP exception. He voices a come-home-America policy in Afghanistan based on non-feasibility, economics and war-weariness — all valid points — but without parsing COIN, which he sees as a success in Iraq.) The candidates speak in generalities, when they speak at all.

I think that's because if Republicans were to discuss the past decade's wars — what worked, what didn't, whether the USA should fight for constitutions that enshrine Shariah (Iraq's and Afghanistan's)

-- they would have to discuss the president whose tenure was dominated by these wars. And the last thing they want to discuss is George W. Bush.

This is a grave political mistake. The fact is, President Obama has continued much of the Bush war agenda in both Iraq and Afghanistan — an agenda polls indicate most Americans don't support. For much of Obama's term, key war-making personnel were Bush holdovers, from Defense Secretary Bill Gates to Gen. David Petraeus. The war plan for "Obama's war" in Afghanistan came off the Bush drawing board.

Even Obama's withdrawal from Iraq was on Bush's schedule. Opponents, including most GOP candidates, seem to forget that Obama agreed with them. After all, he pleaded with Iraq to allow some U.S. forces to remain.

How does this play out in Election 2012? Without a GOP strategy to confront the essentially non-conservative mistakes of the Bush presidency, I predict GOP defeat. Come November, having failed to repudiate George W. Bush's bailouts and stimulus spending, Mr. GOP will be unable to make the clear case for free markets, let alone for repealing socialized medicine. Reverting to Republican "good manners," he won't argue against leaving a redistributionist and collectivist in the Oval Office, either (and forget about the phony birth certificate). He'll probably think he has an ace in the hole — foreign policy, traditionally the Republican strong suit.

But, no. Failing to have distanced himself from key Bush policies, the GOP candidate has failed to distance himself from Obama's, too. Then Obama shows his cards, the pieces de resistance: the hit on Osama bin Laden (operationally insignificant, but no matter); the killing of Libyan leader Moammar Gadhafi (never mind the USA actually supported al-Qaida allies to get it done); more drone-killed hilltop jihadis than Bush ever got. In a campaign endgame, such strokes could give Obama the empty but winning boost.

Sure, Iraq's al-Maliki can clam up about everything, but we know better. Or do we?

Chalk up another one for Islam in the PR battle

2/6/12

Even after all these years, journalist-socialite Sally Quinn still embodies a Washington way of thinking – a heart-of-Georgetown, A-list set of salon-tested assumptions "everyone" knows that provides attitudes for any occasion.

Take the surreal state of the U.S. Military Academy at West Point.

One day, William G. "Jerry" Boykin, a highly decorated retired Army general and ordained minister, and a founding member and leader of Delta Force, was scheduled to speak at a West Point prayer breakfast. The next day, following a campaign to stop Boykin's appearance by what the New York Times describes as "liberal veterans' groups, civil liberties advocates and Muslim organizations," Boykin was *not* scheduled to speak at West Point. "In fulfilling its commitment to the community," West Point announced, "the U.S. Military Academy will feature another speaker for the event."

Quinn's reaction? West Point didn't go far enough. Fire whoever is responsible for inviting Boykin, she wrote in her online Washington Post column "On Faith," because his criticism of Islam makes him "notorious." Why, it's nothing less than blasphemy, as everyone who is anyone would agree – and who else is there?

No one, at least not at West Point. You can bet your last bullet the replacement speaker will not have identified, studied and himself experienced jihad – in military terms, the enemy threat doctrine – as Lt. Gen. Boykin has. This makes Boykin's abrupt cancellation an information-war victory for the Muslim Brotherhood something few in Washington or West Point will even notice.

Muslim Brotherhood? Isn't that in Egypt? How does the Muslim Brotherhood figure into a story about West Point?

Prominent in the stop-Boykin coalition is the Council on American-Islamic Relations (CAIR), known mainly for sound bite-ready spokesmen who present an Islamic point of view on TV. More important is CAIR's place in the Muslim Brotherhood constellation of front groups as an entity founded by members of the Muslim Brotherhood's Palestinian franchise, the jihad terror group Hamas.

This revelation emerged during the 2008 Holy Land Foundation terror-financing trial in a document authored by the Muslim Brotherhood itself. It attests to the presence in the United States of multiple Muslim Brotherhood front groups, including CAIR, which remains an unindicted co-conspirator in that case. The FBI cut off official contacts with CAIR in 2008.

Such information is documented in "Shariah: The Threat to America," a book Boykin and I and 17 others, including former CIA director James Woolsey and former Reagan Pentagon official Frank Gaffney, co-authored in 2010. I wouldn't be surprised if the book played some animating role in the Battle over Boykin at West Point, won by CAIR and celebrated in all the best bastions impregnable to fact.

That includes Quinn's Washington Post column. Not only should Boykin's West Point sponsor be fired, she writes, "that person should ... say 'I'm sorry.'"

If Georgetown were a revival tent, a chorus of "Amen, sister" would rise over N Street. But no. Indeed, some animus toward Boykin may form in reaction to the evangelical brand of Christianity he expresses on faith and war in churches across the country. Back in 2003, following the publication of snippets of these talks, the Pentagon investigated Boykin's invocations of "Satan" as the enemy, and his attesting to his faith in the Christian "real God" over his enemy's "idol." In Georgetown, this counts as full-blown culture clash – enough to deflate the bubbles in the sparkling Vouvray.

"He has said that 'there is no greater threat to America than Islam,'" Quinn continues, building her case. Luckily, she isn't arguing in a Shariah-run courtroom, because her testimony would then be worth half of a man's – one reason for Boykin's concerns about Islam's impact.

Then Quinn quotes "Shariah: The Threat to America": "And in a study he co-authored, (he said) 'most mosques in the United States already have been radicalized, that most Muslim social organizations are fronts for jihadists.' How could this happen?" She means the West Point invitation, natch.

Quinn is quoting a description of the book by others, but never mind. What's extremely interesting here is that she isn't contesting the veracity of these documented claims. Conventional Washington-to-West Point wisdom is conditioned to see them as so absurd as to be beneath consideration. Doesn't everybody? Ridiculous. Stoo-pid. Just typing them out – regardless of their accuracy – elicits guffaws of programmed outrage.

I would say the Muslim Brothers have done their public-relations job well, but frankly, this information operation was over before it began.

Invasion of the Body Snatchers

5/4/12

Remember the sci-fi cult classic "Invasion of the Body Snatchers"? The 1956 movie is about a small town where extraterrestrial "pods" take over the townspeople. Even pillars of the community change into zombielike clones, as revealed by their blank stares and abnormal impulses. Outwardly, though, the "pod people" remain unchanged.

The town doctor, played by Kevin McCarthy, figures out what's going on, but, as the movie progresses, there are fewer real people to warn. Soon, they've all gone over to the Other Side! The climactic sequence features McCarthy, the last free man, running across a rugged landscape and onto a crowded highway to warn the rest of humanity.

"Let him go—they'll never believe him," say his erstwhile neighbors, now pod people.

"Stop! Listen to me! You're next!" he shouts to people in cars, barely dodging traffic.

Brakes squeal, horns blare. Angry drivers ("You're drunk!") wave him away. Needless, to say, he can't make them understand.

True confession: I can relate. Sometimes, gearing up for a weekly column — particularly when it's another entry in the annals of the Islamization of the West — feels a lot like running onto the highway yelling, "Stop! Listen! It's coming! You're next ..." The feeling gets stronger still when sizing up what I can describe only as body-snatched impulses in real-life pillars of society. I refer to people in positions of responsibility — in uniform, even — who, by all appearances, are "normal" until — wham! -- their eyes go glassy and you realize you're looking at ... a pod person.

Am I kidding? I don't know how else to explain the memorandum sent out last week by the Joint Chiefs chairman, Gen. Martin E. Dempsey. (Well, I do, but bear with me.) Could it have been sent out by a pod person who just *looks* like a Joint Chiefs chairman? It's the general's signature, all right, and his official seal. But the memo itself is from another planet.

In this memo, our highest-ranking military officer orders the entire United States military to purge its educational and training classes, files and rosters of instructors to ensure that no members of the U.S. military are ever again instructed in the basic principles of Islamic jihad. The body snatchers call such allegedly offending educational material "anti-Islam," but it covers study of Islamic-style war. Given the unchecked threat of such war, both violent and covert, to spread Shariah (Islamic law) until a new global caliphate exists, the question is whether eliminating instruction in the enemy threat doctrine is something that a "normal" Joint Chiefs chairman would do. The answer is no. "Invasion of the Body Snatchers" strikes again.

It all started this time (there was an earlier round last fall) due to one elective course — "Perspectives on Islam and Islamic Radicalism" — offered at a military staff college in Norfolk, Va. According to Wired online, this course included guest lectures by Maj. Stephen Coughlin (U.S. Army Reserves). Coughlin is an expert in Islamic law and jihad doctrine (he and I are among the 19 co-authors of "Shariah: The Threat to America"), whose rigorously sourced briefs are legendary in Washington security circles and beyond. Coughlin's contributions alone would make the whole course worth taking.

When I read that the general's deputy for education, Lt. Gen. George Flynn, described the course as "inflammatory," my eyes widened in horror: Oh, no — that's what a pod person would say! Joint Chiefs Chairman Dempsey canceled the course, then ordered that top-to-bottom purge. Clearly, only an im-pod-ster would do that.

Dempsey wrote that he was concerned the military was teaching material "inconsistent with the values of our profession, and disrespectful of Islam." A new review would "ensure our Professional Military Education programs exhibit the cultural sensitivity, respect for religion and intellectual balance that we should expect in our academic institutions."

How about teaching material consistent with the values of free inquiry and with respect for veracity instead? What is urgently needed is a review to ensure military education offers unflinching threat analysis based on meticulously sourced facts and research. That's what a "real" Joint Chiefs chairman would demand, not a "politically correct" curriculum designed to subordinate U.S. national security interests to a policy of not offending Islam.

Wake me when this horror flick is over.

Eurabia

The Eurabian alliance

3-03-03

Just one more thing about France. Considering all the analysis of the country's motives for trying to thwart a U.S.-led invasion of Iraq, one gathers that France is out to prove its "relevance"; that French president Jacques Chirac is "bent on securing his place in history"; that France wants to counterbalance American might by taking its rightful place at the head of a united Europe. In other words, it seems that all of France's histrionics — what was it foreign minister Dominique de Villepin said, straight-faced, at "this temple of the United Nations" about France always standing "upright in the face of history before mankind"? -- boil down to one big power grab.

But where's the muscle? With Britain, Italy, Spain, Denmark, Hungary, the Czech Republic, Poland, Portugal, Albania, Bulgaria, Croatia, Estonia, Latvia, Macedonia, Romania, Slovakia and Slovenia -"New Europe"—joining President Bush's "coalition of the willing," you'd think the old cheese stands alone (except for Germany and Belgium). France, however, doesn't share this impression. So, what backs up Chirac's big talk? Robert Kagan, strategist of the new book "Of Paradise and Power" might answer that nothing does.

His nifty theory on what really separates the United States and Europe — that the United States fully expects to exercise power in an anarchic, Hobbesian world, while Europeans believe they have evolved "beyond power" into a "world of laws and rules and transnational negotiation" — assumes that traditional notions of "power" in Europe are increasingly beside the point.

This notion suggests that what we're witnessing in France is a matter of, well, gall, both insupportable and unsupported. But I'm not so sure.

France may have something besides vetoes and resolutions up its sleeve, something that trumps NATO and, if necessary, the EU — or at least allows the French to think so. That "something" is its deeply layered, binding relationship with the Arab-Muslim world.

It seems that what helps make the French so cavalier about the Atlantic alliance is its place in a bona fide Mediterranean bloc. This goes beyond the lucrative oil concessions and weapons contracts with Iraq we hear about. It involves a complex relationship at every level — economic, educational, religious, artistic, legal, demographic — between France and the Arab-Muslim world, a surprisingly overlooked collaboration that now includes the rest of the EU nations in what is officially known as the Euro-Arab Dialogue. Over roughly 30 years, this Dialogue has led to a change in European, and particularly French, culture of a magnitude at first difficult to grasp. The historian Bat Ye'or — perhaps as great a prophet as she is a path-breaking historian — pinpoints the origins of this transformation in a stunning article, "European Fears of the Gathering Jihad". It all began, she writes, with the terms of a terrible bargain struck between Europe, largely at France's instigation, and the Arab League countries around the time of the Arab oil embargo of 1973: oil and business markets for Europe in exchange for anti-Israel policies for the Arab world.

"The Europeans tried to maintain the Dialogue on a base of economic relations, while the Arab countries tied the oil and business markets to the European alignment on their anti-Israeli policies," she writes. "However, the Dialogue was not restricted to influencing European foreign policy against Israel and detaching Europe from America. It also aimed at establishing ... a massive Arab-Muslim presence (in Europe) by the immigration and settlement of millions of Muslims." The goal? As Ye'or sees it, "to integrate Europe and the Arab-Muslim world into one political and economic bloc, by mixing populations (multiculturalism), weakening the Atlantic solidarity, and isolating America."

This sounds like a Dialogue worth listening to. It helps explain the French vision, as described in The New York Times by former Chirac adviser Pierre Lellouche, of "Europe as a bridge between the developing and developed world." It indicates that continental Europe is not the extent of French designs. And it helps explain why France is such a "stability"-booster in the neighborhood of Iraq and other dictatorships: Any changes war could bring to Arab-Muslim regimes, from retooling to rebirth, could also change the Dialogue — which is not something France wants to hear.

Such revelations should also clue us in to another reason the ex-communist proto-democracies of New Europe are with the United States. Because the Euro-Arab Dialogue never extended to Eastern Europe,

Euro-Arab ties don't exist there. (As members of the Eastern Bloc, these same countries once toed a reflexively anti-U.S., anti-Israel line, but such dogma has gone the way of the U.S.S.R.) Absent this special relationship, there have been none of the major influxes of Muslim immigrants into these countries that have transformed the demographics of Old Europe.

The Israeli newspaper Haaretz has mentioned some of these same points in an essay exploring why the upsurge of violent anti-Semitism that swept Western Europe last year largely missed Eastern Europe. Interesting to see what else they tell us.

Ludicrous moments from a somber season

8-29-03

This summer, there was no so-called silly season. There was too much menace, from Iraq to Indonesia to northern Virginia, for the media to muster the enthusiasm to obsessively tally shark attacks, assiduously track global warming, or chronicle even the most vapid celebrity breakups as if they mattered.

But if there was no silly season, there may have been a summertime spike in the ludicrous, from California recall reports of Arianna Huffington's measly $771 two-year federal tax bill (but what did she pay the accountant?) to a Washington Post front-pager parsing the finer points of identity politics — as in why no self-respecting "Latino" wants to be known as "Hispanic."

Then there were outrages du jour that barely broke the media haze. Maurice Gourdault-Montagne, an advisor to French president Jacques Chirac, offered up this bit of Frenchery about the Bush push for the European Union to outlaw Islamic Jihad and Hamas, two terror groups behind last week's bus bombing in Jerusalem: "If we find that Hamas and Islamic Jihad are indeed terror groups opposed to peace, we may have to change the EU's stand. However, we must not limit ourselves to one, clear-cut, position."

If they are terror groups? If they are opposed to peace? After all the many innocent people Hamas-murdered and Hamas-maimed (ditto for Islamic Jihad) in the name of eradicating Israel from the world map, a bout of sputtering might be the first line of response to such amoral prattle. Better to sputter, though, than to dodge behind a figleafy distinction between the "military" and "political" wings of Hamas and Co., which the French have done, shunning the former and tolerating the latter.

This week, The Middle East Media Research Institute (www.memri.com) posted an article by Dr. Abd Al-Aziz Al-Rantisi, "The False Holocaust — the greatest of lies funded by the Zionists," that gives us all a gander at the world according to "political" Hamas. "It is no longer a secret that the Zionists were behind the Nazi's murder of many Jews, and agreed to it, with the aim of intimidating (the Jews) and forcing them to immigrate to Palestine," Al-Rantisi writes — I mean raves. "Every time they failed to persuade a group of Jews to immigrate to Palestine, they unhesitatingly sentenced them to death." Al-Rantisi also believes the gas chambers of the Third Reich were a myth, but never mind. "When we compare the Zionists to the Nazis," he concludes, "we insult the Nazis."

And when we compare "political Hamas" to political anything, we insult ourselves. This isn't political, it's diabolical — and in reality, alas, no mere aberration of the summer season. No doubt there's more double-talk in store from the Gourdault-Montagnes of the world, who disguise such anti-Western venom as parlor-ready political discourse, masking their own motives, it seems, in the process. Which is one reason the next entry in the summer memory book — the obituary of a notable British explorer — is at least a little different.

Sir Wilfred Thesiger, dead at age 93, was by all accounts the last of his kind when it comes to pre-modern desert exploration. He rode camels here and roughed it there, covering vast stretches of the Arabian Peninsula back when it was still uncharted, even by Standard Oil. His August death prompted suitably lengthy and predictably respectful obits in the British papers, but only Saudi Arabia's Arab News got to the more curious heart of the matter.

According to a fellow explorer, Thesiger was not just an eccentric reactionary opposed to "progress, education and cars" — odd enough — he was also "able to travel to fulfill his antipathy to Western values." How's that? Here is an example: After Eton and Oxford, naturally, dear Thesiger trekked around Abyssinia with tribesmen "whose social standing," the Arab News reports, "was measured by the number of men they had killed." From his autobiography, Thesiger is quoted as having written about the experience: "I knew that this moonlight meeting in unknown Africa with a savage potentate who hated Europeans was the realization of my boyhood dreams."

At least the man was forthright about his antipathies, not to mention his dreams. Of course, there are those who dream of a home where the buffalo roam; others who dream of April, or even August, in Paris — a dream deferred this summer as many Americans, in the travel story of the season, steered clear of France. Which certainly wouldn't have pleased Thesiger much.

After all, all those Americans bypassing France look like they're fulfilling their affinity for Western values.

French fashion?

1/16/04

When Jacques Chirac announced his intention to unveil Islamic schoolgirls in France by barring the hijab, or head scarf, from state-run schools, he raised some provocative questions. Why would a French president whose power as a global broker derives from his close ties to the Arab-Muslim world (and distance from the United States and Israel) act to restrict Islam's burgeoning place in French society?

Why would the European leader behind the international opposition to the war in Iraq — dubbed by at least one Arab media outlet "the Western Saladin" — suddenly seek to sweep a big chunk of Islam out of the French public square?

Sure, Mr. Chirac took the ecumenical approach and barred Jewish yarmulkes and "obvious" Christian crosses from the schools as well, but it was the scarf-wrapped-girl multitudes in increasingly Muslim France that caused presidential concern. There hasn't been a good explanation of his decision, but the untamed uproar in the Arab and Muslim world makes it pretty clear that the priciest dates on sale next Ramadan won't be called (as they were this year) "Chiracs." Indeed, some analysts see hijab-trouble ahead for France, with Walid Phares predicting that "a myriad of jihads," both non-violent and violent, "can and will take place."

Meanwhile, does banning Muslim head scarves in French public schools infringe on freedom of religion? Most clergy, along with such watchdog groups as Freedom House and the U.S. Commission on International Religious Freedom, have already said yes, huffily. But here's where things get intellectually gooey. If the head scarf is a feature of Islam, and Islam has a history of repressing non-Muslims, then is the head scarf a symbol of religious repression? If so, how can Mr. Chirac be curtailing religious liberty by restricting a symbol of religious repression?

Also worth wondering is whether a head scarf is a religious "symbol" in the first place. This sounds like a question for the muftis on call at "Fatwa Corner" at www.islamonline.com, a fundamentalist Web site tracking every wrinkle of the hijab controversy. There, a reader learns that the head scarf is not a symbol of Muslim faith, but rather "an ordinance from Allah to protect [girls_] chastity." In other words, unlike yarmulkes and crucifixes, the hijab doesn't function as a sign of piety, as so many assume. It is wrapped around a girl's head and upper torso to serve a purpose. As one Web site scholar puts it, "If a girl is approaching puberty, there is the fear that her not wearing hijab may cause young men to be tempted by her, or her by them ... The parent or guardian has to make her wear hijab so as to prevent means that may lead to evil or immorality."

Such a revelation should give the hijab a new look. It certainly offers insights into the ongoing culture clash. While most Westerners wince at the dowdy uniformity of the hijab, all the while hoping to convince themselves to accept it as a symbol of feminine modesty, Muslims regard it as a functional means of safeguarding young girls and women from the untrammeled sexual impulses of men. This belies a fairly unevolved set of manners and mores (not to mention an almost literal state of war between the sexes) that reflects the culturally entrenched repression and abuse of women in Islamic society. Little wonder that Turkey and Tunisia, two Islamic societies with a somewhat more modern bent, have long banned the hijab in public places.

Not too long ago, I received an e-mail from an American woman married to a "basically enlightened Lebanese husband." From him, she wrote, she was surprised to learn that "the concept of controlling lust, anger, etc., is not taught in the Arab world." Rather, what in the West are matters of self-control and personal responsibility, are in the Arab world outwardly and "socially controlled." Her husband has commented, she continued, "that some Arabs come to the U.S. and lose their manners — once outside the controlling environment they have none."

My correspondent offers one explanation of the enduring nature of the hijab, the abaya and burqa in Islamic society. But what about in France — not to mention Paris, the city of light, Balenciaga and Yves St. Laurent? Such uniforms reflect both women's second-class status within Islam, and Muslims' newly expanding place in the Western world.

All of which may help explain why, despite my own hankering for a little more modesty (and a lot more style) across the board, the hijab remains a symbol of repression and extremism — a definite fashion-don't.

When is a scarf not just a scarf?

1/26/04

My e-mailbag was brimming with responses to last week's column about Jacques Chirac's proposed ban on Islamic headscarves — along with jumbo crucifixes and all yarmulkes — in France's public schools. "Good grief," one correspondent declared, concluding a negative critique, "it's just a scarf!"

Good grief, it's anything but. And I say that not so much to reprise last week's arguments, but rather to consider intervening developments — such as the reaction of Grand Mufti Sheikh Abdulaziz bin Abdullah al-Sheikh to a newspaper photograph of a leading Saudi Arabian businesswoman without her headscarf.

"This," said the grand mufti, Saudi Arabia's leading religious authority, referring to the head-exposed Muslim woman, "is prohibited for all. I severely condemn this matter and warn of grave consequences.

I am pained by such shameful behavior in the country of the two holy mosques. What was published in some newspapers about this being the start of liberating the Saudi woman ... such talk is null and void. One's duty is to obey sharia by complying with orders and shunning that which is forbidden." Not doing so, he continued, will "cause the doors of evil to open before the people of Islam."

The doors of evil? This sounds like a melodramatic mouthful from an old Saturday serial, but then again, maybe the mufti has a point. That is, if women were ever to achieve equality throughout Islam — and that means achieving a range of extremely basic rights, from the ability to vote to being able to get a driver's license — maybe the whole of Islam would unravel. Sharia, or Islamic law, which codifies the inequality of women and non-Muslims, would be shredded, and the hoary hierarchy would lurch if not topple.

A big "if," but not inconceivable. This may explain something about the intensity of the opposition to France's hijab ban among Muslim activists, from France's officially recognized Council of the Muslim Faith to Britain's extremist group Al-Muhajiroun. The question is, in rejecting the Muslim headscarf, do Western governments affirm secular values — namely, Western civilization's highly evolved traditions of tolerance, equality and liberty? Last week, I wrote that, given Islam's tradition of repressing women and non-Muslims, a result of the twin precepts of jihad and dhimmitude, the headscarf as a trapping of that tradition could well be banned from secular schools without sacrificing Western principles. I still think so. But to what end?

This week, French education minister Luc Ferry noted that beards, too, if they were determined to be signs of faith, could be outlawed under the school ban on religious symbols. This prompted author and Islamic expert Robert Spencer to explain on his Web site (www.jihadwatch.org) why he believes the French approach — under consideration or in effect in Belgium and a large part of Germany — is way off the mark. In an entry dubbed "A close shave for French Muslims?" Mr. Spencer writes: "Instead of going after the root of the problem, [the French] are targeting minutiae. They can't or won't get Muslims to renounce the sharia and accept Western principles of tolerance and equality: instead, European Muslim groups are loudly denouncing assimilation. So the French instead go against the outward manifestations of the Islamic rejection of those things. But does [the French government] really think that beardless, bareheaded Muslims will not try to institute an Islamic state in France?"

I still don't have a problem with the French ban on headscarves or even beards in their public schools. After all, my own secular school uniform, an L.A.-does-Great Britain costume of blue blazers, pleated skirts and saddle oxfords, included a haircut code for boys that banned beards — as if — and stipulated sideburn length. But Mr. Spencer raises a thought-provoking point: that France's actions — and similar actions contemplated across Europe — are strictly cosmetic patches to mask the underlying conflict between the West and Islam, between a European Christianity that is contracting and a European Islam that is expanding.

And what of secularism? Also this week, an octogenarian French priest was fined nearly $1,000 for a letter to parishioners that railed against a Muslim "ideology that threatens the whole world" and called the Koran a "manual for the extension of the kingdom of the devil." Assuming that secular France wishes to police the religious speech of its priests, as Mr. Spencer notes, it should also police the religious speech of its imams. Will it? Should it? It would seem that the real battle over liberty, equality and fraternity has yet to begin.

An open letter to Germany's chancellor

1/13/06

Good morning, Madame Chancellor.

Here you are, Germany's Angela Merkel, on your first trip to Washington, D.C., preparing for your meeting with President Bush. As you look out of your Blair House window over Lafayette Square toward the White House, consider the historicity of the era: the beginning of Mr. Bush's fifth year leading his country, and the beginning of your first year leading your country in the so-called War on Terror. Or is that the War on Guantanamo Bay? I get them confused.

That's because in just about every account of your American trip — biggish news in Europe — it is prominently mentioned that Guantanamo Bay is prominently high on your list of, well, prominent concerns. Trouble spots. Global things you lose sleep over.

This is, with due respect, bizarre. Iran is going nuclear, Europe is going Islamic, Russia is going off the reservation, China is a fearsome thing, and your big concern is sending what is called a "clear message" to Mr. Bush about Guantanamo Bay, the tropical jail where the United States keeps jihadis on ice — and keeps the rest of the world safer as a result. But that's not what you say. "An institution like Guantanamo can and should not exist in the longer term," you told the German news magazine Der Spiegel this week. "Different ways and means must be found for dealing with these prisoners."

I have a suggestion: How about if we ship all these guys — unflushed Korans and all — to Germany? Maybe "72 Virgins" Airlines would cut us a deal. Then you — Germany — can parole them to Lebanon.

That, of course, is just what you did just before Christmas with

Muhammad Ali Hammadi, the convicted Hezbollah killer of Petty Officer Robert Dean Stethem. In case you didn't know, Mr. Stethem is one of our American heroes, a courageous young Navy diver who became an early casualty of the war on Islamic terror. In 1985, at age 23, he was beaten to an unrecognizable pulp by Hammadi and his gang, shot through the head and dumped onto a Beirut runway during the Hezbollah hijacking of TWA Flight 847.

But, as his brother Kenneth reminded President Bush in a letter this week posted by Michael Ledeen at National Review Online, "He wouldn't give in to the demands of the terrorists," who wanted him to scream into a transmitter for airplane fuel. "He would not allow the honor and dignity of America to be intimidated by the fear and pain that Hammadi and terrorists everywhere represent."

Such is the Hezbollah terrorist that you, Madame Chancellor, set free. And funny thing: Shortly after, your own German hostage in Iraq, Suzanne Osthoff, was released from captivity. Which is quite a coincidence. But so was the fact that after the hostage-takers said Ms. Osthoff would be killed unless Germany stopped training Iraqi security forces, the Iraqi government announced, according to the news Web site Deutsche Welle, that Iraq would be seeking security training elsewhere. And there was more. Osthoff says Germany paid a ransom to secure her freedom, maybe as much as $5 million, according to a German wire service report translated online by Transatlantic Intelligencer. In other words, despite your refusal to be "blackmailed" over Ms. Osthoff's release, Germany seems to be a country terrorists can do business with — including, very possibly, Robert Stethem's killer, and his Hezbollah masters with Iraqi terror connections.

But doing business with terrorists doesn't buy peace. It just buys more business. I'm guessing that publicly confronting President Bush over Guantanamo is, along these same lines, business as usual — doing jihadists' bidding in a craven bid to spare Germany a 9/11, a 3/11 or a 7/7. It's just a hunch; but it fits a dispiriting pattern of surrender.

Such a pattern never marked Robert Stethem, as his brother's letter reminded the president: "You have truly said that 'We are in a fight for our principles, and our responsibility is to live by them,'" Kenneth Stethem wrote. "Robert lived by them. Robert also died by them. ... I hope that his example, and the example of the other heroes like him, can inspire you to understand why allowing Germany to release Hammadi was a wrong. Justice was not done. Robert was not honored and Americans are not safer by allowing Hammadi to return to Lebanon and Hezbollah."

Of course, Germany isn't safer either, nor is any other Western nation. This is the "clear message" I certainly hope you hear from President Bush.

We mustn't rile the terror-mongers

7/10/06

Just in time for the one-year anniversary of 7/7, a poll conducted for The Times of London indicates that 13 percent of British Muslims believe that the four Islamic suicide bombers who murdered 52 people in London last July should be regarded as "martyrs."

With a Muslim population in Britain estimated at 1.6 million, this means that some 208,000 British Muslims regard these killers with what can only be described as a worshipful attitude. Which is despicable. But Mother England, it seems, is home to an awful lot of despicable people.

One of them, surely, is Anjem Choudary, who made related news this week. Choudary is a former leader of Al Mujahiroun — a defunct, jihad-inciting group, whose venomous pronouncements on Islamic supremacy have earned him a strange prominence in the British media. He refuses to condemn the 7/7 attacks, says Muslims shouldn't help police combat jihad terror, and advocates sharia (Islamic law) for Britain. During a BBC "Newsnight" appearance this year, the host asked Choudary why he didn't simply move to a sharia state like Iran.

"Who says you own Britain, anyway?" Choudary replied. "Britain belongs to Allah. The whole world belongs to Allah. ... If I go to the jungle, I'm not going to live like the animals, I'm going to propagate a superior way of life. Islam is a superior way of life."

In a way, the 39-year-old Essex man was just found guilty of a charge connected to propagating that "superior way of life." It all started last February when Choudary organized a march on the Danish Embassy in London to protest Muhammad cartoons first published in a Danish newspaper. This wasn't one of those anti-Danish protests in which people were killed — hundreds died around the Islamic world in this year's Days of Cartoon Rage — but it was definitely murder-minded. "Behead Those Who Insult Islam," said one placard. "Slay Those Who Insult Islam," said another. "Kill Those Who Insult Islam," and (for variety) "Butcher Those Who Mock Islam," said others. Hundreds of demonstrators marched through London, praising the 7/7 killers, or calling for the murder of journalists who publish Mohammed cartoons.

And the police stood by.

More accurately, they made sure the protest went off smoothly, as the Times Online reported. "People who tried to snatch away (the placards) were held back by police," the newspaper said. "Several members of the public tackled senior police officers guarding the protesters, demanding to know why they allowed banners that praised the 'Magnificent 19' — the terrorists who hijacked the aircrafts used on Sept. 11, 2001 — and others threatening further attacks on London."

Why, indeed. The "Newsnight" show on which Choudary

subsequently appeared included news footage of an English bobby vigorously silencing such a citizen, described as a van driver, who, according to the televised report, had angrily criticized the Muslim protesters. It is tragically enlightening.

"Listen to me, listen to me," said the policeman, shaking his finger at the van driver. "They have a right to protest. You let them do it. You say things like that you'll get them riled and I end up in (trouble). You say one more thing like that, mate, and you'll get yourself nicked (arrested) and I am not kidding you, d'you understand me?"

Van driver: "They can do whatever they want and I can't?"

Policeman: "They've got their way of doing it. The way you did it was wrong. You've got one second to get back in your van and get out of here."

Van driver: (bitter) "Freedom of speech."

This vignette wasn't law and order in action. It was desperate, craven appeasement. As the bobby put it, "You say things like that, you'll get them riled." And we mustn't get them riled. Let Choudary and his band of thugs praise mass killings, threaten more attacks and advocate murder by beheading on London streets in broad daylight — but don't get them riled.

Still, Choudary did end up in a British court of law, and this week a British judge handed down a verdict. Choudary has been found guilty of ... staging a demonstration without giving the required six days' written notice.

Tsk, tsk. That'll be $1,400 in fines, please — easy enough to pay since Choudary, the Online Sun reports, receives more than twice that per month in government handouts. All of which makes Pax Britannica seem quite cheap at the price.

Should Muslim students get special treatment in U.K. schools?

2/23/07

I saw something eerie this week. It wasn't an apparition exactly, but rather a head-spinning blur of headlines about global jihad that, rather incredibly, began to take on the unmistakable shape of a British old school tie.

How? Maybe I should start by explaining it was the old school tie that came to mind first in the form of a new publication on British education: Namely, a 72-page manifesto (sorry, "guidance") from the Muslim Council of Britain on how British state schools might better accommodate children from the Muslim community, which, according to the 2001 census, makes up 2.7 percent of the British population.

id I say "better" accommodate their Muslim pupils? I mean accommodate them much, much better. In fact, if the British were to adopt half of the MCB's recommendations for making British schooling Muslim-friendly, they might as well re-issue the 19th-century boys' school classic as Abdullah Brown's School Days. At the crux of the MCB document is a call for special treatment for Britain's Muslim students that is so special as to reorient the entire British system according to Islamic law.

he report kicks off with a British poll finding that religion "appears to be more important" to young Muslims than to young people of "white British or mixed heritage." It seems to follow, then, at least according to MCB logic, that Muslim religious requirements should also supersede those of "white British or mixed heritage young people," not to mention those of the Church of England. And, so, in this report, they effectively do.

Muslim girls should be allowed to wear the hijab instead of regulation uniforms — of course, "schools may wish to specify the colour." (Thanks awfully.) Muslim boys should be allowed to grow beards "following the example of the Prophet Muhammad," not school grooming guidelines. Muslim children should receive "halal meals," a suggestion which entails a slew of other "suggestions" for staff training and food preparation and storage, and Muslim children should be allotted prayer rooms, perhaps segregated by sex.

That's not all. "Muslim pupils who wish to pray will need access to washing facilities to perform Wudu, which includes the washing of the hands, mouth, arms to the elbow and feet." Washing facilities?

he guidelines continue. "This state of purification becomes nullified when one goes to the toilet or breaks wind." Heavens. Such, er, nullification calls for more washing — "private parts," this time. "Hence pupils will need to use water cans or bottles that are easily accessible from a storage area in or near the washing area."

hen comes Ramadan. Rather than simply informing schools how to accommodate pupils' private fasting, the MCB also explains how schools might participate in the holiday. Urging them to schedule tests, meetings, swimming ("the potential for swallowing water is very high") and sex education — even reproductive science lessons — some other time, the report also urges schools "to build on" the Ramadan spirit and participate in nightly fast-breaking meals.

Muslim students should be allowed to take Arabic as a foreign language, and perhaps study "the art of Qur'anic recitation" instead of music. And on and on. The MCB isn't asking the British taxpayer to create the perfect sharia state exactly, but rather the perfect sharia state school system.

And what does all of this have to do with that blur of jihad stories mentioned at the top of the column? First, consider the headlines. In Pakistan, a liberal-minded minister (and wife and mother of two) was assassinated for not wearing a veil. (The shooter reportedly said, "I have no regrets. I just obeyed Allah's commandment.") Also in Pakistan, barbers received threatening letters warning them against continuing their "anti-sharia work" — cutting customers' beards. (One barber told the Associated Press that two dozen barbers have responded by asking customers not to request shaves.) In London, a Muslim father killed his wife and four daughters (ages 16, 13, 10 and 3) because, according to the Telegraph, "he could not bear them adopting a more westernised lifestyle."

What is quite eerie about these horrific crimes is the striking fact that the perpetrators, who acted to avenge various infractions of Islamic law, would likely feel right at home in a British state school that had adopted the MCB's recommendations. In other words, the outlaws and the advocacy group are working in their different ways to enact Islamic law. Which should teach us all a lesson — if we bothered to learn it.

Britain's silence ammo for a Sharia-run future

8/1/08

Strange, the apparent lack of public alarm in Britain over an extensive new poll showing that significant minorities of Muslim students at some of Britain's better colleges and universities embrace the most threatening aspects of Islam. These include the conviction that killing in the name of religion can be justified (32 percent), belief that men and women shouldn't mix freely (40 percent), support for Sharia (Islamic law) in Britain (40 percent), and support for a global caliphate (33 percent) based in Sharia, among other repressive tenets.

Of course, the poll, conducted by the online research company YouGov and commissioned by the conservative Centre for Social Cohesion, came out just this week. Still, having recently visited England and interviewed a string of political, media and religious figures, I'm going to guess that these horrifying numbers — and they are indeed horrifying, despite the emphatic disclaimer that the majority of polled Muslim students support secularism and democratic values — will kick up little cultural dust. After being plastered across a news cycle's worth of papers, they will be regarded as so much political wallpaper that people gaze upon without seeing — or, at least, without reacting.

Fear or outrage would be considered Islamophobic, of course, and isn't there a law against that? Concern for British common law would be called nationalistic, and that's got to be a crime against multiculturalism. Calling for any action would be labeled xenophobic-slash-mean-spirited. Better to read and weep, silently.

One early exception was a laudably passionate outcry from columnist Minette Marrin writing in the venerable Sunday Times. Marrin's concern was palpable; she ticked off many of the poll's disturbing statistics, noting also the perils to be found within Muslim uncertainty over key questions. For example, she wrote, "When asked how supportive, if at all, they would be of the introduction of a worldwide caliphate based on Sharia, fully 42 percent said they weren't sure. That's quite some uncertainty." She added: "One in five wasn't sure whether Islam is compatible with the western notion of democracy. Insecure young people can be swayed by extremists.

And then she acknowledged the all-important and consistently avoided problem: "The question is how to stand up to the extremists."

Did the columnist next call for a campaign of zero-tolerance for Islamic law? A new immigration policy designed to stop or even reverse the growth of the Islamic demographic in Britain as a means of preventing the democratic implementation of Islamic law in Britain?

Not a chance. "First," she wrote, "I think, we should abandon all discussion of what Islam truly is." In other words, just stop the conversation, PC-halting as it already is.

Her logic? "Questions of true (Islamic) doctrine are insoluble," she declared, felling with one deconstructive swoop the objectively knowable facts of Islamic law, which is rooted in Islam's mainstream teachings.

She went on: "Clearly, for lots of Muslims Islam is not a doctrine of gentleness, tolerance, sexual equality, forgiveness, democracy and all the rest. For countless others it clearly is. What follows inescapably from this," she wrote in the very next sentence — and here we must pause to stretch our neck muscles to soften the approaching trauma of journalistic whiplash — "is that religious people and their views should not be officially recognized in groups. Religion should not be allowed a public space or public representation." She added: "This is hard for those of us who used to love the muddled Anglican compromise; it means the disestablishment of our national church — if it doesn't self-destruct first."

Huh? It's not easy to read between these lines, but it seems possible that Marrin just might believe that the anti-Western and even violent outlook of too many of Britain's best and brightest Muslims is in fact traditional Islamic doctrine. Shutting down discussion of Islam, eradicating all religion, even British core Anglicanism, from the public square — which is essentially what former French President Jacques

Chirac did in 2003 when he banned the kippa and cross along with the hijab from public schools — allows the British to avoid this postmodern abyss.

But it leaves another gaping hole.

Anthony Glees, a professor of security and intelligence studies at London's Brunel University, has underscored the importance of the survey. "The finding that a large number of students think it is OK to kill in the name of religion is alarming," he said, adding: "There is a wide cultural divide between Muslim and non-Muslim students. The solution is to stop talking about celebrating diversity and focus on integration and assimilation."

Excuse me, but integration and assimilation into what? Not a Britain that abandons all discussion of what Islam actually is — along with all vestiges of what Britain ever was.

Sharia continues to strangle free speech

6/19/09

COPENHAGEN, Denmark — I am being patted down by a female Danish security officer in the basement of the parliament building in Copenhagen and I have a thought. I have just triggered the metal detector — my heels, I'm sure — en route upstairs to the Landstingssalen, formerly the parliament's upper house. There, I am scheduled to deliver a speech at the invitation of the Danish Free Press Society, or Trykkefrihedsselskabet. (Say that three times fast — or slow.)

Indeed, I am holding the text of my 20-minute address inside a folder in one of my hands, now rigidly outstretched as I am being searched. The speech is called "The Impact of Islam on Free Speech in the U.S.," but as I am checked for bombs and knives and whatnot, my thought is of the impact of Islam on free society everywhere.

Such a thought surely tops the heights of "political incorrectness," I know. But what should I do — not express it? Not think it? Not even notice that Western civilization, in skewing to accommodate the jihad threat of Islam within, has already traded away too much precious freedom?

As the security officer continues patting me down, I follow this forbidden train of thought to the realization that it is only due to the incursions of Islam into the West — Islam with its death penalty for criticism of Islam — that I am now standing here under guard. Here we are (for there is a long line behind me by now), participants in a conference to consider Islam's censoring impact on free speech, and Danish security is doing its best to prevent Islam from censoring the speech of anyone here permanently. This strikes me as an exceedingly hard way to prove a point.

Not that there are many people likely to try outside the elegant, security-ringed conference room upstairs. In PC lingo, security in the basement is looking for "terrorists" or "extremists" — those postmodern designations for perpetrators of Islamic jihad that, presto, turn everything Islamic into something generic. Still, with Islam comes jihad, and with jihad comes Islamic law (Sharia), no matter what "experts" tell you. And because Islam is a growing presence in the West, Western countries must now and presumably forever expend vast sums of money and manpower to manage — not defeat, just manage — the jihad that can break out in acts large and small at any time. Increasingly, this also means deferring to Sharia.

Finally, my pre-conference frisk is over. Hallelujah, I am no threat to society and allowed to pass. I go on to meet for the first time the great author Wafa Sultan, and meet again the great Dutch parliamentarian Geert Wilders, the two most illustrious speakers on the conference roster.

Both Sultan and Wilders, of course, live under unrelenting, permanent and Islamic threat of death for their critiques of Islam, in a very real way suffering every day for defying Sharia's prohibition against criticizing Islam. But does the outrageousness of their plight resonate with their fellow citizens? I don't think so. I think we've all grown much too used to it, and dully complacent. But imagine if I had written, circa 1970, that for his critique of communism, Ronald Reagan lived under unrelenting, permanent and communist threat of death in his beloved California, that he couldn't travel the streets of Los Angeles without a massive security retinue, that he could no longer even sleep in his own home. Wouldn't Americans have become rightly agitated over the communist enemy within?

I think the answer would have been yes, but the point is, no such mortal homeland danger existed at that time for those who spoke against the leading threat to Western-style liberty. Today, a mortal homeland danger does exist. I won't tell you what it was like to slip in and out of the Wilders security bubble during the course of his stay in Copenhagen, but suffice it to say, it is both a veritable shame and an outrage that his life depends on that bubble, and that for speaking his mind in defense of Western-style liberty he has lost his own freedom.

The same goes for Wafa Sultan, who, for attacking the repressiveness of Islamic law (under which she existed for 30 years in Syria), also lives privately a similarly wary, hunted life that necessitates protective security measures.

Remember, this is happening in the "Free World." Whether in Denmark, Holland or the United States, the heavy hand of Islamic law is pressing in on its leading critics, squeezing the freedom out of their existence. It is time to say enough — literally enough, for example, and stop Sharia by stopping Islamic immigration — and throw off the rising chokehold of jihad-advanced Sharia. I guarantee it will take a lot more effort than just patting down the occasional free speechnik, but I also guarantee that for the sake of free speech it is worth it.

Can 'Eurabia' be far behind?

7/30/10

The battle over whether to admit Turkey into the European Union seems eternal, at least among the EU's rulers. Among the peoples of Europe, when granted the rare chance to go to the ballot box — increasingly window-dressing as far as the EU's soft totalitarians are concerned — there is little argument. In fact, there is bona fide consensus: NO to Turkey becoming a part of Europe. Why? Because, culturally and historically, it is not.

Tell that to British Prime Minister David Cameron, who just visited Ankara to present himself as Europe's leading booster for Turkish EU membership (a move the United States has meddlesomely supported), pandering so low a prayer rug could give him cover.

Dubbing himself Turkey's "strongest possible advocate for EU membership and for greater influence at the top table of European diplomacy," Cameron gave a speech that also attacked "those who willfully misunderstand Islam" and who "see no difference between real Islam and the distorted version of the extremists."

Of course, such a description likely irked Cameron's host, Turkish prime minister Recep Tayyip Erdogan. Erdogan has repeatedly criticized those who make the distinction between "moderate" and "extremist" Islam. "These descriptions are very ugly," Erdogan said in 2007. "It is offensive and an insult to our religion. There is no moderate or immoderate Islam. Islam is Islam, and that's it." Further, Erdogan in 2009 specifically rejected descriptions of Turkey as being an example of "moderate Islam." Enlarging on a theme, Erdogan in 2008 told Turks living in Europe that assimilation is "a crime against humanity."

But Cameron aimed to please. And no doubt he did, especially with his stunning denunciation of Israel for its blockade of Gaza, a defensive measure that Israel devised after Hamas terrorists were elected to govern Israel-ceded Gaza in 2005 and — no surprise to any student of jihad — decided to continue their charter-commanded war on Israel, raining down nearly 10,000 rockets onto Israeli civilians. Dubbing Gaza a "prison camp," Cameron also attacked Israel for the May shipboard battle to defend its blockage that pitted Israeli commandos, lightly armed with paintball guns and emergency sidearms, against trained fighters with ties to the Turkish government, specifically to Erdogan's ruling AKP party.

Little wonder that before the day was over — at some point after Britain hired itself out, as Cameron put it, for the job of "paving the road from Ankara to Brussels" — Erdogan had hailed a "golden age" of Turkish-British relations.

Of course, giving EU membership to Turkey would be a political move with more than political consequences. Demographically alone, it would accelerate those finishing touches on the Islamization of Europe as Turkey's tens of millions of Muslims entered a largely post-Christian, secular European society, bringing a weighty Islamic influence on European law. Could the total transformation to "Eurabia" be far behind?

This is the salient question that is never asked. Instead, the debate is deceptively framed as a civil rights issue, as though the EU were a pointlessly exclusive Neanderthal society, or supposedly obsolete men's club.

"We know what it's like to be shut out of a club," Cameron said, referring to Charles de Gaulle's efforts to block British entry into the European organization. "Europe can either decide to become a global actor or it can fence itself off as a Christian club," Erdogan has said.

Never mind the EU's deliberate omission of "G0d" or "Christianity" in its 439-page constitution. And never mind Turkey's having "fenced itself off" into the most exclusive "club" of all: the supremacist Organization of the Islamic Conference (OIC). Turkey is also a signatory to the Cairo Declaration of Human Rights in Islam, a distinctly Islamic version of the United Nations' Universal Declaration of Human Rights that is informed by Sharia (Islamic law) rather than what the West recognizes as universal human rights. The Cairo Declaration declares that the Muslim community's role is to "guide" humanity, a point that isn't "clubby" but is downright imperialist.

But there is another implication to the debate: that Western identity is merely an atavistic expression of petty insularity. Free will, free conscience — the evolution of individual liberty — is the fruit of Judeo-Christian civilization, one that Islamic doctrine is unable to produce.

Tragically, it is also one that Westerners are throwing away.

A new 'Silent Night' descends on Austria

12/23/11

Ah, to be in Vienna at Yuletide. Streets sparkle with the lights of the *Christkindlmarkts*, the traditional markets that spring up for the season. Skaters circle the rink outside the picturesque *Rathaus* (City Hall). Merrymakers warm their hands on cups of *gluhwein* (mulled wine). What could possibly be missing?

Freedom of speech.

Freedom of speech no longer exists in Austria, as definitively proven by the Vienna high court. This week, a judge upheld the conviction against Elisabeth Sabaditsch-Wolff on the following charge: "denigration of religious beliefs of a legally recognized religion." In simplest terms, this means that Elisabeth Sabaditsch-Wolff speaks the truth about Islam, and in Austria, as in other nations across the Western world currently transitioning to sharia (Islamic law), speaking the truth about Islam is not tolerated, and, more and more, is against the law.

What did my friend Elisabeth say that the Vienna high court ruled *verboten*? Elisabeth was convicted in February 2011 of "denigration" of Islam because in the course of a seminar she was teaching on Islam she stated that "Muhammad had a thing for little girls."

This statement is demonstrably true. According to an authoritative Islamic text (hadith), Muhammad married his wife Aisha when she was six years old. According to the same hadith, Muhammad engaged in sexual intercourse with his "wife" when she was nine. This, at the very least, constitutes "a thing" for little girls. It also constitutes child rape under Western law and Judeo-Christian-derived morality. In all too many Islamic societies where Mohammed's example is emulated, such child rape in "wedlock" is not a crime; indeed, it is permissible under sharia.

In fact, the court didn't contest this. In both Elisabeth's initial trial and her recent appeal, the factual basis of her statement didn't come under judicial attack. Elisabeth is right, and the court knows it. What the Vienna court has twice defined now as being outside the law of Austria is the negative opinion her remark conveyed regarding Muhammad's record of deviance from Western traditions forbidding sexual intercourse with children. (Brava, Elisabeth.) It is wrong, according to the Austrian court, to look down on sex with children if the alleged perp, centuries ago, was the Islamic prophet.

As Henrik Rader Clausen put it, live-blogging the proceedings for the blog Gates of Vienna, Elisabeth, in the court's eyes, expressed "an excess of opinion that can not be tolerated. It is a ridiculing that cannot be justified." Cannot be tolerated, cannot be justified by whom, by what? The answer is by Islamic law. It is literally against Islamic law to criticize or expose Islam or its prophet (Muhammad) in any adverse way. This prohibition against freedom of conscience is now part of Austrian law as well. That the verdict upheld against Elisabeth Sabaditsch-Wolff actually imperils the most innocent and vulnerable among us — little girls whose molestation the courts have implicitly excused as a religious rite — only underscores the depravity of the Vienna high court.

Where, exactly, does this leave all of the rest of us in that community of nations whose calendars, despite the press of Islamization, still culminate in Christmas? I offer in response a clarifying quotation that pegs our existential whereabouts exactly. It comes from Afshin Ellian, a Dutch columnist, law professor, and professor of citizenship, social cohesion and multiculturalism at the Leiden University, who in 1983 fled Ayatollah Khomeini's Islamic Revolution in Iran.

In early 2010, Ellian, commenting on the trial of Dutch parliamentarian Geert Wilders for allegedly anti-Islamic statements, had this to say:

"If you cannot say that Islam is a backward religion and that Muhammad is a criminal, then you are living in an Islamic country, my friend, because there you also cannot say such things. I may say Christ was a fag and Mary was a whore, but apparently I should stay off of Muhammad."

Merry Christmas.

The Forbidden Columns

Articles that some outlets refused to print

Where were you born, Obama?

12/12/08

Roger Kimball may have tagged it first: The real news out of Chicago this week wasn't Illinois Gov. Rod Blagojevich's arrest on cartoonishly lurid charges of corruption stemming from his alleged attempts to sell President-elect Barack Obama's now-vacant U.S. Senate seat. The real news out of Chicago this week was that President-elect Barack Obama had nothing to do with it.

And I mean nothing to do with any of it. There was an almost comical aspect to the spectacle of journalists across the mainstream media (MSM) suddenly, as if on command, assuming pretzel positions in a contortionist's effort not to seem at all curious, for instance, about the discrepancy between David Axelrod's recent declaration that the president-elect had discussed Senate-seat replacements with Blagojevich, and Obama's more recent declaration that he had done no such thing.

The MSM instantly agreed: Obama had nothing to do with it. Such a message took Obama out of the story even before the story itself was clear.

This mantra, this strategy should be familiar by now. Whether it is Jeremiah "G — d — - America" Wright, William "We didn't do enough" Ayers, or now, Rod "F — - him" Blagojevich, Obama is never a player, never even a responsible presence in controversies involving associates past and present. In the media-filtered version of events, he's just not even there. But in no story is what we may one day come to think of as Obama's invisible man-hood more obvious than in the still-roiling controversy over Obama's birth certificate.

What controversy? Anyone who relies solely on MSM outlets (and most conservative outlets) may not even know that Obama has, to this day, not authorized the state of Hawaii to release his Certificate of Live Birth — the "long form" — to prove that he is a "natural born citizen" (NBC), a Constitutional requirement of all presidents.

Instead, We, the People, have online access to an Obama document known as a Certification of Live Birth, which, as Randall Hoven explains at American Thinker blog, is a computer-generated short form that is not even accepted by the Hawaii Department of Home Lands as adequate verification of Hawaiian identity. (The Home Lands Department requires "information that is found only on the original Certificate of Live Birth," or long form.) Further dimming the online document's Holy Grail aspects, it has been altered — the certificate's number has been redacted — which, according to a statement printed on the document, actually invalidates it.

But that's not all. Back on Oct. 31, Hawaii's director of health, along with the registrar of Vital Statistics, released a statement verifying that the Hawaii's Department of Health has Obama's "original birth certificate on record in accordance with state policies and procedures."

Well, that's just great. But no matter how many times this statement from "Hawaiian authorities" is cited as the NBC clincher, it doesn't prove a thing. It turns out, as Hoven reports, that Hawaii issues birth certificates even for babies born elsewhere, so simply having an original Hawaiian birth certificate "on record" doesn't answer the key questions. Namely: What exactly does this original birth certificate say? And why doesn't Obama simply authorize the document's release and be done with the question?

This is some of the background to the birth-certificate controversy. According to the same MSM reporting that omits Obama from everything, however, the controversy is the sole, self-inflicted creation of people unreasonable enough — no, kooky enough — to be concerned about the issue. This includes citizens who have gone to court (up to the U.S. Supreme Court) in more than a dozen states with various NBC-related complaints, all of which could be resolved by the release of Obama's original birth certificate. It also includes followers of radio shows or Internet forums including KHOW's Peter Boyle in Denver, the blog Atlas Shrugs and the news Web site WorldNetDaily.com, which have aggressively covered the story.

In the MSM's no-Obama version of events, though, such efforts and interest are mocked as the freakiest kind of lunacy. And this same MSM argument has lately been trumpeted by prominent conservative voices. "Shut up about the birth certificate," David Horowitz wrote this past week.

Shut up? Is he kidding? Apparently not. Horowitz went on to tell "fringe conservatives" and "birth-certificate zealots" that their "continuing efforts" to "deny Obama his victory" are "embarrassing and destructive." NRO's Mark Krikorian, in turn, congratulated Horowitz for "stomping on the ridiculous, bitter-ender efforts to disqualify Obama from the presidency." Michelle Malkin, too, pooh-poohed the "birth-certificate hunters," describing them as having "lurched into rabid Truther territory."

("Truthers," by the way, are people who believe the United States engineered the attacks of 9/11.)

I disagree. I think it is nothing less than good citizenship to seek to verify that Obama is a "natural born citizen" since our elites, which include the major political parties and the MSM, failed to bring the matter to its extremely simple resolution long ago. But while important, this isn't just a story about whether we as Americans are right or wrong to ask our president-elect the question about his original birth certificate. It is about whether our president-elect is right or wrong not to answer it.

Once again, Barack Obama is treated as though he were not even a part of this story. Those who seek to resolve the birth certificate controversy draw the fire, but not the man who causes it. Talk shows, court battles and blogs can air the issue, but it is only Obama who can put it to rest. And he can do it simply by authorizing the release of his original, "long form" birth certificate — and quickly, preferably before the Electoral College meets to validate his election on Dec. 15, but certainly before his term of office begins on Jan. 20, 2009.

Unless, of course, he has something to hide.

What Obama's hiding and the media are ignoring

7/30/09

Barack Obama's birthday is Aug. 4, and I hereby urge the president to bestow a party favor on the nation that elected him: a verifying look at the original "long-form" version of his birth certificate. It's important to grasp the weird fact that this simple request, requiring nothing more than a nod of the presidential head, ranks as fightin' words to American journalists.

Right wing, left wing, these ladies and gentlemen of the Fourth Estate seem to want nothing less than to gain access to the one piece of evidence that could lay the "natural born" issue to rest once and for all. The media have made their aversion to proof perversely clear: Whatever Obama does, their jarringly unified message is that he certainly should not direct the state of Hawaii to make public his original, long-form birth certificate.

Even though such a presidential directive would instantly dispense with the divisive question of whether President Obama's still-secret, long-form birth certificate contains compromising information, it's unlikely we'll get a peak. The entire controversy would disappear forever if there were nothing more sensational on that document than the name of the Hawaiian hospital where baby Barack came into the world. Such mundane info is the kind of thing that's missing from what We the People have been provided to date: brave-new-world-like Internet images of the short-form Certification of Live Birth (COLB) that the Obama campaign made available in 2008 online.

I emphasize the web-projected, liquid-crystal display nature of the imagery that the mainstream media (MSM) have unquestioningly relied on, even as they have imperiously dismissed all questions regarding its veracity and provenance as "Internet-fueled rumor." In MSM eyes, the Obama campaign document becomes the rock-solid truth, while questions about it amount to "Internet-fueled rumor." To be sure, there is COLB-corroborating evidence available — contemporaneous announcements of baby Barack's arrival in local Hawaiian papers are usually cited as the clincher — but none of it is definitive. The president's maternal grandparents could have been the ones who placed the birth announcement in the papers, regardless of whether their first grandchild was in state residence. Even the oracles of the Hawaiian health department, periodically trotted out to pronounce that all is as should be with the president's top secret birth papers, leave us with nothing concrete. Why won't the president just give us a look at the thing and be done with it?

This is the mystery behind the unease "out there," unease the MSM are now simultaneously picking up on even as they try to squelch it. And this is true particularly after CNN's Lou Dobbs raised the issue in a historically resonant manner: Dobbs trusts that Obama is a natural-born citizen but would like the president to verify his status regardless.

And why not? It is no accident that history and literature are replete with rocky tales of doubtful succession, of the maladjustment brought on by pretenders to thrones. There is something in human nature that yearns for the rightful leader. And there is something in our Constitution that requires it. So why won't this president, who, after all, promised the American people an unprecedented level of transparency, reveal his original long-form birth certificate? Unheeded, the "natural born" controversy will roil indefinitely, further fired by the vagaries of Hawaiian law — specifically, Section 338-17.8, titled "Certificates for children born out of State" (WorldNetDaily.com) -- which makes state birth documentation available to children born out of state, even born out of the country.

None of this is healthy, not the president's suspicious secrecy and not the MSM's protective incuriosity. It almost seems as if someone has something to hide.

Arizona's Fight for Our America

5/2/10

Three cheers aren't enough for Arizona. It's the first state to defend American citizenship on the basis of identity, and American sovereignty on the basis of borders. In an age of blurred identities and undefended borders, Arizona has put itself in a good, old-fashioned state of revolt against the postmodern, global-minded state of being foisted on us by internationalist elites up to and including President Barack Hussein Obama.

That's the effect, anyway, of Arizona's new immigration law, which, as George F. Will has aptly pointed out, "makes what is already a federal offense—being in the country illegally—a state offense." Only in our time, with identities blurred, borders undefended and elites internationalized, could this be controversial. Among other things, the new law requires state law enforcement to verify a person's immigration status in the course of "lawful contact."

Far from heralding the deployment of jackbooted terror squads among the tumbleweed and sprinklers, Arizona's new law acknowledges that American citizenship does and (wow) should exist, and affirms that sovereignty, ignored at the federal level, is the responsibility of a state overrun by illegal aliens mainly from neighboring Mexico.

Given our psycho idea of "normal"—alien-strained schools, bankrupted hospitals, advancing bilingualism and "sanctuary cities"—this new immigration law has aroused Establishment wrath.

Moving across the spectrum from Right(ish) to Left, this ranges from the tense chorus of tut-tutting from the pro-amnesty Republican underbelly (Jeb Bush, Karl Rove, Tom Ridge), insta-calls for boycotts of Arizona from California officials, denunciations from Left-wing national pols and pundits (Nancy Pelosi, E.J. Dionne) a possible Justice Department investigation from President Obama, and, of course, much razzing from La Raza and other Che-idolizing open-borders and Reconquista agitators. There's another reason. Arizona suddenly poses an unexpected threat to the status quo of permissible lawlessness, the illegal demographic transformation of this country into a linguistic and cultural extension of Latin America. This out-of-control movement has been tolerated if not facilitated by our political leadership for several decades under the dangerous influence of what we know as multiculturalism, the school of thought that has widely delegitimized U.S. identity altogether. Maybe more than anything else, Arizona's law restores a civic sense that there exists such an identity, and it is, and should be, legally protected. Thus, the multiculti rage.

A second bill pending in Arizona concerns another legal aspect of American identity, namely the constitutional requirement that our presidents be "natural-born" and not "naturalized" Americans. Both laws may be seen as state-level attempts to safeguard the nation according to principles set forth in the Constitution because authorities have failed to act responsibly at the federal level.

The "natural born" bill would require presidential candidates running in Arizona to submit proof of their constitutional eligibility to the Arizona secretary of state. In the case of President Obama, one such proof would be his long-form, circa 1961, birth certificate. This original form includes, for example, the name of the hospital where a person was born, as well as that of the attending physician—information not included in the computer-generated short form that has appeared online and is of recent vintage.

Just as the state's new check on immigration status seems appropriate, so, too, does this potential requirement that presidential candidates prove their "natural born" bona fides, a requirement that, according to WorldNetDaily.com, is also under consideration in state legislatures in Georgia, New Hampshire, Oklahoma, South Carolina and in the U.S. Congress.

I've never understood the derisive wrath targeting Americans troubled by Obama's refusal, for reasons unknown, to release his long-form birth certificate and end the divisive natural-born controversy—partly, of course, because I am one such American. Another so troubled is Army Lt. Col. Terry Lakin, who, taking seriously his oath to preserve and protect the Constitution, has laid it all on the line: Lakin has stopped obeying military orders, including deployment orders to Afghanistan for his second tour, pending release of the president's original birth document proving his constitutional eligibility to be commander in chief. Unconscionably, the president prefers to see Lakin court-martialed rather than show his old paperwork. Why?

Unanswered, the question consigns us to that limbo of uncertainty—of blurred identities, undefended borders and internationalized elites. But identity matters. The law matters. And the Constitution matters above all.

Truth falling down the memory hole

11/19/10

Wikipedia, the widely read, online, multi-authored encyclopedia, features an entry on the term "memory hole," which originated with the prescient (if not also clairvoyant) George Orwell. The Wikipedia definition begins:

"A memory hole is any mechanism for the alteration or disappearance of inconvenient or embarrassing documents, photographs, transcripts or other records ... particularly as part of an attempt to give the impression that something never happened."

Wikipedia itself may have just offered a good example of how the mechanism works when unknown, unknowable site authorities "took down" a new entry on Lt. Col. Terrence "Terry" Lakin's challenge to President Barack Obama's eligibility to hold office almost as soon it went up. I read a screen shot of the entry and it is factual and non-inflammatory. Did Lakin's page go down the memory hole? Wikipedia readers who seek information about Lakin are redirected to a synopsis of his case within a composite entry on the larger Obama citizenship controversy. Not all but much of the same information is available there, only now, instead of appearing under a biographical entry titled "Terrence L. Lakin," it is included within "Barack Obama Citizenship Conspiracy Theories."

I linger over this incident not only because Lakin supporters have dubbed this week Terry Lakin Action Week, urging American citizens to take the occasion to call their congressional representatives about the case, or even because Lakin, a decorated, 18-year Army officer and physician, faces an upcoming court martial at Fort Meade, Md., on Dec. 14, for refusing to follow orders to redeploy to Afghanistan due to his conviction that the president hasn't proven his eligibility to hold office. Those are both timely reasons to think about Terry Lakin. But there is a larger question here that his sensational case should point us to consider.

Essentially, Wikipedia's editing decision reflects one point of view regarding the Obama "natural-born" citizenship matter — the point of view, as polled by CNN in July, of the 4-in-10 American voters who believe Obama was "definitely born" in the United States. That relatively low percentage of convinced Americans surprised me given the near-100 percent figure that would surely apply to mainstream (read: liberal) and conservative media, with "alternate" exceptions. Rounding out the poll, 29 percent believe the president was "probably born" in the United States; 16 percent think he was "probably born" in another country; 11 percent think he was "definitely born" in another country and only 2 percent had "no opinion." This demonstrates that the topic resonates with practically every American, with a fairly whopping 6-in-10 Americans at least a little uncertain whether Barack Obama was born where he says he was born.

Of course, Obama's failure to release his original 1961 birth certificate (which, contrary to mantra-like misperception, has never been released) is just the beginning. There remains a startling dearth of documentation pertaining to Obama's progress through his 49 years of life that only begins with his birth certificate. A gaping hole — dare I say "memory hole"? -- seems to have consumed all possible Obama records from his education, health, family records, even his pre-presidential political career. But this subject is never taken seriously by the media or the political establishment, including, most glaringly, erstwhile GOP opponent John McCain, who, on being challenged on the eligibility question himself, should have called on Candidate Obama to join him in releasing their bona fides together.

But even to suggest such a thing is to indulge in "conspiracy theories." Not surprisingly, Wikipedia defines this term for us as well, noting that it's "often used dismissively in an attempt to characterize a belief as outlandishly false and held by a person judged to be a crank or a group confined to the lunatic fringe."

In this definition may lie the key to understanding the singularity of the Lakin case. As a senior military officer with an unblemished career, service in war zones, decorations, Pentagon responsibilities including those of flight surgeon for the crew of the Army Chief of Staff, and recommendation for promotion to full colonel, Lakin is neither a "crank" nor a "lunatic." But he has a simple request for the president that drove him to what amounts to a historic act of civil disobedience for which he may well serve time in prison: Release your original 1961 birth certificate so this poisonous issue no longer divides the American people.

Lakin serves the Constitution, Mr. President

12/17/10

Lt. Col. Terrence Lakin didn't rush onto a battleground this week; he walked into a military courtroom. He didn't fire a weapon; he pleaded guilty to disobeying orders related to deployment, and not guilty to the more serious charge of "missing movement." But Lakin put his life — in the sense of his distinguished 17-year career as an Army surgeon, his income, his pension, and his personal freedom — on the line due to his sworn duty to the U.S. Constitution.

All members of the U.S. military take the following oath:

"I, (NAME), having been appointed an officer in the Army of the United States, as indicated above in the grade of _____ do solemnly swear (or affirm) that I will support and defend the Constitution of the United States against all enemies, foreign or domestic, that I will bear true faith and allegiance tot he same; that I take this obligation freely, without any mental reservations or purpose of evasion; and that I will well and faithfully discharge the duties of the office upon which I am about to enter; So help me G0d."

To Lakin, "true faith and allegiance" were more than words; they were a call to action. And so, because the current President of the United States has never released the paperwork necessary to establish his legitimacy as a "natural-born citizen," Lt. Col. Lakin took action.

Over the course of a year, he sought assurances of the president's eligibility from both the military and his congressional delegation.

Receiving none, Lakin questioned his 2010 redeployment orders, believing that as a senior officer ordered back into a war zone—and, not incidentally, ordered to bring along copies of his own birth certificate—he had every right to ask his commander-in-chief to prove his bona fides. Hoping to force the issue into the open, if necessary in a military court, the Bronze Star recipient stopped following his redeployment order.

Here's the rub as I understand it: The military justice system isn't empowered to consider whether a president, duly elected and certified by the Electoral College, inaugurated and sworn in by the chief justice of the U.S. Supreme Court, is anything other than what the civilian leadership says he is. What this means is that Lakin's beau geste may originate within the military order but it falls into the category of civil disobedience—breaking the law to uphold higher principle. It is a higher principle no one else is upholding. Indeed, Lakin's disobedience highlights the existence of a vacuum of "true faith and allegiance" in the land. A gross abdication of civilian responsibility to ensure the lawful transfer of presidential powers took place long before Lakin received orders to return to Afghanistan.

By sacrificing the service career he loves, Lakin serves the Constitution he loves more. He also does the rest of us a great favor. Through this peaceful action, Lakin has directed our attention to the moral corruption of our most trusted public servants who, rather than expose themselves to political inconvenience, permitted the secrecy of Barack Obama to fester in the first place.

As a presidential candidate born in the Panama Canal Zone, Sen. John McCain was himself challenged during the 2008 presidential campaign to prove his bona fides. He, of course, complied—who wouldn't? As candidate, as GOP party leader, as scion of a military family, as U.S. senator, McCain failed at this crucial point simply, logically, correctly, to invite his opponent, Sen. Obama, to do exactly the same.

Like a house of cards that was never built, the rest of the Senate, the House of Representatives, the White House, the judiciary, the nation's political parties, the Electoral College, and, of course, the Obama-enthralled media all followed suit. And the rest is history.

Or would be, if it weren't for heroic Lt. Col. Terrence Lakin.

This week's court martial verdict, guilty on all counts, settles nothing. On the contrary it leaves the question in boldface: What could possibly be preventing the president from showing the American people his original, 1961 birth certificate? What remains to be seen is whether there exists any authority, any leader in this whole country with the courage of a Lakin to ask.

'Let them eat birth certificates'

5/20/11

One feature that marks a totalitarian regime is media that serve as the government's information service. TASS, Radio Berlin, Voice of Hanoi — these were all government entities that conveyed what the dictatorship wanted. The handout comes, the handout is published. The real danger point arrives when propaganda no longer rankles, but flows naturally. That's when authority carries more weight than evidence, and peer pressure suppresses independent thinking. It's also when captives become subjects.

Watching our free, First-Amendment-protected media react to the surprising release of President Barack Obama's long-form birth certificate, I have to wonder: What exactly is the difference?

I exaggerate, but not much. It's been three weeks since Obama first made his long-form birth certificate public on April 27, 2011. Why, suddenly, did he do this, and not in 2008, 2009 or 2010 when this first of the missing bona fides became a focal point of deep national consternation? Why did Obama send lawyers to courtroom after courtroom to keep this simple document hidden — and now mass-produce it on Obama 2012 campaign t-shirts?

Why did Obama prefer to see Army Lt. Col. Terrence Lakin throw away his military career and go to prison for five months rather than, presto, authorize the document's release? The answers have something to do with political inroads Donald Trump was quite unexpectedly making simply by asking natural, obvious questions about Obama that neither Big Media nor someone of un-ignorable celebrity had ever asked before. But that's not the whole story.

We have the long-form birth certificate now — or at least another highly questionable PDF of a scan of a copy of a document to stare at online (and, almost ghoulishly, on those Obama 2012 campaign T-shirts) -- but we don't have all the answers. Certainly we didn't get them from the "off camera and only pen and pad, not for audio" White House briefing on the document's release. That's because the media don't think, can't think to ask for them. Having spent years fending off the rare query about the long-form birth certificate like angry cats snarling that the president had already released his birth certificate, they didn't even seem to notice what chumps the new Obama document — the one they said had already been released — showed them all to be.

Either that, or they channeled their anger at ... Donald Trump. At that moment the non-declared GOP presidential front-runner, Trump got off his helicopter in New Hampshire also on April 27 to discuss his big coup, which is how he viewed the release of this first document in Obama's hidden paper trail. To say the media didn't share Trump's positive views on transparency is the understatement of the year.

First question to Trump: You're taking "credit" but a lot of people say what you caused was a distraction.

The president plays games for three years and Trump caused the "distraction"? And "distraction" from what — White House talking points? Remember, this is supposed to be a professional journalist talking.

Second question to Trump, who said he still wanted to know what took Obama so long: Why is it relevant?

Again, this isn't supposed to be a member of Obama's re-election team, at least not officially. Another question: What are your qualifications to assess it (the birth certificate)?

Another question: Who cares (whether Obama releases his academic records)?

Who cares?

These aren't questions from reporters who follow facts where they lead. These are people who have circled the wagons, and woe to anyone outside. Meanwhile, back at the simultaneous White House briefing, the transcript shows what happened when one journalist haltingly attempted to do his job:

"Q. And this is going to sound — I mean, you can just anticipate what people are going to — remain unconvinced. They're going to say that this is just a photocopy of a piece of paper, you could have typed anything in there. Will the actual certificate be on display or viewable at any -- (laughter.)"

Laughter. That was the answer.

Evidence is a joke to media in thrall to authority, those whose incuriosity about the many mundane documents Obama has mysteriously withheld from us leads to copy fit only for a palace pamphlet. From the transcript: "Q. Dan, was there a debate about whether or not this deserved being discussed by the White House .... was there debate about whether or not this was worthy of the White House?" Let them eat birth certificates.

Why wasn't Obama in contempt of court?

2/10/12

One thing I've learned while researching my new, nearly finished book is that both history and news, history's so-called rough draft, are not written by the "victors" as much as they are censored, twisted and reconfigured by what I can best describe as "the mob."

I'm not referring to the Mafia. What I'm talking about is a mob-like amalgam of sharp elbows and big mouths who dictate acceptable topics, their narrative flow and an approved range of opinion – the consensus-makers. Defying consensus, breaking what amount to Mafia-like vows of "omerta" – silence – and delving into the verboten, is the worst possible crime of anti-mobness, punishable by eternal hooting and marginalization.

Few transgress. Which explains the news blackout on an extraordinary chain of recent events that took place in and around a Georgia courtroom and pertained to challenges to President Obama's eligibility to be a presidential candidate in Georgia in 2012. In the end, the president defeated the challenge. He will be on the Georgia primary ballot come March. But therein lies an amazing tale.

Already I can feel the chill hiss of "birther" at the mere mention of these events, all because I haven't included the mob-requisite catcalls that are "supposed" to go along with such accounts. But there's nothing to mock here.

Last month, after Administrative Law Judge Michael Malihi denied motions by President Obama's lawyer Michael Jablonski both to dismiss proceedings against the president and to quash a subpoena, three attorneys made history. For the first time, attorneys were permitted to enter evidence into the court record challenging Barack Obama's constitutional eligibility to be president.

Georgia state law stipulates: "Every candidate for federal and state office ... shall meet the constitutional and statutory qualifications for holding the office being sought." Plaintiff attorneys Van Irion and Mark Hatfield, who is also a Georgia state representative, argued that President Obama, an American citizen, fails to meet these qualifications because he is not a "natural born" citizen, the constitutional requirement for the presidency. This is due, they argued, to the uncontested fact that his father, Barack Obama Sr. of Kenya, was a British subject, not an American citizen. A third plaintiff attorney, Orly Taitz – object of an eternity's worth of "two-minute hates" within the media mob – introduced evidence that the 44th president of the United States has engaged in what appears to be identity fraud.

Such evidence, as gleaned from a partial list of exhibits introduced in the hearing and published at the American Thinker website, included affidavits from security professionals and other documentation attesting that Obama is using a Connecticut Social Security number (he never lived in Connecticut); that Obama's purported Social Security number was never issued to him; and that – my favorite – his Social Security number "does not pass E-Verify." Another affidavit from an Adobe Illustrator expert maintains that Obama's birth certificate, released last spring to much hype and ballyhoo, is a computer-generated forgery.

Frankly, I was unimpressed with the presidential defense in pre-hearing arguments. For example, Jablonski tried to deflect the Social

Security issue – which, after all, raises serious questions of fraud – by pointing out that "nothing in the Constitution makes … participating in Social Security a prerequisite to serving as president." (So what's a little felonious fraud?) On the "citizenship issue," Jablonski declared the issue was "soundly rejected by 69,456,897 Americans in the 2008 elections, as it has been by every judicial body" since. Is he saying that a lot of votes or previous court actions nullify the legal merits of any new proceeding? I'm no lawyer, but that doesn't seem like much of a legal argument.

The day before the hearing, Jablonksi announced he and the president would "suspend further participation" in the proceedings; Brian Kemp, the Georgia secretary of state, retorted that Jablonski and his client would "do so at your own peril." On hearing day, the defense and defendant didn't just rest; they didn't show up, defying the subpoena summoning Jablonski and the president to court. (The Atlanta Journal-Constitution later styled the president's rejection of his subpoena as a boycott.) Contempt of court, anyone? How about just a headline?

Nope. Headlines could wait – at least until the story came out "right," which it did when both the judge and secretary of state ruled this month in favor of President Obama.

Obama's on the Georgia ballot; "birthers" lose again. The narrative is locked down.

This time around, though, it doesn't feel as if Obama really won.

Silence of the lapdogs

3/22/12

Warning: This column contains news of evidence of possible forgery and fraud in the long-form birth certificate of the president of the United States and – bonus – his Selective Service registration card.

I figure the warning is necessary to prevent Americans, particularly Americans who work in news media and politics, from hurting themselves on any hard, sharp facts that might poke through my discussion of what is surely the biggest scandal to emerge around the seemingly dodgy docs Barack Obama is using to verify his identity.

I refer to the logic- and history-defying news and political blackout of the March 1 press conference called in Maricopa County, Ariz., by Sheriff Joe Arpaio's Cold Case Posse.

I ask you: Have you read in your local paper about the technical evidence that led the posse's three retired criminal investigators and two attorneys to conclude that the birth certificate image White House officials uploaded at the White House website on April 27, 2011, did not originate in a paper format, but rather was created (forged) as an electronic file on a computer?

Have you seen on network or cable news the video clip (one of six posse videos at YouTube) re-creating exactly how an additional fraud might have been committed to forge the president's Selective Service registration card? Heard even conservative talk radio discussing the posse's discovery that immigration files in the National Archives recording overseas arrivals into Hawaii are missing from the week of Obama's 1961 birthday? Or about the retired mailman's affidavit attesting that the mother of ex-Weather Underground terrorist Bill Ayers enthusiastically told him that she helped with "foreign student" Barack Obama's education?

I know my ears pricked up when, watching the posse's press conference online, I heard lead investigator Michael Zullo explain that the 1961 Hawaiian newspaper listings of Barack Obama's birth confirm nothing because the posse "can prove beyond a doubt" that these newspapers announced arrivals of foreign babies as well as native-born. Zullo also announced the posse had "documented evidence of two adopted individuals who were breathing three years prior" and were similarly listed as newborn infants. Heard anything about that?

I know the answer. You have read, seen and heard nothing – and certainly not a peep from any representatives in Congress. The unique exception seems to be poor Republican Rep. Cliff Stearns of Florida, whose mere mentions (better than nothing) of "examining the evidence" get him insta-hammered by the media and White House alike. Obama's communications director, Dan Pfeiffer, one of the presenters of the birth certificate at the White House last spring, actually had the gall to call into question via tweet Stearns' fitness to conduct congressional investigations into the Obama administration's decision to funnel $535 million into Solyndra, the bankrupt solar company. Why? Because Stearns dared to express interest in evidence amassed by veteran law enforcement professionals under Arpaio, himself a 30-year federal law-enforcement official and five-time-elected sheriff.

"1984"-style, we mustn't question. We mustn't look. We certainly mustn't look at questions that cross the narrative of authority. What are we, free people?

Apparently not. One editor told me the problem is the evidence of fraud might prove to be true! A very famous conservative figure told me that if the president were proved to be an identity thief, "that would alienate too many people" from the Republican Party!

I am reminded of Groucho Marx's answer to the question, Are we mice or men? "Throw some cheese on the floor and we'll find out."

Recently, Breitbart.com's new editor at large, Ben Shapiro, was on Mark Gillar's radio show, "Tea Party Power Hour," promoting his conservative media organization's "vetting Obama" campaign. Gillar asked Shapiro if "vetting" Obama would include investigating Obama's birth and/or Selective Service documents. Absolutely not, Shapiro replied, explaining that he didn't believe this was an issue. "I am discouraging people from spending time on this," Shapiro said, emphasizing once again that he himself did not believe there were irregularities in the documents since, as he put it, he knew Media Matters would be listening to the interview.

The walls have ears? Shapiro's concern almost makes Media Matters sound like a secret police outfit with a gulag for journalists who ask too many questions. In reality, it's an ideologically driven, left-wing attack group funded by ideologically driven, left-wing George Soros.

Shapiro continued, quite candidly: "It's an issue on which people are being marginalized very easily and very quickly at this point."

Marginalized by whom? The Soros-funded attack machine? The liberal-dominated "mainstream media"? Fox News-dominated conservative media? The Obama White House?

Clearly, something has us all on lockdown. That's much, much scarier than even the amazing possibility that some con artist might be pulling off the biggest scam in history.

Disowning birth certificates, disowning truth

4/20/12

Below is this week's syndicated column: "Is Obama Disowning His Online Birth Certificate?" It takes in the shifting strategy of the Obama defense team in fending off challenges to Obama's eligibility to appear on presidential primary ballots. Obama's eligibility is a signal concern for the nation which should be the subject of informed, serious debate on the front pages, on news shows, and also, most important, in the Congress. Such debate is non-existent. Such concern is non-existent, too. It doesn't seem to matter to the citizenry that a fraudster may be completing one term in the White House while seeking another.

I recently had the occasion to discuss the matter with a very famous American conservative.

Famous Conservative said to me: Tell me what columns of yours are getting a big response lately.

I had earlier written this column about the Georgia ballot challenge hearing in which President Obama *ignored a subpoena* for the certified copy of his birth certificate (among other documents). This column elicited a great response from readers, many of whom asked me the same question: why this important story wasn't being covered in the media.

They're really interested in this whole eligibility story, I said.

Famous Conservative: I'll bet they are.

Me: Aren't you?

FC: No.

Me: No? Why aren't you?

FC: If this were happening back at the time of the election, maybe.

I told FC this *is* an election (ding-dong).

FC: Exactly. But this will alienate the people we need to defeat him at the polls.

I made some naive-sounding comment (which I thoroughly subscribe to) about the seeking the truth regardless of the outcome, adding that the truth would likely alienate plenty of people from Obama, too.

Impasse.

New tack for Famous Conservative: If this were true, why hasn't Rush or Hannity taken it on?

Me: They're afraid.

FC: (Scoffs.)

Me: Look, Rush won't talk about a lot of things: Islamization, for one. Sharia. Muslim Brotherood, those kinds of things. He has a comfort zone.

FC: (Disbelief.)

Impasse.

FC: Well, maybe if some respected conservative journalist were to examine the story —

Me: (What am I, chopped liver?) Who, for instance?

FC: John Fund, Daniel Henniger ...

Hey boys, have at it. But there's a problem. According to the FC (1) the truth will alienate voters so we mustn't seek the truth; and (2) it can't be true anyway because otherwise Rush, Sean, John and Dan would be all over the story. Of course, if FC's conservative journalists subscribe to #1 or some variation thereon as partisans or Republicans, we'll never get to #2. Meanwhile, across the journalistic aisle, the MSM has the another, equally heavy stake in preventing the truth from outing. They want Obama re-elected.

What's wrong with this picture? Conservative logic, conservative morality.

Needless to say, I didn't make any inroads with FC although FC's spouse shares my concern in the subject, so that's something.

The column:

Almost exactly one year ago – with Donald Trump on top of presidential polls and author Jerome Corsi on top of Amazon's best-seller list, both for asking where President Barack Obama's "real" birth certificate was – Judith Corley, the president's personal attorney, flew to Hawaii. She went there to pick up two certified copies of the president's long-form birth certificate from the Hawaii Department of Health.

At least, that's what then-White House Counsel Robert Bauer told us last April 27 at a White House press briefing called to unveil the new, certified document. Multiple copies were passed out to the press, while NBC's Savannah Guthrie became the one witness I know of to touch the certified document. (She reported she "felt the raised seal.") A computer image of this Obama long-form birth certificate appeared on the White House website, where now you and I can download it for ourselves as proof of the president's bona fides.

The Forbidden Columns

Or is it?

It is this same Internet image that the Cold Case Posse, a group of lawyers and former law enforcement professionals assembled by Maricopa County, Ariz., Sheriff Joe Arpaio to vet Obama's identity documents, has concluded is most likely a forgery. At its March 1 press conference, the posse further explained that it believed the online image *originated* as a computer file. In other words, a paper document did not exist before the image appeared on the White House website.

If the posse's mind-blowing findings are correct, what is it that Judith Corley couriered back to Washington? And what is it that Savannah Guthrie touched?

I find such questions most intriguing – even if the rest of the media do not – particularly after last week's court hearing into Obama's eligibility to appear on the ballot in the New Jersey presidential primary. After literally dozens of such eligibility cases since 2008 (evidently, the media are waiting for a discernible story trend to emerge before they pounce), I can report, having watched a video of the New Jersey hearing online, that the president's team is making progress. Only now it's *away* from his long-form birth certificate.

The curious fact is, President Obama's attorney, Alexandra Hill, couldn't have been more adamant about not citing the online birth certificate as a means of proving the president's identity in this recent challenge – and after everyone went to so much trouble to get it! Indeed, she called the Internet image "legally irrelevant," arguing that New Jersey law doesn't specifically call for a birth certificate to qualify a presidential candidate for the ballot.

Exactly how a presidential candidate demonstrates he is at least 35 years old and "natural born," the constitutional requirement New Jersey upholds, Hill didn't say, but Administrative Law Judge Jeff Masin found her arguments persuasive to the point of preventing an expert witness from offering testimony that the online image is a forgery.

Even though the Obama team entered no documentation of the president's identity into the record – not even that "certified" birth document Obama's personal lawyer traveled so far to retrieve – Judge Masin managed to find that the president was both born in Hawaii and "natural born."

Neat, huh? But note the shift in legal tactics. If, in New Jersey, the online birth certificate was "legally irrelevant," in January's Georgia eligibility hearing, the president's lawyer, Michael Jablonski, considered it legally decisive. Jablonski cited "the documents evidencing the birth of President Obama" that are available online to try to quash a subpoena that "commanded" Obama to come to court and bring "any and all birth records" with him (among other documents).

A golden opportunity to show off that certified, hand-couriered birth doc from Hawaii, and be done with it, no? No. When Administrative Law Judge Michael Malihi refused to quash the subpoena, Jablonski and Obama ignored it. They just didn't show up. Not to worry: Flouted subpoena and all, and without any evidence from the Obama team, Judge Malihi found that the president was both born in Hawaii and "natural born," too.

Amazing how that works, and no matter what the president's lawyers do – so long as they don't enter tangible evidence of the president's identity into the court record.

As for that new birth certificate that came online last April? Since government and media have abdicated their responsibility to help determine whether it's the real McCoy or a forgery, what else is there to do but wish it a happy first birthday?

Repeat after me: The identity thief is a Socialist

4/13/12

"Only Voters Can Stop the Insidious Spread of Socialism" – syndicate title – got through on Townhall, not Exmainer (at least I couldn't find it).

Now that Election 2012 is shaping up as a contest between President Obama and Mitt Romney, an observation and a prediction.

Our nation heads into a presidential campaign with an incumbent whose online birth certificate and Selective Service registration card are almost certainly forgeries, and this is a nonissue. (Don't ask about the subpoena from a Georgia court that Obama ignored. Everyone else did, too.)

That's the observation. The prediction is that unless voters come to view Barack Obama as a "socialist" – even a "democratic socialist" – and, as such, an existential threat to our (in theory) constitutional republic, President Obama, funny papers and all, will be re-elected in November.

The two stories are related. Both turn on the relative power of "evidence" vs. "narrative." By evidence, I mean the facts and clues that support an argument or hypothesis. By narrative, I mean propaganda. For example, there is evidence of fraud in Obama's identity documents, but such evidence does not fit the narrative that Obama's identity documents are authentic. In the face of narrative, We the People are supposed to ignore the evidence. All of our officials and elites do.

Similarly, there is plentiful evidence of Barack Obama's socialist beliefs and ties – Stanley Kurtz's 2010 book "Radical-in-Chief: Barack Obama and the Untold Story of American Socialism" meticulously lays it out – but the narrative insists that Obama is anything but a socialist. And, as with the evidence of identity fraud, woe and besmirching to anyone who mentions it.

Now, what do I mean by socialism? Too often, and sometimes by design, defining socialism becomes an absurdly contentious exercise. If we narrowly define socialism as "government ownership of the means of production," however, we'll never know what hit us until it's too late. I found it helpful to learn that Alexander Solzhenitsyn recognized there was no "single precise definition of socialism" out there. This is probably due to vagaries of time and place, and to the fact that, short of a violent revolution, socialism is a complex, messy work in progress. What's vital to identify is the direction of that progress. If the progress tends toward increasing economic collectivism and political centralization, the movement is socialist. If the progress is in the other direction, the movement is known as capitalist.

By leaps of collectivism and bounds of centralization, Barack Obama has been taking the country in a socialist direction since he took office. I would add, however, that this is the direction the country has been moving since 1933. That's another story.

But it's all part of a story we're not supposed to discuss in concrete terms. This must change this year, or else. Or else what? More and more socialism. That means less and less freedom.

On Oct. 12, 2008, Joe the Plumber – who, today, as Samuel Wurzelbacher is running for Congress – prompted candidate Obama to repeat the socialist mantra, in Obama's words, that "when you spread the wealth around it's good for everybody." If you recall, this led to an intense, frenzied media vetting – of Joe the Plumber. Obama and his ties – for example, to the socialist New Party and the socialist front organization ACORN – went *unreported* in the print and television mainstream, even as new evidence was exploding like fireworks on mainly conservative Internet news sites and blogs, particularly in those final weeks of the campaign.

To date, Mitt Romney has balked at labeling President Obama or even his policies as socialist, probably calculating that the label distracts from his arguments. I implore him to reconsider lest Obama's and the Democrats' stealth socialism finish off the country once and for all.

What's fascinating, meanwhile, is that Obama is underscoring his own socialism by disavowing it – even as no one in the political arena is accusing him of it. Psychologists probably would call this phenomenon "projection."

Joel Gehrke of the Washington Examiner noted that twice last week Obama defended his economic ideas against charges of socialism – charges no one is actually making. This week, Gehrke picked up on the president's stated denial that he is trying to "redistribute wealth," even as Obama touted a plan to do exactly that with the "Buffett Rule." This rule, as Obama explained to Joe the Plumber back in 2008, "spreads the wealth around" by taxing millionaires at a higher rate to pay for "investments" (a deceptive word for government programs). These "investments," Obama told a Florida audience, "haven't been made as some grand scheme to redistribute wealth from one group to another. This is not some socialist dream."

That's the narrative, of course. Who really believes it's supported by the facts?

Obama's eligibility saga continues unreported: the dirtiest secret of all

6/8/12

Earlier this spring, President Obama's attorney Alexandra Hill went to court in New Jersey over a challenge to her client's eligibility to appear on the 2012 presidential primary ballot.

New Jersey citizens, represented by attorney Mario Apuzzo, made two claims: that Barack Obama has not proved he meets the conditions for presidential eligibility (namely, that he is a "natural born citizen"), and that the proof Obama released attesting to his bona fides (an Internet image of his long-form birth certificate) is fraudulent.

Hill's argument? A presidential candidate has no obligation under New Jersey state law to prove his eligibility, period.

Administrative Law Judge Jeff Masin agreed with Hill and ruled in Obama's favor. He further asserted that, absent such an obligation, the Internet image of Obama's birth certificate – the same image Sheriff Joe Arpaio's Cold Case Posse investigators believe to be a forgery – is "legally irrelevant."

The upshot for New Jersey? As the president's attorney put it, "you could have Mickey Mouse" on the presidential ballot so long as he received the requisite 1,000 petition signatures.

While such exercises may more closely resemble a tax cheat's search for loopholes than a court ensuring the rectitude of a presidential primary, our elites consider it all a big yawn, something to endure until those awful people (denigrated as "birthers") go away. This is the dirtiest secret of the great, non-reported Obama eligibility saga: The integrity of our leaders and our Constitution doesn't matter to those citizens who are actually responsible for upholding it.

On the contrary, there is an unchecked rush to abdicate responsibility – a manifestation of "the death of the grown-up," as I titled my first book. The following questions, asked last week by the three judges who heard the New Jersey case on appeal [video here], typify the official attitude:

"Why is it incumbent on New Jersey to resolve this issue?"
Subtext: Voters, schmoters.

"What statute of New Jersey says he (Obama) has to prove his eligibility?"

Subtext: Please make it someone else's problem.

"Why won't Congress and (the Electoral College) protect the integrity of the election?"

Subtext: It's not our problem.

"Why don't we accept at face value that they made that determination (after the 2008 election)?"

Subtext: It's no one's problem anymore. Can we go home yet?

"Do you agree that we need not reach the issue of natural born citizen?"

Subtext: We don't want to walk that scary plank, whatever we do.

Surprise, surprise, the appeals court upheld President Obama's eligibility. The judges, along with Obama's counsel, agreed that any eligibility questions should be kicked upstairs to Congress and the Electoral College – and after the November 2012 election.

That'll be the day. Of course, the best way to settle the matter would be for Congress to investigate immediately: Is President Obama eligible to run for re-election? What's up with that funky online ID of his? No junior high school would hire a P.E. teacher on the strength of that.

That'll be the day, too. Congress has shirked its responsibility since 2008, when the U.S. Senate affirmed Sen. John McCain's eligibility to become president but not then-Sen. Barack Obama's.

Why not?

As I've previously noted, some media outlets that subscribe to this column have informed me they won't run anything I write on the eligibility subject.

No doubt other writers are similarly censored – sometimes even after publication. For example, on March 5, 2012, Floyd and Mary Beth Brown's syndicated column, "Sheriff Joe Exposes Forgery of Obama's Selective Service Registration," appeared at Townhall.com. Then it was taken down. On March 24, 2012, John Mariotti published a piece at Forbes.com called "Is There an Impostor in the White House?" That was taken down, too. As WND noted, Geraldo Rivera's May 24, 2012, WABC radio interview with "birther Lord Christopher Monckton" is still listed in the WABC archive, but the audio file of the show is no longer there.

Why isn't it?

Leaving all these questions hanging is unhealthy. And it's not enough to promise to do better in the future, as former Republican Rep. Pete Hoekstra of Michigan, now running a Senate primary campaign, recently suggested. Advocating a department to check presidential credentials next time around, Hoekstra said: "I hate to say it, but I think the debate is over. We lost the debate in 2008 when our presidential nominee said, 'I ain't talking about it.' ... I'd love to ... say that I'm going to fight it, we're going to beat it and we're going to win it. I think it wasn't fought and we lost it."

It wasn't fought and we lost it. What a great motto for the shirkers of responsibility today, and the subjects of tyranny tomorrow.

Question: Where was Obama born? Answer ...

6/13/12, blog entry

I don't know.

What I do know is that Obama's life "story" reeks of fraud, as independent investigators pull chunks and shards of evidence from the Obama deep, attempting to piece them together as a way through what should be a clear roadmap of a man's early life but is instead a maze of purposeful deception. It is a maze thick with irony beginning with the notion that the same man who wrote two (count 'em, two) autobiographical volumes before age 47 won't release one single document attesting to his identity, his family, his education, his travels, his careers. (No, I don't count the dodgy computerized images that have appeared, presto, before our eyes, high-tech-smoke-and-mirrors style.) It is a maze whispering with rumors as well, sometimes leading to dead ends.

In the past four months, I have written four columns syndicated by Universal Uclick devoted to the eligibility saga as it wends its way through different state courts and Sheriff Joe Arpaio's Cold Case Posse investigation, as well as the attendant issue of gross media and political irresponsibility in failing to address the story in any serious, professional way. These columns are: "Why wasn't Obama slapped with contempt of court?" (2/09/12), "Why the silence about Obama's historic scam?" (3/22/12), "Is Obama disowning online birth certificate?" (4/19/12), and last week's "Spineless officials choose to ignore Obama's fraud" (6/07/12). Some of my weekly-like-clockwork outlets chose not to publish these four columns, a fact which itself has aroused commentary of its own, with Roger Kimball and Thomas Lifson, for example, addressing the supremely important issue of censorship and self-censorship such "spikes" reveal.

A fifth column, "Only voters can stop insidious spread of socialism" 4/12/12, which makes plain reference to the Obama document fraud, sneaked through. Before these 2012 columns, the last time I wrote about the eligibility issue in a column was to cover last year's White House press conference at which the long-form computer image was unveiled— "Let Them Eat Birth Certificates" 5/20/11. That column appeared in some places and not others.

While this is merely my bird's eye of the story — and there is a busy, sharp-eyed flock of independent writers, investigators, lawyers, and concerned citizens out there trying to solve the mysteries — I think the story is starting to seep slowly into a new layer of consciousness. For example, after Frank Gaffney, noted national security expert and former Pentagon official who served in the Reagan administration (and one of my 19 co-authors on the Team B II Report, *Shariah: The Threat to America*) chose for the first time to devote one of his hour-long radio shows to the topic, WorldNetDaily.com, leader of the pack on the eligibility issue, wrote up the interview, which then made it into the Washington Times 24/7 email alert.

Will the newspaper proper take on the story? Will *any* newspaper proper take on the story? There is another irony to the whole Obama eligibility story in the fact that with the 40th anniversary of Watergate upon us (as the Washington Post is busy reminding us), the new platitude in Washington to bemoan the demise of investigative reporting. And how! But it is not just a lack of financial resources, as former Post exec ed Leonard Downie Jr. tells us. We are witnessing a colossal failure of imagination and professional duty. Perhaps more than ever, fealty to ideology shapes news-gathering, while the word of authority (Dear Leader) takes precedence over evidence — over logic itself. A high mental hurdle blocks most people from even seeing the issue, a hurdle that has arisen in the pin-drop hush on the subject in all mainstream circles. This week, The American Thinker blog, another rare stalwart in the quest for answers on the eligibility issue, published an essay in which Nick Chase tracks his own progress in thinking to a point where he could finally vault that hurdle and address the evidence himself despite what he calls "the cone of silence." Unbound, he's attested to the fraudulence on the online long form over five essays since April. A fine example.

More please.

Ohio, identity fraud and the presidency

7/8/12, blog entry

On July 2, Susan Daniels, a licensed private investigator and write-in candidate for president in Ohio, filed suit in Geauga County against Ohio Secretary of State Jon Husted. Daniels presents credible evidence that President Obama is fraudulently using a Connecticut Social Security number, and, as a result, calls on the court: 1) to prohibit Ohio Secretary of State Hulsted from entering Obama's name on the Ohio presidential ballot in November until it is determined that Obama's Social Security number was properly issued; and further, (2) to order Secretary of State

Hulsted to investigate Obama's fraudulent use of a Connecticut Social Security number.

Jack Cashill's report is here. I just had a chance to listen to Daniels' interview with Mark Gillar here, and read her complaint here. It is all explosive stuff. It fails to explode inside the media bubble only because that media bubble, Left and Right, is a vacuum hermetically sealed against reality. That doesn't mean, however, that the pressure stops building.

What the media, Right and Left, are not telling the American people is this: Daniels discovered in 2009 that, since the 1980s, Barack Obama has been using a Social Security number issued in the late 1970s by the state of Connecticut. Daniels' evidence begins with the three-digit prefix -- 042 -- which tags the number as having originated in Connecticut. (The Social Security agency abandoned state prefixes shortly after Daniels' findings began to surface. Connected? Another question that should be investigated.)

This 042-number is linked to, among other things, Obama's 1980 Selective Service Registration card (alleged to be a forgery by Sheriff Arpaio), his Massachusetts driver's license from his Harvard Law School days; and his 2009 tax return. But Barack Obama has no known or traceable connection to the state of Connecticut—notwithstanding the unretracted lie or mistake uttered by Fox's Bill O'Reilly who wrongly stated on the air that Obama Sr. lived in Connecticut for a time and somehow that explained everything. Obama Sr. never lived in Connecticut.

There's more. Daniels also flags the entirely anomalous appearance of two birth dates associated with the 042-number: 1961 (Obama's birth year) and 1890. Out of "thousands" of Social Security numbers Daniels has checked as a P.I., she says she have never seen a second birth date attach itself to a number.

How could this be so? Why is it so? Daniels' suit places the responsibility of answering these troubling questions with Ohio Secretary of State Husted—and that means not permitting the Obama defense team to wiggle out of such charges by asserting, as the president's lawyer did in Georgia this year when the Social Security issue came before the court: "Nothing in the Constitution makes ... participating in Social Security a prerequisite to serving as president."

Not exactly a ringing endorsement of his client's bona fides.

Daniels' challenge is probably unique among the well over Obama 100 eligibility lawsuits filed to date because it focuses exclusively on the fraud angle. That is, Daniels' case in no way bears on the Constitutional "natural-born" issue, or even matters related to the Obama birth certificate, which Arpaio's team and many experts also believe to be a forgery.

What next? Daniels tells Gillar that a response—a hearing date—from the court may be expected no later than 28 days after her complaint is served to Husted. That gives the forces of suppression and secrecy a scant month to cook up more suppression and secrecy.

Will it work ... again?

Forty-five percent

7/22/12

Cold Case Posse lead investigator Mike Zullo explaining more anomalies in the White House illustration known as the president's "birth certificate." Even though the media isn't reporting the story, 45 percent of the American people get the idea.

From YouGov polling:

> Polling conducted last week suggests that whatever remaining effect of the release of the birth certificate that persisted through January is completely gone today. From June 30-July 2, 2012, YouGov surveyed 1000 Americans and asked whether "Barack Obama was born in the United States of America." In the table below, I present these results, alongside the earlier polls that I presented in my January post.

	"Barack Obama was born in the United States": Full Sample			
	April 2011		Jan. 2012	July 2012
	Before release of birth certificate	After release of birth certificate		
True	55%	67%	59%	55%
False	15%	13%	17%	20%
Not sure	30%	20%	24%	25%

> These polls demonstrate that the public is back where it was before Obama released his long form birth certificate. In April 2011 55% of the public believed that Obama was born in the United States. Today 55% of the public believes that he was born in the United States.

Which, to engage in some fancy math, means 45 percent of the American people do not believe he was born in the United States.

I would infer that this means 45 percent of the American people are not persuaded by the document showcased online at the White House website as proof of Barack Huseein Obama's brith in Hawaii. Which, logically speaking, tells us that 45 percent of the American people understand on some level that they are victims of a gigantic fraud.

This reflects an extraordinary crisis with legal and constitutional implications, whether the media and government ignore it or not.

Honolulu greets the posse

7/2712

I'm sorry to report that the substantive findings of the latest press conference held by Maricopa County, Ariz., Sheriff Joe Arpaio's Cold Case Posse will not be appearing on Fox, on CNN or in the Washington Post. They will not be appearing in the media, period. I guess the nation's press corps is too busy submitting its work to Obama and Romney campaign officials for "quote approval" – as the New York Times recently confessed in an outbreak of candor – to report on anything.

To remain a free people, a new kind of do-it-yourself journalism is in order. For starters, I recommend every American seek out and watch the two Cold Case Posse press conferences on YouTube. You report and you decide. It's better that way.

The bottom line is this: The posse investigation has amassed extensive computer forensics and other evidence that the Barack Obama birth certificate posted on the White House website is a forgery. Again, I urge readers to review the case for themselves. What I want to focus on today is something at least as bad as document fraud. I want to focus on document fraud cover-up.

Listening to posse lead investigator Mike Zullo describe the investigation's itinerary during the posse's recent trip to Hawaii, a picture of statewide stonewalling emerges. Dead ends guarded by hunkered-down public officials. The same non-answers to the simplest questions. Canned responses. If CNN, Chris Matthews, Obama press secretary Jay Carney, Rachel Maddow, the Huffington Post and the Los Angeles Times all didn't know so much better, a neutral observer might say it sounded like a conspiracy – an agreement between at least two people to do something shifty.

Kapiolani Medical Center was the first stop for Zullo and Detective Brian Mackiewicz. That's where the birth certificate says Obama was born. Why visit? A retired doctor told the posse that when he was a medical resident at Kapiolani in 1970, it was common practice for a nurse to record by hand the name of every expectant mother as she entered the delivery room. After the register was filled, it was filed in the hospital library archives. Those archives are open to the public – with permission from Kapiolani.

One thing Zullo makes shockingly clear in his recent presentation is the legal flimsiness of a Hawaiian birth certificate under the best of circumstances. A Hawaiian birth certificate is evidence only of information on file with the state; it is not evidence that this information is true. Hawaiian law spells this out by categorizing its state-issued birth certificates as "prima facie" evidence. This makes corroborating evidence – such as infant vaccine records, scene-setting baby pictures or, in this particular case, a delivery-room entry log – essential. There is zero such corroborating evidence in our Obama files. All we have is that posse-disputed online image floating before our eyes.

Now, imagine the laurels that would come to the hospital librarian who brandished a maternity log with Stanley Ann Dunham's name inscribed in 1961 in the investigators' faces – the follow-up high-fives on "Good Morning America," the round of applause on David Letterman's "Late Show," maybe even a thank-you note from Barack and Michelle for finally putting Arpaio's Cold Case Posse on ice.

Instead, the reply to the posse's request from Kapiolani was: The hospital wasn't in the business of investigating birth certificates but was in the business of saving lives. (How unrehearsed.) "They all but threw us out," Zullo recalled.

It was a similar story at the Hawaii Department of Health, where two uniformed policemen were called in after the investigators showed their credentials and asked to speak to state registrar Alvin Onaka. (The cops looked quite irritated at having been called, noted Zullo.) "Mr. Onaka doesn't speak to the public," the investigators were told. Translation: Mr. Onaka was hiding in his office. Fortunately, Deputy Attorney General Jill Nagamine deigned to give the posse 15 minutes.

Were the two certified copies of the birth certificate that Obama's personal attorney is said to have brought back to Washington identical to the image posted at the White House website? Nagamine wouldn't answer the question, repeatedly invoking a Hawaiian statute she said prevented her from talking about the copy of the White House birth certificate Zullo had with him.

He tried a different tack. Say, for instance, he had to release his driver's license, Zullo said. And that Nagamine scanned his license into a computer. Before the public could view it, however, she changed or added information. "Is that still my driver's license?" he asked Nagamine.

Hawaii's deputy attorney general replied: "But you still have a driver's license."

No, you don't. You have a forgery.

So what do we have in Hawaii – and in the White House?

'Outing the Muslim Brotherhood'

7/28/12

Be alarmed: The U.S. government continues to be "advised by organizations and individuals that the U.S. government itself has identified in federal courts as fronts for the international Muslim Brotherhood."

So wrote Rep. Michele Bachmann, R-Minn., in a lengthy, heavily footnoted answer to a query last week from Rep. Keith Ellison, D-Minn. He was seeking more information about the reasons Bachmann plus four other House Republicans – Louis Gohmert (Texas), Trent Franks (Ariz.), Lynn Westmoreland (Ga.) and Thomas Rooney (Fla.) – requested Inspector General investigations into "potential Muslim Brotherhood infiltration" of the government. (See all of the letters here.)

Yes, that would be the same Muslim Brotherhood whose leaders are sweeping to power in the Middle East – most recently in Egypt. There, the new president, Mohamed Morsi, fired up voters this spring by declaring: "The Koran is our constitution. The Prophet Muhammad is our leader. Jihad is our path. And death for the sake of Allah is our most lofty aspiration." That, by the way, is the Muslim Brotherhood's motto.

Brotherhood-linked groups in the U.S. still take a low-key approach, at least publicly. Thanks to the FBI discovery of a key Muslim Brotherhood document, we know what they're up to, even who some of them are. The document, entered into evidence during the landmark Holy Land Foundation terrorism finance trial, presents the Brotherhood plan for "civilization-jihad" against the U.S. It describes the group's "grand jihad" to destroy "the Western civilization from within ... so that it is eliminated and (Islam) is made victorious over all religions." Further, it declares Brotherhood support for "the global Islamic state wherever it is." It also lists 29 of "our organization and the organizations of our friends" – i.e., front groups. Among them are such well-known Islamic organizations as the Islamic Society of North America, or ISNA, and the Council on American Islamic Relations, or CAIR, both of which remain unindicted co-conspirators.

What is beyond shocking – beyond reason – is that such anti-American Brotherhood-linked groups and individuals have variously engaged, particularly since 9/11, with the U.S. government. Is it a coincidence that U.S. policy has since become receptive to, if not openly supportive of the Muslim Brotherhood? This is the serious question these House Republicans want answered.

"Influence" can be an intangible thing, but sometimes there are signs. For example, someone, something, somehow managed to convince Director of National Intelligence James Clapper to testify before the House Intelligence Committee in 2011 that the Muslim Brotherhood was a "largely secular organization" without "an overarching agenda."

This is a laughable statement – unless spoken in earnest by the DNI. Then the question becomes: Is it possible that in Clapper's chain of information there is, in fact, disinformation? Other questions Bachmann and her colleagues have concern the Homeland Security Department, where, for example, Mohamed Magid, head of ISNA, the largest Brotherhood front group, according to the U.S. government itself, also serves as a member of Homeland Security's Countering Violent Extremism Working Group.

Are there national security implications in the influence of Brotherhood front groups on Justice Department and FBI policies on terrorism? Bachmann & Co. want to find out. How about the ongoing relationship between domestic Brotherhood front groups and the Organization of Islamic Cooperation, or OIC? As Bachmann notes, this foreign bloc of 57 Muslim nations "claims jurisdiction over Muslims in non-Muslim lands, defines human rights as Shariah, and advocates that Muslims not assimilate into the cultures of non-Muslims." What of Secretary of State Hillary Clinton's decision to team up with the OIC to pass a U.N. resolution to restrict free speech deemed to be "defamation" of Islam? Such an effort flouts the First Amendment and also reverses U.S. policy. Could malign influence be a factor?

These five Republicans have also expressed concern over media reports that Clinton's longtime top aide Huma Abedin has family relations (late father, mother, brother) with ties to Muslim Brotherhood groups. Her mother, for example, reportedly belongs to the Muslim Sisterhood, a group the new first lady of Egypt also reportedly belongs to. Are such reports true? Do they have security implications? These are questions Americans have a right to know.

"For us to raise issues about a highly based U.S. government official with known immediate family connections to foreign extremist organizations is not a question of singling out Ms. Abedin," Bachmann writes. "In fact, these questions are raised by the U.S. government of anyone seeking a security clearance."

I'm guessing the bit about Abedin is the only piece of this complex story most readers have heard of. It has come to dominate and distort the response to a rational and patriotic effort to bring more transparency to government decision-making in order to ensure that it remains Muslim Brotherhood-free.

Why would anyone want to stay in the dark about that?

Brennan: Jihad apologist to lead fight against it?

2/14/13

We all know what happens when the fox guards the chicken coop – or do we?

This is not a rhetorical question. Do we Americans understand what happens when a wily predator is custodian of defenseless clucks? Our state of psychological disarmament makes us unable to recognize even such an obvious threat. I can't think of another explanation for why the country hasn't melted down the Capitol switchboard with phone calls to U.S. senators beseeching them not to confirm John Brennan as the next director of the CIA.

What's so scary about Brennan, currently President Obama's top adviser for counterterrorism?

More than any other Obama administration official, Brennan has openly cultivated groups in this country that I describe, with good reason, as being of the jihadist persuasion. Simultaneously, Brennan misinforms or dissembles about the nature of jihad itself. How can such a man helm America's premier intelligence institution, which, at least ostensibly, is engaged in thwarting jihad?

Consider Brennan's interactions with the Islamic Society of North America (ISNA). Despite evidence presented (and later upheld) in federal court during the landmark 2008 Holy Land Foundation trial, which established ISNA as a Muslim Brotherhood organization and financial supporter of the terrorist organization Hamas (a wing of the Muslim Brotherhood), Brennan has continued to meet with ISNA officials and participate in ISNA events.

At ISNA's annual conference in 2009, for example, Brennan delivered the keynote address. In 2010, Brennan spoke at a "town hall" with ISNA president Ingrid Mattson. As former FBI agent John Guandolo wrote recently in a paper he shared with me, Brennan continues to grant ISNA leaders access to senior government officials and support their appointments to key intelligence positions. (Guandolo and I are among the 19 co-authors of "Shariah: The Threat to America.")

"The current president of ISNA, Imam Mohamed Magid, sits on the Homeland Security Advisory Council, which reports directly to (Homeland) Secretary (Janet) Napolitano," Guandolo writes. "With the support of John Brennan, Imam Magid works with the National Security Council, which has publicly applauded this Hamas supporter."

Guandolo was referring to praise heaped on Magid in 2011 by then-deputy national security adviser Denis McDonough. McDonough is now Obama's chief of staff.

If this all sounds surreal, welcome to our world. Here, the leader of a group that the U.S. government has designated a conspirator to promote and finance Islamic terrorism is tapped to advise the same government on how to defuse Islamic terrorism – or, rather, what the government prefers to call "extremism."

The flip side to this affinity for Muslim Brotherhood groups is hostility toward officials who dare to unmask them. Last year, a reporter asked Brennan to assess extremely alarming evidence of Muslim Brotherhood penetration of the U.S. government brought forward by five House Republicans led by Rep. Michele Bachmann – "the National

Security Five," as Newt Gingrich would dub them. Brennan's reaction was to dismiss the charges and the elected representatives. "I have no idea what it is that they are making reference to," Brennan said, "and I'm not even going to try to divine what it is that sometimes comes out of Congress."

His reaction is much the same when it comes to what is called, in military parlance, the "enemy threat doctrine." Take jihad. We must not "describe our enemy as 'jihadists' or 'Islamists,'" Brennan said in 2010, "because jihad is a holy struggle, a legitimate tenet of Islam, meaning to purify oneself or one's community."

This notion of "jihad" as self-help is often disseminated by dupes in ignorance. It is deception, or "taqiyya," however, when voiced by those who know better. Nonviolent jihad barely shows up in the Quran. (Sorbonne Ph.D. linguist Tina Magaard came up with only one appearance of spiritual struggle in her detailed textual analysis of the Quran – as opposed to 50 references that invoke violent aggression.) Meanwhile, the first definition of "jihad" in the authoritative Sunni law book "Reliance of the Traveller" reads: "Jihad means to war against non-Muslims."

If intelligence expert Brennan knows this, he doesn't like to talk about it. When he was pressed in 2010 by a member of the Washington Times editorial page for an example of armed jihad in history, Brennan packed up his papers and abruptly left the meeting. I recently watched a video of the meeting, which is on YouTube, and his behavior is very strange.

So are his ideas about Islam and jihad. "Al-Qaida has perverted Islam and has corrupted the concept of Islam," Brennan declared in a 2010 press conference, thereby obscuring the clear Quranic imperatives on waging jihad that drove Umar Farouk Abdulmutallab, the so-called underwear bomber, to try to bring down a passenger plane over Detroit on Christmas Day 2009. Why does Brennan, a counterterrorism expert, say such things?

Guandolo offers two possible reasons: 1) Brennan is "functionally incapable of reasonable … thought on this matter," or 2) he is "intentionally misleading U.S. government leaders on al-Qaida's stated objectives and how they marry up to the requirements of Shariah (Islamic law)."

Either reason disqualifies John Brennan to be CIA director. Still, not one single senator has raised this crucial matter during confirmation hearings.

There is something else. Guandolo has gone public with an allegation that Brennan, while CIA station chief in Saudi Arabia in the 1990s, converted to Islam. This allegation is based on anonymous sources within the government who, Guandolo says, "have direct knowledge" of the conversion.

Given Guandolo's own counterterrorism expertise as an FBI subject-expert in Islam and professional observer of the Muslim Brotherhood, his charges carry heft. Detractors try to undermine them by resurrecting an inappropriate sexual relationship Guandolo had as an FBI agent with an FBI informant during a high-profile corruption investigation. This might be relevant if, for example, Guandolo were running for office as a traditional-values candidate. He is, however, trying to get information he discovered using his skills as an investigator into the public square for evaluation.

He's halfway there – that is, the story has entered the pubic square via talk radio, the blogosphere and the news media, including WND.com, MSNBC, TheBlaze, The Atlantic, U.S. News & World Report, the Daily Mail and Al Arabiya. Will it be evaluated? It should, for what Guandolo believes it tells us about Brennan.

"Why has (Brennan) kept this piece of information secret?" Guandolo writes. "The reason appears to be self-evident. ... Mr. Brennan's conversion to Islam was the culmination of a hostile campaign by a foreign intelligence service. ... Someone who has been recruited by a foreign government has necessarily demonstrated he is susceptible to easy manipulation by others and should certainly not lead one of America's intelligence agencies."

Case closed, I'd say. But what about the chicken coop?

Who Blacklisted Whom?

Elia Kazan's last Oscar

1/29/99

When the board of the Academy of Motion Picture Arts and Sciences voted unanimously to give director Elia Kazan an Honorary Oscar, the news seemed to signify a historic shift in Hollywood. After all, hadn't Mr. Kazan, now 89, been demonized for almost half a century in the arts community for cooperating with the House Committee on Un-American Activities? This immigrant of a Greek rug dealer may well have won two Oscars for directing Gentlemen's Agreement and "On the Waterfront," and made Broadway history with such landmark productions as "A Streetcar Names Desire" and "Death of a Salesman" but -- as the Hollywood line – the man "named names."

That meant, as far as his peers were concerned, Mr. Kazan was on the wrong side o the struggle the anointed Left and the oppressive Right. And because villains were black hats, not laurel wreaths, Mr. Kazan's golden years have not been burnished with the glowing testimonials a man of his superior achievements could have expected.

Until now. Is it possible that Hollywood's decision t honor Mr. Kazan reflects a new understanding of the concerted Communist efforts to infiltrate Hollywood in the 1930s and 1940s, and the Blacklist era that followed? Not really. That is, Mr. Kazan's career may be about to be officially inducted into the celluloid pantheon, but the man remains typecast as the bad guy who made good movies.

The question is, is it right to continue to brand Mr. Kazan an "informer," as recent press reports do, for telling Congress the truth about his 1930s experiences in a Communist Party cell and giving out the names of former comrades? Had Mr. Kazan revealed the identities of erstwhile associates, in, say, the pro-Nazi German-American Bund, it's unlikely the New York Times would persist with this sneering semantic slap. But it is one of the tragic peculiarities of the Cold War that while the West prevailed in the long struggle with Communist totalitarianism, the arts-and-lettered set remains emotionally in thrall to those who supported the Moscow-dictated Party line, including the so-called "unfriendly" witnesses who famously refused to cooperate with Congress. To put the matter into its shocking historical context, such faithful Party members remained loyal to Stalin, through purges, show trials, the famine in the Ukraine and the Katyn Forest Massacre. And that's a lot to be unfriendly about.

In light of this record, the reverence accorded Mr. Kazan's ideological opposites is bizarre. Most famously represented by the Hollywood Ten, they routinely get the wings-and-halo treatment from the Hollywood guilds and associations for their historic stands. N such occasions, there is always plenty of speechifying about McCarthyism, witch hunts and Amendments 1 and 5, but, as Kenneth Lloyd Billingsley reports in "Hollywood Party," his excellent new history of the era, there is precious little mention of anyone's former association with the Communist Party during its secretive efforts to use Hollywood to promote its socialist message, and, more important, to squelch scripts and careers associated with anti-Communism.

Which is what Elia Kazan ultimately decided to expose. Would a greater good have been served by his silence? This is a question Kazan asked himself before testifying in 1952, seventeen years after he had broken with Communism. "Wasn't what I'd been defending up until now by my silence a conspiracy working for another country?" he writes in his memoir, A Life. "Was the question really what the 'comrades' said it was, the right to think what you will and say what you believe? Or did it have to do with acts, allegiances, and secret programs?" What Mr. Kazan came to was this: "I believe that this committee, which everyone scorned – I had plenty against them, too – had a proper duty. I wanted to help break open the secrecy."

They say history belongs to the victors; not in Hollywood it doesn't. Under secure and sunny skies, Blacklist veterans still fulminate to warm applause about "reactionaries" such as Mr. Kazan (who, by the way, never voted for "Ronnie"). As for Mr. Kazan, he never wavered in his convictions, having discovered long ago what the Cold War was like on the front line. After his congressional appearance, he embarked for Europe to shoot "Man on a Tightrope," the true story of a circus troupe that escaped the Communist Bloc, elephants and all. On the first day of production, East German radio broadcast a roll call of the mainly German cast and crew, calling on them to cease work for Mr. Kazan or risk "revenge without limit." Only one man left. The tough bravery of the crew was a tonic to the American director, whose testimony, though born of conviction, had taken its personal toll.

The Washington Post's Richard Cohen says Mr. Kazan in being honored now "not because his anti-Communism doesn't matter, but because it does – and it is triumphant." On what Hollywood marquee is that one playing? Mr. Kazan is being honored because he was great; because he is old; and because Hollywood has some inkling that he may have been right, although there is no one yet articulating that fact. Perhaps one day, Hollywood will acknowledge the realities of the conflict of the century, and Mr. Kazan's last Oscar will stand not only as a symbol of artistic genius but also of true liberalism, as tangible as a hunk of rubble from the Berlin Wall.

One fell out of the cuckoo's nest

3/26/99

After accepting a special Oscar for his monumental directing career, 89-year-old Elia Kazan told the world he would just slip away now. Not so fast. Mr. Kazan himself may have left the Hollywood limelight for more secluded haunts, but the clamorous debate his award set off, a jarring and insistent coda to the Cold War, demands further attention. Too many central questions remain unanswered – and unasked.

The climactic event of Mr. Kazan's real-life morality play has by now been widely reprised, typically with a hasty rundown of the Hollywood blacklist era during which Mr. Kazan named names of old friends (or, in the alternate version, old enemies). The moral momentum of these grossly superficial stories builds solely from Mr. Kazan's act of giving names to the House Un-American Activities Committee, ultimately turning on his refusal to apologize or recant, and whether such a man should be honored with an Academy Award. In light of this blinkered, nearly universal viewpoint, the aged, once-blacklisted Hollywood Stalinists, having roused themselves to mount a protest against Kazan and his award, found a more or less sympathetic spotlight for the duration of the controversy, a brighter beam than many of them ever knew during their careers.

And such nice people. Take screenwriter Abe Polonsky, who along with fellow scribe Bernard Gordon organized the anti-Kazan protest that ultimately divided the Oscar audience between those who rose to applaud Kazan (Warren Beatty, Meryl Streep), and those who sat in silence (Nick Nolte, Ed Harris). (There were of course those who had it both ways, sitting *and* applauding, such as Steven Spielberg.) "I'll be watching, hoping someone shoots him [Mr. Kazan]," the 88-year-old Mr. Polonsky told the New York Post before the ceremony. "We must protest everything Citizen Kazan stood for," said 81-year-old Gordon, attacking Kazan for supporting HUAC's reign of terror. Robespierre complexes notwithstanding, these are the men who got much of the good ink in this affair, and not just in the pages of the Village Voice (which, in typically subtle fashion, depicted on its most recent cover a sweaty Kazan grasping a rat-shaped Oscar). The New York Times' Maureen Dowd, as accurate a barometer of mainstream liberalism as any, wrote up an approving interview with Gordon, smearing Kazan's brand of anti-communism as scuzzy. More disappointing still have been the tepid defenses mounted on Kazan's behalf (with some striking exceptions, such as a robust essay from Arthur Schlessinger Jr.). Our Man in Hollywood Charleton Heston could say only that it would be fiercely unfair to penalize artistic Kazan because of political Kazan – a weak-tea defense of the battle scarred anti-communist which practically echoed Steven Spielberg's position. "What he did was wrong," Mr. Spielberg told the Los Angeles Times. "But it didn't make his films wrong for me."

But did Mr. Kazan in fact do wrong? Consider some questions commonly overlooked during the debate. Who and what stood to benefit from Mr. Kazan's silence? Answer: America's Stalinists and their beloved Party, the malevolent source of most of this century's human suffering and devastation. And why the Communist fetish for secrecy anyhow? And on whose orders was the secrecy maintained?

Kazan, old now and beyond the fray, fortunately has recorded his thoughts on the matter in detail in his compelling autobiography, "A Life." I couldn't behave as if my old comrades didn't exist and didn't have an active political program," he has written. "There was no way I could go along with their crap that the CP was nothing but another political party, like the Republicans and the Democrats. I knew very well what it was, a thoroughly organized worldwide conspiracy. This conviction separated me from many of my old friends."

Still does. Ninety-yea-old director Edward Dmytryk, another former Communist who made political history by breaking ranks with the so-called Hollywood Ten – hence the name of his own illuminating but obscure memoir "Odd Man Out" – elaborated on these questions in his 1996 book. "To realize its ambitious programs," he explained, "the Party needed the willing cooperation of a large number of outsiders, and ... the unaware liberals were its greatest asset ... So, like the cuckoo, [party organizers] laid their eggs in other birds' nests and depended on those birds to hatch their chicks and nourish their fledglings. This was one of the chief sources of the Party's surprising power, and exposure was the greatest danger it faced .... And that was the reason for their tight membership secrecy, and why naming names was the ultimate sin."

And *is* the ultimate sin. The lamentable lesson of the Kazan controversy is that while Mr. Kazan may have won his career-capping Oscar, Messrs. Polonsky, Gordon et al seem to have won all too many

Americans – unaware liberals at heart – over to their position that naming names is the crime of the century. Heedlessly, too many of us fail to consider the moral responsibility such men bear for their historical devotion to the likes of Stalin – through the many purges, the show trials, the famine in the Ukraine, the Nazi-Soviet Pact, and the Gulag. As Mr. Dmytryk has put it, "What thousands of confused liberals have believed ... was that one must allow a seditious Party to destroy one's country rather than expose the men and women who *are* the Party. In other words, naming names is a greater crime than subversion. That's what I call the 'Mafia Syndrome,' and I find no shame or indignity in rejecting it."

Nor should we, any of us. But it is our bizarre historical lot that having won the geopolitical phase of the Cold War, the cultural front remains a sphere of the Hollywood Left. Yes, Elia Kazan, accompanied by his wife, Frances, and phalanxed by an impressive bodyguard made up of Martin Scorcese and Robert De Niro, came before all Hollywood to collect his well-deserved statuette. But he had to slip into the auditorium through a side entrance to avoid the gauntlet of 500 picketers outside. And while no outbursts punctured his televised moment, his reception, as they say, was decidedly mixed. Hardly a lionizing moment to bask in. Is this the triumphalist Western world we hear tell of? Not so long as we keep such courageous anti-communists as Elia Kazan out in the cold.

Edward Dmytryk

7/9/99

One of the more peculiar legacies of the epic struggle known as the Cold War is the fact that while the West may have won its geopolitical phase, the cultural sphere remains fixedly under the influence of the Hollywood left. Nowhere is this bizarre condition better reflected than in the popular understanding of the Hollywood Blacklist, the mid-century intersection of politics and culture.

Consider the reception accorded director Elia Kazan on receiving his special Oscar earlier this year. It largely ranged from hostile and grudging, to merely ambivalent. Such reactions derive from the misbegotten notion that those, such as Mr. Kazan, who "named names" - i.e., disclosed the identities of secretly organized Americans who were willing participants in a conspiracy guided by Moscow - committed a crime far greater than those who engaged in the conspiracy itself. And so it is that the "informers," the disillusioned ex-communists who acquired their wisdom the hard way, have been culturally ostracized, while the informed-upon have been embraced, even celebrated - certainly never held responsible or called upon to explain their zealous allegiance to the likes of Joseph Stalin through purges, show trials, the Ukraine famine, the Hitler-Stalin pact and the gulag.

A bizarre condition, indeed. Director Edward Dmytryk, who died last week at age 90, once came up with a good name for it: "What thousands of liberals have believed since [the Blacklist] was that one must allow a seditious party to destroy one's country rather than expose the men or women who are the Party, In other words, naming names is a greater crime than subversion. That's what I call the 'Mafia Syndrome,' and I find no shame or indignity in rejecting it." This quotation comes from Mr. Dmytryk's fascinating memoir, "Odd Man Out," perhaps the most illuminating and intelligent account of the Blacklist period.

Published when Mr. Dmytryk was 87, the book tells the story of the director's experiences as a Communist in Hollywood who rapidly became disillusioned with the party after a series of eye-opening experiences, ranging from his astonishment at learning that Arthur Koestler's "Darkness at Noon" was forbidden reading to party members, to his final rupture over party efforts to compel him to change and reshoot the script of "Cornered" (incidentally, a pretty good, noirish, post-World War II movie). While Mr. Dmytryk may well have thought that his involvement with the party was over, his life had already taken an unalterable turn leading first to one kind of infamy as a member of the so-called Hollywood Ten, the group of famously uncooperative witnesses called upon to testify before the House Committee on Un-American Activities, and later to another kind of infamy as the only member of the Hollywood Ten to break ranks.

In recent years, Mr. Dmytryk would say, somewhat ruefully, that his obituaries would primarily remember him for his relationship to the Hollywood Ten, not for his direction of such memorable movies as "Murder, My Sweet" with Dick Powell, and "The Caine Mutiny" with Humphrey Bogart. He was right. The career in movies that Mr. Dmytryk pursued since 1922 (when he worked as a 14-year-old messenger boy at Paramount Pictures) was indeed overshadowed by his very much unplanned role as a warrior of the early Cold War, with certain newspapers, namely the Los Angeles Times, passing along the fearsomely ugly judgments of nameless "critics."

But if, in this bizarre era, Mr. Dmytryk's outspokenness as a former Communist and an anti-communist did take something away from his artistic legacy, it added another legacy, one that eventually may even transcend all others. One day, perhaps, Edward Dmytryk will be widely recognized not only as an accomplished Hollywood director, but also as a man of history who rose to the exacting demands of a dangerous era with integrity, intelligence and courage.

Elia Kazan, freedom fighter

10-3-03

Elia Kazan, who died this week at age 94, is remembered for two things: for having directed masterpieces on stage and screen, and, in the parlance of the Left, for having "named names" before the House Committee on Un-American Activities in 1952.

He was long recognized for the former; but he should have been equally celebrated for the latter. For what was "naming names" but lifting the operational anonymity of Americans who served the hostile interests of a foreign power bent on dominating the world? Regardless of this hard historical truth, the potshots flew for a half-century at the mention of Kazan's name, with no-talent Lefties scoring easy ink well into their dotage just for taking aim at Kazan the "informer," the "Judas" and the "heel." Never did they account for — and never were they asked to account for — their own shameful careers as shills and agents of what was, in truth, an aggressive Stalinist conspiracy to infiltrate and twist the entertainment industry into a propaganda tool for the Soviet Union.

What goes unacknowledged is how very successful this conspiracy was, and how potent its repercussions remain. Communist success in Hollywood lies not so much in the movies that have engraved the Leftist demonology of Big Business, the CIA and suburbia onto our collective consciousness, nor in movies that baldly extolled the supposed virtues of Communism. The very best measure of the smashing success of Communist infiltration of Hollywood is the near-total absence of movies, black-and-white or color, that chronicle the primary drama of the last century: the struggle for freedom against totalitarian communism.

In his book "Hollywood Party: How Communism Seduced the American Film Industry in the 1930s and 1940s" (Prima Lifestyles, 1998), Kenneth Lloyd Billingsley plumbs this massive cultural chasm. Thousands of Germans risked their lives to break out from behind the Berlin Wall and find freedom in the West, he writes, but only a single Hollywood offering — "Night Crossing" from Disney — ever dramatized this scenario. Screen heroes with "progressive" politics abound, but who can name a single anti-communist good guy?

By Billingsley's count, not one Hollywood film has ever showed the Ukraine famine, the Moscow show trials or the Hungarian uprising against the Soviet military. Both the epic drama of Prague Spring and the Soviet-backed crackdown on Poland's Solidarity movement are backdrops for just one film apiece: the former in a short sequence in "The Unbearable Lightness of Being" and the latter in "To Kill a Priest," which, as Billingsley points out, "failed to detail the politics involved." As screenwriter and Communist Party official Dalton Trumbo bragged in a 1946 article for "The Worker," major anti-Communist books of the

1930s and 1940s, such as Arthur Koestler's "Darkness at Noon" (literally verboten to Hollywood Communists, as ex-communist director Edward Dmytryk revealed), Victor Kravchenko's "I Chose Freedom," and Trotsky's biography of Stalin, never made it to the screen. How could they?

As Billingsley reports, story analysts and talent agents working for the Communist Party were perfectly placed to block the progress of such anti-Communist material.

One result is that the Cold War experience has never been blended into our cultural narrative. Lore-less, it remains politics alone, a not-fully-incorporated appendage of our history. Meanwhile, having to some large extent robbed us of the cultural legacy of that mighty global struggle, Hollywood communists left only the spiritually stunting cult of what has become known as political correctness in its place.

In the end, it was this coercive political orthodoxy — lockstep, collectivist "liberalism" that brooked no dissent — that drove ex-Communists such as Kazan to break silence, earning him the eternal enmity of the anti-anti-Communists. Which is something to ponder in our own time, as a gathering movement of anti-antiterrorism builds. In his new book, "Onward Muslim Soldiers" (Regnery), Robert Spencer highlights an undeniable parallel between yesterday's anti-anti-Communism and today's anti-antiterrorism: both movements see in the United States the chief villain of the world.

And "just as twentieth-century leftists prostrated themselves before the progressive' Soviet Union and its satellites, so too does the twenty-first century Left prefer Islam — with its presumed, romanticized history of 'tolerance,' despite all evidence to the contrary — to the West," he writes. "Just as the Left was anti-anticommunist, so too then are they anti-antiterrorist."

This is not to suggest how Elia Kazan — who, by the way, never voted for Ronald Reagan — would have come down on the war on Islamic terrorism. Still, this Constantinople-born son of a Greek rug dealer well understood the differences between Islam and the West. His favorite among his own movies, "America, America," is about a Greek Christian boy's near-endless struggle to leave behind the repression of Ottoman (Islamic) Turkey for freedom in the United States.

Elia Kazan, R.I.P.

Why were real spies treated like Hollywood fiction?

7/16/10

Just how entertaining was that Russian spy ring story that came in with a flurry of late-June arrests and went out with a Russo-American agent swap last weekend?

Two thumbs up, judging by the reviews, or was that news coverage? Sometimes it was hard to tell. In fact, something about the way the startling fact that allegedly post-Cold War Russia was running a ring of deep-cover agents in this "reset" era was put over made it seem as though there was little distinction between spy fact and spy fiction. Or, rather, that the main significance to spy fact was its place in our pop-culture attic of spy fiction.

"Details of the Russian spy network, outlined in two FBI complaints and a government press release, tell a spy story that is part John le Carre and part Austin Powers," reported Newsweek. "Russian spy case 'right out of a John le Carre novel'" headlined the Christian Science Monitor. "A sensational summer spy tale that already seemed ripped from the pages of Le Carre or Ludlum," explained the New York Daily News. The real-life events had their reference points not in historical experience but in genre fiction.

Little wonder that the news story found its own storybook femme fatale in Anna Chapman (nee Kushchenko), the comely "flame-haired" agent whose intercepted distress call to ex-KGB papa triggered the string of FBI arrests. Chapman's web-handy glamour portraits only enhanced a story already seen as more celluloid than microfilm, more Hollywood script than criminal complaint. "Do we have any spies that hot?" Jay Leno, 60, asked the vice president, holding up a sultry Chapman pic. "Let me be clear," replied 68-year-old Joe Biden. "It was not my idea to send her back. I thought they'd take Rush Limbaugh."

It was all one big laugh riot. Or maybe it was all one big Hollywood publicity stunt given the spate of spy-related Hollywood products now flooding the market. Indeed, New York Times' television critic Alessandra Stanley decided, in a spy show round-up, that the country is now in a "giddy Spy vs. Spy mood." Giddy? "They may live among us, posing as lawn-mowing, hydrangea-growing suburbanites," Stanley wrote. "They may be reporting intimate secrets back to Moscow, although it's hard to know what those 11 would-be spies infiltrated besides Facebook. Ex-K.G.B. agents do die mysteriously of polonium poisoning from time to time, but Kremlin-sent assassins are not likely to blow up New York office towers or unleash chemical weapons in our subways."

Don't be so sure. That is, the not-so-mysteriously poisoned Russian ex-agent Alexander Litvinenko, whose slow, excruciating 2006 death by polonium poisoning is attributed to orders from Russia's Vladimir Putin, made numerous claims that terrorism attributed to al Qaida and other jihadist groups is, in fact, backed by Russian security services, the original hell-font of global terrorism. In 2005, for example, Litvinenko told a Polish newspaper that top al Qaida leader Ayman al-Zawahiri was trained by the FSB (successor to the KGB) for six months in 1997, after which he was sent to Afghanistan where he penetrated the top ranks around Osama bin Laden.

Some plot. Almost as perfectly thrilling as the Times-noted upcoming AMC series "Rubicon" about "an intelligence analyst who stumbles on a high-level government conspiracy" (snore), or the upcoming NBC series "Undercovers," which, according to the same Times review that dismisses the occasional polonium poisoning, focuses on "a pair of caterers, a husband and a wife, who are retired agents coaxed into coming in from the cold and using their chef toques as covers." Get it?

Well, we didn't either. That is, as Bill Gertz, noted national security correspondent for the Washington Times, reported this week, a number of current and former national security officials are "critical of the speedy exchange with Moscow" less than two weeks after the Russian spies' arrests because it effectively blocked U.S. intelligence from learning key facts about "Russian espionage and influence operations."

"We gave up the opportunity," said Rep. Pete Hoekstra, Michigan Republican. "Now that these people are out of the country, it's game off, not game on. We will get no additional insights or information from them."

And that means this is one story without an ending.

Polish plane crash investigation under suspicion

8/13/10

It's never been clear what really happened on that foggy morning of April 10 when a Polish airplane crashed on a Russian runway, killing all 96 people aboard including Polish President Lech Kaczynski, cabinet ministers, military service chiefs, intelligence officials, the central bank president, parliamentarians, historians, decapitating the conservative government and gutting the country's elite.

Given the occasion—the 70th anniversary of the Soviet Union's long-denied massacre of 22,000 Poles at Katyn Forest—and given many of the crash victims' dedication to exposing Soviet-era treachery and opposing Putin-era Russian expansionism, was the crash, as reported, an epically tragic accident?

Even as the Russians immediately cited "pilot error" (they did wait, as former CIA officer Eugene Poteat has noted, until after the plane had gone down), they also pledged to Poland a joint, transparent investigation. But four months later, Russian obfuscation casts doubt on both notions: pilot error and Russian cooperation. Little wonder that Polish parliamentarian Antoni Marcierewicz, a member of the late president's conservative Law and Justice Party, has recently announced a parliamentary probe into the crash, which he calls a "crime."

What sort of crime? I caught up with the story's latest twists at BigPeace.com (where I am a contributor) in a post called "Polish Airplane Crash Cover-Up?" After seeking attribution for the post's more sensational clues from a Polish journalist, I believe that "cover-up" might turn out to be the least of the problem.

Point one. Russia hasn't turned over the plane's black boxes to Polish investigators. This may well follow an odd, post-crash agreement between the two countries, whereby Russia provides Poland with recordings of the black boxes and Poland controls the recordings' release (typical Russian-Polish agreement). But it also hoists a red flag over the entire investigative process. After all, "who" might have done "what" to a black box in a Russian recording studio?

Meanwhile, writing in the Polish newspaper Nasz Dziennik, some Polish pilots have challenged the authenticity of the recordings. Among other aeronautical reasons, they cited the length of the transcript, which appears to exceed the 30-minute capacity of a black box tape. The pilots also noted the transcript is missing the signature of the sole Polish expert involved. Further, Polish Radio RMF has reported that one of the Russian-made black-box recordings contains a 16-second gap.

Good thing no non-partisan, international team of investigators is examining this international mystery, right? Much better that the United Nations, for example, is currently squeezing Israel for defending its lawful naval blockade on Gaza (and concurrent offers to shuttle seaborne humanitarian aid to Gaza via land). With former KGB officer Vladimir Putin having personally taken charge of the crash investigation, why worry?

Point two. The Polish newspaper Fakt reported that three days after the crash, the air traffic controller on duty during the fatal crash disappeared. The Russians say he retired — and no, they don't know where he is.

Uh-huh.

At the website of the Institute of World Politics where he teaches, ex-CIA officer Eugene Poteat writes that Russians "stripped the 97 dead passengers of personal effects, luggage, laptop computers, flash drives, cell phones, sensitive papers, names, telephone numbers, correspondence, documents, and top secret military and diplomatic codes — a coup for Russia's intelligence service. ... The Russians delayed for weeks before returning the less sensitive items, but kept items of intelligence value. The bodies were shipped to Moscow for 'autopsies.' No Polish medical people were permitted as witnesses.

... The bodies were returned to Poland in sealed coffins for burial and families of the victims were not permitted to open the coffins."

And why was that? Some survivors are exploring the autopsy process to find out, with one parliamentarian's widow planning to exhume her late husband's corpse to learn more about the crash circumstances.

"Poland has no doubts about Russia's good will in investigating crash," read a headline from the Russian wire service Itar-Tass on Aug. 7. The story quoted a Polish minister complaining about gaps in Russia's evidence — not that this minister for a moment doubted Russia's investigatory good will. For its part, Russia maintains it has already handed over everything to Poland. "There is nothing more to transfer," said Deputy Prime Minister Sergei Ivanov.

At least nothing more that wouldn't lift the fog on this mystery.

Commie plot that put us in the red

10/19/11

The most amazing aspects of the accelerating American submission to the state are: 1) how matter-of-fact we are in contemplating massive government interventions, such as President Barack Obama's latest stimulus "jobs" plan, and 2) how virtually no one notices the blatant Marxist overtones. When someone does, a la "Joe the Plumber" at the end of the 2008 campaign season, he or she is mocked off the stage.

President Obama demonstrated how this is done in January 2010 when, during an unusual White House meeting with congressional Republicans about his pending health-care legislation – another massive government

intervention into the private sector – he declared: "If you were to listen to the debate, and, frankly, how some of you went after this bill, you'd think this thing was some Bolshevik plot."

I remember cringing when a smattering of applause arose from the GOP ranks, as though some Republicans actually believed the president had delivered a punch line revealing the absurdity of considering "Obamacare" a government apparatus for seizing control of the lives of citizens – which it is. And that's no joke.

I wish any Republican had replied: "Not necessarily a 'plot,' sir, but a program that is indeed 'Bolshevik' in conception, design and purpose nonetheless. Government control of private sector activity, as the American people well know (or should), is aptly described as 'Bolshevik' – or Marxist, socialist, collectivist, statist and, for that matter, fascist, too. Indeed, nationalized health care was one of the first programs enacted by the Bolsheviks after they seized power in 1917."

But, no. Among the many deep psychological factors repressing such a factually devastating response is pure historical ignorance. This isn't entirely our fault. That is, the truth about Bolshevism and closely related creeds barely makes it into our curricula – another Bolshevik plot, if you ask me. Indeed, the shocking intelligence history of communist plotters who secretly sabotaged our government barely dents our understanding of history even now, some 20 years after secret archives in Moscow and Washington opened, somewhat, to disgorge incontrovertible proof of pro-Soviet agents operating in the highest reaches of power.

But if nationalized health care is a demonstrably Bolshevik program, "stimulus spending" is what you might call a genuine Bolshevik plot. Why? One of the Kremlin's greatest agents you probably never heard of played a leading role in introducing stimulus spending as a macroeconomic policy for the first time in U.S. history during the Franklin D. Roosevelt years.

The agent's name was Lauchlin Currie, and, as M. Stanton Evans writes in his indispensable 2007 book "Blacklisted by History," he ranks "among the most influential Soviet agents ever in the U.S. government, if only by virtue of his portfolio in the White House dealing with affairs of China." Currie, an administrative assistant to FDR, was instrumental in the U.S.-government-wide communist plot to turn China red.

But that's not all he did. Currie pops up in nine KGB cables translated by American cryptographers in what is known as the Venona Project, which became public in 1995. From these and other archival sources we have learned that Currie passed secret documents and shared sensitive political intelligence with Soviet spymasters. Equally as damaging, Currie used his stature as a senior Roosevelt aide to shut down investigations into the activities of other American traitors operating inside government.

While I haven't seen mention of Currie's economic activities in KGB documents, how does stimulus spending sound now on discovering that this bona fide Soviet agent was its leading proponent? In "Roosevelt, the Great Depression and the Economics of Recovery" (University of Virginia Press, 2005), Elliot Rosen, professor emeritus of history at Rutgers, writes: "The initial rationale for public expenditure as a stimulus to the economy was provided by Currie, who won a wide and influential audience in the Roosevelt administration." As assistant research director for the Federal Reserve, his position before moving to the White House, "Currie provided an economic rationale" for deficit spending. "Wartime aside," Rosen writes, "no precedent existed for budget unbalance." Not surprisingly, another Currie project was to push for the "abandonment of the concept of annual budget balance."

So that's where balanced budgets went, and stimulus spending came from. Think of it: One agent of communist influence in high places, and the U.S. economy was revolutionized.

If only Americans could learn to recognize a Bolshevik plot when they see one.

Is Russia covering up real cause of plane crash?

12/29/11

'Tis the season for media list-mania, and (true confession) I always am mildly surprised upon viewing Top 10 story lists to find that I've forgotten some humdingers. Osama bin Laden was killed in 2011?

In fact, given a tally of my own columns, jihad is the top story of 2011, just as it has been since at least 2001. Not that the media see it that way, of course; they see the spread of Islam's law and call it "diversity" in the West or "Arab Spring" in the Middle East. They are blind to its implications, they apologize for its depredations and, in general, they commit professional malfeasance by misrepresenting the facts. Then again, at least they cover it.

The same isn't true for the following story, which I submit is the great unsolved mystery of 2011. What really happened in the forest at Smolensk, Russia, when a Polish aircraft carrying Poland's national leadership crashed in April 2010, killing all 96 people on board, including Poland's president and first lady?

The answers Russia presented in its 2011 crash report are wholly unsatisfactory. Indeed, the Moscow-controlled crash investigation seems to have been designed to suppress or tamper with evidence to exonerate Russia of all responsibility for an accident, or any guilt for a crime. Like a tired rerun of an old horror movie, the Russian pattern of investigation into the 2010 Smolensk crash is the Russian pattern of investigation into the 1940 Katyn Forest massacre.

It's hard to overstate the significance of that fateful flight by those Polish leaders, now deceased. They lost their lives trying to commemorate the 70th anniversary of Katyn, the mass murder of 22,000 Polish officers and intelligentsia killed by Stalin in 1940 to make way for a pro-Soviet, communist Poland. After Nazi German troops discovered their graves in 1943, Stalin denied responsibility for this crime against humanity. Roosevelt and Churchill let him, thus joining in a Big Lie;

Stalin's successors lied about it until Boris Yeltsin came along in 1995. The 2010 anniversary was to be a public, ceremonial Russian admission of guilt. That those who cared so much about Katyn were killed — and quite possibly assassinated — nearby is one of history's darkest ironies.

The Russians assert that Polish pilot error, supposedly induced by pressure to land from the Polish president himself, caused the crash. Poles, particularly those associated with the late president's conservative Law and Justice party, see something far more sinister. In this worst-case scenario, Russian air controllers incorrectly informed Polish pilots they were on the proper glide path when that wasn't true. On purpose? If so, the world has witnessed mass assassination of a government. And done nothing.

I don't claim to judge the evidence. But it's clear an impartial investigation is warranted, due to a Moscow-run investigative process marked by irregularities. These include the red flag that Russia has refused to return the black boxes of the Polish plane to Poland. Other irregularities, as summarized in a November 2011 Polish document known as the Smolensk Status Report, include the fact that crash evidence was crudely destroyed (including by bulldozers), tampered with and lied about. (Russian investigators claimed no radar video recording existed, for example, but then cited it in the crash report.) The document notes that some Russian pathological reports on victims included descriptions of organs that had been surgically removed before the crash.

A glaring discrepancy concerns the cockpit voice recording (CVR). To prove the pilots were under third-party pressure to land, the Russians reported that a Polish crew member twice says "he will go crazy" if the plane doesn't land. Both the Polish Investigation Committee and the Polish Prosecutor's Office publicly contended that no such statement was made and that the Russians altered the CVR to create the statement.

In 1952, Congress investigated the Katyn Forest massacre and proved Soviet guilt; in 2010 and 2011, there were calls in Congress for an independent investigation into the Smolensk crash. Such an investigation is urgently required in 2012, and not only to solve the mystery of a vexing crash. We must find out whether the West has once again been party to a Big Lie out of Moscow.

Joe McCarthy was right all along
(As printed in *Dispatch International*)

1/24/13

WASHINGTON, D.C. — Most Europeans are unlikely to be familiar with the facts behind the American term "McCarthyism." They probably know it describes something very bad in American politics – the "Communist witch hunts" of more than half a century ago. They may also know that simply uttering the term, like casting a spell, stops all debate cold by associating someone with the eponymous Joseph McCarthy. As the story goes, he was himself very bad. After all, he conducted those long ago "Communist witch hunts," ruining his name in perpetuity. This probably exhausts general knowledge.

But here's a secret: Most Americans know little more than this same familiar but *completely false* narrative. In recent years, stunning revelations from archives in Washington and Moscow have confirmed that McCarthy's investigations – and those conducted by other officials before and after – netted not innocent and imaginary "witches," but secret cadres of hardened Communist agents determined to bring down the American republic. Surely, this makes Joe McCarthy a great patriot and deserving "the plaudits of a grateful nation."

So wrote M. Stanton Evans, the consensus-smashing, revisionist biographer of McCarthy in *Blacklisted by History: The Untold Story of Senator Joe McCarthy and His Fight Against America's Enemies* (2007). Evans was attempting to convey the significance of just one particular Soviet intelligence operation, circa 1945, that McCarthy was instrumental in bringing to light, circa 1950.

Even a few details about this operation, named initially as the *Amerasia* affair after a pro-Communist journal of the day, will add a little needed context to modern-day perspective on the so-called McCarthy era.

Amerasia's editor, Phillip Jaffe, came under FBI surveillance in 1944 after the contents of a confidential OSS memo appeared in his magazine. (The OSS was the precursor to the CIA.) The FBI soon learned Jaffe was in possession of hundreds of stolen, secret US government documents, plus a photographic set-up. The magazine ran no photographs, so the FBI plausibly believed it had come across an active espionage operation. Further surveillance, including wire-taps, determined that Jaffe was in frequent contact with US Communist Party leader Earl Browder, Soviet "diplomats" in New York, a top Chinese Communist envoy of Mao and US diplomat John Stewart Service (home from Chiang Kai-Shek's China, where, it later emerged, Service roomed with two leading Communist agents, Solomon Adler and Chi Chao-ting).

On June 6, 1945, FBI agents arrested six people, including Jaffe and Service, and seized hundreds of top secret documents, many concerning military matters. An open-and-shut espionage case, it would seem.

An open and quickly shut-down case is more like it. What followed was cover-up, perjury and grand-jury rigging by, among others, high-ranking Washington officials. Some were eager to prevent a national security scandal from engulfing the Truman White House. Others were acting to shield a far wider Communist-led conspiracy mounted by confederates inside the State Department, Treasury, White House and elsewhere in the US government, working not merely to filch secret documents but to ensure, through influence and subversion, the Communist takeover of China. These powerful forces of suppression proved overwhelming. The *Amerasia* case was scuttled, the scandal was buried, and, within a few years, China was Red.

Five years later, McCarthy's laser-beam focus on the still-festering case would be instrumental in follow-up investigations launched by both the Senate and the FBI. These massive probes yielded, as Evans notes, some 5,000 pages of Senate hearings, plus 1,000 pages of exhibits and, from the FBI, 24,000 pages of now-declassified records.

They reveal the workings of a vast, complex influence operation, Evans writes, that "assiduously worked to guide official and public thinking, and hence the course of U.S. policy," in this case regarding the Far East. Other such intricate influence operations, of course, targeted the West. And who was doing this dirty work of Communist-directed subversion from within? Many officials and public figures highlighted by Joseph McCarthy (among others), who, we have since learned from US and Soviet archives, were secret agents and fellow-traveling supporters of Stalin.

McCarthy, as Evans has pointed out, threatened to blow the lid off the official cover-ups and other acts of treason. Thus, he had to be isolated, demonized and destroyed, and so he was. History would be written by the isolators, the demonizers and the destroyers, and repeated by rote for the next half century.

Then along came the declassification of FBI records and releases of intelligence documents, and scholars such as M. Stanton Evans to sift through them. But the far-reaching implications of such research – that anti-Communist "witch-hunters" were *right all along* – have done shockingly little to change the way Americans regard their history. Such hidebound attitudes extend also to American conservatives, who, it would seem, are the modern-day heirs of the anti-Communist legacy. What Evans calls "court history" is that deeply entrenched as national lore.

Will this ever change? "There's no concise answer to that," Evans replied in a recent interview with *Dispatch International*. "There is a mindset, a narrative, a template that has been out there for a long time." The reflex reaction, to date, is to preserve that template rather than assess the new evidence.

Thus, it is minimized or denied. Evans mimics the usual reaction to the specter of historical Communist penetration: " 'Well, this thing was overblown, there wasn't a big problem, these people were persecuted.' The new evidence, he continues, "challenges this so they dismiss it.

We're dealing with an establishment mindset that is impervious to refutation – to fact. It's like throwing popcorn at a battleship."

This hasn't stopped Evans, 78 – once the youngest metropolitan newspaper editor in the USA *(Indianapolis News)*, and formerly a columnist for the *Los Angeles Times* and commentator for CBS News and Voice of America – from reloading and firing again. In fact, following his McCarthy book, which corroborates many McCarthy cases and documents the Washington Establishment's craven efforts to destroy the maverick senator rather than address subversion and cover-up, Evans embarked on a new project. With so much evidence now available attesting to the presence of Soviet agents watching over wartime Washington, Evans set out to write a concise history of what it was these agents of the Kremlin actually accomplished.

The new book, published in November 2012, is *Stalin's Secret Agents: The Subversion of Roosevelt's Government,* co-written with Herbert Romerstein, a leading Cold War expert and longtime congressional investigator. Assessing the achievements of agents of influence, is very different, Evans emphasizes, from standard histories of spying as defined by stealing secrets.

The series of history-changing events Evans and Romerstein identify as having been subverted by Soviet agents is itself history-changing, demanding a rewrite of much of the history of World War II. Despite the familiarity with which we regard the era, in many ways, Evans and Romerstein are pioneering a new field of study. The best way to approach it with what Evans himself calls his *Law of Inadequate Paranoia*: "No matter how bad you think something is," he says, "when you look into it, it's always worse."

It's time to slay the dragon of 'McCarthyism'

2/21/13

Freshman Republican Sen. Ted Cruz of Texas is just the latest in a long series of public figures to be reviled for "McCarthyism" following his recent questioning of Chuck Hagel, President Obama's nominee for secretary of defense. The response? Conservatives have rushed to defend their own against the charge. To understate the case, that's not enough. It's time to debunk McCarthyism itself.

No matter how much evidence vindicating the late Sen. Joe McCarthy comes out, what we call McCarthyism remains anathema in American life. Simply to utter the word is to deep-freeze debate, even thought itself. Even as we learn about the history-changing extent to which American traitors working for the Kremlin penetrated and subverted the U.S. government (including many individuals investigated by McCarthy), the unsupportable fact remains that nothing in American public life is worse than to be compared to the man best-known for his uncompromising fight against the secret, massive assault on our nation. When will we realize it's time to make amends and honor his memory?

Liberals and also conservatives who should know better continue to fall for the poisonous bait. Last summer, for example, conservative cries of "McCarthyism" erupted after Senate Majority Leader Harry Reid aired an anonymous charge that Mitt Romney had not paid taxes. Romney adviser Eric Fehrnstrom called Reid's accusation "baseless" and "shameless," and compared it to so-called McCarthyism. The Hill newspaper's write-up of Fehrnstrom's comments perfectly sums up society's ignorance on the issue:

"This reminds me of the McCarthy hearings back in the 1950s," Fehrnstrom said, referring to former Republican Sen. Joseph McCarthy of Wisconsin, who led a controversial search for communist sentiment during the Cold War. "I would ask (Reid) one simple question: 'Have you no sense of decency, sir? Is there nothing that you won't do to debase yourself and the office you hold in the name of dirty politics?'"

"Baseless" and "shameless" were indeed apt descriptions for Reid's smear tactics, but they don't describe the exhaustive investigations mounted in the middle of the 20th century by teams of Red-hunters, including McCarthy's, in the House and Senate. As for their quarry, it was not, as The Hill delicately stated, "communist sentiment during the Cold War." Literally hundreds of Soviet agents taking orders from the KGB and related Soviet intelligence agencies to bring down the American republic had become deeply embedded in the U.S. government in the 1930s and 1940s. Most of them remained undiscovered, and many were active well into the 1950s.

After World War II, Red-hunters in Congress did their best to expose this communist menace – a menace that we now know, following declassification of some FBI and intelligence files in Washington and Moscow, was much worse than we thought. Thanks to Joe McCarthy, many Americans whom the left angelicized as "free thinkers" or "liberals" were finally unmasked as hardened Soviet agents. These would include, to take 10 examples from M. Stanton Evans' masterpiece, "Blacklisted by History: The Untold Story of Senator Joe McCarthy and His Fight Against America's Enemies," Solomon Adler, Cedric Belfrage, T.A. Bisson, V. Frank Coe, Lauchlin Currie, Harold Glasser, David Karr, Mary Jane Keeney, Leonard Mins and Franz Neumann.

As for "Have you no sense of decency, sir?" This tiresome catchphrase may quiver with righteousness on history's eternal wavelength, but it is probably the biggest crock of all. As Evans writes, Army counsel Joseph Welch famously hurled the question as an accusation at McCarthy. McCarthy's transgression, we are supposed to believe, was outing Welch's young legal associate, Frederick G. Fisher Jr., as a former member of the National Lawyers Guild, a notorious communist front group.

The truth is quite different. Six weeks earlier, Welch himself was quoted in the New York Times, confirming that Fisher had belonged to the communist front and that, as a result, Welch himself had "relieved (Fisher) from duty." Welch's hearing-room histrionics, in other words, were a lot of hot air. But they worked. To this day, the truth remains lost to most people, while this thinnest fiction is immortal.

Many other charges against McCarthy similarly disintegrate on examination. The problem is, there is far too little examination. Even this week, when the National Review took up editorial arms to defend Ted Cruz from croaky cries of "McCarthyism" coming from Democrats in Congress and cable TV hosts, the editorial explained how it was that Cruz had not engaged in the "M-word." It further declared Cruz "has not, as Senator McCarthy was reputed to have done, slandered an honorable man by cavalierly associating him with an odious and politically radioactive 'ism.'"

"Reputed" by whom, and according to what facts? Failing to unmask the McCarthyism libel for what it is and always was – bunk and agitprop designed to demonize conservatives, from Joe then to Ted today – does exactly what conservatives continue to take pains to disavow. It slanders a patriot – Joe McCarthy – by cavalierly associating him with an odious and politically radioactive "ism."

It's time to thank the man instead.

Immigration, Amnesty & the Border

Creeping amnesty

4/10/06

So there I was, thinking that the only "imminent" threat was the Islamization of the Western world, a historic shift well underway in Europe. Yes, it remained clear that out-of-control immigration in the United States jeopardized the future of our nationhood. But after Sept. 11, the present danger had become creeping sharia: the gradual — and not so gradual — acceptance of Islamic law by Western and, therefore, non-Islamic societies.

But then came last month's massive, mainly Mexican street protests against border control and in favor of amnesty for illegal aliens, mainly Mexican, who have crossed into this country since the last time Uncle Sam granted amnesty in 1986. Back then, it was amnesty for less than 3 million. Today, 20 years later, these protestors, along with George W. Bush, want to see some 12 million illegal aliens "earn" citizenship (amnesty). In another 20 years, will a new, amnesty-seeking illegal population number 48 million?

In light of the post-protest retreat — I mean, "deliberations" — in the U.S. Senate, such a colossal figure looks increasingly plausible. After all, what does an illegal alien or two (or 48 million) have to lose? We are, as we are repeatedly lectured, "a nation of immigrants" who do the work that "Americans" won't do. In fact, maybe just forget about "Americans." If We, the People, get anything like Amnesty 2006 — with provisions to attain an increasingly Hispanic demographic — the United States will change from being a neighbor of Latin America to becoming a part of it.

All of which is to say that creeping sharia, both at home and abroad, is still a present danger. But so is creeping amnesty. And strikingly, the amnesty scenario begins to mirror, if even in a cracked way, some of the demographic changes that historian Bernard Lewis predicted will turn Europe Islamic by the end of this century. That is, as America increasingly loses its European-descended majority on one side of the Atlantic, Europe, too, increasingly loses its European majority on the other. In a National Review Online piece called "American Dhimmitude," the Center for Immigration Studies' Mark Krikorian likened illegal aliens' demands on the U.S. government to "the same kind of challenge that aggressive outsiders are making against other parts of the West, including Muslim immigrants in Europe and, in its most extreme form, Palestinians in Israel."

One blogger, Freedom Folks (hat tip Michelle Malkin), took this concept a step further. Reporting on craven decisions by several American public schools to ban American flags and other patriotic symbols that presumably offend or inflame student-advocates of illegal alien "rights," Freedom Folks referenced "dhimmitude," the subservient condition of non-Muslims under Islamic rule, and wrote: "Welcome to the beginning of Mexitude right here in the U.S. of A. ... Think dhimmitude, but substitute Colorado for Kandahar and La Raza for The Religion of Peace (Islam)."

There are other parallels. Both Mexican and Islamic supremacist movements harken back to chimerical Golden Ages — the purely mythical Aztlan kingdom said to comprise the American Southwest, and the mythically tolerant Andalusia of Islamic Spain. Both groups seem to thrive on crazy conspiracy theories. For example, we've all heard from the Arab-Muslim world that Sept. 11 was an Israeli and/or CIA plot; I found similar claptrap online at the separatist (and Palestinian suicide-bomber honoring) "news" site, La Voz de Aztlan, where publisher Hector Carreon, writing from "Los Angeles, Alta California" (Imperial Spain's, then Mexico's, name for the region before it was ceded to the United States in 1848), declared that Nicholas Berg's decapitation by jihadists in Iraq was a stunt engineered at Abu Ghraib. La Voz de Aztlan, by the way, is one of the organizations calling for a nationwide, pro-amnesty boycott on May 1.

Small wonder that some organizational solidarity exists between Islamic and Mexican radical groups — as seen, for example, when the Council on American-Islamic Relations (CAIR) joins a "pro-immigrant" rally at the U.S. Capitol. International A.N.S.W.E.R. (Act Now to Stop War & End Racism) — which, as the Washington Times reported, was the hard-left coalition behind last month's pro-amnesty march in Los Angeles — has a steering committee that includes, along with "civil justice" and "socialism and liberation" groups, the Mexico Solidarity Network, the Nicaragua Network, the Free Palestine Alliance and the Muslim Student Association. It all begins to make sense, in a leftist, anti-

American, open-borders coalition sort of way.

My question: Why does George W. Bush seem to have signed onto this coalition?

Backlash nation and the high cost of citizenship

5/8/06

"Backlash" is one of those words with an iffy reputation, connoting an angry or even unreasoned reaction to a benign or just plain immutable reality. Like a tantrum, a backlash is widely regarded as an emotional spasm that inevitably subsides, leaving the supposedly benign or just plain immutable reality to unfold unmolested. Meanwhile, backlash is cluck-clucked as unenlightened (Backlash to Feminism), mean-spirited (Angry White Men Backlash), xenophobic (Dubai Ports Backlash) — or, in the case of the burgeoning reaction against the illegal-alien amnesty movement, all of the above.

But by whom? Backlash opponents. More often than not, "backlash" is the word mainstream liberals use to describe the sound the silent majority makes when it finally gets around to piping up. The family unit is shattered: That's progress. Somebody says, "Uh, maybe it was better when it wasn't shattered": That's backlash. The nation's borders are breached by millions of illegal aliens, who not only provide an immorally cheap labor force, but also more than 29 percent of prisoners in Federal Bureau of Prisons facilities: That's progress. Somebody yells, "Hey, put up a fence": That's backlash. The following headline in The Washington Post, summing up reaction to May Day amnesty demonstrations, crystallizes this cracked-prism vision. "After Protests, Backlash Grows: Opponents of Illegal Immigration Are Increasingly Vocal."

Who, the Post seems to wonder, do these increasingly vocal "opponents" think they are — illegal aliens?

Of course, such "opponents" not only became "increasingly vocal" this week, some of them actually went to the polls. In Herndon, Va., voters elected what the cultural mainstream would probably dub the nation's first Backlash Legislature — a new city council and mayor who oppose Herndon's "day-laborer center," that law-flouting tax-payer-funded facility that opened last year to match up illegal alien workers with employers of illegal aliens. The Herndon vote seems highly significant: With one exception, no incumbent was re-elected who didn't oppose the center — and all new council members, including the new mayor, oppose the center. According to the Post report, last year's 5-2 majority in favor of the facility now becomes a probable 6-1 majority against. Not surprisingly, the online edition of The Washington Post headlined the election story "Immigrant Backlash in Herndon."

But this is no fit of pique. Indeed, it could be part of an ad hoc movement. According to the National Conference of State Legislatures, 463 immigration bills have been introduced just this year in 43 states, "the biggest crop of state immigration proposals ever recorded," the Post writes. Most of the measures, the newspaper continues, "are designed to get tough on illegal immigrants, on employers who give them jobs and on state officials who give them benefits" — in other words, to fill the breach left by Congress ever since a patriot-lite Senate failed to pass Rep. Tom Tancredo's eminently sensible immigration bill (complete with border fence) that came out of the House last year.

Will these get-tough — or, at least, get-tougher — state measures pass? The answer will tell us a lot about whether what we're witnessing is a passing "backlash," or a durable national movement, kicked off by the Minutemen Project, that has emerged from the vacuum on border protection and national preservation left by our leaders in Washington.

I'm not sure if it's simply because I'm looking, but I feel as though I'm seeing more anecdotal reports of American citizens taking local action, whether it's a story out of Arizona — "Sheriff's posse to patrol desert" — or from Connecticut, where the appearance of infectious diseases among illegal alien populations has convinced the Board of Health in Milford effectively to ban local restaurants from employing illegal workers. The fact is, if Americans can find a sustainable level of outrage and concern to drive such reform at the state level, we, as a nation, might actually have a chance to survive the hand wringing, no-can-do gridlock in Washington.

Of course, a sustainable level of outrage and concern is no small feat for the extremely comfy people that we are. Then again, times being what they are, the extreme comfort levels to which we have grown accustomed could well become a thing of our past. Which wouldn't necessarily be a bad thing. Surely, it's time to wean ourselves of immorally cheap labor and immorally cheap goods. Surely, it's time we learn that some things cost more than we want them to, even — no, especially — American citizenship.

Lost in Mexico

5/30/06

Did you hear about the last-minute amendment the Senate slipped into its mammoth immigration "reform" bill? The Senate voted something like 99 to Jeff Sessions to relocate the Statue of Liberty to the U.S.-Mexico border. And why not? If you won't fence 'em, join 'em — or, rather, let 'em join you. Isn't that what Bugs Bunny always said, or is that Bill Frist? I get them confused.

Not that it's fair to single out the Senate majority leader as the only joke who can't get a grip on the dangerous chaos of U.S immigration. There's every other American politician, up to and including George W. Bush, who supports the contents of the Dissolve America Now bill — oops, I mean the Senate's "comprehensive" immigration reform legislation.

The bill's crazy provisions for allowing 66 million new legal immigrants into the United States by 2026 (twice the population of Canada) aside, the Senate bill grants citizenship rights to 10 million to 20 million mainly Mexican illegal aliens who have sneaked into the country since the last U.S. amnesty for illegal aliens in 1986. It also waives any penalties for employers who have been illegally employing them. Such provisions only create conditions for ever greater, ever denser waves of new illegal immigration. This isn't exactly what a rational being would call fixing the problem. And don't even ask about the multi billion-dollar price tag on ballooning social services; the Senate hasn't.

What we're left with is not a nation, but a honey trap. If a body can just make it across the border, the Senate guarantees amnesty will always be the light at the end of the tunnel. And who knows? Maybe next time around, such as in 2026, the amnesty bill will be written in Spanish. After all, with 10 percent of Mexico already here, what's to stop 20 or 40 or 60 percent of Mexico from following? Not a law. Not a fence. Certainly not a border. Who needs a border, anyway? This, I'm afraid, is the rhetorical question driving too many of our public servants to abdicate their duty.

But why? Why does the American political establishment — with few genuinely patriotic exceptions — want to destabilize the American nation? If this were a Democratic era — a Kerry presidency, a Reid Senate, a Pelosi House — I would understand. I wouldn't like it any better, but the eradication of U.S. borders and, ultimately, the nation's core European identity is the sort of policy that follows from the West-corroding multiculturalism once uniquely associated with the left.

But this is a rock-ribbed Republican moment. Plus, it's a time of war. Sad to say, it's also time for a national shrink, someone to answer the question: Why are we killing ourselves?

The first patient, of course, would be the president himself. The Wall Street Journal's Peggy Noonan has pegged the president's obvious disinterest in securing the border either to a crass effort to placate the Hispanic vote (which, despite GOP dreams, trends heavily Democratic), or to "being lost in some geopolitical-globalist abstract-athon" that disconnects the administration from "the low concerns of normal Americans."

This bubble comes to mind on reading reader e-mail from Arizona, for instance, about home invasions and other illegal-alien crime the president seems callous to, even as he seems to view immigration law enforcement as gratuitously brutish or, as the Center for Immigration Studies' Mark Krikorian puts it, as "uncompassionate and un-Christian." This is particularly the case, Mr. Krikorian writes at National Review Online when it comes to Mexico, which he believes Mr. Bush regards as a "cousin" nation like Britain or Israel.

Familial feelings for corrupt and non-cooperative Mexico may seem puzzling until one reads Newsweek's contribution to the couch session, a story highlighting Mr. Bush's affection for the Mexican-born women who have always tended him and his family. OK: So Mr. Bush regards housekeeper Paula Rendon as his "second mother." That's nice. But does that mean the rest of us have to regard 100 million Mexicans as fellow citizens?

Of course, the end of America as a national idea is being promulgated by forces greater than any one man. From the anti-American left to bottom-line Big Business, from global elites to media elites, there is less and less any notion of a nation. Such amnesia may be fine for them. But then there's the rest of us. Is America something we can just forget?

The NFL drops the ball on border security

2/19/07

All civilizations fall. That's what "they" say, and who can argue? Even from the vantage point of the American Superpower, the historic record — from Greece to Rome, from Mongols to Moguls, from the Age of Spain to Pax Britannica — looks less than encouraging, particularly when you consider society's nasty self-destructive streak. But if the end is clear — let's hope it's not near — the causes will drive historians of the future crazy. I can hear them now: "They had unprecedented freedom. They had massive nukes. They had great lawns and a thousand different kinds of potato chips. What went wrong?" Solving the riddle won't be easy. But some day, when historians wonder about the decline and fall of, well, us, I hope they examine Super Bowl XLI in the year 2007. It marked a crucial turning point.

How can that be? Nothing happened on the field or on screen to cause our sunken but stable culture of idolized thuggishness, bad pop stars and crude commercialism to spin out of control and plummet to the ground. There wasn't a wardrobe malfunction in sight. What historians will need to examine instead is something that didn't materialize on game day.

That something is a recruitment ad for the U.S. Border Patrol that the

National Football League refused to print in-game programs distributed at the stadium and over the Internet because it was "controversial."

There is a hefty chunk of symbolism to ponder here, beginning with the staggering concept that a recruitment effort on behalf of the U.S. Border Patrol can be considered "controversial" by any American organization. More alarming still is that the organization here is professional football, hobbyhorse to red-meat America, the kind of people — the kind of men — who are stereotypically supposed to have retained their atavistic reflexes when it comes to defending hearth and home.

The Border Patrol ad in question lists an agent's prospective duties in protecting that last line of defense for the United States — our border. By any measure, this is an affirmative mission that should have a salutary effect on any civilization with even halfway healthy reflexes. The first duty listed in the ad is to "prevent the entry of terrorists and their weapons into the United States." Next, to "help detect and prevent the unlawful entry of undocumented aliens ... and apprehend violators of our immigration laws." And finally, to "play a role in stopping drug smuggling along our borders."

This is controversial? The answer is yes, if the NFL is talking. As NFL spokesman Greg Aiello put it to The Washington Times, "The ad that the department submitted was specific to Border Patrol, and it mentioned terrorism. We were not comfortable with that."

Tsk, tsk. Isn't that just too bad. But is the NFL really saying it isn't "comfortable" with supporting government efforts to prevent terrorism at the border?

Aiello went on. "The borders, the immigration debate is a very controversial issue, and we were sensitive to any perception we were injecting ourselves into that." The key phrase here is sensitive to "any perception." It becomes clear that the NFL is not focused on the American perception.

The fact is, the ad wasn't "injecting" anything into the immigration debate. The ad's substance concerned not, for example, the pros and cons of "guest worker" programs, but defending the border and upholding the law. And who could be "sensitive" about that? All I can think of, besides terrorists and drug smugglers, is illegal aliens and their families back home. Considering that the NFL hopes to add a Mexican franchise to its roster, maybe Mexico is where the NFL thinks discomfort and sensitivity over "the borders" come from. Which isn't exactly going to win a trophy for being all-American. But maybe there's more than a supranational business decision to consider. The NFL has revealed something new about the state of the border in the popular imagination. Even as one large constituency of the country wants to mark our southern border with a fence, making it more tangible, another wants to make the border more elastic, making it less meaningful, even less defensible. This political struggle has had the effect of making the border itself controversial, a development the NFL was somehow mindful of in its decision to rebuff the border agency.

Next question: When a nation's border becomes controversial, how long does its sovereignty last? And what happens to the civilization? All of which is precisely why future historians of American decline shouldn't overlook what didn't happen at Super Bowl XLI.

Cultural takeover

6/8/07

As Prime Minister Tony Blair prepares to leave 10 Downing Street, "Mohammad" is the second most popular name in Britain.

As President Bush is finally deserted by his long-suffering conservative base, "Jose" is not the second-most popular name in the United States. But Spanish, as yet unofficially, is America's second language.

Such developments represent two obviously different phenomena — the impact of Muslims and Hispanics on societies once aptly summed up as English-speaking peoples. What is similar is the phenomena's transformative effect: Britain is increasingly defined by its accommodation of a tiny (3 percent) Islamic minority; the United States is increasingly defined by its accommodation of a large Hispanic minority (14.8 percent), some considerable number of whom are here illegally.

Is this a shocking turn of events? You bet. Of course, to anyone who remembers the "Behead Those Who Insult Islam" posters displayed in London last year, the Islamization of Britain may seem long obvious. But that doesn't mean it isn't startling to see, quantified, in a government tally of baby names, a reliable indicator of the increasingly Muslim future of Britain.

Similarly, to anyone beset by bilingualism, both in business and the business of daily life, the Hispanization of America is currently a fact. But that doesn't mean there isn't an almost tangible gut-check, say, in reading about the extent to which 2008 American presidential candidates, Republicans and Democrats alike, are gearing up Spanish-speaking drives within their English-speaking campaigns to vie for Spanish-speaking voters.

Rep. Tom Tancredo, Colorado Republican, is the principled exception, believing, as he has said, that where a bilingual individual gains an advantage, a bilingual country suffers from irreparable fragmentation because the disappearance of a common language leads to the end of a common culture. If the Senate effectively legalizes 12 to 20 million mostly Spanish-speaking illegal aliens — a mainly Mexican bloc which, ironically, is anything but "diverse" — the common language (English) and common culture (American) slip that much farther away. It's inevitable. This Spanish-speaking demographic is simply too massive to assimilate — even assuming the multicultural states of America were still in the assimilation business, which we're emphatically not.

And that's shocking, too. But more than shocking, this whole issue is depressing and distressing — although I know I'm not supposed to say so. Whenever anyone has the bad taste to point out markers of cultural transformation, the rest of us are supposed to play it very cool, expressing only the most noncommittal reaction, if any at all. We're not supposed to flinch, and we're certainly not supposed to lament such changes, or mourn what is being lost, or, heaven help us, do anything to stop or reverse them, such as demanding the enforcement of existing immigration laws that would both encourage the repatriation of illegal aliens and discourage more from coming.

The socially acceptable position, the one that qualifies as politically correct wisdom suitable to be shouted from rooftops (or written in the Wall Street Journal editorial page), is to accept phenomena such as the Islamization of Britain and the Hispanization of the United States as givens, as progress, as proof of one's own moral goodness. Anything less than regarding these wholly optional changes, ours to make or not, as national destiny — international destiny? — is denounced as malicious bigotry.

In this way our conception of ourselves as an existing culture — open to modification and growth, yes, but not irreversible transformation — has been grossly undermined. Not only are the traditions and characteristics (English-speaking? non-Muslim?) of our societies now regarded as being retrograde embarrassments, we are also supposed to cheerfully maintain our societies in a perpetual state of ethnic and/or religious flux. The irony that goes unremarked is that the homogenous — dare I say, non-diverse? — nature of Islamic and Hispanic countries sending forth immigrants remains immutable. Which is why it won't matter much to the world if the United States ever becomes the 18th Spanish-speaking country in the Western Hemisphere, and if Britain ever becomes the 57th nation in the Organization of the Islamic Conference.

Except, that is, to those who would lament the passing of the English-speaking peoples. Mr. Bush and Mr. Blair obviously don't belong to such a group, but who does? The group exists in shamed silence, having bought the PC line that cultural self-preservation — Western self-preservation, that is — is nothing but an exercise in crude racism. But is it really? If we never hear any answer but "yes," it's time to get out the handkerchiefs and weep, silently.

Is 'decency' enough for citizenship?

6/15/07

Now that the president has tried to revive the comatose Senate amnesty bill, at least as big a question as whether he can bring it back to life is why on earth he would want to?

Sure, he wants a win because he hasn't had one lately. Sure, he wants a (gulp) legacy because it's that clock-ticking time in his second term. But why this particular attempted win, which his political base sees only as betrayal? Why this hoped-for legacy, which would eliminate him from any conservative pantheon?

"It's a very emotional issue." That's what the president says by way of describing the acid turmoil his "comprehensive" immigration reform push has caused, particularly among conservatives. He's right on one level, but I get the impression he makes the point to dismiss his opponents' objections as volcanic eruptions of feeling, rather than legitimate and reasonable arguments.

At the same time, immigration reform is a very emotional issue for Bush himself. Too emotional. When it comes to illegal aliens — in particular, illegal aliens from Mexico — the man seems to be governed by his gut. And that, of course, is no way to govern.

I say this having gone back over the immigration file that has piled up during this administration. A strong emotional thread connecting Bush to the issue comes through stories about his beloved Mexican-born housekeeper/nannies, and through stories about his political associates with Mexican roots, such as Attorney General Alberto Gonzales, or campaign aide Israel Hernandez, "whom," Newsweek noted last year, "Bush hired after hearing his family story."

Bush just loves those family stories. No one needs a shrink's couch to imagine the inspiring effect of immigrant success stories on an Establishment scion like Bush, who, while he may have had to struggle for his Texas twang, never had to struggle for much else — at least anything essential. From the big chair on the hacienda porch, with that "sense of Southwestern noblesse" Newsweek's Howard Fineman fancifully attributes to Bush's possible notion of himself as a hacendado (landowner), the president's admiration seems to know few bounds. "When you grow up in Texas like ... I did," Bush recently told McClatchy Newspapers, "you recognize the decency and hard work and humanity of Hispanics."

A lovely testimonial, but hardly a criterion on which to offer amnesty to some 12 to 20 million illegal aliens, even if they are mainly Hispanic. Half the world's population are undoubtedly just as decent, hard-working and humane, but that doesn't qualify the non-Hispanic billions (who haven't broken innumerable U.S. laws) for citizenship — at least not yet.

But the rosy — better, hazy — view from the hacienda porch doesn't take this in. Instead, Bush not only imagines comprehensively reforming the illegal, mainly Hispanic millions into citizens, but also "assimilating" them into Americans. The president doesn't seem to have noticed that the multicultural states of America long ago junked the "assimilation" process as being "Eurocentric," "racist" and worse. Nope, he's still talking about "this system's capacity to assimilate newcomers" as though it's the Statue of Liberty's birthday — her 50th birthday in 1936. This "capacity to assimilate," he says, "has been one of the great, powerful traditions of America. It works, and it will work this time."

It will? Question from McClatchy: "Do you think we assimilate immigrants as well as in previous waves?"

Bush's answer: "Absolutely."

Obviously, Bush hasn't ridden a rush-hour bus where no English is spoken, or listened to a business office recording asking "oprima el numero dos." But not even the presidential bubble excuses him from failing to notice the cultural transformation this country has undergone over the past half century. From his inviolate state of oblivion, Bush views "a backlash against newcomers" as being the only conceivable threat to the assimilation process — and more. "I am deeply concerned about America losing its soul," he said, bemoaning the country's opposition to illegal — illegal — immigration. "I am worried that a backlash to newcomers could cause our country to lose its great capacity to assimilate newcomers."

America's soul has been gasping for survival for ages. This has nothing to do with Bush's "backlash" bogeyman — which, frankly, sounds like another slap at Americans who want U.S. sovereignty upheld. Maybe Bush is just being emotional. But it's clear where his emotions lie, and it's not with conservatives. And I don't think they stop at the border, either.

Arizona's fight for our America

4/30/10

Three cheers aren't enough for Arizona. It's the first state to defend American citizenship on the basis of identity, and American sovereignty on the basis of borders. In an age of blurred identities and undefended borders, Arizona has put itself in a good, old-fashioned state of revolt against the postmodern, global-minded state of being foisted on us by internationalist elites up to and including President Barack Hussein Obama.

That's the effect, anyway, of Arizona's new immigration law, which, as George F. Will has aptly pointed out, "makes what is already a federal offense — being in the country illegally — a state offense." Only in our time, with identities blurred, borders undefended and elites internationalized, could this be controversial. Among other things, the new law requires state law enforcement to verify a person's immigration status in the course of "lawful contact."

Far from heralding the deployment of jackbooted terror squads among the tumbleweed and sprinklers, Arizona's new law acknowledges that American citizenship does and (wow) should exist, and affirms that sovereignty, ignored at the federal level, is the responsibility of a state overrun by illegal aliens mainly from neighboring Mexico.

Given our psycho idea of "normal" — alien-strained schools, bankrupted hospitals, advancing bilingualism and "sanctuary cities" — this new immigration law has aroused Establishment wrath. Moving across the spectrum from Right(ish) to Left, this ranges from the tense chorus of tut-tutting from the pro-amnesty Republican underbelly (Jeb Bush, Karl Rove, Tom Ridge), insta-calls for boycotts of Arizona from California officials, denunciations from Left-wing national pols and pundits (Nancy Pelosi, E.J. Dionne) a possible Justice Department investigation from President Obama, and, of course, much razzing from La Raza and other Che-idolizing open-borders and Reconquista agitators.

There's another reason. Arizona suddenly poses an unexpected threat to the status quo of permissible lawlessness, the illegal demographic transformation of this country into a linguistic and cultural extension of Latin America. This out-of-control movement has been tolerated if not facilitated by our political leadership for several decades under the dangerous influence of what we know as multiculturalism, the school of thought that has widely delegitimized U.S. identity altogether. Maybe more than anything else, Arizona's law restores a civic sense that there exists such an identity, and it is, and should be, legally protected. Thus, the multiculti rage.

A second bill pending in Arizona concerns another legal aspect of American identity, namely the constitutional requirement that our presidents be "natural-born" and not "naturalized" Americans. Both laws may be seen as state-level attempts to safeguard the nation according to principles set forth in the Constitution because authorities have failed to act responsibly at the federal level.

The "natural born" bill would require presidential candidates running in Arizona to submit proof of their constitutional eligibility to the Arizona secretary of state. In the case of President Obama, one such proof would be his long-form, circa 1961, birth certificate. This original form includes, for example, the name of the hospital where a person was born, as well as that of the attending physician — information not included in the computer-generated short form that has appeared online and is of recent vintage.

Just as the state's new check on immigration status seems appropriate, so, too, does this potential requirement that presidential candidates prove their "natural born" bona fides, a requirement that, according to World Net Daily, is also under consideration in state legislatures in Georgia, New Hampshire, Oklahoma, South Carolina and in the U.S. Congress.

I've never understood the derisive wrath targeting Americans troubled by Obama's refusal, for reasons unknown, to release his long-form birth certificate and end the divisive natural-born controversy — partly, of course, because I am one such American. Another so troubled is Army Lt. Col. Terry Lakin, who, taking seriously his oath to preserve and protect the Constitution, has laid it all on the line: Lakin has stopped obeying military orders, including deployment orders to Afghanistan for his second tour, pending release of the president's original birth document proving his constitutional eligibility to be commander in chief. Unconscionably, the president prefers to see Lakin court-martialed rather than show his old paperwork. Why?

Unanswered, the question consigns us to that limbo of uncertainty — of blurred identities, undefended borders and internationalized elites. But identity matters. The law matters. And the Constitution matters above all.

Protecting our American identity

5/21/10

Excellent news: Most Americans approve of Arizona's new immigration law. And by wide margins. According to Pew, the overall number is 59 percent. The New York Times poll came in at 60 percent. According to the NBC/Wall Street Journal poll, that overall number is higher still: 64 percent. These solid majorities show stirrings of a surprisingly resilient national survival instinct.

I say "surprisingly" because that instinct—in some cases perhaps no more than a reflexive urge to hold the line—has been subjected to decades of steady, acidic corrosion in the "politically correct" re-education camps we know as our nation's school systems. There, we all learn (or are all taught, anyway) that borders are "divisive" and immigration laws are "discriminatory." In other words, it's either "We are the world" or you are a racist. The moral blackmail that begins in kindergarten doesn't stop.

But if we think past it for a minute—a quiet, reflective minute, away from our minders—the logical notion that borders necessarily divide (nations), and immigration laws necessarily discriminate (between citizen and non-citizen) is still likely to coalesce. And that's excellent news. Who knows? With Arizona as our shining state in a desert, the electorate might even come to realize that without borders and without immigration laws, there is no nation and there is no citizenship, and that we had better beef up both—and fast.

No wonder our transnational elites and rowdy, open-border agitators are so unnerved by what's going on in Arizona. And they make a lot of noise telling us so. In fact, when I sat down to write the week's column, I falsely assumed Arizona was getting hammered from all sides. After all, headlines scream, municipalities in Northern California (the usual - Berkeley, Oakland, San Francisco), Boston, Seattle and Austin have voted to boycott Arizona businesses. Los Angeles, too (which prompted an Arizona energy official to offer, tartly, to help turn off the lights in L.A., which buys 25 percent of its power from the state).

Rumors of sports boycotts float. Assistant Secretary of State Michael Posner even complained about Arizona on the subject of human rights to totalitarian China, for Pete's sake.

Still, Arizona is really only getting it from one side. (As noted in the Pew poll, even a strong majority of Democrats favor essential provisions of the Arizona law, with almost half supporting the law itself.) The anti-Arizona side, however, is the one with mainstream media access and Washington political clout. It's the same side that almost reached critical mass under George W. Bush, with his "comprehensive immigration reform"—shamnesty - plan, and it hasn't leveled off under Barack Obama, now gunning for similar legislation.

"In the 21st century, we are defined not by our borders, but by our bonds," said the President of North America, I mean, the United States, in an appearance with Mexican president Felipe Calderon this week. We want "a border that will unite us instead of dividing us," Calderon said in turn. This was somewhat less imperialistic than Calderon's 2007 line, "Where there is a Mexican there is Mexico," but the gist is clear. Neither president wants a border, both want amnesty for millions of mainly Mexican illegal aliens, and Arizona makes them mad.

That's because nothing could be worse for such "citizens of the world" than Arizona's immigration law—except, maybe, Arizona's other restorative new law, which, to further the principle that "public school pupils should be taught to treat and value each other as individuals and not be taught to resent or hate other races or classes of people," now prohibits courses, for example, that "promote resentment toward a race or class of people," or "advocate ethnic solidarity instead of the treatment of pupils as individuals." (It will be almost amusing to watch Leftists slam a law against teaching racial resentment and hatred as "racist.") The fact is, the Arizona legislature is onto the multicultural masquerade—the non-Western grievance industry pretending to be "education." The party's over.

It all fits, really. The state that wants to protect American identity to ensure that all of its citizens, regardless of race or origin, have one. Call it the Spirit of Arizona. And let's hope it's catching.

Media In the Tank

A vote against the entrenched media

10/22/04

"Absolutely," most reporters want John Kerry to win the election, declares Newsweek's Evan Thomas, commenting on the media bias he says translates into "maybe" five extra points for the Democratic ticket at the polls. That's down from the 15 points Thomas first predicted Fourth Estate favor would bestow on Kerry-Edwards, but even five points could tip a race as close as this one.

Which is a chilling thought — but also a golden opportunity. It means that a vote for Bush-Cheney is not only a vote against Kerry-Edwards, but also a vote against Kerry-Edwards-CBS-CNN-New York Times. Are you incensed over Dan Rather's crude attempt to influence the presidential election with a sheaf of pathetic forgeries? Appalled by "Nightline's Ted Koppel for using dictatorship-vetted sources in communist Vietnam to contradict the testimonies of decorated American veterans?

Outraged by ABC's head-office directive to its reporters to go easier on John Kerry than George W. Bush, and not "reflexively and artificially hold both sides 'equally' accountable"? Don't get mad, vote Republican.

The fact is, never before have mainstream media (MSM) organizations — and I mean the hunters and gatherers of news, not its cooks and consumers — sunk so deep in the tank for a Democratic ticket. The election is days away but vital questions about Kerry remain not just unanswered in MSM outlets, but unasked — evidence of the efficiency with which the only-selectively adversarial media have embraced the role of Democratic star-maker, not newsmaker.

"It's up to Kerry to defend himself, of course," ABC News political director Mark Halperin admits in a "1984"-style directive leaked to the

Drudge Report. "But as one of the few news organizations with the skill and strength to help voters evaluate what the candidates are saying..." — gee, thanks a lot — "now is the time for all of us to step up and do that right."

And how's that done — by covering for Kerry? Given what we still don't know about the candidate after his practically incessant blathering, including three debates, this becomes the inescapable conclusion. And I don't just mean de-emphasizing such Kerry facts as his inexplicable failure to attend three-quarters of his public Senate Intelligence Committee hearings. Or failing to ponder the coincidence that Kerry cousin C. Stewart Forbes' company won a $900 million contract from Vietnam after Sen. Kerry pushed to normalize relations.

Here we are, on the brink, possibly, of electing a man who, as an American officer, parlayed with the enemy, and there have been no questions, no stories in response. No thoughts, no curiosity. We contemplate a new wartime leader whose political epiphany — the famous Christmas in Cambodia, "seared, seared" into Kerry's memory — never happened. Stories in the MSM? It's tough to find even one.

We consider trusting our very lives to a man who has consistently hewed to the wrong side of history, favoring appeasement and disarmament over democratic principle and strength, but we know nothing of his current thinking on those old positions.

How, for instance, does this American presidential candidate explain his place of honor in a Vietnamese war museum dedicated to an American defeat? Does Kerry believe the anti-war movement in which he figured so prominently bears any moral responsibility for the mass brutality — executions, re-education camps, boat people — that marked Hanoi's victory? Indeed, does Kerry still believe North Vietnam "liberated" South Vietnam, and that the conflict itself was not a front in the Cold War? We saw valedictory comments from Kerry on Ronald Reagan's death, but we have no idea whether he still reviles the Reagan years as a "moral blackness."

We don't know because no one in the MSM has asked him. This glaring failure makes a mockery of the media. It leaves us gasping for facts. It also explains the volcanic eruption of alternative sources of campaign information — Swift Boat Veterans for Truth, the newsies of the blogosphere, and a slew of independent ads and documentaries, including "Stolen Honor." Such activity has injected vital blasts of oxygen into otherwise stilted coverage.

But in the land of the free and the free press, we shouldn't have to rely on the unique gumption of, say, a John O'Neill, the Swiftee spokesman who went so far as to write a best-selling book about John Kerry, "Unfit for Command" (Regnery), to publicize crucial information the MSM ignored. I remember well the veritable news blackout on the

Swift Boat vets when they first assembled last spring in downtown Washington. The Associated Press didn't even send a correspondent, calling the group's press conference "old news" — before it happened.

Whatever the final tally on Election Day, we, the people need to take a good hard look at the MSM scorecard the day after.

NYT imam series not even Journalism 101

3/13/06

Way back when I was a cub reporter, I got hold of a book about the "art" of interviewing. It was a thin book — no use spending thousands of words to tell a reporter, cub or old Grizzly, to bone up on a subject and let natural curiosity take its course.

That thin book came to mind on reading a three-part series in The New York Times about an imam named Reda Shata, who presides over the Islamic Society of Bay Ridge in Brooklyn, N.Y. As far as the art of interviewing goes, the reporter got it exactly backward: Thousands of words; negligible expertise; and no curiosity.

Both the New York Post and the New York Sun have already pounced on the most egregious flaw of omission: not a mention, in 11,000-plus words, of the day in March 1994 when a man walked out of that same Bay Ridge mosque and, inspired by the anti-Jewish sermon of the day (delivered by a different, unidentified imam), armed himself and opened fire on a van carrying Hasidic Jewish children. Ari Halberstam, 16, was killed. The Times series, as it happened, concluded on the 12th anniversary of his death.

Such journalistic jaw-droppers abound: not only gaping holes, like the one above, but also dead ends that leave countless questions that the female reporter, it seems, never thought to ask. For example, she notes, over six months of interviews, the Egyptian-born imam refused to shake her hand. "He offers women only a nod," she writes. Why is shaking hands with a woman "improper"? What does the imam think about sexual equality? She doesn't tell us. In Belgium last year, she doesn't mention, the female president of the parliament made headlines for canceling a meeting with an Iranian delegation over this same refusal to shake a woman's hand (the parliamentarian's own); while in Holland, the English-language blog Zacht Ei reported, a Muslim man lost a month's worth of welfare benefits for not only refusing to shake hands with female municipal employees, but also refusing to acknowledge their presence. This is supposed to be "the story of Mr. Shata's journey west," but the story bypasses such landmark issues.

Instead, we get a load of happy talk: "Married life in Islam is an act of worship," Mr. Shata says. So impressed were the editors of The

New York Times by this load that they ran the quotation, not just above the fold, but across the very top of the front page over a gold-bathed family photo four columns wide. Does Miss Reporter ask the imam to reconcile this ecstatic notion with the Islamic custom of arranged and forced marriages, the spate of spousal abuse and "honor killings" within European Muslim communities — as recounted in clarifying detail in Bruce Bawer's important new book, "While Europe Slept" — or the tradition of polygamy, which exists to this day in portions of Islamic society?

No, no and no. She writes: "One Brooklyn imam reportedly urged his wealthier male congregants during a Ramadan sermon last year to take two wives. When a woman complained about the sermon to Mr. Shata, he laughed. 'You know that preacher who said Hugo Chavez should be shot?' he asked," referring to a comment by Pat Robertson about the Venezuelan leader. "'We have our idiots, too.'" One clumsy feint and presto — The New York Times loses all interest in polygamy, from Mohammed's Mecca to Bloomberg's New York.

Then there was the series' look at terrorism. "What I may see as terrorism, you may not see that way," Mr. Shata says. What does he mean by that? The reporter doesn't tell us. Hamas is a powerful symbol of resistance, he says; the assassinated Hamas founder Sheik Ahmed Yassin was the "martyred" "lion of Palestine," he sermonizes; and yet the imam says he condemns all violence. How does he square that? She doesn't tell us. And when he sanctions violence against soldiers, not civilians, how does he define "soldier" and "civilian"? She doesn't tell us that, either.

When asked about a 2004 sermon that "exalted" a female suicide bomber as a "martyr," Mr. Shata seems "unusually conflicted," the reporter writes. He declines to comment for fear of "(inviting) controversy," and alienating New York rabbis he has "forged friendships with." And there the question lies: She just lets him slip away. All the news that's fit to print, apparently, doesn't include the heart of the matter.

Going gaga over Ahmadinejad

10/1/07

Some years ago, when our teenagers were tots, my husband and I took them to a puppet version of "Goldilocks and the Three Bears." Or was that "The Three Bears and Goldilocks"? Turns out, we were seeing "the other side" of the old story. Here, Goldilocks was no wandering lass improbably meeting up with an even more improbable household of bears, but a human interloper vandalizing the home of her fellow mammals.

When the bears came home from their walk, happened upon Goldilocks' mischief and chased her out of the house, they were acting in fright, not anger, and had no thought of, say, devouring the heroine — which is often the conventionally climactic possibility in this and other such fairy tales. The puppets made it clear that the whole incident resulted from a lack of communication. Everyone — bears, children — should listen to one another because, as the puppets sang in conclusion, "there are two sides to every story."

This really burned me up. First, the kids in the theatre were too young to have their Goldilocks narrative down pat, and, therefore, too young to have it messed with. And who did these puppeteers think they were injecting a dose of moral relativism into age-old tales? It's not that Goldilocks is a rallying figure exactly, but there's a disconnect here. For kids still grappling with moral absolutes known as right and wrong, it's very confusing to contend with the "alternate" message: essentially, that there is right and right again. For the preschoolers in the audience, this was just the beginning of their postmodern education.

It's no coincidence that this anecdote comes up in the aftermath of Iranian President Mahmoud Ahmadinejad's obscene caper across New York City — from Columbia University (with a threatened detour to Ground Zero), to the United Nations, and to the Intercontinental Hotel where he hosted a dinner for 50 American guests from academia and the media. The same childlike ethos of right and right again — moral relativism — of the PC puppet show was the institutional rationale that permitted Ahmadinejad's terrible public relations triumph over America. I fear it has only convinced him that he can win more.

He came, he raved, he hosted the media. Question: Couldn't news stars Brian Williams and Christiane Amanpour and Time magazine's Richard Stengel and whomever else supped with Iran's jihadist-in-chief have told him, if not where to go, that they had to wash their hair? Alas, no. Not the president, not the State Department, not Columbia, not the media, could think of a single reason to say no to this thug — this sworn enemy of our country fighting a covert war against U.S. troops in Iraq, this largest sponsor of terrorism in the world, this Holocaust-denier seeking the nuclear tools for another Holocaust — and deny him an American showcase on the world stage.

That's because they don't know a single reason. Decades of multiculturalism, positing that all cultures are equally valuable, except, of course, for Western culture (which is the pits) have undermined our ability to make distinctions, to understand that being open to everything — including Ahmadinejad's presence — is not the same as preserving a tolerant society.

"If we are not prepared to defend a tolerant society against the onslaught of the intolerant," Karl Popper wrote, "then the tolerant will be destroyed and tolerance with them."

From the puppet theatre to the Ivy League, we are not prepared. Instead, we act as though Ahmadinejad has his point of view, and we, or, rather, the U.S. government — as, for example, Scott Pelley of "60 Minutes" carefully pointed out in his A-jad interview (I've never heard a reporter say "sir" more times) — has its point of view. "This is America at its best," according to Columbia president Lee Bollinger. No, it's America at its morally paralyzed.

Transforming Ahmadinejad into a grand old statesman, some have noted, has parallels to the notorious 1933 Oxford Union resolution declaring "That this House refuses to fight for King and country." Among Britain's enemies, Churchill later noted, "the idea of a decadent, degenerate Britain took deep root and swayed many calculations."

This is the recurring danger. But this time the decadence is more widespread and the degeneracy more entrenched. Why? The Oxford resolution was passed by college students — very young people. Ahmadinejad was admitted into the country, hosted by Columbia, and respectfully received by the media on the say-so of supposedly seasoned adults. Which should make us all cry out: Where have all the grown-ups gone?

Media's O-colored glasses blank out leftist truth

10/31/08

Only three weeks ago I wrote about the presidential race's "third candidate." By that I meant the phenomenon of Barack Obama's hard-left affiliations just then bursting into public view and catching up with the front-runner as the candidates headed into the campaign's final stretch.

Turned out, of course, this was not a "candidate" the prObamedia was ever going to cover, not even as evidence of Obama's lifelong association and collaboration with radicals — self-identified communists, even — gained definition and detail, mainly on Internet journals and blogs. At the beginning of Obama's life, for example, there was "Frank," Obama's boyhood mentor who appears in his 1995 memoir "Dreams from My Father." Accuracy In Media's Cliff Kincaid has identified "Frank" as Frank Marshall Davis, a known Stalinist in a Soviet-sponsored communist network in Hawaii. But Obama obscures Frank's identity in his book, even, as Sean Hannity has reported, going so far as to drop passages about "Frank" from the more recent, recorded version of the book. Why? The media never asked.

Later in Obama's life there was Mike Klonsky, an unreconstructed

Marxist and erstwhile leader of an honest-to-goodness Maoist splinter group in the United States. Klonsky, like his buddy, ex-Weatherman William Ayers, spreads Marxism through education "reform." As the National Review Online's Andrew C. McCarthy reported, Obama directed nearly 2 million foundation dollars to fund Klonsky's ideas in the 1990s. More recently, Klonsky wrote a "social justice education" blog on the official Obama campaign Web site — at least until a blog named Global Labor and Politics pointed this fact out. Klonsky's musings were summarily scrubbed from the campaign Web site in June. Why? The media never asked.

And so it goes. The assorted radicals — from ACORN to Ayers, from anti-white Jeremiah Wright to Saudi-adviser Khalid al-Mansour to former PLO associate Rashid Khalidi — who have peopled Obama's ideological passage from rising leftist to post-ideological cipher, have been lost in the blur to a media focused solely on their own prize: Obama in the White House.

Such focus has created a drastically blinkered journalism, particularly in these final weeks. Take the fact that the supposedly "post-racial" Obama once funded Afrocentric, race-focused education programs supported by Jeremiah "G — - D — - America" Wright. That was a juicy blend of hypocrisy and extremism (dug up by Stanley Kurtz), but the media just averted their eyes.

Or how about good, ol' William "America Makes Me Want to Puke" Ayers, whose own relationship with Klonsky (the Maoist mentioned above) goes back to the days of the SDS (Students for a Democratic Society)? Obama worked closely with Ayers to fund radical programs (such as Klonsky's) in Chicago, endorsed Ayers' work, and launched his political career in Ayers' home. This is the ideological and literal bomb-thrower Obama brushed off as just "a guy in my neighborhood." But the media saw nothing to it — not even a piece of Obama's questionable pattern of collaboration with a series of people best described as unregenerate leftists.

But Colin Powell endorsed Obama, right? We heard all about that. Guess who else endorsed him? Anti-white, anti-Semite Louis Farrakhan, the Ahmadinejad-lite speaker of Iran's parliament Ali Larijani, Hamas and the pro-Hamas National Association of Muslim American Women. Did we hear about that? No.

And what about this one? Obama — potentially the next leader of the Free World, after all — once belonged to a socialist party called the New Party (and there are giant scans of a 1996 New Party News story claiming Obama as a member, courtesy the blog New Zeal). Smoking gun for the media, no?

No. The media didn't consider this worth any ink, not even after Joe the Plumber prompted Obama to let slip, clearly and unequivocally, his antipathies to basic capitalism: "When you spread the wealth around," Obama famously said, "I think it's good for everybody."

Despite the code of silence (omerta) maintained by the prObamedia (prObamerta), these stories and others like them have still come out in dribs, drabs and funny feelings, infusing the body politic with enough uneasiness about Obama's ideological affinities for the left to keep John McCain surprisingly and perhaps even resiliently competitive.

Despite the disgrace of our free-but-self-caged press, many voters have managed to learn for themselves that Obama has spent a lifetime associating with the kind of anti-Americans and subversives that, by rights, make him ineligible for a federal security clearance — something Daniel Pipes has noted. Many voters understand that when you "spread the wealth around" you are enacting a basic premise of Marxism, or communism, or socialism, or something once upon a time derided as plain old commie-pinko. But that was a long time ago, and the fact is, we just don't know how many Americans are still put off, if not outraged, by such things.

And maybe this becomes the most important question to be settled on Nov. 4: How many Americans still consider mixing with and supporting bomb-throwers and radicals to be un-presidential? How many Americans still consider a Marxist basis for economics to be, in fact, downright un-American?

That such questions need to be asked, that such answers are in doubt, indicates the extent to which we have already changed as a people, and that is not a hopeful thing. Perhaps the miscalculation many conservatives made throughout this campaign was in assuming that Obama's alliances and working relationships with leftists and leftist causes were things most Americans would vigorously and automatically reject.

Then again, maybe they still will.

Cronkite's offensive history

7/24/09

It's time for a post-Cronkite post-mortem, but not on the late "icon" himself — the "most trusted man in America," the "voice of God," "the gold standard," the "proxy for a nation," or, in plainer English, the lush-lived celebrity "anchor" who died this month at age 92. No, the Cronkite post-mortem that's needed is for the zombies who conjured up the hollow rapture and the living dead who fell for it.

Harsh words? You bet. But I don't know how else to begin to assess a nation that sees fit to celebrate, crown, even worship a man who said his "proudest moment" was when he declared on CBS, having misinterpreted the 1968 Tet offensive as a victory for North Vietnam, that the Vietnam war was unwinnable for the United States. "If I've lost Cronkite, I've lost middle America," almost every Cronkite obituary approvingly quoted President Lyndon B. Johnson as having said in response — never mind that Cronkite was flat-out wrong in his reporting.

This was the infamous "stalemate" broadcast in which Cronkite editorialized in unprecedented manner: "It is increasingly clear to this reporter that the only rational way out then will be to negotiate, not as victors, but as an honorable people who ... did the best they could." Despite his obit-omnipotence, Cronkite alone wasn't responsible for LBJ's offer again to negotiate with Hanoi, his decision not to run for re-election, the ultimate flagging of America's commitment to South Vietnam, or one million-plus boat people who fled the communist regime, but the famed broadcaster was without doubt a key influence in persuading the nation, particularly its elites, to accept, if not court, American defeat in Vietnam.

So, to use his own words, was Walter Cronkite an honorable journalist who did the best he could?

No. What may — may — have resulted from forgivable misimpressions due to the "fog of war" long ago crystallized into obdurate lies. Cronkite never clarified the record, never admitted that the Tet offensive — the Vietcong's surprise holiday attack on cities across South Vietnam — resulted in a military and political fiasco for North Vietnam.

This was becoming apparent even before the dust had settled in 1968, as we learn in Peter Braestrup's indispensable "The Big Story", one of the signal historical works of the 20th century, which meticulously analyzes the media's failure to assess Tet correctly as a defeat for North Vietnam. Even Leftist journalist Frances Fitzgerald in her Pulitzer Prize-winning "Fire in the Lake" reported that Tet had "seriously depleted" Vietcong forces and "wiped out" many of their "most experienced cadres," noting that such losses drove "the southern movement for the first time into almost total dependency on the north." Her conclusion: "By all the indices available to the American military, the Tet offensive was a major defeat for the enemy."

And the enemy agreed. In a 1995 interview with the Wall Street Journal, Bui Tin, a member of the North Vietnamese general staff who in 1975 personally received the unconditional surrender of South Vietnam, called North Vietnam's losses in Tet "staggering." Communist forces in the South, he explained, "were nearly wiped out by all the fighting in 1968. It took us until 1971 to re-establish our presence, but we had to use North Vietnamese troops as local guerillas. If the American forces had not begun to withdraw under Nixon in 1969," he added, "they could have punished us severely." And who knows? If Cronkite had not used Tet to nudge for negotiations, maybe American forces would not have begun to withdraw.

Bui Tin said North Vietnamese commander Gen. Vo Nguyen Giap told him Tet was "a military defeat though we had gained the planned political advantages when Johnson agreed to negotiate and did not run for re-election."

Well, who could blame him? The president had "lost Cronkite."

And so be it. The president lost Cronkite, the United States lost Vietnam. But why are the rest of us still stuck with Cronkite's Orwellian packaging as "America's most trusted newsman" 41 years after he totally and calamitously and obstinately blew Tet? The ongoing genuflection before "Uncle Walter" reveals something mighty weird about this body politic—something beyond the ken of a mere journalist, something more in the line of work of a really good shrink.

Media sheepish about lion's murky past

8/27/09

Something about the death of a famous liberal person turns the media into grieving widows whose dictum against speaking "ill" of the dead eliminates all sober analysis of the life in question. Once, death in the passing parade came to us, more or less, in "just-the-facts, ma'am" obituaries.

Now, breaking, live and for the duration, a celebratory loop plays on about even the most mixed and controversial public lives. Notice I said "mixed" and "controversial," restrained terminology to describe the life and times of Sen. Ted Kennedy, whose death triggered a media dump of Hallmark-curlicued tributes that all begin with "lion of the Senate"—as though that were his official title—and finish with "the end of Camelot," as though that were his actual residence, not the tagline of an ancient PR campaign.

Question: How does the 1969 death of Mary Jo Kopechne—whom the married, panicked and first-term Sen. Ted Kennedy left to drown in 7 feet of Chappaquiddick water—apply to the "lion" from "Camelot"? Answer: It doesn't.

Remember? Don't speak ill of the dead. Kennedy fixture Ted Sorensen's gloss in Time magazine is typical, depicting "the Chappaquiddick incident" as merely ending Kennedy's "bright prospects for still higher office." The "Chappaquiddick incident" ended more than presidential prospects. It ended the life of a woman unlucky enough to have depended on Ted Kennedy. But it didn't end Kennedy's political career as it should have—and would have any non-Kennedy's.

ABCNews.com, maybe more perversely still, paints Kopechne's death as the reason Kennedy became the "lion of the Senate" in the first place: "But oddly, the darkest moment in Kennedy's career ... ultimately transformed him into one of the most highly regarded politicians in Congress." A dainty segue back to the "lion of the Senate," no?

Remember: Don't speak ill of the dead — and particularly "not at this time," which, in truth, describes a summer that has taken a toll on our celebrity class. From Michael Jackson to Walter Cronkite, deaths of the rich and famous have led the season's news as much as health care and town-hall meetings. Add Farrah Fawcett, Robert Novak, Don Hewitt, and now, Dominick Dunne (RIP), and it becomes clear that this was a summer in which death did not take a holiday. It also claimed Saudi billionaire and serial-libel tourist Khalid bin Mahfouz.

Not everyone gets the star treatment from the media — in fact, Mahfouz, world-famous bane of the free press, didn't get an obituary. (This is likely due to media fear of being sued from the grave: Don't speak ill of the dead, or else.) But Michael Jackson was a cash cow the media milked for everything they could, ignoring — that is, not speaking "ill" of — Jackson's freakish life to elevate the pathetic, unsavory pop idol to national iconhood and reap maximum ratings.

In showering approval on Walter Cronkite, the media were showering approval on themselves, or at least on their notion of their own importance. Oh, and about the fact that Cronkite misreported the 1968 Tet Offensive as an American defeat?

Don't speak — you know the rest. It's an old story by now. But there is so much the media consider "ill" in Kennedy's life — thus, unmentionable — that we are not getting a straight story. Besides the "Chappaquiddick incident," there were the decades of public debauchery. His political career was indeed at times momentous, but "controversial" is a mild word for it.

The first legislation he managed as a U.S. senator, the 1965 Immigration Act, effectively tipped the immigrant pool of this nation from Europe to the Third World. His despicable and notorious slander of Judge Robert Bork not only spearheaded the assault on Bork's 1987 nomination to the Supreme Court, it opened the sewer gates to slime politics.

We get scant consideration of such consequential facts. We get an emotional rush. This would matter less if the man were quietly going to his rest. But Democrats have already seized on the Disneyfied Kennedy — The Lion-Senator — as the posthumous mascot of nationalized health care, and will be adding Kennedy's name to health-care legislation.

This would make zero political sense if the media told the whole mixed and controversial truth. But they haven't marked the passing of a consequential scion of a power-wielding, privileged American family. They have showcased the debut of a cartoon superhero. The eyes and ears of democracy have failed us again.

Our best defense against Sharia: 'South Park'

4/23/10

The creators of "South Park," Trey Parker and Matt Stone, get it. They get the free-speech significance of the Danish Muhammad cartoons epitomized by Kurt Westergaard's bomb-head Muhammad.

They even get it across.

"It's so sad, the whole Muhammad, the whole Danish cartoon thing," said Stone, Parker seated beside him during a joint interview with the entertainment website Boing Boing.

Don't laugh. "Boing Boing" here goes where "elite" media fear to tiptoe, let alone tread. The subject was the 200th episode of "South Park," which, in unusually clean if satirical fashion, focused on Islam's fanatical, and, to Western sensibilities, ridiculous prohibitions on depictions and criticism of Muhammad, who is at one point presented in a bear suit disguise. (Now you can laugh.) Stone continued: "It's like, if everyone would have just, like, (done what they) normally they do in the news organizations, (and) just printed the cartoons…" "Everyone would have rallied together," interjected Parker.

"Now that guy (Westergaard) has to be hiding and all this (bleep) because everyone just kind of left him out to dry. It's a big problem when you have the New York Times and Comedy Central and Viacom basically just (wimping) out on it. It's just sad. I was, like, really sad about the whole thing."

This — despite the grubby vall-speakish patois of the astronomically successful Hollywood postmodern — is a singularly powerful statement. It is powerful in its sincerity, and it is singular in its, well, singularity. No other American "name" I can think of, no one tops in pop culture, has spoken out against (or even mentioned) the Islamic threat to Western freedom of expression as exemplified by the Sharia dictates against "Muhamtooning." Certainly no one has produced creative content about it. Rather, such dictates have been religiously followed — no pun whatsoever intended — just as though our society were itself officially Islamic. This makes "South Park"'s message the closest thing yet to a mainstream declaration of independence from Sharia. For rejecting both the threat of violence and the emotional blackmail emanating from Islam over critiquing Islam's prophet, the two "South Park" creators deserve a medal.

"They're courageous — no doubt that they are," said Bill O'Reilly of Fox's "The O'Reilly Factor" this week. He was discussing the Islamic death threats against Parker and Stone that, naturally, followed the recent "South Park" Muhammad episode. The threats came in a jihadist video (caption: "Help Us Remove this Filth") portraying the writer-producers as likely victims of Islamic violence along with Ayaan Hirsi Ali, Salman Rushdie, Geert Wilders, Kurt Westergaard and Lars Vilks. A photo of the slain body of filmmaker Theo van Gogh, his head nearly cut off on an Amsterdam street in 2004 by a jihadist assassin, served as an example.

Rather than praise Parker's and Stone's courage, however, O'Reilly went on to disparage their judgment.

"Was it the smart thing to do in light of the Danish cartoonist and van Gogh?" he asked. "It's harmless to me," he continued about the episode in question. "But if you are a hardcore jihadist any mention of Muhammad in any kind of way, particularly if you poking fun at him, is a capital offense."

According to whose law, Bill — Islam's or ours? Or is our law now Islamic? Those are the question citizens of the Western world need to hear discussed.

But not on the O'Reilly Factor.

"See, I would have advised them not to do it," O'Reilly continued, "because the risk is higher than the reward."

One reason there is such a high "risk" is because media people such as O'Reilly left Westergaard and now the "South Park" creators, as Parker put it, "out to dry." All media in American should have reproduced Westergaard's cartoon, just as all media in American should now applaud Parker and Stone for their defense of free speech against Sharia.

Surely, it is O'Reilly's responsibility as a leading broadcaster to do that small bit to keep the airwaves free.

Alas, this man of the folks doesn't see it that way. "You don't want to give in to the intimidating forces of evil," he said. "But you got to deal with reality. And these people are killers and they will kill you."

In other words, shut up about Muhammad, and everything will be fine — or at least Islamic.

Tragedy exposes 'the Big Lie'

1/14/11

The suppression of the facts is by no means the most dangerous aspect of any Big Lie. After all, facts don't go away even amid efforts to suppress them. All sorts of inconsistencies, impossibilities and clues remain behind, and sometimes in plain sight, for anyone who cares to look. The real threat the Big Lie poses to society comes when it is not stopped in its tracks, exposed and trashed for what it is — a lie — but rather accepted, accommodated and, indeed, treated as if it were the truth. At that point, a Big Lie is a big success, having created an alternate reality that turns its very targets into hapless accomplices.

Unfortunately, that last bit describes most Republicans' supine reaction to the reaction — the Big Lie — about the Arizona massacre. Much has already been written about the heinous movement on the Left to blame conservative politicians, political groups and pundits — but mainly Sarah Palin — for causing the crime, for creating the conditions unique to the crime, with "heated rhetoric" and "violent imagery." Without even examining the violence (note to liberals: I use the word metaphorically) this specious argument does to the First Amendment, I say this argument is a Big Lie.

Violent imagery ("battleground states," for goodness sake) and figures of speech are not only unexceptional in politics across the board, they are prevalent in ghoulish excess on the Left. I recommend that every reader visit Michelle Malkin's website to view her greatest-hits gallery of berserk Leftist "violence," from "Abort Palin" bumperstickers, to Bush assassination imagery, to our own President Obama's unforgettably thuggish rhetoric from the 2008 campaign trail: "If they bring a knife to the fight, we bring a gun."

Then there is the ongoing lie within the lie (which is how Big Lies are constructed) about Sarah Palin's infamous list of "targeted districts."

Assorted MSM outlets have displayed her political map that put swing districts in the cross-hairs; none of these outlets have reproduced the official Democratic Congressional Campaign Committee map that similarly "targeted" such districts in 2009 with bull's-eyes, featuring, for example, "Targeted Republican Thaddeus McCotter — Michigan's 11th District." If I can find it online, why can't they?

Such evidence, of course, would (metaphor alert) kill the Big-Lie drive to judge Republicans guilty of the Arizona crime and thereafter sentence them to a kind of peer-pressured censorship. Robust and, lately, winning conservative debate is (metaphors ahead) the target here; the weaponry doesn't matter to the Left. Which means facts don't matter, either. To wit: "So far, there's no connection between alleged murderer Jared Lee Loughner and the extremes of the Tea Party movement," writes the Washington Post's Jonathan Capehart, arguing for "Republican leaders to tamp down the rhetoric." He continues: "But that's beside the point...."

Really?

In the end, though, what's worse than the Big Lie itself is the failure to reject and expose it — the failure, in this case, to identity the lie as a naked influence operation to mute conservative political expression. This failure is the crime Republicans are guilty of each time they stoop to defend themselves within the phony terms of the lie itself.

When House Speaker John Boehner canceled all House votes this week, including the all-important first round on repealing Obamacare, the message was: Yes, maybe there is a bona fide link between congressional debate in Washington and the internal monologue that drove a man to kill in Tucson. Sarah Palin, too, protested way too much in her response to the Left's "blood libel" against her. It's not a civics lesson that's required to bring the Left to "reason." Where there are no facts, there is no reason, and any painstakingly logical arguments against disreputable falsehoods only further extend the charade.

A great unmasking is what's needed here. Having twisted an unspeakable crime into a gag for their opposition, the Left must be called out, and it's the job of the Right to do it. Otherwise, as with every Big Lie, silence turns everyone into a Big Liar.

Spiking the Examiner

7/28/12

News flash: The Washington Examiner spiked my syndicated column on the Muslim Brotherhood and why five House Republicans — Reps. Michele Bachmann, Trent Franks, Louie Gohmert, Tom Rooney and Lynn Westermoreland — were correct to call on Inspectors General to investigate MB influence on US government policy-making. And therein lies a tale. (The column is reprinted in this book under "Forbidden Columns.")

If the newspaper's online search function is accurate, it is even more perplexing to note that the Examiner hasn't run a single news story on the media-politics feeding frenzy, led by Sen. John McCain, directed at Rep. Michele Bachmann for raising questions about strong indications of Muslim Brotherhood penetration of the Washington policy-making chain. The geyser of Left-cum-GOP-Establishment hysteria arose from Bachmann et al pointing out in a letter to the State Department IG that Huma Abedin, a top advisor to Secretary of State Hillary Clinton, has close family members involved in MB-associated groups and movements, which are dedicated to the destruction of the West. Indeed, it was on the mention of Huma Abedin that the Examiner told me the paper turned down my column (full column reprinted below).

A little backstory.

I have noted before with dismay that the Washington Examiner automatically spikes any syndicated column I write regarding what might be referred to as President Obama's identity issues.

These include: the debate over the constitutional requirement that the president and vice president be "natural born"; this same debate as it enters court in eligibility challenges litigated from New Jersey to Georgia to the US Supreme Court; and related pieces of "natural born" legislation introduced in some state legislatures, including Arizona's. Since April 27, 2011, when Obama published a highly problematic illustration of a birth certificate on the White House website, the debate has taken a darker turn. There is now extensive evidence that fraud and forgery took place in the creation of the White House birth certificate. What that means to the Examiner is that it now also auto-spikes columns about this evidence and other sensational news coming out of the Cold Case Posse investigation mounted by the renowned Sheriff Joe Arpaio.

Regrettably, Townhall.com has this year decided to spike columns on this same subject by myself and others. In fact, the silence on this epic story extends across the public square, from Left to Right, from CNN to Fox, from Democrats to Republicans. When, earlier this year, this began happening to my column in a more systematic way, I was shocked. Others, too. I will note for the record that concerned scribes expressed outrage and alarm over such censorship, for which I remain grateful.

It is a more than passing strange sensation to write about what clearly seems to be important news in our country's history involving Americans from different states, from different walks of life—lawyers, judges, detectives, computer experts, government officials including the president, and more—knowing full well that some outlets won't run it because the subject is verboten in the public square. I have even come to expect this treatment on the subject, which must be some dangerous stage of complacency.

In a way, then, I almost welcome this latest, very different spike as a salutary jolt of alarm.

Here's how Examiner editorial page editor David Freddoso explained why the column didn't appear:

> We opted not to use it this week. We also passed over other syndicated columnists' offerings about the insinuations against Huma Abedin. The reason is simply that there is no hint of proof that she has done anything improper.

But the five House Republicans made no such claim. Amid their broad concerns about MB influence on US government policy-making, the members raised a red flag over Huma Abedin, Deputy Chief of Staff to the US Secretary of State. Why? Abedin's family members have been deeply involved with groups and movements dedicated to the destruction of Western civilization. This concerns the five House members. As it should, in my *opinion* – which is what my fact-based *opinion column* argued. What we learn from this escapade is that such an opinion is not considered printable at the Examiner.

Meanwhile, as former federal prosecutor Andrew C. McCarthy writes:

> A person is not required to have done anything wrong to be denied a high-ranking government position, or more immediately,

the security clearance allowing access to classified information that is necessary to function in such a job. There simply need be associations, allegiances, or interests that establish a potential conflict of interest.

To sample some of what McCarthy has further reported:
1) Saleha Abedin, Huma's mother, is a member of the Muslim Sisterhood.

2) Saleha is also a board member of the International Islamic Council for Dawa and Relief. **The IICDR has been long banned in Israel for supporting Hamas.**

3) Moreover it turns out that Huma Abedin herself was, until late 2008, a member of another of her mother's Islamist organizations, the Institute of Muslim Minority Affairs.

Huma's parents actually started this institute in Saudi Arabia in the 1970s, McCarthy explains, "with the backing of Abdullah Omar Naseef."

Who is Naseef?

McCarthy: "Naseef is a former secretary-general of the Muslim World League, which, as I've previously explained, has long been the Muslim Brotherhood's principal vehicle for the international propagation of Islamic supremacist ideology. Under the auspices of the MWL, Naseef not only backed the IMMA" — which, remember, was Huma's parents' Saudi project — "Naseef founded the Rabita Trust, which ...**is a specially designated international terrorist organization under federal law.**"

Can't you just hear the background-checker? *So, Huma, your folks were in business with a guy who started a designated terrorist group, your mom's on a board of a group banned in Israel for supporting Hamas, and you want top secret clearance to work alongside the SecState...HAHAHAHAHA.*

And there's even more, so much more. But let just this much sink in while I note that I sent this information (and more) to the Examiner, asking the editorial page editor to examine the evidence for himself, and, I hoped, run my column belatedly this week.

No soap.

Response: "I've had a look, and I will not be using the column."

I've had a look, too — the newspaper's lack of columns on this whole controversy, the newspaper's lack of *news* on this whole controversy — and I will not be using the Examiner.

What's Whiter Than the GOP? The Media

8/31/12

Ah, to be a member of Big Media when the white Republicans gather to nominate their white ticket for the White House. It's like shooting white elephants in a white convention center, what with their unbearable whiteness of being — so "non-diverse," as Big Media strenuously signal their audiences.

Gallup tells us Republicans are 87 percent white and Democrats are 63 percent white. But even when Republicans are not white — which occurs despite Big Media efforts to fool viewers (conservative websites observed that NBC failed to post speeches by non-white Republicans at its website, while MSNBC cut to its pundits on such non-white occasions) -- they might as well be white. That's because "white" is the media's slam on the GOP, their hectoring, subtle-as-a-sledgehammer message: Republicans are too "white" to deserve any decent person's vote. Perhaps veteran ABC and PBS political editor turned Yahoo! News Washington bureau chief David Chalian blurted out the storyline best: "(The Romneys) are happy to have a party with black people drowning."

This, it turned out, was a race-bait too far. Chalian lost his job after his comment went viral. But who will take his place? Someone just like him. Probably someone who looks like him, too — and those dread, white Republicans.

That's the dirty secret. Big Media are castigating the party of Lincoln and Reagan for displaying, as the Los Angeles Times put it, "a distinctly pale hue" while "the United States has become an increasingly more diverse country," but the newsrooms of America are just as pale if not actually more so. According to 2012 figures from the American Society of News Editors (ASNE), minorities make up 12.32 percent of newsroom employees. That leaves 87.68 percent of the writing and editing jobs in white hands. That means newsrooms are lily-whiter than the GOP!

Some news organizations take this to the limit. While Time magazine dings the GOP for being "a mostly white, aging party (doing) its best to avoid looking like it," the National Association of Black Journalists (NABJ) gave Time its 2012 Thumbs Down Award for, among other grievances, not having a single full-time black correspondent.

The media also hold a slim white edge over the GOP in the racial composition of television newsroom managers. According to a 2011 NABJ study, white people — mainly white men — hold 88 percent of these decision-making jobs, leaving 12 percent to minorities. As for news anchors and presidential debate moderators? To build on a title of a Salon.com piece about the GOP convention, welcome to the "Heart of

Whiteness."

Stunningly, these same Caucasian newsies are blind to their own skins. How else, for instance, could "NBC Nightly News" anchor Brian Williams in July have asked Mitt Romney "to confirm or deny" whether he was looking for a running mate who is "an incredibly boring white guy"?

"You told me you were not available," quipped Romney.

But Williams and the rest of his mainly white media brethren (also sistren) seem to regard their core liberalism as their camouflage. It is the shield and spear they carry in the Left's push to demonize people of one color (white) and a particular sex (male) in order to delegitimize a glorious political philosophy — small-government, low-tax, anti-statist conservatism. This philosophy is what draws together Republicans and their delegates, not their "whiteness."

What the Left and its media acolytes are trying to do is poison the wider appeal of the Republican message by depicting it as race-based and retrograde. This is a dirty operation. It is also the height of hypocrisy, given that it is being led by a bunch of truly "angry white men" against what is purported to be another.

GOP membership is 53 percent male and 47 percent female. (The Democrats are 45 percent male and 55 percent female.) But take the perfectly liberal New York Times. While it perseverates on the GOP becoming "a smaller, older, whiter and more male party" from the confines of its mainly white and male newsroom, it publishes 80 percent male-written op-eds, according to a recent byline survey cited in the Columbia Journalism Review. Meanwhile, the newspaper's own "party" of readers, according to the Pew Research Center in 2010, is 59 percent men and 41 percent women. Call in the "gender gap" police!

Comedy Central's Stephen Colbert — a major "news" source for young adults — sarcastically razzes Mitt Romney for his "bold" choice of a running mate who is "white, Christian and male." But with an audience that is largely white, likely majority-Christian and, says Pew, 65 percent male, how does Colbert rate as "bolder"?

The answer is that "The Colbert Report," like the rest of what passes for news media, is much, much further to the left. They are so far to the left they can't imagine anyone can see their acid hypocrisy and ideological warfare play out in living color.

Media refuse to interrogate Obama on his chicanery

March 21, 2013

I found myself in a group conversation that included one of the more instantly recognizable media figures -- someone who personifies the phrase "mainstream media." Since this isn't something that happens every day, why not make the best of it? Why not ask this VIMP (Very Important Media Person) a question or two on the topics that I frequently criticize the press for not covering?

The problem was how to do so without unduly alarming the poor thing. My favorite kinds of questions might be distressing to VIMPs who never ask them, or even seem to think of them. I didn't want to scare off her (or him) without eliciting an answer. I had to consider carefully while my VIMP remained at hand in a perpetual state of high-definition recognition.

There was no doubt about what was uppermost on my list: Had this journalistic personage ever had the curiosity to download and examine the online document posted at the White House website that purports to be President Obama's long-form birth certificate? Had he (or she) ever weighed any analysis or investigation that concludes the online document is a digitally created forgery? Or did this exemplar of the Fourth Estate simply take the White House at its word?

Speaking of taking the White House at its word, a second subject I hoped to introduce concerned the many unanswered questions about the Benghazi attack. Did she (or he) consider the Obama administration adequately transparent about Benghazi and its many-layered cover-up? Maybe I should say many-layered "aftermath" so as not to be too shocking.

From the ongoing chatter, it became clear such topics would have the allure of stink bombs. So much conventional wisdom flowed about A-list topics such as "Obama and Boehner" and "what would Israel do about Iran?" that I felt as if I were in a rerun of a Sunday news show. At one point, the timing of the killing of Osama bin Laden came up. Why, after knowing the al-Qaida leader's whereabouts for eight or nine months, did Obama suddenly order a strike on May 2, 2011? It was all-around baffling.

this point, I might have introduced my topic of interest. I could have noted that the death of bin Laden erased the birth certificate issue from the news, where, thanks to Donald Trump and author Jerome Corsi, it actually was commanding new levels of scrutiny that had prompted the White House to release its online document at a press conference on

April 27, 2011. A few days later, boom -- bin Laden was dead. Wasn't that a little bit interesting? Imagining in response the cold, revolted stare reserved for unwelcome bugs, I said nothing.

I knew it would be hard to launch such a conversation without any context, which too often describes the condition of public discourse on the many issues that go uncovered or incompletely covered. In this instance, I was once again struck by the fact that my own local outlet, the soon-to-be-defunct daily Washington Examiner, had followed a blanket policy to reject any column I wrote about the Obama eligibility issue. Accordingly, the paper refused to run the column I devoted to that April 2011 press conference that the White House called exclusively to mark the release of Obama's online birth certificate. In the here and now, I would have to explain everything. I could never claim his (or her) attention for so long, so I let the moment pass.

Rather amazingly, a question did come up as to whether this in-the-know VIMP had ever seen Obama's college records. "No, why?" the VIMP replied, as if the question concerned looking at instructions for using a doorknob. Later, the VIMP's tradecraft became evident: "I don't think anything matters about Obama before the day he began serving as president." Here, most likely, was the answer to my question: No, the VIMP wasn't interested in eyeballing Obama's online identity artwork. Rich man, poor man, beggar man, fraud, it didn't matter. Nothing pre-presidency did -- not even, I was told, consideration of Obama's mentors, beginning with communist Frank Marshall Davis, and not even when it came to trying to parse Obama's political ideology.

OK, so what about Benghazi? The Sept. 11, 2012, attack on the U.S. compound in Benghazi, Libya, during which four Americans, including Ambassador Christopher Stevens, were killed, definitely took place on Obama's watch as commander in chief. Did my VIMP believe there was any journalistic spadework still to be done to unearth the facts about what was happening in Washington during and after our Benghazi compound was attacked?

In a word, no. Blaming the fiasco on "negligence," this leading journalist declared there was no more to be seen, heard or spoken about. In so doing, this VIMP gave a pretty good impersonation of the three monkeys of oblivion who together symbolize blindness, deafness and dumbness."It's not important." Naturally, if it's not important, administration lies and cover-up become wasted efforts not worth spending time on.

Richard Nixon would have really liked this character.

I found myself in a group conversation that included one of the more instantly recognizable media figures -- someone who personifies the phrase "mainstream media"; Since this isn't something that

Intelligence? Secrets?

Karl Rove and WMD

4/9/10, blog entry

Former Bush speechwriter Joseph Shattan has picked up on an notable point in Karl Rove's book, namely Rove's admission that it was all his fault that information regarding the presence of WMD in Iraq (and subsequent removal to Syria) was never put out by the White House. Shattan writes at the American Spectator:

> About four years ago, around the time when Democrats were heatedly charging that Bush had "lied" about Saddam Hussein's weapons of mass destruction in order to build a case for war (after all, they argued, if the weapons had existed, why weren't we able to find them after liberating Iraq?), I was having lunch with Dr. Laurie Mylroie, one of America's leading students of terrorism in general, and Iraqi terrorism in particular. Laurie was beside herself with anger. Why wasn't the Bush administration citing Gen. James Clapper, the Director of the National Imagery and Mapping Agency, who said that satellite imagery proved conclusively that shortly before the war's outbreak, Iraq had transferred its weapons of mass destruction to Syria? Why wasn't it quoting Gen. Georges Sada, deputy chief of Saddam's air force, or Gen. Moshe Ya'alon, Israel's chief-of-staff, both of whom also claimed that Saddam's weapons had been transferred to Syria? Why was it so tongue-tied, so unsure of itself, so unwilling to answer its critics? Didn't anybody in the White House realize that if the Democrats' charges went unanswered, they would fatally undermine the entire case for the war?
>
> By this time, however, I had left the White House, so I had to tell

Laurie the truth: Her revelations about Generals Clapper and Sada (though not Ya'alon) were news to me, and I had no idea why the White House wasn't citing them.

Given this background, readers will understand the mixed feelings with which I reacted to Karl Rove's assertion, in a chapter entitled "Bush Was Right on Iraq," that Clapper, Sada and Ya'alon all maintained that Saddam had transferred his weapons of mass destruction to Syria on the eve of the war. On the one hand, I recalled the old saw, "Better late than never." On the other hand, I couldn't help feeling that history might have turned out differently had Karl spoken out sooner.

To his immense credit, Karl makes no effort to deny that he screwed up, big time. "So who was responsible for the failure to respond [to the Democrats' assault]?" he asks. "I was. I should have stepped forward, rung the warning bell, and pressed for full-scale response. I didn't. Preoccupied with the coming campaign and the pressures of the daily schedule in the West Wing, I did not see how damaging this assault was. There were others who could have sounded the alarm, but regardless, I should have."

I wonder. It seems hard to imagine that the damage of this assault, day in, day out, wasn't visible to the point of being overwhelming, particularly to someone as sensitive to political currents as Rove. Maybe it wasn't so much preoccupation that led to silence on the issue as a (bad) campaign decision to stonewall — although that doesn't make sense, either. And what about "the others" who could have sounded the alarm and didn't? Were the following a doomed political policy, or were they just "proccupied," too?

Then there are stories like this one from the AP at MSNBC on July 8, 2008, that the White House never, ever presented to the American people:

> Secret U.S. mission hauls uranium from Iraq
>
> Last major stockpile from Saddam's nuclear efforts arrives in Canada
>
> The last major remnant of Saddam Hussein's nuclear program — a huge stockpile of concentrated natural uranium — reached a Canadian port Saturday to complete a secret U.S. operation that included a two-week airlift from Baghdad and a ship voyage crossing two oceans.

> The removal of 550 metric tons of "yellowcake" — the seed material for higher-grade nuclear enrichment — was a significant step toward closing the books on Saddam's nuclear legacy. It also brought relief to U.S. and Iraqi authorities who had worried the cache would reach insurgents or smugglers crossing to Iran to aid its nuclear ambitions. ...

Closing the books on Saddam's nuclear legacy? When were they ever opened? Not by the Bush administration.

Monster intelligence machine still won't protect us from the real threat

7/23/10

A clarifying bomblet drops in the final paragraph of the opening installment of the big Washington Post series on what is best described as National Intelligence Sprawl:

"Soon, on the grounds of the former St. Elizabeth's mental hospital in Anacostia, a $3.4 billion showcase of security will rise from the crumbling brick wards. The new headquarters will be the largest government complex built since the Pentagon ..."

National security meets mental hospital: How tragically appropriate. And yes, these inmates will definitely be running the asylum — some of the Post-estimated 854,000 Americans with top secret clearance now filling massive new government complexes all over the country — another unwanted legacy of 9/11.

Some of my conservative brethren worry that the Post series reveals national security secrets. The question is, with nearly a million people possessing top secret clearance, how many secrets are left to reveal? Is it possible that our national security apparatus has gotten too big not to fail?

The Post series focuses on the gargantuan-ness that, more than ever, bloats the intelligence realm. Last year's budget was $75 billion, 2-1/2 times larger than the budget was on 9/11. At least 20 percent of the government organizations pitted against terrorism, the Post reports, have been "created or refashioned" since 9/11, while many that previously existed have ballooned to historic size.

For example, the Pentagon's Defense Intelligence Agency went from 7,500 employees in 2002 to 16,500 today. Since the 2001 attacks, 17 million square feet of new office space has been built or is now under construction in the Washington area alone.

I feel safer?

As the intelligence budget increased by tens of billions, the Post reports, "military and intelligence agencies multiplied. ... In all, at least 263 (government) organizations have been created or reorganized as a response to 9/11." In round numbers, U.S. intelligence activity is now spread among 1,200 government organizations supported by 2,000 private corporations at 10,000 locations across the country. But still we must endure the indignities of shuffling shoeless through full-body scanners at our airports just to have a nice flight, maybe. Our great halls and institutions remain defended by state-of-siege-like installations. And we continue to adapt, accommodate and accept the "post-9/11 world," and seemingly forever now that these massive new government bureaucracies and new industries will attempt to retain indefinite support. Why?

The reason is this: In all of these scores and hundreds and thousands of organizations created and boosted and buffed up since 9/11 there is one thing they all forgot.

Islam.

I will bet my bottom dollar that in all of the hyper-burgeoning bureaucracies there is no single office organized to study, in Pentagon parlance, the "enemy threat doctrine" of jihad, which has, whether it is admitted or not, driven this intelligence boom in the first place. Similarly, I will bet there is no program designed to investigate the historical, canonical goals of jihad movements: namely, the spread of Islamic law (Sharia), and the attendant condition of dhimmitude that Sharia imposes on Islamized and Islam-dominated populations, even as such dhimmitude is an enabler of jihad. Instead, what we see in this frantic, government-led explosion is an Orwellian study in mass denial, a hamster-in-a-cage approach to what was first masked as "terror" and is now disguised as "transnational violent extremists" despite the fact that the threat is precisely and guilelessly presented by perps the world over as Islamic jihad.

Such is life in the politically correct, multiculturally dictated (read: dishonest) world.

Here's my idea for a brand new approach.

First, hire a crack team of true experts to catch military and security officials up on the fundamental doctrinal issues by which all of our strategy — military, immigration, education and intelligence — should be informed. For example, on jihad as enemy threat doctrine, Maj. Stephen Coughlin; on jihad history and Islamic anti-Semitism, Andrew Bostom; on dhimmitude through the ages, Bat Ye'or; on revaluing the West, Ibn Warraq.; on repositioning our military forces, Gen. Paul Vallely (USA ret.).

That should get us going all right and save the taxpayer trillions. Heck, we could run the whole thing out of my house. Oh, and one more thing: Turn St. Elizabeth's into a top secret rest home for several hundred thousand indefinitely furloughed intelligence analysts.

And they call this our intelligence community?

10/8/10

Reading Patrick Poole's splashy coverage of the FBI's VIP treatment of Kifah Mustapha—a known Hamas operative and unindicted co-conspirator in the landmark Holy Land Foundation terror financing trial—will make your head spin with the dizzying question:

How could the same officials charged with securing the nation against the very terrorism Mustapha's activities supported (as laid out in court documents filed by federal investigators) have possibly invited him into the top-secret National Counterterrorism Center (NCTC) and the FBI's training center at Quantico during a six-week "Citizen's Academy" hosted by the FBI as "outreach" to the Muslim community?

"The plugs had to be pulled on our (watch) system" just to get Mustapha in the NCTC door, Poole, writing online at Big Peace, quoted a Department of Homeland Security official as saying. After all, "the NCTC has Kifah Mustapha on the highest watch list we have."

Unbelievable. So who pulled those plugs? Wouldn't it be great to get a bunch of national security pooh-bahs into one room to try to find out?

It would be—and so it was. This week, a passel of senior national security officials assembled for a Washington conference on domestic intelligence sponsored by the Bipartisan Policy Center. First up was James Clapper, director of National Intelligence. During question-and-answer session, I asked him about FBI "outreach" to Mustapha.

"I think the FBI will be here later," Clapper boldly punted (laughter in the room). Meanwhile, he continued, there is "great merit in outreach, to engage as much as possible with the Muslim community."

Subtext: It's no big.

When later asked about the government policy of eliminating the terminology of Islamic jihad from intelligence analysis and collection, Clapper affirmed it to "acknowledge sensitivities"—a process begun under George W. Bush and recently extended by Homeland Security adviser John Brennan. "There's plenty of terminology cut there (to convey) the meaning and the message that we need to."

The director of national intelligence's meaning and message of choice: "homegrown violent extremism."

Between panels, I spoke to panelist Sean Joyce of the FBI. What did the FBI executive assistant director for national security think about the Mustapha incident?

"We don't comment on individuals," he told me.

OK. How about commenting on a blanket policy regarding FBI tours for unindicted co-conspirators and terrorist group operatives?

"Again, we don't comment on individuals."

It's not every day a former director of Central Intelligence Agency is standing by, so I asked Michael Hayden for his opinion of the speak-no-Islam issue. "People I trust" — uh-oh — "say to be careful not to use the term 'jihadist' because it does have a broader use across the Islamic world," he said.

So what? That doesn't affect its accuracy as a description of the enemy!

However, he continued, not using the word 'Islamic' "obfuscates the issue (and) neuters our understanding" of Islamic terrorism — "however perverted it might be." Hayden added: "This is in no way a comment on the Islamic faith."

But it is in some way a comment on American intelligence. Political correctness stymies it.

Of course, NCTC Director Michael Leiter was quick to insist "there was no PC-ness" on his watch. "If someone is inspired by Islamic ideology—" he began, then stopped. "Let me rephrase that: al-Qaida ideology …"

Poor baby.

Later, I had an opportunity to ask Leiter what he thought about the FBI bringing Mustapha into NCTC.

"Ask the FBI," he suggested, helpfully.

But isn't NCTC your shop? I asked.

"Actually," he explained, "the building isn't owned by us. Three organizations have offices there. …"

When I pulled myself up off the floor, he was still talking: "It's more complicated — talk to the FBI. They've got a lot more information than I do."

The FBI better be good, right? After all, on taking my Mustapha question, FBI Director Robert Mueller, the conference's final speaker, said he'd been briefed to expect it. "I'm not sure I agree with the predicate of your question," he said, "and we're not going to debate it here."

He continued, discussing the Citizen's Academy program, which he described as "exposing the FBI to a variety of communities."

"Exposing" is right.

He, too, said he wouldn't discuss individuals, but added, meaningfully: "We do look into the individuals that we invite into the Citizen's Academies."

I think the man who pulled the plugs had spoken.

Chatting with 'Big Sis' about toughening up

11/26/10

A few days ago, I got to do what many Americans would like to do — ask Department of Homeland Security Secretary Janet Napolitano a thing or two. Before I report on what I asked and what she said, I must note there were "ground rules" in effect. The conversation itself between a small group of mainly conservative-minded journalists and Napolitano was free and even easy, but reporting on any aspect of the exchange required after-the-fact approval from DHS Assistant Secretary for Public Affairs Sean Smith.

This rankles. It is also something new in my personal experience. Sure, I have conducted scores of one-on-one interviews "on background," a term which, in brief, I define as a means to acquire an understanding of a story from a source unwilling to be quoted directly, at least at first. Follow-up conversations may or may not be "on the record." But I have never participated as a member of a group so bound, and I have to say I don't like it.

First of all, it's a phony setup. Telling 15 or 20 people in a room a secret is obviously no way to keep one, no way to keep anything confidential. There are simply too many people involved, each with his own private pipeline to public access. Something else is afoot. Making the journalist into a kind of co-conspirator? Or, as bad, a supplicant begging for morsels of information?

The point, we are told, is to allow for a no-holds-barred exchange — attractive on its face, maybe, but in the end, when you actually have to go back and ask for permission to print a government official's response to questions every American has the right to ask, the exchange is very much barred. In sum, the state is managing the news.

So why did I participate? Curiosity. I wanted to see "Big Sis" in person. I was curious also how an event billed as "off the record" — which to my understanding means "total blackout, didn't happen, can't use it" — could be selectively switched to "on the record" by government diktat. I wanted to see how our brave new world works.

I didn't "clear" my impressions of Napolitano the person, so I'll have to leave them "off the record." I did e-mail the press secretary for permission (gag) to report two particular points Napolitano made. What follows is how I played along with the state, almost as a lark. (PS. I don't claim it's pretty).

"Hi, Sean - Good to hear from you.

"Two main points I'd like to be able to write up:

"1) After the main discussion I had the opportunity to ask the Secretary whether she envisioned this security situation ever abating — for example, whether she could foresee conditions under which the current scanners might be removed. Or whether, as she told us earlier, it would be necessary for Americans to toughen up, stay involved (indefinitely) ... I would like to be able to report that I spoke to the Secretary on this topic and that she indicated that in the future the current scanner technology could someday be replaced by less obtrusive technology, including less obviously invasive security checks that might not require taking off shoes, etc. ..."

The answer came back from on high: "Yes, but you should also put into context that there are no current plans to move off the current technologies and procedures."

Context so ordered.

(I will not convey my second question because the e-mailed answer—"I'd like to see how you formulate it"—ratcheted state control outside the bounds of my experiment.)

Napolitano's vision of our techno-future, however, is devastating. If, as she makes clear, our government has no conception of a plan to end this untenable security situation stemming from the jihad in progress, our government has admitted defeat, and is merely managing the aftermath of capitulation. In its colossal failure of imagination and responsibility, the government has abandoned its primary purpose—to defend the citizenry. Thus, every time we the people go to the airport (now and apparently forever the nation's forward front) we are expected to "toughen up" and make up a pathetic first line of defense—unarmed, unshod, de-toothpasted and, now, disrobed by scanners and violated by government workers—until, happy day, the technology is "less obviously intrusive."

There's no managing that news. It stinks.

Assange's WikiLeaks scandal: blood on his hands, or egg on their faces?

12/3/10

I am still working out why I watch the high dudgeon sparked by Julian Assange and the WikiLeaks dump of a quarter-million State Department cables that has given rise to the most heated, bloodthirsty chorus I have ever heard in Washington, notably from conservatives, and feel strangely numb.

I observe the fits over "sovereignty" lost, and note that some of the same people find such emotion in bad taste when the prompt is our unsecured, non-sovereign border. I hear the arguments that our national security is hanging by a computer keystroke, and note the fecklessness of a U.S. government that hides from us, the people, its own confirmation that North Korea supplies Iran with Russian-made nuclear-capable missiles; China transfers weapons materiel to Iran (despite Hillary Clinton's pathetic entreaties); Iran honeycombs Iraq; Syria supports Hezbollah; Pakistan prevents the United States from securing its nuclear materials; Saudis continue to provide mainstay support to al-Qaida (despite pie-faced denials come from Saudi-supplicating U.S. administrations). Everything good citizens need to know, in short, to see through the dumbed-down, G-rated ("G" for government), official narrative, all "engagement" and "outreach," to throw the ineffectual bums out—all of them—and start from scratch.

But what we're supposed to see in Assange's Internet release of thousands of "classified," mainly non-sensational, if often embarrassing, documents (something journalists usually call a scoop in the singular) is an act of "terrorism," say Republican leaders, with Assange himself, as Sarah Palin would have it, playing the part of Osama bin Laden. Weirdly, I don't recall bin Laden himself inspiring as many public calls for "execution." Nor did the arrests of the notorious traitors CIA analyst Aldrich Ames in 1994 or FBI agent Robert Hanssen in 2001 ratchet up a fury approaching the emotional pitch over Assange that has drowned out all other news this week, including the murder of six American trainers by an Afghan "policeman."

Why?

These six unnecessary, punishing deaths may well have resulted from the disastrous statecraft and policies that come under discussion in the leaked cables, but as far as news coverage went they just couldn't compete with the leak frenzy itself. The establishment, Right and Left but mainly Right, coalesced around melodramatic accusations that Assange did have, or would have "blood on his hands."

As I have read my way through some fraction of the leaked record, no evidence for this frequently leveled charge yet appears, certainly none that begins to compare to the blood already spilled to implement a hopelessly misguided U.S. foreign policy that, from the Bush administration to the Obama administration, determinedly ignores Islam in its prosecution of wars in the Islamic world. Exhibit A, at least this week, is the six dead Americans in that Muslim-on-infidel "training accident" mentioned above. In our attempt to remake Afghanistan in more or less our own image, we shut our eyes to all eruptions of Islam, hostile, undermining and antithetical to our utopian goals, that continually and inevitably warp our exhausting and disappointing effort.

More see-no-Islam evidence comes straight from the leaked cables. As noted by the British newspaper The Guardian, Anne Patterson, the former U.S. ambassador to Pakistan, vainly conveyed to Washington her conviction that no amount of aid money would persuade the Pakistan army (motto: "Faith in Allah, fear of Allah, and jihad in the path of Allah") to stop sponsoring what you might call similarly jihad-centric groups: the Taliban, the Taliban-allied Haqqani and Hekmatyar networks, and the Mumbai attackers. I say "vainly" because the aid money doesn't stop—nor does Pakistan's covert support for America's jihadist enemies.

This may sound like sticking coin after coin into a jukebox playing our own funeral march, but that's official U.S. policy, as supported from the pro-war Right to the Obama Left. More than that, it's part of the shambles WikiLeaks confirms U.S. foreign policy to be. Could this be why the establishment condemns WikiLeaks as the worst thing ever? The Pakistan cables alone should stop the presses, start a debate and inspire congressional hearings: "Pakistan: Ally to Spend Billions on, or Enemy to De-nuke?"

But the reaction instead is to kill the messenger—literally, say many. The more I read, however, the more I wonder whether the raging rhetoric is less about blood on WikiLeaks' hands than about egg on the faces of others, including a secretive Uncle Sam.

WikiLeaks spurs Big Brother to strike

12/10/10

WikiLeaks is exposing the way our government conducts "business." It is not a pretty process. Sometimes Uncle Sam limps along like a powerless giant, as when secretaries of State Condoleezza Rice and Hillary Clinton vainly plead with China to stop facilitating the military rise of Iran. (But don't let that stop you from buying that made-in-China flat-screen TV for Christmas. Great price.) Sometimes Uncle Sam slimes around like the mob, as when shutting down opposition to the Copenhagen climate accord is his racquet and bullying is his game.

The rock-bottom worst of the revelations, however, shows Uncle Sam patronizing the American people, lying to us about fundamental issues that any democracy catastrophically attacked and supporting armies abroad ever since doesn't merely deserve to know, but needs to know. Our democracy demands it, if it is to remain a democracy.

Most pundits, certainly on the Right, disagree. As Commentary editor Gabriel Schoenfeld wrote in the WSJ this week: WikiLeaks "is not informing our democracy but waging war on its ability to conduct diplomacy and defend itself."

Funny, but I feel more informed—and particularly about what a rotten job the government knows it's doing in conducting diplomacy and waging war on democracy's behalf. I know more about the government's feckless accommodation of incomparable corruption in Afghanistan; its callousness toward Pakistani government support for the Taliban and other groups fighting our soldiers in Afghanistan; its inability to prevail upon "banker" China to stop facilitating the military rise of Iran (mentioned above but worth a reminder) and its failures to prevail upon aid-recipient Pakistan to allow us to secure its vulnerable nuclear assets.

One running theme that emerges from the leaked cables is that the U.S. government consistently obscures the identity of the nation's foes, for example, depicting the hostile peoples of Saudi Arabia and the Gulf States as "allies." It's not that such hostility is a secret, or even constitutes news. But the cables reveal that our diplomats actually recognize that these countries form the financial engine that drives global jihad, or, as they mincingly prefer to call it, "terrorism." But they, with the rest of the government, kept the American people officially in the dark.

Then came WikiLeaks, Internet publisher of leaked information, prompting the question: What is more important — the information theft that potentially harms government power, or the knowledge contained therein that might salvage our national destiny?

Whether such information was originally "classified," the body politic should be electrified by the fact, as revealed by the leaked cables, that nations from Pakistan to Afghanistan to Saudi Arabia are regularly discussed as black holes of infinite corruption into which American money gushes, either through foreign aid or oil revenue, and unstaunched and unstaunchable sources of terror or terror-financing. If this were to get out — and guess what, it did — the foreign policy of at least the past two administrations, Democrat and Republican alike, would be unmasked as a colossal failure.

And maybe that's what behind the acute distress over WikiLeaks. Last week, I put it down to political embarrassment; this week, a new, more disturbing factor has emerged. The state power structure, the establishment more or less, believes itself to be threatened. Its fearful response has been quite startling. First, there were calls for WikiLeaks editor Julian Assange's execution; these have simmered down to calls for trial. Amazon and PayPal cut off service to the WikiLeaks website. Then, in a twist or kink perhaps beyond even Orwell's ken, Assange was arrested without bond this week on an Interpol warrant over very fishy-sounding charges about "unprotected" sex in Sweden — a country, we may now ironically note, of draconian laws governing sexual intercourse and no laws whatsoever governing violent Islamic no-gone-zones.

Things went completely "1984"-ish when the federal government weighed in, actually warning federal employees not to read the WikiLeaks materials — still "classified," after all. Creepier still, the Library of Congress followed suit, voluntarily blocking the WikiLeaks site from library computers. Now, universities are warning students not to post public comments about WikiLeaks on Facebook or Twitter — lest Big Brother takes note and holds a federal employment grudge.

Suddenly, it's not about secret information anymore, or diplomatic relations. It's about control. The atmosphere chills.

The CIA should be a bit more 'CAIR' less

8/12/11

This week, a three-day conference hosted by the CIA on "homegrown radicalization" was supposed to have taken place at CIA headquarters. It did not. The conference was abruptly canceled — or, softening the blow, "postponed." Question: Did pressure from what we might (and should) call a certain "homegrown radical" group — the Council on American Islamic Relations (CAIR) -- make this happen?

Here is what we know.

On Monday, July 18, CAIR issued a press release headlined: "CAIR Asks CIA to Drop Islamophobic Trainer." It revealed that CAIR national executive director Nihad Awad wrote a letter to now-former CIA director Leon Panetta to that effect. The rest of the release is more opaque. In referencing an NPR report that slammed one counterterrorism trainer by name, former FBI agent John Guandolo, for "allegedly smearing" an "Ohio Muslim" in a presentation, CAIR noted that an entirely different trainer, unnamed, was "scheduled to hold a similar session in August for the CIA." (Full disclosure: Guandolo and I are among 19 co-authors of "Shariah: the Threat to America.") The August CIA "session" appears to be the driver of both the CAIR release and letter asking the CIA, as the headline put it, to "Drop Islamophobic Trainer."

On Friday, July 22, an email from the CIA informed hundreds of confirmed attendees that the whole August "radicalization" conference was off (much to the consternation of those who had already purchased non-refundable airline tickets). "The sponsors — in partnership with the Department of Homeland Security — have decided to delay the conference so it can include insights from, among other sources, the new National Strategy for Counterterrorism, in an updated agenda," the email said. The goal "is to ensure that conference participants receive material that is as current and comprehensive as possible."

Pretty lame, even for the CIA. But there is more to groan about. "Updated agenda" is Washington-speak for gutted agenda. With the new White House counterterrorism strategy as a source of insights du jour, the holes in the original conference lineup will be filled to the brim with the see-no-jihad mush that the strategy dishes up.

It gets worse. I am hearing from multiple sources that pressure brought by CAIR, as publicly announced by CAIR, played a crucial role in the CIA decision to pull the plug on its conference. This means, to repeat, that a "homegrown radical" group appears to be influencing what is known in the strategy world as the "information battle space" at the CIA.

The fact is, no matter how many times Bill O'Reilly plays "no-spin-zone" host to CAIR spokesmen, CAIR co-founder and national director Nihad Awad, the man who asked the CIA to drop the "Islamophobic" trainer, has been identified by the FBI as a member of the terrorist group Hamas, which is an offshoot of the Muslim Brotherhood. The same goes for CAIR co-founder Omar Ahmad. Both men have long been involved in a veritable constellation of Islamic front groups affiliated with the Muslim Brotherhood, whose 1991 "explanatory memorandum" calls on Brothers to "understand that their work in America is a kind of grand jihad in eliminating and destroying the Western civilization from within and 'sabotaging' their miserable house by their hands and the hands of the believers so that it is eliminated and G0d's religion is made victorious over all religions."

The FBI has been following what clearly became a Muslim-Brotherhood-Hamas-CAIR (and more) nexus since 1993. (CAIR was founded in 1994 and Hamas was designated a terrorist organization by the United States in 1995.) After this linkage became public record during the landmark Holy Land Foundation jihad financing trial (in which CAIR was labeled an unindicted co-conspirator), the FBI finally ended all formal contacts with CAIR in 2008.

This policy holds. In March 2011, under questioning by Rep. Louis Gohmert (Texas Republican) before the House Judiciary Oversight Committee, FBI director Robert Mueller confirmed, albeit grudgingly, that "we" — the FBI — "have no formal relationship with CAIR because of concerns with regard to the national leadership."

So what's wrong with the CIA? Congress should — must — find out by investigating how it is that a Muslim Brotherhood and Hamas creation such as CAIR, which the FBI broke relations with, appears to exert so much influence on the CIA's information battle space. I think Lewis Carroll already told us this story, but when he was writing, the rabbit hole wasn't such a dangerous place.

Shine a light on America's Afghan-Iraqi rathole

11/18/11

When the Commission on Wartime Contracting in Iraq and Afghanistan closed shop on Sept. 30, it reported its "sobering but conservative" estimate that U.S. taxpayers had lost between $31 billion and $60 billion in waste and fraud of the $206 billion Uncle Sam has spent on contracts and grants in Iraq and Afghanistan. Of course, that's not all. According to the commission's final report, "a similar amount could be lost due to unsustainable projects and programs."

These staggering, if "conservative," figures are the result of three years of the commission's work, including 25 hearings and eight reports to Congress. What the commission neglected to mention in its final press release, however, was that it was trucking all of its records to the National Archives where, as The Wall Street Journal reported, also on Sept. 30, they would be sealed for 20 years.

News traveled slowly up Capitol Hill. "We learned of this development after the fact," the two original Senate co-sponsors of the commission, Claire McCaskill and Jim Webb, wrote in a Nov. 7 letter to the archivist of the United States, David S. Ferriero. Noting that the commission hadn't thought to ask or even inform Congress about deep-freezing the documents for the next two decades, the senators asked "that the National Archives make a full disclosure of the commission's files and records as quickly as possible, consistent with protections for privacy, proprietary information and other applicable laws."

There, as they say, the matter stands. And what an outrage. Locking up vital public records and throwing away the key is not behavior becoming to a democratic republic; it is a peremptory and arbitrary act of authoritarianism. With the "overclassification" of government documents rampant, it fits into a democracy-imperiling trend. "Simply stated," the senators wrote, "we need to live in the light."

Amen — no matter what crawls out from under the piles of paper. The fact is, these wartime contracting expenditures are not for run-of-the-mill public works projects flawed by cost overruns, fraud and waste. They form the foundation of a failed American foreign policy to use our armies to build nations in regions culturally and religiously hostile to our principles. In increasing desperation, as these documents no doubt attest, that foreign policy has become one of bribery on a grotesque scale.

I don't know what else to call a 2009 USAID agricultural project that started as a $60 million initiative to distribute vouchers for wheat seed and fertilizer in the north — generous enough — and ended up, "under pressure to inject $1 million each day into a dozen or so key terrain districts," dumping $360 million into the south and east not just for seeds and fertilizer but also "cash-for-work" — hmm — and something dubiously called "community development."

Or how about the U.S. mission to train and equip Afghan National Security Forces at a cost to American taxpayers of $6.4 billion a year? "Such costs far exceed what the government of Afghanistan can sustain," the commission determined, "so it is unclear how those costs will be funded in the future."

Uh-oh.

"Meanwhile," the report continues, "$11 billion of facilities constructed by the U.S. Army Corps of Engineers (USACE) for (Afghan

National Security Forces) are 'at risk.'"

Needless to say, $11 billion worth of facilities is a terrible thing to waste.

Then there's a category called "Diversion of U.S. Funds" — as in diversion of funds to the enemy. No official estimate here, the commission reports; it's anyone's guess. While the opium trade is considered to be the primary funding for the jihadists, guess who's next on the list?

You are. "During a March 2011 trip to Afghanistan, experts told the commission that extortion of funds from U.S construction projects and transportation contracts is the insurgents' second-largest funding source."

This record must be open to citizens, scholars and journalists — not to mention the Justice Department fraud squad — ASAP. Otherwise, the bucks won't stop anywhere, ever.

It's time to stop keeping secrets

12/9/11

Last month, I noted that Democratic Sens. Claire McCaskill of Missouri and Jim Webb of Virginia had written to national archivist David S. Ferriero on Nov. 7, asking him to open the records of the Commission on Wartime Contracting in Iraq and Afghanistan, which Ferriero has summarily sealed for 20 years. Guess what? Webb's office tells me it still hasn't received a reply. Where's WikiLeaks when you need it?

It's been about a year since the furor crescendoed over Wikileaks. Actually, "furor" is too mild a term. This was baying for blood. (Charles Krauthammer and Mike Huckabee talked about "execution," while Sarah Palin practically called in a drone strike herself.) Then and now, I consider the revelations of lying, incompetence and betrayal of foundational principle, as revealed by the Wikileaks organization's massive dumps of classified documents, to be a public service.

We heard an awful lot about "blood" being on WikiLeaks' hands, but it all seemed to come down to egg on officials' faces. The fact is, a government of the people, by the people and for the people — whose officials, as information security experts Elizabeth Goitein and William Leonard recently wrote in The New York Times, "made 77 million decisions to classify information" in 2010 alone — should have the shutters yanked off so the sun can shine in.

Unfortunately, we just get more shutters. For example, the Obama administration just sealed the court records on the murder of federal agent Brian Terry, whose killers, Mexican drug smugglers, used weapons from a failed federal program to smuggle arms into Mexico. As Judicial

Watch noted: "No one will know the reason for the confiscation of public court records in this case because the judge's decision to seal it was also sealed."

That's about as secret as it gets. What WikiLeaks was dealing with was classified information that the 4.2 million Americans with security clearances already could read.

Yes, you read that number right, but I'll write it again to make sure it sticks. In its first public count ever, the intelligence community reported to Congress in September that 4.2 million Americans have security clearances, with nearly 1.2 million of those being "Top Secret." Suddenly, the charges against Bradley Manning, the Army private who allegedly leaked tens of thousands of classified documents and whose pretrial hearings begin next week, fall into a new and quite sprawling context.

Manning faces life in prison for charges related to divulging national secrets. But literally millions of Americans have access to the same "secrets" that Manning is alleged to have downloaded from a government server known as SIPRNet and passed to WikiLeaks for publication on the Internet. And his civilian defense attorney, David E. Coombs, is arguing that the news those documents contained was not harmful to national security.

Maybe most of the documents shouldn't have been classified in the first place. Maybe most of the information they contained shouldn't have been denied to Us the People by our elected leaders.

Coombs also claims that the government is denying his client access to exculpatory evidence proving the leaks did no national harm, evidence to which Manning is entitled by law in order to mount his defense. So far, the government is—you guessed it—keeping that evidence a secret.

In a request filed in court last month (released in partly redacted form), Coombs asked for copies of several internal reviews of the WikiLeaks material that he said were conducted by the White House, the Defense Intelligence Agency and the State Department. All of them, Coombs claims, conclude the leaks weren't harmful to the nation because they conveyed dated information, low-level opinions or previously disclosed information. Quoting a published report, Coombs continued: "A congressional official briefed on the reviews stated that the administration felt compelled to say publicly that the revelations had seriously damaged American interests in order to bolster legal efforts to shut down the WikiLeaks website and bring charges against the leakers."

More lies? More hypocrisy? The government must release its reviews so we can begin to find out.

Come to think of it, lies and hypocrisy, along with incompetence, were the major revelations of WikiLeaks. Which tells us the real dangers to U.S. national security are our own foreign policymakers who shield themselves from public scrutiny with too much secrecy. And no one should go to jail for life for telling us that.

Iraq WMD in Syria?

7/22/12, blog entry

In the Daily Beast, as linked on Drudge, a fairly wide audience will read, matter of fact, that there is now some concern about securing WMD in Syria that just might have come from Iraq in the run-up to the Iraq War.

Impossible — Bushliedpeopledied! At least, that was the mantra the Left used like a leg-hold trap to clamp down on the Bush adminstration. They couldn't shake it. Stranger still, they didn't try,

But here we are in 2012 entertaining the possibility that the CIA is chasing down WMD in Syria that might have Iraqi provenance.

> DeSutter also said she would want the U.S. and international community to secure any remaining nuclear-related equipment from the al-Kibar reactor destroyed in 2007 by Israeli jets. Also unclear is what, if anything, Iraq transferred to Syria before the 2003 U.S. invasion. "That is the wild card," said DeSutter.
>
> Whether or not sensitive weapons technology was moved to Syria is a hotly disputed question in the intelligence community. James Clapper, now the Director of National Intelligence and formerly the director of the National Geospatial Intelligence Agency, said in 2003 that he believed materials had been moved out of Iraq in the months before the war and cited satellite imagery.

And not just James Clapper. In addition to Clapper, Gen. Georges Sada, deputy chief of Saddam Hussein's air force and Gen. Moshe Ya'alon, Israel's chief-of-staff, also claimed that Iraqi WMD was moved to Syria. And satellite imagery is not the only evidence of the movement of WMD materials out of Iraq. In 2008, MSNBC reported on the successful secret transfer of 550 metric tons of "yellowcake" from Iraq to Canada.

Headline:

"Secret U.S. mission hauls uranium from Iraq"

"Last major stockpile from Saddam's nuclear effort arrives in Canada"

Last major nuclear stockpile? Were there others?

We have no answers to these questions. In fact, we were lucky to get this much information. I've written before on the inexplicable failure of the Bush administration to trumpet such findings. Karl Rove actually discusses this weird silence in his memoir, offering a lame if not also non-credible explanation that he was just too busy with the upcoming campaign to find time to refute (or task others to refute) the poisonous "Bush lied, people died" mantra that permanently damaged the Bush presidency. In Bush's own memoir, he doesn't even give the short shrift to the subject that Rove did, simply stating that he was "sickened" about the nonexistence of Iraqi WMD.

The "last" of which was shipped to Canada, and some of which now might turn up in Syria.

Media oddly silent on WikiLeaks proceedings

12/14/12

Some thoughts about Army Pfc. Bradley Manning's pretrial hearing, which concluded this week.

Manning, of course, is charged with leaking hundreds of thousands of classified documents to the website WikiLeaks and, at his trial in March, will be pleading guilty to certain charges while rejecting the military's contention that he "aided the enemy" in doing so.

Manning was in court this month seeking dismissal on the grounds that since his arrest in May 2010, he has been subjected to unlawful pretrial punishment. Certainly the conditions Manning and his civilian lawyer David E. Coombs described in often dramatic testimony were inhumane, especially for someone not convicted of anything—two months in a dark "cage" in Kuwait; nearly nine months in solitary confinement in Quantico, Va.; orders to stand for inspection naked.

Oddly, the mainstream media and conservative media have been cool, if not callous, to the whole story. This is hard to understand on many levels. To begin with, the media are the main consumers—beneficiaries—of WikiLeaks documents presumably leaked by Manning. Among the first 115 editions of The New York Times in 2011, for example, 54 of them contained stories sourced to WikiLeaks, The Atlantic Wire reported. That's almost half. The Grey Lady, however, had to be publicly browbeaten by online criticism and her own ombudsman into sending a correspondent to cover even one day of hearings on this biggest leak case in history. Could the media's aversion to the story be related to their noted adulation of President Barack Obama, who has already prosecuted more leak cases (six) than all other presidents combined (three)?

As for conservatives, it was only two years ago that pundits were openly calling for the 'execution' of Julian Assange, WikiLeaks' founder and publisher. Now, with Manning's pretrial proceedings under way, their silence is notable.

I, too, am both a consumer and beneficiary of WikiLeaks, only I've never harbored bloodlust for Assange, nor outrage over WikiLeaks. As far as I've been able to tell, these document dumps jeopardize only the deployment of U.S. government lies, not U.S. troops, and, personally, I would like to see many more such revelations.

But not just as a journalist. As an American citizen, I am extremely alarmed by a government colossus that not only routinely withholds its own dealings and deliberations from Us, the People, but increasingly believes it can take possession of our dealings and deliberations in the form of cellphone and email interception, black boxes on our cars, cameras everywhere and other invasive control techniques once relegated to Orwellian satire or Communist spying apparatuses. In other words, it's not as if WikiLeaks happened in a state of informational transparency befitting a democratic republic. Ours is an era of increasingly dictatorial information control.

But back to Bradley Manning, the media's invisible man. Should he, as Barack Obama's government is pressing, go to jail for life for releasing about 250,000 diplomatic cables to which as many as 3 million Americans with security clearance already had access? Is it even possible to consider such widely available documents secret? We're not discussing, for example, the documents passed to Kremlin agents by the infamous Rosenberg ring that helped the Soviet Union construct an atomic bomb. This release of truly sensitive information not only aided the enemy, intelligence archives now tell us, but also gave Stalin the confidence to back the invasion of South Korea, kicking off a war that claimed nearly 50,000 American lives and those of about 2 million Korean civilians. This left much blood on the hands of the Rosenbergs, who were executed as traitors.

And WikiLeaks? We haven't seen any evidence of such enemy aid, not even resulting from disclosures of Iraq and Afghanistan war logs Manning is alleged to have released. Which isn't to say that Manning didn't give someone something — but I would call it heartburn to the powers that be. Is life in prison really the appropriate punishment?

Of course not — that is, not if national security is the chief concern. But the prosecution of Bradley Manning doesn't seem to be about national security. It's about power — the power to control the information that constitutes an inattentive American public's understanding of events, now and in the future.

Frankly, our world abounds with information leaks and spills that pose grave threats to national security and will never be punished. You could argue, for example, that Bill Clinton's "leaking" as president created the Chinese military threat. Clinton, in effect, ran a WikiLeaks of his own when his administration declassified some 11 million pages of military data. As journalist Richard Poe has written, federal investigators later determined that these documents helped China modernize its missile technology and nuclear know-how (including "suitcase nukes".

Journalist Bill Gertz and others have also chronicled how the Clinton administration permitted top-secret weapons technology to flow to Beijing in exchange for campaign contributions. Far from being considered an enemy of the state, of course, Clinton is lionized and petted, while his equally corrupt wife is the No. 1 Democratic hopeful for 2016 -- if, that is, President Obama doesn't run for an unconstitutional third term.

And speaking of Obama, wasn't it he and Vice President Joe Biden who disclosed the top-secret fact that members of Navy SEAL Team 6 killed Osama bin Laden? Some SEAL parents believe releasing this information led SEALs to be targeted by a strike in Afghanistan that resulted in the deaths of 17 SEALs and 13 other service members.

Obviously, Clinton and Obama are presidents, not privates. A president can release whatever information he wants. And a president can seek to jail citizens for life for the same. But that doesn't make it the right thing to do—not even if the "free press" ignores it.

No Constitution, No Borders, No USA

6/14/13

At what point does it become clear that we no longer inhabit America?

When we "Press 2," not "1" for English?

When a National Social Security Number syncs an electronic identity that the government hospital provided us at birth to track us till death?

When borders are no more, but the Surveillance State always knows where we are?

Ours is the age of dislocation before realization: The United States of America no longer exists. Why? How? The answer is simple, tragic and outrageous: Government officials, elected and unelected, with precious exceptions, no longer preserve, protect and defend the U.S. Constitution. Instead, they do whatever it takes to beat it, flout it and ignore it. Worse, We, the People, let them.

This can't go on. Otherwise our country-'tis-of-thee becomes a melody to be forgotten, a mirage of a tradition more storybook than real every day. Nowhere is this more the case, of course, than in Washington,

D.C., where absolute unaccountability corrupts absolutely, where echoing down the cool, white marble halls of power, hollow men and women trample sovereignty and citizenship in a pathway to American betrayal. And I haven't even gotten to Congress, busy, busy "reforming" the illegal alien crisis they antiseptically refer to as "immigration," while considering passage of a $940 billion "farm bill," 80 percent of which will fund food stamps. These two laws alone can institutionalize the lawlessness of the land and make countless more Americans wards of the state.

Meanwhile, there is in Washington a faceless power-mongery that lives and works in the shadows. City by city, rural state by rural state, its mechanisms of "immigration," "refugee resettlement," and socialist government programs overwhelm a near-impotent citizenry with alien cultures, religions, languages and traditions.

There is no "melting pot" out there, nor is there even residual belief in one -- particularly not on the part of the state. Most of our new peoples will never embrace American constitutional virtues en masse to perpetuate them because their own sponsor, their own lifeline, is the mega-state that brought them here and supports them.

This goes for newcomers from the Hispano-sphere, 75 percent of whom, Pew reported in 2012, believe the U.S. government isn't big enough and want more government services. It also goes for Muslim "refugee resettlement" populations, willfully deployed by this same power-mongery to displace and erase what we may one day look back on as just another indigenous culture that Washington overlords destroyed.

Then there is the faceless power-mongery that transforms the country, ironically, in the name of "national security." How can "national security" be achievable in an America without borders? It is a post-9/11 fact that more than one million Americans, government employees and contactors, now have "top-secret" access. They monitor our electronic lives, and collect all of our telephone numbers, something we have learned from the completely unauthorized but vital disclosures of Edward Snowden. This mass monitoring, we are told repeatedly, is what it takes to prevent "another 9/11."

Never mind those pinprick jihad attacks in Boston, Arkansas or Fort Hood. In fact, never mind jihad, period. This same Surveillance State has officially eliminated jihad as a subject to be taught or studied by security agencies and the military. In this way, every one of us becomes a suspect.

"Why do you need every telephone number?" NBC's Andrea Mitchell asked Director of National Intelligence James Clapper. "Why is it such a broad vacuum cleaner approach?"

"Well, you have to start someplace," Clapper replied.

Incredibly, this deaf, dumb and blind vacuum cleaner approach is touted as effective enough to have prevented 9/11 in the first place. So stresses former CIA and NSA chief Michael Hayden, a booster of the warrantless "data mining" of the PRISM program and the mass collection of all Americans' telephone records.

The mendacity of this rationale is as appalling as the hyper-state it enables. Just ask the airline ticket taker in Boston who, constricted by "political correctness" forced herself to tell the al-Qaida hijackers to "have a nice flight" rather than investigate their strange pre-boarding behavior.

If our leaders really wanted to prevent "another 9/11," they would have long ago admitted the obvious: that the world of Islam, from its terrorists to its kings, is engaged in the latest historical cycle of jihad to extend the reach of Islamic law (sharia). They would have decided that "profiling" isn't worse than terrorism. They would have halted Islamic immigration not only to stop more jihad cells from forming but also to prevent Constitution-endangering, pro-sharia demographics from forming, too. They would have sharply curtailed travel, and particularly return travel from jihad nations such as Chechnya and Pakistan. They would have long ago blocked U.S. institutions, including colleges, media organizations and banks, from accepting millions of dollars from sharia-ruled dictatorships. They would have closed down mosques in America where jihad is preached and supported.

Above all, they would have secured our borders rather than leave them open all these post-9/11 years. Of course, that would mean re-establishing and defending those borders, both literally and figuratively.

That's one thing Washington, D.C., will never tolerate.

Big Brother (Uncle Sam) Rewrites History -- Again

6/21/13

The narrow boxes through which we find ourselves entering public debate over the rise of a totalitarian government surveillance infrastructure are driving me a little crazy.

"Edward Snowden: Hero or traitor?"

Pick one, now, the question demands, before we learn anything else, think anything more. In this way, our attention is focused onto Snowden, the man, not Uncle Sam, the secret megastate. We wade into a vortex of emotions whirling around loyalty to the republic: a republic with sovereign borders, or so we hope; that runs by rule of law, or so we think; where citizenship is precious, or so we imagine.

What Snowden's revelations confirm, however, is that such a republic no longer exists -- except as a mirage that powerful Surveillance State officials spin as reality.

Tap, tap -- answer the question! "Hero or traitor?"

"Traitor!" some cry, never noticing that Snowden's leak makes him a "traitor" to the Surveillance State, not the republic of memory. But such a gaffe is fine with our Big Brothers, from President Obama and FBI Director Robert Mueller to former Vice President Dick Cheney.

Listen the next time they insist that it is only the current state of mass surveillance that can preserve our folkloric republic, its residual form currently being liquidated by "immigration-reforming" U.S. senators, whose "hero" or "traitor" status we might also weigh. Listen the next time they argue that only PRISM, only stockpiling hundreds of millions of cellphone conversations, emails, texts and other personal records, can prevent a fiery cloud of new 9/11s.

Now they are even telling us that the first 9/11 could have been prevented altogether had the mass surveillance infrastructure been in place at the time.

This is a whopper too far, and with the gravest implications. Big Brother is rewriting our history again, after having withheld too many facts from We, the People, about 9/11 all along.

This new Big Lie about 9/11 is that the Snowden-leaked programs of data mining and cellphone collection might well have led authorities to identify two key Saudi hijackers in San Diego and roll up the whole al-Qaida plot. As former Florida Sen. Bob Graham, who served as co-chairman of the Congressional Joint 9/11 Inquiry, has made abundantly clear, this particular pair, Nawaf al-Hazmi and Khalid al-Mihdhar, was already well known to U.S. intelligence authorities for ties to the embassy bombings in Kenya and Tanzania and other hostile activities. Indeed, the CIA had even listened in on conversations at an al-Qaida safe house in Yemen that referenced the pair as far back as December 1999 -- no PRISM necessary.

For reasons unknown, the CIA did not nominate them to any U.S. terror watch lists, and they were able to live and take flying lessons and consort with other Saudi nationals in the U.S. in plain sight up until the 9/11 attacks.

Why? Are we looking at government incompetence as usual? Or how about more special U.S. treatment for Saudis? In Graham's excellent book "Intelligence Matters," he recounts the instructive experience of U.S. immigration official Jose Melendez-Perez, who, following an alarming entry interview at Orlando airport with a Saudi man named Mohammed al-Qahtani, barred al-Qahtani's entry into the country.

"Many of the other agents thought Melendez-Perez was risking his career because ... it is made clear to customs officials in their training that Saudis are different," Graham writes. "He told me he was taught that a Saudi ... is to be treated with deference and special respect." Graham continues: "Melendez-Perez's instincts proved correct. Waiting outside the airport for al-Qahtani's arrival was Mohamed Atta."

Not a byte of data mining necessary.

Meanwhile, the information linking 9/11 hijackers to other Saudis in California is information that congressional investigators developed themselves. The FBI, as Graham has long attested, withheld evidence from Congress' Joint Inquiry -- and, later, the 9/11 Commission. Why? More Saudi cover-up, it seems. It doesn't stop. For example, the 28-page section of the 9/11 Commission's final report on "sources of foreign support for some of the Sept. 11 hijackers," remains classified, another bone of Graham's contention.

In 2011, reporters Anthony Summers and Dan Christiansen broke the news in the Broward Bulldog that the FBI withheld more information from the Congress' inquiry: its investigation into another Saudi 9/11 support network, this one in Sarasota, Fla. The FBI rejected the claim, insisting the agency had informed the 9/11 Commission about its investigation at the time, which it also claimed had gone nowhere.

"This assertion by the FBI was not credible," Graham wrote in a sworn declaration dated May 31, 2013 attached to a new Freedom of Information Act request by the reporters. Graham contacted 9/11 Commission co-chairmen Thomas Kean and Lee Hamilton and reported that neither of them had ever heard of an FBI investigation in Sarasota, either.

More important, as Graham states, the FBI's failure to call attention to "documents finding 'many connections' between Saudis living in the United States and individuals associated with the terrorist (attacks) ... interfered with the Inquiry's ability to complete its mission."

This stonewalling continues under the Obama administration. In his sworn declaration, Graham names names. These include CIA Director John Brennan, who fobbed him off, and deputy FBI Deputy Director Sean Joyce, who has blocked Graham's efforts to pursue the Sarasota story at every turn. Graham states that Joyce advised him that he, Joyce, had instructed the FBI agent in charge of the Sarasota investigation (since transferred to Honolulu!) not to speak to Graham.

"I am troubled by what appears to me to be a persistent effort by the FBI to conceal from the American people information concerning possible Saudi support of the Sept. 11 attacks," Graham writes.

Also troubling is watching the U.S. government hide and twist history -- the shocking subject of my new book, "American Betrayal" -- in real time. We can't let them do this to us again.

Iraq and the Doomed 'Democracy' Project

In Iraq, is democracy in the eye of the beholder?

4-21-03

After roughly 100 Iraqi exiles, sheiks and clerics gathered in a fortified and air-conditioned tent in Iraq this week to begin piecing together their country's future, U.S. Central Command headquarters released a 13-point summary of the meeting. This included the outcome of the historic first vote in Saddam-free Iraq (the Iraqi proto-body voted to meet again in 10 days) and a string of high-minded resolutions.

Point one said "Iraq must be a democracy;" point three said "the rule of law must be paramount;" and point four stated that the country "must be built on respect for diversity including the role of women." No word as yet on how "respect" for "diversity including the role of women" translates into legal or political rights; maybe that comes at the next meeting.

Meanwhile, there's something positive to be said about the plain-spoken certitude with which some of these democratic building-blocks are being laid out, at least on paper. But such energy is lacking in another key point on the list. Point six is downright phlegmatic which it comes to noting, merely, that "the meeting discussed the role of religion in state and society."

It did, did it? Well, what did "the meeting" say? Nothing that could be distilled into a declarative point of consensus. Which shouldn't be surprising. The most intractable problem facing democratic reform in Iraq (or anywhere else in the Muslim world) is how to reconcile that founding principle of democracy - the separation of church and state - with Islamic law, which is predicated on the inseparable union of religious and political power.

"Those who would like to separate religion from the state are simply dreaming," a conference participant told the New York Times, echoing a line that resounds with much of Iraq's Shi'ite Muslim majority. At least one Iraqi Shi'ite cleric at the big-tent planning session, Sheik Ayad Jamal al-Din, however, disagreed. "Dictators may not speak in the name of religion," he said, calling for a "system of government that separates belief from politics." (Let's hope such a "system" is an improvement on a dictatorship that is secular.) Sheik al-Din's is a rare voice of dissent. More typical is the comment of another Shi'ite imam to Agence France Presse: "Our objective is to set up an Islamic state, because this is the supreme ambition of all Arab and Muslim countries. All Muslim countries would like to see their governments applying sharia (Islamic law)."

This doesn't bode well for democracy, fledgling or otherwise. As Islamic scholar Ibn Warraq explains in his book "Why I am Not a Muslim," Islamic law "tries to legislate every aspect of an individual's life. The individual is not at liberty to think or decide for himself; he has but to accept G-d's rulings as infallibly interpreted by the doctors of law, " or clerics. Another problem is that Islamic law limits, or even "denies the rights of women and non-Muslim religious minorities." Which, of course, is no way to run a democracy.

We have already begun to see elements of sharia re-introduced into post-Taliban Afghanistan, where, as Freedom House's Nina Shea has warned, a "theological iron curtain" is dropping across the country, even as the United States pours in hundreds of millions of political and economic reconstruction dollars. Will that happen in Iraq? It's too soon to tell, of course - but not too soon to make ourselves acutely aware of the possibility.

Nor is it too soon to develop a really good nose for similar developments elsewhere. Citing an article in the Israeli newspaper Makor Rishon, Cybercast News Service reports that the new Palestinian constitution - the creation of which is considered a prerequisite for reforming the Palestinian Authority - defines not a democratic republic, but an Islamic state. Not a good sign. And this week in France, La Republique found itself taking an unexpected step closer to sharia, European-style, with the surprising electoral success of the Union of Islamic Organizations, an Islamist group that preaches Islamic law for France, which between 5 and 10 million Muslims now call home. Having won a big chunk of seats on the new Islamic council created by the government to foster "an official (read: moderate) Islam for France," the decidedly un-moderate group has earned its place at the government table.

This prompted surprisingly tough talk from Interior Minister Nicolas Sarkosy: "It is precisely because we recognize the right of Islam to sit at the table of the republic that we will not accept any deviation. Any prayer leader whose views run contrary to the values of the republic will be expelled." And there was more: "Islamic law will not apply anywhere," he said, "because it is not the law of the French republic."

Not yet, anyway. But who knows what can happen in a democracy.

Islam's consistency with democracy

11-24-03

No doubt President Bush's Whitehall speech will be remembered for its "three pillars" — Bush's metaphorical framework for the peace and security of free nations. Maybe more significant, however, are the two "Ifs."

If No. 1: "If the Middle East remains a place where freedom does not flourish, it will remain a place of stagnation and anger and violence for export," Bush said. "As we saw in the ruins of two towers, no distance on the map will protect our lives and way of life."

If No. 2: "If the greater Middle East joins the democratic revolution that has reached much of the world, the lives of millions in that region will be bettered, and a trend of conflict and fear will be ended at its source."

The two "Ifs" take us to a crossroads, staring down uncharted paths through what I take to be our relationship with the Islamic world. After all, the only non-Islamic country in the Middle East, Israel, long ago joined the "democratic revolution" Bush invoked. (The president himself indicated the Islamic-ness of his two conditions when, soon after stating them, he noted, critically, "We're told that Islam is somehow inconsistent with a democratic culture.")

If No. 2, obviously, is the preferred destination for all nations resting on Bush's three pillars. But how to get there from here, and how to avoid the blind alleys along the way?

According to Bush, "the most helpful" action "is to change our own thinking" — namely, to change what he called "a certain skepticism about the capacity or even the desire of Middle Eastern peoples for self-government." As he put it, "It is not realism to suppose that one-fifth of humanity is unsuited to liberty. It is pessimism and condescension, and we should have none of it."

This rather muscular line drew applause, bulging as it does with an infectious vigor. Still, as someone unconvinced that Islam is consistent with "democratic culture" — if democratic culture includes freedom of worship, freedom of speech, and equality of men and women before the law — I would say the concern is not so much that "Middle Eastern peoples" are incapable of self-government, but rather that the governments they would likely form would little resemble the kinds of democracies that now coexist, finally, in peace and relative harmony.

Why? The president talked about a "freedom deficit" in the Middle East that has denied nations "the progress of our time." Such a "deficit" refers to a range of freedoms — democratic culture — that is conspicuously lacking in Muslim lands. But more than a freedom deficit divides Islam from the West. In the absence of freedom, a noxious culture of anti-Jewish and anti-American hatred and delusion has become deeply entrenched, encouraged, nurtured and fueled by governments, mosques, state-run media, and school systems.

The ministry of education in the Palestinian Authority encourages this culture of hatred and delusion when it produces, for example, a new textbook urging jihad and martyrdom onto 11th-graders. Hezbollah satellite television (available worldwide) nurtures it when, as during this Ramadan season, it broadcasts a 30-part, Syrian-produced exercise in anti-Semitism called "Diaspora" for the holidays. One episode, partly translated (along with a video clip) at www.memri.org, depicts a group of rabbis and other Jews engaged in the act of ritual murder.

(Head rabbi to accomplices: "You, pour lead in his mouth. You, stab his body with a knife before the lead kills him ... ."). Al Riyadh newspaper — also according to www.memri.com — fuels it by fantastically attributing Islamic terrorism to Israel, declaring that "Mossad agents recruit young Arabs to act as Islamists in order to shake the faith and social foundation of the Middle East." This sanity-challenged theme has endless variations, dating back to reports across the Muslim world of joint Mossad-CIA complicity in the attacks of 9/11. A secret ballot can do a lot for the freedom deficit, but something more drastic is needed to plug the reality gap.

Something more drastic, of course, has taken place in Iraq, where as the president also noted, 150 free newspapers now circulate, textbooks are propaganda-free, and incitement-as-government-policy has ended. But laying this groundwork for democracy has cost us greatly, requiring far more than merely "changing our own thinking." Even so, now that Saddam Hussein is gone, everyone's thinking about what's possible in the Middle East has changed. Will it evolve from a place where freedom doesn't flourish to a place where democratic culture takes root? The answer is unclear.

What *is* clear is that any change for the better requires the end of state-sponsored incitement in the Muslim kingdoms and dictatorships of the Middle East — in the media, in the textbooks and in the mosques.

Understanding Condi

10/28/05

If Condoleezza Rice ever does run for president, the following line may become very familiar:

"The only problem, of course, was that when the Founding Fathers said, 'We the people,' they didn't mean me."

For the past few years, the most powerful woman on earth has been delivering this clincher. And it gets a gasp every time. I first read it in a speech Ms. Rice gave last week in Birmingham. Of course, it's a dramatic, even melodramatic, statement—a testament to the continuing expansion of liberty provided by our 218-year-old Constitution. But Ms. Rice drops it in by way of illustrating the historic flaws of democracy, American-style; and this she drops in by way of dismissing the current flaws of democracy-building in the Muslim world.

It's an awkward exercise, but she's bent on it. "We should note that unlike in our Constitutional Convention, the Iraqis have not made a compromise as bad as the one that made my ancestors three-fifths of a man," she said. Is it politically incorrect to find this statement offensive? Yes, slaves were indeed counted as a fractional person in pre-abolition censuses that determined how many representatives a state would send to the House of Representatives. (Slaveholders, not slavery opponents, wanted a slave to count as one person to augment their state's political power.) But it is the miracle of that 18th-century document that it contained the blueprint for abolition. By contrast, the 2005 Iraqi Constitution (also the 2003 Palestinian Authority constitution and the 2004 Afghanistan constitution) contains provisions for a sharia state under which all men are not created equal, and freedom of conscience is denied.

But that's not what Ms. Rice sees, and it's her prism that counts. While the president works his way through a string of "isms" (fascism, totalitarianism, communism, Nazism) to place the ideology of Islamic terrorism into context, the Secretary of State studies something else: the lessons of the civil rights movement. In the transformation of her hometown of Birmingham from, as she put it, "a place called 'Bombingham,' where I witnessed the denial of democracy in America for so many years," the Secretary of State seems to see the blueprint for the democratization of the non-democratic, particularly Muslim world.

This Rice Doctrine grows from the segregated South: "Across the empire of Jim Crow, from upper Dixie to the lower Delta, the descendants of slaves shamed our nation with the power of righteousness and redeemed America at last from its original sin of slavery," Ms. Rice said. "By resolving the contradiction at the heart of our democracy," she continued, "America finally found its voice as a true champion of democracy beyond its shores."

In this worldview, it's not, say, the 700,000 casualties of the Civil War plus one assassinated president who redeemed that original sin of slavery, but rather the civil rights movement that helped overturn Southern segregation laws a century later. Indeed, it was only at this relatively late date, if I'm reading Ms. Rice's words correctly, that America could finally sally forth as a "true champion of democracy" — which makes you wonder who it was who went to Belleau Wood in 1918, St Lo in 1945, and Chosin Reservoir in 1950.

The implication seems clear: American democracy wasn't all that much to be proud of until the civil rights leaders Ms. Rice calls the "impatient patriots" — Martin Luther King and Rosa Parks, for instance — came along. This supports one of her main policy points; namely, that even in America "democratization is a long and difficult process, not a singular event." So much for the miracle at Philadelphia.

Such a view of American unexceptionalism makes it perfectly okay to support other "impatient patriots" (her phrase again) in Afghanistan, Iraq and the Palestinian Authority. They, like our Founders, she might say, permit anti-democratic tendencies to mar their nascent democracies (sharia on the books, bomb-toting terrorists on the ballots), but no one should balk. Only "cynics," as Ms. Rice said—the same people she said "once believed that blacks were unfit for democracy"—argue "that the people of the Middle East, perhaps because of their color or their creed or their culture or even perhaps because of their religion, are somehow incapable of democracy."

In this mix 'n' match take on history, facts about clashing belief systems have no place, and fears for freedom under sharia are "cynical" or worse. But when debate is stopped cold by pushing the hot buttons of racism and bigotry, realpolitik gives way to feelpolitik—maybe the ultimate doctrine of pre-emption.

When democracy isn't democratic

12/26/05

Not to curdle the Christmas pudding or anything, but it's hard to see how Uncle Sam comes out a winner in any of the elections that have just taken place, however historically, in the Arab world.

This isn't to contradict President Bush, who said, referring to Iraq's parliamentary elections, we're seeing "something new: constitutional democracy at the heart of the Middle East." Sure, campaign posters and ballot boxes are new. But the emerging nature of this constitutional democracy — from Iraq to Egypt to the Palestinian Authority (PA) — calls into question whether, as the president also said in referring to Iraq,

"America has an ally of growing strength in the fight against terror."

For that statement to be true, Arab voters would need to be electing brave anti-jihadists, right? They would be dunking their fingers in purple ink for reform-minded advocates of equality and freedom of conscience, not to mention peace with Israel. But with nearly two-thirds of the ballots counted in Iraq, the initial headlines tell a different story.

"Parties Linked to Tehran Gain in Iraq," reported The New York Sun.

"Secular candidates not doing well," reported the Los Angeles Times.

Apparently, that's putting it mildly. So far, election returns indicate that the Shi'ite Muslim religious coalition, the United Iraqi Alliance (UIA), has overcome internal tensions and weak projections to win a dominating bloc of parliamentary seats. That means that the democratic enterprise in Iraq appears to have empowered proponents of sharia law with alarmingly close ties to the terror masters of Iran.

Little wonder, then, that something approaching jubilation is the reaction in Tehran. "We share this victory with the Iraqi nation because we paid a price for its preparation," said Ali Akbar Hashemi Rafsanjani, the former president of Iran, making reference to the Iran-Iraq War (1980-88). Usually described as Iran's "pragmatic conservative" in the Western media (not necessarily saying much), Mr. Rafsanjani continued: "It is a victory because the results were the opposite of what the Americans were seeking."

If out of democratic Iraq emerges a sharia state allied with Iran, Mr. Rafsanjani would be right. Which would make President Bush wrong — not about the need to fight in Iraq, but about the transformative powers of the democratic process (emphasis on process). In other words, what we see in Iraq and in the rest of the Muslim world is that the political freedom to vote doesn't guarantee election results that we in the West would in any way equate with political freedom. Amid claims of Shi'ite election fraud, one liberal party candidate, Mithal al-Alusi, told The New York Sun: "We may have just traded the Ba'athist fascists for the religious fascists."

This isn't to say scrap the war, or give credence to hate-Bush Democratic carping. But there is a deepening disconnect between Western democracy theories and Muslim democracy realities that urgently needs to be confronted and assessed.

And not just in Iraq. A similar story unfolded in Egypt where, contrary to Washington's wishes and projections, November elections also yielded results that were more democratic, but not more liberal. As the San Francisco Chronicle reported, "Most liberal, secular reformers lost their seats, while a banned Islamist party" — the Muslim Brotherhood (MB) — "became the most important opposition bloc in parliament.

The MB platform? "Islam is the solution." As political analyst Hala Mustafa told the Chronicle, "It was a complete defeat for the liberal political tendencies."

Then there's the Palestinian Authority. Election Day lies ahead (January 25), but primary victories for Hamas already underscore the inability of foreign-made democratic machinery to produce anything akin to homegrown democratic candidates. Instead, we get People's Choice terrorists — convicted killer Marwan Barghouti, "mother of martyrs" Miriam Farhat, and "Hitler" (aka Jamal Abu Al-Rub), a real crowd-pleaser known for public execution-style slayings of suspected Israeli "collaborators." And these are People's Choice terrorists with attitude: When the European Union, rather surprisingly, discussed ending aid to the PA if Hamas won parliamentary seats next month, Hamas leader Khaled Mashaal responded with Sons-of-Liberty-style rhetoric about the dangers of "playing with the values of democracy and freedom."

All of which is why I beg to differ when the president says, "the terrorists know that democracy is their enemy." From the PA, where sharia-supporting terrorists are winning primaries, to Egypt, where sharia-supporting terror-ideologues are being elected, to Iraq, where sharia-supporting terror-state-allies are being elected, democracy is not their enemy. It is vox populi. And just because the people have spoken doesn't mean we should applaud what they say.

Why they fight.
(No, really — why?)

5/1/06

No one has ever adequately explained why the jihadist "insurgency" fights on in Iraq. Really. It's not enough to say these Islamic fanatics want to drive "infidel" U.S. forces out of Iraq, or that they want to bring down the Iraqi government. It is by remaining in Iraq that the United States has built up a democratically elected but Islamic government in Iraq — and an Islamic government is the goal of every good jihadist. In other words, our Islamic enemies should be at peace with the Iraqi government because its constitution makes Islamic law supreme. "No law that contradicts the established provisions of Islam may be established," says Article 2. That single line contains the blueprint for a sharia state, and if there's one thing a jihadist apparently likes, it's a sharia state.

Recently, Sayyed Ayad, a liberal member of Iraqi parliament who favors the separation of church (mosque) and state, spoke in Washington.

When I asked him what could be done under Iraq's constitution to foster democracy, not sharia, his answer was chilling. Pointing out that Iraqi voters chose this sharia-supreme document, he said: "They have to try it for 10 or 20 years, and then change it." Maybe.

Which leads me to another point no one has adequately explained: Why exactly American troops fight on in Iraq. Sure, the objective is to destroy the hellions of the insurgency — a killing machine more aptly and derisively described by the late journalist Steven Vincent as "paramilitary death squads." And I still believe the goal of killing jihadists "there," not "here," is entirely commendable. But even after their destruction, does an American victory lie in making Iraq safe for sharia?

The same question applies to Afghanistan, where another democratically mandated sharia state has been established thanks to the U.S. of A — as the world finally noticed when an Afghan Christian "apostate" named Abdul Rahman had to flee to Italy rather than face Islamic "justice" in the courts or on the street.

Maybe this all proves that Islam and democracy don't mix. Then again, maybe they mix just fine; it's the mixture itself — sharia for the people — that clashes with liberty as defined in the Western world. This is the lesson we seem determined not to learn. But in making such ignorance inviolate, we end up making the world safe for sharia.

Certainly, we didn't put up all those ballot boxes across the Middle East to mandate a rollback of freedom. But in failing to assess the ideology central to Islam that makes Western notions of liberty fatally heretical, this is increasingly what is happening. Which gives a head-hurting circularity to our policy. Maybe such dizzying confusion should make us welcome the advent of the Iraq Study Group, a presidential advisory council created, as The New York Times put it, "to generate new ideas on Iraq."

But new ideas on "Iraq" are the last thing we need, particularly as generated by a bipartisan snooze of a group that includes James Baker, Vernon Jordan, Charles Robb, Sandra Day O'Connor, Alan K. Simpson, Lee Hamilton — I can hardly tap out the other names because they're so solidly and venerably uninspiring (with the notable exception of Rudy Giuliani).

Framing their study around "Iraq" reveals how blinkered government thinking is. Iraq is only a small piece of our troubles in this period of resurgent Islamic jihad, from Osama bin Laden's cave to downtown Tehran, from worldwide Danish cartoon protests to Tel Aviv falafel stands, from Paris banlieus to Zacarias Moussaui's courtroom hot seat.

Squeezing big brains for "new ideas" about winning Iraq is sort of like planning the Normandy invasion to win France. We need something bigger. We need new ideas about Islam.

My list of idea men and women would include Hirsi Ali, Bat Ye'or, Bruce Bawer, Andrew G. Bostom, Walid Phares, Daniel Pipes, Wafa Sultan, Ibn Warraq, and other experts and observers unbowed by the strictures of political correctness that strangle debate on Islam — its teachings, its demands, its history. Iraq would figure into such a curriculum, but from a broader perspective that would allow us to size up the global battlefield in terms of the two great threats to the Western way of life: the spread of sharia through active jihad (war, terrorism), and the spread of sharia through Islamization (demographics, multicultural correctness). Of the two, the second — quiet jihad — is the more serious threat, as the continuing Islamization of Europe shows.

We need an Islam Study Group.

Forget false democracy, stop real terrorism

6/12/06

Got to hand it to the new Iraqi prime minister, Nuri Kamal al-Maliki. Here's a guy who, less than two months on the job, has discovered the real enemy of his country. It's not, of course, Abu Musab al-Zarqawi — he's dead. It's not other mass murderers of jihad who blow up markets and shoot up schools, who kidnap and maim and chop off heads. It's neither Baathist party holdouts nor "sectarian" violence. It doesn't come from Al Qaeda, and it doesn't come from Iran.

The enemy of Iraq comes from Haditha.

Haditha, of course, is the Iraqi town where American troops are alleged to have killed civilians on Nov. 19, 2005. If American society were not suicidal and self-loathing, this singular incident would be seen in the context of the greater war effort. If American society were not suicidal and self-loathing, the rush to judgment would halt in the imagined tracks of fellow Americans on patrol among hostile, even murderous townspeople. But no. American society is indeed suicidal and self-loathing, so Haditha is portrayed as the culmination of the war even as we giddily judge ourselves guilty as thrillingly charged. But that hardly excuses al-Maliki.

The New York Times reported his reaction to Haditha on its front page. The prime minister "lashed out at the American military," the newspaper wrote, "denouncing what he characterized as habitual attacks by troops against Iraqi civilians." The Times quoted al-Maliki as saying violence against civilians had become "a daily phenomenon" — the next edition of the paper corrected this phrase to "regular occurrence" — by many American troops who "do not respect the Iraqi people." al-Maliki went on: "They (the Americans) crush them with their vehicles and kill them just on suspicion. This is completely unacceptable."

Wrong.

What's completely unacceptable are al-Maliki's hyperbolic remarks. Iraq, drenched in American blood, littered with American limbs, is a land of American sacrifice. The goal of this sacrifice is a stable and peaceable Iraq that is no party to Islamic terrorism. Frankly, this is all very generous of us because, as far as strictly American interests go, we could certainly achieve an Iraq that is no party to Islamic terrorism without bothering with the stable and peaceable part — and at much less American sacrifice.

This fact makes me wish to reconsider al-Maliki's ungrateful and slanderous statements — at least as far as his apparent dissatisfaction with our presence goes. After all, the American mission has indeed been accomplished. Saddam Hussein no longer poses a threat to the region. His WMD programs, such as they are, have been destroyed. The idiotic U.N. Security Council resolutions, all 17 of them, have been upheld. Now the hydra-head of jihad in Iraq (Zarqawi) has been killed. Our only failure — to create, say, Switzerland in Iraq — is, to say the least, not for want of trying. It is high time to redefine the mission: What we should aim for is an Iraq that is not a terrorist threat, not an Iraq that is a democratic paradigm.

Would such a change in mission mark a defeat for the United States in the so-called war on terror? Only if we failed to rethink our overall strategy, particularly as it pertains to our assessment of Islam. That is, if Jeffersonian democracy remains a strategic goal for Iraq, anything short of that goal will be scored as a failure. But what if we accept the politically incorrect fact that our failure to establish liberty and justice for all in Iraq — namely, freedom of conscience and equality before the law — is due to the nature of Islamic culture, not to the efficacy of American efforts? If, five years after Sept. 11, we finally faced the fact that liberty in Islam — defined, literally, as "freedom from unbelief" — has nothing to do with liberty in the West, we could finally understand why an Iraqi constitution enshrining sharia is wholly incompatible with everything our own democracy stands for, and is thus not something worth dying for.

Such a reassessment would remove the "political transformation" of the Muslim Middle East from our war strategy. This would let us focus on the formidable military task of fighting jihad in Iraq and beyond — eliminating, deporting and containing the threat as needed. This is a global war with many fronts, from Iran to Syria to Gaza to quite a few neighborhoods in Toronto, London and elsewhere. It is time to arrive at new ways and means to fight on them.

Limitations of limited war

10/20/06

The worst thing about the upcoming elections is, when it comes to war and peace, they turn on a deficient choice. Stay the course versus cut and run. Keep up your dukes versus cry "uncle."

For anyone who wants to fight to win, the choice is clear enough, if also non-compelling. Sticking to offense is intuitively better than giving up, but it doesn't inspire stirring campaign slogans. As in: "Vote Republican — at least terrorists' overseas phone calls will continue to be intercepted." Then again, intercepting terrorists' overseas phone calls is considerably better than not.

But to what end? Here's where the deficiency shows up. What if "the course" is wrong? And what if its destination is a) unreachable or, worse, b) wholly imaginary?

As an Air Force pilot noted in an e-mail to me, he doesn't recall hearing the president define "victory" for Iraq or Afghanistan. Me neither. Terms like "security" and "stabilization" just aren't substitutes. Guided by the false god of democracy, blind to the zealotry of Islamic culture, we have locked onto a course with no rational endpoint. Even as we pursue "security," "stabilizing" the Shiite-dominated, sharia-guided Iraqi government — and, thus, creating a natural Iranian (Shiite) ally — makes zero strategic sense. But, see here, say supporters of the president's Iraq policy: If we don't secure and stabilize the Shiite-dominated, sharia-guided government in Iraq, that same government falls, America suffers defeat in jihadist eyes, and Shiite-Sunni war breaks out in full force.

Well, which scenario is better for the US of A? I vote for civil war. It seems obvious when Shiite and Sunni jihadis — and their Islamic world sponsors — are busy slaughtering one another, they have much less time to plan their next attack on Americans, in the region or stateside. This isn't to say there's no role for American forces in the Middle East. But that role may be, as a marine captain home from Afghanistan and Iraq put it to me, far from booby-trapped Iraqi cities, perhaps in Kurdistan, where they can keep a lid on Iraq while preparing for the next stage of the war on jihad, against Iran and Syria. Assuming there is a next stage.

Such a redeployment is no defeat. But it would represent a drastic change in war aims and in the Bush belief in the magical properties of Western-style liberty for truly all. The fact is, democratizing Islamic cultures into secular wonders of ecumenical productivity just ain't going to happen. The sooner we acknowledge this, the better for us. And above all, this war should be, as they say in our therapeutic culture, all about us.

What would a war policy "about us" look like? First, as a matter of national security, it would call for energy independence. It also would be designed to keep jihad out of the West, and emphatically not to bring democracy to lands of jihad. Such a mission would necessarily engage the military in the Middle East, destroying or neutralizing myriad Islamic threats, from Iran to Al Qaeda, from Syria to Hezbollah. Maybe what I envision darkly doesn't sound like the kind of "limited war" the West has exclusively waged for a half century. But it doesn't sound like the kind of "limited war" the West has fought without definable end for half a century, either. And here I'm thinking back to Korea, the very first "limited war" fought to stalemate, not victory, by the last total warrior, Douglas MacArthur — at least until President Truman fired him for the general's not wanting to fight to stalemate.

Since I began reading William Manchester's biography of Douglas MacArthur, I've been wondering what the famed general would say about today's plight. In a 1951 newspaper interview, MacArthur described his multinational (mainly American, of course) forces in Korea as being "circumscribed by a web of artificial conditions ... in a war without a definite objective. ... The situation would be ludicrous if men's lives were not involved."

It all sounds alarmingly familiar. And what was achieved in this limited war? Roughly 54,000 American servicemen dead for stalemate. Fifty-odd years later, we still have stalemate, and we still have American troops in South Korea (incredible) arrayed against Kim Jong Il, son of North Korean war leader, Kim Il Sung. Now we have NoKo nukes there, as well. Which should make us think hard: What will a limited, ill-defined war on terror look like ... in 50 years?

How to win the winnable war? Oil

12/1/06

Did anybody really need a leaked memo from the National Security Agency to figure out that Iraqi prime minister Nouri al-Maliki is incapable of stopping the carnage in Iraq?

Given that his political power depends on factions allied with Shiite militias behind much of the carnage, Maliki has never fit the white hat and brass star in this wretched desert saga. Insult to injury, he even left the president in Jordan this week, cooling his heels, as they say, when Maliki postponed a summit meeting after the memo leaked.

Then again, what about Bush? Why hasn't he been able to bring order to Iraq with the U.S. military? Here's the answer: As a creature of Shiite thug-o-crats, Maliki's hands are tied. As creatures of political correctness, we have tied our own hands.

And almost literally. The PC rules of engagement imposed on

American soldiers have as much to do with the chaotic limbo our troops find themselves in as failed political policies. Closely held, these rules — burdensome constraints, really — have become obvious to everyone, including our foes. News reports tell us potential targets in Iraq must be engaged in hostile acts, or show "clear intent," before our men and women can take a shot at them. Mosques where insurgents seek shelter and store arms are no-go zones for American soldiers. We don't even shut down mosque loudspeakers that broadcast incitement against our troops. Marine Maj. Jeffrey O'Neill put it this way to the Christian Science Monitor: "Many would ask, What other war would we allow the enemy to broadcast calls for our defeat for the sake of cultural sensitivity?"

The answer is no other war, at least no other war fought to win. But we don't even know what victory looks like — unless anyone seriously believes victory looks like just another basic death-to-America-and-Israel sharia state dominated by Shiites with ties to jihadist Iran. Next to such a prospect, chaotic limbo doesn't look good, but it does postpone that sure-to-be nasty shock of recognition.

But is our choice only "victory" or else? (Forget Plan B, soon to come from the blue-ribbon lunatics — I mean, "realists" — of the Iraq Survey Group, who are expected to argue that it's in America's national interest to "solve" Iraq by seeking help from the terrorist likes of Iran and Syria.) And what is "or else," anyway?

"Or else" refers to the cataclysm that's supposed to occur should we decide that remaking Islamic culture isn't our strong suit or in our national interest, and thus refocus our mission so as to ensure that Islamic culture doesn't remake us. Depending on its purpose and execution, withdrawal — or better, redeployment — wouldn't necessarily lead to cataclysm.

Here's an "or else" scenario from Nawaf Obaid, an adviser to the Saudi government, that actually sounds promising — not a term that usually springs to my mind to describe Saudi scenarios. Contemplating what he would call an unwelcome American withdrawal from Iraq, Obaid writes that the Saudi government just might fill the breach out of "religious responsibility" to Iraq's Sunni minority. Saudi Arabia, "the de facto leader of the world's Sunni community," Obaid writes, just might decide to support Iraq's Sunni fighters, just as Iran has been supporting Iraq's Shiite fighters, to avert a possible "full-blown ethnic cleansing."

Imagine: Sunni Saudi Arabia vs. Shiite Iran — and nary an American soldier ordered to pull his PC punches in the crossfire. But there's more. Obaid continues: King Abdullah might also "decide to strangle Iranian funding of the (Shiite) militias through oil policy. If Saudi Arabia boosted production and cut the price of oil in half, the kingdom could still finance its current spending. But it would be devastating to Iran, which is facing economic difficulties .... The result would be to limit Tehran's ability to continue funneling hundreds of millions each year to Shiite militias in Iraq and elsewhere."

I like. If Saudi Arabia "strangled" Iran's economy, that would also strangle Iran's capacity to fund its nuclear blackmail program, not to mention Hezbollah and other murderous proxies. And what was that the Saudi adviser said about cutting the price of crude oil in half?

A Saudi-Iranian, Sunni-Shiite rift over Iraq sounds like a win-win situation for the United States, maybe even better than the Sino-Soviet rivalry of the Cold War. This time around, instead of nuclear weapons to build in the interim, we would have something even more liberating to work on — energy independence.

(Sectarian) war is the answer

12/15/06

Funny thing about the recent op-ed by Nawaf Obaid in The Washington Post outlining likely Saudi actions if the United States withdraws from Iraq: namely, that Saudis would both support Sunnis in Iraq (versus Shiites supported by Iran) and manipulate the oil market to "strangle" the Iranian economy.

I think it sounds peachy, this let-them-devour-each-other strategy — which I'm guessing many Americans mutter to one another in frankness, if not also in confidence.

After the column appeared, not only did the Saudi government disavow it, but Obaid was fired from his job advising the Saudi ambassador to the United States, Prince Turki al-Faisal. Hmmm, thought Saudi-ologists.

Before anyone could say, "shifting desert sands," Turki resigned his post in Washington, hightailing it back to the so-called kingdom for reasons unknown, but possibly concerning machinations related to securing the post of foreign minister long held by Turki's ailing brother, Prince Saud al-Faisal. The post is also coveted by former Saudi ambassador to the United States, Prince Bandar bin Sultan. Hmmm again.

But now it seems the Obaid column "reflected the view of the Saudi government," after all. At least, that's the way The New York Times tells it.

Meanwhile, the Associated Press is reporting that "private" Saudi money is already supporting Sunni forces in Iraq. According to the Times, this private funding could easily become official Saudi policy. While Saudi leaders say they have so far withheld support from Al Qaeda-led Sunni groups in Iraq, the newspaper explains, "if Iraq's sectarian violence worsened, the Saudis would line up with Sunni tribal leaders" — Al Qaeda or no Al Qaeda. Meanwhile, we already know Iran is backing, if not guiding, Iraqi Shiites. So what should we do?

I propose two options, neither of which has occurred to Iraq Study Groupies calling for peace parleys with Hezbollah boosters and Holocaust deniers, or to hawkish proponents of "winning" Iraq (or at least Baghdad) with more troops. But maybe that's because neither group dares to reckon with the two greatest obstacles to our efforts in the region: namely, Islam (culturally unsuited to Westernity) and our own politically correct ROE, or rules of engagement (strategically unsuited to victory).

The first option is military, but it carries a seemingly insurmountable cultural override. The fact is, the United States has an arsenal that could obliterate any jihad threat in the region once and for all, whether that threat is bands of IED-exploding "insurgents" in Ramadi, the deadly so-called Mahdi Army in Sadr City, or genocidal maniacs in Tehran. In other words, it's a disgrace for military brass to talk about the 21st century struggle with Islam as necessarily being a 50- to 100-year war. Ridiculous. It could be over in two weeks if we cared enough to blast our way off the list of endangered civilizations.

As a culture, however, the West is paralyzed by the specter of civilian casualties, massive or not, that accompanies modern (not high-tech) warfare, and fights accordingly. It may well have been massive civilian casualties in Germany (40,000 dead in Hamburg after one cataclysmic night of "fire-bombing" in 1943, for example) and Japan that helped end World War II in an Allied victory. But this is a price I doubt any Western power would pay for victory today.

So, the military solution — which isn't the same as boosting ROE-cuffed troop levels in Baghdad — is out, unless or until our desperation level rises to some insupportably manic level. The great paradox of the "war on terror," of course, is that as our capacity and desire to protect civilians in warfare grows, our enemy's capacity and desire to kill civilians as a means of warfare grows also. Our fathers saved us from having to say, "Sieg Heil," but what's next — "Allahu akbar"?

Not necessarily. There's another Middle Eastern strategy to deter expansionist Islam: Get out of the way. Get out of the way of Sunnis and Shiites killing each other. As a sectarian conflict more than a thousand years old, this is not only one fight we didn't start, it's one we can't end. And why should we? If Iran, the jihad-supporting leader of the Shiite world, is being "strangled" by Saudi Arabia, the jihad-supporting leader of the Sunni world, isn't that good for the Sunni-and-Shiite-terrorized West? With the two main sects of Islam preoccupied with an internecine battle of epic proportions, the non-Muslim world gets some breathing room. And we sure could use it — to plan for the next round.

'Success' in Iraq

12/22/06

Sure, let's go ahead and say this new "troop surge" being bandied about Washington comes off, and tens of thousands of additional American troops pacify enough of Iraq to pull off what President Bush this week called the Iraqi dream — "a stable government that can defend, govern and sustain itself."

OK. So then what? It's not hard to imagine that the United States would take the first opportunity to wish that dream-come-true government well in defending, governing and sustaining itself, and then high-tail it back home. But that's no strategy. That's an escape hatch. What happens after that? Looking back on, lo, our many costly years of liberation and occupation in Iraq, what would it turn out that we had actually won? In other words, what, in this best-case scenario, is "victory" supposed to look like?

This is an important question. But it's one that is never, ever asked, let alone discussed. For reasons I can't altogether explain, tunnel-vision on Iraq has led to a kind of dead-end thinking on Iraq. Amid what amounts to a group failure of imagination on the part of our Big Brass and Deep Thinkers, no one takes into account, or even seems curious about, what exactly "victory" in Iraq might mean, or, more important, might gain for the United States of America and friends.

To the president, victory must seem self-evident, which is why he will say things like, "Success in Iraq will be success." Taking the opposite tack, the new secretary of defense explains also that "failure would be a calamity." But neither of them — and no one else, either — offers much more in the way of hard detail. "Success" may well be the stabilized Iraqi government the president waxes pre-nostalgic about, and "failure" may well be the absence of that "success," but none of this talk counts for enlightening debate.

What I want to know is what happens if this much-discussed American troop surge actually manages to secure Iraq, which then emerges as a natural ally of Iran and perhaps Syria? Will we salute U.S. efforts that brought into the (Islamic) world another Shi'ite-dominated, pro-Hezbollah, anti-American, anti-Israel Shariah state with lots of oil? To me, such "success" sounds more like the "failure" that is usually described, roughly, as the loss of American face or the transformation of Iraq into a terrorist haven. In the aftermath of any "victory" in Iraq that benefits Iran more than the United States, our face wouldn't look so hot with all that egg on it, and the world would surely have a new terrorist haven.

So maybe "more troops" to shore up the Iraqi government doesn't give us a bona fide win in the so-called war on terror — which is, of course, what this intervention in Iraq was supposed to achieve in the first place. That's not a failure of our great military; it's a failure of our best intentions. The next question is, what can we salvage from battle for the United States?

The only way we can even try to answer this question is to take a longer, wider view that takes in more than just the map of Iraq, which remains, after all, the arbitrary creation of Anglo-French diplomats carving up conquered land masses after World War I. We need to refocus this 21st-century war effort of ours around the specific needs of the United States as it fights against what we persist in calling "terror," but which really comes down to the expansion of Islam and Islamic power — via terrorism, both gangland (al Qaeda) and state (Iran), oil, massive demographic movement, and the resulting introduction of Shariah (Islamic law) — into the West. If we were to acknowledge this over-arching mission and recognize its urgency, "stabilizing" Iraq — which now means spending American blood and treasure to try to quell millennia-old Sunni-Shiite barbarism — might not figure prominently in the fight.

Stopping Iran and its allies in mass murder from becoming a genocidal nuclear outlaw and world-class menace; stopping the liberty-sapping spread of Shariah into the heretofore non-Muslim world; stopping U.S. aid to countries that foment jihad against us; stopping our addict-like dependence on Islamic oil: These are the urgent missions of our day. They are grand objectives on whose success the future of the West turns. I'm increasingly dubious we can make the same case for "success" in Iraq.

Elevated morality won't win Iraq

1/29/07

I find myself in political limbo.

I don't agree with the president and I don't agree with his opponents. I'm not convinced by the argument for sending 21,000 additional troops mainly to Baghdad, and I'm downright incensed at Senate Foreign Relations Committee voting along (Democratic) party lines (plus GOP Sen. Chuck Hagel of Nebraska) to declare this same so-called troop surge to be against "the national interest."

he president's argument fails to convince me that the effort required to secure Baghdad, which comes down to American troops quashing sectarian street violence, is worth the price. It's hard to imagine that an increased American presence, which is necessarily temporary, will win more than a pause in the violence, which goes back centuries. But I'm also unconvinced that the mission itself is of strategic value to the

United States. My great concern, as I have written before, is that it's very possible that renewed American fighting in Baghdad, if successful — which, as Americans, we must hope it to be — will not only stabilize the chaotic capital of Iraq, but will also entrench its Shiite-led, pro-Hezbollah, anti-Western government. This suggests that victory n Iraq may deliver not a new brother for the anti-terror coalition, but rather a perfect ally for Iran. And what kind of American victory is that?

A victory for democracy, I guess. In his State of the Union address this week, President Bush was still chanting the democracy mantra, insisting that "free people are not drawn to violent and malignant ideologies" — this after a whole lot of free people cross the Islamic world have democratically shown themselves to be drawn to just such ideologies. Even so, Lt. Gen. David Petraeus, whom Bush has tapped to execute his new Iraq strategy, has noted the limited transformative powers of democracy. Addressing the Senate Foreign Relations Committee this week, the general said, "The elections that gave us such hope actually intensified sectarian divisions in the population at the expense of the sense of the Iraqi identity."

He could say that again, and, in a way, even about our own elections. With Senate Democrats pushing through that non-binding resolution opposing troop surge (mentioned above), it might well be argued that recent U.S. elections brought about "divisions" that have fractured the American identity. Debate is one thing, but, as Sen. Richard G. Lugar (Indiana Republican), who himself considers the troop surge "dubious," pointed out, "Official roll call votes carry a unique message." And, in this vote's case, that message goes straight to our enemies, who will hunker down to wait for a divided America to up and crumble. This is a disgraceful way for lawmakers to send troops off anywhere.

It also reveals the blindness of Bush's political opponents, who see no mission of strategic value to the United States in Iraq. For example, if, as Al Qaeda claims, there are some 12,000 Al Qaeda terrorists in Iraq, it is obviously a mission of strategic value to the United States to eliminate them, and to do so with as little loss of American life as possible.

This would likely require U.S. air attacks, and such attacks would likely entail Iraqi civilian casualties. Just the thought of such casualties seems to render such a mission unthinkable to both Bush opponents and the Bush team, which now presides, for example, over a recurring battle for Baghdad's Haifa Street, where enemy fighters keep returning to fire at American and Iraqi troops from positions in high-rise buildings. Is it just me, or does anyone ever wonder why, if pacifying Baghdad is so darn vital, those buildings are still standing?

It is the great irony of our time that even as our stone-age enemies seek to inflict as many civilian casualties as possible, we in the postmodern West seek to inflict none. Which is extremely nice, but what is it they say about nice guys? And how nice, really, is it? Citizens of the 21st century, we pat ourselves on the back for an elevated morality even as we expect our brave volunteers to risk life and limb to protect both ourselves and, in effect, our enemies also. This does nothing but prolong the state of war and the suffering that goes with it, which is surely neither nice, nor morally uplifting. Maybe such a mindset is relatively new to the American identity, but the limbo of unresolved conflict it consigns us to promises to be with us for a long time.

In Iraq strategy applying logic is ... illogical

3/23/07

Here's a conundrum: The craziest thing about America's role in the world is its reliance on logic. As in: "See how reasonable we are? That'll fix you." Such certitude animates the more naive notions masquerading as grand strategy, from a belief in winning Iraqi "hearts and minds," as expressed by Gen. David Petraeus four years after Saddam Hussein was toppled, to a faith in "the appeal of freedom" for Muslims in Europe, as expressed by historian Bernard Lewis now that the continent's Islamization is well advanced.

Belief and faith may seem like strange words to choose in talking about logic and reason. But they go a long way to explain an increasingly irrational attachment to the world as it should be — logical and reasonable — that ignores the world as it is. On second thought, better to say that the craziest thing about America's world role has less to do with its logic than with stubbornly insisting such logic works the same way everywhere.

The "surge" strategy in Iraq exemplifies such thinking. It goes like this. More U.S. troops, mainly in Baghdad, will create stability and security. Such nonviolent conditions will allow Iraq to function as a bona fide state. And such bona fide statehood will allow Iraqis to come to their senses.

Actually, such a strategy seems designed to allow Iraqis to come to our senses — to come around to a way of doing things that makes American sense. But is that really, well, logical?

Writing in Commentary magazine, Arthur Herman expounds on the general's strategy to engender Iraqi support for the U.S. mission, which, according to our lights, is the perfectly reasonable position. As the general's counterinsurgency manual states, "Some of the best weapons do not shoot." Herman explains: "They come instead in the form of meetings held with local leaders, wells drilled, streets repaired, soccer leagues organized. In the current surge, one of his stated goals is to get American soldiers out of Baghdad's Green Zone to meet, eat with, and even live with Iraqi families."

Given the dangers American soldiers have had meeting, eating and especially living with Iraqi forces, I have to ask, Is he kidding? But no. This is the strategic logic of American benevolence. As in: "We're so strategically nice it's only logical that everyone like us." Is it really? Are the same criteria for reasonableness common to every culture? PC aside, of course not. A couple of little-noticed stories out of Iraq this week should drive the point home. One was a report about the de facto return to Iraq of the "jizya," the Islamic tax on non-Islamic (in this case, Christian) worship, last seen in the Fertile Crescent before the Ottoman Empire ended in 1918. The other was about the increasing enthusiasm with which the U.S.-backed Iraqi government is participating in the Arab League boycott of Israel. According to a U.S. Commerce Department document reported on by the Jerusalem Post, the number of such cases quadrupled, from 8 to 31, between 2005 and 2006. Furthermore, U.S. companies doing business in Iraq are actually coming under Iraqi pressure to comply with the boycott.

Such practices constitute religious bigotry — and, from the Western side of the cultural divide, "illogical" or "irrational" are the most polite words for them. But if such examples are, in fact, logical and rational expressions of Arab-Islamic society, how can American troops organizing soccer leagues compete? Clearly, the American logic of a "hearts and minds" strategy relies on wishful thinking.

The same may be said of the survival strategy Bernard Lewis laid out in the 2007 Irving Kristol Lecture, which he recently delivered at the American Enterprise Institute. Having described the energized process by which Shariah-following immigrants are Islamizing Europe, Mr. Lewis arrived at his conclusion. Did he suggest that Islamic immigration be stopped? That Shariah practices be stringently outlawed? No. He merely offered a "hearts and minds" strategy to win Islamic converts to Westernism via, simply, "the appeal of freedom." The idea of Western freedom, he explained, "is perhaps in the long run our best hope, perhaps even our only hope, of surviving this developing struggle."

So, like American troops, all Europeans have to do to prevail is be themselves. Maybe they, too, should meet, eat, even live with Shariah-following families. Freedom, soccer leagues — who could ask for anything more? The logic of it all is self-evident.

And that's precisely why it makes no sense.

When a civilization no longer inculcates an overriding attachment to its own survival, it no longer survives as a civilization

3/30/07

Quick — somebody promote Lt. Cmdr. Erik Horner for good instincts. "We not only have a right to self-defense but also an obligation to self-defense," the second-in-command officer of the USS Underwood said, referring to the surrender by 15 British sailors in Iraqi waters to Iranian forces last week. "[The British] had every right to defend themselves rather than allow themselves to be taken. Our reaction was, 'Why didn't you guys defend yourselves?' "

Better to ask why the larger Western world didn't teach these sailors to defend themselves, both as their personal right and their societal obligation. And speaking of societal obligations, could someone please explain why the sailor-mother of a three-year-old — now imprinted on history for performing the hostage-squirm in a Muslim headscarf — was required on this mission in the first place? But I digress (sort of).

When a civilization no longer inculcates an overriding attachment to its own survival, well, it no longer survives as a civilization. In peacetime, the disintegration appears more theoretical. In wartime, the holes really begin to show.

Sticking with Britain as an example, when Tony Blair long ago brought forth his "Cool Britannia," multiculti, domestic agenda, the ensuing debate was a "culture war," not a real war. It might have politically divided Britain, but the country seemed to remain intact. When the government of Britain recently responded to a recognized act of war against its military personnel by threatening diplomacy, a kind of emptiness to the whole British enterprise was exposed.

Or was it? At a certain point, people probably stop realizing they're even looking at holes. This is something that comes through in another story, not about victims in uniform, but about a bona fide hero — an American hero. This is an American hero of demonstrable bravery who was recently awarded the Distinguished Flying Cross by Britain — the first American to be so honored since World War II.

While serving as an exchange officer with an English Naval Air Squadron in Iraq, Marine Maj. William D. Chesarek Jr. was flying a British Lynx helicopter accompanying British forces on the ground. It was June 2006, just one month after another British Lynx had been shot down by an Iranian-smuggled missile, killing five on board. Maj. Chesarek realized British forces below him were under attack. The attackers, according to a report on marinecorpstimes.com, were "using large hostile crowds for cover."

The report continued: "Given the serious threat to the forces on the ground, and the inability to return fire given the crowds of protesters, Maj. Chesarek elected to fly repeated passes at very low level, under heavy small-arms fire and at least one near-miss from an RPG, in an attempt to disperse the crowds." And he flew these extremely dangerous passes for five long hours. He also evacuated a seriously wounded British soldier, undoubtedly saving the man's life.

Major Chesarek's courage is exemplary; his official recognition for bravery deserved. So, what's wrong with this picture?

There is a gaping hole in it due to the "large hostile crowds" the enemy was using for cover. As I understand the report, Maj. Chesarek didn't fire his machine gun to destroy, or even scatter the enemy for fear of hitting those same crowds. I'm guessing this "inability" to return fire was a restriction written into the rules of engagement, which have been officially hamstringing coalition soldiers since the war in Iraq began. More distressing, it was a restriction that wasn't even overridden by the "serious threat" to allies under fire.

This is incredible. This seemingly immutable restriction suggests that, according to current military and civilian thinking — which together reflect a pretty clear consensus of elites — the lives of allies under fire are of no greater value or significance than the lives of enemy sympathizers. And the enemy knows this, in Iraq and beyond, no doubt reveling in the safe haven of our fantastic objectivity.

Such rules and restrictions, the product of politically correct developments in Western culture, foster a non-combative theory of combat. Surrender is an expression of this culture; so are rules of engagement that risk the lives of our people. Such a culture, whether acting by the book or by consensus, hardly supports a soldier's right and obligation to self-defense, let alone unleashes the warrior in pursuit of anything resembling victory. Which isn't to say this cultural trend is irreversible. But we must learn to see the holes before we can plug them up.

The 'limited' war for 'hearts and minds'

4/30/07

Someday, when the war in Iraq has become a historical episode, we will tally up the lessons learned — if, that is, we ever learn any. Here are two worth mastering because failing to do so probably means we will no longer exist.

1. Nation-building in a war zone is nuts. Nation-building in an Islamic war zone is suicide.

When the United States embarked on its most successful cases of nation-building in Germany and Japan, both countries lay in ruins, their cities and infrastructure devastated, their populations decimated.

These appalling conditions worked wonders toward opening both countries to all manner of Americana: democracy, deNazification, demilitarization and, in Japan's case, not just a constitution practically written by Gen. Douglas MacArthur, but also baseball. In other words, Total War was followed by Total Pacification.

In Iraq, we have fought a Limited War for Limited Pacification, which has resulted in a perpetual, if limited, war zone. At about $200 million a day, this war may not sound very "limited," but consider where "Sunni insurgents," "Shiite militias" and assorted thugs and jihadi groups go at night after a hard day's maiming and killing and IED-ing. They go home to safe houses. Now, ask yourself whether, say, a George Patton or a Curtis LeMay would allow them to wake up again, chow down breakfast and return to maim, kill and IED another day.

The answer is no, not on your life. Such generals would have seen to it that the enemy's home, his neighborhood, his entire town if necessary, was destroyed, doubtless killing innocent (and not innocent) civilians in the process. Total War. It's ugly and barbaric, but it leads to Total Pacification, not to mention Total Victory, which is supposed to be the point. Limited War is ugly and barbaric, but it just leads on and on. And where is the moral purity in war unending?

The Limited Warrior struggles for the answer, and comes up with ... Hearts and Minds: The superpower that doesn't want to use its super powers will instead make everyone like it a lot. To that end, Gen. David Petraeus, our top commander in Iraq, has ordered troops out of their well-fortified bases into "outposts" in Iraq's most dangerous enclaves. (One such outpost was recently struck by suicide bombers, killing nine Americans and wounding 20.) Often described as the linchpin of Gen. Petraeus' counterinsurgency strategy, this outpost-plan is supposed to "establish regular contact with Iraqi civilians and win their allegiance," according to The New York Times.

Win their allegiance — is he kidding? I hate to be the one to break it to Gen. Petraeus, not to mention President Bush, but the fact is, in an Islamic war zone, an "infidel" army just isn't going to win Islamic allegiance. There are many religious and cultural reasons I could offer in explanation, but instead I'll turn to the underreported story of the week: two findings contained within an extensive new poll of Muslim opinion conducted in four major Islamic countries Egypt, Indonesia, Morocco and Pakistan.

According to WorldPublicOpinion.org, more than half of those polled in Indonesia, and three-quarters of those polled in Egypt, Morocco and Pakistan believe in the strict application of Sharia, or Islamic law. Nearly two-thirds of all respondents expressed their desire to see the

Islamic world united in a caliphate.

Which brings me to Lesson 2.

With numbers like these, portraying jihadist war goals (Sharia, caliphate) as belonging to a "tiny band of extremists" is nuts. Persisting in this PC fantasy as part of the narrative and strategy of the "war on terror" is suicidal.

But such PC fantasy fuels hearts-and-minds efforts that go beyond "allegiance"-winning outposts in Iraq as the United States now weirdly cheers on world Islamization to curry Islamic favor. As said by House Foreign Affairs Committee Chairman Tom Lantos at a recent Kosovo hearing "Here is yet another example that the United States leads the way for the creation of a predominantly Muslim country in the very heart of Europe. This should be noted by both responsible leaders of Islamic governments, such as Indonesia, and also for jihadists of all color and hue. ... The United States stands foursquare for the creation of an overwhelmingly Muslim country in the very heart of Europe."

Aren't we nice? Aren't we lovable?

Or are we just too dumb to live?

Doing the 'bump' with Iran

5/7/07

Marvelous, isn't it, that Secretary of State Condoleezza Rice traveled to an Egyptian resort for a summit on stabilizing Iraq that was attended by, among other "neighbors" and interested parties, Iran and Syria. I mean, who better to discuss stabilizing Iraq than the very countries that are actually trying to de-stabilize it?

Such wily statecraft. Now I see how it works: Only honest-to-goodness state sponsors of terrorism like Iran or Syria can really understand what it takes to stabilize a country, since it's only honest-to-goodness state sponsors of terrorism like Iran and Syria that really understand what it takes to destabilize it — what it takes to smuggle into Iraq men and munitions, including deadly IEDs; what it takes to organize and sustain resistance to our utopian efforts. Iranian and Syrian expertise on such matters will prove invaluable to those same utopian efforts, right? After all, as Rice put it, "Iraq's neighbors have everything at stake here. Iraq is at the center of a stable Middle East or an unstable Middle East. We should therefore align our policies in ways that contribute to stability."

"Therefore." Isn't that brilliant? Never mind that Iran and Syria are in many ways responsible for the unstable Middle East Rice is talking about. Let's "therefore align our policies" just the same. Meanwhile, why haven't we thought of talking with terror-states before?

At least we're starting at the top with Iran. In time for the conference, the State Department issued its annual global terrorism survey, crowning Iran the leading state sponsor of terrorism in the world. (Congrats, Mahmoud Ahmadinejad!) Let's hope Condi remembered to take along a copy to present to Manouchehr Mottaki, the Iranian foreign minister she was supposed to "bump" into somewhere or other at the resort — at the conference table, or was it the pool? Or was he supposed to "bump" into her? What was it the president said again?

"Should the foreign minister of Iran bump into Condi Rice, Condi won't be rude; she's not a rude person. I'm sure she'll be polite," said Bush. "She'll also be firm in reminding the representative of the Iranian government that there's a better way forward for the Iranian people than isolation."

Polite ... firm ... better way forward. Clearly, the Great Satan lives. As Condi later roared, all fire and brimstone, "If we encounter each other then I am certainly planning to be polite and see what that encounter brings."

Phew. Americans can thank goodness for that. If there's one thing we want to be with the leading state sponsor of terrorism in the world, it's polite. Maybe Rice could politely inscribe the terrorism report to the Iranian foreign minister. Maybe he could politely inscribe it back to her. I can see it now, that old Iranian proverb: "Dear Condi — Never give a sucker an even break."

Enough sarcasm. No amount of metaphorical acid dropped on this sorry event can cover up either the futility or the shame of negotiations with the jihadist state of Iran and its fellow state sponsor of jihadist terrorism, Syria. And such negotiations, whether via "bumping into," or "on the sidelines," were exactly what the breathless run-up to the Egyptian conference was all about. "That meeting," explained Undersecretary of State Nicholas Burns, "will be important because Secretary Rice will be seated around a table with the Syrian foreign minister, and we hope and think with the Iranian foreign minister."

Yuck. Since when does an Iranian foreign minister, let alone a Syrian foreign minister, count as the belle of the ball? There's something unseemly about this diplomatic courtship, which follows not a single concession on Iranian and Syrian support for Hezbollah and assorted Palestinian terror groups, their deadly interference in Iraq, or their failure to corral Al Qaeda operatives. In the case of Iran, this all-too-hot political pursuit rages on despite its flouting international rules governing its nuclear program, and its barbaric call for the genocidal eradication of the state of Israel.

But there's something else. American soldiers now die and are maimed because of such belligerence. Not so very long ago, Beirut CIA station chief William Buckley, Navy diver Robert Stethem, and Marine

Col. William Higgins all fell to Iranian-sponsored, Hezbollah terrorism, suffering horrendous beatings and torture before they died, unavenged.

When will it occur to our leaders that Iran is already in a state of war with us? Surely, that's nothing to be "polite" about.

Petraeus and PC-policy-making

5/21/07

"This fight depends on securing the population, which must understand that we — not our enemies — occupy the moral high ground."

—Gen. David Petraeus, May 10

Oh, they must, must they?

With his single sentence, Gen. David Petraeus reveals what's wrong with our Iraq policy. Success depends not on our own actions, but on a politically correct expectation of how Iraqis will react to those actions. It seems that victory depends on something over which we have no control — the point of view and behavior of people in Iraq.

Consider the "surge." Even if our troops achieve the goal of "securing the population" by securing Baghdad, success still rides on subsequent Iraqi behavior: whether murderously competing Iraqi sects decide to come together and sing "Kumbayah" — what you might call a big "whether."

Somehow, I'm practically alone among conservatives in believing this to be a dangerously ill-conceived policy (Surrender-crats aren't worth discussing here), and I think I know why. The Iraq policy itself is an outgrowth of another dangerously ill-conceived policy of our leaders to avoid any rational assessment of the Islamic culture that informs the point of view and behavior of people across the Fertile Crescent in the first place.

In other words, most people with even an elemental understanding of institutional Islamic antipathies toward non-Muslims and non-Muslim culture would balk at spending blood and treasure for Gen. Petraeus' "hearts and minds" strategy. Such a criterion, sadly, disqualifies our deeply Islam-challenged elites, all of whom seem to have missed the fact that "moral high ground" in Islam makes room for suicide-bombing terrorists. No wonder our guys are having trouble.

Still, we persist in ordering American forces onto Iraq's meanest streets to "win over the trust and allegiance of the civilians," as a Weekly Standard report on Gen. Petraeus' counterinsurgency plan recently put it. What goes unconsidered is why, after all the lives and limbs our troops have already lost in Iraq, after all the lollipops our troops have already passed around Iraq, Iraqi "trust" and "allegiance" aren't already ours for the asking. Could it be that most of the Muslims who make up about 99.99 percent of the Iraqi population simply don't trust infidel armies? Could it be that they only offer allegiance to fellow-Muslims?

Such questions never enter into PC policy-making. The problem, PC-policy-makers maintain, is ours alone. Maybe we did topple Saddam Hussein, fight Islamic terror troops, and bring democracy and air conditioners to a benighted land. But that's not enough to win "hearts and minds," or so the PC-theory goes. And that's where the new counterinsurgency strategy comes in — killing the enemy, while, as the Standard wrote, "spending time with the [Iraqi] people, getting to know them, and building relationships with them."

Is this a war plan, or a Miss Universe contest?

Recently, I came across a heart-stopping story from "A Man Called Intrepid," William Stevenson's book about World War II intelligence operations. It concerned a ghastly, brilliant British air raid on Copenhagen in spring 1945. The objective, next door to a school, was a Gestapo prison. There, Danish underground leaders were being tortured, thus compromising the entire underground network, bonafide nuclear secrets, and potentially resulting in the diversion of 200,000 German troops to fight American forces. The air raid was a stunning success. It was also a terrible tragedy. Not only did the British lose 10 airmen, but 27 teachers and 87 children were killed, with many more civilians badly injured.

The battlefields then and now have few parallels, but imagine, for a moment, that 87 children were killed in an important air raid in terror-riddled Baghdad, not Nazi-occupied Copenhagen. Imagine, also, the ensuing mayhem and media amplification of an "irreparable blow to the battle for Iraqi 'hearts and minds.' "

Now, back to the historical account: One of the raid's planners, Ted Sismore, later returned to the bombed school in Copenhagen to offer an explanation. "The parents of the dead children, to his astonishment, gave him comfort. They wanted me to know the raid was necessary.' "

The Danes knew his heart, and were of one mind. This could hardly be more different from Iraq for many reasons, including cultural ones separating Islamic and Western cultures. Gen. Petraeus decrees Iraqis "must understand that we — not our enemies — occupy the moral high ground." But does their political-religious culture even permit such an understanding? We must face up to this question if we ever want a winning war plan.

*Identifying with jihadists —
in the U.S. military*

6/1/07

"If I were a Muslim, I'd probably be a jihadist. The thing that drives these guys — a sense of adventure, wanting to be part of the moment, wanting to be in the big movement of history that's happening now — that's the same thing that drives me, you know?" No. I don't know. And I sorely wish I could tell him so — "him" being David Kilcullen, senior counterinsurgency adviser to Gen. David Petraeus, senior U.S. commander in Iraq.

With this bizarro depiction of jihadists-as-swashbucklers, Lt. Col. David Kilcullen, an Australian Army officer "on loan" to the U.S. government, should probably have been sent back with: "And I suppose if you had been a German during a certain world war, you would have been a Nazi, eh? Who more than those Third Reich 'guys' wanted to be in 'the big movement of history'? Grr. Thanks, mate, but no thanks. Go play Abu Robin al-Hood down under."

Of course, Kilcullen made his outrageous comment almost six months ago to The New Yorker's George Packer and is still on the job. But when a key counterinsurgency adviser in Iraq identifies with jihadists, it's not just a matter of surrealism — hallucinations — at the top. As they say at NASA when things are about to fall out of the sky: Houston, we've got a problem.

Why? Such remarks convey either noncomprehension or indifference to the evil nature of jihad. Or both. Such neutrality, if that's the word for it, also marks Kilcullen's discussion of his big, formative idea: lessons drawn from what he refers to as "an Islamic insurgency in West Java and a Christian-separatist insurgency in East Timor."

In the latter case, the language is jarring for what Serge Trifkovic has described this way: "In the motivation, patterns and perceptions of the actors on the ground — killers and victims alike — East Timor was an Islamic jihad against Christian infidels" that left as many as 200,000 East Timorese dead.

In Kilcullen's Islam-blind view of the world, such events become plain-vanilla conflicts without moral distinction, differentiated only by the advent of global media coverage — a large obstacle, he maintains, to winning counter-insurgencies. Indeed, he compares Indonesia's role in East Timor (where Indonesia ultimately failed, he says, due to global media) with the U.S. role in Iraq. This is a weirdly shocking way to see the American struggle against varyingly jihadist factions — particularly for someone advising the U.S. military.

It's hard to say what's worse: ignorance of jihad, for which there's no excuse at this advanced stage of war, or indifference to it, for which there's never an excuse. Both attitudes deeply imbue U.S. war policy. As Kilcullen would (and has) put it, "the Islamic bit is secondary." Far more important to this Australian anthropologist are what he calls "social networks." Packer writes: "He noted that all fifteen Saudi (9/11) hijackers had trouble with their fathers."

Oh, brother — as if half the people in the world don't have trouble with their fathers (but don't hijack airplanes for Allah).

The New Yorker story continues: Although "radical ideas" lead young men to become jihadists, "the reasons they convert, Kilcullen said, are more mundane and familiar: family, friends, associates."

Sounds like our problem is a cell calling plan, not jihadist Islam. Little wonder Kilcullen is also down on the phrase "war on terror." That's because, as Packer writes, the concept (elliptical as it is) "suggests an undifferentiated enemy" engaged in global jihad. David Kilcullen strives to "disaggregate" insurgencies by disconnecting the Islamic dots linking various terror-states and terrorists. He prefers to see jihadist movements in terms of so many local grievances. It's as if he has taken the defunct Bush doctrine — You're with us or you're against us — and changed it to: You're really not with anyone, and certainly not anyone Islamic.

To what end? Difficult to say, particularly when, according to the New Yorker, his example of "disaggregation" is the Indonesian province of Aceh. Here, he maintains, Western tsunami aid and resentment of outsiders prevented Aceh from "becoming," as the article put it, "part of the global jihad" — a funny sort of victory to claim in a place where, increasingly, sharia rules.

Of course, maybe the man "disaggregates" sharia, too, reducing it to so many differentiated social networks. Just the thing, as Kilcullen might say, for family, friends and associates with that jihadist sense of adventure.

Why not disarm Iran?

6/22/07

A reader recently e-mailed me about casualties sustained by his nephew's Stryker unit in Iraq after an attack by an Iranian-manufactured fragmentary device. "Why," he wrote, "are we not leveling the plants in Iran that manufacture these weapons?"

Well, that would make too much sense. It's obvious Iran is at war with us — and not just in Iraq, where its agents and proxies kill and maim Americans by arming and organizing some of our many foes there. Throughout the region, from Hamastan (Gaza) to Hezbollah-land (Lebanon) to Taliban strongholds in Afghanistan, the Islamic Republic of

Iraq and the Doomed 'Democracy' Project

Iran, along with Syria, is pursuing its war against us, and our interests. But we pretend, as a matter of policy, not to notice.

Why?

I don't claim to know the whole answer, but fear must surely figure into it — fear of wider war, which I guess is natural, but also fear of a deeper truth, which is more difficult to overcome. That deeper truth starts with the realization that our strategic interests do not lie within the borders of Iraq. After all, what do we get even if the "surge" succeeds in establishing security in Baghdad and even if — and this is the impossibly big "if" — the Iraqis manage to establish a functional government?

The answer, under the best of circumstances, would seem to be a Shiite state that not only enshrines sharia (Islamic law) above all, but also promises to be a natural ally of Iran. Which doesn't exactly sound like an ally in the war on terror, or whatever we're calling it these days. Worse, even if we ultimately manage to have established "the new Iraq," we still won't have addressed the greater problems posed by the old Iran and Syria.

And why is it that all we can hope to get out of our costly, lengthy Middle Eastern war is just another Western-hostile Sharia State? Here comes another difficult realization: It turns out that bringing democracy to Islam just brings democracy to Islam. In other words, ballot booths don't change the illiberal aspects of Islam; they merely provide for them to be voted into office. At the end of the election day, it's still an Islamic culture — whether it's in Iraq, the shrinking Palestinian Authority, Afghanistan, or elsewhere. As such, it functions more or less according to guidelines laid out in a supremacist theology that fails to recognize the equality of women and non-Muslims, and, in its political manifestations, is doctrinally ill-suited to Western alliances that are anything but fleetingly expedient.

Of course, this realization is the Big No-No, the stake through the heart of multicultural teachings that give life to platitudes that everyone — every culture, every religion, every people — is the same, or, rather, wants the same things. (How many times have we heard the president or the secretary of State talk specifically about the normalcy of theoretical "Muslim Moms and Dads," even as actual "Muslim Moms and Dads" were celebrating mass murder committed by their suicide-bomber offspring?) For most, if not all, of our leadership, civilian and military alike, this is the blow to be warded off at all costs. As in: Live multiculturally or die.

And so, it seems, we crouch defensively over Iraq as though the secret to our national security lies within these lines on a map drawn by colonial powers in the early 1920s. We hone in on its provinces, its cities, its sects, its militias, its religious rivalries, its turf battles. We freely risk our men's lives and limbs in its dangerous neighborhoods, along bomb-mined streets, past booby-trapped houses, where we seek to destroy (or arrest) hunkered-down enemy fighters — as though our men were worth less than their civilians. Our soldiers learn to tell tribe from tribe and gang from gang, as though it were really our business. And in Baquba this week, where we have massed troops against 300 to 500 Al Qaeda fighters dug in among civilians (because they know we value our men less than their civilians), we are attempting to tell thug from thug. According to The New York Times, our men are equipped "to take fingerprints and other biometric data from every resident who seems to be a potential fighter."

And here lies another part of the answer for my letter-writing reader as to why Iran continues to fire away at us with impunity: In waging war through a microscope, we have lost sight of the big picture.

Iraq's only a battle in the war

9/7/07

The worst possible outcome of next week's congressional hearings on Iraq — already dubbed "Petraeus Week" after Gen. David Petraeus's dramatically anticipated testimony on whether "the surge" is working in Iraq — would be a political haggle over whether the surge is working in Iraq.

Let's just say the surge — defined as a military plan to enhance security in targeted sections of Iraq — is working. As even The Washington Post owned up, "If there is one indisputable truth regarding the current offensive, it is this: When large numbers of U.S. troops are funneled into areas, security improves." No one needs four years at West Point or even two hours watching "Battleground" to figure that out. The cavalry rides in, things get better.

But there are other, more significant questions to hash out: namely, whether the strategy behind the surge still makes national security sense for the United States. That is, should a functioning state of Iraq — the ultimate goal of the surge (aside from the president's mirage-like vision of Iraq as a "friend" and "ally") — remain the overriding objective of U.S. foreign policy?

I have long argued no, and not only because majority-Shiite Iraq is likely to end up a client-state of Shiite Iran, although that's a huge reason. There's also the fact that our gargantuan efforts to build an Iraqi society that never before existed do nothing whatsoever to ward off jihadist state threats — Iran, for instance — in the wider region.

This is the deepest chink in the president's Iraqi-centric policy. As we minutely focus on Iraq, sect by sect, tribe by tribe, and now, literally, retina by retina, we have lost sight of the big bad world beyond, not to mention what's in it for us. And "tunnel vision" doesn't begin to describe the microscopic range of debate we can expect between proponents of "surge" and "withdrawal."

In a recent interview, Michael Ledeen, author of the new book, "The Iranian Time Bomb" identifies the main problem with the conventional wisdom: "What drives me crazy is that even our most brilliant analysts — among whom I count some very close friends — still aren't talking about the regional war. They still talk about Iraq alone. And down that road only misery lies." As for Congress, he adds: "They're debating the wrong question. We have to win the war, but the real war, not the battle for Iraq.

And what is that "real war"?

Jed Babbin, author of the book, "In the Words of Our Enemies", has written this formulation: "Let's be very clear: whether Iraq becomes a democracy is not determinative of our success or defeat in this war. Iraq is only one campaign in the war against the nations that sponsor terrorism. Victory isn't an Iraq that can defend and govern itself. Victory is defined as the end of state sponsorship of Islamic terrorism, which means forcing Iran, Syria, Saudi Arabia and others out of that business. Nothing more is needed, and nothing less will defeat an existential threat to America."

Daniel Pipes writes in terms of losing the occupation but winning the war by keeping U.S. troops in Iraq, but removing them from the deadly cities — perhaps to a base in Kurdistan, I would add, the closest thing to democracy in Mesopotamia — "to influence developments in the world's most volatile theater." These include, Pipes writes, containing Iran and Syria; assuring the flow of oil; fighting international terrorist organizations, including Al Qaeda.

Such a proposition is always undone by the word "bloodbath," as though Americans are eternally obligated to serve as buffers between the warring Islamic tribes of Iraq — which is both cracked and a good way to tie up American forces for the next several centuries.

"Peace in Iraq has to be built on a Shiite-Sunni consensus, not a constant balancing act by us," Thomas Friedman writes. This begs the question: Should we stand on one foot until Iraq finds equilibrium? Surge architect Frederick Kagan apparently thinks so. The United States, he writes, should continue to serve as "the bridge between Sunni and Shia" in Iraq. Why? "If we remove this bridge now, it is unlikely that the Iraqis will be able to continue on a path to real reconciliation."

Maybe the United States needs to get out of the real reconciliation business, and fast.

There's a world of trouble outside Iraq. At the very least, it's debatable whether building bridges between Sunnis and Shiites inside Iraq should remain American Priority No. 1. So let's debate it.

Stop treating Sharia-supreme Iraq like post-war Japan

2/15/08

Condoleezza Rice and Robert Gates penned an op-ed this week to say it's time to negotiate "a basic framework for normalized relations with the Iraqi government." This, they wrote, will "set the basic parameters for the U.S. presence in Iraq," which must extend past 2008 "for progress in stabilizing Iraq to continue."

Has the administration's policy of "surge till they (Iraqis) merge" changed to "keep surging because they're not merging"? Unclear. At the same time, the new framework they envision will not set troop levels, make security commitments or authorize permanent bases in Iraq — "something neither we nor Iraqis want," they added.

Me neither. U.S. forces should not ordinarily be engaged in nation-building — sorry, nation-stabilizing — nor should they ever be engaged in Sharia-nation-stabilizing, which is my core problem with our overall strategy in constitutionally Sharia-supreme Iraq as well as constitutionally Sharia-supreme Afghanistan (not to mention the constitutionally Sharia-supreme Palestinian Authority), but that's another column.

Meanwhile, Rice and Gates are calling for more of the same — for U.S. "help" to fight Al Qaeda, develop Iraq's security forces and halt Iranian interference. After that? They write: "In addition, we seek to establish a basic framework for a strong relationship with Iraq, reflecting our shared political, economic, cultural and security interests."

If your next question is, "What 'shared' political, economic, cultural and security interests?" I second it. The only unanimous expression of Iraqi political will I know of was a parliamentary vote in favor of Hezbollah in its 2006 war with Israel. Economically speaking, Iraq is not only an increasingly enthusiastic OPEC player, it enforces the Arab boycott on Israel. And when it comes to "common" cultural interests, Iraq is, as mentioned above, a Sharia-supreme state where one writer was recently found guilty of "blasphemy." Given the Shiism Iraq shares with nuke-seeking Iran, how many security interests does that leave us in common?

Not that many. Maybe this accounts for the secretaries' flat tone of understatement regarding a U.S.-Iraq future. It certainly speaks to my own concern that when we finally walk away from "democratic" Iraq, we are unlikely to leave behind a staunch U.S. ally. If — when? — this comes to pass, what lessons will we take away?

Frankly, the same lessons we should have taken into Iraq. Writing in the winter 2007-08 issue of The Objective Standard, John David Lewis offers an illuminating analysis of another U.S. occupation, this one thoroughly successful, in Japan (1945-1952). President Bush, of course, frequently refers to the democratization of Japan as a model for the democratization of Iraq (and the wider Islamic Middle East). But, as Lewis' must-read essay makes historically clear, the president has been comparing apples and oranges.

It isn't just that the total defeat and utter devastation of Japan nullifies the comparison with Iraq (which it does). There is something else. There is the completely different U.S. approach to Japan's animating, warlike state religion of Shintoism, which, not incidentally, bears striking similarities to the animating, warlike state religion of Islam.

In 1945, our government was of one mind regarding state Shintoism. Lewis quotes Secretary of State James F. Byrnes, who wrote: "Shintoism, insofar as it is a religion of individual Japanese, is not to be interfered with. Shintoism, however, insofar as it is directed by the Japanese government, and as a measure enforced from above by the government, is to be done away with. ... There will be no place for Shintoism in the schools. Shintoism as a state religion — National Shinto, that is — will go. ... Our policy on this goes beyond Shinto. ... The dissemination of Japanese militaristic and ultra-nationalistic ideology in any form will be completely suppressed."

And it was, with fabulous results.

Obviously, there have been no analogous U.S. efforts to "de-jihadize" Islamic public culture even as the United States has spent lives, limbs, money and years trying, essentially, to stop the jihad in the Islamic Middle East — not even, to take a manageable example, in the U.S.-funded Palestinian Authority, where state-run media continue to incite Islamically motivated violence against Jews and Americans. And then there are all those U.S.-fostered constitutions that enshrine Sharia law — just the sort of ideological concession our forebears would never have made.

Bottom line? History shows that the conditions that drove the model transformation of Japan do not exist today with regard to the Islamic Middle East. We're going to need another strategy — for starters, an immigration policy and new laws to halt the creep of Sharia — to ward off the Islamization of the West.

Iran's betrayal leaves U.S. suffering pulp fiction

3/7/08

I can't think of a point of historic comparison to the figurative bed we have made for ourselves in Iraq — particularly now that our Iraqi allies have welcomed our Iranian enemies right into it.

Maybe the way to understand international affairs is to turn not to history but to pulp fiction — namely, the old love triangle. The good guy (us, natch), has been betrayed by the love object he supports and defends (Iraq), having been left to watch and stew as she gallivants with his rival (Iran).

In real life, of course, Iran is responsible for many of our nearly 4,000 war dead in Iraq, many of our nearly 30,000 war-wounded in Iraq, along with murders, kidnappings and torture of Americans throughout the Middle East over the past quarter-century through its terrorist proxy Hezbollah.

This all makes Iranian President Mahmoud Ahmadinejad's visit to Baghdad a stinging Mesopotamian slap across the American face. And don't forget that Iran's leader, the classic heavy in our plot, was quite possibly a participant in the 1979 Iranian seizure of the U.S. Embassy in Tehran and ensuing 444-day hostage crisis.

As a potboiler, such triangle stuff works. As post-9/11 U.S. foreign policy, it's certifiably insane. We are living and dying for a ward-like "ally" who is happy to cozy up to our worst enemy. Weirdly enough, no one seems to notice.

So let's review. Mahmoud Ahmadinejad — nuke-seeking Holocaust-denier, homosexual-and-apostate-slayer, and wannabe destroyer of both the Great (United States) and Little (Israel) Satans — was just this week the honored guest of the Iraqi government. And yes, that would be the same Iraqi government the U.S. taxpayer is supporting to the tune of $200 million a day.

The countries share more than a border. As USA Today pointed out, "Saddam Hussein was replaced by a new crop of Shiite leaders, many of whom were groomed during years of exile in predominantly Shiite Iran. Many of Iraq's Kurdish leaders have also spent years in exile in Iran and retain close ties there." And some, including Iraq's senior religious leader, Grand Ayatollah Ali al-Sistani, have never given up Iranian citizenship.

This may explain why Iraqis rolled out the red carpet (literally) for Ahmadinejad, but not why we are sappy enough to pretend nothing significant happened — beginning with the infuriating fact that Ahmadinejad, on his ceremonial arrival in Baghdad, required minimal security compared to the furtive security gauntlet American leaders must run. There's a reason, of course: Iranian-supplied bombs and rockets endanger American presidents, not Iranian ones.

At the Iraqi presidential palace, Ahmadinejad was greeted with multiple kisses from Iraqi President Jalal Talabani. An Iraqi military honor guard—make that a U.S.-trained Iraqi military honor guard—saluted the two leaders. An Iraqi military band—make that a U.S.-trained Iraqi military band—also played the Iranian and the Iraqi anthems. "Call me Uncle Jalal," Mr. Talabani told Ahmadinejad. "Iraqis don't like Americans," Ahmadinejad told the world.

And so went Iran's "brotherly" visit to Iraq, as if U.S. protests (and U.S. casualties) over Iran's violent subversion of the country didn't exist. There were political meetings, gas, oil and electrical agreements, and an Iranian interest-free $1 billion loan. To cap things off, Iraq and Iran issued a joint statement condemning Israel, America's bona fide ally in the region, for taking belated action in Gaza to stop Hamas from firing Iranian-supplied rockets into Israeli towns. (Did I mention Hamas gets Iranian support?)

It's not a question of which side Iraq is on. Certainly, as Iraq becomes what Radio Free Europe analyst Kathleen Ridolfo described as "economically, if not politically subordinate to Iran," that becomes increasingly clear. More disturbing is why we think we're on the same side—why we think there's a future for us in this and similar relationships.

The fact is, this unsuitable ménage isn't unique to Iraq. Desperately naive American courtships across the Middle East follow similar patterns of hypocrisy, deceit and danger. From Saudi Arabia to Egypt, artificial, if costly, American "alliances" are mocked and trashed by such countries' aid and abetment of jihad. Just this week, the Washington Times reported that oil-rich Qatar is massively underwriting Hamas. At the same time, Qatar—which hosts a colossal pre-positioning base for the U.S. military—is supposed to be a "moderate" Islamic ally of ours. What next—permanent U.S. military bases in a Shiite-Kurdish satellite of Iran? I wonder whether we will ever walk out on these destructive relationships and recover our self-respect.

Whose side is Iraq really on?

3/10/08

I can't think of a point of historic comparison to the figurative bed we have made for ourselves in Iraq-particularly now that our Iraqi allies have welcomed our Iranian enemies right into it.

Maybe the way to understand international affairs is to turn not to history but to pulp fiction-namely, the old love triangle. The good guy (us, natch), has been betrayed by the love object he supports and defends (Iraq), having been left to watch and stew as she gallivants with his rival (Iran).

In real life, of course, Iran is responsible for many of our nearly 4,000 war dead in Iraq, many of our nearly 30,000 war-wounded in Iraq, along with murders, kidnappings and torture of Americans throughout the Middle East over the past quarter-century through its terrorist proxy Hezbollah.

This all makes Iranian President Mahmoud Ahmadinejad's visit to Baghdad a stinging Mesopotamian slap across the American face. And don't forget that Iran's leader, the classic heavy in our plot, was quite possibly a participant in the 1979 Iranian seizure of the U.S. Embassy in Tehran and ensuing 444-day hostage crisis.

As a potboiler, such triangle stuff works. As post-9/11 US foreign policy, it's certifiably insane. We are living and dying for a ward-like "ally" who is happy to cozy up to our worst enemy. Weirdly enough, no one seems to notice.

So let's review. Mahmoud Ahmadinejad – nuke-seeking Holocaust-denier, homosexual-and-apostate-slayer, and wanna-be destroyer of both the Great (United States) and Little (Israel) Satans – was just this week the honored guest of the Iraqi government. And yes, that would be the same Iraqi government the US taxpayer is supporting to the tune of $200 million a day.

The countries share more than a border. As USA Today pointed out, "Saddam Hussein was replaced by a new crop of Shiite leaders, many of whom were groomed during years of exile in predominantly Shiite Iran. Many of Iraq's Kurdish leaders have also spent years in exile in Iran and retain close ties there." And some, including Iraq's senior religious leader, Grand Ayatollah Ali Sistani, have never given up Iranian citizenship.

This may explain why Iraqis rolled out the red carpet (literally) for Ahmadinejad, but not why we are sappy enough to pretend nothing significant happened-beginning with the infuriating fact that Ahmadinejad, on his ceremonial arrival in Baghdad, required minimal security compared to the furtive security gauntlet American leaders must run. There's a reason, of course: Iranian-supplied bombs and rockets endanger American presidents, not Iranian ones.

At the Iraqi presidential palace, Mr. Ahmadinejad was greeted with multiple kisses from Iraqi President Jalal Talabani. (Blech.) An Iraqi military honor guard-make that a US-trained Iraqi military honor guard saluted the two leaders. An Iraqi military band-make that a US-trained Iraqi military band-also played the Iranian and the Iraqi anthems. "Call me Uncle Jalal," Mr. Talabani told Ahmadinejad. "Iraqis don't like

Americans," Mr. Ahmadinejad told the world.

And so went Iran's "brotherly" visit to Iraq, as if US protests (and U.S. casualties) over Iran's violent subversion of the country didn't exist. There were political meetings, gas, oil and electrical agreements, and an Iranian interest-free $1 billion loan. To cap things off, Iraq and Iran issued a joint statement condemning Israel, America's bona fide ally in the region, for taking belated action in Gaza to stop Hamas from firing Iranian-supplied rockets into Israeli towns. (Did I mention Hamas gets Iranian support?) It's not a question of which side Iraq is on. Certainly, as Iraq becomes what Radio Free Europe analyst Kathleen Ridolfo described as "economically, if not politically subordinate to Iran," that becomes increasingly clear. More disturbing is why we think we're on the same side-why we think there's a future for us in this and similar relationships.

The fact is, this unsuitable *ménage* isn't unique to Iraq. Desperately naive American courtships across the Middle East follow similar patterns of hypocrisy, deceit and danger. From Saudi Arabia to Egypt, artificial, if costly, American "alliances" are mocked and trashed by such countries' aid and abetment of jihad.

Just this week, The Washington Times reported that oil-rich Qatar is massively underwriting Hamas. At the same time, Qatar-which hosts a colossal pre-positioning base for the U.S. military is supposed to be a "moderate" Islamic ally of ours. What next permanent U.S. military bases in a Shiite-Kurdish satellite of Iran? I wonder whether we will ever walk out on these destructive relationships and recover our self-respect.

Condi is a dangerous incompetent

4/4/08

I wonder if Condoleezza Rice was surprised by the headlines over her comment to The Washington Times that America suffers from a national "birth defect" — namely, the practice of slavery at the time of the nation's founding.

Make that the first founding. She said she considers the civil rights movement to be the nation's "second founding." The secretary of state made another point. She said "one of the primary things" that attracted her to the candidacy of George W. Bush "was not actually foreign policy." Rather, she explained, "it was No Child Left Behind." She continued: "When he talks about 'the soft bigotry of low expectations,' I know what that feels like."

Rice has actually said all of this before, including more emphatic remarks on No Child Left Behind and "soft" bigotry. "I've seen it. Okay?" Rice said in 2005 to The New York Times. "And it's not in this president. It is, however, pretty deeply ingrained in our system and we're going to have to do something about it." Rice offered as an example her own high school teacher who suggested she was junior college material.

Maybe someone should inform the secretary of state that being underestimated, turned down or shunted aside is, alas, part of the human experience, not the exclusive function of race. But it's probably too late for that. As secretary of state — not, say, secretary of education — Rice has long been doing "something about it" on the world stage. Instead of different states and school systems, she's been working with different countries and belief systems. Suddenly, things about the Rice Doctrine — better, the No Country Left Behind Doctrine — begin to fall into place.

I've written before about how Rice makes faulty comparisons between the evolution of democratic principle (all men are created equal) in the United States and the introduction of democratic procedure (ballot boxes) to the Middle East, always ignoring both the miracle of our 18th-century Constitution, which contained the blueprint for abolition, and the dispiriting reality of 21st century Islamic constitutions, which charter Sharia states where freedom of conscience (among other things) doesn't exist. I've written also about how she sees the transformation of her once-segregated hometown of Birmingham, Ala., as the blueprint for democratizing the Islamic world. Hers is a worldview personal to the point of autobiographical, as when she explains how, as a daughter of Birmingham (or "Bombingham," as she has called it), she can relate both to Israeli fear of Palestinian bombs, and Palestinian "humiliation and powerlessness" over Israeli checkpoints, which she sees as a form of segregation. What she never seems to realize is that such "segregation," far being the sort of prejudice she remembers, is actually an Israeli line of defense against the ultimate prejudice of Palestinian bombs.

Considering her remarks about America's "birth defect" — an egregious term for any secretary of state to use about a nation that has brought more liberty to more races, colors and creeds than any in history — I am struck anew how deeply Rice's vision of race in America, or, perhaps, in segregated Birmingham, affects her vision of America in the wider world. It is as if Rice sees American influence as a means by which to address what she perceives as disparities of race or Third World heritage on the international level.

This would help explain her ahistorical habit of linking the civil rights movement to the Bush administration's effort to bring democracy to Iraq and Afghanistan. Indeed, in a 2003 speech to the National Association of Black Journalists, she argued that blacks, more than others, should "reject" the "condescending" argument that some are not "ready" for freedom. "That view was wrong in 1963 in Birmingham and it's wrong in 2003 in Baghdad," she said. In 2006, she made a similar point. "When I look around the world and I hear people say, 'Well, you know, they're just not ready for democracy,' it really does resonate," Rice told CBS's Katie Couric. "It makes me so angry because I think there are those echoes of what people once thought about black Americans."

There's something shockingly provincial at work here. In seeing so much of the world through an American prism of race, Rice has effectively blinded herself to historical and cultural and religious differences between Islam and the West. To put it simply, neither Baghdad nor Gaza is Birmingham. And nothing in all of history quite compares to Philadelphia.

Iraq war architects shrug off truth

5/2/08

So there I was, listening to a few of the major "architects" of the war in Iraq — Paul Wolfowitz, formerly No. 2 man at the Pentagon under Donald Rumsfeld; Douglas J. Feith, formerly No. 3 man at the Pentagon under Rumsfeld; Peter Rodman, another former senior adviser to Rumsfeld; and Dan Senor, former senior adviser to Paul Bremer of the Coalition Provisional Authority (CPA). They had assembled at the Hudson Institute in Washington, D.C., for a discussion of Feith's new book, "War and Decision: Inside the Pentagon at the Dawn of the War on Terrorism," but what they were drawn to discuss was what went wrong with the war in Iraq.

A rather large topic. Would it cover, perhaps, such grand themes as the multicultural Big Lie that insists Western ways may be grafted — presto! — onto Islamic cultures? Or maybe the difficulties inherent in the Western-style, humane projection of power against seventh-century terrorist barbarians? No.

The main discussion I heard turned more or less on one extremely narrow point of historic contention. It concerned the CPA rule of Iraq, which came to an end almost exactly four years ago. Wolfowitz and Feith, and Rodman to a less explicit degree, agreed that this period of American governance — that is, the interlude before Iraq officially became sovereign — was the fatal flaw, the fly in the ointment, the monkey wrench, the skunk at the garden party, the bad penny and overall cause of all of America's troubles in Iraq. It wasn't the overweening Bush administration plan for Jeffersonizing the Fertile Crescent, or our leaders' misreading of the "democratic ally" potential therein. It was the 14-month-reign of the CPA that caused all our woes. The CPA, the argument goes, in effect created the Sunni insurgency, which later gave rise to the Sunni-Shiite wars, and which ultimately required the added infusion of American troops known as the surge.

If I'm following this theory correctly, there is absolutely nothing in Iraqi history, politics, religion, sectarianism or culture that manifested itself in the bloody insurgency that followed the removal of Saddam Hussein. According to Feith & Co., it was only the American face on (and muscle behind) initial efforts to bring order, civil society and air conditioning to Iraq that made the newly ejected-from-power Sunnis (and others) organize, shoot, stab, blow up, maim and make violence a fact of Iraqi life to this day, four years into Iraqi sovereignty.

This sounds a bit like the asinine theory that tells us U.S. foreign policy made 19 jihadists attack us on 9/11. But isn't there also something a little goofy about the notion that if only the United States hadn't run an occupation government for a year, everything in Iraq would be hunky-dory? Not surprisingly, the CPA's Senor didn't agree with the Feithian proposition, arguing that the lack of a U.S. counterinsurgency strategy was a bigger problem. He didn't get much argument that this was a problem; indeed, Wolfowitz agreed the United States was, as he put it a trifle breezily, "pretty much clueless on counterinsurgency."

The classic clueless moment, however, came later in answer to a question from the floor: Did the administration ever tell Syria, Iran and Saudi Arabia to bar combatants from crossing their borders into Iraq — or else? And if not ("not" is clearly the answer since these borders have been Grand Central Station for jihadists), why not? Wolfowitz owned up that the United States had said something or other at some point, but, overall, the consensus on the dais came down to a big, shrugging non-answer.

I got one of those answers myself, at least from Feith. I asked: What did these gentlemen think the United States would ultimately get out of Iraq in exchange for our massive investment of blood and treasure? And had they learned anything to make them doubt the president's often-repeated promise that Iraq would become an "ally" in the "war on terror"? Shrug. Not interested in answering.

Looking back, there was a narrowness in the scope of discussion that time constraints alone can't explain. It was as though the men believed every clue to heartbreak in Iraq could be found in the chain of events as they had already occurred — in papers already generated, debates already argued, rounds of infighting already waged, decisions already executed. In other words, to these men, there would seem to be nothing new worth pondering — like, for instance, the havoc Islamic ways wreak on Western-style nation-building.

Shrug.

America's global influence spread too thin

8/22/08

I hate to say it, but both John McCain and Barack Obama are wrong in their approaches to Iraq. On Aug. 18, McCain said, "The lasting advantage of a peaceful and democratic ally in the heart of the Middle East could still be squandered by hasty withdrawals and arbitrary timelines." A day later, Obama mused, "Iraqi inaction threatens the progress we've made and creates an opening for Iran and the 'special groups' it supports."

Before I explain, it's worth noting that the era in which the United States has the dubious luxury of focusing on one kind of war at a time, plus Afghanistan, plus too much face time in that so-called "peace process," is over.

It almost seems like bad form to critique the Iraq policies of the men who would be president. Iraq has taken a back seat to Georgia in driving the news cycle, while the candidates are having enough trouble this month picking veeps and keeping up with events coming out of Russia.

But Iraq is probably the direct catalyst of the transformation in stature and capacity of the United States on the world stage, even if the recent crisis in Georgia is what revealed it.

That transformation has manifested itself in what is a new experience for the United States: We are being ignored. Of course, we are used to being reviled, even as we are also used to seeking approval. We are used to being accommodated, taken advantage of, and even, on historic occasions, feared. We are not used to being ignored, and especially not by Russia.

So, what's going on? Here's the short answer via another question: Would Russia be ignoring the United States if practically every U.S. man under arms (even every woman) weren't irretrievably tied up on the quixotic mission of transforming Iraq into a Western-style democracy? I don't think so. We can't follow Teddy Roosevelt's advice to speak softly and carry a big stick if our stick is stuck in sand. I'm not sure if we've become a superpower with the power shut off, exactly, but I do know that Russia is always happy to advance under cover of darkness.

But back to Iraq. McCain, of course, is wrong for believing Iraq is a "democratic ally," peaceful or otherwise. Obama is wrong for believing Iraq is able or even cares to block the "opening" for Iran and the "special groups" or militias, it supports. And the disastrous implication behind both assessments is that there is something worthwhile the United States can reasonably expect to extract from its costly Iraqi investment — namely, a democratic ally and bulwark against Iran.

I don't believe this for many reasons, most of which I've written about before. My sense is that a democratic ally and bulwark against Iran doesn't enshrine sharia in its constitution; doesn't have a prime minister practically itching, as Nouri al-Maliki put it to Der Spiegel, to "prosecute crimes committed by U.S. soldiers against our population"; doesn't have 42 percent of a population which, according to a 2008 BBC poll, believes attacks on U.S. troops are acceptable; doesn't make the U.S. soldiers who protect it pay OPEC prices at the pump; doesn't express solidarity with Hezbollah; doesn't participate in the Arab boycott of Israel. And that's just for starters.

Now, thanks to a Middle East Media Research Institute (MEMRI) report on Iraqi reactions to negotiations over the terms of the continued presence of U.S. troops in Iraq — the long-haggled-over Status of Forces Agreement — we have even more Iraqi attributes to factor into our grand strategy, if only our leaders would pay attention.

According to MEMRI's analysis of Arab press reports this summer, "the agreement was intensely opposed by most elements in Iraqi politics," with Prime Minister Maliki going so far as to visit Iran in June "to assure the Iranians that the agreement with the U.S. would not be detrimental to Iran. During the visit, he stated that all influential political elements in Iraq supported rapprochement with Iran in all areas, and that Iraq would not allow its territory to be used as a base for attacks against Iran."

Well, that's nice — for Iran. Now, tell me again how U.S. interests are being advanced by propping up the Maliki government?

From the Iraqi religious world, the reaction to the U.S. side is no friendlier. "Shiite religious scholar Grand Ayatollah Ali Al-Sistani voiced opposition to the agreement, arguing that 'any agreement that harmed Iraq's sovereignty in any way was considered a violation of sharia,'" MEMRI writes. "Another three Shiite scholars in Najaf also condemned the agreement, warning that signing would constitute a violation of Islam and bring about a popular intifada. Abd Al-Aziz Al-Hakim, the head of the Supreme Council for Islamic Revolution in Iraq (the largest Shiite group in the Al-Maliki government), also criticized the agreement, since it stipulated a continued presence of U.S. forces."

Condoleezza Rice flew to Baghdad this week to "see what we can do from Washington to get closure" on the agreement. Lots of luck on that. Because with "allies" like these, who needs ... Russians?

Hardly comfortable for U.S. on Iraq's SOFA

12/23/08

Here's your hat, what's your hurry — but since you're still hanging around, why don't you knot your shoelaces together and soak your head?

That's the unsubtle Iraqi subtext to the agreement the United States recently and triumphantly inked with Iraq widely known as the Status of Forces Agreement, or SOFA.

Officially, the pact is titled "Agreement between the United States and the Republic of Iraq on the Withdrawal of United States Forces from Iraq and the Organization of Their Activities During Their Temporary Presence in Iraq," but I guess AUSRIWUSFIOTATTPI is a hard sell.

Actually, the whole thing is a hard sell, or surely would be if Americans really knew that in the interest of a treaty, the Bush administration has gone so far as to trade away, among other things, some of our troops' constitutional rights.

Media focus has narrowed mainly on a few points, including: Article 24, Paragraph 1, which stipulates a withdrawal date for all U.S. forces from Iraq of no later than Dec. 31, 2011; and Article 12, Paragraph 2, which states that "Iraq shall have the primary right to exercise jurisdiction over United States contractors and United States contractor employees." This means, of course, that as of Jan. 1, 2009, when the agreement goes into effect, all U.S. contractors will be under Iraqi law 24/7, just as though they were tourists vacationing in a foreign country rather than employees of the U.S. government working in a war zone.

But there's so much more to be sick about in this 18-page document, which I only recently found in its entirety online via one of the closer analyses out there by Chris Weigant writing at Huffington Post. (Contrary to my conclusions, Weigant thinks the agreement bodes "a pretty good outcome, all things considered.")

Weigant begins his analysis with Article 4 ("Missions"), aptly noting that "Iraq gets veto power over American operations." But that's putting it mildly. Paragraph 2 reads: "All such military operations ... shall be conducted with the agreement of the Government of Iraq ... shall be fully coordinated with Iraqi authorities." Paragraph 3 reads: "All such operations shall be conducted with full respect for the Iraqi Constitution and the laws of Iraq...." And there's more: "It is the duty of the United States Forces to respect the laws, customs and traditions of Iraq...."

What's up with that? This is the neither the first nor the last time in this agreement that the "laws, customs and traditions" of Iraq are declared "the duty" of Americans in Iraq to "respect." For example, Article 3 also declares: "While conducting military operations ... it is the duty of members of the United States Forces and of the civilian component to respect Iraqi laws, customs, traditions, and conventions" and "it is the duty of the United States to take all necessary measures for this purpose."

Has such a "duty" ever been written into a U.S. treaty with another country? Is it even constitutional? I doubt it. After all, the "duty" of United States Forces anywhere is to the U.S. Constitution alone, not to the laws of another country. Given that Iraq's constitution above all enshrines Sharia (Islamic law), this would also seem to mean that it is now "the duty" of U.S. troops and other Americans in Iraq to "respect" Sharia as well.

This isn't just grotesque, it poses a colossal moral and strategic problem if and when Iraqis deem American actions in Iraq to clash with the strictures of Iraqi law. Combined with the huge concessions our government has made regarding legal jurisdiction over Americans in Iraq, this new American "duty" to Iraq is at least humiliating if not also potentially disastrous.

The jurisdiction article (Article 12) opens by repeating this same troubling stipulation: namely, that it is "the duty of the members of the United States Forces and the civilian component to respect Iraqi laws, customs, traditions and conventions," which, of course, include Sharia. It goes on to place U.S. contractors and their employees wholly under Iraqi legal jurisdiction, and to place "United States Forces" and "the civilian component" under Iraqi legal jurisdiction should they commit "grave premeditated felonies" off base and off duty.

The predicament of U.S. contractors aside, it appears that the U.S. government has surrendered key constitutional rights of our fighting men and women. Now, it's bad enough to read, for example, in Article 5 ("Property Ownership") that the Bush administration has agreed to transfer to the Iraqi government everything "connected to the soil" that the United States has built — bases, buildings, facilities of all sorts — for free.

Or, even more significantly, in Article 27, Paragraph 3, that "Iraqi land, sea and air shall not be used as a launching or transit point for attacks against other countries." After all, U.S. bases in Iraq for just such potential actions against Iran or Syria were once ballyhooed as a strategic rationale for our prolonged presence in Iraq. But what about this new "duty" of American troops to "respect" the laws of Iraq, and even, in some circumstances, to be subject to them?

It all starts New Year's Day.

Iraq is victorious ... over the 'foreign' U.S.?

7/3/09

I've been stewing over something really lousy that Iraqi Prime Minister Nouri al-Maliki has been saying since June 20: that Iraqis have won a "great victory" over the "foreign presence in Iraq."

That "great victory," as he calls it, is the June 30 withdrawal of U.S. troops from Iraq's cities. That "foreign presence," as he calls it, is the United States — the thousands of mainly young American men who have fought a vicious enemy under the harshest conditions for more than six long years, with 4,321 Americans killed, many thousands wounded, often grievously so, and some small, tortured number wrongfully ensnared by the U.S. military justice system in apparent deference to Iraqi political considerations.

"Ingrate" doesn't begin to describe this al-Maliki creep — or, as all too many conservatives and Bush loyalists persist in thinking of him, our Iraqi "ally." But let's skip the labels and stick to the implications of the Iraqi prime minister's rhetoric: He has transformed long-term American sacrifice on Iraq's behalf into a residual "foreign presence" over which he now declares Iraqi victory.

The mind reels — both at the import of Maliki's words and the tepid U.S. non-reaction to them. Asked whether he found Maliki's "terminology acceptable," Gen. Raymond Odierno went all political, talking-pointing to Iraqis' "progression in their capacities" blah, blah. The post-withdrawal "expert" assessments I've seen haven't even mentioned Iraq's "victory." Typically, John Nagl, president of Center for a New American Security, a Left-wing defense think tank with close ties to the Obama administration, is still mooning over "the strategic imperative of establishing an enduring relationship" with Iraq. Someone should break it to him that Iraq isn't going to enter into an "enduring relationship" with a "foreign presence." Like love, U.S. defense policy is blind.

This could explain why the United States has entered total pushover mode in Iraq, as dictated by the U.S.-Iraq security agreement (Status of Forces Agreement, or SOFA) negotiated by the Bush administration, all in support of Maliki's narrative of victory over ... us.

The New York Times describes "a drastically reshaped American military posture has emerged, largely because of Mr. Maliki's insistence," and notes that the rapid dismantlement of bases and outposts often is carried out "during the dark of night." Transport and resupply convoys are taking place at night, too — all, presumably, in order to bolster Maliki's claims of "victory." As one of Maliki's political cronies put it, "They (U.S. troops) will be invisible for the people. They will turn into genies."

"Genies?" Does that mean Maliki has the USA plugged up in a bottle?

Certainly, we don't talk like free agents. Among the 150-plus bases and outposts the United States has closed in Iraqi cities this year are some U.S. commanders still considered crucial. About one such base, Brig. Gen. John M. Murray told the Times: "This is one we wanted. The Iraqi government said 'no,' so now we are leaving."

This doesn't sound exactly Patton-esque, but would that we were leaving the whole sorry country. Meanwhile, the Times reports, "decisions on what Americans remain where — doing what — ultimately now rest with the Iraqis, and the Americans have deferred in negotiations."

Me, I feel sick.

But apparently not Lt. Col. Timothy M. Karcher, commander of forces departing Sadr City: "We will be gone in whatever way the Iraqi government tells us to be gone." Now, there's a rousing war quotation for you. Quick — someone write a new verse to the "The Caissons Go Rolling Along."

The Times report continues: "The Americans have been strikingly sensitive" — naturally — "to Mr. Maliki's political position, emphasizing Iraqi primacy in all public remarks." For example, "they have declined to specify how many American troops will remain in cities, seemingly fearful of undercutting Mr. Maliki's public declarations of a full withdrawal."

What, no "Kick Me" stickers? Sorry to interrupt the old Fourth of July weenie roast, but doesn't it bother a single American out there that the United States is just kind of hanging around Iraq, full-metal rent-a-cops, waiting for some word, any word, from the self-anointed victor over the United States?

Of course, the main point here is not what we perceive as Maliki's ingratitude, or his disgraceful disregard of those Americans and allies who have fallen in Iraq. The main point of the prime minister's shocking statement is this: Iraq is not on the same side as the United States.

I'm afraid this will shock most Americans, but just let it sink in; it will explain a lot about the last six years. Meanwhile, the simple fact is, allies don't declare victory over each other. No doubt this presents a problem, at least for those among us who have claimed "victory" in Iraq for (not over) the United States. They and Maliki can't both be right. Someone is being played for a chump.

My suggestion? We should take this Fourth of July weekend to declare U.S. independence all over again — only this time from Iraq.

In Iraq, soldiers are still suffering, dying

7/10/09

The first I heard about what happened to Lt. Col. Timothy Karcher, the last U.S. commander of Sadr City who recently signed over jurisdiction to Iraqis, was from a reader. He e-mailed me about my last column, which argued that "allies" don't declare victory over each other (as Iraq's prime minister Nouri al-Maliki declared "victory" over the United States), and the sooner we realize Iraq isn't our "ally," the better. It also bemoaned the U.S. military's deference to Iraq, quoting top brass beginning with Gen. Raymond Odierno and including Lt. Col. Karcher, in their execution of what I, myself, consider a futile U.S. policy to Westernize Islamic cultures.

"I appreciate your fervor and feelings about Mr. al-Maliki's comments, but I must say that your biting commentary regarding the quote from Lt. Col Karcher has driven me to reply," he wrote. "You may not be aware," he continued, but since signing over jurisdiction to the Iraqis, Lt. Col. Karcher suffered a roadside bomb attack and lost both legs. One of his men, Sgt. Timothy David of Beaverton, Mich. — a veteran of six tours in Iraq and Afghanistan — was killed by a second EFP.

I was not aware. This grievous attack received scant coverage. Pieced together, news briefs tell us that on June 28 — two days before Iraq's "victory" celebration, and 10 days after Lt. Col. Karcher signed over jurisdiction to Iraq — the vehicle Lt. Col. Karcher was riding in near Sadr City drove over an explosively formed penetrator (EFP, also called an explosively formed projectile), the particularly lethal, Iranian-made roadside bomb. The blast severed both legs above the knees. After delivering their commander to Baghdad's Combat Support Hospital, his men were hit by a second EFP. It was then that Sgt. David was killed.

Lt. Col. Karcher is now hospitalized at Walter Reed in Washington, DC. Sgt. David , 28, was buried in Beaverton, Mich., this week.

Whether al-Maliki counts this as another "great victory" over the "foreign presence" in Iraq, we don't know. The incident elicited no statements, no calls for an investigation into how and why, shortly after turning over security responsibilities to the 11th Iraqi Army Division, Lt. Col. Karcher was hit. And the official silence blankets both Baghdad and Washington, DC.

It was left to ABC's Martha Raddatz, who has been updating the story's essentials at ABC News' blog, to write that June 28 was a "terrible, terrible day for the soldiers of the 2-5 Cavalry Division." But it was a terrible, terrible day for America as well — or would have been if Americans had known it. And I'm not going to blame Michael-mania for our ignorance.

This kind of thing is invisible on the national radar. It doesn't show up in anyone's vision of Iraq — not that of the Obama administration, which seeks none of the entanglements that an official reckoning of this attack would entail, and not that of the Bush-cons, who persistently see Iraq as a "success." Congress? Dazed. The media? Winding Iraq down — and besides, no "innocent civilians" were killed.

But back to my original e-mail, which having described Lt. Col. Karcher's ghastly fate, asked me "not to disparage the character of individuals who are putting themselves in harm's way," adding: "They do not make the political decisions, but perform the tasks asked of them."

That I know — although being under orders is never a sufficient excuse. But are statements made in harm's way exempt from civilian critique? Of course not. I will say that prior knowledge of Lt. Col. Karcher's injuries would certainly have affected my last column. I would have been 10 times more furious about the U.S. foreign policy, from President Bush's to President Obama's, that has placed our best and bravest patriots in mortal danger for what increasingly appears to be, certainly in these last "democratizing" years, a long and costly misadventure with no discernible benefit to the United States.

When even such patriots, however, engage in PR to promote Iraq as an "ally," cosset al-Maliki's delusional machismo like a dysfunctional family member, or trumpet an ill-conceived mission to Westernize Islamic cultures, I can't help but respond.

That said, there are not adequate phrases to impress upon the Karcher family the depth of my condolences or the sincerity of my wishes for the recovery, body and mind, of Lt. Col. Timothy Karcher.

Our Iraq strategy is now a tale of 'diminishing returns'

8/14/09

Question for Americans: How can we as a nation even consider using our military for another "surge" in Afghanistan when the "surge" in Iraq has left little more imprint on the sands of Mesopotamia than the receding tide?

This, to clarify, is not the antiwar Left writing. I am writing from a pro-military, anti-jihad point of view that has long seen futility in the U.S. nation-building strategy in Iraq, and now sees futility in the rerun in Afghanistan. Problem is, the same blind spot afflicts both strategies: the failure to understand that an infidel nation cannot fight for the soul of an Islamic nation. This, in essence, is what President Bush and now President Obama have ordered our troops to do.

I don't suggest these missions are ever considered in such terms, which implicitly acknowledge intractable differences between Judeo-Christian-based Western cultures and Islamic cultures. Doing so, of course, is a taboo thing—a grievous violation in the PC realm where decisions are made. But the omission helps answer my opening question. I seriously doubt Americans would approve of re-running the surge in Afghanistan if there were an honest reckoning of the religious, cultural and historical reasons why the surge failed to achieve its promised results in Iraq.

Iraq and the Doomed 'Democracy' Project

This is not to say the U.S. military failed. On the contrary, the U.S. military succeeded, as ordered, to bring a measure of security and aid to a carnage-maddened Islamic society. Given U.S.-won security, surge architects promised us, this same Islamic society was supposed to then respond by coming together in "national reconciliation." They were wrong. Not only did Iraqis fail to coalesce as a pro-American, anti-jihad bulwark in the Islamic world (the thoroughly delusional original objective), they have also failed to form a minimally functional nation-state. And the United States is now poised to do the same thing all over again in Afghanistan.

I write this as the volume of talk of an Afghanistan "surge" is getting louder, drowning out the quiet undercurrent of eye-opening reports now emerging on post-surge Iraq. Late last month, for example, the New York Times reported on a bluntly revealing memo written by Col. Timothy Reese, an adviser to the Iraqi military's Baghdad command. In it, Reese urgently argues that the United States has "reached the point of diminishing returns" in Iraq due, among many other things, to endemic corruption ("the stuff of legend"), laziness, weakness and culture of "political violence and intimidation."

Reese considers Iraqi Security Forces (ISF) "good enough" —just— to keep the Iraqi government from toppling. That's reason enough, he writes, to leave early, by August 2010 instead of December 2011. Reese describes a "fundamental change" in the U.S.-Iraq relationship since the June 30 handover—a "sudden coolness," lack of cooperation, even a "forcible takeover" by ISF of a checkpoint. While Iraq will still "squeeze the U.S. for all the 'goodies' that we can provide," he writes, tensions are increasing and "the potential for Iraqi on U.S. violence is high now and will grow by the day."

And that's the good news. The Washington Times this week reported on an even more dire prognostication to be published by National Defense University written by Najim Abed Al-Jabouri, a former Iraqi police chief and mayor. Al-Jabouri focuses on problems within the ISF, where, he writes, the divided loyalties of what is essentially a series of militias beholden to competing "ethno-sectarian" political factions could easily drive Iraq to civil war. He writes: "The state security institutions have been built upon a foundation of shifting loyalties that will likely collapse when struck by the earthquake of ethnic and sectarian attacks. Iraq's best hope for creating a long-term stable democracy will come from an independent national security force that is controlled by the state, and not by political parties competing to control the state."

Al-Jabouri insists the United States should exert its "leverage" to revamp the ISF, which, given Reese's evidence of plummeting U.S. influence in Iraq, seems farfetched even if it were a good idea. Which it is emphatically not. An infidel nation cannot fight for the soul of an Islamic nation—a truism that, in a more rational (non-PC) world, might bring surge enthusiasts to their senses.

How a 'surge' fails us, part 1

12/18/2009

This week's syndicated column is the first in a series on the impact of the Iraq "surge" strategy:

The main reason the "surge" in Afghanistan is on is because the conventional wisdom tells us the "surge" in Iraq "worked."

The problem is, the Iraq surge did not work. Yes, the U.S. military perfectly executed its share of the strategy—the restoration of some semblance of calm to blood-gushing Mesopotamian society—but that was only Step One. The end-goal of the surge strategy, Step Two was always out of U.S. control—a fundamental flaw. Step Two was up to the Iraqis: namely, to take the opportunity afforded by U.S.-provided security (see Step One) to bring about both "national reconciliation" and, as the powers-that-were further promised, the emergence of a U.S. ally in the so-called war on terror.

Step One worked. Step Two didn't. The surge, like an uncaught touchdown pass, was incomplete. The United States is now walking off the battlefield with virtually nothing to show for its blood, treasure, time and effort. In fact, another "success" like that could kill us.

Take the state of post-surge U.S.-Iraq investment lately in the news. Remember "blood for oil," the anti-war mantra of the Left? "Blood not for oil" is more like it. Not only did Paul Wolfowitz's prediction that Iraq would pay for its own reconstruction with oil revenue never come true; not only did the United States never get to fill up one crummy Humvee for free; but when Iraq staged one of the biggest oil auctions in history last week, U.S. companies left empty-handed. Russia, China and Europe came out the big winners.

"Strange," said industry experts, which is one word for it. What's also shocking is Iraq's apparent willingness to denigrate the United States by showing favoritism to hostile nations (that sacrificed nothing in Iraq's war), and disregard for American interests in the war's (supposed) aftermath.

Such benefactor-abuse fits a pattern of what you might call Iraqi de-Americanization. At the big Baghdad Trade Fair in November, for example, the United States was "not much evident among the 32 nations represented," the New York Times noted. In fact, of the 396 companies represented, only two or three were American—"but I can't remember their names," the fair company director said. As the newspaper summed up: "America's war in Iraq has been good for business in Iraq—but not necessarily for American business."

Leading the field is United Arab Emirates with investments in Iraq amounting to $31 billion, mostly from the last year, "compared to only about $400 million from American companies when United States government reconstruction spending is excluded."

U.S. government reconstruction spending, of course, equals taxpayer dollars. Beyond our incredible largesse — which (not including the astronomical cost of the war itself) comes to $53 billion, much of which is headed down the drain as Iraqis show little capacity to maintain U.S.-provided public works projects — one market analyst told the Times, "U.S. private investors have become negligible players in Iraq." Meanwhile, Turkey, the nation that prevented U.S. troops from transiting through during the initial invasion, has become a major commercial player in Iraq. Likewise Iran, the nuke-seeking, genocide-promising nation that fomented much of the war, particularly the IED war, on U.S. forces in Iraq.

The sour experience of FedEx is revealing. This fall, the shipping company announced it was suspending operations to Iraq. "The reason is that Iraqi officials gave RusAir, a Russian airline, exclusive rights to cargo flight," the Times reports. "FedEx was one of the very few American businesses that braved the risks of working not only on American bases but also in the Red Zone, back when it was particularly dangerous to do so. Now that the danger is much less, its business is being thwarted by an upstart Russian come-lately."

Emphasis on "Russian." And, with the oil auction, emphasis on "Chinese." "We all know that China is on track to become a major economic as well as technological power," an Iraqi oil ministry spokesman told the Washington Post.

And the United States? More like an old shoe now than anything else. Which reminds me: After that Iraqi "journalist" threw his shoes at then-President Bush, The Scotsman newspaper reported that the Istanbul-based shoe manufacturer received orders from around the world, including an incredible 120,000 orders from Iraq.

What's that old Middle Eastern saying — The shoe of my enemy's enemy is my shoe?

The 'surge' and 'success,' part 2

12-29-09

Belowis the second part of a three-column series assessing the ~~benefit, gain,~~ outcome of six-plus American years in Iraq as we rev up to do it all over again in Afghanistan — only with much more exciting logistics.

So much for the lack of post-surge U.S. business benefits in Iraq, as I wrote last week. Now, what kind of post-surge ally is Iraq?

No kind.

I write in wonder that the ultimate failures of the surge strategy—which include the failure of anything resembling a U.S. ally to emerge in post-Saddam Iraq—have never entered national discourse. Rather, the strategy that "won Iraq" has been mythologized as a "success" to be repeated in Afghanistan.

It's not that there aren't hints to the contrary—as when U.S. ambassador to Iraq Christopher Hill arrived at the Iraqi parliament in early December and "some deputies," the New York Times reported, "demanded he be barred from the building." Or when 42 percent of Iraqis polled by the BBC in March 2008 still thought it "acceptable" to attack U.S. forces. Or when Prime Minister Nuri al-Maliki, as U.S. forces transferred security responsibilities to Iraqi forces in June, obstreperously declared "victory" over those same U.S. forces! Such incidents convey hostility toward the United States inside Iraq, but there's more. Of greater consequence are the positions against U.S. interests Iraq is taking in world affairs.

Take the foundational principle of freedom of speech, continuously under assault by the Organization of the Islamic Conference (OIC) in the international arena. The OIC includes the world's 57 Muslim nations as represented by kings, heads of state and governments, with policies overseen by the foreign ministers of these same 57 nations. Describing itself as the "collective voice of the Islamic world," the OIC strives to extend Islamic law throughout the world, and to that end, is the driving force at the United Nations to outlaw criticism of Islam (which includes Islamic law) through proposed bans on the "defamation of religions"—namely, Islam. This is a malignant thrust at the mechanism of Western liberty. Where does post-surge Iraq come down in this crucial ideological struggle?

An OIC nation, Iraq is, with other OIC nations, a signatory to the 1990 Cairo Declaration of Human Rights in Islam. This declaration defines human rights according to Islamic law, which prohibits criticism of Islam. Indeed, Iraq's U.S.-enabled 2004 constitution enshrines Islamic law above all. Little wonder Iraq consistently votes at the United Nations with the OIC and against the United States on this key ideological divide between Islam and the West, most recently in November.

Then there's Iran.

Iran may be a menace to the West, but it is also Iraq's largest trading partner. Heavily involved in Iraq's reconstruction, Iran has masterminded extensive loan, tourism and energy programs in Iraq while maintaining close connections to Iraq's dominant Shiite political parties. This disastrous fact should dampen—at least enter into—assessments of the surge strategy's "success."

But it doesn't. Not even the fact that Bank Melli—the Iranian terror bank outlawed by the U.S. Treasury as a conduit for Iran's nuclear and terrorist programs—operates a branch in Baghdad gives pause to one-surge-fits-all enthusiasts. The Bank Melli example is particularly egregious because the bank funds Iran's Revolutionary Guard Corps' Qods Force, which is responsible for innumerable American casualties in Iraq—American sacrifices on behalf of Iraq. Guess we're supposed to look the other way. But that's like applauding the Status of Forces Agreement (SOFA) between the United States and Iraq without noticing that the agreement prohibits the United States from attacking Iran (or any other country) from Iraq. Iraq's pattern of hostility to U.S. interests continues vis-a-vis Israel, a bona-fide U.S. ally against jihad terror. Whenever Israel strikes back at jihad—whether at Hamas in Gaza or Hezbollah in Lebanon—post-Saddam Iraq is quick to condemn the Jewish state, which, not incidentally, it also continues to boycott with the rest of the Arab League.

Additionally, Maliki's public refusal even to criticize Hezbollah in 2006 prompted Dan Senor, a former Bush administration advisor in Baghdad, to write in the Wall Street Journal: "It wasn't supposed to be this way. We had thought that a post-Saddam Iraqi government would be less susceptible to Arab League pressure. ... This change of tone was to be a model for the region."

And why did "we" ever think this? Such was—and is—the deceptive power of the see-no-Islam fantasy.

On to Afghanistan.

Victory? Really?
How the surge failed us, part 3

12/30/09

There's at least one more aspect to consider when appraising the past six years in Iraq climaxed by the "surge." This would be the indirect effect of "reflected glory," if such a quaint term applies, and has to do with the sort of state the U.S. helped create in Iraq.

I don't know how to candy-coat reality: Post-surge Iraq is a state of increasing repression, endemic corruption, religious and ethnic persecution and encroaching Sharia. Recent media reports flag just some of these glaring truths that American elites, civilian and military, seem to shy away from.

In October, from Asia News, came the latest news of, to quote the headline, "Sharia Slowly Advancing in Najaf and Basra, for Non-Muslims Too." Here, the Sharia (Islamic law) is invoked to ban alcohol sales and consumption by non-Muslims — namely, Christians, given the eradication and dispersal of Iraq's ancient Jewish population — "on the grounds that Iraq's constitution," as Ahmad al Sulaiti, deputy governor of Najaf, notes, "'bans everything that violates the principles of Islam.'" More on that below.

In November, Reuters highlighted the government crackdown on the media via lawsuits against criticism, and laws enabling the government to close media outlets that "encourage terrorism, violence," and — here's a handy catch-all — "tensions." There are new rules to license satellite trucks, censor books and control Internet cafes. "The measures evoke memories of ... the laws used to muzzle (journalism) under Saddam Hussein," Reuters writes.

In December, the British paper The Observer reported that hundreds of Iraqi police and soldiers descended on Baghdad's 300 nightclubs where they "slapped owners' faces, scattered their patrons and dancing girls, ripped down posters advertising upcoming acts and ordered alcohol removed from the shelves." The official reason? No licenses. But, the paper reports, "the reality is that a year-long renaissance in Baghdad's nightlife may be over as this increasingly conservative city takes on a hardline religious identity." As one club owner said: "This is a political decision with a religious agenda. (Prime Minister Nouri al-) Maliki needs the votes of religious parties ... They (the government) supported us and gave us incentives to reopen the clubs, then when it suited them, they sold us and themselves out to the fundamentalists."

There's a lot of that "selling out to the fundamentalists" going around post-surge Iraq, where, it must be faced, one particularly shocking, unintended consequence of U.S. involvement has been the religious "cleansing" of Iraq's ancient Christian populations. In 2003, 1 million Christians lived in Iraq. Six years later, after successive waves of violence and intimidation largely unchecked by either Iraqi government action or U.S. intercession, more than 500,000 Christians have fled the country. It is a crisis that inspired Christian leaders to assemble in Baghdad in December for a conference piteously titled: "Do Christians Have a Future in Iraq?"

This anti-Christian persecution is a large part of why the U.S. Commission on International Religious Freedom recommended in December 2008 that the State Department name Iraq a Country of Particular Concern (CPC) — its dread Saddam-era designation. (Recommendation denied.) In May, to strengthen human rights in Iraq, the commission's Iraq report included suggested amendments to Iraq's constitution, which, not incidentally, boil down to abolishing the constitutional supremacy of Islamic law. (And yes, U.S. legal advisers helped write this same Sharia-supreme governing document.)

For example, the commission suggested deleting the line in Article 2 that says no law may contradict "the established provisions of Islam." It suggested revising the "guarantee of 'the Islamic identity of the majority' to make certain that this identity is not used to justify violations" of human rights. It also suggested that "the free and informed consent of both parties (be) required to move a personal status case to the religious law system," and "that religious court rulings (be) subject to final review under Iraq's civil law." Another suggestion was to remove "the ability of making appointments to the Federal Supreme Court based on training in Islamic jurisprudence alone."

Good ideas — if religious freedom is the objective. But it is not the objective in Iraq, or in other Islamic countries.

Which should make the United States, founded and defined by such freedom, look before nation-building, and ask: Do we really want Americans to "surge" and risk death to build nations such as this to stand as monuments to "victory"?

Anyone surprised that Iraq is the 'new Iran'?

1/29/10

"The real danger in Iraq is Iran. It controls Iraq with a firm fist." So said Iraqi parliamentarian Ayad Jamal Aldin to Bloomberg.com last month in London. "It was through (Grand Ayatollah Ali) al-Sistani that Iran was able to invade Iraq."

"Could you please elaborate on that?" I asked Aldin this week in Washington, D.C., where the leader of the new anti-corruption Ahrar Party was making the rounds. This point — that post-Saddam, post-surge Iraq (initial thanks to top cleric and Iranian citizen al-Sistani) is effectively a satellite of Iran — goes against the victory-narrative of the policymakers and pundits who have urged the Obama administration to repeat mistakes the United States made in Iraq again in Afghanistan.

The answer (through an interpreter) was a chilling geopolitical lesson taught from the perspective of an Iraqi Shiite cleric from Najaf, who, from the beginning, as I reported in 2003, has called for the separation of religion and state in Iraq. An amalgam of apparent contradictions difficult to unravel in one interview — Aldin is considered pro-Western but would support the anti-Western objectives of the Arab League (including the boycott of pro-Western Israel); says "people need nightclubs" even as he believes alcohol consumption "undoubtedly leads one to Hell;" wears the black turban of those who claim descent from Muhammad and penny loafers — Aldin is nonetheless an insightful, implacable opponent of Iranian influence in Iraq, which, as he describes it, is in full and malevolent ascendance.

First things first: Aldin is grateful to the United States for removing

Saddam Hussein. This was a boon, he says, not just for Iraq but for humanity. But due to the U.S. backing "the Iranian men," the net American effect has been to create "a new Iran — Iraq — with its capital in Baghdad."

For example, think back to the big Iraqi oil auction last year — a bust for U.S. oil companies. Aldin explains their being empty-handed with a question: "Is there any U.S. oil business in Iran? No." He continues: "Iraq is the second Iran. The difference between the two is that the new Iran is supported and defended by the U.S. The old Iran is boycotted and sanctioned by the U.S." But there's "no meaning" to such measures because more than the notorious Iranian terror-bank Bank Melli operates in Iraq. A multitude of Iranian banking concerns, he says, operate freely in Iraq under Iraqi names.

Do they laugh at us over things like this? I asked. "No," he replied. "People think the U.S. must be in some big conspiracy." In other words, we just couldn't be as dumb as we really are.

What about China and Russia, the big winners in the oil auction?

"We don't need China and Russia," he replied. "Iran does. Iran needs China's and Russia's support at the United Nations. Iran doesn't have much to give, so Iran gives them Iraqi oil contracts to get their support at the U.N."

Makes sense.

"Iran's objective is to drive the U.S. out of the Middle East," Aldin says. And, he says, Iran works with al-Qaida and the Taliban to do so. Testing him on another Washington myth, I asked: But Shiite Iran wouldn't work with Sunni al-Qaida and Sunni Taliban, would they?

"They all have one enemy," he said. "The U.S. — Shia and Sunni differences don't matter to them when it comes to the common enemy."

He continued. "There is a saying in Iran: The guard of any caravan is partner with the thieves." That, he says, describes Iran's simultaneous support for the government of Iran and its support for al-Qaida, or anyone else operating against U.S. interests — Baathists, Taliban, anyone.

Al-Qaida and Iran, he says, can control the whole Middle East, between al-Qaida's "southern crescent" (Afghanistan, Pakistan, Yemen and Somalia) and Iran's "northern crescent" (Iran, Iraq, Syria, Lebanon and Gaza). What about Saudi Arabia, I asked.

He doesn't laugh but somehow conveys the impression that he did. Not any kind of a power, in his view. Just rich.

When you tell U.S. policymakers your assessment of Iran in Iraq, what is their reaction?, Deep inside they may realize what has happened, he thinks. But for now, "they're not interested. State of denial."

You can say that again.

We surge, yet Iran wins

4/2/10

What a heady whirl of a month it has been for Iran's Mahmoud Ahmadinejad, the world's most fabulous jihad-kingpin and leading proponent of genocide. Everyone seems to want a piece of him, in a good way, of course. American enemies, American "allies" — they're all palsy-walsy. Where that leaves Uncle Sucker is another matter.

First, the enemies. At the end of February, A-jad was off to Damascus — ah, Damascus in February — for a joint-summit with Bashar Al-Assad to denounce the United States and Israel, and then, a group summit, or "war council" as Arab media called it, with both Assad and Hezbollah's Hassan Nasrallah. All three denounced, for variation, Israel and the United States.

Then it was quick trip back to Tehran for a two-day conference with the Palestinian "resistance" all-stars, as translated by the Middle East Media Research Institute: Hamas head Khaled Mash'al (who told Iranian Ayatollah Khameini "if the resistance breathes … today it is by virtue of Khameini"), Islamic Jihad leader Ramadhan Shallah (who doubles as an entry on the FBI's most wanted list), and PFLP-GC leader Ahmad Jibril (like his colleagues, an all-around great guy). Talk of a third intifada was bandied about while MEMRI notes, "Ahmadinejad made particularly virulent anti-Israel statements."

MEMRI ought to know; the group translates scores of them. A-jad's remarks no doubt thrilled the genocide-eager crowd: "Zionist regime … purge the region of your existence … insult to all humanity … racist group… not committed to a single human principle … their presence on even a single centimeter of Palestine and the region leads to … consecutive wars … Zionists are the source of all wars … end of its road … downward slope … completely dead end … completely eliminated. …" Brilliant stuff. Another speech like that, and they'll all be ready for the "peace process."

As MEMRI notes, "Iran has been noticeably ratcheting up its efforts to arouse the Palestinian resistance organizations against Israel," thus boosting "its position in the Islamic world." But in spite of Gen. David Petraeus' assertion that the Israeli-Palestinian issues "set the strategic context within which we operate in the Central Command (region)," there are in fact other contexts involving Iran that have nothing to do with Israel, and everything to do with us. I'm talking about Iran's relationships with our putative (non-Israel) allies in the region, the ones American troops have actually died for, Afghanistan and Iraq.

In March, Afghanistan's Hamid Karzai visited A-jad in Tehran to make merry for the Nowruz holiday; then, following Karzai's three-day visit to Beijing, Karzai reciprocated, giving A-jad what the New York

Times called "the red-carpet treatment" in Kabul where he "delivered a fiery anti-American speech inside Afghanistan's presidential palace." That would be the same presidential palace that is ultimately protected by U.S. troops. With Karzai at his side, A-jad "accused the United States of promoting terrorism."

Kind of takes the bounce out of the "surge" to have your own puppet pull your strings.

And what did Karzai say back? According to Radio Free Europe/Radio Liberty, Karzai riffed on brotherly love, praising "Tehran for spending hundreds of millions of dollars in rebuilding roads, providing electricity, education and health care in parts of Afghanistan." No mention of Iran's generous military assistance, including IED assistance, to the Taliban.

RFE/RL continued, noting suspicions in Kabul over Iran's "investments in Afghan media and support for Afghan Shi'ite communities, in particular the Hazaras," who "now enjoy a major share in the Afghan government and are also making significant progress in education and private sectors — partly because of generous assistance from Iran's clerical regime."

Great. Anyone want to bet that Iran won't be the big winner again at the end of America's latest "surge"?

Back to A-jad's busy whirl. Even as he was shaking Kabul's dust from his boots, he was preparing to receive a delegation from Iraq. Seems that Iraqi Prime Minister Nouri al-Maliki is trying to build a parliamentary bloc large enough to transform his whisker-close, second-place-finish in March elections into ultimate victory — and what better place to do Iraqi political horse-trading than in Iran? Last week, Maliki delegations visited A-jad in Tehran and Moqtada al-Sadr in Qom.

Gee. Maybe someday, if we "surge" long enough, Afghanistan's elections can be worked out in Iran, too.

Good riddance to 'ungrateful volcanoes'

11/29/11

The last hot meal to be served at Camp Victory, the largest of 505 military bases once operated by the United States in Iraq, was a Thanksgiving dinner on Nov. 20. Cooks served more than 2,000 pounds of turkey and more than 3,000 pounds of mashed potatoes to 6,000-plus military personnel.

Doing the dishes this time also meant shutting down the kitchen.

That's because Camp Victory, one of only 10 U.S. bases still in operation, will be closed soon. According to the agreement signed in 2008 by President George W. Bush and implemented by President Barack

Obama, the U.S. military in Iraq is coming home.

Praises be. So what if the U.S. withdrawal comes only after Obama was unable to convince Iraq to extend its welcome under tenable conditions? I'll take it, and give thanks. I am very sorry Camp Victory troops are on cold rations until they finally return stateside next month, but I am thankful to be able to see the day when they will have left Iraq – taking all of their Christian religious posters and symbols from base chapels with them, according to the New York Times.

This withdrawal will mark the end of a misguided misadventure to convert, in a zealously secular and even philo-Islamic way, a member of the Islamic world to the ways of the West. Despite the courage, dedication and sacrifice of American and allied troops, despite the so-called surge, despite the endless (and endlessly expensive) attempts to win Iraqi "hearts and minds," it was a flop.

The top American spokesman in Iraq, Gen. Jeffrey Buchanan, can spin all he wants – "It's not about winning or losing but making significant progress" – but this eight-year "counterinsurgency" didn't work. It was a failure – unless, of course, you're Iran. To borrow from the great Winston Churchill, also unenthralled with the British misadventure in Iraq in the year 1922, we have been paying billions of dollars "for the privilege of living on an ungrateful volcano out of which we are in no circumstances to get anything worth having."

In Afghanistan, meanwhile, no preparations for departure are so clearly evident. For the time being, the U.S. military's per diem costs – an estimated $350 million just to get U.S. forces fed and in the field every day – are still effectively open-ended. In fact, Afghan President Hamid Karzai has just presided over a gathering of the clans, a "loya jirga" assembly of some 2,000 Afghans, who have produced a list of conditions for a continuing American presence.

Here, culled from different news sources, is a list of the loya jirga's conditions:

1) No more immunity from Afghan law for U.S. forces;
2) No more night raids by U.S. forces;
3) No more "arbitrary" detention of Afghan suspects;
4) No more U.S. detention centers;
5) Transfer Afghan detainees to Afghan detention centers;
6) A capped 10- year limit to any pact with the United States;
7) Afghans must lead all security missions after 2014;
8) The United States should commit to training role and "support";
9) No More U.S.-run "parallel" structures to handle contracting and other matters; rather, America should support Afghan institutions; and
10) No U.S. attacks on neighbors from Afghan soil.

Can you say "rent-a-cop"?

No wonder Karzai is so enthused. "I absolutely agree with it," Karzai said of the loya jirga's list of terms, as McClatchy Newspapers reported. "We would never allow any foreign country to use our soil for causing harm to our neighbors," he added. Love thy non-infidel neighbors, Iran and Pakistan – the default-affinity that is a basic stumbling block to U.S.-Afghan alliance.

But still Karzai wants more. "The U.S. wants military installations from us. We will give those to them. But we have conditions for this.

We will benefit from this. Our soldiers will be trained. Our police will be trained. We will benefit from their money."

It's one thing for yet another "ungrateful volcano" to scheme so, cold and numb to the blood and sacrifice of tens of thousands of Americans, even in this season of Thanksgiving. What I want to know is why we put up with it.

GOP candidates walk a tightrope on Iraq

1/6/12

On Dec. 31, 2011, Iraq's Nouri al-Maliki declared a national holiday to celebrate the withdrawal of U.S. forces from Iraq. Funny way to say "thank you" for all the blood and treasure, no?

Not that Maliki was saying thank you. He wasn't even saying good riddance. He was saying, in effect, it was all a dream. Or, in the Associated Press' words: "The prime minister sought to credit Iraqis with the overthrow of Saddam Hussein and made no mention of the role played by U.S. forces that invaded Iraq in March 2003."

No mention, huh? I guess it was just a trillion-dollar mirage, a figment, a never-never fantasy best dropped from speeches, polite conversation, maybe history books. Then again, silence suits the American political classes fine. Amazingly, following the U.S. withdrawal, the questions, "What was that all about?" or, "What went wrong in Iraq?" or even, "Did something go wrong in Iraq?" (never mind, "What is going wrong in Afghanistan?") don't rise even to the level of conversation-enders. They don't rise, period, not even among GOP presidential candidates, beyond the odd sound bite.

Famously, of course, Ron Paul calls for withdrawal of U.S. troops everywhere, a rollback of the international security force the U.S. military has become, certainly since entering World War II. While Paul's constitutional position is strong, his misunderstanding of Islam undermines his rationale for me; indeed, it transforms his policy into submission. The aftermath of withdrawal under a Paul presidency could be as dangerous as it would be under more Obama.

I support withdrawal from guaranteed recidivist hellholes such as Iraq and Afghanistan as a means to shore up the wall against the spread of Shariah (Islamic law) in the West rather than, in effect, continuing to fight/accommodate Shariah culture in the Islamic world. This is a no-win struggle in which only a see-no-Shariah utopian could still engage. It is this Islam-blind engagement that is the simple but devastating flaw of the Bush-Obama counterinsurgencies (COIN). But it continues to get a national pass.

Indeed, most GOP candidates tend to promise more of the same Bush-Obama COIN. (Jon Huntsman is the other main GOP exception. He voices a come-home-America policy in Afghanistan based on non-feasibility, economics and war-weariness — all valid points — but without parsing COIN, which he sees as a success in Iraq.) The candidates speak in generalities, when they speak at all.

I think that's because if Republicans were to discuss the past decade's wars — what worked, what didn't, whether the USA should fight for constitutions that enshrine Shariah (Iraq's and Afghanistan's) -- they would have to discuss the president whose tenure was dominated by these wars. And the last thing they want to discuss is George W. Bush.

This is a grave political mistake. The fact is, President Obama has continued much of the Bush war agenda in both Iraq and Afghanistan — an agenda polls indicate most Americans don't support. For much of Obama's term, key war-making personnel were Bush holdovers, from Defense Secretary Bill Gates to Gen. David Petraeus. The war plan for "Obama's war" in Afghanistan came off the Bush drawing board.

Even Obama's withdrawal from Iraq was on Bush's schedule. Opponents, including most GOP candidates, seem to forget that Obama agreed with them. After all, he pleaded with Iraq to allow some U.S. forces to remain.

How does this play out in Election 2012? Without a GOP strategy to confront the essentially non-conservative mistakes of the Bush presidency, I predict GOP defeat. Come November, having failed to repudiate George W. Bush's bailouts and stimulus spending, Mr. GOP will be unable to make the clear case for free markets, let alone for repealing socialized medicine. Reverting to Republican "good manners," he won't argue against leaving a redistributionist and collectivist in the Oval Office, either (and forget about the phony birth certificate). He'll probably think he has an ace in the hole — foreign policy, traditionally the Republican strong suit.

But, no. Failing to have distanced himself from key Bush policies, the GOP candidate has failed to distance himself from Obama's, too. Then Obama shows his cards, the pieces de resistance: the hit on Osama bin Laden (operationally insignificant, but no matter); the killing of Libyan leader Moammar Gadhafi (never mind the USA actually supported al-Qaida allies to get it done); more drone-killed hilltop jihadis than Bush ever got. In a campaign endgame, such strokes could give Obama the empty but winning boost.

Sure, Iraq's al-Maliki can clam up about everything, but we know better. Or do we?

The Murdoch Problem

Saudi moneybags has become crimson sugar daddy, Hoya honey pot and Fox News policy maker

12/19/05

There's one good thing about the news that Alwaleed bin Talal, the richest Saudi prince in the world, just bought Harvard and Georgetown universities — or, at least buried them up to their ivy in $40 million.

It gives everybody reason to relive a McAuliffe moment. McAuliffe, of course, was Gen. Anthony C. McAuliffe, who, in response to a Nazi invitation to surrender during the 1944 Battle of the Bulge, sent back a one-word reply: "NUTS."

In kindred spirit, but in a very different war, Rudy Giuliani gave the United States a McAuliffe moment after he realized that Mr. Alwaleed's $10 million donation to help rebuild the Twin Towers after 9/11 was in fact the price of principle. Having signed his hefty check, Mr. Alwaleed spoke his nasty piece: basically, that the United States had it coming — "it" being 9/11 — given America's support of Israel.

Rudy didn't say "nuts," but he immediately returned the money. "Not only are those statements wrong," Mr. Giuliani said, "they're part of the problem."

Sigh. That was then. Now, Mr. "Part of the Problem" is a Crimson sugar daddy, a Hoya honey pot, whose millions will buy a colossal expansion of Saudi-friendly Islamic studies at the heart of the Ivy League and inside the Beltway.

Smart. Not that anybody ever said a man worth $23.7 billion wasn't smart. But Mr. Alwaleed explains his largesse this way: "Bridging the understanding between East and West is important for peace and tolerance." Funny how that bridge goes only one-way. We won't ever, for example, see a Saudi prince (or anyone else) plunk down cold cash to expand — or even establish — Christian studies in Saudi Arabia, where exercising freedom of a non-Islamic religion is a crime.

This doesn't stop Mr. Alwaleed from chattering about "bridges between East and West." Maybe that's because, as a mega-mogul of the East with major holdings in the West, he crosses them all the time.

Take his media holdings. In the West, they include a sizeable stake in Rupert Murdoch's News Corporation, which owns Fox News, "fair and balanced" pride of any parent company. And Mr. Alwaleed takes pride — pride of ownership, anyway — in Fox as well. "During last month's street protests in France," he bragged to an audience at a Dubai media conference, according to Middle East Online, "Fox ran a banner saying: 'Muslim riots.' I picked up the phone and called Murdoch" — Rupert — "to tell him these are not Muslim riots, these are riots out of poverty. Within 30 minutes," the prince recalled, "the title was changed from 'Muslim riots' to 'civil riots.'"

I guess money — oops, I mean, peace and tolerance — talks. Why else, as noted by Accuracy in Media (AIM), would News Corporation's Harper Collins have published the prince's "authorized biography"? In the DVD documentary accompanying the book — a royal bonus — Rupert Murdoch makes a cameo appearance (presumably "authorized") to praise Mr. Alwaleed, dismissing Mr. Giuliani's rejection as so much "politics."

Mr. Murdoch might well have added that not everyone is too proud to take the prince's, well, princely sums. In 2002, Mr. Alwaleed contributed $27 million to a Saudi government telethon that raised more than $100 million for the families of Palestinian "martyrs." Like Harvard and Georgetown — like Andover ($500,000), like the Carter Center ($5 million) — no Hamas or Al Aqsa alums or legacies (survivors?) were about to give any bucks back.

And why should they? Harvard may have a record of Arab gifts gone wrong, including a $2.5 million donation the divinity school returned following revelations of the donor's anti-Semitic, anti-American leanings. "But," as the Boston Globe noted, "problems with the Alwaleed donation do not seem probable."

Here's one. Prince "Crimson bin Hoya" is now not only one of American academia's most generous benefactors ever, he's co-owner of ART TV network, the Saudi company that includes what Steven Stalinsky of the Middle East Media Research Institute (MEMRI) has described in the New York Sun as "the anti-American, anti-Semitic, pro-Jihad Arabic TV channel Iqra."

That's putting it mildly. Programming, Mr. Stalinsky writes, includes telethons — the notorious terrorist fundraiser (mentioned above) of 2002, and an August 2005 fundraiser for "Jihad in Palestine"; lectures that endorse suicide bombing and exhort Muslims to triumph over the West by the "slitting of throats and shattering skulls"; 9/11 conspiracy theories blaming the United States, Israel and the Vatican; children's shows that instruct parents to teach their children to pray for "martyrdom"; a soap opera with Jews casting spells on Muhammad; and talk shows on wife-beating. I'd say it's about time Rupert picked up the phone.

As for Harvard and Georgetown — NUTS.

Fox's fairly imbalanced pro-Muslim influence

2/5/10

Should Fox News register with the State Department as a foreign agent — an agent of Saudi Arabia?

First off, is that a farfetched question? Not when a leading member of the ruling family of the Sharia-totalitarian "kingdom" of Saudi Arabia, Prince Alwaleed bin Talal, has made himself the second-largest shareholder of Rupert Murdoch's News Corp., Fox News' parent company.

Just as Steven Emerson believes that American universities using Saudi mega-millions (many from Alwaleed) to set up Islamic studies departments should register as Saudi agents, I believe an American news channel part-owned and part-influenced by the Saudi prince should, too.

Alwaleed's long march through U.S. institutions is a mainly post-9/11 progression greased by his purchase of about a 5.5 percent stake in News Corp. in 2005, and his purchases, I mean, gifts, of $20 million apiece to Georgetown and Harvard Universities, also in 2005.

There have been other eye-catching displays of Alwaleed's largesse — $500,000 in 2002 to the Council on American Islamic Relations (CAIR), a Hamas- and Muslim-Brotherhood-linked entity, and a whopping $27 million, also in 2002, to the families of Palestinian "martyrs," aka suicide bombers. These, along with Alwaleed's self-described "very close relationship" with Murdoch son and apparent heir-apparent James, a left-wing global-warmist with virulently anti-Israel views, should only deepen Americans' concerns about Fox's ties to "the prince." Recently, Murdoch and Alwaleed have discussed expanding their business relationship through the Murdoch purchase of a substantial stake in Rotana, Alwaleed's huge Arab media company.

Before entering his Murdoch association, Alwaleed gave a remarkably candid interview in 2002 about what Arab News described as his belief that "Arabs should focus more on penetrating U.S. public opinion as a means to influencing decision-making" rather than boycotting U.S. products, an idea of the moment.

The Arab News reported: "Arab countries can influence U.S. decision-making 'if they unite through economic interests, not political,' (Alwaleed) stressed. 'We have to be logical and understand that the U.S. administration is subject to U.S. public opinion. We (Arabs) are not so active in this sphere (public opinion). And to bring the decision-maker on your side, you not only have to be active inside the U.S. Congress or the administration but also inside U.S. society.'"

And active inside U.S. society living rooms — even better. Alwaleed would seem to have hit on a Fox strategy some time after Rudy Giuliani refused to accept, on behalf of a 9/11-shattered New York City, his $10 million check-cum-lecture that essentially justified the al-Qaida attacks as having been a response to U.S. foreign policy. This was "such an egregious, outrageous, unfair offense that I would have nothing to do with his money either," Sean Hannity said at the time on Fox News' "Hannity & Colmes," his remarks (and those of other Fox personalities) recently re-examined by the left-wing group Media Matters. "This is a bad guy," Hannity said. "Rudy was right to decline the money." Bill Sammon called Alwaleed's check "blood money," adding, "we're better off without it."

How terribly ironic that this same "bad guy" is now a News Corp. blood-money bags, a boss who must be handled with care as, for example, Fox host Neil Cavuto did in a deferential interview with Alwaleed last month.

How does this influence Fox News coverage? It's impossible to say. Alwaleed has bragged that it only took a phone call to ensure that Fox coverage of Muslim rioting in France not be described as "Muslim" rioting in France, a boast News Corp. has never denied. This week, security analyst Joseph Trento, in light of recent negotiations between Alwaleed and Murdoch, mused online whether his own recent interview on "Fox & Friends" didn't appear in Fox's online video cache because he had told host Steve Ducey that "Saudi Arabian money was still financing al-Qaida." The doubt itself is damaging.

Meanwhile, spokesmen for terrorism-linked and Alwaleed-endowed CAIR still appear on Fox shows, for example, while Dave Gaubatz and Paul Sperry, likely Fox guests as conservative authors of the sleeper-hit book "Muslim Mafia" (an expose of CAIR and the Muslim Brotherhood), get zero airtime. The more important question becomes: How does Alwaleed's stake in News Corp. affect what Fox News doesn't cover?

FOX News rebukes Wilders and anti-Islamization

3/12/10

When Glenn Beck, Charles Krauthammer and Bill Kristol, each from their respective Fox News perches, branded Dutch political phenom Geert Wilders as beyond the political pale, it was shocking and outrageous for several reasons. One: I've grown used to Fox News and all other media ignoring not just the Wilders story but also the cultural story of the century, the Islamization of Europe. Something Wilders, a great admirer of Ronald Reagan and a committed supporter of Israel, is dedicated to halting and reversing. The survival instinct of the Dutch, who, earlier this month gave unprecedented electoral victories to Wilders and his party, is a strong indicator that this civilizational transformation is not irreversible. But covering the Islamization of Europe usually makes for bad news. Worse, according to the powers-that-be, is that even halfway competent reporting on the subject puts Islam in a bad light as it exposes what happens to Western-style liberty when Muslims enter a host country in sufficient numbers to extend sharia (Islamic law).

Better safe (politically correct) than sorry (subject to potential boycott or worse), our media prefer, frittering away precious powers afforded by the First Amendment. This motto seems to go double at Fox ever since Rupert Murdoch sold what is now a 7-percent stake of Fox's parent company, News Corp., to a scion of the sharia-dictatorship of Saudi Arabia, Prince Alwaleed bin Talal. For the Fox commentators, supposedly punditry's bulwark of Western values, to bring it up just to slap it down — and without factual care (to say the least) — was disappointing but also irresponsible.

Two: Readers may recall that I've questioned Talal's ownership stake before. This week, much too synergistically, after Murdoch's and Talal's all-stars warned Fox viewers about the Wilders threat, in effect, to Islam in Europe, Murdoch was in Abu Dhabi, along with Talal and 400 other media executives, announcing that key components of the News Corp. empire were moving into the Islamic world, into the United Arab Emirates.

Remember the UAE, notorious for enslaving Bangladeshi boys as camel jockeys, support of Hamas? It was the UAE whose ministers and princes were hunting with Osama bin Laden, preventing the Clinton White House from taking a cruise missile shot at the jihad kingpin. It was the UAE that was one of three countries (Saudi Arabia and Pakistan) to recognize the Taliban. And it was the UAE's Dubai Ports World that was thwarted in a pre-tea-party populist uproar about these connections and more. (More than half of the 9/11 hijackers, including two UAE citizens, were deployed to the United States from Dubai.) The UAE is "not free" now, says Freedom House, and never has been.

What impact does the Islamization of News Corp. have on "fair and balanced" news stateside? I don't know. But when one of the big bosses is a Saudi prince, it doesn't exactly encourage reporters to doodle spoofs of the Danish Motoons on their notepads, let alone engage in "offensive," PC-busting debate in the news room or on the air.

Three: Regardless of cause or effect, the fact remains that in classifying Wilders as a fascist (Beck), denouncing his views as "extreme, radical and wrong" (Krauthammer), and slandering him as a "demagogue" (Kristol), Fox's opinion-leaders expressed themselves in terms that surely thrilled not just Murdoch's Islamic prince-cronies, but also the 57-nation Organization of the Islamic Conference (OIC). This is the organization driving the advance of sharia in the world, as, for example, at the United Nations, where it leads an endless campaign to outlaw all criticism of Islam — such as Wilders' — under the PC-sensitive rubric of banning "defamation of religion."

Now, one thing you don't want to do in this life is thrill the OIC, particularly on its smooth drive to extend sharia that is only now, according to OIC plan, unexpectedly blocked by Geert Wilders. And it certainly hurts to see Fox pushing in the wrong direction.

Did Saudi Prince Buy Fox's Silence?

2/16/12

Have you heard about the 23-year-old Saudi journalist who tweeted an imaginary conversation with Muhammad? It went something like this: He loved Muhammad, he hated Muhammad, he couldn't understand Muhammad, he wasn't going to pray for Muhammad. If this isn't exactly a disquisition on faith and doubt a la "The Brothers Karamazov," remember, we're just talking Twitter.

If you haven't heard of this young man, whose name is Hamza Kashgari, it could be because you're watching too much Fox News. As of this writing, almost a week after the Kashgari story broke, I haven't found a single story about it at the Fox News website. (You try: www.foxnews.com.) Meanwhile, CBS, NBC, ABC, MSNBC and CNN have all reported the Kashgari story, clueing in their viewers on how far totalitarian Islam, Saudi style, will go to exert its control over the human spirit. But not Fox.

Say — you don't suppose the fact that Prince Alwaleed bin Talal owns the second-largest block of stock (7 percent) in News Corp., Fox News' parent company, not to mention a new $300 million stake in Twitter (almost 4 percent), has anything to do with Fox's silence on this Saudi black eye of a story? After all, it was Saudi dictator King Abdullah — Alwaleed's uncle — whom press accounts credit with ordering the tweeting journalist's hot pursuit and imprisonment. And it is Saudi Arabia's adherence to Islamic limits on free speech that is driving Kashgari's ordeal.

Maybe it has become institutional Fox thinking to let such news slide for fear of offending the Saudi prince — or for fear of risking the kind of exposure that might remind viewers of Fox's connections to Saudi regime interests via Alwaleed.

As I've argued in the past, it is these connections that make it incumbent upon News Corp. to register as a foreign agent. (So, too, should universities that accept Saudi and other Islamic millions to open departments of Islamic studies.) Fox's silence on this bell-ringer of a story reinforces the sneaking suspicion that, conscious or not, there may be an Alwaleed effect on Fox coverage which, in a conflict of interest, actually serves the House of Saud before Fox viewers.

Prediction: I don't believe Hamza Kashgari will be executed or even face hard time for his Twitter "blasphemy." Despite widespread enthusiasm for his demise among his fellow Saudis — at last count, a Facebook page titled "The Saudi People Demand Hamza Kashgari's Execution" had a whopping 23,000 members — I'm guessing Kashgari's already publicized repentance will be accepted by Saudi poobahs. The crisis will likely end in a gesture of royal magnanimousness. The new "moderation" of the Kingdom — see, they don't kill you for tweeting! -- will become the story of the day, maybe even "fair and balanced" enough for Fox News to cover it.

That would make it a win-win situation, at least when it comes to Islamic law enforcement: Saudi Arabia gets international "modernization" brownie points, and no one dares break Shariah inside the country anyway, particularly given the bloodthirsty scorn of the Saudi public. (Remember that Facebook community of execution-for-"blasphemy" enthusiasts.) No "blasphemy," no "defamation," no problem.

This same issue is part of a much larger story, a terrifying point of parley between the Islamic world, as represented by the Saudi-based Organization of Islamic Cooperation (OIC), and the Free World, as led, still, by the USA. Why terrifying? Any accommodation of Islamic so-called blasphemy law is an unconstitutional erosion of American free speech.

I'm mortified to report that the USA, as represented by Secretary of State Hillary Clinton, is working itself into sync with the Saudi, OIC and, apparently, Fox position that silence on Islam is golden. Last summer, Clinton, while meeting with the OIC in Turkey (where they throw journalists who cross the state in jail) to discuss "defamation" of Islam, promoted a de facto censorship of Islam's critics by calling for "some old-fashioned techniques of peer pressure and shaming, so that people don't feel that they have the support to do what we abhor."

Funny, but I don't think Fox covered the secretary of state's menacing comments about free speech. Not even a tweet's worth.

Is Saudi prince steering News Corp. coverage?

1/11/13

Ever since Al Gore sold Current TV to Al Jazeera, the network founded and funded by the oil-rich emirate of Qatar, the former vice president has drawn continuous fire in conservative media. Fox News, the New York Post and The Wall Street Journal, for example, have all castigated Gore, a man of the Left and leading avatar of "global warming," for such hypocrisies as timing the deal to avoid Lefty tax hikes and bagging $100 million in greenhouse-gas money.

These same news outlets share something else in common: They all belong to Rupert Murdoch's News Corp. That means they also belong to Saudi Prince Alwaleed bin Talal.

Alwaleed owns the largest chunk of News Corp. stock outside the Murdoch family. Shortly after his purchase of 5.5 percent of News Corp. voting shares in 2005, Alwaleed gave a speech that made it clear just what he had bought. As noted in The (U.K.) Guardian, Alwaleed told an audience in Dubai that it took just one phone call to Rupert Murdoch — "speaking not as a shareholder but as a viewer," Alwaleed said — to get the Fox News crawl reporting "Muslim riots" in France changed to "civil riots."

This didn't make the "Muslim" riots go away, but Alwaleed managed to fog our perception of them. With a phone call, the Saudi prince eliminated the peculiarly Islamic character of the unprecedented French street violence for both the viewers at home and, more significantly, for the journalists behind the scenes. When little owner doesn't want "Muslim" rioting identified and big owner agrees, it sets a marker for employees. Alwaleed's stake, by the way, is now 7 percent.

We can only speculate on what other acts of influence this nephew of the Saudi dictator might have since imposed on Fox News and other News Corp. properties. (I have long argued that News Corp. should register as a foreign agent, due to the stock owned by a senior member of the Saudi ruling dynasty.) Alwaleed hasn't shared any other editorial exploits with the public. But that opening act of eliminating key information from News Corp.'s coverage of Islamic news might well have set a pattern of omission.

Recently, such a pattern of omission in News Corp.'s coverage of the Gore-Al Jazeera deal seems evident. I say "seems," because I can't be entirely certain that I haven't missed something in my research. But judging from online searches of news stories and audio transcripts, two salient points are missing from at least the main body of News Corp.'s coverage.

One is reference to the noticeable alignment of Al Jazeera with the Muslim Brotherhood, the global Islamic movement whose motto is, "The Koran is our law; jihad is our way; dying in the way of Allah is our highest hope." The second (with an exception noted below) is reference to Al Jazeera's superstar host and ideological lodestar, Yusuf al-Qaradawi, a leading Muslim Brotherhood figure. The influence of al-Qaradawi at the network and in Qatar — where, according to Freedom House's 2012 press report, it is against the law for journalists to criticize the Qatari government, the ruling family or Islam — can hardly be overestimated.

Strange omission? This relationship between the Qatari-controlled network and the Muslim Brotherhood organization has been observed for years. Back in 2007, for example, Steven Stalinsky reported in The New York Sun that various Arab commentators referred to Al Jazeera as "the Muslim Brotherhood channel" and the like. What's more, reference to the relationship appears at least in passing in coverage of the Gore deal at mainstream media sites such as USA Today and the Seattle Times. More discussion is available at some conservative outlets, including Rush Limbaugh and The Blaze. (Searches at Breitbart and the Washington Examiner, like News Corp. sites, yielded nothing on these same points. Call it, perhaps, "the Fox effect.")

Given the rise of Muslim Brotherhood parties in the revolutions of the so-called Arab Spring — undeviatingly cheered on by Al Jazeera — the network's Muslim Brotherhood connection, which extends to Al Jazeera's sponsors inside the Qatari ruling family, is a crucial point to miss. Especially when it seems to be missed across the board.

The same goes for failing to mention Al Jazeera's leading personality, Yusuf al-Qaradawi, in the Gore deal coverage. This longtime "spiritual guide" of the Muslim Brotherhood hosts one of Al Jazeera's most popular shows, "Sharia and Life." Among other poisonous pronouncements, al-Qaradawi has called for Americans in Iraq and Israelis everywhere to be targeted by terrorists ("martyrs") who would then find a place in Islamic paradise. Given Al Gore's refusal to sell his network to Glenn Beck's The Blaze TV due to political differences, Muslim Brother Al-Qaradawi and his Shariah ideology become highly relevant. Then again, maybe one man's news story is just another man's clipping on the cutting-room floor.

Meanwhile, the one story I found in News Corp. coverage of the Gore deal that mentions al-Qaradawi — a column by Gordon Crovitz —

neglected to note al-Qaradawi's place in the Muslim Brotherhood. Particularly given current events, this is a little like forgetting to mention that Hermann Goring was in the Nazi Party.

Could normal editorial discretion or plain ignorance be at work here? I suppose so. Still, there is that tie-in between News Corp. and the House of Saud to consider, a partnership I find more troubling than Gore's deal with the Qatari emirate. Not only does Alwaleed own a stake in News Corp., Murdoch owns an even more substantial stake (18.97 percent) in Alwaleed's Arabic media company Rotana.

Within the Alwaleed-Murdoch-Rotana galaxy is a 24-hour-Islamic outlet called Al Risala, which Alwaleed founded in 2006. The channel's director and popular "tele-Islamist" is Tareq Al-Suwaidan, widely reported to be a leader of the Muslim Brotherhood in Kuwait. The station's "Supreme Advisory Committee" includes Abdullah Omar Naseef, who, according to former federal prosecutor Andrew C. McCarthy, is "a major Muslim Brotherhood figure" involved in the financing of al-Qaida.

Al Risala, then, would seem to fit right into the Al Jazeera-Qaradawi-Muslim-Brotherhood lineup.

We know Alwaleed has influenced Fox editorial matters before. Could that Alwaleed influence – even his very presence – account for why News Corp. hasn't hit harder on the Muslim Brotherhood and al-Qaradawi angles of the Gore-Jazeera deal?

Obama

Obama skirts the 'L' word

2/8/08

Something went by in a blur on the road to Super Tuesday. The National Journal ranked Sen. Barack Obama the No. 1 liberal U.S. senator of 2007. Sen. Hillary Clinton came in somewhat less left-wing at No. 16.

Horrors. According to his press notices, Obama isn't supposed to be any kind of a liberal at all — let alone "Number One" — but rather the great non-partisan hand-holder and country re-maker. As in: "We (have to) decide to join hands and remake this country." (My response: Why? It's pretty well-made already.) Turns out he's not so non-partisan after all, at least not according to the, well, non-partisan criteria first devised by the National Journal back in 1981.

Not that you have to be a political scientist to figure this out. Just take a look at Obama's endorsements from MoveOn.Org, Ted Kennedy and more than 80 lawyers representing detainees at Guantanamo Bay. Or his positions on illegal aliens, raising taxes on "the wealthy" or talking Muslim world leaders into taking our side in the "war on terror" (despite the fact that some of them are busy abetting or even waging that same war against us).

Once upon a time, such positions could only be staked out on the far left. With Obama occupying them, however, they become the dreamy landscape of non-partisan epiphany. As the Washington Post campaign blog The Trail noted: "(His) is a platform that, delivered by others, might well be viewed as hewing to long-standing, traditional liberal notions. Yet Obama wraps it into his message of national transformation, making it sound part of a whole new package, and by the time he gets to his trademark crescendo conclusion, every person in the arena is standing

..."

Guess it's not easy to stand and think "liberal" at the same time — especially with trademark crescendos dancing in your head. The disconnect has served the Obama camp well, allowing it to run far on thin and gaseous vapors of non-partisan "hope" and "change." That's why nobody at Obama headquarters was enthused by Obama's solid ideological victory as Top Senate Liberal for his votes as a leading anti-war senator supporting the withdrawal of American troops from Iraq, amnesty for illegal aliens, and a host of liberal initiatives on health care, education, energy and the budget. Such a record sounds downright McGovernesque. But don't mention that out loud. After all, Barack Obama is a presidential candidate who likes to say, "There's not a liberal America and a conservative America — there is the United States of America." What if it got out that there is also a very liberal Barack Obama?

We don't know the answer to that, because it is "hope" and "change," not liberalism, that Obama is supposed to stand for. Maybe that's why, as Obama spokeswoman Jen Psaki told the National Journal, Obama is "the only candidate who's shown the ability to appeal to Republicans and the ability to appeal to independents."

The fact is, being Top Senate Liberal isn't part of the official narrative of the Obama movement. And the campaign seems to want to keep it that way.

Dismissing the National Journal senate rankings, Obama spokesman Bill Burton told ABC: "The tendency of Washington to apply a misleading label to every person and idea is just one of the many things we need to change about how things operate inside the Beltway."

Here's hoping we never find out how an Obama administration would "change" freedom of labeling. But misleading? On the contrary, "liberal" aptly describes Obama's point of view (not to mention Mrs. Clinton's). But notice the difference between Republicans and Democrats when it comes to political labels.

Republicans struggle over who will wear the "conservative" mantle, while Democrats strike a "Who, me?" pose when it comes to carrying the "liberal" flag. The National Journal put it this way: both Democratic presidential contenders "have emphasized their liberal policy positions. But neither has embraced the liberal label the way Republican presidential candidates have proudly stamped themselves conservatives."

This goes, of course, for John McCain, whose claims to conservatism are unconvincing to many conservatives. Incidentally, the National Journal doesn't help much in this regard. Turns out McCain missed too many votes in 2007 to score a ranking. I'd say that's lucky for him, as he grabs at that conservative mantle. He might have given Sens. Clinton and Obama some pretty stiff competition.

Obama's truthiness about Farrakhan

3/1/08

Transfixed by the two-candidate "horse race," maybe we didn't focus precisely on what happened in the home stretch of the last Democratic debate when Barack Obama tried to pick and nuance his way through a straight-ahead question from MSNBC's Tim Russert.

Q: Do you accept the support of Louis Farrakhan?

The question arose because the longtime racist and anti-Semitic leader of the racist and anti-Semitic Nation of Islam had delivered a two-hour speech devoted mainly to praising Obama's candidacy.

Here is Obama's answer: "You know, I have been very clear in my denunciation of Minister Farrakhan's anti-Semitic comments. I think they are unacceptable and reprehensible. I did not solicit this support. He expressed pride in an African-American who seems to be bringing the country together. I obviously can't censor him, but it is not support that I sought. And we're not doing anything, I assure you, formally or informally, with Minister Farrakhan."

"Minister" Farrakhan? The honorific seems unduly deferential applied to a demagogue who, just to recall a few pearls of his noxiousness, has labeled Judaism a "gutter religion," said "the white man" is "the anti-Christ," and suggested the post-Katrina failure of the New Orleans levees was a "white" plot to flood "black" neighborhoods. But what is most important here is to note Obama's failure to take a stand on Farrakhan support: "I obviously can't censor him" — whether Obama could censor him wasn't the question — "but it is not support I sought."

Kind of tepid, no? Russert tried again.

Q: Do you reject his support?

Here is Obama's second answer. "Well, Tim, you know, I can't say to somebody that he can't say that he thinks I'm a good guy." (This, of course, was just another way of saying Obama couldn't censor Farrakhan.) The presidential candidate continued: "You know, I — you know, I — I have been very clear in my denunciations of him and his past statements, and I think that indicates to the American people what my stance is on those comments."

Again, Russert hadn't asked Obama about "his stance" on "those comments." The question was about Farrakhan as a package deal. Did Obama accept his support? Did Obama reject his support?

So far, no answer. And this was incredible. Before a national audience, Obama, whose very candidacy has come to symbolize a promise of "post-racial" "unity" in America, failed to reject the support of arguably the most racist and divisive figure in America.

Russert tried another tack, this time raising the ties between

Farrakhan and Obama's pastor, the Rev. Jeremiah A. Wright Jr. of Chicago's Trinity United Church. Russert noted that Wright, whom Obama has called his "spiritual mentor" and "sounding board," has not only traveled with Farrakhan to visit Moammar Gadhafi in Libya — some junket. Wright has also said that Farrakhan "epitomized greatness." Just last year, Wright's church, known for a creed aptly described as black separatist, bestowed on Farrakhan the Rev. Dr. Jeremiah A. Wright Jr. Lifetime Achievement Trumpeteer award.

Does the Farrakhan-Wright relationship explain the reason Obama appeared unwilling to denounce Farrakhan altogether — not just his more notorious statements? Alas, such a question remained unasked. Obama launched into a lengthy discussion about Israel's security ("sacrosanct"), the civil rights movement, even Dr. Martin Luther King Jr.'s birthday, without mentioning Farrakhan or Wright again.

None of which escaped his opponent's notice. "I just want to add something here," Hillary Clinton said. She explained that under similar circumstances during her first Senate race in New York she had repudiated the support of a political party she described as anti-Semitic. "I rejected it," Clinton said in one of her genuinely better debating points. "I said that it would not be anything I would be comfortable with ... I have no doubt that everything that Barack just said is absolutely sincere. But I just think, we've got to be even stronger."

Clearly, Obama had to say something stronger. So he did: "Tim, I have to say I don't see a difference between denouncing and rejecting. ... But if the word 'reject' Sen. Clinton feels is stronger than the word 'denounce,' then I'm happy to concede the point, and I would reject and denounce."

One could ask, Reject what? Denounce what? But the more interesting question is why was it so hard for Senator Post-Racial Unity to reject Minister Racism and Divisiveness?

What if McCain had been palling around with a terrorist?

10/20/08

We interrupt regular column writing to ... imagine John McCain ahead in the polls.

Imagine that McCain had spent the last 20 years in the pews of a white supremacist church that supported an apartheid-like separationism from black people, and also that, until a few months ago, McCain had proudly claimed the church's white racist pastor as his "friend, mentor and pastor" — even taking the title of his best-selling

2006 memoir from one of this man's sermons. Imagine further that, in the 1990s, McCain had directed foundation funding toward a white-separatist educational program supported by this same pastor.

Now imagine McCain — this same imaginary McCain whose polls indicate imminent victory — had only lately left this church, brushing off his relationship with the racist pastor by pleading ignorance of the man's vile views.

All of these McCain hypotheticals, of course, are mirrored in Barack Obama realities related to his relationship with the Rev. Jeremiah "G—d—America" Wright. The foundation funding I refer to, detailed in a recent scoop by Stanley Kurtz, is the $200,000 that Obama, as chairman of the Chicago Annenberg Challenge foundation, approved for a local organization that promoted black separatism as taught by such Afrocentric theorists as Jacob Carruthers, who, Kurtz writes at National Review Online, sought to use "African-centered education to recreate a separatist universe within America, a kind of state-within-a-state." Carruthers, and many others from his organization, the Association for the Study of Classical African Civilizations (ASCAC), which, Kurtz writes, "takes as its mission the need to 'dismantle the European intellectual campaign to commit historicide against African peoples,' were featured speakers at Wright's church.

Interesting, no? Worth a question or two into Obama's more or less political relationship with Wright, no? Or views on Afrocentrism, no? Or into his media-honed reputation as the candidate of post-racial integration, no?

No.

Let me demonstrate why not by harkening back to our McCainian world of pretend for an unreality-check.

Imagine — and this may be the hardest thing to swallow — that the press corps (panting adjunct to this imaginary McCain campaign), assorted pundits, politicians and practically anyone else with a microphone or blog, say none of this matters. Or say it is "racist" to discuss these shocking facts. Weirder still, imagine that Obama, imaginary McCain's trailing opponent, says the very same thing — more than passing strange given the happenstance that Obama is black and thus a key symbol of the imaginary pastor's vicious animus.

It is mind games like these that we need to play on ourselves to puncture the bubble of complacency and conditioning that has swathed and protected Obama not merely from the consequences (as in voter-rejection) from his Jeremiah Wright relationship, but from his relationships with a veritable pantheon of anti-American extremists. A partial list includes the racist Jeremiah Wright, the radical William Ayers, the former PLO spokesman Rashid Khalidi, the redistributionist and voter-fraud-perpetrating ACORN, and the out-and-out socialist New

Party. These are the people and groups, from the farthest reaches of the anti-American left, that have shaped and driven this man who would be president.

Obama's association with the New Party is probably new to most readers. Despite person or persons unknown having engaged in the Stalinist technique of "scrubbing" (erasing) online New Party records that claim Obama as a New Party member, the blog politicallydrunk.blogspot.com has recently located documentation indicating Obama was indeed a member of the Chicago branch of this socialist party.

This may come as a big yawn to big media, but it is, as our little game of pretend shows, outrageous. Just imagine if McCain had once belonged to a far-right extremist party, and, naturally enough, had had his 1995 political coming-out party in the living room of the likes of Timothy McVeigh. Imagine, like ex-Weatherman William Ayers, that McVeigh's treasonous goals to destroy the U.S. government hadn't diminished over the years — indeed, that he called himself a "radical, rightist, small "f" fascist" the same year McCain's political career was launched in his home — but that he had merely abandoned violent means to revolution in favor of "educational reform."

(Ayers, of course, in real life, called himself a "radical, leftist, small 'c' communist" in 1995, the same year Obama debuted as a political candidate in Ayers' home. In 2006, with Venezuelan strongman Hugo Chavez looking on, he declared, "La educacion es revolucion.")

Now imagine that McCain had also served as the first chairman of McVeigh's foundation, distributing money to radical, rightist, small "f" fascist causes. (Again, this mirrors Obama's real-life gig as chairman of the Chicago Annenberg Challenge foundation that Ayers co-founded.)

Would the media and political consensus insist none of this mattered to voters? That it was "racist" or "negative" even to bring it up? And, further, that such a candidate's comfort with and receptivity to anti-American extremists was not an automatic disqualifier for the presidency?

The answer to all of these questions is "no." Indeed, it's a sure thing that a reflexive, righteous and widespread consensus against my imaginary candidate would have formed among the media and political establishment, thus disqualifying him from becoming his party's presidential nominee, let alone the next president of the United States....

We now return to regular programming.

Look who's endorsing Obama now

10/24/08

Colin Powell got all the airtime, sure, but his isn't the only Barack Obama endorsement worth talking about lately.

There was Ali Larijani, for example, the Hezbollah- and Hamas-supporting speaker of Iran's parliament, who voiced Iran's preference for a "more flexible and rational" Obama over John McCain — not that he got what you could call a media roll-out. Nor did America's own anti-white, anti-Jewish Louis Farrakhan, who recently heralded an Obama presidency as the coming age of the "the Messiah." There was a newsflash for fluffy-con endorsements at home and abroad, arcing and sputtering on a thin mix of elitism and naiveté, but virtually no one seems to have noticed an Obama endorsement that came in from the National Association of Muslim American Women (NAMAW).

Big yawn? Hardly. In its endorsement, the Columbus-based Muslim women's group described itself as "pro-family" and "pro-life." But, given the record of NAMAW chairwoman and CEO Anisa Abd el Fattah, it is also pro-Hamas.

As Patrick Poole has reported, Fattah has published Hamas-ian writings contending, for example, that Zionism "violates ... every norm of decency known to the human species." Fattah has also co-authored two books with Hamas spokesman and chief political adviser Ahmed Yousef ("The Agent: The Truth Behind the Anti-Muslim Campaign in America and Al-Aqsa Intifada"). And yes, that would be the same Ahmed Yousef, who, on behalf of Hamas, endorsed Barack Obama back in April.

Both Fattah and Yousef (who fled the country in 2005 to avoid prosecution in the terrorism-related Fawaz Damra trial) used to work for the United Association for Studies and Research (UASR), an innocuously named organization founded by Hamas chieftain Mousa abu Marzook that has been described as "the political command of Hamas in the United States." The UASR, along with an interlocking network of Islamic organizations, has been designated by the government as both an unindicted co-conspirator in the Holy Land Foundation terror-financing trial, and an affiliate of the Muslim Brotherhood, the Egyptian-founded organization that seeks to install the Sharia (Islamic law) worldwide. Other groups so designated include the Muslim American Society (MAS), which the government said was "founded as the overt arm of the Muslim Brotherhood in the United States," and the Council on American-Islamic Relations (CAIR), of which Fattah, it so happens, was a founding board member. (Fattah, according to her online biography, as Poole has noted, also helped develop the American Muslim Council, which was founded by convicted terrorist financier Abdurahman

Alamoudi.)

No candidate, of course, has control over what groups or persons decide to go public with endorsements. McCain, for example, recently received an endorsement from a jihadist blogger at an Al Qaeda linked Web site predicting that McCain's determination to fight global jihad would "exhaust" America, thus serving jihadist goals. It is also true that the Obama campaign has, for example, rejected Hamas support. But such endorsements should be weighed, and particularly when there is evidence the Obama campaign may have engaged in a quiet, if uneasy brand of "outreach" to such pro-jihad domestic groups as those listed above.

Earlier this month, several news organizations reported that Minha Husaini, the Obama campaign director of Muslim outreach, participated in a non-advertised September meeting in hotly contested Virginia with about 30 Muslim leaders. Among them were Nihad Awad of CAIR and Mahdi Bray of MAS — both leaders of groups the government has designated as unindicted co-conspirators and Muslim Brotherhood affiliates. Also present was Johari Abdul Malik, the imam of Dar Al-Hijrah Mosque, aka "the 9/11 mosque" because two of the 9/11 hijackers worshipped there. (So did Ahmed Omar Abu Ali, an Al Qaeda member now serving a 30-year sentence for plotting to assassinate President Bush, and also Hamas chieftain and UASR founder Mousa abu Marzook.)

Another person attending the meeting was Mazen Asbahi, the former Obama director of Muslim outreach who quickly resigned in early August after news broke about his ties to unindicted co-conspirators. This was not his first post-resignation campaign-related event. At a luncheon during the Democratic National Convention, Investor's Business Daily reported Asbahi as saying that his resignation was a "strategic decision," and "that he was participating in campaign conference calls on Muslim outreach."

The Obama campaign has pleaded ignorance concerning the September meeting, with campaign spokesman Ben LaBolt telling NBC News producer Jim Popkin that campaign staffers, including Husaini, wouldn't have "attended if they were aware of the complete list of attendees." The campaign had no comment on Asbahi's presence, and, oddly, wouldn't allow reporters speak with Muslim outreach director Husaini.

What are voters to make of this? Did Obama campaign staffers abandon the event on learning who was there? The meeting went on as scheduled. Did the campaign later denounce these controversial, to say the least, groups in media statements? Apparently not. One unidentified meeting participant told Popkin that "some in the Obama group knew ahead of time that top CAIR officials would be in attendance," adding:

"There was some hope it wouldn't get out" into the media.

That, of course, should never have concerned a campaign for whom media scrutiny resembles cupcake frosting. But "out" it is, thanks to a few journalists still on the job. If any questions remain, though, they are questions voters will have to answer for themselves.

You elected a man, not a moral judgment

11/07/08

If we really inhabited a "post-racial" world, the news of the week would be that a Democrat has won the White House. But since we don't inhabit such a world, there is much more to the news, even more than that an African-American, far-left Democrat has won the White House.

The New York Times' Thomas Friedman clued us in the morning after, waxing rhapsodic (or something): "And so it came to pass that on Nov. 4, 2008, shortly after 11 p.m. Eastern time, the American Civil War ended, as a black man — Barack Hussein Obama — won enough electoral votes to become president of the United States. A civil war that, in many ways, began at Bull Run, Va., on July 21, 1861, ended 147 years later via a ballot box in the very same state."

As befitting a Pulitzer-Prize winner, Friedman was only just warming up ("For nothing more symbolically illustrated the final chapter of America's Civil War than the fact that" blah blah...). But there were others taking up a similar battle cry. Madeleine M. Kunin, former governor of Vermont (and, as she also bills herself, eternal "first woman governor" of Vermont) declared at the online Huffington Post that the election of Barack Obama "is, in a sense, the culmination of Lincoln's quest — a more perfect union."

And, well, so it came to pass that in those earliest hours of the new era that Spike Lee went on MSNBC to tell us will heretofore be known as AB (After Barack, natch, with all past millennia relegated to BB, Before Barack), the Civil War ended, and Lincoln's "more perfect union" was achieved. What next — or, perhaps, why bother? That is, who could ask for anything more?

One answer is Menachem Rosensaft, who, elsewhere on Huffpo, pushed the election results into a somewhat different cosmic direction. "On Nov. 4, 2008, at 11 pm," he wrote, "Robert Kennedy finally won."

I rubbed my eyes but Rosensaft continued: "Forty years after his assassination shattered dreams and brought his quest to change America to a sudden, brutal halt, Robert Kennedy reached the goal that had been denied him in life."

Now I was starting to get it. Candidate Obama, whom the media permitted to remain a political cipher behind the flowing messiah robes, is now President-Elect Obama, magic mirror of historical redress.

No doubt this would present where's-the-beef style problems for the average president, but Obama isn't destined to be the average president — or so we have been led to believe. Or, rather, so we have led ourselves to believe.

In a particularly trenchant post-election column, author Shelby Steele explained how it was that a candidate he describes as "quite unremarkable" regarding public policy (an amalgam of "old-fashioned Keynesianism" and "recycled Great Society") was able, first, "to project an idealized vision of post-racial America," and then "have that vision define political decency."

Once these visions were set, Steele writes, "a failure to support Obama politically became a failure of decency."

In this way, the white voters who became Obama's political base were vested in the success of Obama's vision — or, rather, in the vision of Obama's success. Longing to "escape the stigma of racism," as Steele calls it, white voters became "enchanted" with Obama because their support for him provided evidence and certification of their own now self-evident state of "post-racial" enlightenment.

But, as Steele further explains, there's an inherent contradiction to this unusual, if not historically unique, relationship. "When whites — especially today's younger generation — proudly support Obama for his post-racialism, they unwittingly embrace race as their primary motivation. They think and act racially, not post-racially. The point is that a post-racial society ... seduces whites with a vision of the racial innocence precisely to coerce them into acting out of a racial motivation. A real post-racialist ... would not care about displaying or documenting his racial innocence. Such a person would evaluate Obama politically rather than culturally."

Bingo. Here Steel demystifies the great and perplexing divide between those who care supremely about documenting and displaying their own "racial innocence" — and I would put the mainstream media, Obama voters and most politicians including John McCain into that category — and those who don't. These latter "real post-racialists" see Obama as a man, not an icon, as a politician who emerged from a hotbed of anti-American radicalism, not a sacred totem of enlightenment better suited to a glass case at the Smithsonian than the boisterous tussle of the political arena.

For almost two years, Obama has been, in Steele's words, evaluated culturally. This has resulted in reverential media non-coverage and now post-election judgments and metaphors that are already beginning to defy satire. Of course, Barack Obama didn't end the Civil War, isn't the reincarnation of RFK, and benefits from, but didn't bring about, the long-entrenched social changes that facilitated his political rise. As he now heads to the White House, it's crucial that he finally be regarded as a politician, not a messiah, and as a man, not a moral judgment. Otherwise, the cultural juggernaut he seems likely to unleash will be unstoppable.

Just answer the Hil question, Mr. President-elect

12/5/08

Interesting thing happened this week. Somebody in the mainstream media (MSM) actually asked President-elect Barack Obama a good question. It concerned how Obama could square his campaign attacks on Hillary Clinton's foreign policy with his selecting her as secretary of state. Let's just say Obama didn't much like this new experience.

But besides making history as a bout of insubordination against the praetorian guardlike duties of the Obamedia, the question was also newsworthy enough to kick off a column by Dana Milbank in the Washington Post. Milbank set it up this way:

"Peter Baker of the New York Times pointed out to Obama that he once held a different view of his nominee to be secretary of state. 'You belittled her travels around the world, equating it to having teas with foreign leaders,' Baker recalled. 'And your new White House counsel said that her resume was grossly exaggerated when it came to foreign policy. I'm wondering whether you can talk about the evolution of your views of your credentials since the spring.'"

Baker would ultimately buff the edges of the resulting give-and-take with Obama in his article — this was, after all, the New Obama Times — but Milbank, thankfully, retained the verbatim sharpness:

"'Well, I mean, I think —' Obama began. 'This is fun for the press to try to stir up whatever quotes were generated during the course of the campaign.'

"'They're your quotes, sir,' Baker pointed out.

"'No, I understand. And you're having fun,' Obama continued. 'And there's nothing wrong with that. I'm not faulting that.'"

Milbank placed this exchange in the context of the return on the Clintonistas, who, at last count, will hold nine key positions in the Obama White House. "Obama," Milbank wrote, "who campaigned against the Clinton way of doing things is now engaged in the veritable restoration of the Clinton administration."

But something deeper and more serious than personnel decisions is on display here. What is revealed is Obama's tactical denigration of a basic, legitimate and even screamingly obvious question as so much "fun" that he, the serious new president, may disregard and deride as frivolous.

The roll-the-tape, clip-file fact is, however, candidate Obama belittled candidate Clinton's foreign policy judgment and experience throughout the primary season. Any reporter with the minimal moxie to ask the president-elect why he would now decide to make Clinton the face of American foreign policy is simply (barely) doing his job.

But even this journalistic ABC is debatable in today's Obamedia. Time magazine's Joe Klein, while traveling abroad ("I'm in Europe on my way to Afghanistan"), was moved to blog against the "inanity" of the Obama-Hillary press conference questions, particularly the Baker question. Klein asked:

"What sort of journalist expects the president-elect to tell the 'inside story' of how he selected Hillary Clinton? (Those sorts of stories," he continued, "if told at all, are wrenched from aides on background — and reported only after consulting multiple sources.) And what's the point of raising the nasty things Obama and Clinton said about each other during the primaries? Did the reporter expect Obama to say, 'Well, I still believe her resume is overblown, that's why I appointed her ... oh, and by the way, she still thinks it's dumb to talk to the Iranians without preconditions.'"

This is nothing less than breathtaking. Because, as Klein has effectively admitted, there is no plausible, logical or even grace-saving answer to the why-Hillary question, Klein sees no reason at all to ask it. This hyper-protective rationale opens a window onto a mindset that has long baffled me: Reporters like Klein simply don't want to put politicians like Obama (or, for that matter, Clinton) on the spot. Their litmus test appears to be: If it doesn't promise a good Obama answer, it's not a good Obama question. Indeed, according to Klein, there were much "better" questions reporters could have asked at that same Obama-Hillary press conference, a few of which he thoughtfully provided, including:

"Are you still going to call it the Global War on Terror?"

"What are you going to do about Robert Gates's staff of Bush administration holdovers?"

"Could you give us a better sense of what the vice president's role will be in your Administration?"

Is he kidding?

Let's just say these aren't exactly queries born of zapping neurons, let alone a detectable pulse.

Elsewhere in the MSM, CNN's Campbell Brown of "No Bias, No Bull" reacted to the Obama-Baker exchange with far more lively sarcasm and fervor.

"I mean, really," Brown said, "how silly of that reporter to dare ask you, Mr. President-Elect, how it is that you completely mocked Hillary Clinton's foreign policy experience just a few months ago, and yet today, you think there is no one more qualified than she to lead your foreign policy team." Brown went on to nail Obama's "fun" response as "an attempt to delegitimize" the question.

"But it is a legitimate question," she continued, adding: "Annoying questions are about more than just the press 'having fun.' Annoying questions are about the press doing its job and the people's right to know."

Could this mark the decline of Obamedia-mania? Don't hold your breath. Paradoxically, though, even as the conservative punditry glows with a strange rapture over President-elect Obama's emerging Cabinet, there is at least a limited revolt in progress among the MSM.

Of course, we still don't have an answer to that one good question.

President's stimulus plan is an Obamanation

1/23/09

"That we are in the midst of a crisis is well understood," President Barack Obama told the nation on Inauguration Day. The president can say that again, and no doubt will. But the "crisis" itself is anything but well understood.

What we know for certain is that on or around Sept. 18 — oddly enough, as AIM's Cliff Kincaid has pointed out, during the polling high point of John McCain's pathetic presidential campaign — Bush administration Treasury Secretary Henry Paulson convinced former President Bush to abandon all remaining free-market principles and come up with hundreds of billions of bailout dollars from Congress. This not only saved Paulson's "buddies on Wall Street," as CNN's Lou Dobbs put it (not to mention Chinese interests, as Kincaid notes), but also endowed George W. Bush with the unexpected legacy of kick-starting the socialization of the U.S. economy.

We have been in "crisis" ever since, and, despite massive government interventions, markets remain what they call volatile. But mysteries abound. Maybe chief among them a set of September statements by Bush about the possibility that the point of crisis had been precipitated by what he called "illegal market manipulation." As Kincaid asks, "By whom or what? The President didn't say."

Nor has anyone else. This has left tantalizing questions hanging. Alas, curiosity seems to be a casualty of the crisis — or at least of our media-churned crisis mode, a condition that more closely resembles panic.

Still, such a state gets results, which is surely what White House Chief of Staff Rahm Emanuel meant in November when he said, "You never want a serious crisis to go to waste." Such panic passed the Bush bailout bills in October, it boosted Obama's presidential campaign in November, and it now promises to drive forward Obama's colossal expansion of the Bush bailout strategy, lately euphemistically rebranded as the new president's "American Recovery and Reinvestment Plan."

A question for Obama, then, becomes, how does he maintain a national state of lightly constrained but motivating hysteria? Talking about it helps, as he did on Inauguration Day. The new president didn't simply note our understanding of being "in the midst of a crisis." No, he actually compared our current economic woes to the extremis and near-dissolution of the nascent nation in the its very first winter of war "when," as Barack Obama put it, "the snow was stained with blood." Your 401K plan has taken a hit? Welcome to Valley Forge.

Not surprisingly, The New York Times headline the following day was typical: "Obama Takes Oath and Nation in Crisis Embraces the Moment." But there was another attention-getting headline in that same Times edition, this one on the business page. No, not the story titled "Bank Crisis Deepens: No Quick Fix Likely from Obama Team," a headline that ingeniously gives both juice to the crisis and time to the Obama team. Rather, the column next to it was titled, "It's Bad, But 1982 Was Worse."

What's that? Times writer David Leonhardt, having solicited what he called a "broad measure of the job market ... stretching back to 1970" from economists at the Bureau of Labor Statistics, comes to a shocking conclusion. His research, he writes, "shows, for starters, that the economy is not yet as bad as it was in the early 1980s. It's not even that close to being as bad. The ranks of the unemployed and underemployed, controlling for the size of the population, were much larger in 1982 than today."

Other "indicators of crisis," as Obama called them in his inaugural, were worse back then as well. "Home sales," Leonhardt writes, at their worst in 1982, "were 30 percent lower than they are even now." Additionally, inflation was in double digits, as was the prime interest rate, which peaked at 21.5 percent.

I found myself wondering how Ronald Reagan, entering office in 1981 with high inflation (12 percent) and unemployment (7.5 percent) higher than today (7.2 percent), and a contracting GDP approached hard times. In what turned out to be his first inaugural address, he, too, used the word "crisis" to describe "the economic ills" Americans were suffering. Noting that these ills were a long time coming and wouldn't go away "in days, weeks or months," he said: "But they will go away.

They will go away because we, as Americans, have the capacity now, as we have had in the past, to do whatever needs to be done to preserve this last and greatest bastion of freedom."

"In this present crisis," he continued, "government is not the solution to our problem."

There's a twist. In this present crisis, according to the Obama administration and its stimulus-package trillions, government isn't just the solution, it's our only hope.

That's change for you.

Is this the job of the president of the United States?

1/30/09

It all just went by in a flash: The very first TV interview Barack Obama gave as president went to Saudi — backed, Dubai-based Al-Arabiya television. Missed it? The interview aired too late Monday night to make the morning papers (in most of the United States, anyway), transforming its initial burst of coverage into a second-day follow-up story (at least in the United States). It was as if the people (Americans) who put Obama into office were so much, well, chopped liver.

Is that halal? Couldn't say. But the target audience for this first Obama interview was anything but kosher. The whole event, however, was a huge surprise.

According to Time magazine, Al-Arabiya reporter "(Hisham) Melhem's bosses in Dubai got a feeler from the White House on Sunday." That image alone — a White House "feeler" to "bosses in Dubai" is sci-fi fantastic. That is, it's easy to see why Obama would bypass Fox News, for example, but how could he do this to his Main Squeeze Media (MSM)?

On Monday, the White House contacted the Washington bureau of Al-Arabiya, but even then Melhem wasn't expecting anything greater than an interview with the new envoy to the Middle East, George Mitchell. "Would you like to chat with the president about 5 p.m. today?" a White House caller asked the reporter. And that was how this precedent-shattering interview came about.

But why did it come about? I'm guessing Barack Now-You-See-Hussein-Now-You-Don't Obama chose to sit down for this first interview before the Muslim world for an important reason. He wanted to appeal to what he seems to regard as his new constituency.

No kidding. Obama spoke quite deliberately about the requirements of his new "job" as commander in chief, many of which are unprecedented. "My job is to communicate the fact that the United States has a stake in the well-being of the Muslim world, that the language has to be the language of respect."

That's the job of the president of the United States?

"I have Muslim members of my family. I have lived in Muslim countries," Obama continued, simply speaking about his Islamic connections, indulging in what he condemned as "scare tactics" on the campaign trail. Now these connections are job credentials. "My job is to communicate to the American people that the Muslim world is filled with extraordinary people who simply want to live their lives and see their children live better lives."

That's the job of the president of the United States?

Obama continued. "My job to the Muslim world is to communicate that the Americans are not your enemy. We sometimes make mistakes. We have not been perfect. But if you look at the track record — as you say, America was not born as a colonial power — and that the same respect and partnership that America had with the Muslim world as recently as 20 or 30 years ago, there's no reason why we can't restore that."

What golden age of American-Islamic "respect and partnership" (circa 1979 or 1989) Obama is talking about I have no idea. But mark his words to describe Islam and the United States: "People who just want to see their children live better lives" versus a country that isn't "perfect" and sometimes makes "mistakes." This is one reprehensible way for an American president to frame the relationship between the repressive, jihad-exporting Sharia cultures of Islam and the liberty-and-justice-for-all-based USA.

"I'm not going to agree with everything that some Muslim leader may say, or what's on a television station in the Arab world," he continued, quite possibly but also quite opaquely referring to the genocidal yearnings and hatreds expressed from Iran to Syria to the Palestinian Authority by both leadership and state-run media. "But I think that what you'll see is somebody who is listening, who is respectful" — there's that word again — "and who is trying to promote the interests not just of the United States, but also ordinary people who right now are suffering from poverty and a lack of opportunity. I want to make sure I am speaking to them as well."

This wasn't just one of those beacon-of-freedom pep talks U.S. presidents have given in the past. This was something different. Indeed, not since Napoleon has a leader of a Western superpower made so unabashed a political pitch to the people of the Muslim world.

Commenting on CNN, Islam apologist Reza Aslan called himself "giddy" over the interview, explaining: Obama "is essentially setting himself up as a bridge between the Muslim world, between the United

States and the Middle East. It's a grand gesture, and I think it's going to be taken very well."

In the Muslim world, anyway. But again, that's precisely where Obama was aiming. At one point, the interviewer mentioned Osama bin Laden and his henchman Ayman al-Zawahiri.

"They seem nervous," Obama interjected.

When asked why they should be "more nervous," the president replied: "Well, I think that when you look at the rhetoric they've been using against me before I even took office, what that tells me is that their ideas are bankrupt."

Excuse me, Mr. President: You mean before they used rhetoric against you, their ideas were not bankrupt? But I digress. What's worth noting here is the possible glimmering of a presidential inference that he, Barack Hussein Obama, poses an alternative to Al Qaeda in the eyes of the Muslim world. (Mehlem insists Obama doesn't put Hamas and Hezbollah in the same category as Al Qaeda.)

Obama continued: "There's no actions that they've taken that, say, a child in the Muslim world is getting a better education because of them, or has better health care because of them. ... And over time, I think the Muslim world has recognized that that path is leading no place, except more death and destruction."

Mehlem later interpreted these comments as I did above — as the Obama alternative to Al Qaeda for Muslims. As Mehlem put it to theatlantic.com, "He's closing down Guantanamo, sending Mitchell, pulling out of Iraq, and ... I hope he would show Palestinians and Israelis tough love. Do you want to tell me that bin Laden and all these nuts" — excluding Hamas and Hezbollah, in Mehlem's eyes — "are not going to be nervous about him?"

In other words, the new president of the United States is vying for the affections of the Muslim world, and this is making jihadists "nervous." Aslan's comments seemed to underscore this same point. "I'm sure that wherever Zawahiri and bin Laden are right now, they're scrambling to try to figure out a way to answer this comment. When the president of the United States says, 'My family is Muslim,' what are you supposed to respond to that? How do you — how do you criticize that?"

I'll agree that it does tend to leave one speechless.

Churchill, Obama and Bush

3/6/09

Even before Barack Obama was inaugurated, the question of what to do with the bust of Winston Churchill on display in the Oval Office arose. The valuable bronze by Sir Jacob Epstein had been loaned by the

British government to George W. Bush in mid-2001 — before Sept. 11, contrary to recent reports — and had gazed with weary wisdom over the Oval Office ever since. Not that Winnie was alone.

Busts of Lincoln and Eisenhower rounded out the trio of wartime leaders President Bush had chosen to watch over him at work even when the nation was at peace.

The Lincoln bust remains in the Obama Oval Office. I haven't received definitive word on the fate of the Eisenhower bust, but I strongly suspect it's gone.

So, definitely, is the Churchill bust, its unceremonial crating and return to the British Embassy generating a diplomatic flap and many mainly British news stories wondering, whither the "special relationship"?

There is some pathos to this reflexive plaint given that what makes this relationship special of late is the fact that the CIA considers the likeliest source of a terrorist atrocity against the United States to be British citizens traveling on the visa-waiver program — British citizens of Pakistani descent, that is. Either way, the relationship is necessarily different when some potentially lethal percentage of the British citizenry is no longer what you could call on our side. Or should I say "our" side to denote the postmodern shambles of conceiving of sides, "ours" or "theirs"?

I don't mean to go abstruse on anyone, but there is a muddle here onto which the fate of the Churchill bronze shines a welcome if cauterizing beam. Indeed, packing up and returning Churchill to the British reveals more than the current state of U.S. ties with Britain. When President Obama declined the British offer to extend its loan, when President Obama indicated he wanted the bust out of the Oval Office, indeed, out of the White House, he sent a much more significant message.

Namely, he demonstrated how completely our world has turned.

The London Telegraph attempted an explanation:

"Churchill has less happy connotations for Mr. Obama than those American politicians who celebrate his wartime leadership. It was during Churchill's second premiership that Britain suppressed Kenya's Mau Mau rebellion. Among Kenyans allegedly tortured by the colonial regime included one Hussein Onyango Obama, the President's grandfather."

In other words, such family lore is supposed to render the British titan who roused the Free World against Nazi Germany and warned the Free World against the Communist U.S.S.R. as popular with the new president as Guantanamo Bay. For the record, though, the Mau Mau story is a historic impossibility, at least according to the known timeline of events. As noted by the blogger Papa Whiskey via the Jawa Report,

Obama's grandfather was jailed and tortured between 1949 and 1951. That's the story according to his widow, Obama's "Granny Sarah." Of course, Granny Sarah is also a primary source of the claim that Obama was born in Kenya, so who really knows? Obama himself has offered conflicting accounts in both cases.

In his memoir "Dreams of My Father," Obama describes his grandfather's detention as lasting "over six months" before he was found innocent (no mention of torture).

Whatever the case, Churchill didn't become prime minister for the second time until the end of 1951. The Mau Mau Rebellion didn't begin until the end of 1952, one year after Obama's grandfather's release.

It seems that what we are seeing in the return of the Churchill bust is less a personal vendetta against Churchill the man and more an open breach in the Western continuum out of which a new orientation toward the Third World will become increasingly apparent. Having achieved a Washington-like apotheosis in the American imagination, Churchill serves not only as the preeminent symbol of resolve, courage and faith against the enemies of Western civilization. He serves as a symbol of Western civilization, period. One of President Obama's first acts as president was to consign that symbol to a box and send it packing.

Somewhat complicating our understanding of the incident is the fact that even as George W. Bush may have retained the knickknacks of that same civilization, the 43rd president did more to break with it maybe than any previous president, certainly more than any previous Republican president. Yes, he ordered the military to war upon attack by Islamic terrorists on Sept. 11, 2001, to fight ill-defined "extremism." But Bush was first and always an internationalist, a globalist, with no national calling, for example, to stem the massive illegal Hispanic influx that has transformed large swaths of the United States by replacing their Western, English-speaking heritage with a Third World, Spanish-speaking culture.

In countless ways, President Obama is merely extending and expanding policies already initiated by his predecessor. From securing the border, which neither man has considered a priority, to securing a Palestinian state, which both men have considered a priority, to a shared belief in bailout packages that are nationalizing the economy, a neutered lexicon with which to address Islam, and legalizing millions of illegal aliens, there is in both leaders a transformational impulse, intensified and now recognized as radicalism in Obama's case. Does this Bush-Obama nexus represent the place where what we once called "white guilt" and "black rage" overlap? It's possible.

In the end, Bush kept Churchill in the room with him, perhaps to mollycoddle the Right. From the beginning, Obama did not, perhaps to avoid being mistaken for a "sellout." I refer to the new president's concern as expressed in his first memoir where he wrote about his maneuvering as an undergraduate at Occidental College:

"To avoid being mistaken for such a sellout, I chose my friends carefully: the more politically active black students, the foreign students, the Chicanos, the Marxist professors and structural feminists, and punk rock performance poets. We smoked cigarettes and wore leather jackets. At night in the dorms, we discussed neocolonialism, Frantz Fanon, Euro-centrism, and patriarchy. When we ground out our cigarettes in the hallway carpet, or set our stereos so loud that the walls began to shake, we were resisting Bourgeois society's stifling constraints. We weren't indifferent or careless or insecure. We were alienated."

Maybe he still is. Only now Barack Obama is taking that "alienation" out on the nation. Increasingly, this is how I interpret President Obama's open, aggressive war on capitalism that is designed to wrest control of the economy from the private sector and transfer it to the government. I call that Marxism. Like the symbolic repudiation of Churchill, Obama's Marxist attack on free markets plays to the same factions of the radical left he once set out to ingratiate himself with as a young man.

"When the native hears a speech about Western culture, he pulls out his knife," wrote Frantz Fanon, the seminal theorist of anti-Western Third Worldism Obama mentioned above. When a Marxist, Third World-tilting president of the United States sees a bust of Winston Churchill, he sends it packing. He may have proven once again to the Left that he's no sellout, but that doesn't mean he hasn't just alienated an awful lot of the American people.

Jack Bauer meets Barack Obama

3/27/09

Editor's note: While the "24" references and characters below are fictional, the message to Iran attributed to "the President" below is directly quoted from President Barack Obama's message to Iran of March 20, 2009.

The following takes place in an unseen episode of "24."

Tony Almeda, glowering, is watching the President live on a television in a coffee shop across the street from the White House.

The President (on screen): "In particular, I would like to speak directly to the people and leaders of the Islamic Republic of Iran. Nowruz is just one part of your great and celebrated culture...."

Without taking his eyes off the screen, Tony punches in a number on his cell.

Jack Bauer answers. "Yeah," he breathes, also watching the president on a mirror server uploaded to his monitor.

The President: "Over many centuries, your art, your music, literature and innovation have made the world a better and more beautiful place...."

Tony: "Are you watching the President?"

Jack, making his way to his car as he downloads a frame grab to his PDA: "Copy."

Tony, walking toward the White House: "What's he talking about, 'innovation'? Does he mean the high-tech armor-piercing roadside bombs Iran "innovated" to kill and maim hundreds of U.S. troops in Iraq?"

Jack, now speeding across the 14th Street Bridge into downtown Washington: "Copy. And notice the specific reference to 'the leaders of the Islamic Republic of Iran.' The president is directly addressing A-jad and the mullahs, and thus in some unprecedented way America is now legitimizing the 1979 Khomeini revolution."

Tony: "Copy that, too. Are you thinking what I'm thinking?"

Jack: "Copy. No American president would ever, could ever, lower himself and our nation to grovel like this to that vicious Islamic regime. Unless — Tony, someone's gotten to the president. He's in trouble."

Tony, eyes narrowing as he peers at the White House: "Copy."

The President (on Jack's car radio): "We know that you are a great civilization and your accomplishments have earned the respect of the United States and the world...."

Jack parks near the White House and joins Tony by the fence.

Jack: "Someone must be forcing the president to make this broadcast, Tony, forcing him to grovel to the mullah-ocracy. We need weapons, surveillance equipment, thumbtacks, quick." Punches in a number on his cell."

Jack: "Chloe?"

Chloe, also watching the president on television: "Jack!"

The President: "We seek instead engagement that is honest and grounded in mutual respect...."

Jack: "The president is being coerced into surrendering to Iran."

Chloe: "I know. I'm watching. How else could he talk about 'mutual respect' with a regime obsessed with Holocaust denial, nuking Israel and destroying America?"

Jack: "Copy."

Chloe: "Jack, who could be making the president do this?!"

Jack: "We don't find out for a few more episodes, Chloe. You know that."

Chloe: "OK. Listen, I just accessed encrypted Secret Service bandwidths to confirm the President's children are at school, but what about the First Lady? Do we have a visual?"

Tony, urgent: "Jack, I think I see the First Lady being held by weird-looking hostiles in white coats in that untamed thicket over there."

Jack, looking up: "No, that's just the First Lady with her chefs in the new White House organic vegetable garden. Chloe, I need the most current CIRG logs and recognition codes for entry in the Oval Office."

Chloe: "I'm on it, OK. I've downloaded them to your PDA."

Jack: "Copy. We're on it."

From a duct over the Oval Office, Jack and Tony hear the President wrapping up as Jack noiselessly drills an eyehole in the plaster wall.

The President: "With the coming of a new season, we're reminded of this precious humanity that we all share."

Jack, under his breath: "Precious humanity we share? What about the regime's hanging of homosexuals and stoning-to-death of adulterers? Tony, just recently a 25-year-old Iranian blogger named Omidreza Mirsayafi died during his two-year prison term for 'insulting' Ayatollah Khomeini and criticizing the government."

Tony: "The President must be under incredible duress. We've got to save him."

The President, concluding: "Thank you and Eid-eh Shoma Mobarak."

An Aide: "OK. All clear. Thank you, Mr. President. We'll get you up on YouTube within the hour."

The President: "I want it out on Al Jazeera, too."

Aide: "Of course."

Surreptitiously, Jack peers into the room.

The President: "Thank you all. That was great. I've been wanting to do that for a long time. Now, when is the Islamic Republic of Iran's actual Independence Day — or whatever they call it? Maybe we can send them a cake, or pie, or something."

Tony: "How many hostiles, Jack?"

Jack is still surveying the apparently peaceful scene when the First Lady enters.

First Lady: "Hi, honey. Want some organic broccoli?"

Jack: "No hostiles, Tony. Or maybe all hostiles." Punches in a number on his cell.

"Chloe, download the reverse quadralinear coordinates to my PDA so we can get out of here. The President of the United States just groveled to Iran because he wanted to. And that makes this whole thing one lost episode."

Mr. President, visit Pvt. Long's family, not 'where Islam began'

6/5/09

The last thing "President Hussein" did not do before flying Magic Carpet One to "the Kingdom" was ....

OK. Hang on a sec. I'm just trying to get into the Islamo-spirit of being a citizen of what the 44th president called, and I quote: "one of the largest Muslim countries in the world." Yes, Barack Obama was talking about the United States, which, with somewhere between 2 million and 3 million Muslims tops (not all of whom are citizens) doesn't exactly sound like Mecca for Islam, literally or figuratively.

So why did the president say this bizarro thing? Was it just one more super-corny, proto-crypto-Islamic slip, a la his visits to, as Obama put it on the campaign trail, "all 57 states" (the Organization of the Islamic Conference has 57 member states)? Or the "five pillars" of his economic plan (Islam has "five pillars")? Or was it more prosaically the case that the teleprompter was taking the day off?

We just don't know. But don't expect the White House press corps to find out, particularly not after the State Department warned media traveling with al-POTUS (President of the United States) to Saudi-land not to stray from either pre-planned coverage or their hotels at the risk of "arrest and detention by Saudi authorities." Yes, these were the ground rules dictated by Saudi Arabia and agreed to by the U.S. government — and, apparently, all major media. Are we dhimmi or are we dhimmi?

But I digress.

Taking it from the top: The last thing President Obama did not do before leaving for Saudi Arabia, "addressing" the Muslim world from Cairo, and commemorating D-Day in Europe (in that order) was condemn a bona-fide jihadist attack on a Little Rock, Ark., Army-Navy recruiting station that left U.S. Army Pvt. William Long, 23, dead, and U.S. Army Private Quinton Ezeagwula, 18, wounded. The killer was Abdulhakim Mujahid Muhammad, 23, an American convert to Islam originally named Carlos Bledsoe. Muhammad had recently returned from studying jihad in nearby Yemen — nearby, that is, to Saudi Arabia, President Obama's first stop abroad.

The horrific shooting took place Monday morning when the soldiers, both of whom had just completed basic training, were taking a break outside the office. The hours passed, then the entire day, but no statement came from these soldiers' commander-in-chief (Obama). Never mind that just the week before, as Michelle Malkin has pointed out, President Obama personally condemned the murder of abortionist George Tiller within hours of the crime ("I am shocked and outraged by this heinous crime ..."). The Justice Department also issued a timely statement condemning Tiller's murder, additionally dispatching federal protection to abortion clinics. But there was nothing on Monday from Washington for these U.S. soldiers who had come under fire in a sleepy shopping mall on U.S. soil, and no federal assistance was put forward for the country's recruiting stations, long subjected to harassment, vandalism and now worse.

The silence was even more noticeable on Tuesday when President Obama held a press conference in Washington to announce his selection for secretary of the Army. While blah-blahing about preparing our soldiers "to meet the challenges of our time," the president failed to note the "challenge" of homegrown jihad that had tragically cost Pvt. Long his life and put his comrade in the hospital. And then Obama was off on his own jarringly personal mission of perpetual outreach to the Islamic world, this time setting out in Sharia-ruled, oil- and jihad-exporting Saudi Arabia. "I thought it was very important to come to the place where Islam began and to seek his majesty's counsel," Obama said on Wednesday.

The place where Islam began? Spare us. How about the president instead going to the place where Islam ended the life a U.S. soldier, an unexpected casualty of jihad in the young man's own back yard?

Little Rock is where the president of the United States should have traveled this week to address the Muslim world. There, he should have declared that the 21st century era of Islamic jihad is over, that Pvt. Long had not died in vain, that his memory would be served by a new American resolve to join with its kindred allies in liberty to contain and ultimately reverse the militarily- and demographically pressed advance of Sharia (Islamic law) across the non-Muslim world.

But such a pilgrimage to the heart of America to denounce jihad obviously doesn't interest Barack Obama. Not when he could make a pilgrimage to the heart of Islam where jihad is a sacred institution. Finally, on Wednesday afternoon, as criticism of the president's silence began to achieve a critical Internet mass, a statement came from the White House: "I am deeply saddened by this senseless act of violence ..." it said.

"Saddened"? "Senseless"? What dishwater-weak words to use about what the shooter himself is said to have described as an Islamically motivated attack on U.S. troops. Of course, from the president's bully pulpit in Cairo, such talk is sure to go down smoothly with his newest, most sought-after constituency.

Obama's war for Socialism. Yes, Socialism

7/16/09

At some point of embittering clarity, Americans will open their eyes to the glaring significance of the Obama era and see the Power Grab Years for what they are. Whether this realization comes in time to stave off the eradication of the United States as we thought we knew it, or whether it comes too late, I predict it will surely come.

If it comes in time, the realization that the nation dodged history's bullet will produce massive waves of relief. If it comes too late, the understanding of our fallen state will live on as the lost lore, not of a subject people exactly, but of a self-subjected people. That's because in this strange historical instance, the American people, beginning with but not limited to those of us who voted Barack Obama into the White House, seem to have agreed to shoulder the heavy, costly yoke of exponentially increasing government control of our lives.

Make that exponentially increasing executive branch control of our lives—even more alarming given the cult of President Obama's personality already evident. With a rubberstamp Democratic Congress, it is the Obama White House that calls the shots, and it doesn't let dissenters forget it. As much as anything else this week, what cast me into this particular abyss of speculation was the stunning news that after Sen. Jon Kyl, R-Ariz., declared the Obama administration's stimulus spending plan ineffective and urged a halt to further stimulus spending, the White House dispatched four Cabinet secretaries—Transportation's Ray LaHood, Agriculture's Tom Vilsack, Housing and Urban Development's Shaun Donovan, Interior's Ken Salazar—to write letters to Republican Arizona Gov. Jan Brewer enumerating every dime of federal monies that would no longer flow to her state if Sen. Kyl had his way.

As LaHood snarkily put it to Gov. Brewer, "If you prefer to forfeit the money we are making available to your state, as Senator Kyl suggests, please let me know."

What did the White House expect the governor to do next? Make Sen. Kyl an offer he couldn't refuse? Or, as Mark Steyn, detecting the whiff of extortion in the air, asked: "Why not just break his (Kyl's) legs in the Senate parking lot?"

Muscular politicking on steroids is the Obama way, whether the administration is bullying Chrysler bond-holders, wresting control of the Census from the Commerce Department, or empowering, at last count, as many as 31 "czars" to oversee various aspects of federal policy, from Gitmo closure "czar" Daniel Fried to executive pay "czar" Kenneth Feinberg, many without Senate confirmation. In explaining the full White House press on government-controlled health care, top Obama strategist David Axelrod could have been describing the Obama White House MO in general: "Ultimately, this is not about a process, it's about results." Which is just another way of saying the ends justify the means.

But what are those ends? My guess is that socializing the engines of wealth and creation in this county is itself a means to an end — the consolidation of a new power structure derived from a government-dependent population and animated by the kind of identity politics exemplified by Sonya "wise Latina" Sotomayor, whose self-contradictory Senate testimony this week, by the way, perfectly tracks Axelrod's playbook. In the meantime, however, as the administration expands its control over the private sector, as it formulates foreign policy in harmony with that of Castro's Cuba, Chavez's Venezuela, and Ortega's Nicaragua, it's no stretch to say that Barack Obama is reshaping the USA in a distinctly socialist mold, something closer to a dictatorial workers' paradise than to cowboy-friendly Reagan Country.

But there exists a potent taboo against the S-word and other terminology essential for analysis. Jeb Bush's aversion to the term is typical. "Is Obama a socialist?" Tucker Carlson recently asked him in Esquire magazine.

Bush said he didn't know, and called the president a "collectivist." Same difference? Perish the thought. "Socialism is pejorative in America," Bush explained. "So people stop listening. People are tired of it. That word won't stick. It's a turnoff. It doesn't help."

"It's a turnoff"? It had better not be a turnoff. Because if we don't talk about it, we won't think about it — until it's too late.

Only voters can stop the insidious spread of Socialism

4/13/12

Now that Election 2012 is shaping up as a contest between President Obama and Mitt Romney, an observation and a prediction.

Our nation heads into a presidential campaign with an incumbent whose online birth certificate and Selective Service registration card are almost certainly forgeries, and this is a nonissue. (Don't ask about the subpoena from a Georgia court that Obama ignored. Everyone else did, too.)

That's the observation. The prediction is that unless voters come to view Barack Obama as a "socialist" — even a "democratic socialist" — and, as such, an existential threat to our (in theory) constitutional republic, President Obama, funny papers and all, will be re-elected in November.

The two stories are related. Both turn on the relative power of "evidence" vs. "narrative." By evidence, I mean the facts and clues that support an argument or hypothesis. By narrative, I mean propaganda. For example, there is evidence of fraud in Obama's identity documents, but such evidence does not fit the narrative that Obama's identity documents are authentic. In the face of narrative, We the People are supposed to ignore the evidence. All of our officials and elites do.

Similarly, there is plentiful evidence of Barack Obama's socialist beliefs and ties—Stanley Kurtz's 2010 book "Radical-in-Chief: Barack Obama and the Untold Story of American Socialism" meticulously lays it out—but the narrative insists that Obama is anything but a socialist. And, as with the evidence of identity fraud, woe and besmirching to anyone who mentions it.

Now, what do I mean by socialism? Too often, and sometimes by design, defining socialism becomes an absurdly contentious exercise. If we narrowly define socialism as "government ownership of the means of production," however, we'll never know what hit us until it's too late. I found it helpful to learn that Alexander Solzhenitsyn recognized there was no "single precise definition of socialism" out there. This is probably due to vagaries of time and place, and to the fact that, short of a violent revolution, socialism is a complex, messy work in progress. What's vital to identify is the direction of that progress. If the progress tends toward increasing economic collectivism and political centralization, the movement is socialist. If the progress is in the other direction, the movement is known as capitalist.

By leaps of collectivism and bounds of centralization, Barack Obama has been taking the country in a socialist direction since he took office. I would add, however, that this is the direction the country has been moving since 1933. That's another story.

But it's all part of a story we're not supposed to discuss in concrete terms. This must change this year, or else. Or else what? More and more socialism. That means less and less freedom.

On Oct. 12, 2008, Joe the Plumber—who, today, as Samuel Wurzelbacher is running for Congress—prompted Candidate Obama to repeat the socialist mantra, in Obama's words, that "when you spread the wealth around it's good for everybody." If you recall, this led to an intense, frenzied media vetting—of Joe the Plumber. Obama and his ties—for example, to the socialist New Party and the socialist front organization ACORN—went *unreported* in the print and television mainstream, even as new evidence was exploding like fireworks on mainly conservative Internet news sites and blogs, particularly in those final weeks of the campaign.

To date, Mitt Romney has balked at labeling President Obama or even his policies as socialist, probably calculating that the label distracts from his arguments. I implore him to reconsider lest Obama's and the

Democrats' stealth socialism finish off the country once and for all.

What's fascinating, meanwhile, is that Obama is underscoring his own socialism by disavowing it—even as no one in the political arena is accusing him of it. Psychologists probably would call this phenomenon "projection."

Joel Gehrke of the Washington Examiner noted that twice last week Obama defended his economic ideas against charges of socialism — charges no one is actually making. This week, Gehrke picked up on the president's stated denial that he is trying to "redistribute wealth," even as Obama touted a plan to do exactly that with the "Buffett Rule." This rule, as Obama explained to Joe the Plumber back in 2008, "spreads the wealth around" by taxing millionaires at a higher rate to pay for "investments" (a deceptive word for government programs). These "investments," Obama told a Florida audience, "haven't been made as some grand scheme to redistribute wealth from one group to another. This is not some socialist dream."

That's the narrative, of course. Who really believes it's supported by the facts?

Obama: political phoenix

6/22/12

Are we watching the meltdown of Barack Obama, soon to become a radioactive pile from which voters will run come November? Or are we instead witnessing the stirrings of a kind of political phoenix heretofore unseen in American history?

By any traditional measure, news in the past week or two alone should sink Barack Obama's chances for a second term. First, Obama biographer Stanley Kurtz reported new and definitive proof that, as a 34-year-old embarking on his political career, Obama belonged to the anti-capitalist – indeed, socialist – New Party, a phase of his political development he has not only never repudiated but also has hidden from the American people. By any traditional measure, such news would at least intensify any Obama meltdown. But wait. Kurtz and other researchers discovered this fact back in 2008, only to be smeared by the Obama campaign as not wrong but "crackpot." They were right all along and deserve an apology. (Don't hold your breath.)

Do Obama and his campaign get away with lying about this key entry in the president's political resume? Does Obama get away with having masked his early efforts to socialize America? So far, even against the backdrop of imploding European socialism, the answers are "yes."

Next, there was the president's Rose Garden amnesty of June 15. That's when the president seized legislative powers by declaring a brand-new law to exempt an entire class of illegal aliens – those 16 to 30 years old – from deportation laws enacted by Congress. Frankly, revolutions have started over shorter dictatorial overreach. As kids in elementary school should know, but aren't taught – no time with all those sex-ed and "green" energy requirements – the executive branch doesn't make law; it executes it. Even Barack Obama has repeatedly made the point.

What changed? The conventional wisdom, assuming the White House is in political "panic," explains this presidential diktat as a desperate act of pandering to anti-immigration-law Hispanic voters. No doubt. But as Mark Krikorian noted at National Review Online: "One needs to ask why the White House thought it could get away with such a shocking power grab. And the answer is that no one stopped them before, so they figured ... they could go further."

Was the White House right? Opposition hasn't coalesced – let alone any volcanic eruptions of good, old-fashioned outrage – and that's putting it mildly. Thus, 130-plus days from the election, the New Party emeritus president has grabbed powers that not only tighten the already constricted job market for the American unemployed, but make mincemeat of the Constitution, trample national sovereignty and advance the erosion of our once-beloved English-speaking culture (the love that really dares not speak its name). Meltdown, right?

Nope. The only villain of the piece to emerge is Neil Munro of the Daily Caller, who interrupted the president's press audience (no questions, please) to hurl the issue of jobs for Americans (not for foreigners already illegally exploiting the U.S. taxpayer) into the mix. Off with his head, cried the PrObamedia, echoes reverberating. To his everlasting credit, Munro's editor, Tucker Carlson, defiantly announced he would instead give Munro a raise. The echo-chamber narrative, however, was set. Obama did the right thing, "everyone" said, notwithstanding all that rude, right-wing "heckling."

Which brings us to this week. After House Republicans on the Oversight and Government Reform Committee took the unprecedented step of voting Attorney General Eric Holder in contempt of Congress for withholding documents relevant to its investigation of the Fast and Furious "gun-walking" operation, President Obama invoked "executive privilege," dropping the dubious mantle of secrecy over all the documents in question.

This time, House Republicans and media conservatives hit the roof. But what of the great national echo chamber?

It hit the mute button. The Washington Post, still brushing Watergate anniversary confetti from its hair, reported on Page A1 that this assertion of presidential privilege at the climactic moment of Congress' 16-month investigation simply "reignited a long-running Washington debate over the limits of White House power." In other words, ho-hum. The story sits low in the New York Times' online queue, with a headline winding up the perfect PrObamedia pitch: "House Panel Vote Steps Up Partisan Fight on Gun Inquiry." "Partisan fight," of course, is New York Times-ese for "heckling."

So is the president melting down or rising like a phoenix? For a socialist with dictatorial inclinations – or is that a dictator with socialist inclinations? – he's shockingly buoyant in the polls. Watch out, lovers of constitutional liberty: Unless We, the People, make ourselves heard, this rara avis could still take flight.

Peering into the Cultural Abyss

Felony neglect

3/9/01

The Associated Press posted a round-up of tragedies averted at American schools after 15-year-old Charles Andrew Williams went on a 10-minute shooting rampage at his Santee, California, high school, killing 14-year-old Bryan Zuckor and 17-year-old Randy Gordon, and wounding 13 other boys and girls.

Within 48 hours, 23 American schoolchildren had been arrested or detained for threatening various acts of violence including a bomb plot at a middle school. Among the suspects were three students from the California School for the Deaf, a 15-year-old Catholic schoolboy from Davenport, Iowa, and a 15-year-old honor student from Camden said to have threatened to kill off a high school clique during wood shop.

Bomb plot and middle school; honor student, murder, and wood shop: Still there persists a sense of horror and disbelief at the linkage. How about eight-years-old, loaded handgun and talk of "bloodbath"? That chilling combo came together on Monday in a Philadelphia elementary school before authorities took the second-grader into custody. As disturbing as such accounts are, in the five short years since a Washington-state boy killed three fellow students, the unthinkable has become, if not an everyday event, an everyday threat.

So it comes as little surprise to learn that on the same day a 14-year-old Catholic schoolgirl in Pennsylvania made headlines for shooting a 13-year-old classmate in the shoulder, the AP reported: a 12-year-old Philadelphia schoolboy WAS ARRESTED for carrying a .22-caliber pistol to school; a Florida sophomore was charged with possessing a semiautomatic handgun; another Florida teen was charged with bringing a sawed-off revolver to his old high school; a 16-year-old boy in Washington state was arrested after making threats and brandishing a gun during a Junior Reserve Officers' Training Corps session; and a 14-year-old Wisconsin boy, having fled school while being disciplined, returned with a gun. And, finally, an Indianapolis couple, Calvin and Shawnee Sistrunk, were charged with felony neglect after their 6-year-old daughter had taken a loaded handgun to kindergarten on March 1.

Felony neglect. There seems to be a lot of that going around as details emerge to fill in some of the blanks surrounding the more notorious child crimes. In Charles Andrew Williams' case, the Linus-in-the-school-play reports were quickly overshadowed by revelations of a sad life of maternal estrangement, paternal laxity, uprootedness, being bullied at school, and drug and alcohol abuse. Experts say there is no reliable "profile" of a schoolyard killer, but there is an all-too-familiar look to the private world of the Williams boy, as there is to the public tragedy for which he is responsible. Worse still, there's little doubt that this same kind of private world will again combust in a similar tragedy. As a Santee girl told reporters, "It makes you wonder when it will end."

There is understandable despair in the girl's reaction, a numbness that Americans can't help feeling whether directly affected or watching from afar. But this is a time to keep outrage raw and real if ever we are to stamp out such barbarities as schoolyard massacres, and not just accommodate ourselves to them. It's an open question whether we're up to the challenge, or will instead learn to "cope" with some measure of murder on campus, to adjust to it as though it were just another pitfall of postmodern life. President Bush reacted to the Santee shooting, not by blaming the gun lobby as his predecessor always did, but by sanely emphasizing character development and the importance of teaching children right from wrong. This is vitally important, but there's more to consider.

Writing in the Los Angeles Times, author Judith Rich Harris noted, "Modern children live two almost independent lives: their lives at home with their parents and siblings and their lives outside the home, where the important people are their peers." Maybe this is as good a time as any to challenge the undisputed primacy of the peer group, which derives its influence from high school as we know it. Maybe it's time also to reassess the vast, impersonal secondary school, where galaxies of adolescents are pulled by the irrational forces of clique-life and pop-culture, and where the adult lessons of right and wrong often become distorted by teen tunnel-vision.

And about pop culture. The lack of remorse noted in the Williams boy may have more than a little to do with his affinity for the nihilism of punk rock and his idolizing Kurt Cobain, the Nirvana singer who committed suicide in 1994. "Over and over, he played the song, 'In the End,' " the Los Angeles Times reported, "which features the lyrics,

'I had to fall/To lose it all/But in end/It doesn't even matter'"

Maybe it didn't to Charles Andrew Williams — but it does, one hopes, to the rest of us.

America's magazines and the 'ick factor'

3/23/01

One of the more outré commonplaces of modern life is the mandatory voyeurism of the supermarket check-out line. The inevitable wait to pay transforms even the most distracted shopper, however briefly, into a captive audience for a nearly cinematic pastiche of glossy sexual intimacy and abandon complete with X-rated subtitles about rather improbable anatomical maneuvers and other heat-seeking measures. And heaven help the parent whose grade-schoolers pipe up that they want to try out "the most incredible bedroom trick of all" — plugged, of course, in giant letters beneath an abundant plunge of cleavage.

But can it be that the check-out line, forced gauntlet of sex (not to mention sugar) that it is, has become slightly less tawdry of late? Inside. com, an internet magazine that tracks the publishing trade, recently reported on a "newfound primness" in the salacious world of women's magazines that dawned recently when Cosmopolitan and Glamour, two industry leaders in lowness, effectively banned the word "sex" from their covers. "Over the last six months, "writes David Carr, "the two magazines — which had been in an arms race over coverlines that had all the linguistic subtlety of a gynecological exam — have defaulted to 'Whoa Baby' romance novel motifs."

Let's be clear: The "Whoa Baby" motifs Mr. Carr cites — practically straight-faced — as evidence of a "newly demure" mag-world sensibility are still about as out of place in a grocery store as thong-flashing in the Oval Office.

In fact, these "more chaste" magazine cover lines remain emphatically tasteless to the point of being unquotable in the kind of newspaper that may linger a few days in the family den. But that doesn't mean that there hasn't been a discernible change.

Why? Nope — a renaissance of decency is hardly underway in the women's magazine world. But sales are down — in 2000, almost 10 and 11 percent for Cosmopolitan and Glamour respectively. Does that mean — stop the presses — that sex isn't selling the way it used to? Could be. Inside.com cites "ennui" as partially inspiring the fall-off. "I think that beyond the 'ick' factor, there is the boredom factor," explained Elizabeth Crow, a longtime executive in the magazine trade. "Once you're found out how to supersize your sex life four different ways, the fifth is not all that interesting."

Be that as it may, don't underestimate that "ick" factor. Jane Pratt, eponymous editor of Jane, said that halfway through 2000 she toned down her magazine's bluntly sexual cover lines about comparative vibrator shopping and the like because "the readers didn't like it and they told us so.

They thought it was low brow, something they wouldn't be proud of having on the coffee table." Particularly not next to that Martha-Stewart-inspired floral-foam-filled ice bucket full of pussy willow branches decked with blown and decorated Easter Eggs.

Of course, it's not just readers who have made their sexual dissatisfaction known. Supermarkets are hearing from all those long-suffering shoppers—who, after all, are dropping in for pull-ups and frosted pop tarts, not come-ons and air-brushed hot tarts. Their complaints, along with the laudable efforts of such groups as the American Decency Association (an offshoot of Donald E. Wildmon's American Family Association), are getting an encouraging response. Many grocery stores across the nation, including such chains as Ohio-based Kroger's, Massachusetts-based Big Y and Maryland-based Giant Food, have actually taken some of the more strumpety mags and dropped them behind the Mother-Hubbard-like shields once reserved for pornographic men's magazines. There, of course, they can ooze suggestively from month to month all they like, but the casual observer has only to look at their names. As Donald D' Amour, CEO of Big Y, told Fox News recently, "People don't need to have to give their 6-, 7- and 10-year-olds sex education every time they go to a checkout counter."

Indeed. It's bizarre, to say the least, to live during an age when Mr. D' Amour's words are actually debatable, and not just as obvious as looking both ways before crossing the street. But that's what happens when everything is waved into the mainstream and nothing is restricted to its margins—where shopping for dinner with the kids routinely includes an explicit menu of sexual specials as well. Considering the uphill movement to give those gamey gal mags some cover and maybe a zone of their own—an encouraging development, to be sure—it becomes clear, once again, that it's much harder to restore a sense of order and place to a society than it ever was to abolish them.

But that doesn't mean it isn't well worth the effort.

Dodging balls, bugs, and 'brilliance'

5/11/01

The worst thing about living in a period of cultural decline is not having to ride out the pop-toxic tide of cultural waste yourself, but having to ride it out with your children. Since what was once marginal is now mainstream—red-light sexuality, for example, or the obsession with explicitly violent peril—even the most casual scan of the public airwaves demands a close eye on the cultural periscope plus a quick-trigger finger on the off-button to torpedo the inevitable barrage of incoming smut and violence. Viagra ads at 12 o'clock. Pedophilia jokes at 8 o'clock. The songsters of necrophilia, suicide and mayhem around the clock. Talk about battle fatigue.

But finally, some good news. Educators and tastemakers are hunkering down to draw some lines, establish a few boundaries and remind people what is off-limits and what is not. There's just one problem: These folks haven't a clue. How else to explain a week in which society has taken protective measures to ward off the triple scourge of dodgeball, Mother's Day and Bugs Bunny?

Take dodgeball. Seeking measures to prevent future Columbines and Santees, education "experts" are banding together to bring the weight of their assorted specialties to lobby, not against Mortal Kombat and other ghoulish video games that accustom youngsters to realistic blood-lettings, and not against death-metal "music" groups that sink young spirits and warp their ambition, but rather against an old recess game played with a big rubber ball. "This [dodgeball] is something that should not be used in today's classrooms, especially in today's society," Diane Farr, a "curriculum specialist" told the New York Times. "With Columbine and all the violence we are having, we have to be very careful how we teach our children." It may sound like a joke, but this is the voice of the cutting-edge: Dodgeball in elementary school today, mass murder in high school tomorrow.

Then there's that other threat to children's well-being, Mother's Day—and, while they're at it, Father's Day. At a ritzy private elementary school in Manhattan where tuition starts at $15,000 in pre-K and tops out at almost $20,000 by grade 6, educators now conclude that both holidays may be harmful to children. As the official school mailing explained, "The recognition of these holidays in a social setting may not be a positive experience for all children."

But since when, as the New York Post's Andrea Peyser wondered, did "the biblical commandment -- 'Honor thy father and thy mother'—become a threat to children's emotional well-being?" Since the dictates of political correctness exploded the definition of family, that's when. As a school official put it to Ms. Peyser, "There may be two fathers, two mothers, the mother may not have custody, it could be a grandmother..." Here, in order to accommodate the "non-traditional" family, the traditional model will be taking its Hallmark holiday observance underground—but all for the greater good.

Which brings us to the corporate decision to keep certain cartoons featuring Bugs Bunny under lock and key. From the front-page of the

Wall Street Journal comes a report detailing the tortured machinations at the highest levels of Time Warner AOL over what to do with one dozen cartoon shorts featuring Bugs at his worst—that is, at his most politically incorrect—during a planned retrospective of the bunny's life work on Cartoon Network. These include a World-War-II-era cartoon entitled, "Bugs Nips the Nips," which lambastes the Japanese—who were once, it is said, our mortal enemies (look it up). In another "sensitive" cartoon, Bugs addresses an awkwardly hulking Eskimo as a "big baboon"— which, sad to say, is not entirely out of character for this particular bunny (ask Elmer Fudd). Then there's the one in which Bugs does Al Jolson impersonation in blackface—an entertainment genre about as antique and relevant to modern times as soft shoe numbers and Mack Sennett shorts. But not even Cartoon Network's plans "to ensure kids wouldn't be likely to see" Bugs at His Most Insensitive by screening offending episodes in the dark of the night (with disclaimers scrolling across the screen during the entire broadcast) convinced AOL Time Warner executives to release them.

But how comforting is it, really, to know that AOL Time Warner is doing its bit to save society from that wascally wabbit? What's most fascinating about the conglomerate's quandary is that while this is same company that most infamously brought us "Copkiller," along with an near-endless assortment of pop-profanities, it is only Bugs and his "disturbing cartoon content" that sent executives into a pre-emptive panic of censorship. You have to wonder, though, whether anyone but the professionals could ever think that Bugs Bunny—or dodgeball or Mother's Day—could make society's problems worse.

When "viewpoint discrimination" in our schools was not nearly so gnarly a notion

6/22/01

Let's see if we can sort out the field of battle. The Boy Scouts remain besieged by the Forces of Tolerance—that special, ultra-liberal kind of "tolerance" that comes to a skidding, rubber-burning halt at the Scout-den door.

Dedicated to the eradication of the 91-year-old private organization's principles of rectitude that bar homosexuals from joining up, the Scouts' opponents include not just homosexual activists, or maybe People for the American Way, but also large swaths of what has to be called the establishment. These include school districts in at least a dozen cities, from New York to Minneapolis, charities such as United Way, labor unions, teacher unions, the PTA and Steven Spielberg, all of which have withdrawn support and privileges to starve out the Scouts until, presumably, they are a social menace (read: "morally straight") no more.

Hoping to cushion the impact of all this broad-mindedness, Sen. Jesse Helms, North Carolina Republican, sent in a rider-to-the-rescue last week, an amendment that passed, 51-49, to deny federal funds to schools that bar Scouts access to facilities enjoyed by other groups. Not to be outdone, Democrats answered with a measure from Sen. Barbara Boxer, California Democrat, that passed, 52-47, to ensure that no schools deny access to any student group, including the Scouts, "based on that group's favorable or unfavorable position concerning sexual orientation."

What could be more, as they say, "inclusive"? But look how the battle has shifted: from trying to save the Scouts, who, after all, want as little to do with "sexual orientation" as possible, to ensuring that schools sanction any group with any "sexual orientation."

This sort of pressure is testing schools across the nation, often to unpredictable effect. In one of the more bizarre cases to date, a Southern California school district last week decided to ban all 29 of its service and social clubs rather than recognize a Christian club, the Fellowship of Christian Athletes — no doubt another one of those morally straight scourges that help left-wing activists raise money. With this decision, the district ended a lawsuit filed by a former student to gain club status for the Christian group. Under the new rules, the Christian group will be treated on the same basis as other non-academic and non-athletic clubs, gaining after-school access to facilities, possibly for a fee.

Is this good? The Christian group, enjoying a new, if lesser, equality, seems to think so, although the other clubs are still smarting over their new non-status. "If people aren't happy with [it], they can go to the Christian group and thank them for it," school board President Dore Gilbert rather churlishly told the Orange County Register. Then he said something much more interesting. "I don't want a crack in the door that then becomes a swinging gate that allows any group official club status. ... If you start allowing certain groups on campus, they might not be as brotherly as a Christian club."

How intriguing: Could Mr. Gilbert believe that unfettered, unfiltered inclusiveness is not always a good thing? That there could be something worse for a student body than a — gasp — religious jock's club? Maybe a total ban was the only way to maintain any control over club activity. As Judy Selz, an official with the American Association of School Administrators put it to the Los Angeles Times, "Local school districts can no longer be as sensitive to local community preferences as they used to be. It's either everything or nothing."

Everything or nothing. It may be a measure of the sloppiness of the so-called culture wars that Ms. Selz was actually bemoaning a 6-3 Supreme Court decision holding that a New York state school may not prevent an evangelical children's club from meeting after school on the premises—the kind of "everything" that probably appeals to those among us who still have a soft spot for freedom of religion, not to mention freedom of speech. "This case opens it all up," education law expert Rob DeKoven told the newspaper. "This case says schools cannot engage in any viewpoint discrimination." Really? Ominously, the New York state district that was the defendant in the case is considering the California option of shutting down all after-school groups, including Girl Scouts and the 4-H Club, rather than allowing the children's Christian club to meet on campus.

Maybe once upon a time "viewpoint discrimination" in the schools was not nearly so gnarly a notion. That was back when a "morally straight" Scout color guard drew cheers, not jeers (as one did at last summer's Democratic National Convention), avowed homosexuals didn't try to be scout leaders, and Bible class wasn't such a big deal. Many bemoan those days, but they're gone. Today, it looks like the best thing to hope for is everything.

When PC parades are too 'mainstream'

6/29/01

There she was, partaking of that quintessential *fin* (and debut) *de siècle* event known as the gay pride parade, when she was overcome with revulsion and embarrassment at—what else?--something revolting and embarrassing.

There, in midtown Manhattan, in the middle of the day, in full sight of children and even politicians, was something so horrific that Sarah Schulman, author and lesbian activist, never attended a gay pride parade again. It was a gay-pride float sponsored (shriek) by Coors beer.

Coors beer—wasn't that the official brew of the Nicaraguan contras? Not that Ms. Schulman's reaction had a thing to do with Old War politics.

According to the Wall Street Journal, her objections were more basic. This was a matter of survival—of gasping for cultural existence amid the ever-swelling waters of the mainstream, which are fast-subsuming a cause that once thrived where Coors (let alone FleetBoston Financial Corp., US Airways Group Inc. and Viacom Inc.) dared not go, and certainly not with holiday floats. As Ms. Schulman put it, "A political movement simply can't have corporate sponsorship."

Unless, of course, the "movement" has arrived.

That's the hard truth for Ms. Schulman and other homosexual activists turned off by the ardent embrace of American corporations. In San Francisco, for example, corporate sponsorship of the city's "pride festival" has expanded to cover one-third of its $1 million budget. Hewlett Packard alone has upped its "pride" ante to back celebrations in San Jose, Denver and Atlanta. But some people, alas, are never happy. "Critics complain that the pride parades are more about partying and selling rainbow-colored flags and teddy bears," the paper reported, "than about protesting continued discrimination."

Isn't acceptance, and even approval, what "pride" is all about? There's no better measure of both than widespread teddy-bear-trafficking, that's weird badge of significance in contemporary America, where every event, gay or grim, to capture national attention strikes the populace as an irresistible call to amass vast public stockpiles of stuffed animals.

Although perhaps not Brooklyn's "Gay Shame" rally. This is one of a growing number of events organized to protest the crass (naturally) commercialization of pride parades of the apple-pie persuasion. According to the Journal, Brooklyn's "renegade group, whose slogan is 'It's a movement, not a market,' will stage a more sober affair, with speeches about prison reform and civil rights for transgender people."

Don't miss it.

Besides Mother Marketplace, the Journal noted that some are also protesting "further assimilation" into the mainstream. "For example, some people resent attempts to make the parades family-friendly by censoring bare skin and bawdy behavior." Here's the rub: As the mainstream fills and swells to carry along chunks of humanity historically left in a kind of high and dry isolation, those chunks change, at least a little, if only because of their new center-stream position—on a float parading down Main Street, for example, with the local chamber of commerce. Frankly, pushing to expand the already "inclusive" mainstream a tad more (how much skin is left to bare?) bears less resemblance to a weighty political cause than to the truculence of the spoiler. Maybe realizing that the movement has hit the end of the line is the source of this evident hard-core restlessness and discontent.

A somewhat different kind of malaise afflicts other equally triumphant cultural movements. Take liberated women. The female executive may be as much a part of American business as corporate "pride," but she, too, has an argument with success: The mainstream hasn't changed enough for her, either. "So Where Are the Corporate Husbands?" the headline to a hefty feature in the New York Times recently wondered. "For Women at the Top, Something is Missing: Social, Wifely Support." This is not a joke. Marie Knowles, a woman who last year climbed down from the sky-scraping heights of having been executive vice president and chief financial officer of Atlantic Richfield oil company, describes executive women who have to compete with executive men assisted by "corporate wives" as nothing less than "disadvantaged."

Disadvantaged? How, one wonders, besides just rolling along, might the mainstream be expected to level this playing field? Could be that teddy bears or even bare skin might help. Executive grousing aside, the cultural mainstream is now so wide and deep, it has hit the point where nothing makes much of a splash. Remember Comedy Central's "South Park"? When that scatologically inclined cartoon show began airing a few years ago, its naughty words and stories were fresh bait to hungry critics. Last week, an episode featured one particular four-letter word 162 times to zero critique.

"No one cares anymore," co-creator Matt Stone told the New York Times.

"The standards are almost gone."

He almost sounds disappointed. But this is no cause for despair; it's probably cause for a parade.

Hemming about Hemings

7/20/01

By rights, the unanimous finding of a blue-ribbon panel of scholars should have renewed American curiosity over whether Thomas Jefferson and his slave Sally Hemings had a child together, if not recast the two-century-old debate altogether. Remember when this allegation was said to have been settled, as Pulitzer-Prize-winning historian and resume-craftsman-extraordinaire Joseph J. Ellis put it, "beyond a reasonable doubt"? That was back in 1998, after a retired pathologist named Eugene Foster analyzed DNA samples from the Jefferson and Hemings families to conclude, as the resulting Nature headline read, "Jefferson Fathered Slave's Last Child."

But did he? After weighing the evidence, both scientific and historical, a commission of 12 professors led by Robert F. Turner of the University of Virginia announced in April that, given the two dozen-plus Jefferson males (with DNA markers in common) roaming Virginia at the time in question, there simply can be no grounds for certainty. "The commission agrees unanimously that the allegation is by no means proven," the summary of the report reads, "and we find it regrettable that public confusion about the 1998 DNA testing and other evidence has misled many people." With the exception of one low-key dissent, the professors' conclusions "range from serious skepticism about the charge to a conviction that it is almost certainly false."

Alas, most people will have to go online to follow the fascinating detective work that went into this landmark study (the full report is available at www.mindspring.com/~tjshcommission). It is a frustrating fact that while the original Jefferson-DNA story made a massive media splash—perhaps exceeded that year only by the re-election and impeachment of Bill Clinton—subsequent retrenchments and emendations to the initial story have made nary a media blip.

For instance, almost immediately after the Nature story broke, sparking one of those fabled follow-up frenzies, Dr. Foster and his co-authors admitted their evidence was inconclusive and even "misleading" for not having clarified the fact that then-65-year-old Thomas Jefferson was only one of a family-treeful of possible fathers for Sally's last child, Eston Hemings. As reported in Science magazine, two of the more plausible sources of Jeffersonian DNA, for example, Thomas's younger brother Randolph (12 years his junior) and Randoph's son Isham, were completely ignored by the Foster study because, as Dr. Foster told the magazine, "they weren't suspects."

This crucial phase of the Jefferson-Hemings story went grossly unreported.

But back to Joseph J. Ellis—Foster booster, Jefferson expert, and, not incidentally, Clinton-impeachment opponent. Mr. Ellis, it may be remembered, had something of a cottage industry in 1998 for his camera-ready comparisons of Thomas Jefferson and Bill Clinton (along with Sally Hemings and Monica Lewinsky), which surely greased the old Clinton spin machine before, during and after the election and subsequent impeachment proceedings. Typical of his impeachment-era analysis is the following: "The dominant effect of this news [the Foster study] will be to make Clinton's sins less aberrant and more palatable ... I think he's [Thomas Jefferson is] going to help Bill Clinton in his impeachment hearings." Mr. Ellis grew positively lyrical on the subject, writing, "The Foster study seems impeccably timed to arrive like a comet that has been winging through space for 200 years before landing squarely in the middle of the Clinton impeachment inquiry."

Sigh. Of course, as it is now well known, Mr. Ellis is prone to flights of fancy, most notoriously about himself. Following a report last month in the Boston Globe, Mr. Ellis admitted to fabricating an extensive Vietnam War record, roles in both the anti-war and civil rights movements, even a stellar student football career—all lies, which he wanted everyone, himself included, to believe in. No word, incidentally, in the media on Mr. Ellis's starring role in riding that Jefferson comet through space into the middle of the Clinton impeachment inquiry.

Not that it was all lies, but it was certainly something he wanted everyone to believe in.

The transformation from Green Mountain State to Green Activist State is all but complete

8/24/01

VERMONT — As much a part of late summer here as tender corn, crickets and the faint but startling snap in the mornings, is the sudden desolation of the summer camps that ring the pleasant lakes and ponds of this scenic state. Those seasonal hives of youthful activity are just about emptied now by the convoys of shiny family cars come to retrieve all campers, bringing the summer season to an end again too soon.

No more do the campfire sounds of African drums carry across the cow fields; no more do the smells of communal vegetarian meals catch the breeze at twilight. Alas, the interactive workshops on gender issues, world hunger, globalization, and environmental degradation are over now. Even the treehouse on the pine-covered hill in Hartland where Buddhist monks — Brother Clint and Brother Michael from the nearby Maple Forest Monastery — once led campers in a rousing round of chanting, is quiet. Homeschool Political Activist Theater Camp is over for another year.

Sigh. You might say the old New England idyll isn't what it used to be.

In fact, it's tough to imagine even Robert Frost bringing this sort of material back to earth. ("The Road Not Taken to the Recycling Center"...?) Not that terra firma is necessarily the preferred destination. While most kids lucky enough (read: sufficiently affluent) to go to camp in Vermont take home the same Calamine-coated memories of archery, boating, and hiking familiar for generations, there is a new contingent of campers for whom "world issues" and "community building" trump woodlore and camaraderie every time.

At Homeschool Political Activist Theater Camp (can't wait to hear the song) happy — or, rather, "concerned" — campers arrive "with world issues that tug at them," co-founder Nancy Theriault explained to the Valley News, "mega issues like environmental degradation, saving the whales and living in a violent society." These mainly local kids also have "personal concerns," she added, such as "discrimination against teens" — which was a new one on me. No wonder their campfires are never wasted on mere s'mores. These enlightened teens use a "crackling campfire ... to bring up a world issue of personal importance and [share] a song, poem or a work of art that speaks to the issue."

And what, pray tell, does it say? The story goes on to describe a 12-year-old girl who "stands in the firelight and sings a song for a dying whale in her clear voice." (No mention on whether this made neighborhood cows nervous.) Another camper reads a poem "that expresses the pain of growing up in a perilous world" — very painful — while another "quietly strums her guitar in counterpoint." Dying whales, pain and bar chords: Clearly, a good time was had by all.

There is nothing new, of course, about summer camps with social consciences. Homeschool Political Whatsis may be only two summers old, but Camp Thoreau in lovely Thetford Center, for example, is a local institution. In addition to expounding on the glories of its private lakeside setting, Camp Thoreau's literature sets forth its mission, in part, as helping campers overcome their "prejudices such as racism, sexism, classism, and homophobia" as they "participate in & appreciate the value of collective work." Good old collective work. No wonder Camp Thoreau is nicknamed "the Commie camp."

Then, of course, there's the real McCoy. The New York Times recently ran a sentimental-journey-to-the-land-that-time-forget-style memoir about Camp Kinderland, a camp in Massachusetts for red-diaper babies who have, presumably, outgrown the diapers. (Tantrums, however, have been known to recur. Two years ago, during a UPS strike, a hapless delivery man was roundly condemned by counselors and campers as a "scab" for bringing in packages from home.) Founded in 1923, Camp Kinderland, after struggling through the dark days of the Reagan administration and the fall of the Soviet Union, is now actually "booming" according to the article's author, Ivy Meeropol — Kinderland alumna and, whaddya know, granddaughter of Ethel and Julius Rosenberg.

Vermont has never had that kind of pedigree — historically, that is. Now, however, the transformation from Green Mountain State to Green Activist State is all but complete. This is hardly news, given that most people know that Vermont has long put the nuts in granola (think of the state's re-distributionist Act 60 and civil union). Still, there remains something shocking about the change, about all those slender white church spires, forest-banked rivers and Holstein-dotted fields having become little more than a backdrop for a population lurching Left faster than any known laws of evolution.

It should come as no surprise then that, come spring, Homeschool Political Activist Theater Camp hopes to be taking its show on the road — to Cuba. Which is a pity. Camp Kinderland is so much closer.

Can rock gods save the queen?

6/4/02

Burbling on about the historic spectacle of Queen Elizabeth's Golden Jubilee and the centrality of tradition is probably best left to Britishers. But there's one aspect of the jubilee celebration that, far from being anachronistic, spotlights a more universal and thoroughly postmodern phenomenon.

After months of puzzling over why "the Party at the Palace" — next week's rock concert at Buckingham Palace marking the queen's half-century on the throne — has held such a ghastly fascination for me, I've finally figured it out. First, the palace announced the headliners: Eric Clapton, Phil Collins, Aretha Franklin, Elton John, Tom Jones and Paul McCartney. Rod Stewart and Tony Bennett have since signed on, along with newer acts including Atomic Kitten and Mis-Teeq. "There appears to be a fervent hope that 30-year-old Dido will perform and lower the average age of the cast," the London Telegraph noted.

Next came the royal rock video put together by Sir Michael Peat, Keeper of the Privy Purse, for what was billed as a palace press "presentation." This included tracks by the Beatles, decibels cranked — natch — along with a half-century's worth of queenly imagery welded to concert clips by Cliff Richards, Jimi Hendrix and Freddy Mercury of Queen (the group, not the monarch). Talk about a bad trip. According to the Telegraph, Sir Privy Purse wasn't hoping "to show the Palace was 'with it,' but simply to impart information." For instance: Friends don't let queens go to rock concerts?

This month, courtiers announced they'd snagged rocker and reality-TV-millionaire Ozzy Osbourne, fresh from his addled display (sorry, smash success) before a fawning press corps at the White House Correspondents Dinner this spring. Did the queen herself make the request?

"The queen was said to have been kept informed of who had been invited, though not necessarily consulted," the Guardian reported, which makes you wonder what the point of a crown really is. As one palace official put it, "We have taken the very best of advice, mainly from the BBC."

Et tu, Beeb? Here, apparently, are more results of that advice: "Queen to sing yeah, yeah, yeah," headlined the Telegraph this week, heralding the biggest story since Ronald Reagan was shoehorned into singing "We Are the World." "The Queen is to join Sir Paul McCartney on-stage," the newspaper reported, "and 'almost certainly' sing along" during a performance of All You Need Is Love. Noting that the song opens with the French anthem — odd choice right there for a British jubilee — the paper also provided the first lines for easy reference: "Love, love, love.

Love, love, love. Love, love, love...."

Stop. This must be a put-on, or maybe a government sting operation — or even a royal coup masterminded by Prince Charles to reveal that the Empress Has No Judgment. If not, this pending union of rock royalty and royalty royalty is so attractively awful it must mean something. After all, while Lennon and McCartney and The Rest didn't go to war against the queen, per se, they did attack the vast British middle class who hung her image in the parlor — sans irony — in obeisance to fealty, honor, duty and other soul-senses made obsolete by the rock revolution. Surely, culturally significant sparks are flying as the aged advocates of Wild Abandon prepare to meet the immutable keeper of the Stiff Upper Lip. But no. There has been no discernible tut-tutting, no Letters to the Editor wondering what the country is coming to, not a single feather ruffled or otherwise displaced. No one has noticed anything amiss about an event that will bring together a man who bites bats with a woman who has a Royal Taster. The cultural revolution isn't just over, it's forgotten.

This wasn't the case in 1977 during the queen's last jubilee, when the Sex Pistols (remember them?) prompted vestigial clucks of outrage with their banal if nasty punk anthem, "G-d Save the Queen." The song was actually banned for a time from the land and the airwaves, prompting a performance on the Thames that ended in a few cheap thrills and several arrests. Those were the days when no rock star worth his authenticity would have dared cross the palace moat — nor would he have been asked. Boundaries like that don't exist anymore.

Which may, in the end, be the moral of this concert. As the queen is a symbol, so too is her no-boundaries jubilee. Such a phenomenon, however, is by no means limited to the British realm — or even to the realm of culture. A no-boundary world is all around us, from bar-to-boardroom vulgarity in the language, to the line-crossing improprieties in the Catholic Church, to the very porousness of our national borders. Which leads where? Keep an eye on Ozzy and Elizabeth to find out.

Destiny's prefabricated child

2/26/02

It's a pretty new place in town — let's call it Colette's — one more birthday-party factory where scores of children assemble for some hasty pizza and sheet cake, romp, and leave, balloon in one hand, party favors in the other. Across the country, this annual drill of the middle class, the birthday ritual, has relocated from the home and been reduced to its pre-packaged parts in a spirit of egalitarianism (the whole class comes) and convenience (Mom and Dad have no responsibility beyond hauling home presents).

Once upon a time, in the not-too distant past, Junior presided over a select group of friends (the number determined by adding his age plus one) that gathered around the dining-room table in a house dressed up and battened-down for the occasion. While Junior may wear the same kind of party hat today, his place at the table has changed: Still the birthday-king, he is no longer the child-host, who, year by year, would be seen assuming a greater role within the family, within the home, where his parents, not "fun-staffers," officiated.

Colette's actually makes me nostalgic for the birthday-party factories that once, as recently as the last paragraph, made me nostalgic for birthdays at home. After all, birthday-party factories produce a dependable product—paper hats, Crisco frosting and noise—while Colette's, it turns out, is in another business entirely.

My first clue came in an invitation in which my daughter, then 6 years old, was cordially invited to attend a pajama party—"please wear your favorite jammies"—at Colette's, "the place to jump, jam & party, additional parking in rear." That sent my eyebrows up—not the additional parking in rear, but the jumping, jamming & partying. I needed to know more.

So, in my eternal quest to stamp out all the fun in my daughter's life, I called the place to find out what a pajama party for a bunch of little kids would entail. The children would arrive wearing bathrobes and slippers, I was told, and file into a giant bedroom—"with a phone and everything"—that was outfitted with a stereo system stocked with CDs by Britney Spears and the Backstreet Boys. After a sufficiently fabulous "jump, jam & party" session, they would all sit down for cake and ice cream.

But by then it would be too late. What Colette was describing was a teen training session, a parentally guided intro to adolescence accompanied by the continuously looping soundtrack of pop angst (interrupted only by phone calls from other adolescents). I actually shivered when I saw that behind the birthday-candle smoke and mirrors, Colette's was in the nefarious business of turning 6-year-olds into 17-year-olds.

Not that she is alone in this industry. It's becoming increasingly difficult to ward off the social and cultural pressures forcing children, and particularly girls, into the rigid pose of the teenager who is more closely bonded to peer group than to family, who is more Destiny's Child than Daddy's Girl. The pressures come from all over, from department stores, where retailers push high-cut and low-cut styles onto the 6X set (known as "tweens"), to concert venues, where Nickelodeon, for example, has sponsored national "Kiddiepalooza" rock 'n' roll tours. In an excellent book, *"Ready or Not: Why Treating Children as Small Adults*

Endangers Their Future and Ours," author Kay S. Hymowitz analyzes this phenomenon, noting the complicity of parents who have ceded their influence to pop cultural dictates of what is hip and what is nerdy. Where the home was once seen as a haven from the marketplace (not to mention the setting for birthday parties), it is now, thanks to television and the Internet, a 24-hour bazaar of bad attitude sanctioned and financially supported by all too many parents.

Such as the ones who chose Colette's for their daughter's sixth birthday celebration, starring Britney Spears and the Backstreet Boys. This music of adolescent yearning and oh-so-fragile feelings is beyond wrong for youngsters; it is indecent. Why introduce "the reason I breathe is you" to little ones who still relish a good round of "Frere Jacques"?

Children need to be molded and guided, introduced to what is good and protected from what is bad. Whatever you do, they'll still become teenagers. My daughter, poor thing, didn't get off to an early start. Dear, old mom telephoned her regrets.

Lost in The Matrix

5-27-03

It's a recurring question: How do movies influence behavior?

Fashion designers expect movies to influence taste, otherwise they wouldn't be hanging "Matrix"-y trench coats on the racks this fall. CEOs think movies influence consumption, otherwise they wouldn't pay to place their products on a movie set. Movies affect the way people talk (cuss), comb their hair (or not), kiss and make up.

Almost everyone admits a link between reel people's habits and real people's habits except Hollywood, particularly when it comes to the connection between screen violence and street violence.

"I don't know what the links are," said producer Joel Silver.

Mr. Silver, of course, is the man behind "The Matrix" series, in which anti-gravitational bouts of violence punctuate human efforts to liberate themselves from an omnipotent computer network — the Matrix. The producer was reacting to a Washington Post article about several murder cases in which "The Matrix" has emerged as "a central theme." Not possible, according to Mr. Silver. The movie, he said, is "a wonderful fantasy story that doesn't take place in the real world" — a catch-all description roomy enough to include "Snow White."

"I can't comment on what makes people do what they do," added Silver.

Not everyone is tongue-tied. A poll of parents commissioned by Common Sense Media, a new media monitoring group, finds that 80 percent believe movies (such as "The Matrix") -- along with television, music and video products — promote violence in their children. Not all of which remains under control.

Rachel M. Fierro, currently defending Josh Cooke, a 19-year-old Virginia man accused of murdering his parents, described her client as being "obsessed" with "The Matrix." According to a court-appointed psychiatrist, Mr. Cooke "harbored a bona fide belief that he was living in the virtual reality of 'The Matrix'" when he allegedly gunned down Mom and Dad. So, too, did Vadim Mieseges, who, police say, described himself as having been "sucked into The Matrix" before killing and dismembering his landlord in California. He was found not guilty by reason of insanity. Tonda Lynn Ansley, who, curiously, also murdered her landlord, later told authorities in Ohio she "lived" in The Matrix. She, too, was found not guilty by reason of insanity. Maybe pleading not guilty by reason of "The Matrix" would have been more appropriate.

There's more: "Wake up! Free your mind, you are a slave to the matrix 'control,'" Washington sniper suspect Lee Boyd Malvo wrote from a Virginia jail cell this year. "The outside force has arrived. Free yourself of the matrix 'control' ..." Blah, blah — you get the picture.

No word on whether the suspect's defense team will enter an insanity plea. But maybe that's beside the point. While a significant legal decision on the sniper case lies ahead, the Matrix-ing of the culture is already here. The movie's inspirational role in a rash of murders makes all the headlines, but its wider impact probably lies with the law-abiding population.

The fact is, even though most of us will never see a single "Matrix" movie, all of us live with their influences — what one (approving, if ironic) write-up said becomes "our characteristic pose in the history books: sullen, dystopian, jaded." It's bad enough when you pay to study that pose on a two-dimensional movie screen, but perfectly awful to encounter it, say, in a three-dimensional clerk at the hardware store.

However, that is our lot, to live in a time when the biggest cultural influence of the day isn't, alas, "Lives of a Bengal Lancer" with Gary Cooper (characteristic pose: courageous and downright noble), but is "The Matrix Reloaded" with Keanu Reeves — one more numbing dump of violence and a very pretentious foray into darkness that is embarrassingly empty.

It is also, as demonstrated by the murder cases to date, quite potent. Experts may not directly pin crimes to "The Matrix" — or "Natural Born Killers" or "The Basketball Diaries," to name other movies associated with murder cases — but they tend to believe, as the Post pointed out, that movies "with suggestions of hidden evil and uncertain reality" encourage violent behavior in the mentally ill "by helping unhealthy fantasy worlds to flourish."

Which isn't so edifying for anyone else, moviegoer or homebody.

Not that movies have to be edifying, exactly. But we find ourselves at a strange bottleneck, a stranglehold of the sullen, dystopian and jaded — a cultural matrix in need of an overhaul.

Madonna meets middle age

9-22-03

In times like these — times of heightened discord and possibly tectonic upheaval — there's little reason to linger on a culture-blip like the publishing launch of a series of kiddie books by Madonna. No doubt there are contrasts to be drawn between the semi-retired pop queen's latest and most dubious incarnation as a tea-sipping sort of Mrs. Miniver who writes children's books, and her extremely sordid, extremely lucrative career as a pop-exhibitionist. (Said career in pop-exhibitionism includes one prior publishing lark as a porno-spread subject and author in a book called "Sex.")

Still, anyone who has successfully parried the thrust of all recent media hoopla — equal parts pretentious and nauseous-making — over Madonna and the kissing pop tarts on MTV will understand the reflexive instinct to shield the eyes from all Madonna news. But the pop-ostrich in me just couldn't resist something Madonna said — a real mouthful — to the Times of London Sunday magazine.

It was about her 7-year-old daughter, Lourdes, and Madonna's long career of mass-marketing her own vulgar sexuality. Quoth Madonna (given her current and slavish pursuit of English toff-dom, she's bound to do a lot of quothing): "I protect her from sex full stop. She's not aware of sex, nor should she be. You know, we've had little conversations about where babies come from, but sex is not, and should not be, part of her repertoire right now." Full stop?

Given that Madonna is one of the pre-eminent despoilers of youthful innocence, this, as her new compatriots might say, is crust. That is, there's Bill Clinton — whose lasting legacy is American youth's working knowledge of oral sex — and, of course, several generations of relentless promoters of sex, drugs and rock and roll; nonetheless, it is Madonna who first shredded virginity and wedding dresses into pop mega-hits, displaying a leave-us-alone exhibitionism that wreaked havoc on girlhood. Well and good that Madonna has had "little conversations" with her daughter about where babies come from; but what about the conversations about where Mommy's riches come from?

Later, Madonna says. She says she someday plans to tell Lourdes her career as a sexual provocateur was all an act, which may or may not be comforting. "I'd explain that's me putting on a show. I'm playing a character, it's not really me. I'm being an actress. This may work for

Madonna-the-delusionist. Indeed, the 45-year-old wife and mother may have moved on permanently to floral prints, matching pumps and a kiddie book that is rooted, Madonna is quick to emphasize, in her seven-year study of Jewish mysticism.

The rest of us, meanwhile, remain stuck among her true spawn — little girls and big, baby Britneys and Madonna-wannabes, who believe that exhibitionism is liberation, that the birds and the bees equal "hooking up," and, almost worse of all, that bra straps and navels are outerwear. Thus, has sexuality — to borrow a phrase from the late Sen. Daniel Patrick Moynihan — been defined down, down, down. Little mystery here — let alone mysticism.

No wonder Madonna hopes to protect her wee one. Which is precisely what many of us spend our own children's early years trying to do: We resist the extent to which sexuality, particularly female sexuality, has been snatched from its traditional time and place in human development — as a rite of passage to adulthood, to marriage, to having children — and grafted onto girlhood.

The sexualization of childhood may not have started with Madonna, but under her pop influence, and under that of her pop descendants, it became pretty irreversible. Madonna says she has no regrets. But neither does she appear to understand her own leading role in coarsening the culture against which she now guards her daughter.

She does admit that what was cast as a crusade for sexual honesty in the 1980s and 1990s was really something of a scam. "Was I really trying to liberate people?" she asks rhetorically. "Or was I just being an exhibitionist and basking in the glory of being able to do what I wanted. I think that probably was mostly what it was."

So do I. But while she exhibited and basked and did what she wanted — and grew wealthy beyond exaggeration — she could always take shelter in an impervious cocoon of wealth and cultural influence. (The multitudes she influenced to bare all and do all, alas, had no such protection.) Now that she has moved on a little bit, wearing specs and writing children's books, maybe she is finally trying to hide her tracks. We know for sure she is trying to hide her daughter. Not that she can, of course. Which is too bad, because the real Madonna — the notorious global persona — isn't too savory an influence on anybody's growing girl.

Censorship across the divide: #%$^ that!

2/2/04

My husband received the following letter from a waggish friend: "I just wanted to wish you and yours a happy holiday. I'll leave it at 'holiday' to avoid running afoul of the ACLU ...

"On second thought, I withdraw 'holiday.' It derives from 'holy day,' which clearly presents problems. And 'season's greetings,' a well-known dodge, suggests other difficulties. With global warming, what is a season? So I'll just say, 'Timely greetings to you and yours.' Uh, wait. 'Yours' implies possession of the female. Maybe it should be, 'Timely greetings to you and those who, through their own free choice, the same choice we cherish in Roe v. Wade, choose to be associated with you.'

"Nor will I mention the so-called 'new year.' After all, other cultures celebrate their new year at other times. Who are we imperialists to demand our own?

"I find this time of year so difficult. Don't you?"

In a word, yes. Everyone has a war story from the Yuletide front, where Christmas comes under such heavy fire that Americans wave the pre-emptive white flag of "Happy Holidays" to avoid giving what is known as "offense" and receiving what feels like censure. Not that "Christmas" is the ultimate unmentionable. A story recently made the rounds about a Virginia teacher who spoke the utterly non-denominational (in fact, traditionally superstitious) injunction "God bless you" over a sneezy student. Said student, sniveling wretch, proceeded to inform on the teacher for this act of New Blasphemy, for which the teacher was, incredibly, reprimanded.

Such developments make New York Governor George Pataki's posthumous pardon of Lenny Bruce's obscenity conviction all the more, well, offensive. Lenny Bruce, of course, was a comic celebrated since his fatal drug overdose for being the first performer to stand on a stage and give voice to all of those words that are usually represented in print by typewriter symbols. (He also found fun in St. Paul's sex life, Eleanor Roosevelt's anatomy and Jacqueline Kennedy's reaction to her husband's assassination.) Pataki saw fit to call the pardon "a declaration of New York's commitment to upholding the First Amendment."

What is there to say when four-letter words get a commitment to uphold the First Amendment, but "Merry Christmas" (not to mention "God bless you") is an offense punishable by sensitivity training? And how strange that Lenny Bruce's expletives deleted so long ago were effectively restored in the same month the Supreme Court effectively censored G-rated political speech by upholding the McCain-Feingold campaign finance reform act?

Confusing? The reaction to the Bruce pardon by Ronald K. L. Collins, a First Amendment scholar and pardon proponent, is unlikely to clarify things. "You see, there is a God," said Collins to The New York Times upon hearing the news. (A letter to the editor only deepened the muddle by describing Bruce as having "died for our sins.") The New York Times, by the way, has practically run more stories on the Bruce pardon than on the capture of Saddam Hussein. Funny how the same paper — along with the rest of Big Media — has put a veritable gag order on the recent doings of the obvious heirs to Lenny Bruce, those foul-mouthed comedians who have come out to raise money for Howard Dean.

It took the New York Post's Deborah Orin to report in any detail on the "X-rated, epithet-ridden" comedy-fund-raiser held for the Democratic front-runner last month in New York City. The event included Judy Gold calling President Bush "this piece of living, breathing s — -"; Janeane Garofalo deriding the Medicare prescription-drug bill Bush recently signed as the "you can go f — - yourself, Grandma, bill"; and Sandra Bernhard insulting Condoleeza Rice "in racial terms with a 'Yes Massa' accent at another Dean fund-raiser the same night." Dropping the n-word for blacks, David Cross "joked" that Republicans are racists, while Vice President Dick Cheney's daughter Mary was derided as "a big lezzie." Dean, "fuming," according to his aides, did nothing to stop the session. Republicans, Orin wrote, "say that if anything like this had happened at an event where a top Republican was present and did nothing to stop it, the media would rage about it for weeks."

The fact is, censorship is no less a part of our society because comics are free to cuss and soil; indeed, the lines that cannot be crossed without social sanction are as indelible as ever. The difference lies only in the location of the lines. With four-letter-language — and insults against Republicans — you're on terra firma; when it comes to holiday greetings, you're on your own. H — — N — Y — -.

Mucking out the media barn

12/3/04

Taking a break from reading 676-page "I Am Charlotte Simmons," Tom Wolfe's primal scream of a public service announcement that depicts college as more Hefner mansion than ivory tower, I happened to scan an article about a new trend in architectural preservation. Rural shacks, sheds and ramshackle barns are no longer seen as demolition targets, The New York Times reports, but rather as favored facades for contemporary arts and leisure activities among professionals with second homes.

Naturally, an old barn becomes an art studio, but a pigpen also becomes a poolside cabana, and a 19th-century chicken coop becomes a 21st-century space for a film production company and a business making "waterproof postsurgical booties for dogs."

How antiseptic life on these old farms has become. No muck, no sweat. No remnants of the herd life that once defined the landscape. It's an interior world now, of stretched canvas, computer disks, videotape, clean towels and tiny rubber boots. This may be a leap, but I can't help comparing this postmodern version of "clean" living to the destiny of Wolfe's brave new collegians. How will they ever sweep away the dirt of the sordid, subhuman life they lead at his novel's Dupont College?

This isn't to say that Wolfe's book about sex and the college kid is a shock, exactly. You would have to live somewhere over the rainbow, beyond the range of the satellite dish, not to be familiar with the pulsating, orgiastic media sac in which parents set their teens to gestate, where they suck up the noxious currents of scatologically idiotic Hollywood and sexually berserk MTV until society deems them fit for four years of "higher education." This is the point at which we meet them in the book. What follows — the phenomenon of "hooking up" and related degradations described in this investigation of the decline of a freshman woman — is not what's new. But in the Wolfeian accumulation of detail, much of it clinical, and the torrential rain of expletives, there is an unavoidable tsunami of revelation, all of it crashingly depressing. College as we know it becomes something to rethink, particularly at $40,000 per annum.

That's because "I Am Charlotte Simmons" is a cautionary tale, a sexually and emotionally frank work of polemical fiction that should shake the young even as it speaks to their parents. But will they listen? Explicit as the book is about unconstrained bodily functions (not all sexual), it's a definite rap on the 1960s revolution that sanctified promiscuities from "free love" to hooking up. Which seems to irritate reviewers peering into the book from the Left. They seem to resent the fact that this massive tome is no "Sex and the Dorm" or "Desperate Coeds," even if it shares certain themes in common with both "Sex and the City" and "Desperate Housewives." But where "Charlotte Simmons" is disturbing and dispiriting, "Sex" and "Housewives" are supposed to titillate and lead on.

And they do more than that. Like the crime show "CSI," their kin in coarseness, "Housewives" et. al. expand the boundaries of accepted, even expected, talk and behavior. A ratings squib on "CSI: Miami" noted that 22.26 million viewers is a lot of people to hear a character remark, "Where there's vomit, there's bile. Where there's bile, there's DNA." Television crimesolvers from Peter Wimsey to Columbo never thought to mention such goos, which probably says less about their reticence than about the contemporary pose of full-frontal exposure.

According to Newsweek, one "Housewives" script called for a character to shame her TV husband by publicly announcing he "cries after he — ." (I omit the verb, if only to keep my byline Google-pure.) According to the magazine, the actress "blanched when she first read the scene. 'Honestly, I was, like, I can't say that line,' she says. But she did," the story continues, "and with the kind of glee (the character) reserves for a perfect soufflé."

"But she did" is hardly the end of the story. In overriding instinctive modesty or even the irrelevant tug of good manners, this actress did more than force herself to imagine and project an image of sexual humiliation. She also passed it on to the rest of us. She pushed the envelope where we think and live. She ensured such yuck will come across the TV screen more easily next time — and also in real life.

Vomit, bile and explicit ick. Frankly, it's a heap for poor Charlotte Simmons to have to muck out alone.

Bob Guccione's pornographic legacy

1/14/05

For about 24 hours, my hat was off to the seven members of the board governing the Jackson-George Regional Library System in southern Mississippi. They had decided, officially, not to make room on the shelf in any of their eight libraries in Jackson and George Counties for one of the best-selling books in America today, the book that Publishers Weekly named best book of 2004: "America (The Book)," a mock-textbook in mock-civics by mock-anchorman Jon Stewart and the writers of "The Daily Show."

Or maybe I should write: a "textbook" in "civics" by "anchorman" Jon Stewart and the writers of "The Daily Show." All of those quotation marks, of course, convey the nudge-nudge nihilism that is comedian-cum-author Stewart's stock-in-trade. Not that it was Stewart's brand of "comedy" (see, I can do it, too) that brought on the ban, briefly, but a visual aid in the pages of the book. On page 99, the book features a photograph of the nine justices of the Supreme Court posed to reveal what the skin mags not all that long ago taught us to call "full-frontal nudity." USA Today elaborated on the phrase to describe the poses as "full-frontal, sagging nudity." Which could be further amended to "full-frontal, sagging, puckered, spreading nudity."

The photos are fakes, of course, with naked bodies culled from a nudist Web site superimposed to match the familiar faces of the court. Cutouts of the justice's black robes hang nearby, with a caption instructing readers to "restore their dignity by matching each justice with his or her respective robe." It was all too much for Wal-Mart, which decided not to sell the book in its stores (although it is available at Wal-Mart online). And it was too much for the Jackson-George librarians.

"We're not an adult bookstore," said library system director Robert Willits. "Our entire collection is open to the public. If they had published the book without that one picture, that one page, we'd have the book."

Of course, they do have the book, now, after news of the ban triggered a wave of sentiment, local and national, in favor of circulating the book. The board has reversed itself, and "America (The Book)" has already been checked out in seven out of eight branches.

But it was nice while it lasted. The ban, I mean. For a minute there, it seemed that Babbitt was alive and well in Mississippi, striking a quixotic blow for the kind of middle-class morality that once strived to cordon off the public square to keep it neat and clean — sterile, even, in that wholesome way that once drove true artists out of bounds and into paroxysms of creativity. In the age of the Internet and wireless communication, such boundaries are nothing less than quaint and nothing more than window-dressing, just a handsome-prince fantasy in a reality of cultural degradation.

The same day I happened on the library story, I came across a lavish profile in Vanity Fair of pornographer Bob Guccione. It is an exercise in hagiography, depicting the 74-year-old former Penthouse publisher as "the fallen king," "one of the greatest success stories in magazine history" blah, blah, done in by "Reagan-era censorship, the Internet, and a series of expensive dreams." In other words, no typography of irony here. (Save that for "democracy" in Jon Stewart's "America.") Lamented son Bob Jr.: "He wanted so much to be acknowledged for something other than pornography."

But what a pornographer he was. Having launched Penthouse in 1969, "Bob outraunched Playboy by displaying genitalia and pubic hair in a magazine," a colleague told Vanity Fair approvingly. "That had never been done before." Certainly not in a magazine that plied the mainstream, both as a widely available mass publication, and as a mass influence on a wide variety of publications.

Which is where "America (The Book)" comes back in. The Guccione article alludes to a hazard of the porn trade: jaded customers, which were already a concern for magazine pornographers by the middle 1970s. Simply having lived through the several decades since — even through a brief description of those decades — makes us all, to some extent, jaded customers. Which means that no one, not even in Mississippi, is shocked by nudity alone. What is troubling is the, well, naked intention to level a pillar of our democracy — the law — and leave behind vicious little images of humiliation and shame, discomfort and exposure. Which is a kind of pornography in itself, I would argue, but one Americans seem happy to consume.

This gives Bob Guccione another legacy after all: "America."

Bobby Short was much more than a saloon singer

3/25/05

Every so often, my dad laughs about a kid with whom he served in the Army during World War II. This fellow wasn't a big pal; just a guy he knew from New Jersey, 18 or 19 years old. One day, kidding around, this young GI started to dance my dad, also 18 or 19 years old, around the barracks singing, "Cheek to Cheek" — a perfect if unconventional standard by Irving Berlin, introduced by Fred Astaire in "Top Hat." Now consigned to the rarefied, quite narrow stratum of cabaret, this was the kind of tune that was playing in the head of the American enlisted man circa 1943.

This anecdote occurred to me this week at the news that Bobby Short had died, age 80. As the cabaret singer nonpareil — he preferred the job description "saloon singer" — Bobby Short and his passing were duly noted with deservedly generous obits and glowing appreciations. His flair, his sophistication, his giant musicality made all the papers, as did his high-society status as a New York institution, commemorated on film by another New York institution, Woody Allen, who featured the pianist in "Hannah and Her Sisters." His elegance in a dinner jacket, his insouciance with a song, all received their due. But his salient contribution to society — high, low and otherwise — went completely unmentioned.

That contribution was the leading role Bobby Short played in saving the American popular song. Once upon a time, the music Bobby Short played for the mink-and-mimosa set — the marvelously vital and enchanting songs of Rodgers and Hart, Cole Porter, the Gershwins, Noel Coward, Frank Loesser, Duke Ellington, Harold Arlen and many others — flowed along just fine in the meat-and-potatoes mainstream, dancing GIs included. Then came the rock 'n' roll flood that washed away everything that came before it. "I barely kept the wolf from the door!" Bobby Short told one reporter, recalling the 1960s as the most difficult time in his life. But just as the Irish monks on their windy crags preserved the texts of Western civilization through the Dark Ages, Bobby Short at his piano in the Cafe Carlyle on the Upper East Side of Manhattan preserved the American standard through the Rock Ages — albeit more glamorously.

Twice a night, five nights a week, six months a year, starting in 1968 — the year of the Tet Offensive, "Hair" and Richard Nixon — Bobby Short played, sang and breathed life into the American popular songbook that the new rock culture had slammed shut.

And he didn't just play, sing and breathe life into the 100 most familiar songs of the genre — the showstoppers and signature tunes that make up the less adventurous repertoires of more pedestrian performers.

On the contrary, Bobby Short sought out tunes no one had heard before (and there are hundreds) — or at least hadn't heard since the 1930s when they were cut from the overlong scores of pre-Broadway shows playing out of town. On sides one through four of "Bobby Short Loves Cole Porter," for example, he never sings the familiar Porter tunes "Night and Day" or "I Get a Kick Out of You," but he does sing the freshly effervescent "Rap Tap on Wood," "How's Your Romance?" and "Let's Fly Away." His albums and set lists always contained some "new" gem, something a musicologist might have dug out of the vaults. Indeed, along with the unsurpassable zest and grace that made him a dazzling performer, Bobby Short approached the pop oeuvre with the care and diligence of the archivist.

Sure, the modern mainstream left Bobby Short high and dry. But having managed to paddle into the posh pond of the Carlyle, he was able to lure all the big fish in New York — the movers and socials, the royals and shakers — to hear him play the songs he so infectiously adored. (And me. I got there twice.) That swank boite of a living laboratory kept this music going, endowing it with presence and cachet in a time otherwise dead to it. I'm not sure anyone else could have done it. Younger cabaret singers notwithstanding, I'm not sure anyone else can do it now.

Bobby Short, R.I.P. "Easy Come, Easy Go"? (As that song by Eddie Heyman and Johnny Green says.) Hardly. This was, as Cole Porter's tune states, "At Long Last Love." And, to borrow a title from a new (to me) Rodgers and Hart song, "How Can You Forget?"

One more thing. Heading uptown to see Bobby Short may well have been a bow to Western civ, but a pilgrimage to the Carlyle was nothing but fun.

Laura Bush: No laughing matter

5/9/05

Lovely Laura Bush: yuk-yuk, or just yuck?
The event under consideration — the first lady's monologue at the White House Correspondents' Dinner — weighs in alongside flotsam and jetsam, but the question has hefty ramifications. It may be the ultimate "litmus test," a chance to reveal something more vital than mere politics, and certainly less easily defined: the state of public taste and judgment.

This should come as something of a relief to those among us weary of the well-worn Red State, Blue State divide. Better to carve up the world between those who found Laura Bush's jokes funny, and those who didn't.

Or, rather, those who found Laura Bush's jokes an ornament to the White House, and those who wished a grownup had happened by the East Wing to yank them from the script and throw in some nifty new adventures of Barney.

Why? When a woman happens to be first lady, "funny" at any expense isn't part of the job description, not when "funny" comes at the expense of her husband's image. And I don't mean "image" as in public relations product. I mean "image" as in public symbol. World leader. Commander-in-chief. In these explosive times, with tens of thousands of soldiers under arms. Which is a sobering thought, or should be.

In other words, feet of clay are fine, but there's no reason to bring the barnyard into it. Whoopi Goldberg steered a Democratic fund-raiser into the gutter last summer with a crude pun on the Bush family name, prompting Republican accusations that John Kerry didn't "share the same values" as the rest of America.

But what about the rest of the Bush family? Laura Bush is no stand-up comic, but that's all the more reason certain sorts of "jokes" should be automatically, reflexively, unquestioningly ruled out for her public delivery. Jokes that link the president's hands and the underside of a horse, for instance. Jokes that create a regrettably indelible image of the first lady, the vice president's wife, the secretary of state, and a Supreme Court justice together at Chippendale's, waving dollars bills at male strippers. Even jokes that make a "Mommie Dearest" out of former first lady Barbara Bush. Such material won't pull more than a PG rating these days, but a first lady in any era should be mature enough to avoid all "adult" material.

Once upon a time, such discretion was a no-brainer, an obvious rule that needed no articulation, much less conscious thought. No more — which is why there seem to be more people, including conservatives, applauding Mrs. Bush than sitting on their hands. We live in a society that prizes the guffaw above all, where "lighten up" is a commandment and anything really does go. But it goes for no reason. That is, I can think of no reason to motivate a first lady to mock a president in front of a White House press corps that makes a career of doing so on a daily basis. "George," she said, "if you really want to end tyranny in the world, you're going to have to stay up later." The hilarity of her moment passes, but something has changed.

Exactly what it is that has changed is difficult to explain. After all, the whole thing was "just" a joke. But Laura Bush is not Joan Rivers. Splashing into the media mainstream to join the derisive fun, decoupling fateful words from mortal purpose, is a risky proposition for the wife of a superpower leader. One day, "ending tyranny" is Mr. Bush's raison d'etre; the next day, it is Mrs. Bush's punch line.

The day after that — who knows? The lingering air of uncertainty is hardly worth the media snickers, even if the first lady did manage to "humanize" her husband, as The New York Times so admiringly put it. Certainly, she knocked him down some pegs, which in our age is much the same thing. But imagine other presidencies, particularly in wartime. Would we have said Eleanor humanized FDR by doing a stand-up routine about Franklin always "fearing fear itself"? Or that Pat Nixon humanized Richard by wondering where the heck the peace was that Dick said was "at hand"? Or that Nancy Reagan humanized Ron by teasing him about tearing down that old wall?

"Lighten up," they say, in a programmed response. No thanks. A laugh-track nation doesn't really offer serious comic relief.

Replacing duty and honor with 'South Park'

5/13/05

I do while perusing the morning Internet is read the military obituaries in the British press, mainly The Daily Telegraph.

Invariably, these write-ups mark the passing of a veteran of World War II in the kind of scope and detail, as critic James Bowman has noted, rarely found in an American paper. Sometimes, I feel compelled to save them in a file. Last summer, there was Wing Commander David Penman, 85, one of five Lancaster bombers pilots (out of 12 who started on the mission) to return in 1942 from a daring, low-flying, daylight raid on a German engine plant; the year before that, there was Capt. Philip "Pip" Gardner, the Victoria Cross-winning tank commander captured at the fall of Tobruk. His death at age 88 left only 15 (now 14) surviving VC-holders. Just this week, there was 84-year-old Petty Officer Norman Walton, who, after the cruiser Neptune was sunk in a minefield off Libya in 1941, endured three days in the water and two on a raft to become the sole survivor out of 765 crewmembers. A boxer of some success after the war, Petty Officer Walton thwarted two muggers with a left hook and a head-butt at age 82.

But there is more to these tales than derring-do. There is usually a line, maybe two, that offers the modern-day reader an almost shocking glimpse of a mode of behavior based on virtues unconstrained by the strictures of modern-day hipness, smarts and irony. For example, in his account of the final moments of the Neptune, Petty Officer Walton described clinging to the side of a raft in cold, heavy seas thick with oil. "We saw the ship capsize and sink, and gave her a cheer as she went down."

Was it a huzzah, maybe? Hip, hip, hooray? In their struggle for survival, these doomed sailors could still muster a salute that would save not their lives, but their gallantry. Only I can see it now: Jon Stewart on "The Daily Show," ripping this beau geste into ironic little bits.

Then there was Lt. Col. Duncan Campbell, 91, who was awarded two Military Crosses in 1940 in the East Africa Campaign. Walking ahead of the two infantry companies he was leading on a strong Italian position, the Telegraph reported, "he ensured that his C.O. did not lose sight of him in the rough terrain by singing the theme song from the film 'Sanders of the River' at the top of his voice amid the crack of rifle bullets and the noise of shell explosions." (I gather "Sanders of the River" is a cinematic ode to Empire along the lines of the 1939 version of "The Four Feathers.") It's almost difficult to read about such dazzling bravery without also imagining a Monty Python-esque parody popping up like a jack-in-the-box to deconstruct it between the lines. But such was life before the "Desperate Housewife" and the "South Park" conservative, a time when the cultural mainstream — the all-enveloping mass media — treated duty and honor like dependable anchors rather than balls-and-chains.

That was a good half-century or so ago. In the interim, the sensibility these men expressed as deeds in their youth has died a death for which there was no obituary. A flood of affluence, the Baby Boom, the forces of political correctness and celebrity worship have seen to that. Which is not at all to say that their virtues no longer exist.

The bravery and sacrifice and commitment of our armed forces, most obviously, prove otherwise. But I think it's fair to say that such virtues exist despite the mainstream culture rather than because of it.

This, in itself, is a testament to the innate resilience of something very good. But word is that the future of the very conservatism that has always prized such virtues lies in the hands of "South Park Conservatives," after the book by the same name by Brian C. Anderson. Very basically, the theory posits that the rank vulgarity institutionalized by the cartoon "South Park," which degrades and desacralizes absolutely everything, will inspire young conservatives to smash the stultifying tyranny of political correctness. If you're picking sides, P.C. vs. South Park offers about as much choice as the Iran-Iraq War — which, remember, after eight years of carnage, left both sides still afloat.

Such stalemate on the cultural high seas is probably where we are, and certainly where we're heading. But I wonder who will give a cheer when we sink?

Searching for accurate information in sex education

6/6/05

Last month, a federal judge found the Montgomery County School Board's sex-education pilot plan in Maryland so flagrantly in violation of the First Amendment that he had to hand down a restraining order. (Either that or hand in his gavel forever.) With the sex-ed plan's legal route blocked, the school board ditched the whole idea for now, along with the citizens committee that waved it through in the first place, despite plenty of flapping red flags.

OK, there were two really big red flags. Judge Alexander Williams Jr. called one "viewpoint discrimination" because, as he wrote, the new curriculum for 10th graders was supposed to teach that "homosexuality is a natural and morally correct lifestyle — to the exclusion of other perspectives." Also outrageous was the way the curriculum promoted certain religions to the exclusion of others. In touting "the moral rightness of the homosexual lifestyle," the judge wrote, the curriculum suggested that "the Baptist Church's position on homosexuality is theologically flawed," and reminiscent of the racial prejudice of the segregation era. At the same time, the curriculum applauded Reform Jews, Unitarians and Quakers for promoting an activist homosexual political agenda. If you're wondering when religious prejudice or favoritism became a subject fit for the public schools to preach — I mean, teach — the answer is never. And that's what the court ruled.

But imagine if the school board had been smart enough to reel in those First Amendment red flags on which this particular sex-ed course was hung out to dry. Would Montgomery County teens be sitting down to become both "informed" and desensitized by the course's instructional video on how to apply a condom to a cucumber? Would these kids be reflecting on their curriculum's no doubt scholarly treatment of all manner of sexual experimentation? In this hyper-sexualized culture of ours, I'm afraid the answer has to be yes.

But kudos to the parents in Montgomery County who banded together to stop this sex-ed train on its way out of the station. After it retools, the same basic train will undoubtedly chug away in the fall. My question is, do we like where it's going, and, if not, how do we get off?

It's a track we've been stuck on for a long time — since 1930, in fact, when the Second Circuit Court of Appeals "forever changed the course of obscenity law," writes Rochelle Gurstein in her illuminating book "The Repeal of Reticence" (Hill and Wang, 1998). It was then, in an acclaimed case, that the court ruled that sex-education material could no longer be considered illicit. According to Judge Augustus Hand, "accurate information, rather than mystery and curiosity, is better in the long view and is less likely to occasion lascivious thoughts than ignorance and anxiety."

But, as Gurstein points out, "accurate information" did more than remedy "ignorance and anxiety." After all, she explains, "ignorance and anxiety" were only part of the human condition. "Equally important," she writes, "were considerations of the inherent fragility of intimate life, the tone of public conversation, standards of taste and morality, and reverence owed to mysteries. These defining characteristics of the reticent sensibility had been lost."

"Lost" isn't the word. Something more forceful (pulverized? mutilated?) is in order to describe the, well, fallen condition of a world in which — just to take a random example — a new Simon & Schuster teen title, "Rainbow Party," that recounts a tale of an oral group sex party for the "young adult" set. (Thanks, Bill Clinton.) I'm both happy and resentful to report that so-called rainbow parties — reportedly a real-life trend — are a new one on me: happy that I've lived multiple decades without an inkling; resentful that I'm now and forever stuck with the knowledge. Who needs it?

More important — what does making such berserk sexual adventurism a mass-cultural commonplace do to the individual human psyche? Are we better off so limitlessly coarsened? Are our children? Certainly, the publishing industry is better off. According to The New York Times, publisher Judith Regan, among others, has capitalized on sex-in-the-citified sensibilities to inaugurate a "growing and increasingly racy genre of how-to sex books ... extolling the excitement that could come from oral sex, anal sex, fetishism and S&M."

So glad to hear what now constitutes "racy." What we really need, though, are some new definitions of pornographic, obscene, lewd — categories the courts told us decades ago don't really exist. I think they do. And I think we've wallowed in them long enough.

The real taboo

10/9/06

What may be most revolting about ex-Rep. Mark Foley is what shows through his debasing IM sex talk with teenage boys: the congressman's absolute lack of what was once known as restraint, inhibition, a sense of social taboo. In this same absence of restraint is the absence of a moral compass guided by maturity.

On a different level (one removed from sexual malfeasance), there's something somewhat unseemly about the media's unblushing — dare I say shameless? — reportage. They may claim a fig leaf by acting in the "public interest," but that doesn't completely cover up a practically carnal zeal for smutty details. And let's not even think about the IM-leaker's as-yet secret ecstasy. Restraint, inhibition and social taboo have become dirty words in the decades since the 1960s, but the culture that lets it all hang out, it seems, doesn't have much inside.

I say this as the rapid-response conventional wisdom insists the Foley fiasco will discourage GOP voter turnout in November, particularly among all-important, so-called "values voters," thereby vaulting Democratic majorities into Congress. If so, this is a 21st-century twist on Bread and Circuses any Roman emperor would applaud. In the ancient tradition of distracting Ye Olde Populi from events of national import, sex-scandal-focused GOP voters are expected to stay home because of Mark Foley's appalling lack of traditional values, helping to elect Democrats who are more likely to eschew such values in the first place. And the war goes on — or not, with Democrats in charge.

All of which is to say that Foley's transgressions (first, overlooked by the House GOP leadership, and later, set to explode at election-time by persons unknown) are unlikely to resonate culturally even as they have become political dynamite. That's partly because the GOP in smithereens is never a victory for "values." It's also because Foley is less a creation of his "traditional values" GOP than he is a creature (cretin) of his time — our sex-drenched time. It's also because society's ire is directed not at his (homo)sexuality, but at his exploitation of youth and power. Such context doesn't excuse Foley's monstrous behavior, but it helps explain why his fall, why the Republicans' possible fall, won't usher in an era of cultural restoration.

Meanwhile, cultural restoration isn't what this election is about. It can't be. Culture wars, such as they are, necessarily become secondary political issues in times of war. And these are certainly times of war, even if leaders on both sides prefer to mask them in less momentous terms, as when they exhort us not to triumph over Islamic jihadism, but rather to fight against "terror," or, lately, "extremism."

Come to think of it, maybe such rigid adherence to euphemism is a bona fide show of restraint. But in this case, "restraint" is not mature. Restraining the libido (which Foley did not amid a culture that does not) comes down to a matter of mind (or morality) over matter — a display of forbearance which is by definition mature. Intellectual restraint — self-censorship — in matters of war and peace belies a lack of will or confidence that defines the unformed uncertainty of immature man.

Then again, maybe war-talk "inhibitions" simply show how "repressed" we are as when we observe the "social taboo" of denying the Islamic nature of our foe. I'm playing around with these 1960s cliches to try to illustrate a key aspect of our social condition: Sexually untrammeled, we have become intellectually moribund. We continue, tiresomely, to highlight sexuality in the culture, even as we continue, perilously, to stifle debate that touches on non-Western topics such as Islam. Are the two related? You bet, because they both carry the stamp of approval from the school of political correctness that was established amid the sexual revolution and the rise of multiculturalism. What we might regard as sexual liberationism and multiculturally rigged reason are on track to roll back the Enlightenment that produced Western civilization as we know it today.

This symbiosis may in the end help explain why, in the midst of a global war to determine the fate of Western civilization (as in whether Western civilization will continue to have a fate), American voters and politicians alike appear poised to turn all-important midterm elections into a meaningless referendum on a sexual predator already ostracized, while still failing to debate, examine, or even recognize urgent facts before us.

For a culture with few taboos, we sure have a lot of hang-ups.

For whom the bell weeps

9/21/07

I love Ernest Hemingway.

That's a switch for this column, but not for me. Ever since sophomore year in college, I've hung his picture near my desk — his youthful passport photo, which made the cover of The New York Times Magazine on the publication of a letters collection, which I framed — and that's a long time ago.

Haven't read him much for nearly as long, although I did take "A Moveable Feast" on a trip to Paris, "The Garden of Eden" to the south of France, and "For Whom the Bell Tolls" to Spain (where the bag the book was in was stolen outside Cadaques), but that's also a while back. Lately, he crosses my mind only when I exchange the occasional glance with his photo on the wall.

But then I began reading about his relationship with his legendary editor Maxwell Perkins, and his lifelong publisher, Charles Scribner's Sons, in a new book called "The Lousy Racket" (Kent State) by Robert W. Trogdon. I now realize how much the path-breaking writer's experience in the 1920s and 1930s says about us as a society, both then — when Hemingway's writerly urge to use the rare profanity presented his publishers with a legal and moral nightmare; and now — when four-letter language is shoptalk, ads for sexual performance aids are as much a part of the national past time as home plate, and even children have become consumers of what can only be called pornography.

And whose nightmare is that? The answer is all of us little people who no longer have gatekeepers like Maxwell Perkins to keep what Laura Ingraham, author of the new blockbuster "Power to the People" (Regnery), calls "pornification" at bay. Of course, the absence of gatekeepers is only part of our predicament, as Hemingway's experience also reveals. Included in "The Lousy Racket" are fascinating exchanges between Hemingway and Perkins over the writer's (quite sparing) use of bad language, or the occasional raw scene. Perkins would invariably argue for their elimination on the grounds that even one four-letter word would bring down the censors, leading to the book's repression, or — and this is even more significant — the public losing interest in it. This last bit suggests that censorship in the first half of the 20th century wasn't merely the superfluous law of the land; it actually reflected the sensibility of most people, maybe even the Hemingway-reading crowd.

I found this discussion of particular interest because in the course of bringing my own new book, "The Death of the Grown-Up" (Editor's note: To buy at a discount, see sidebar at bottom of column) to market, I came up against a very different set of attitudes. In describing our state of cultural decline, I found myself quoting foul language — sometimes spelling it out for shock value, sometimes using dashes to spare the reader. During the copy-editing process, I was urged to spell everything out, or, conversely, spell nothing out. (I stuck with my original style.) Never, of course, was I urged not to use the profanities in the first place. That's not our world.

But do we like it that way, really? I was reminded of this question on reading about a gathering of girls — wealthy, Upper-East-Side-of-Manhattan 12- and 13-year-olds — orchestrated by The New York Times to document the youngsters' reactions to a rancid new TV show called "Gossip Girl," which chronicles the sex- and drug-obsessed lives of spoiled teens. I don't think the show uses profanity, but it certainly features profane behavior. For example: Boys in blazers smoke marijuana and talk about sampling their fathers' Viagra. The martini-swilling teen heroine engages in "smoldering" sex scenes with her best friend's boyfriend. Yuck.

Not that these young flowers of American privilege blushed. Projecting a sometimes gigglesome ennui, they explained how closely the show tracks their little world. (Sometimes it's wonderful not to be able to afford $28,000 tuition.) You have to wonder about their parents, who not only groomed the girls to be consumers of such smut, but also made them available to go on the record about it. There was something sad about the brazen, pointlessness of it all.

Long ago, Hemingway wrote to Perkins that "it is good for the language to restore its life that they (censors) bleed out of it. That is very important." And maybe it was — although personally, I've never felt cheated by the constraints your basic Dickenses and Tolstoys and, reluctantly, Hemingway operated under. But if it was necessary to restore vigor to the language then, what do we do now, when the life it too often describes — unremarkably profane, unnoticeably shameless — no longer has much meaning?

Making the West disappear

10/19/07

Earlier this week, I took a trip down memory lane to Yale, where I happily attended college almost 25 years ago in the second decade of its co-ed existence. Which meant that I was plenty old enough to be the mother of the undergraduates I was addressing in the traditionally genteel setting of a "master's tea." The tea, attended by about two dozen, was in beauteous Branford, one of Yale's 12 residential colleges, all carved stone and grassy courtyard.

All power-washed carved stone and weedless grassy courtyard, that is. At least it felt that way. After a renovating overhaul, Yale's patina of age, of passing time, of history itself no longer quite imbues this rigorously spruced-up campus the way it once did, lessening the more tangible links to Yale's storied past.

Maybe it was the disappearance of some of the eclectic book collections from reading-room shelves that was jarring. Or maybe it was the plentiful new crop of plaques prominently advertising — I mean, attesting to — alumni generosity that gave the old place a practically nouveau feel. Or maybe it was the absence of rep-tie-and-blue-blazered old dears flapping about campus. Clearly, that once-mighty Ivy ascendancy isn't just down, it's out like the cuckoo. Time flies when the culture is changing.

Still, none of this completely accounts for the interplanetary gulf between myself and some of the students when it came to what, for cuckoo-me, is a bedrock notion: namely, that Western culture — for its enshrinement of liberty, freedom of conscience, equality before the law and the like — is a Good Thing.

The point of my talk — based on my new book, "The Death of the Grown-Up: How America's Arrested Development Is Bringing Down Western Civilization" (linked below) — was to explain why perpetual adolescence is not just a cultural drag, but also dangerous to our way of life. I argued that the leveling of adult authority over the past half century or so was accompanied by a leveling of cultural authority. This brought on the age of multiculturalism, a time when Western Civ (like the adult) no longer occupies its old pinnacle atop the hierarchy of cultures. The multiculti conception of equally valuable cultures (except for the West, which is deemed the pits) depends on a strenuous non-judgmentalism. This non-judgmentalism expresses itself in a self-censoring adherence to political correctness. Such non-judgmentalism, such PC self-censorship, is infantilizing because it requires us to suppress our faculties of analysis and judgment.

Case in point: Our society's refusal to analyze and judge the anti-Western teachings of mainstream Islam for fear of giving offense to the grandees of PC, or to Muslims, or both. This refusal, I maintained, is a brewing civilizational crisis.

Having made ourselves into a self-censoring society, I explained to the students at tea, we now find ourselves confronting an Islamic system that demands such censorship as a point of law. Look what happened to Silvio Berlusconi when, as prime minister of Italy after 9/11, he mounted a heartfelt defense of Western civilization for having enshrined liberty, freedom of conscience, equality before the law and the like — which, he also pointed out, Islam most certainly did not.

The voluble Italian was dumped upon by the world, Western and Islamic. He swiftly recanted to satisfy both the censoring dictates of PC, which outlaws non-Western critiques, and the censoring dictates of Islam, which outlaws criticism of Islam. Berlusconi's example shows how easily an adolescent, PC society can slip under Islamic law into the hush of dhimmitude.

At this point in the presentation, I expected to hear that Islam wasn't all bad; that I oversimplified. What emerged instead was that the West wasn't all good; that I oversimplified. As the Yale Daily News later put it, "Some students said West blamed Americans for censoring themselves in thought but ignored the censorship she employs in her own speech by concentrating only on the positive aspects of Western civilization."

Sounds like "some students" believe that the freedoms existing here — which don't exist in Islam — are somehow voided by "negative" Western aspects. Or maybe that the negatives, which apparently loom larger than any Islamic threat, simply invalidate any positive conception of the West, and maybe any conception of the West as an identifiable, defensible culture, period. Little wonder the Yale newspaper used quotation marks to set off the West as "The West." It's good; it's bad — whatever.

I hope I'm wrong. But all of sudden the campus renovations that had scrubbed away Yale's past seemed to be all too apt a metaphor.

Sweeping away the traditional from the public square

11/26/08

Americans may have just embarked on these most ritualistic weeks of the year stretching between Thanksgiving and New Year's Day, but something is clearly different this time around.

It isn't that the customary rites show signs of change. Americans roasted ceremonial turkeys by the million on Thanksgiving Day to sustain themselves as they hunt and gather goods to disperse during Hanukkah or on Christmas morning. There will be fewer big-ticket items and more discounted goods given this year, but that's not the difference. Nor am I sensing resistance to red and green, nor a break in the continuous loop of "Silver Bells" and "Silent Night" that, by melodic rote, choreographs the patterns of holiday behavior.

In other words, everything promises to look and sound what you might call traditional. But the fact is, "traditional" is out. The rock-solid assumptions on which society is built have gone wobbly, while the guideposts to "traditional" behaviors are, of course, long gone.

That's the lesson of the poisonously volcanic aftermath to Proposition 8, the ballot measure defining marriage as between one man and one woman, which California voters approved on Election Day by a margin of 52.5 to 47.5 percent.

How can "traditional" be out when what is now being labeled "traditional marriage" won at the polls?

To begin with, framing husband-wife nuptials as "traditional" marriage already implies the existence of alternative forms of wedlock. Indeed, the very act of throwing open the definition of marriage to a vote reveals how dramatically notions of the traditional have already changed, transformed beyond even recognition to prior generations.

In a state that Barack Obama won, 61 percent to John McCain's 37 percent, "traditional marriage" also triumphed, clearly but not overwhelmingly, due to strong support — exit polling indicates — from church-going voters, senior citizens, Republicans, a slim majority of Hispanic voters, and a whopping 70 percent of black voters. Yet the question remains: despite the will of the California electorate, how has tradition fallen from favor?

Tradition as pariah is the message of the past weeks of protests, boycotts, firings, condemnation and revilement of supporters of Prop. 8, not only by same-sex marriage activists but also by leading figures in the political, media, educational and entertainment establishments. This message tells us that the public square no longer enshrines, protects or even recognizes the traditional. Indeed, this central clearing house of society, where custom, rites, communication and conduct are vetted and approved, has aggressively ejected tradition and its supporters, going so far as to stigmatize the sacred, time-tested conception of marriage as being indecent, if not anathema.

And such cultural whiplash has been weirdly accepted if not welcomed by the traditionalists, if their overwhelmingly apologetic reactions to their own political and moral ostracism are any measure. Sure, they belong to a majority backed by thousands of years of civilization, but those who dared to vote, or worse, contribute money to "restrict" marriage to one man and one woman now seek to make amends and apologize for their loudly derided beliefs. From Scott Eckern, the musical theater director in Sacramento who, having been "outed" for contributing $1,000 to support Prop. 8, resigned under pressure, to Marjorie Christoffersen, co-owner of a well-liked Los Angeles eatery, whose $100 donation in support of "traditional" marriage brought hundreds of protestors to the restaurant, the response has been one of guilty contrition.

Not coincidentally, both Eckern and Christoffersen are Mormons. The brunt of the protests and public opprobrium has been directed at Mormons, whose church strongly supported Prop. 8, with many of its followers donating generously to the campaign. Of course, other churches support "traditional" marriage, including black churches, but anti-8 activists are not boycotting businesses owned by black supporters of Prop. 8. In a shameful display of easy-mark bigotry, anti-8 activists have instead seized on the weakest link in the pro-8 chain — Mormons — for public flaying. Indeed, anti-8 protestors continue to plan boycotts against enterprises owned by Mormon supporters of Prop. 8, from Cinemark Theaters to A1 Self-Storage. Some anti-8 activists are pushing a boycott of the upcoming Sundance Film Festival for its ties to Utah, headquarters of the Mormon church.

The point here doesn't seem to be simply to win fair and square at the polls, which, frankly, is a darn good bet for same-sex marriage proponents come 2010. This year's large black turnout, inspired by Barack Obama and said to have put Prop. 8 over the top, is unlikely to be duplicated in an off-year election. A lower black turnout might well clear the way for a fairly speedy democratic repeal of Prop. 8. No, this current anti-8 effort seems to be about something else. Something different. Something more like cleansing the public square, ostentatiously, of tradition and its followers.

I wonder whether just hanging a bunch more holiday lights will keep everyone from noticing.

'Hedge Fund Man' for president

5/8/09

I have seen the future of conservatism and ... he is a hedge fund manager.

I refer to hedge fund manager Clifford S. Asness, and I'm only halfway kidding. Or maybe I'm not kidding at all. The fact is, Asness this week launched the single most lucid and inspiring counter-attack against the Obama administration's brazen assault on capitalism as seen in its Chrysler bankruptcy shakedown.

Basically, the White House Chrysler plan picks economic losers and winners according to a naked political calculation that penalizes bondholders and rewards the union bosses of the United Auto Workers. It's that simple, that appalling, and that anti-capitalist. The hedge funds, seeking not to surrender the protections afforded their investors by the bankruptcy court process, quite naturally balked at the Obama administration's blatant power grab on behalf of what amount to union cronies. As Asness explained, "Some bondholders thought (the White House plan was) unfair. Specifically, they thought it unfairly favored the United Auto Workers. ... So, they said no to the plan and decided, as is their right, to take their chances in the bankruptcy process."

Their "right"? Hah. With a remarked-upon display of anger, President Obama publicly castigated bondholders for opposing his plan, deriding them as "speculators" who refused "to sacrifice like everyone else," and who only opposed the White House deal to "hold out for the prospect of an unjustified taxpayer-funded bailout."

It was after this that Asness penned what stands as the first post-Obama capitalist manifesto, now making the rounds on the Internet.

"I am indeed fearful writing this. It's a really bad idea to speak out," Asness admits in a preamble that reads like a bulletin from capitalism's trenches where white-shoe comrades, as Asness writes, remain "anonymous for fear of going on the record against a powerful president." Possibly, Asness was also thinking about bankruptcy lawyer Tom Lauria's recent charges that the White House had pressured the firm Perella Weinberg to "withdraw its opposition to the (White House) deal under threat that the full force of the White House press corps would destroy its reputation if it continued to fight." (The White House denies the charge; Perella Weinberg says economic considerations compelled it withdraw its opposition.)

Asness, whose $20 billion company AQR Capital Management is not involved in the Chrysler mess, went on to describe the bankruptcy process ("the rules of the game lenders know before they lend") which the president's plan upends, along with the fiduciary obligation money managers have to manage their clients' money apolitically. Then he gets to his bottom line: "The President's attempted diktat takes money from bondholders and gives it to a labor union that delivers money and votes for him. Why is he not calling on his party to 'sacrifice' some campaign contributions, and votes, for the greater good? Shaking down lenders for the benefit of political donors is recycled corruption and abuse of power."

I don't know who Asness is aside from being a highly successful hedge fund manager — an occupation for which I don't even know how to pack a briefcase. But he is speaking truth to power, which is exactly what the American people need to hear. "The President screaming that the hedge funds are looking for an unjustified taxpayer-funded bailout is the big lie writ large," he writes. "Find me a hedge fund that has been bailed out. Find me a hedge fund, even a failed one, that has asked for one. In fact, it was only because hedge funds have not taken government funds that they could stand up to this bullying. ... The President's comments here are backwards and libelous. Yet somehow I don't think the hedge funds will be following ACORN's lead and trucking in a bunch of paid professional protestors soon. Hedge funds really need a community organizer."

Contrast this fiery defense of capitalism — the latest cause of the "culture war," according to Arthur Brooks, the new head of the American Enterprise Institute — with the gag-inducing mush almost simultaneously offered by Jeb Bush, Eric Cantor and Mitt Romney during a political event during which, as the Washington Post noted, these proto-presidential hopefuls "did not directly attack President Obama, rarely used the word 'Republican,' and engaged in a healthy dose of self-criticism."

"You can't beat something with nothing," burbled former-presidential brother Jeb Bush during this GOP-lite squish-o-rama. "And the other side has something. I don't like it, but they have it, and we have to be respectful and mindful of that."

The "other side" has something, all right — possession of the economy, which is nothing to "respect." It is something to oppose.

As Asness does. "This is America," Asness concludes. "We have a free-enterprise system that has worked spectacularly for us for 200-plus years. When it fails it fixes itself. Most importantly, it is not an owned lackey of the Oval Office to be scolded for disobedience by the President."

Could there be a pulse in the body politic? Be still, my political heart. This is the vital spirit of rebellion that just might lead conservatives to declare: Hedge Fund Man for President.

Opposing Sotomayor is the Right's thing to do

5/28/09

Frank Ricci is "just" a fireman, and not, like Supreme Court Justice nominee Sonia Sotomayor, a federal judge. He is "only" a white male, and not, like Sotomayor, a Latina. And while he works in New Haven, Conn., he certainly didn't attend Yale Law School as Sotomayor did.

For one thing, he's dyslexic. That's why Ricci spent more than $1,000 to pay an acquaintance to make recordings of the educational materials Ricci needed to master in order to pass a 2003 test that was specially drawn up for the New Haven Fire Department. The test was to determine who was eligible for 15 lieutenant and captain promotions. After months of intensive study, Ricci scored sixth highest out of 77 candidates. Because the results were deemed racially unacceptable — none of the 19 black test-takers made the cut — New Haven mayor John DeStefano Jr. decided to junk all the test results and promote no one.

That was six years ago. This April, the Supreme Court heard Ricci v. DeStefano, a case that Sotomayor, as part of a three-judge panel, upheld on appeal against Ricci and the 17 other firemen who joined his complaint. Better to perpetuate group grievance, Sotomayor's decision tells us, than to ensure equality of opportunity. Better to pick winners and losers from the bench than to safeguard the rights of the individual to life, liberty and a fair shot at a promotion.

And better to advocate a kind of racial and sexual supremacism than to safeguard for one and all the kind of justice that is blind. "I would hope that a wise Latina woman with the richness of her experiences would more often than not reach a better conclusion (as a judge) than a white male who hasn't lived that life," Sotomayor said in her Judge Mario G. Olmos Law and Cultural Diversity Lecture at UC Berkeley's law school in 2001.

The cavalier condescension toward the "white" and the "male" in this statement is breathtaking. And in Ricci v. DeStefano, Sotomayor showed us precisely how she implements it: by upholding discrimination against the expendable, those such as Ricci and his co-plaintiffs who don't have black skin. This is reverse discrimination, and among activist judges such as Sotomayor and Democrats on the left, such as President Barack Obama, it is not only acceptable, it is a sterling credential.

But no one on the right is supposed to mention it, or so the conventional wisdom would have it. That's because Sotomayor, in addition to being a Latina — or, rather, as a function of being a Latina — is also a sacred cow. As a woman (check one) with parents from Puerto Rico (check two), she is by accident of birth virtually above criticism, a condition of neo-royalty that is death to a democratic republic.

Worse, she is seen in these sacred terms by far too many Republicans, thus revealing the extent to which they, too, have bought into the dehumanizing givens of identity politics.

In other words, it's one thing for Sen. Charles Schumer, D-N.Y., to say, "They (Republicans) oppose her at their peril." It's quite another to hear the very same theme echoed by GOP professionals. "Republicans who pick a fight with an up-from-the-bootstraps Hispanic woman do so at their own peril," said GOP consultant Phil Musser. "If Republicans make a big deal of opposing Sotomayor, we will be hurling ourselves off a cliff," said former George W. Bush aide Mark McKinnon. "It's a bad visual. It's bad symbolism for the Republicans," said Matthew Dowd, another former Bush aide. "You want to be careful," said GOP chairman Michael Steele. "You don't want to be perceived as a bully."

Such shallow, pointless politicking, devoid of philosophical principle, reveals the crisis in conservative circles: namely, the lack of understanding of what is required to mount the philosophical arguments against the leftist social engineering, as practiced by Sotomayor and as promulgated by Obama, that has derailed the lives of countless Frank Riccis, stripping them of the protections of the Constitution in the name of perpetual resentment and unslakeable grievance.

Making this moral, conservative case isn't jumping off a cliff. It isn't "bad symbolism" and it isn't bullying. It's leadership based on fundamental, core principles. We'll find out if there is anyone left with any such principles when the Senate confirmation hearings for Sotomayor begin.

When did opposition become 'racism'?

9/18/09

South Carolina Republican Rep. Joe Wilson may have unexpectedly ignited an explosion of race rhetoric with two words in the House chamber — "You lie" — but I can snuff it out with two words in a newspaper — "Jimmy Carter."

The former president threw rhetorical kerosene on the political flames this week when he twice advanced the lowdown argument that political opposition to Barack Obama — in town halls, faltering presidential poll numbers, the colossal anti-Obama demonstration in Washington — boils down to "racism."

The allegation is contemptible but, particularly in the wake of the Wilson story, has been pushed by journalists on the Left and Democratic U.S. Representatives mainly from the Black Congressional Caucus.

Evidence of racism is so thin, though, the racism-ists must invent lurid details. The New York Times' Maureen Dowd writes that when she heard Wilson say "You lie" she felt as if, "fair or not," she heard him say: You lie, boy! Georgia Democrat Rep. Hank Johnson draws a straight line from Wilson's remark to "folks putting on white hoods and white uniforms again and riding through the countryside intimidating people." Yeah. En route to Bellevue.

It would almost be funny if it weren't so grotesque. Of course, Jimmy Carter, who last appeared in this column after he laid red roses on the grave of Yasir Arafat before resuming his pursuit of face-time with Hamas terrorists, is no stranger to grotesque. Certainly after Osama bin Laden this week actually endorsed Carter's anti-Israel book, "Palestine: Peace not Apartheid," the former president needed a good, unctuous wallow in sanctimony to deflect our attention from his new fan. But Carter went too far — even for him.

"I think an overwhelming portion of the intensely demonstrated animosity toward President Barack Obama is based on the fact that he is a black man," Carter told NBC. There exists the belief "among many white people, not just in the South, but around the country," he continued, "that African-Americans are not qualified to lead this great country. It's an abominable circumstance, and grieves me and concerns me very deeply."

What's "abominable" here is the spectacle of a former president attempting to asphyxiate democratic debate with the stranglehold charge of "racism."

It won't work. As promised above, I can stop it by mentioning the man's name. Fact is, the Americans who are now apoplectic about President Obama were once apoplectic about Jimmy Carter, and, later, Bill Clinton. (Some of us still are.) And please — no American president, not even Richard Nixon, has ever been reviled to the gruesomely mock-violent degree that George W. Bush was. "Racism" had nothing to do with any of it.

In other words, it is not "racism" we are seeing breaking out around the country, it is political opposition. The Left is responding to vital signs on the Right, a stirring in the ashes of eight disorienting Bush years, that indicate there is a political fight to be had over the direction of this country.

And the best thing that Joe Wilson did for that fight was to stop apologizing while he was ahead.

But it is for this reason — his refusal to submit to House Democrat pressure to participate in a show-trial-style mea culpa circus after the president accepted his personal apology — that the public pillorying continues.

And is it ever ugly. Under cover of "racism" charges, the assault on the last unprotected victim group in America is rejoined. That victim, of course, is the white male. Or, as his politically correct tormentors like to taunt him repeatedly, "middle-aged white guys." These are certainly one of Maureen Dowd's favorite targets — "white Republican men afraid of extinction," she calls them with the sadistic complacency of one who plays to society's approved prejudices. "Just it gives off a strange vibe," says MSNBC's David Shuster about the "older white men, all Republicans, sitting there" in Congress.

Wonder what Shuster says about the "older white men" at the Continental Congress? Or what Dowd says about such "middle-aged white guys" as Leonardo da Vinci, Louis Pasteur, Robert Browning, Thomas Edison and Clark Gable? As the academic leftists have reeducated us to believe, she would call them all dead white males.

Of course, you know something's changed when the tocsin of demonization targets live ones.

Few Pulitzers on the right side

4/16/10

Just as the Pulitzer Prizes come around every year, a conservative columnist comes around after them, dusting off the hard fact, as measured in an ever-expanding set of tally marks, that conservatives rarely get to pop a champagne cork over one of their own. Take the Pulitzer Prize for commentary. Since George F. Will won in 1977, William Safire (1978), Vermont Royster (1984), Charles Krauthammer (1987), Paul Gigot (2000), and Dorothy Rabinowitz (2001) have won as well, and good for them. But that's six conservative columnists in 33 years.

This year's winner, Kathleen Parker, is sometimes seen as Rightish, but, with a penchant for smacking down social conservatives, she is perhaps too enlightened, Pulitzer-ainly speaking, to count. As Parker herself put it: "It's only because I'm a conservative-basher that I'm now recognized after 23 years of toiling in the fields, right?"

Hard to say. But it fits the Pulitzer pattern. The best to way to win a Pulitzer still seems to be by "pleasing liberals with stories that advance their agenda," as L. Brent Bozell III wrote in 2007. The chosen winners "demonstrate again the stranglehold that liberals and leftists enjoy when it comes to garnering recognition," as George Shadroui put it in Frontpagemag.com in 2004. It is "the main business of the Pulitzer committees to hand out the Prizes to other liberals, both in the press and in the arts," noted the New Criterion in 1992. And the conservative grumbling goes back farther than that.

With good reason. According to the conditions set by press baron Joseph Pulitzer himself when he created his eponymous awards a century ago, it turns out that we — meaning we conservatives — was (stet) robbed. That is, according to Pulitzer's intentions, these prizes should really be going to conservatives.

I stumbled onto this scoop quite by chance after first leafing through an old essay by the great American writer Kenneth Roberts, author of a remarkable series of historical novels including "Northwest Passage" and "Oliver Wiswell." Roberts was discussing what was already in the early 1930s an enduring mystery to him: why the Pulitzer Prize for novels (later fiction) was consistently awarded to books "that would have seriously affected Mr. Pulitzer's blood pressure if he were still alive."

Intrigued, I continued reading. According to the World Almanac Roberts consulted (a Pulitzer property, he notes), Pulitzer wanted to honor "the American novel published during the year which shall best present the wholesome atmosphere of American life, and the highest standard of American manners and manhood." Wholesome? High American standards? Writing at a time of proletarian chic, Roberts went on to list a series of prize-winning books that had little wholesome or even American about them.

I found that the original playwriting criteria were similar. According to a 1918 New York Times report on early Pulitzer winners, the drama prize was meant for the New York-produced play that "shall best represent the educational value and power of the stage in raising the standard of good morals, good taste and good manners."

The current Pulitzer Web site makes some note of its board "growing less conservative over the years in matters of taste," adding: "In 1963 the drama jury nominated Edward Albee's 'Who's Afraid of Virginia Woolf?,' but the board found the script insufficiently 'uplifting,' a complaint that related to arguments over sexual permissiveness and rough dialogue. In 1993 the prize went to Tony Kushner's 'Angels in America: Millennium Approaches,' a play that dealt with problems of homosexuality and AIDS and whose script was replete with obscenities."

Well, as long as it was "replete."

Regarding editorial writing (the commentary prize didn't kick in until later), the original criteria were more nebulous — "the test of excellence being clearness of style, moral purpose, sound reasoning, and power to influence public opinion in what the writer conceives to be the right direction."

Maybe some of the first Prize winners, a pair of 1917 editorials from the Louisville Courier-Journal, can clue us in to what that "right direction" was. Written in support of U.S. involvement in World War I, one is called "Vae Victis" — Woe to the Vanquished — and the other, "War Has Its Compensations."

I think it's safe to say the Pulitzer Prize wasn't dreamed up for Lefties. Meanwhile, Kenneth Roberts somehow garnered his well-deserved Pulitzer — two months before he died in 1957.

Honors' behavior a result, not a standard

1/7/11

That was fast. Sunday, the Virginian-Pilot posted a montage of lewd, "morale-boosting" videos that Capt. Owen P. Honors starred in, directed and broadcast to the crew of the USS Enterprise dating back to 2006-2007 when he was the ship's executive (number two) officer. Tuesday, the Navy fired Honors, now captain of the ship, citing a "profound lack of good judgment and professionalism."

Not, take note, conduct unbecoming an officer and a gentleman.

So, now what? With the Navy, the Washington Post reports, set on a "broader investigation into whether senior Navy officials knew about the 4-year-old videos, and why they failed to take disciplinary action against Honors," we once again seem to be embarking, rudderless, into the dangerous waters of the hydra-headed purge, gathering, sharpening, steeling, lusting for suspects. But of what crime? Not the one I would charge the unfortunately named Capt. Honors with.

The post-Tailhook Navy fetish, of course, remains sexually oriented — or, more accurate, sexual-orientationally oriented. (In the guise of an aviator persona, Honors lets fly some homosexual putdowns in the video, and later encounters same-sex couples in the shower.) As one retired vice admiral put it to the Post, "What bothers me is that Capt. Honors' behavior set a standard that allowed for sexual innuendo."

Funny. What bothers me is that Capt. Honors' behavior didn't set any standard at all. This should come as little surprise. Perhaps the greatest triumph of the Left in the last 25 years has been the junking of military standards regarding the sexes, a set of traditional attitudes that was slow to dismantle itself in the wake of the 1960s sexual revolution. Indeed, the military could be, and was, seen as a bulwark against the social changes wrought by a metastasizing feminism in the civilian world that would go on to kill, among other things, such concepts as "mixed company" and its prohibitions on "bad language" and other social shields. These had allowed for the existence of now-lost refuges such as reticence and discretion, which, in turn, provided shelter for a kind of privacy and intimacy that is all but unimaginable in our over-exposed world of TMI (too much information).

Which is more than sad. I think it has driven people a little berserk. Indeed, there is something quite possibly certifiable in the behavior of an aircraft carrier executive officer simulating masturbation on a "movie night" video to boost his crew's morale.

"It's nothing worse than 'Saturday Night Live,'" one defender of Capt. Honors commented online. That's true and not unrelated. As sex roles were rewritten to check male dominance and expand the female role, and as women, in effect, were used to destroy the ideal of "officer and gentlemen," other lines were crossed and blurred. The entire culture became increasingly conditioned to break any and all of the old molds, adopting an "irreverence toward uptight, oppressive, hypocritical, old-fashioned norms of social propriety," writes Brian Mitchell, in his history-jeremiad against and titled "Women in the Military: Flirting with Disaster." By now, this means that putative defenders of "old-fashioned norms," such as 49-year-old Capt. Honors, are unwilling, ill-equipped and even unaware as to how to do so. Indeed, the powers that promoted Honors to the captain's bridge would punish anyone who did.

Discussing the Tailhook investigation, Mitchell writes: "No one seriously expected them to be officers and gentlemen anymore." And, institutionally, no one expected more or better of the brave, new women, either. Indeed, after no raunchy female misconduct at the infamous 1991 Tailhook convention was prosecuted, after even some exonerated men continued to be punished, the true object of that historic purge became all too clear: not to check "Animal House"-in-uniform across the board, but instead to target and eradicate traditional attitudes as the basis for criminal behavior—"sexism"—in violation of Pentagon policy.

In large part, this prefigured approval for open homosexuals in the military. Now, consequences emerge. A society that rejects officers and gentlemen, it seems, is going to get crude clowns helming its nuclear-powered aircraft carriers. And who is left in command who can figure out how that happened?

Race should not color our outrage over crimes

3/29/12

Is there any interest in discovering the facts about the killing of Trayvon Martin by George Zimmerman? Facts, after all, can undermine ideology. They have the power to dispel fantasy. They can put the brakes on error. They lead, sometimes, to logical conclusions. All of which means, in this particular case, that when the facts come out, they might well undermine "the cause."

We simply don't know all of the facts yet. We can say with certainty, however, that the cause is not justice, no matter what the protesters, agitators and officials say. The cause is not truth, either. The cause is social strife, division, leverage, power and—you never know—violence and revolution, all of it drawn and driven by an outrage-stoked engine of racial grievance.

Even if the facts of this case were to prove that Zimmerman acted in self-defense when he killed Martin—a scenario supported by a police report obtained by the Orlando Sentinel that says Zimmerman had a bloody or broken nose and a head wound, and that an eyewitness "unequivocally" identified Zimmerman as having been under assault by Martin—that wouldn't change the cause.

The rationale for protests, sit-ins, outrage among far-left elected black officials and the mass donning of memorial "hoodies" would disappear, but that wouldn't change the cause, either. Seemingly, nothing could. This killing was initially depicted as a white-on-black crime of "racism"; square-peg-into-round-hole style, it must always be depicted thus.

Further, it must be seen as emblematic of the state of crime in America today—American blacks living in fear of American whites. Who cares, as author and radio host Larry Elder recently wrote, citing 2010 Justice Department statistics, that "in murders involving a single black victim and a single offender, 90 percent of the time it is a black perpetrator who murders the black victim"? Who cares, as former Republican Rep. Virgil Goode of Virginia pointed out in a 2010 article in Human Events, that blacks commit crimes against whites at an exceedingly higher rate? "According to the FBI's latest National Crime Victimization Survey," Goode wrote, "blacks were over 50 times more likely to commit a crime against whites than vice versa."

It is the real-life fear and grief behind such alarming statistics, seldom reported, that can turn a hoodie into a cause for alarm for blacks and whites alike. As a costume for middle-aged black legislators in statehouses and the U.S. Congress, however, it's supposed to make a nation hang its head in shame.

Such is the point of political theater where the script has little to do with fact. News of Zimmerman's multiracial background (his mother is a native of Peru; his father is white; he has black relatives) hasn't dented the white-racism angle for agitators. Similarly, the unresolved questions about the fateful encounter that left Martin, 17, dead and Zimmerman, 28, reportedly with injuries haven't slowed the rush to the microphone by a bevy of officials and self-appointed spokesmen.

The shooting was a "hate crime" (Democratic Rep. Maxine Waters of California), an "assassination" (Philadelphia Mayor Michael Nutter). "Blacks are under attack," said Jesse Jackson. According to those Justice Department statistics cited above, that is true—but overwhelmingly by other blacks.

What is under attack here is due process. It is an attack, I regret to say, carried forward even by the president of the United States, who, subtle as a club, ramped up the race narrative when he said: "If I had a son, he'd look like Trayvon."

Would he also look like Tyrone Woodfork? The black 20-year-old has been charged with first-degree murder and other crimes related to the invasion March 12 of the Oklahoma home of Bob and Nancy Strait (both white). Nancy, 85, was sexually assaulted and beaten to death. Bob, 90, a veteran of the invasion of Normandy and married to Nancy for 65 years, suffered a broken jaw and ribs.

Despite the violence and cruelty of this particular crime, it is strictly a local story. One distraught neighbor set up a Facebook page called "Justice for Bob and Nancy Strait." When I last looked, it had 60-some followers.

All of which means — what? Victims of violent crime, both black and white, abound. Their undeserved suffering and grief are things that everyone wants to prevent. In the Trayvon Martin case, what also hurts is the cold, political calculation to divide us as a nation for nefarious ends. What hurts in the Bob and Nancy Strait case is the silence.

For the record, President Obama has not mentioned that Nancy Strait looks like his grandmother.

When women fight, civilization loses

1/25/13

And so it came, the coup de grace. The final "barrier" to "opportunities" for women in combat is no more. With a stroke of their pens, Secretary of Defense Leon Panetta and Joint Chiefs Chairman Gen. Martin E. Dempsey decreed that no battlefield mission or military role is off-limits to the female sex. The defense secretary and the general thus liberated mothers, daughters, sisters and wives to kill and be killed in the infantry, commando raids, even in Obama administration "overseas contingency operations." In so doing, they also slashed away at that last institutional protection for the space that separates men and women, where civilization once grew.

It (civilization) has been struggling there for decades, as social engineers and radical feminists — all heirs to Marx — have been cutting away at elemental human instinct, social grace, language and thought itself. This overhaul of manners and mores, the family structure and marriage — even private aspects of the relationship between men and women — has been successful to a point where the cultural argument against women in combat (women in the military being a lost cause) is rarely voiced, not even on the right. (I watched Fox News on women-in-combat announcement day, listening in vain for just one culture warrior.)

We are left to make only the utilitarian arguments — body strength and speed, unit cohesion, even urinary tract infections and other hazards that front-line deployment pose to females. These are compellingly logical points, but they are unlikely to reverse an ideological juggernaut. When the secretary of defense says putting women in combat is about "making our military ... and America stronger" and no one says he's lying to further a Marxian ideal via social engineering, the cultural argument is lost, and the culture it comes from is bound and gagged, hostage to what we know as "political correctness."

I still see threads of the cultural argument in emails and some blog responses to the Pentagon's latest whack at creating "gender neutrality." It erupts like a reflex against the conditioning to deny differences defined, at their essence, by muscle mass and womb. Such conditioning erodes the male protective instinct—which, surely, is what war is supposed to arise from—and the female nurturing instinct, which surely is what a civilization depends on.

No more. Women with wombs and without manly muscle mass now count as Pentagon-approved "warriors," modern-day knights in Kevlar, soon to be humping 80-pound packs over mountain and desert.

Or maybe not. Didn't Gen. Dempsey indicate that dropping some of those old-fashioned strength and speed requirements might be in order? "If we do decide that a particular standard is so high that a woman couldn't make it," Dempsey said last week, "the burden is now on the service to come back and explain to the secretary, why is it that high? Does it really have to be that high?" Of course not! Why train Navy SEALs when Navy OTTERs will do as well?

And what about their children, when these front-line warriors bear them? And their pregnancies, when they decide it's better for their mission, for their country, to terminate them? Don't think Daddy Government, once again, won't be a steady provider to his womenfolk.

And why not? "It is women who pass on the culture," my daughters' pediatrician—a font of human wisdom after six of his own kids and endless patients—used to tell me, his voice rising over baby girls screaming. But what kind of "gender-neutral" culture will they pass on?

Rather, what kind of gender-neutral culture have women already passed on? After all, this penultimate shift at the Pentagon (will the NFL be next?) is just the tail end of something, not the beginning—the rewiring of the human spirit. In other words, the whole movement in the name of "equal rights" has no more to do with women being legally able to apply for a credit card and other aspects of equality before the law than ordering women into combat is about making the military and America stronger.

No, it's about behavioral manipulation and transformation—the Equal Rights Amendment by executive fiat. These changes have been a long time coming. In my lifetime, I have watched even post-1960s standards of femininity, for example, plunge to a point where female tendencies toward privacy, intimacy and modesty have given way to norms of clinical-style revelation and numbing brazenness—and I'm talking about today's "nice" girls, the ones who soon will be considered eligible for Selective Service.

Yes, I know, only 15 percent of our all-volunteer military is female—

even after decades of active government courtship to woo women into the ranks and make "a force that looks like America" (not Obama's Cabinet), as Bill Clinton has put it. But don't think this "opportunity" for the few comes without strings to the many. As Army Col. Ellen Haring pointed out on "PBS NewsHour" last week, "With full rights come full responsibilities."

And then what? Will gender-neutral raw recruits soon be brawling outside the bar (with the man "beating the snot" out of the woman, as one Iraq veteran recently suggested to me in an email)? Will gender-neutral male soldiers be trained out of their protective instinct toward women? Do we want to live with the results?

One senior officer with multiple tours in Iraq and Afghanistan wrote this to me: "I would never want my mother, sisters, wife or daughter to have to experience the ravages of combat or, worse, become a prisoner of war. It goes against every fiber of my being."

Yesterday's man. For a better tomorrow, we need more like him.

Scales of Injustice

Justice has not been served in the Loiuma police brutality case

7/13/01

NOW that it has been announced that Abner Louima stands to collect $8.7 million from the city of New York and its police union after suffering a grievous assault in the bathroom of a Brooklyn police station in 1997, the temptation is to let this terrible case close once and for all. Even after Mr. Louima has paid off his recurring-dream team of lawyers, ranging from Johnnie Cochran to Barry Scheck, he will be a wealthy man. His attacker is behind bars.

There can be little purpose, for example, in continuing to ponder the sadistic passion that drove a New York City policeman named Justin Volpe to torture the defenseless Haitian immigrant with the broken handle of a broomstick, a crime for which Volpe is now serving a 30-year-sentence.

But there is every reason to examine the calculated legal maneuvers that seem to have led to a miscarriage of justice no less outrageous: namely, the conviction of another New York City policeman named Charles Schwarz for the crime of restraining Mr. Louima during his torture session at the hands of Justin Volpe. Did Charles Schwarz do this heinous thing? While the 36-year-old ex-Marine is probably padding his cell in a federal penitentiary in the Midwest at this very moment, serving out another day of his 15-year-sentence in solitary confinement for his own safety, the gut-wrenching fact is there is no evidence that he did.

That's right. No evidence. After sifting through the cold ashes of the once-blazing media firestorm ignited by the Louima case, one imperishable truth remains. No one—not even Mr. Louima—has ever identified Charles Schwarz as having been in the station-house bathroom on the night of the attack. Indeed, Justin Volpe has stated that another policeman arrived on the scene of his crime, one named Thomas Wiese. Days after the attack took place, Thomas Wiese himself, acting against his lawyer's counsel, admitted to investigators to having been on the scene—although, he maintains, he arrived after Volpe's assault on Mr. Louima was over. In a bizarre twist—no, wrench—of logic, prosecutors chose to interpret Thomas Wiese's potentially self-incriminating statement, which has since been corroborated by Thomas Bruder, Volpe's partner on the night in question, as evidence of a conspiracy on the part of the policemen to cover up for Charles Schwarz.

(Indeed, Wiese and Bruder, along with Schwarz, were subsequently convicted on conspiracy charges stemming from the case and sentenced to five years apiece.)

But the jurors who convicted Charles Schwarz never heard any of this information. To be sure, they heard quite a lot—stunning recantations (including a mid-trial shocker as Volpe changed his plea from innocent to guilty) and conflicting testimonies (including radically shifting versions of events from Mr. Louima)--but no such compelling evidence of Charles Schwarz's innocence. This hard fact of the Louima case has haunted many of its jurors, driving no fewer than five to come forward and admit that had they just heard Volpe's testimony, they would have acquitted Schwarz. Two have signed affidavits to that effect.

But there is more to the story. As columnist Nat Henthoff, one of Charles Schwarz's more muscular champions, has sagely pointed out, "the *prosecutors* knew that Volpe had identified Wiese as the second man—and that Wiese had admitted he was that man. Why didn't the government—in the interest of justice—put that information in this case?"

Why, indeed. In his appeal on behalf of Charles Schwarz last December, defense attorney Ronald Fischetti went so far as to charge federal prosecutors with misconduct in their relentless campaign to convict his client. Alluding to the so-called "blue wall of silence," a code of conduct critics ascribe to the police as a technique for concealing wrongdoing, Mr. Fischetti said the federal government "erected its own wall, federal blue, behind which witnesses were intimidated, coached, homogenized and hidden, so that the theory on which investigators went public days after the Louima assault would be sustained."

No matter, it would seem, who had to suffer for it. Coincidentally or not, a couple of days before Mr. Louima and his lawyers concluded their settlement agreement with New York City, Charles Schwarz's legal team won a not- insignificant legal victory. The appeals court hearing the Schwarz case ordered prosecutors to turn over all the tapes and transcripts of the dozens of interviews police investigators conducted with police officers following the Louima attack—evidence that had been withheld from the defense throughout all the legal proceedings.

What will the defense find? Oral arguments begin on July 19. Having already learned what went wrong in the station house, we may soon begin to find out what went wrong in the courtroom.

Eating our own

5/14/07

On the 60th anniversary of VJ-Day in 2005, Marine Capt. Randy Stone, a military lawyer serving in Iraq, became a presidential poster boy. Capt. Stone's two grandfathers fought at Iwo Jima, so George W. Bush, in a celebratory speech, turned the whole family into a gold-braided rhetorical flourish to depict the continuity of American character and courage from one war to another.

"Capt. Stone proudly wears the uniform just as his grandfathers did at Iwo Jima," said Bush. "He's guided by the same convictions they carried into battle. He shares the same willingness to serve a cause greater than himself. ... Randy says, 'I know we will win because I see it in the eyes of the Marines every morning. In their eyes is the sparkle of victory.'"

That was then. I wish the president would look into Capt. Stone's eyes now as the officer finishes up his first week of Article 32 hearings, the military's equivalent of a grand jury proceeding, to determine whether dereliction of duty charges against him will go to trial. What would Bush see? I can only imagine that if I were Capt. Stone, in the uniform my grandfathers wore, with their convictions and willingness to serve, that "sparkle of victory" the 34-year-old Marine once talked about would be lost in the hard-eyed look of the betrayed.

Capt. Stone is the first of four Marine officers to be charged with dereliction of duty for failing to investigate "properly" 24 civilian deaths in Haditha in November 2005. Having reviewed the facts — what you might call his politically correct job as battalion lawyer — Capt. Stone determined no further investigation was warranted. In other words, he came to a politically incorrect conclusion. (So did his superiors, but he's the guy on trial — another story.) Capt. Stone could get three years in prison. Three enlisted Marines are charged with unpremeditated murder. They could get life. At least eight other Marines may have been granted immunity to testify. The whole case exudes the terrible, rotting stench of eating our own.

Described in the heavy-breathing press as "the biggest U.S. criminal case involving civilian deaths in the Iraq war," the incident sounds less like a war crime than, well, a war.

Here's what happened: A convoy of Marines trolling insurgent-riddled Haditha was hit by a huge IED. A Humvee was destroyed. One Marine was killed (split in two). Two other Marines were wounded (one grievously). There was a lot of shooting at an approaching Iraqi car. There was a lot of shooting at two nearby Iraqi houses where Marines heard, as The New York Times put it, "the distinct metallic sound of an AK-47 being prepared to fire." As one Marine witness explained, "the squad leader thought he was about to kick in the door and walk into a machine gun." In the end, no additional Marines had died, but 24 Iraqi civilians, including some children, had been killed.

And here lies a hunk of the politically correct outrage fueling prosecutorial fires. According to a leaked report chiding Marines for not investigating further, Army Maj. Gen. Eldon A. Bargewell was apparently appalled by "statements made by the chain of command" that "suggest that Iraqi civilian lives are not as important as U.S. lives, their deaths are just the cost of doing business. ..." Maj. Gen. Bargewell was also apparently exercised by the Marine consensus that "civilian casualties were to be expected" due to such insurgent tactics as hiding among civilians. "Although this proposition may accurately reflect insurgent tactics," he wrote, he heard it so often "that it almost appeared rehearsed."

Rehearsed? Notice the contorted way military brass disparages the exculpatory reality of the Iraqi battlefield.

Meanwhile, three cheers for the Marines. If only someone would mention to the Waughian-named Maj. Bargewell that when the "business" is war, the chain of command darn well better consider "U.S. lives" more important than "Iraqi civilian lives" (many "civilian" in name only), or guess what? Too many U.S. lives will be lost and the United States won't win.

Victory, however, isn't the objective of our increasingly PC military. This is becoming more and more apparent as the war continues. Which calls into question our very capacity — not military, but psychological — to wage war. It also calls into question our continuity with our forbears — Capt. Stone's grandfathers, for instance. They might know the uniform but, watching their grandson's show trial, I doubt they'd recognize much else.

Killed by the rules

8/17/07

Now that Marcus Luttrell's book "Lone Survivor: The Eyewitness Account of Operation Redwing and the Lost Heroes of Seal Team 10" is a national bestseller, maybe Americans are ready to start discussing the core issue his story brings to light: the inverted morality, even insanity, of the American military's rules of engagement (ROE).

On a stark mountaintop in Afghanistan in 2005, Leading Petty Officer Luttrell and three Navy SEAL teammates found themselves having just such a discussion. Dropped behind enemy lines to kill or capture a Taliban kingpin who commanded between 150-200 fighters, the SEAL team was unexpectedly discovered in the early stages of a mission whose success, of course, depended on secrecy. Three unarmed Afghan goatherds, one a teenager, had stumbled across the Americans' position.

This presented the soldiers with an urgent dilemma: What should they do? If they let the Afghans go, they would probably alert the Taliban to the their whereabouts. This would mean a battle in which the Americans were outnumbered by at least 35 to 1. "Little Big Horn in turbans," as Marcus Luttrell would describe it. If the Americans didn't let the goatherds go — if they killed them, there being no way to hold them — the Americans would avoid detection and, most likely, leave the area safely. On a treeless mountainscape far from home, four of our bravest patriots came to the ghastly conclusion that the only way to save themselves was forbidden by the rules of engagement. Such an action would set off a media firestorm, and lead to murder charges for all.

It is agonizing to read their tense debate as Mr. Luttrell recounts it, the "lone survivor" of the disastrous mission. Each of the SEALs was aware of "the strictly correct military decision" — namely, that it would be suicide to let the goatherds live. But they were also aware that their own country, for which they were fighting, would ultimately turn on them if they made that decision. It was as if committing suicide had become the only politically correct option. For fighting men ordered behind enemy lines, such rules are not only insane. They're immoral.

The SEALs sent the goatherds on their way. One hour later, a sizeable Taliban force attacked, beginning a horrendous battle that resulted not only in the deaths of Mr. Luttrell's three SEAL teammates, but also the deaths of 16 would-be rescuers — eight additional SEALS and eight Army special operations soldiers whose helicopter was shot down by a Taliban rocket-propelled grenade.

"Look at me right now in my story," Mr. Luttrell writes. "Helpless, tortured, shot, blown up, my best buddies all dead, and all because we were afraid of the liberals back home, afraid to do what was necessary to save our own lives. Afraid of American civilian lawyers. I have only one piece of advice for what it's worth: If you don't want to get into a war where things go wrong, where the wrong people sometimes get killed, where innocent people sometimes have to die, then stay the hell out of it in the first place."

I couldn't agree more, except for the fact that conservatives, up to and including the president, are at least as responsible for our outrageous rules of engagement as liberals. The question Americans need to ask themselves now, with "Lone Survivor" as Exhibit A, is whether adhering to these precious rules is worth the exorbitant price — in this case, 19 valiant soldiers.

Another question to raise is why our military, knowing the precise location of a Taliban kingpin, sends in Navy SEALs, not Air Force bombers, in the first place? The answer is "collateral damage." I know this — and so do our enemies, who, as Mr. Luttrell writes, laugh at our ROEs as they sleep safe at night. I find it hard to believe that this is something most Americans applaud. But it's impossible to know, because this debate hasn't begun.

It should. It strikes at the core not only of our capacity to make war, but also our will to survive. A nation that doesn't automatically value its sons who fight to protect it more than the "unarmed civilians" — spies? fighters? — whom they encounter behind enemy lines is not only unlikely to win a war, it isn't showing much interest in its own survival.

This is what comes through, loud and ugly, from that mountaintop in Afghanistan, where four young Americans ultimately agreed it was better to be killed than to kill.

A 'defining atrocity'? Yes, against our Marines

1/4/08

A major story of 2007 was the progressive unraveling of the case against the seven Marines and one Navy corpsman charged in connection with the Nov. 19, 2005, killings of Iraqi civilians in Haditha during a day of intense action. To date, charges against four of the men have been dismissed altogether. Two men have been ordered to a court martial. Two cases are pending.

What a difference a year has made since charges came down at the end of 2006. The New York Times in October mourned — I mean, noted — the shift: "Last year, when accounts of the killings of 24 Iraqis in Haditha by a group of Marines came to light, it seemed that the Iraq war had produced its defining atrocity, just as the conflict in Vietnam had spawned the My Lai massacre a generation ago."

No "defining atrocity"? Gee, that's too bad. The Times went on to lament that the presiding military investigator recommended that murder charges against the ranking enlisted Marine, Staff Sgt. Frank D. Wuterich, be dropped. And this, the newspaper bellyached, "may well have ended prosecutors' chances of winning any murder convictions in the killings."

No murder convictions? Well, boo — the heck — hoo.

This isn't to suggest that the four remaining Marines facing legal proceedings are in the clear. Quite the contrary. Consider the two cases going to military court. The court martial of Lance Cpl. Stephen Tatum, charged with aggravated assault and reckless endangerment, is scheduled for March 28. He could face up to 19 years in prison, a dishonorable discharge and loss of retirement benefits. The court martial of Lt. Col. Jeffrey Chessani, charged with failing to properly report and investigate a possible "law of war" violation, is scheduled for April 28. He could face more than two years in prison, a dishonorable discharge and loss of retirement benefits.

Having survived their war in Iraq, the lives of these American soldiers remain very much in jeopardy. But the most sensational charges against them have fallen apart. Who can forget the March 19, 2006, Time magazine story by Tim McGirk entitled "Collateral Damage or Civilian Massacre in Haditha?" The story answered its own question by describing a vengeful, Marine "rampage."

On May 17, 2006, Rep. John Murtha, D-Pa., piled on to say what happened at Haditha was actually "much worse" than the Time story. Official investigations were still underway, but the ranking member of the Defense Appropriations Subcommittee repeatedly condemned the Marines for having "killed innocent civilians in cold blood."

As if to underscore the point, on May 25, 2006, then-commandant of the Marine Corps Michael Hagee announced he would embark on a grand tour of Marine bases to "reinforce standards and core values." This didn't exactly come off as a vote of confidence in his men.

As 2008 begins, Haditha hysteria still blights the lives of all the men who were implicated, not just the soldiers remaining in legal limbo. But what about the accusers who trumpeted the worst of the charges? Are they accountable for tarnished reputations? Terminated careers? Legal bills? Outrage? Night sweats?

Dream on. McGirk has moved on to a plummy new assignment as Time Jerusalem bureau chief, even as Time has moved away from signal points in the initial report. Via subsequent "corrections," Time asserted that the identity of a key source was grossly misrepresented, and admitted that allegations about a photograph reported as "one of the most damning pieces of evidence investigators have" was based on information from a source who later said "he had no firsthand knowledge" of it.

Murtha refuses to comment on the matter publicly or otherwise; as a defendant in a civil libel suit filed by Staff Sgt. Wuterich, he's appealing a federal court order to be interviewed by Staff Sgt. Wuterich's attorneys.

Hagee, whom Murtha has ID'ed as his source (Hagee denies this), has retired.

End of story? Not necessarily. The week before Christmas, the North County Times of San Diego reported that lawyers for Tatum have asked the military court to order Murtha to submit to interviews about his comments. They also "want to force an interview with retired Marine Corps Commandant Michael Hagee about what Hagee may have said to Murtha or others about the Haditha killings."

The judge has yet to rule on this matter, but I, for one, hope he orders up the interviews. What is said may reveal that the Iraq war has indeed produced its "defining atrocity" — against our own Marines.

Was soldier jailed to appease Iraqi 'allies'?

4/11/08

Recently, I opened an e-mail and read: "I am Sgt. Evan Vela's father. I do no not know if you have followed my son's case but some people have drawn similarities between the Luttrell situation and Evan's."

The father was referring to Marcus Luttrell, whose best-seller "Lone Survivor" tells of four Navy SEALS, Luttrell among them, whose secret mission in Afghanistan was compromised when two Afghan goatherds discovered them hiding deep in Taliban territory. I've written before about the perverse but likely prospect of legal prosecution back home that weighed heavily on the Americans' decision not to save their own lives and their mission by killing the two unarmed Afghans — a "crime" in PC la-la land, even when "unarmed" still means deadly. After releasing the Afghans, the SEALS were overwhelmed by the Taliban, and in the ensuing carnage, not only were three of the four Americans killed, but so were 16 more U.S. special forces, shot down in their helicopter by the Taliban during a rescue attempt. In his book, Luttrell has immortalized the battle, which I think of as Death by Rules of Engagement.

The Luttrell story certainly opens like that of Sgt. Evan Vela, who, as part of an elite sniper squad, was in insurgent-controlled territory south of Baghdad last year when the team's "hide" was discovered by an unarmed Iraqi man who made noise and thrashed about after being captured. Did I mention the American soldiers were heat-exhausted and sleep-deprived after three days operating in 120-degree heat?

Instead of letting the man go and, a la Luttrell's team, getting killed by nearby Sunni terrorists, Sgt. Vela's squad leader made the decision Luttrell and his comrades didn't make. He determined the Iraqi man threatened his team's safety, and he ordered Sgt. Vela to kill the man. Sgt. Vela complied. The Americans returned to base alive. And Sgt. Vela is now serving 10 years in prison for murder.

A recent New York Daily News op-ed on the case was called: "American Sniper Hung Out to Dry." That sums up what happened. But why?

This is where pounding outrage over an injustice to an American soldier — who at least deserves the benefit of the doubt — turns to a sickening sense that what has gone wrong here is even bigger than Sgt. Vela's personal tragedy. It may well be as big as the entire U.S effort to prevail in Iraq.

Let's go back to the scene of the so-called crime: An area outside Iskandariyah, which as recently as last May was Sunni "Triangle of Death"-central.

And let's go back to the victim of the "crime": Genei Nesir Khudair Al-Jenabi, a member of Babil province's pre-eminent tribe. Come the U.S.-led invasion, the Jenabi, like other Sunnis, joined the Sunni insurgency.

And come "the surge," or shortly thereafter (just revving up around the Vela incident), the Jenabi, like other Sunnis, began, via "awakening" councils, to join the United States. At least they started getting paid to stop shooting Americans and start shooting Al Qaeda. Not that it was always easy to make the transition. Lt. Col. Robert Balcavage — who just happens to be the commander of Evan Vela's battalion, and is said by Vela's team leader to have pushed for higher kill rates from snipers — explained it this way last August to the Washington Post: "The Jenabi tribe, the problem they're having is that the Al Qaeda is them."

So let's review. Evan Vela in May 2007 kills a member of "the Al Qaeda is them" tribe who has compromised his squad, and gets convicted of murder in February 2008 in Baghdad.

Baghdad? It was when I heard the court martial was in Baghdad — not stateside, like other such trials — that my initial outrage became the queasy feeling mentioned above, which only intensified on learning that Sgt. Vela's division had actually been ordered back to the United States before the trial began. And the smell of a rat grew stronger still when I read that the Iraqi Minister for Human Rights, Wijdan Salim, attended the trial. "I want to be sure that any American soldier who wrongs an Iraqi will go on trial," Ms. Salim told Time magazine. "(Evan Vela) killed an Iraqi man, an unarmed man. He must be punished."

Well, he was. To the question "why," I can only offer more questions: Is it possible that Evan Vela's Baghdad court martial was all for show? And can his punishment be seen as a sacrificial offering to any of our Iraqi "allies"?

Pardon Sgt. Evan Vela, Mr. President

12/19/08

It's that time again, and I don't just mean Christmastime.

We're now entering the final phase of an outgoing administration. And during this phase, George W. Bush, mere mortal but still president, has the practically supernatural ability to grant pardons. This endows him with the power of life over death, of clemency over conviction. For one month more, President Bush will be able to right wrongs, show mercy and restore faith. For one month more, he will have the opportunity to pardon Sgt. Evan Vela, now serving 10 years in a military prison for what a court martial called "murder" but what I, along with many, many Americans, call war.

I first heard about Sgt. Vela last spring in an e-mail from his father, Curtis Carnahan. "I do not know if you have followed my son's case," he wrote, "but some people have drawn similarities between the Luttrell situation and Evan's."

Carnahan was referring to Marcus Luttrell, whose best-seller "Lone Survivor" tells of four Navy SEALS, Luttrell among them, whose secret mission in Afghanistan was compromised when two unarmed goatherds discovered the Americans hiding in Taliban territory. Fearful of precisely the kind of legal action that would later ensnare Evan Vela and his comrades, the SEALs, as Luttrell tells it, decided not to kill the Afghans, even to preserve their own lives, let along the success of their mission. So the SEALs released the Afghans and abandoned their mission.

It was the tragically wrong decision. Soon, the SEALs were under attack from a large force of Taliban. In the ensuing battle not only were three of the four SEALs gruesomely killed — with only Luttrell living on as the "lone survivor" — but so were 16 additional U.S. special forces who perished in a rescue attempt.

While the Taliban are the clear agents of death in this terrible case, it is our own acid ideology of political and cultural self-sacrifice that is actually responsible. The stunning fact is, the SEAL team faced not one but two enemies that day in Afghanistan: their jihadist opponents in the mountains and their politically correct fellow-citizens in the courtroom. They chose to fight the one enemy they thought they could defeat.

In very similar battleground circumstances, Staff Sgt. Michael Hensley, Evan Vela's squad leader, made a different decision. Of course, Hensley thought he could whip both enemies at once.

A complex saga, the events of that day come down to several salient facts. Operating in Al Qaeda-infested territory south of Baghdad, Hensley and his men were discovered in their "hide" by an unarmed Iraqi man, whom they captured. As the man failed to stop moving and making noise, Hensley was very properly concerned that the Iraqi would reveal the Americans' position to nearby insurgents. It seems that he was also very properly concerned that even this overtly hostile action that he deemed dangerous to his men and mission would not impress his superiors as sufficient cause to kill the Iraqi. In other words, Hensley seemed to sense, as I believe, that where our PC-uber-alles military brass are concerned, the lives of American troops are not as important as their own extremely twisted sense of morality: that it is morally better to risk their troops' lives than to risk marring what they perversely conceive of as their own inner purity.

And there was something else, although I doubt Hensley could have been aware of it. This incident took place in May 2007, just as "the surge" was kicking in and just as Sunni insurgents were "awakening." The resulting trial over the incident, conducted in Iraq rather than in the United States as in the case of all other such trials, would ultimately resemble a platter seeking a sacrificial lamb to serve up to "former" insurgents and Iraqi officials alike. As things turned out, Vela became that lamb.

In any case, Hensley concocted a politically correct, brass-pleasing cover story over the course of several phone calls to the command post — something about the approach of an insurgent armed with an AK-47. He then ordered Evan Vela to kill the man. It was Vela's first "kill."

Long story short: The court martial nightmare our deceased SEALs in Afghanistan feared more than death in battle came true for Hensley and two other members of the squad.

Hensley ultimately served 135 days of confinement and the other soldier connected to the case, Jorge Sandoval, served five months in prison. Only Evan Vela, the young Ranger-trained sniper who carried out his superior's battlefield order, was convicted of "murder." Vela, a 25-year-old husband and father of two small children, is now spending his first of 10 Christmases in the military prison at Fort Leavenworth.

This is a grotesque miscarriage of military justice. It is not the only such travesty to come out of Iraq, but I don't know of another case more deserving of a presidential pardon. Fortunately, two Republican lawmakers from Idaho agree. U.S. Senator George Crapo and U.S. Representative Mike Simpson have recently written letters to the president urging him to pardon Evan Vela.

Our 43rd President frequently expresses gratitude to our troops for their willingness to fight for America's freedom as well as the freedom of foreign, even hostile peoples. I can think of no better way to enshrine that gratitude with a presidential pardon to restore the freedom of one of those very troops — Sgt. Evan Vela.

'See-no-Islam' strategy disgraces fallen soldier

2/19/10

Remember last June when President Obama traveled to Saudi Arabia because, as he put it, "It was very important to come to the place where Islam began and seek his majesty's counsel"?

I argued at the time, gagging, that rather than visiting "the place where Islam began," the president of the United States should have gone to the place where Islam had just ended the life of a U.S. soldier. I refer to the U.S. Army-Navy recruiting center in Little Rock, Ark., where on June 1, Muslim convert Abdulhakim Mujahid Muhammad fatally shot Pvt. William Long, 23, and wounded Pvt. Quinton Ezeagwula, 18. The two soldiers had been standing outside having a smoke.

As usual, the president didn't take my advice, or even my further suggestion that he turn the attack into an opportunity to declare in a major address that the 21st-century era of jihad was over. Instead, he journeyed to lands where jihad is a sacred institution, and in Cairo made another speech entirely, boosting and even preaching on behalf of Islam. His only comment was to call the attack, belatedly, "a senseless act of violence."

Senseless? This was an act of jihad, and both soldiers, along with the fallen and wounded at Fort Hood, should receive the Purple Hearts they deserve. Muhammad himself has made his jihadist intentions against the U.S. military clear, beginning first with his statement to police, and later in collect phone calls to the Associated Press from Pulaski County jail. On June 9, the AP quoted Muhammad calling the attack "a act, for the sake of G0d, for the sake of Allah, the Lord of all the world, and also a retaliation on U.S. military." He wasn't guilty of murder, he said, "because murder is when a person kills another person without justified reason."

Such a definition jibes with Islamic law, which, for example, permits the killing of "non-Muslims at war with Muslims." Muhammad also told the AP he wanted revenge against the U.S. military for its perceived offenses against Muslims and the Koran.

We haven't heard much about the case since Pulaski County prosecutor Larry Jegley asked for a gag order on the gabby jihadi—a step a prosecutor will take, former prosecutor Andrew C. McCarthy tells me, to prevent the jury pool from being "poisoned" and to ward off potential defense claims that a fair trial was not possible.

But lead prosecutor Jegley has now entered bizarro territory, telling the New York Times this week that his team, as the paper put it, "considers (the attack) a straightforward murder case and that they intend to try it without delving into Mr. Muhammad's religious conversion, political beliefs or possible ties to terrorists. 'When you strip away what he says, self-serving or not, it's just an awful killing,' said Larry Jegley ...'It's like a lot of other killings we have.' "

It is? Do "a lot" of middle-class murder defendants in Pulaski County convert to Islam in 2004 and worship at an Ohio mosque frequented by convicted terrorists in 2005 and 2006? Do "a lot" of them travel to Yemen in 2007 where, ABC News reported, "it is believed that Muhammad attended the Damaj Institute, an Islamic institute attended by a number of radicalized U.S. converts (including) John Walker Lindh? Do "a lot" get themselves arrested for overstaying their visa in Yemen, and possessing a fake Somali passport? Do "a lot" finally get deported back to the States in 2008? (Bio highlights courtesy the NEFA Foundation.) Do "a lot" fire on U.S. soldiers at a military recruiting center?

I'm not the only one confounded by the prosecutor's inexplicable and highly disturbing decision to follow a see-no-Islam strategy. Muhammad himself recently wrote to the judge claiming he was encountering legal obstacles to changing his plea to guilty. Avowing affiliation with al-Qaida as a member of "Abu Basir's Army," Muhammad further emphasized the fact that the incident was a "a Jihadi Attack ... justified according to Islamic Laws and the Islamic Religion. Jihad—To fight those who wage war on Islam and Muslims."

This was an act of war against the United States and should be treated as such. Especially for the sake of the fallen, this is no time for the prosecutor to run off the battlefield.

Clemency for the enemy, but not our soldiers?

5/27/10

This Memorial Day Weekend, Americans remember not only our fallen soldiers, but also soldiers currently fighting in hostile lands under atrocious conditions.

But there's another duty upon us as Americans with a debt of gratitude to our armed forces.

We must recognize the travesties of U.S. military justice that have tried, convicted, jailed and repeatedly denied clemency to all too many brave Americans, the same brave Americans who have fought our wars only to be unfairly charged with "murder" in the war zone.

Readers of this column will recall the crushing conviction of Sgt. Evan Vela, a young Ranger-trained sniper and father of two from Idaho, for executing his superior's order to kill an Iraqi man who, at the time, had been compromising his squad's hiding place in pre-"surge" Iraq. Ten years in Fort Leavenworth, ordered not-so-blind justice. (There is evidence that Evan's harsh sentence was a blatant political sop to Iraq's government.) One reason behind my intense dislike for George W. Bush—my own personal Bush Derangement Syndrome—is the former president's callousness toward such Americans as Sgt. Vela, who served their commander in chief well in these difficult times. As the Bush administration drew to an end in January 2009, talk of a presidential pardon for Vela leaked to the media, no doubt elating the Vela family, but, cruelly, nothing came of it.

It never does. And Evan Vela has all too many brothers-in-arms at Fort Leavenworth prison. There serve Vela (10 years), Michael Behenna (20 years), Corey Claggett (18 years), William Hunsaker (18 years), John Hatley (40 years), Larry Hutchins (11 years), Michael Leahy (20 years), Joseph Mayo (20 years), Michael Williams (25 years). Google their names, read their cases and, before recoiling in PC shudders deeper into the hammock, try to imagine the particular hell of war as they and others like them experienced it on our behalf.

If this exercise dampens the barbecue-season kickoff, good. Maybe it will help Americans see the urgent need for clemency in these cases. And particularly given the mind-boggling fact that the United States has released and granted clemency in Iraq to tens of thousands of insurgents, including some of the most dangerous fighters our soldiers were sent to fight in the first place.

Now, the British newspaper The Guardian has reported that Iraq's military is blaming the sharp rise in violence this year on American-released detainees. Maj. Gen. Ahmed Obeidi al-Saedi claims as many as 80 percent of former detainees have joined or rejoined militant groups, adding that 86 former inmates of U.S prisons have been rearrested since March 10 alone.

"We ask them, did they finish their time in prison rehabilitated psychologically and they say, 'No, it was the perfect environment to reorganize al-Qaida,'" the Iraqi general said. Obviously, our men in Fort Leavenworth prison pose no such risks. But they continue to rot behind bars, with neither former President Bush nor President Obama troubled by the injustice of it all, even as clemency spreads across the map to Taliban Afghanistan.

Last week, the New York Times reported that American commanders are informally releasing Taliban fighters on their own recognizance after they "promise" not to fight jihad in the path of Allah again - or PC words to that effect. "This letter right here is a sworn pledge from all of your elders that they're vouching for you and that you will never support the Taliban or fight for the Taliban ever again," one commander told a 23-year-old Taliban seized after Marines found a bomb trigger, ammunition and opium buried on his property.

But no such clemency for our own.

McClatchy Newspapers recently reported that since January of this year, 200 alleged Taliban insurgents had been more released from Bagram prison, including 11 this month. After actually being dressed down by one of these newly freed prisoners, Lt. Gen. John R. Allen, No. 2 man at U.S. Central Command in Florida, "delivered a contrite speech as Afghan leaders and former prisoners munched on fresh fruit and chocolate cake."

"If we detained you unfairly, I am sorry," Allen told the men. "I hope this is a great day for you to return to your families."

Those are the words the general should say to his own men, now prisoners at Fort Leavenworth.

Where is the justice for Michael?

12/21/10

Earlier this month, I received an e-mail update from Scott and Vicki Behenna, whose son, Army Ranger 1st Lt. Michael Behenna, is serving 15 years in Fort Leavenworth military prison over the May 2008 shooting of a known killer in Iraq — a terrorist for whom the Army would actually issue a kill/capture order before realizing he was already dead. By the way, that last detail ranks as a minor outrage compared to the other outrages in this military disgrace of a case.

As for most Americans, December has been a busy month for the Behenna family. But while most families have been busy with Christmas plans, the Behennas have been seeking justice for their 27-year-old son. On Dec. 2, they and Michael's girlfriend (friends since second grade) went before the Army Clemency Board to ask the Board to suspend the rest of Michael's sentence, or at least significantly reduce it given that it's at least 50 percent longer than other combat-related unpremeditated-murder sentences. On Dec. 9, the Behennas wrote, they would be attending the long-awaited appeal of Michael's conviction in military appeals court in Arlington, Va.

"At this point," the e-mail continued, "it would take a miracle to prevent Michael from spending another Christmas in prison. But we count it among our many blessings that we will be able to spend Christmas with our son in the visitation room. We have much to be grateful for as we head into 2011. The support you have given to Michael and to our family has truly been a gift from G0d. Michael's story has continued to grow exponentially as has all the stories of the Leavenworth Ten. Please keep the letters coming for all these brave American soldiers."

Ah, the Leavenworth Ten. Readers of this column should be very familiar with these soldiers. Their continued incarcerations remain a moral blight on the U.S. military, which has frequently and recklessly extended clemency to thousands of Iraqi, Iranian, Afghan and other killers from Gitmo to Camp Bucca to Bagram Prison, even as it continues to imprison these men who went to fight them. One of them, PFC Corey Claggett, suffering from severe PTSD, has been in solitary confinement for over four years. (The superior who gave the unlawful order Claggett followed, however, is free on parole.) How could this be?

I attended Lt. Behenna's appeals hearing, and, listening to the military prosecutor argue to uphold the guilty verdict, it struck me that what drives these prosecutions is less the pursuit of truth through shadow and fire than a free-standing, postmodern kind of righteousness that metastasizes independently from the wartime conditions in which all of these dark and difficult incidents take place.

I urge readers to visit defendmichael.com for details (and Unitedpatriots.org and L10freedomride.com for more general information), but the crux is this: While the prosecution originally argued that Michael shot an unarmed, naked and seated victim, Michael Behenna's defense was and is that he shot and killed in self-defense an enemy who had sprung to his feet, chucking concrete and coming at him. That's what Michael said in his trial. And, of crucial importance to Michael's appeals case, that's what the prosecution's own forensics witness, Dr. Herbert MacDonnell, said the forensics evidence supported. But MacDonnell's key evidence was never disclosed to the jury. And, in seemingly glaring violation of due process, this crucial evidence was never disclosed to the defense until after the guilty verdict came in.

No reason to undermine the guilty verdict, the prosecution insisted. Indeed — and here, an observer of both proceedings told me, came the shift in prosecutorial strategy — whether standing or sitting, the enemy fighter was fully justified in attacking the fully armed American lieutenant, threatening his life. Further, the military prosecutor claimed the situation was such that the American lieutenant had … no … right … to … self-defense.

This is twisted beyond twisted. So, too, is the apparent fact that had the terrorist seized the lieutenant's weapon in a scuffle, Lt. Michael Behenna would be innocent in the military's eyes. He would also be dead.

It's time for our appalling military justice system to go on trial.

Our sanity-defying war

12/29/10

I end the year with a question and one last outrage.

The U.N. believes about 1 million Afghans between the ages of 15 and 64 - roughly 8 percent of the population — are addicted to drugs. The publication Development Asia estimates 2 million Afghan addicts.

Depending on whose figures you read next, some staggering number of these same addicts ends up in the Afghan National Police (ANP).

Fully "half of the latest batch" of police recruits tested positive for narcotics, the Independent reported in March, drawing on Foreign Office Papers from late 2009. Also in March 2010, the Government Accounting Office (GAO) reported, depending on the province, 12 to 41 percent of

Afghan police recruits tested positive. The GAO added: "A State official noted that this percentage likely understates the number of opium users because opiates leave the system quickly; many recruits who tested negative for drugs have shown opium withdrawal symptoms later in their training." The problem was dire enough, the report continues, to place under consideration "the establishment of dedicated rehabilitation clinics at the regional police training centers."

Pederasty, misogyny and corruption aside: This drug-addled ANP is part of the Afghan National Security Forces that the U.S. government fully expects — no, completely relies on — to secure Afghanistan against "extremist networks" and is spending $350 million per day in Afghanistan until that happens.

My question: Who's high here? Illiterate Afghans on drugs, or educated Americans on fantasy?

Like a legion of buttoned-down and uniformed Don Quixotes seeking the impossible COIN (counterinsurgency theory) -- winning Afghan hearts and minds from Islamic loyalties, constructing a heretofore unseen Afghan "city on a hill," training Afghan police (literacy rate 4.5 percent) while simultaneously weaning them from addiction, and don't get me started on "ally" Pakistan — the United States has plunged into a depth of denial only an extravagant "intervention" could reverse.

This American flight from reality skews everything, whether large and obvious, like waging a sanity-defying war, or small and easily overlooked, like starkly refusing to bestow a medal on a deserving fallen soldier. I refer to the appalling fact that Pvt. William Long, slain at age 23 by an avowed jihadist outside an Arkansas military recruitment center in June 2009, has not received a Purple Heart from the U.S. government. When Abdulhakim Mujahid Muhammad fired his AK-47, killing Pvt. Long and wounding Pvt. Quinton Ezeagwula (no Purple Heart, either), he was committing an act of war. The United States refuses to recognize this fact even as Muhammad, in interviews, statements and letters to media, has never shut up about it.

The U.S. failure to recognize Pvt. Long's sacrifice is my year-ending outrage. In many ways it best symbolizes the others that have propelled this column through 2010. In this denial of jihad reality and callousness toward those who bear the brunt of sacrifices most Americans escape, we see symbolized the broader government failures toward the people on every front involving life and death.

Fortunately, the people are not failing Pvt. Long. On a cold and windy December day in Arkansas, at the close of a ceremony honoring Arkansans killed in recent wars, memorial organizer Ron Hopper told a story. As the Arkansas News reported, Hopper, whose son was killed in Iraq, mentioned a jewelry company that automatically makes a present of an engraved silver bracelet to all families of fallen soldiers. When the Long family asked the company to put their son's name on the list, "they were told that since he was not killed in Iraq and Afghanistan, the family was not entitled to one."

"An outraged murmur spread through the room," the report continued. "He may not have been deployed overseas. But he was killed in the Global War on Terror," Hopper declared. "For that reason, we ordered one made ourselves." And he presented a silver bracelet engraved with Pvt. Long's name to his sister, who, tears streaming down her face, announced she would give the bracelet to her mother for Christmas.

The government may be in denial in the sealed corridors of power, but at the VFW on Davis Drive in Searcy, Ark., reality lives, a thing of pain, loyalty and love.

Happy 2011.

The only 'murder' here was of justice

8/5/11

They are the forgotten warriors of the Iraq War, the men whose lives and families and careers blew up in "murder" charges on a vicious battlefield, the pieces coming down in Fort Leavenworth's military prison where the men now serve long sentences. Together, they make up the Leavenworth 10, not always at Leavenworth and not always 10, a group of cold-luck cases still working their way up the ladder of appeals and the clemency process, their families hoping to free them before many more years go by.

They all got bad news recently when word came that the Army Court of Appeals denied Army Ranger 1st Lt. Michael Behenna, 28, a new trial despite the introduction of exculpatory evidence originally withheld by the prosecution. Behenna faces 13 more years of a 15-year sentence for the unpremeditated 2008 "murder" of an insurgent who killed two of his men in post-surge Iraq, an al-Qaida terrorist for whom the Army would issue a kill/capture order before realizing he was already dead.

Why no new trial?

At almost the same time, Assistant Secretary of the Navy Juan Garcia overruled recommendations from the Naval Clemency and Parole Board and from brig officials at Miramar Marine Corps Air Station that Marine Sgt. Lawrence Hutchins, 27, be granted early release. Hutchins has served more than five years on a 15-year sentence that was reduced to 11 years. The sentence was once recommended to be cut to five years, and once thrown out (he spent nine months free starting June 2010). He faces the balance of the 11-year-sentence for conspiracy and unpremeditated "murder" of a man he believed was the killer of Marines and civilians in pre-surge Iraq.

Why no parole?

I put quotation marks of incredulousness around "murder" because this was a war zone — a chaotic, urban war zone in which counterinsurgency theory (COIN), winning hearts and minds, just didn't go according to the book. Those restrictive rules of engagement (ROEs) failed to impress jihadists or their clans with America's good intentions, and the schizoid mishmash of firepower, nation-building, harsh interrogations, bribery, police work and social work made our forces pawns of an untenable policy. These young men shouldn't be the ones to pay for that policy. We should use this week's one-two punch of "military justice" for some national soul-searching. It's the least we can do for men who risked everything for our country.

The two cases are quite different, but they share more than miscarriages of justice. Reading back before the judicial nightmares began is to follow two warriors contending with a basic COIN flaw: the notorious practice known as catch-and-release, the opaque, bureaucratic process by which U.S. forces risked their lives to "arrest" insurgents on the back-alley battlefield only to see them released to kill again for "lack of evidence." In both Behenna's and Hutchins' cases (and others), catch-and-release was the ultimate manifestation of chaotic command and no control, and served as a common trigger of events. Behenna himself had to drive home the very insurgent known to be responsible for the IED (crude, handmade bomb) that recently killed two of his men. He decided to perform one more interrogation himself during which the insurgent rushed him, at which point Behenna fired. This is the self-defense scenario supported by the prosecution's own forensics expert. It was suppressed at Behenna's trial and ignored on appeal.

Hutchins' case is more complex, involving an eight-man plot to "snatch" and kill a "prince" of the insurgency, someone responsible for everything from IEDs to recruiting suicide bombers. Again, it was catch-and-release, and not for the first time, that lit the fuse for this Marine squad. They caught the terrorist and then, on release, had to drive him home. They later decided to fake an incident in which the "prince's" killing would be ROE-lawful. While Hutchins waited in ambush, the wrong man was seized, they all shot at him and then covered up the incident. No Marine was confined for more than 525 days except Hutchins (11 years).

Hutchins also drew a rebuke from Navy Secretary Ray Mabus, who, while Hutchins appealed and sought clemency, slandered him as a premeditated and indiscriminate murderer. Hutchins lawyer, Maj. Babu Kaza, points out that Hutchins was found guilty of neither allegation and that Mabus' unprecedented public comments constitute "unlawful command influence" on the workings of justice.

At least that's what the military calls these nightmares.

Eating our own some more:
Sgt. Derrick Miller

7/31/11, blog post

Sgt. Derrick Miller, 27, of Hagerstown, MD, was convicted this past week of the premeditated murder of an Afghan man in 2010. The husband and father of two was assigned to a Connecticut National Guard unit and attached to the 101st Airborne Division at the time of the shooting in Eastern Afghanistan. After joining the National Guard in 2006, Miller had three combat deployments and had recently been promoted.

From the AP last week:

> FORT CAMPBELL, Ky. - A US Army National Guardsman was sentenced yesterday to life in prison with the chance of parole for the murder of an Afghan civilian.
>
> Sergeant Derrick Miller, 27, of Hagerstown, Md., **shook hands with several soldiers in his unit** after the 10-member military jury delivered the sentence after two hours of deliberation. He was found guilty of premeditated murder.

Clue #1 to smelling yet another rat in our military justice system. Miller is still on good terms with fellow soldiers. Would several soldiers want to shake hands with a "premeditated murderer"?

> His attorney had argued during two days of testimony that **Miller acted in self-defense** when he shot a man last September. The military has identified him as Atta Mohammed but his name was not used in court.
>
> Defense attorney Charles Gittins told the jury that Miller stopped the man for questioning when he **walked through a defensive perimeter** that Miller's unit had set up around a mortar unit.

What was an innocent bystander doing walking through a defensive perimeter?

> **Gittins said Miller believed the man could be a threat** to his unit and that during questioning **the man tried to grab Miller's**

weapon.

> But Specialist Charles Miller, an eyewitness and guardsman from Maryland, testified he heard Miller **threatening to kill the man** if he did not tell the truth and then straddling the man, who was lying on his back, **before shooting him in the head.**

He said, he said — but not much information in between. I decided to email defense attorney Charles Gittins.

Q:Hello, Mr. Gittins,

Saw a brief story about Sgt. Miller's sentencing (first I'd heard of the story). Can you send me any more information about his case?

Best wishes,

Diana West

Charles Gittins replied:

In a contested jury trial at Fort Campbell KY, SGT Miller was sentenced to life in prison with the opportunity for parole (in 10 years) for killing an Afghan civilian when the civilian grabbed his weapon during harsh questioning. The civilian was identified as a possible insurgent who had been walking through SGT Miller's platoon defensive perimeter observing their defensive positions. After the shooting the unit was attacked in a complex attack and the ANA soldiers assigned to the platoon pulled back prior to the start of the shooting and hid behind a building.

The witnesses against SGT Miller were a soldier who originally supported SGT Miller's version of events, but he changed his story when he was threatened with being named an accessory and being placed on legal hold so he could not de-mobilize. The other witness was an Afghan translator who was promised US Citizenship in exchange for his testimony. He was brought to the US in January and has been living on Fort Campbell in a base hotel at $630 per month with a dedicated van to take him wherever he wants to go, and has been fed at taxpayer expense. Basically, the two witnesses had every incentive to testify the way the Government wanted them to — consistent with guilt rather than SGT Miller's claim of innocence. SGT Miller cooperated in every way from the date of the shooting, but his command lacked the moral courage to stand behind him.

I wrote back:

If I say I'm not shocked, it's only because I've been following such cases for years now. But I'd also be exaggerating, because what you describe is shocking in a most disgusting way. Who, in your opinion, is this show trial designed to play to?

Gittins replied:

The Afghans that run that area of the country. This guy [the victim] was an insurgent but no one in the fricking military is willing to say so to the two-faced Afghans. They had a firefight that night that was designed to kill Americans — all the while the ANA soldiers were nowhere to be seen. They disappeared just before the shooting started and the fire on American positions was such that the guys targeted were sure that they [the insurgents] had recon of American positions due to this guy and his two military-aged males accompanying him reporting on the positions.

That we waste ONE American life in defense of that country is anathema. The country is completely corrupt; they are cowards unwilling to defend their own country, and we have gotten so deep in defending an indefensibly corrupt regime we cannot extricate our military in a way that allows us to maintain our honor.

If President Karzai was on fire I wouldn't urinate on him to put out the fire. Feel free to quote me.

CG

How much combat is too much for any human being?

3/15/12

I got to know James Culp, a lawyer who specializes in military defense cases, a little bit around the time he was defending Sgt. Evan Vela, whom I have written about many times. After news broke about an Army Staff Sergeant who allegedly walked off base in Afghanistan and murdered 16 Afghans last weekend, I thought of Jim partly because the Army Staff Sergeant, on his first deployment in Afghanistan after three deployments in Iraq, was said to have suffered a traumatic brain injury in Iraq, which may or may not have had anything to do with his alleged action.

The last case of Culp's I followed concerned Pfc. David Lawrence, a young soldier suffering from mental problems (PTSD and schizophrenia), who was nonetheless prosecuted for murder of a Taliban commander in US custody — even though he had sought help from military psychologists after seven of his fellow soldiers were killed, and even though Army experts ruled he was not criminally responsible for his actions (story here and here). Lawrence is currently serving 12 ½ years at Leavenworth.

Jim sent along some general observations about the strain the US government is imposing on our armed forces after ten years of war, which he gave me permission to post.

> Three and four combat tours are too many for any one person. The amount of combat our Soldiers are being forced to endure is unprecedented in our history. The mental wounds our Soldiers are enduring may be invisible, but they cause catastrophic damage. Sometimes the damage is borne by the warrior alone. The suicide rate of our service members and veterans has never been higher in the history of our nation. Sometimes innocent lives are destroyed by the invisible wounds as well. **It will take another two decades to know the full extent of damage that has been inflicted on the minds of a very few whom we have repeatedly sent back into harm's way in a war where the enemy inflicts daily death and destruction upon our service members, but then escapes retribution or counter-attack by seamlessly blending into the population.** (Emphasis added.)

> It is human nature to desire retribution. We see this in the Afghanistan response to the massacre. It is not irrational to want retribution, to need retribution. What is irrational . . what is maddening . . .is that the deep need for retribution by our fighting men who are consistently ground up like cattle by anonymous IED's planted by an invisible enemy goes un-satiated. This maddening aspect of guerilla warfare is exacerbated ten-fold by overly restrictive Rules of Engagement that are meant to restrict civilian casualties at the expense of the safety of our men and women warriors. I suppose a Soldier or Marine can be put into such a mind altering environment for one tour of duty and be expected to remain relatively sane. Perhaps even two combat deployments under such circumstances. I think the deadly actions of this soldier scream an important question that we are repeatedly finding the answer to the hard way: How much combat, especially guerilla warfare, is too much for one human being?

Army may as well put our soldiers in straightjackets

4/27/12

To keep former Army 1st Lt. Michael Behenna behind bars until 2024 for the "unpremeditated murder" of an insurgent during the war in Iraq, U.S. military prosecutors have resorted to strange and disturbing twists of law, logic and morality. They were all on display again this week in Behenna's final plea before the military's highest court of appeals in Washington, D.C. It was enough to make the gold eagle on top of the American flag in the courtroom shake and then hang its head.

Or so I imagined while listening intently as questions from the five civilian judges began to drill into a central argument advanced by the military prosecutor: that Lt. Behenna had *"lost his right to self-defense"* in the war zone when he embarked on an unauthorized interrogation of Ali Mansur, a suspected al-Qaida cell leader.

Lost his right to self-defense? What does that mean to our soldiers at war, where extenuating circumstances are facts of life?

At the hearing's onset, however, questions from the bench peppering Behenna's defense counsel, Jack Zimmerman, made it clear the judges weren't interested in any such circumstances. For the record, these include the fact that: (1) Behenna, as a 25-year-old platoon leader, lost two of his men very likely to Mansur, who was strongly suspected of organizing attacks against Americans; (2) shortly after Behenna's platoon arrested Mansur, he was released again; (3) Behenna himself, deeply affected by the deaths of his men weeks earlier, was ordered to take Mansur home; and (4) Behenna decided one more interrogation would net the confession necessary to find other al-Qaida members and put Mansur back in jail.

Thus, Michael Behenna, a 2006 ROTC graduate of the University of Central Oklahoma, found himself in a culvert in Baiji, Iraq, in 2008 interrogating Mansur, who, stripped naked, sat on a rock.

Military prosecutors argue Behenna executed Mansur then and there. A court-martial panel (jury) called it "unpremeditated murder" in 2009, and Behenna was sentenced to 25 years in Fort Leavenworth military prison. (That sentence has since been reduced to 15 years.)

According to Behenna's own testimony — *and according to the corroborating hypothesis of one of the prosecution's own expert witnesses* — Mansur rose from the rock and lunged for Behenna's gun. Behenna fired two bullets in self-defense, killing Mansur. And therein lie the seeds of appeal.

One: Military prosecutors didn't inform the defense team about their own expert witness's exculpatory evidence, which is required procedure under the rules of discovery. Two: The instructions to the original panel (jury) were so convoluted that one of the appeals court judges said he'd read them four times and still found them confusing.

Maybe more than anything else, though, what made the eagle in the courtroom droop in despair were the lengths to which the U.S. government was prepared to go to strip this soldier, and by extension all soldiers, of their "right to self-defense," even amid the untenable conditions of urban counterinsurgency (COIN) warfare and its restricted rules of engagement.

A lengthy line of questions on a soldier's right to self-defense indicated considerable interest (incredulity?) among the judges on this key position of the prosecution. Lead prosecutor Army Capt. Steven E. Latino argued that by embarking on the unauthorized interrogation with a loaded gun pointed at Mansur, Behenna lost his right to defend himself — in essence, lost his right to stay alive — even in the event the al-Qaida op attacked him. Indeed, Latino stressed that there was no condition here under which Behenna could have maintained his "right to self-defense."

How twisted Uncle Sam has become. If we take this position to its shocking conclusion, in our government's eyes, a terrorist with American blood on his hands merits more legal protection than does the U.S. soldier who breached protocol, however severely, in hopes of bringing said terrorist to book for killing Americans.

Free Michael Behenna, yes. And free the rest of the "Leavenworth 10" — every one of whom is an Iraq War veteran-victim of unseemly prosecutorial zeal (for courtroom victory over justice), from former Master Sgt. John Hatley and Sgt. Evan Vela, to Pvt. Corey Clagett.

It would make the eagle proud.

Obama should pardon the Leavenworth Ten

5/17/12

Here I am again in the U.S. Court of Appeals for the Armed Forces in Washington, D.C., the highest appeals court for the U.S. military. Last month, I was here to cover Army 1st Lt. Michael Behenna's final appeal. Now I am waiting for Army Sgt. Evan Vela's final appeal to begin. I glance over at Evan's father, Curtis Carnahan, and Evan's wife, Alyssa, sitting together in the otherwise empty first row, and I can't believe it's been more than four years since Curtis first emailed me:

"I am Sgt. Evan Vela's father. I do not know if you have followed my son's case, but some people have drawn similarities between the Luttrell situation and Evan's."

Curtis was referring to Marcus Luttrell, whose 2007 best-seller "Lone

Survivor" tells of four Navy SEALs, Luttrell among them, whose 2005 mission in Afghanistan was compromised when two unarmed Afghan goatherds discovered the SEALs hiding deep in Taliban territory. I had written a column discussing the excruciating fact that the thought of being brought up on legal charges in a military court back home weighed so heavily on these young Americans' minds that they decided not to save their own lives and their mission by killing the two Afghans, but rather to take their chances against the veritable Taliban army the pair would summon against them.

"It was the stupidest, most Southern-fried, lame-brain decision I ever made in my life," Luttrell later wrote of his decisive vote to let the two Afghans go. As a result of the decision the SEALs made on an Afghan mountaintop far from any courthouse, 19 Americans — Luttrell's three SEAL teammates and 16 more special forces — would be killed that same day.

But no one went to court.

In Evan's case, the leader of his elite sniper squad chose the other path. It was May 2007, in insurgent-controlled Iskandariyah, Iraq. When an unarmed Iraqi man compromised the team's "hide" and refused to cooperate quietly, the team leader chose not to risk drawing local insurgents to their position, but instead ordered Evan to kill the man. As a result of this decision, all of our soldiers came home that day.

But then they went to court. Long saga short, Evan Vela became the only soldier convicted of the killing. He was sentenced to 10 years at Fort Leavenworth military prison — the shortest sentence of the so-called Leavenworth 10, as Curtis reminded me this week, using the nickname for a group of veterans who are incarcerated for a variety of desperate, blurry, fog-of-war shootings.

Listening to the procedural review of Evan's case, I am struck again by the ghastly surrealism of their plight — the penalties the U.S. government has forced on its most dutiful sons for not committing, in effect, suicide as the Navy SEALs did in choosing to escape prison rather than death.

Meanwhile, literally thousands of incarcerated terrorists in Iraq and Afghanistan have been granted clemency or otherwise found their freedom. Recently, Ali Musa Daqduq, a Hezbollah mastermind who confessed to kidnapping, torturing and killing five American soldiers in 2007, walked free in Iraq. In December 2011, President Obama turned over Daqduq to an Iraqi court, which released him this month. According to the most basic moral calculus, this is neither fair nor right. As Republican Rep. Allen West of Florida recently wrote to President Obama, it's an "utter betrayal."

I steal another glance at the Carnahans, now focused on the court proceedings. Like the other Leavenworth families, they have been counting off the years by trials, appeals, clemency boards and pleas for congressional support. Back in early 2009, there were flutters in the news about a possible pardon for Evan from outgoing President Bush. Then nothing. No pardon. Which was, to my mind, unpardonable. George W. Bush should have pardoned Evan and the other soldiers, now prisoners, whom he ordered into a confusing, rules-restricted war against an army without uniforms on a battlefield without lines.

And so, the Leavenworth 10 sit in prison: Michael Behenna, Corey Clagett, John Hatley, William Hunsaker, Larry Hutchins, Michael Leahy, Joseph Mayo, Michael Williams, Evan Vela. Newcomer Derrick Miller has joined them. Miller last year drew a life sentence after unsuccessfully claiming self-defense in the killing of a suspected Afghan insurgent who had penetrated his defensive perimeter.

Memorial Day — the day we mourn our war dead — is coming. President Obama, give these men another chance at life. Pardon them.

Petraeus, Help the `Leavenworth Ten' Gain Clemency

3/29/13

Talk is cheap, Gen. Petraeus.

You may not agree. After all, your Washington, D.C., "super lawyer," Bob Barnett, charges you something like $900 an hour for a kind of talk best described as "reputation reconfiguration" or "image management," and that's not cheap. Still, you probably consider it effective.

Judging by your recent coming-out party at a University of Southern California dinner to honor the military – your first public foray since you disappeared in a cloud of Paula Broadwell – whatever advice you've been buying seems to be working. You came, you apologized, you received a standing ovation. The media melted all over again into a puddle of admiration, further obscuring the real reasons you should be not apologizing before a gala crowd, but rather testifying before the American people: those national scandals you have so far successfully left in your dust.

I have previously addressed such scandals and will do so again: lying to the House Intelligence Committee about Benghazi twice; causing death and dismemberment of U.S. forces by directing them to walk the IED-packed roads of Afghanistan as part of counterinsurgency (COIN) strategy to win Afghans' "trust"; your see-no-Islam COIN strategy itself. For the moment, though, as you seek and already seem to have received public forgiveness, there is something else to consider: What you can do to give meaning to your words.

It's not enough to time your first public address in five months to coincide with an op-ed in the Wall Street Journal this week to make the case, in subtext, that it's not just your own next act that concerns you but also the plight of some 3 million returning veterans who may find themselves, as you write, at the bottom of the corporate ladder, underemployed or in dead-end jobs. In conclusion, you write, "Now it is our turn to do our part to help (veterans) build promising futures for themselves and their families."

Here's an idea – gratis – to make us trust the sincerity of your call to help veterans and their families build those promising futures. Take that apparently bulletproof reputation of yours and use it to seek clemency for the so-called "Leavenworth 10."

This tag refers to a group of American soldiers now serving long prison terms mainly at Fort Leavenworth for "crimes" committed on your COIN battlefield in Iraq, and also Afghanistan. Across time and space, from desks in orderly offices peering into ghastly battlefields, obsessed military prosecutors have been able to see "murder" and even "premeditated murder" in the eyes of these soldiers who were blinded by the densest fog of war.

Since it was you who ordered these young men into the hostile urban combat zones in Iraq to win "hearts and minds," since it was you who set them up, unable to tell friend from foe, to earn "trust and confidence" amid hostile outposts in Afghanistan, it should now be you who leads them out of their living hells. Long after the U.S. government has released tens of thousands of insurgents in Iraq and Afghanistan – including Hezbollah mastermind Musa Daqduq, for example – it is time for you, the leading general in these wars, to declare that these young Americans, these American prisoners of COIN, have been punished enough.

I refer, for example, to 1st Lt. Michael Behenna, the elite Army Ranger whose last-ditch interrogation of an al-Qaida terrorist ended when, as forensic evidence indicates, he killed the detainee he was questioning in self-defense. Michael has served roughly four years behind bars, but that's only a dent in his 15-year sentence.

There is Pvt. Corey Clagett, the most junior and the only imprisoned member of an Army squad implicated in following direct orders to shoot captured Iraqi insurgents in Operation Iron Triangle. Corey was sentenced to 18 years; cruelly and unusually, he has already spent nearly seven years in solitary confinement.

There is Sgt. Evan Vela, the first-tour Army sniper whose commander ordered him to kill a captured Iraqi struggling to blow the squad's cover behind enemy lines. He was sentenced to 10 years. There is also Sgt. Derrick Miller, an Army National Guard veteran of Afghanistan, who, during a harsh interrogation, killed in self-defense an Afghan who had penetrated his squad's defensive perimeter. He received life in prison, with the possibility of parole in 10 years.

There are more such men whose names you should know – Marine Sgt. Lawrence Hutchins (sentenced to 11 years), Army Master Sgt. John Hatley (sentenced to 40 years) – whose tragic stories should in truth keep you awake at night, whose families will need your help if ever they are to get a chance to build those "promising futures" you glibly wrote about.

All of these young Americans marched into the crosshairs of COIN, the place where your "hearts and minds" strategy blew up, the place where living among, loving, respecting and bribing Iraqis and Afghans according to COIN's see-no-Islam tenets became life-or-death propositions. These men managed to stay alive. According to COIN, that's their main offense.

You, Gen. Petraeus, could go a long way to change that by pleading for their clemency in the name of healing, even as you plead your own. The war is over in Iraq; it is winding down in Afghanistan. Such humbling efforts would represent a new beginning for them – and for you.

Shutting Up About Islam

Foot-in-mouth disease and little lost Tories

5/4/01

There is something very squeamish-making in the news coming out of England these days—not about foot and mouth disease and little lost lambs, but about foot *in* mouth disease and little lost Tories.

The offending subject is multi-culturalism, but not as the term is most commonly used to describe the inclusion of non-Western works for study as a method of redressing assorted social injustices. In this British political season, the subject relates more literally to Great Britain and its relatively recent transformation, mainly through the influx of large numbers of asylum seekers, into a country of many, not-necessarily-assimilating, cultures.

This fact of British life—and policy of the Labor Party—would seem to make asylum issues an obvious centerpiece of the political campaign, would it not? One of those matters of vital public debate every bit as essential as the topic of British sovereignty in the European community, no?

No. There is a veritable gag order on the subject that all the major parties have actually signed under no duress—or, at least, no more than usual. This agreement, brokered by the august-sounding Commission for Racial Equality, calls for "robust political debate" on every topic under the political sun with just one catch: The debate must be conducted without using any language that might "stir up racial or religious hatred or lead to prejudice on grounds of race, nationality or religion."

Which sounds lovely. But means what? Here's an example: When the Tory party pledged last month to make asylum issues a high priority in the campaign by, for one, ending the racketeering that floods the country with "bogus asylum seekers," the United Nations High Commissioner for Refugees, to the glee of the Labor Party, called foul, charging Tory leader William Hague with breaking his party's commitment, as the Telegraph put it, "not to stir up prejudice with inflammatory language on asylum issues."

Inflammatory language? Apparently, the very mention of the subject is verboten. The British Refugee Council was even more intemperate in its condemnation of the Tories, declaring that it was "extremely dangerous" for political parties "to use this issue in an attempt to get votes."

Without bothering to speculate about what they should do with this issue if not attempt to get votes, that little inter-party agreement to play nice suddenly appears in chilly, new light.

Then there's the case of "the Tory race rebel." That's the newspaper moniker for John Townsend, a retiring Tory Member of Parliament who was practically sent off to re-education camp for initially refusing to apologize for saying that Britain's once "homogenous Anglo-Saxon society has been seriously undermined" by massive legal immigration, which, now barred by law, has given way to equally massive asylum-seeking. This, he went on to say, may help Labor in its quest to weaken the nationalist resistance to total incorporation by the European system, but also gives rise to various social problems associated with relating to different ethnic groups from lands without a tradition of tolerance or the rule of law.

One man's opinion? Not in Tony Blair's or William Hague's Great Britain. Perhaps more than anything, it was the MP's less than euphoric reaction to the population shift that put his head on the block. Leaving Mr. Townsend aside, to say that Britain's Anglo-Saxon society hasn't been transformed by immigration is ridiculous; but to say that the transformation isn't an unameliorated cause for rejoicing and may in fact have created thorny political issues that require serious debate, is apparently impermissible.

And this is a great shame. In shunning open debate, Western cultures are ignoring, even suppressing, crucial questions. Is it evil incarnate to note, mourn or balk at the passing of one historic culture as it gives rise to another?

But, as a Tory official told the Telegraph, Mr. Townsend was "told in the simplest terms: Be quiet or else." He agreed, eventually, but not before the hub-bub had escalated, with one hapless Tory having to issue an effusively abject apology for supporting the remarks in question, and another Tory, the party's senior black member, Lord Taylor of Warwick, threatening to quit the party over the whole brouhaha.

End of story? Hardly. The Telegraph reported this week that Lord Warwick may have been collaborating with Labor all along to embarrass the Tories with racial fireworks, while a former official of the

Commission for Racial Equality has charged that the organization has "turned into a political arm of the Labor Party" to make race an issue in the election. If that's true, of course, it's fair to say that nobody will talk about it.

What's in a name when the name is Muhammad?

11/4/02

At first, I thought the radio-show caller was a put-on. Following the arrests last week of DC-sniper suspects John Allen Mohammed and John Lee Malvo, the caller politely made his request: Would the media please refrain from identifying John Muhammad as John Muhammad? Identifying Mr. Muhammad as "Mr. Muhammad" — the surname the suspected serial killer took as a Muslim convert — might reflect badly on Islam, which, as the caller explained, is a religion of peace, not violence, and whose prophet, of course, was also named Muhammad.

While the radio hosts gurgled over the ramifications of a media-made mix-up between Muhammad the prophet and Muhammad the sniper, I realized the caller — by now revealed as the real Muhammad, I mean, McCoy — had a point. He just hadn't taken it far enough. Not only should we not identify John Muhammad as "Muhammad," we shouldn't call him "John," either. That's the name of a Christian apostle (John, natch). Come to think of it, with such namesakes as these, maybe this prime murder suspect shouldn't be identified, period. In fact, maybe we should just let him go. So much for logic.

What's disturbing about this instinct — the urge to repress a truth that undercuts a belief — is its prevalence. Not that it derives from religious fervor alone. I found myself strangely fascinated by the pains The New York Times, for example, took to guard the Chechens who terrorized Moscow last week against their apparent associations with Islamic terrorism. So far, we know, or think we know, that this Muslim suicide gang sent a videotape to Al-Jazeera proclaiming its intention "to take the lives of hundreds of infidels" was led by a Chechen who London's Daily Telegraph describes as having been "imbued with an unshakable faith in militant Islam" and included "a number of Arab fighters believed to be of Saudi Arabian and Yemeni origin."

To the Times, such telling detail registered only as "gestures and symbols borrowed from extremist Islam." The Chechens, the report wrote with re-capping confidence, were "intent on projecting the image of international Islamic warriors in search of 'martyrdom,'" the idea being to draw Islamic gold into their coffers. In other words, the rebels were faking it. Even considering whether Chechen separatism has been, say, hijacked by Islamic elements, it seems, would take the newspaper too far from a script written for a nationalist movement, not Islamic jihad. The Times' tunnel vision reminds me of the urge to lose the "Muhammad" in John Muhammad's name. It's the same reluctance to face facts, however gruesome — or politically incorrect.

With all the events of the past week, however, nowhere was this mindset more rigidly in force than at Georgetown University. The occasion was a lecture by Bat Ye'or, the foremost expert on "dhimmitude." This is the term the trailblazing historian applies to the institutional humiliations and discrimination suffered historically by the dhimmis, Jews and Christians under Muslim rule.

According to Bat Ye'or, when it comes to non-Muslims, jihad leads to a parlous state of dhimmitude, not a brotherhood of man — and, in a wide-ranging lecture about jihad ideology and dhimmitude practices, she told a Georgetown audience exactly that. Oh, the furor the historian and her facts kicked up. Bat Ye'or and, later, her husband, historian David Littman, were jeered by a sizable Muslim contingent, and, even worse, later denounced — literally — by two lecture-sponsoring Jewish organizations. (See Rod Dreher's first-rate account of the debacle at www.nationalreview.com). The historians' worst crime? "They made offensive implications regarding Islam," organization leaders Julia Segall and Daniel Spector wrote in the Georgetown Hoya in their cringe-making "apology" for staging the event. The students then accused the historians of making "no effort to make a clear distinction between pure, harmonious Islam, and the acts of a few who falsely claim to act in the name of Islam."

"Pure nonsense," replied Bat Ye'or in a letter to the Hoya. "When one studies the Inquisition or the Crusades, one does not feel obliged to make a clear distinction between 'pure' Christianity and those historical events." She went on to note the crucial difference between traditional methods of Western analysis, which weigh evidence and testimonies, and Islam's religion-based interpretation of history, which frames events according to religious dogma. Shockingly, the latter would seem to be the single interpretation valid at Georgetown, where, in Bat Ye'or's experience, "the historical testimony of millions of human victims of jihad is rejected on its face by this doctrinal attitude." Only decades of political correctness and cultural relativism could have brought us to the point where there's even a contest between these alien schools of thought. It should be clear by now that the outcome, still undecided, will be far from academic.

Sorry apologies for speaking the truth

3-10-03

This is a tale of two news stories. They both pertain to Islam and culture clash in the post-9/11 world, but they take place in parallel universes: the first in a world where hard facts are prized like battle stars, the second in a milieu where reality's sharper edges require plenty of padding.

The first story is big stuff: The federal government is making the case that the prominent Yemeni cleric Muhammad Ali Hassan al-Mouyad used the Al Farooq Mosque in Brooklyn to help funnel millions of dollars to Al Qaeda -- $20 million to Osama bin Laden personally, according to what the cleric supposedly told an FBI informant.

(Incidentally, the Al Farooq Mosque is also where Egyptian radical Sheik Omar Abdel Rahman—convicted in the 1993 bombing of the World Trade Center that killed six and wounded more than 1,000 -- served briefly as imam.)

As The New York Times put it, federal authorities see the Yemeni imam's arrest as one of the major financial busts since 9/11 "in terms of both the amount of money involved and the direct connection alleged to Mr. bin Laden himself."

Rita Katz, a specialist in terrorism finance, explained the case's significance this way: "It shows that Islamic clerics are having a lot to do with funding and assisting Al Qaeda."

They are? To be sure, the government says that this particular cleric has. Have others?

And what about the worshippers at Al Farooq? Do some number of them support Al Qaeda in particular, or just "jihad" in general? Or were they all duped into scraping together hundreds of thousands of dollars for some unknown cause?

These and other questions remain not only unanswered but unasked, unspeakable ciphers on the boundaries of acceptable national discourse. There is no help in sight from Brooklyn mosque officials, of course, who profess to be "very, very, very surprised" by the government's charges.

Meanwhile, Yemeni leaders huffily point to Mr. al-Mouyad's respected role as a charitable imam who works in the Yemeni ministry that oversees mosques. (This last bit is not necessarily confidence-building given a recent government-broadcast out of Yemen's Grand Mosque: "O G-d, destroy the unjust sons of Zion and the arrogant Americans. O G-d, shake the ground under them, instill panic into their hearts and disperse them. O G-d, destroy them, for they are within your power.")

Which leaves us exactly where? Left to wonder why the Islamic advocacy groups in the United States fail to rejoice in a successful government sting operation against what certainly appears to be an unholy holy man who gives Islam a bad name. And we're left to wonder why Islamic moderates remain incapable of bringing off a good old-fashioned schism to divide their peaceable selves from their violent-minded co-religionists.

Do such moderates attend the Dallas Central Mosque, where a fund-raiser for five brothers charged with doing business with the Palestinian terrorist group Hamas was held last month? How about the Islamic Center of Greater Cleveland, where mosque officials have decided to retain an imam linked by reports to the federal indictment against suspected Islamic Jihad leader Sami Al-Arian? One has uncomfortable questions, too, about the moderate views of worshippers at the Islamic Community of Tampa Bay, where Mr. Al-Arian remains imam and president.

But such questions aren't being entertained. Which brings us to the second news story, as promised above. It has to do with Lois McMahan, a bespectacled, pearl-necklace-wearing, Republican state representative who declined to take her seat in the Washington legislature this week until after Olympia imam Mohamad Joban finished opening the "session of the House of Representatives in the name of Allah...."

Why? Calling it an "issue of patriotism," she told the Seattle Post-Intelligencer, "The Islamic religion is so ... part and parcel with the attack on America. I just didn't want to be there, be part of that. Even though the mainstream Islamic religion doesn't profess to hate America, nonetheless it spawns the groups that hate America." To Washington state's Sun newspaper, she said, "I'd die for their right to believe what they want to believe; that's America. But the Islamic leaders of this country have not been vocal enough about their criticism of the enemies of this country."

One news cycle later, Rep. McMahan was making headlines again, only this time to recant. "I apologize for offenses given and would like to ask for forgiveness to any whom I have offended," she said, addressing her colleagues from the legislature floor. And soon, she added, she would be delivering her apologies "personally" to the imam on an upcoming visit to his mosque.

What will she say? Something like, "I'm sorry for observing that certain Islamic groups hate America religiously"? Or, "I'm sorry for noticing that Islamic leaders have been tepid in their condemnations of terrorist organizations"? "I'm sorry for raising a serious concern in the hopes of fueling an honest exchange"?

I'm sorry, too.

Holier than thou

5/14/04

When the White House promised to punish the murderers who sawed off Nicholas Berg's head, a spokesman said the crime "showed the true nature of the enemies of freedom."

Wrong. Or, rather, not wrong, but vague, and perilously so. It's not every enemy of freedom who shouts, "Allahu akbar [G-d is great]!" while committing murder in front of a camera. What Mr. Berg's heinous killing showed was the true nature of fundamentalist and unreformed Islam, according to the Koran. "Now when ye meet in battle those who disbelieve, then it is smiting of the necks," says verse 47-4 in the Marmaduke Mohammad Pickthall translation. This and other venerable translations stand until modern Muslims renounce the principle of jihad, or holy war against the "infidel."

Until that happens, pulling the political veil over the face of the enemy is not just a fashionable nod to political correctness. Failing to unmask the brutal face of modern jihad is a possibly suicidal lapse of logic and nerve that dangerously has obscured the wider war on "terror" — which, of course, is the euphemism of choice for Islamic jihad.

Mincing words also contributes to something else, something that has emerged from the flames of the utterly surreal conflagration over Abu Ghraib that still threatens to snuff our entire military mission. Only a politically correct ruling class (including Big Media) that converses in the opaque terms of "war on terror" and "enemies of freedom" — having long learned to ignore assorted truths about sex, test scores, race, religion and body strength — could regard Abu Ghraib with the tunnel vision necessary to shut out all the world — past, present and future. Only the permanently and willfully blinkered can see in the finite abuses at the Baghdad prison — abuses long halted and in the process of being rectified — the epic horror of the age, while a war rages on.

But it is not just prison guards run amok that draw fire. Big guns now train their sights on the interrogation techniques used on all prisoners of the war on Islamic jihad, including top leaders and operatives of al Qaeda. Such a venture reveals a heedless ignorance of the fanatical barbarism of the jihadist enemy we face. That is, our jihad-obsessed enemy — to whom "martyrdom" means paradise and 72 virgins (or 72 white raisins, depending upon the translation), to whom killing as many "infidels" as possible on the battlefield means martyrdom, and to whom marketplaces and hotels and office buildings mean battlefields — has evolved outside the Western tradition and far from the principles of the Geneva Convention.

Not that politically correct lawmakers have noticed. In calling for the administration to abide "unequivocally" by the Geneva Convention regarding all detainees, including terrorists, Sen. Dick Durbin, Illinois Democrat, speculated whether such a declaration would "also serve to help American prisoners." In other words, we'll serve tea and crumpets, and they'll serve tea and crumpets — and not hack off the head of an American Jew who dared to enter Iraq to build radio towers.

And if we can't make nice across the board, we're Nazis — this, according to Sen. John McCain. Telling radio host Don Imus not to downplay the scandal of Abu Ghraib, the Arizona Republican said, "If you go down that slippery slope, OK — you decide, OK, well, this torture is OK — then what's the difference between us and the Gestapo?" One enormous difference — and how dispiriting to need to remind the senator of this — is the motive involved. When the CIA, say, dunks September 11 planner Khalid Sheikh Mohammed into a pool on something called a water-board, as the New York Times breathlessly reported, the CIA is trying to find which shopping mall may contain Osama bin Laden's dirty bomb. When the Gestapo used such techniques (and far worse), the Gestapo was trying to find hidden Jews to kill.

How bizarre: We seem to have become more enamored of our self-image of heavenly stainlessness than we are inspired by our fight to survive. Victory — which is surely just, in that it means liberty and justice for more — takes a back seat on this "high road." From a small spot on the national escutcheon, something for military justice to wipe clean, has erupted a wild epidemic of collective guilt, with stricken pols assuming holier-than-thou poses that would topple in a heap were reality allowed to impinge.

Such as Nicholas Berg's grisly murder. Someone should ask whether it's really necessary to flagellate ourselves into a state of moral chastity before trying to ensure that his short life — like the short lives of hundreds of brave souls killed trying to mend a broken country and save their own — was not lost in vain.

The importance of this crusade

6/4/04

I was nearly finished writing a column on a different topic when news of President Bush's address at the Air Force Academy graduation ceremony flashed on the Drudge Report Web site. "Bush drops 'crusade' from Eisenhower's D-Day message," read the headline.

What? He couldn't; he didn't ... did he? Thanks to instantly accessible archives on the Internet, I quickly found Eisenhower's Order of the Day given to the men of the Allied Expeditionary Force as they prepared to begin the invasion of Normandy on June 6, 1944.

It went like this: "Soldiers, Sailors and Airmen of the Allied

Expeditionary Force! You are about to embark upon the Great Crusade, toward which we have striven these many months. The eyes of the world are upon you. The hope and prayers of liberty-loving people everywhere march with you. In company with our brave Allies and brothers-in-arms on other Fronts, you will bring about the destruction of the German war machine, the elimination of Nazi tyranny over the oppressed people of Europe, and security for ourselves in a free world." And so, stirringly, on.

Sixty years later, facing another global threat from another totalitarian ideology, President Bush saw fit, wisely and importantly, to link essential aspects of our past and present struggles. These include the totalitarian nature of both Nazi fascism and Islamofascism, and the fact that freeing Europe then and the expanding freedom in the Middle East now are crucial to American security. In so doing, Bush invoked the opening lines of Ike's order — but with a shameful, history-defiling cut. "Soldiers, Sailors and Airmen of the Allied Expeditionary Force," Bush said, quoting General Eisenhower. "The eyes of the world are upon you. The hope and prayers of liberty-loving people everywhere march with you."

Missing, of course, is Eisenhower's loin-girding line about those tens of thousands of soldiers, sailors and airmen being about to embark on "the Great Crusade" — the reason "the eyes of the world" are upon them in the first place. This cut may not strike everyone as a reason to tear up Page One. But to me the omission hits at the heart of what is lacking in the so-called "war on terror" — the courage of clarity.

It's possible President Bush didn't drop Ike's language himself. Indeed, his speechwriters might not have given him the choice. They well know that "crusade" was officially outlawed long ago. And by "crusade" I don't mean Christendom's medieval battles to reclaim the Holy Land from Muslim rule. But, of course, neither did Gen. Eisenhower (not in his D-Day remarks, and not in his popular account of the war, "Crusade in Europe"). Neither did President Bush, for that matter, when, in the week following Sept. 11, 2001, he said that "this crusade, this war on terrorism, is going to take a while."

Speaking in terms of a cause may have steadied most Americans at home, but it drove Muslims, Europeans and political correctniks everywhere crazy. A headline in The Christian Science Monitor on Sept. 19, 2001 said it best: "Europe cringes at Bush 'crusade' against terrorists."

It didn't have to cringe long. Rather than inviting citizens of the world to join the new "crusade" against Islamic terror networks — the successor to earlier, victorious crusades against Nazism and Communism — Ari Fleischer, then the president's spokesman, immediately expressed "regret" over unspecified "connotations" the word "crusade" might have had "for anybody, Muslim or otherwise." In other words, America was officially sorry if anyone out there — and I mean "out there" — believed, five days after the fiery collapse of the World Trade Center, that the president of the United States was going send an army of barons to take Jerusalem for the Pope.

Of course, what this was really all about were the terms of engagement — literally. We could not embark on a "crusade" against Islamic jihad, because that term carries echoes of centuries of struggle between the Christian West and the Muslim East. (Never mind that the echoes still have plenty to tell us.) And we may not fight a war against "Islamic jihad," even as Muslims, from "militants" (terrorists) to "spiritual advisers" (terrorist kingpins), claim bloody inspiration from the jihad verses of the Quran. Nope, this is a fight against what the president amorphously describes as "the terrorist ideology," and the religiously based doctrines of fighting and subjugating non-Muslims under Islamic law may not be acknowledged, let alone discussed. Which is preposterous. But it is our lot: a life-or-death struggle to save Judeo-Christian civilization from a masked enemy, a camouflaged ideology and our own willful naiveté.

Our crusade may be quixotic, but a crusade it is, if ever there was one.

Conservative mag capitulates to Muslim group's pressure tactics

4/11/05

What may be most damaging about National Review's act of reference-cleansing is that it helps legitimize CAIR's drive to tar all criticism of Islam as "hate speech" and, thus, squelch it.

If Kafka met Monty Python, and George Orwell edited their collaboration, they might have come up with something like the following real-life exchange.

It took place in an Australian court where two Christian pastors were found guilty of "religious vilification" of Muslims by lecturing to their flock on Islam — a set-up that right away projects grimly satirical possibilities. At one point during the trial, defendant Daniel Scot began to read Quranic verses in his own defense. The Pakistani-born pastor hoped to prove to the judge that his discussion on the inferior status of women under Islam, for example, had a specific textual basis in the Quran.

As he began to read, a lawyer for the Islamic Council of Victoria, the plaintiff in the case, objected. Reading these verses aloud, she said, would in itself be vilification. Scot, ultimately convicted, put it best: "How can it be vilifying to Muslims when I am just reading from the

Quran?"

Like a frustrating dream, the Australian experience echoes a depressingly similar situation in this country. Not in a court, not at a church-sponsored seminar, but in journalism. In the marketplace, literally, of ideas. I'm talking about an online bookstore run under the imprimatur of National Review magazine.

There, "The Life and Religion of Mohammed" (Roman Catholic Books, 2005) by J.L. Menezes, a Roman Catholic priest, used to be for sale. So did "The Sword of the Prophet," (Regina Orthodox Press, 2002) by Serge Trifkovic.

Suddenly, last week, they weren't. It seems that the Council on American Islamic Relations (CAIR) decided National Review shouldn't sell these books. The magazine could have told the, shall we say, controversial Muslim lobby group — three of whose former associates have been indicted on terrorism-related charges, and whose executive director, Nihad Awad, has publicly declared his support for Hamas — to run along and boycott books somewhere else. Instead, National Review whipped those tomes off their e-shelves practically before CAIR could get its "action alert" online. Just a little pressure — including a CAIR letter about the books to Boeing Corp., a big National Review advertiser — did the dirty trick. (CAIR promised to copy its letter to ambassadors of Muslim nations that buy Boeing planes.)

Here's the thing. I am not writing to mount a defense of these eminently defensible books, nasty bits and all, including, according to advertising copy, "the dark mind of Mohammed," his multiple wives (among them a little girl), "rapine," "warfare," "conquests" and "butcheries." Suffice it to say, as crack scholar-author of Islam Robert Spencer has written, "Everything with which CAIR took issue can be readily established from Islamic sources." (And if that doesn't suffice, read his analysis, "CAIR's War Against National Review," at www.frontpagemag.com.) He should know. Not only is Spencer familiar with the books in question, he happens to have written the ad copy for the Menezes book CAIR found so objectionable.

Of greater concern is the philosophical battle National Review declined to fight, and the reasons the magazine declined to fight it. According to National Review editor Rich Lowry's post at National Review Online, because the magazine's book service is put together by an independent publisher, and since the CAIR-provoking copy wasn't written by a National Review staffer, Lowry saw no capitulation in removing the Menezes book at CAIR's behest.

(National Review recently returned "The Sword of the Prophet" to its bookstore.) "In contrast," he wrote, "Robert Spencer and some others on the right feel very strongly that it is important to discredit Mohammed and Islam as such in order to win the war on terror. That's certainly their prerogative, but it is not the tack NR has taken ... ."

This statement reveals an unnerving disconnect. The study undertaken by Spencer and kindred Islamic scholars isn't calculated to "discredit Mohammed and Islam" — as if "discrediting" Mohammed and Islam would convince jihadis to make peace. The fact is, a thorough examination of the expansionist, religious-cum-political ideology of Islam is vital to any successful defense against its jihadist expression. Ignoring facts about Mohammed and Islam, given their role in animating terrorism, would be like ignoring facts about Marx and communism in that earlier ideological struggle National Review championed — worse, even, considering the inspiration Muslims draw from the personal life of Mohammed.

But what may be most damaging about National Review's act of reference-cleansing is that it helps legitimize CAIR's drive to tar all criticism of Islam as "hate speech" and, thus, squelch it. This, of course, was roughly what an Australian court ruled against Preacher Scot. It can't happen here? Maybe not. But the only way to preserve freedom of speech is to speak freely.

The plight of 'Submission'

5/30/05

Phew — that was close. The creators of "24," Fox Television's thriller-diller starring Kiefer Sutherland as counter-terror super-agent Jack Bauer, almost put together a compelling television series rooted in the onerous reality of the war on jihad terrorism. But thanks, apparently, to a few helpful suggestions from the Council of American Islamic Relations (CAIR), they managed to steer clear of all political and historical relevance.

This couldn't have been easy. After all, CAIR didn't even come to their rescue until after the show's season had begun with a couple of episodes that featured a typical Islamic sleeper cell embedded in a typical American sleepy suburb. After these and other obvious blunders — a terse exchange of "Allahu Akbar" between terrorists, for instance — the creative types behind the hit series managed to get their act together and save the world for political correctness. How? Two things: They laid down a suitably distracting Chinese subplot, and cast a bunch of Midwesterners, instead of Middle Easterners, to wear the key black hats. There was the ex-Air Force pilot — obviously blond, obviously disgruntled — who shot down Air Force One; a nefarious ex-marine; and a Patty-Hearst-like commando who just shot whatever.

By this week's season finale, Marwan, the head jihadist, had been comically stripped of all religious identity and motivation, and cloaked in a heavy disguise of moral equivalence. As in: You think we're evil and we think you're evil. This is pretty much what hero-Jack actually said to Marwan, the terror kingpin, who had just that day blown up a train, kidnapped the Secretary of Defense, sent multiple nuclear plants into meltdown and lobbed a nuclear warhead at Los Angeles. Oh well. Marwan was ultimately overshadowed by someone worse — the president of the United States.

Still, maybe the creators of "24" deserve a medal, considering the total silence of their fellow movie- and television-makers when it comes to the war on jihadist terror. War, what war? Culture clash? What culture clash? Freedom — what kind of freedom? Hollywood and the media may be "brave" and "bold" in fearlessly depicting sexuality, violence and the perversions therein, but they're cultural cowards when it comes to depicting, even mentioning, matters of war, Islam and jihad. Call it dhimmitude, Hollywood-style.

While the term dhimmitude, coined by historian Bat Ye'or, refers to the inferior status of Jews and Christians living under Islamic rule, she also points to disturbing signs of dhimmitude throughout the free West. These concerns range from the politically correct fear of giving offense, which curtails freedom of speech (think Fox punting Islam), to the fear of jihadist violence, which curtails freedom of movement, and even the free practice of religion (think armed guards at synagogues).

An unlikely moviemaker who refuses to accept dhimmi conditions is Ayaan Hirsi Ali. She is the amazingly courageous 35-year-old Somali-born ex-Muslim and Dutch parliamentarian whose first foray into screenwriting is a provocative 11-minute film called "Submission." Directed by Theo van Gogh — who was ritualistically murdered on an Amsterdam street last fall, his head nearly severed from his body, a jihadist rant pinned to his chest with a knife — "Submission" depicts the brutalized plight of all too many women at the hands of men under Islam, a political issue championed by Ali. For exercising her freedom of speech, Ali now lives under an Islamically imposed death sentence (fatwa). She also lives under lock and key, guarded 24 hours a day, and transported everywhere in an armored vehicle.

Such is the going price of freedom in Holland, just another ultra-liberal, Western country besieged by jihadists. "This fatwa isn't just directed against me," she explains, "but against Holland, against the entire Western world. We are all targets. In the eyes of radical Muslims, any country in which Muslims can be criticized openly is an enemy of Islam."

Like the creators of "24," who plan to produce at least two more seasons with Jack Bauer, brave Ali also has another project lined up: a sequel to "Submission" about Muslim men. "I don't want anyone else murdered," she told the British newspaper, The Guardian, recently. "But if I stop doing what I'm doing, it will be like another murder. That's the real trauma, perhaps, the thought of going through what happened to Theo van Gogh again. We told each other we would make part two, and the thing that keeps me going is the thought, 'I have to do it, I have to do it, I have to do it.'"

I wonder what keeps Jack Bauer going?

Twisted 'tolerance'

6/27/05

With guns pointed at his shaved and visibly battered head, Australian hostage Douglas Wood said things he didn't mean, parroting words his captors fed him.

In a clip of film that has become a jihadist cliche — masked gunmen, dehumanized captive, Al Jazeera logo — Mr. Douglas called for coalition forces to withdraw from Iraq, a jihadist goal he doesn't share with the thugs who imprisoned him for nearly seven weeks. After his rescue by American and Iraqi forces this week, the 64-year-old engineer made it clear he'd been coerced on tape, that he had not been speaking freely.

"Frankly, I'd like to apologize to both President Bush and Prime Minister Howard for the things I said under duress," Mr. Wood said upon arriving in Melbourne. He also sang out a jubilant chorus of "Waltzing Matilda," Australia's unofficial anthem.

What a twist, then, that this same week, in that same corner of Australia, just as Mr. Wood was exulting in his renewed pursuit of life and liberty, two of his fellow Aussies, Christian pastors Danny Nalliah and Daniel Scot, were finding their own such pursuits derailed — not by vicious criminals in Iraq, but by civilized state statute.

Mr. Wood could breathe freely in Australia and speak his mind once again; but the pastors Nalliah and Scot have been ordered by a tribunal in the state of Victoria to make public statements against their will, their conscience and their faith: namely, to apologize for their teachings on Islam, and to promise never to so teach again. As the first to be convicted of vilifying Islam under Victoria's "1984"-style Racial and Religious Tolerance Act, these men have vowed to go to jail rather than surrender their freedom of speech.

The cases of the kidnapped engineer and the "guilty" pastors are not really parallel. The Victoria state court is not a murderous gang of jihadists. But there's something similarly outrageous about the coercion brought to be bear on these men — coercion at gunpoint in Iraq, or on pain of prison time in Australia — to revoke the precious and essential Western liberty to speak freely. Such liberty is what compelled both pastors to flee their native Pakistan, where "blasphemy" against Islam can be a capital offense. And there's another connection: The Islamic doctrine of jihad that inspires the terrorists in Iraq is precisely what lies at the core of the Australian pastors' lectures and teachings, which are based directly on verses of the Quran and other Islamic texts.

What is car-wreck fascinating here is Judge Michael Higgins' conclusion that simply pointing out what the Quran says now constitutes outlawed speech in Victoria. During court proceedings, when Mr. Scot began to read verses from the Muslim holy book that denigrate women, a lawyer for the Islamic Council of Victoria, the plaintiff, cut him off, explaining that reading such verses aloud is itself an act of vilification. "How," wondered Mr. Scot, "can it be vilifying to Muslims in the room when I am just reading from the Quran?"

How, indeed. As Robert Spencer, author of "Islam Unveiled" (Encounter Books, 2002), has pointed out, at another point in the trial the Australian judge was affronted that Mr. Scot had said that "the Quran promotes violence, killing and looting." Mr. Spencer wrote in FrontPageMag: "In light of Quranic passages such as 9:5, 2:191, 9:29, 47:4, 5:33 and many others, this cannot seriously be a matter of dispute. Muslims have pointed to verses in the Bible that they would have us believe are equivalent in violence and offensiveness, or have claimed that the great majority of Muslims don't take such verses literally; but it takes a peculiarly strong resistance to reality not only to deny that such verses are there, but to charge one who pointed them out with religious vilification."

Mr. Nalliah, who plans to visit Great Britain to campaign against a similar vilification law now under consideration in Parliament, calls Victoria's shockingly totalitarian statute "sharia law by stealth." And so it is. In outlawing criticism of Islam — which, so far, is the effect of the law — Victoria has not only codified a peculiarly strong resistance to reality, it has also adopted the practice of sharia-ruled states. This makes for a startling spectacle — a free people placing a muzzle on speech, a limit on faith and a damper on inquiry. Douglas Wood lost his freedom at gunpoint; Danny Nalliah and Daniel Scot lost theirs by court-ordered political correctness. We know who rescued Mr. Wood; who will save the pastors?

Realpolitik vs. pretendpolitik

8/29/05

Unbowed, if unemployed, Michael Graham issued a thought-provoking challenge as his airtime on "The O'Reilly Factor" ran down to a break. The topic under discussion was the conservative radio host's firing by the Washington, D.C., radio station WMAL — egged on by the terrorist-linked Council on American Islamic Relations (CAIR)

— for having made his case, logically, forcefully, even regretfully that "Islam is a terrorist organization."

Before discussing Graham's final words on "O'Reilly," it's worth mentioning that Graham's argument linking terrorism to Islam is posted at JewishWorldReview.com in a column he wrote after the second London Underground bombing. Sure, the stand-alone scare quote ("I. is a T.O.") collides head-on with 21st-century sensibilities, but Graham builds his argument carefully. He makes the politically incorrect kind of sense, supported by fact (e.g., more than one in four British Muslims said they wouldn't tell police of a planned terrorist attack) and observation (Islamic teachings drive terrorist jihad), that the open-eyed child in "The Emperor's New Clothes" would instantly recognize. But not his bosses at WMAL — not, it seems, after CAIR objected. When Graham refused to "apologize," the ABC-Disney-owned station fired him.

All of which is what he went on "O'Reilly" to discuss, offering a factually reasoned discourse on the controversy. (Good stats, conceded an outgunned Bill O'Reilly.) And then, in closing, Graham said this: "(t)ell me one terrorist attack that's going to be stopped because we stopped this conversation" — that is, by WMAL taking Graham off the air.

An interesting notion. WMAL is no Department of Homeland Security, but given the line the radio station decided Graham crossed over global terrorism (jihad) and its central role in Islam, maybe it's worth wondering whether we are safer because Michael Graham isn't pursuing his on-air line of inquiry. Surely, we are more "sensitive," meaning more guarded, even nervous about what is currently permissible to say, at least according to CAIR's enforcers. Even so, ending a conversation about jihad and Islam doesn't end Islamic jihad. Nor does cutting the talk about links between Islam and terrorism cut the links between Islam and terrorism. The fact is, the train of logic doesn't change its destination no matter how many of us — radio stations, pundits, academics, politicians — hop off.

Still, thanks to WMAL, maybe we really are better protected, at least against the sharp edges and noxious corners of reality. This reality includes the fact that what we know as "terrorism" is directly linked to the centrality of jihad (holy war) and dhimmitude (non-Muslim inferiority) in Islam, no hijackings necessary. But spare us: We live in a politically correct country, one in which the U.S. State Department declares to the world that Americans "believe we are part of one human family, and that the enemy of that family are those who use the name of religion to pursue a violent and hateful ideology that really goes against (what) ... any person of faith believes in, no matter what that faith is."

But what if, as Michael Graham roughly wondered aloud, the violent and hateful ideology runs through Islam itself? In America today, it is considered better to cut the mike, seeking not the truth, but rather a kind of security from the truth. Once the survival strategies of realpolitik are traded in for the pipe dreams of pretendpolitik, such security even feels safe, at least for a time.

Protected against reality, we see only good in any religion because it is a religion. Secure from the truth, we see only liberty and justice in any constitution because it is a constitution. Our only problems stem from "extremism," which not only defines nothing, but also offends no one. Or does it? Out of Great Britain this month came a communiqué from nearly 40 Muslim leaders and groups. Their message? In part to renounce the label of "extremism." They wrote: "To equate 'extremism' with the aspirations of Muslims for Sharia laws in the Muslim world or the desire to see unification towards a Caliphate in the Muslim lands ... is inaccurate and disingenuous. It indicates ignorance of what Sharia is and what a Caliphate is and will alienate and victimize the Muslim community unnecessarily."

In other words, not only does terrorism have nothing to do with Islam, as WMAL seems to have determined, but sharia (repressive Islamic law) and the caliphate (Islamic empire) have nothing to do with extremism, as Britain's Muslim leaders have explained. Clearly, our vocabulary is shrinking as fast the ranks of bold talk-show hosts. But isn't there so much more to talk about?

International caricatures

11/18/05

Last month, on opposite sides of the globe, two assaults on the freedom of speech began.

In Afghanistan, the editor of "Women's Rights" magazine was convicted on "blasphemy" charges after a religious adviser to President Hamid Karzai accused the editor of publishing two "un-Islamic" articles: one criticizing the Islamic practice of punishing adultery with 100 lashes; the other arguing that leaving Islam wasn't a crime.

Such charges may seem as far as the moon to anyone raised in a free-speech society where adultery is a matter of private grief, not public beatings, and where freedom of conscience is a founding liberty.

Speaking of liberty, wasn't it the Taliban, and not the democratically elected Karzai government, who punished people for being "un-Islamic"? Doesn't that new constitution Americans died to enable Afghans to write guarantee protections and freedoms against such totalitarian practices?

Indeed, it does, but that same constitution also guarantees that no law may contradict the law of Islam. And the law of Islam says no messing with Islam. And that's not all: Since March 2004, a new media law signed by President Karzai outlaws anything Islamically "insulting." In other words, hello totalitarian practices, goodbye protections and freedoms. And goodbye Ali Mohaqiq Nasab, the "blaspheming" editor sentenced to two years in jail. By all accounts, this was getting off easy: The prosecutor in the case was angling for a death sentence.

Has anyone heard ringing perorations from the White House on preserving Mr. Nasab's free speech — let alone Mr. Nasab? Emergency deliberations at the international level? Nope; although a United Nations spokesman, when asked by a wire service, did obligingly express "concern." The only action — if paper shuffling counts as action — has come from media organizations that have lodged protests with the Afghan government. The powers that be, meanwhile, are out to lunch. It would be nice if they at least sent Mr. Nasab a file in a cake.

At about the same time Mr. Nasab's "un-Islamic" articles were getting the Sharia treatment in Islamic Afghanistan, Jyllands-Posten, a Danish daily newspaper, was taking it on itself to re-assert the venerable tradition of free speech in Lutheran Denmark. Why and how? Having learned that a Danish author couldn't find an illustrator to depict Mohammed for an upcoming children's book because Danish illustrators were intimidated by Muslim strictures against depicting the Islamic prophet, the newspaper challenged artists to submit drawings of Mohammed for publication. It was a test, said editor Carsten Juste, of whether the threat of Islamic terrorism — and the influence of Sharia — was encroaching on free speech in Denmark.

The paper ended up publishing twelve cartoons of Mohammed to make a liberty-affirming point: Denmark was not subject to the kind of thought control that had sent Ali Mohaqiq Nasab to jail half a world away. Besides, as Flemming Rose, the paper's culture editor put it, "In a democracy, one must from time to time accept criticism or become a laughingstock."

Such criticism is built into Western civilization, but as an institution it is about as "un-Islamic" as it gets. Without recourse to Sharia censorship, Danish Muslims rioted over successive nights in Arhus, Denmark's second largest city, even as their French co-religionists were burning France. Death threats sent several artists into hiding; bomb threats drove the paper to hire security guards. Jyllands-Posten, however, has refused to back down, which just might have something to do with the paper's appearance, according to Brusselsjournal.com, on an al Qaeda Web site listing potential targets.

This story takes another turn, off the streets and into the salons. Eleven Muslim ambassadors to Denmark (including representatives from Egypt, Turkey, Saudi Arabia, Indonesia, Pakistan, Iran and Bosnia-Herzegovina) have tried, unsuccessfully, to meet with Prime Minister Anders Fogh Rasmussen to protest the Mohammed cartoons, which they see, as they wrote in a letter to the prime minister, as a "smear campaign" against Islam.

"The Arab Muslim world must take a stand on this," said Egyptian Foreign Minister Ahmed Abul Gheit, who has announced that "this caricature affair," as one Egyptian diplomat called it, will be high on the agenda in December when the Organization of the Islamic Conference meets in Mecca.

Bless Mr. Rasmussen: "This is a matter of principle," he said. "I won't meet with [the ambassadors] because it is so crystal clear what principles Danish democracy is built upon that there is no reason to do so."

Crystal clear in Denmark. Crystal clear here. Not crystal clear in Afghanistan or elsewhere in the Islamic world. No one should need a crystal ball to see what this says about the future.

Censorship in the name of religion

12/9/05

Now they want to put him to death — Ali Mohaqeq Nasab, the Afghan editor already sentenced to two years hard labor for "blasphemy" against Islam. Now, Afghan prosecutors want to put him to death.

Why? The Muslim editor of "Women's Rights" magazine published articles in post-Taliban Afghanistan that criticized aspects of Islamic law, including the penalties of stoning for adultery, amputation for theft and death for leaving Islam.

"Sometimes the whole religion and the rules of the religion were attacked," explained Muhammad Aref Rahmani, who sits on Afghanistan's council of Islamic scholars.

Attacked? "For instance," Mr. Rahmani told the Chicago Tribune, "he says one woman should be equal to one man, as a witness in a case, which is completely against our religion."

Yes, those seismic vibrations rolling across your eardrums are the sound of culture clash. Under Islamic law, a woman's court testimony is worth half as much as a man's — another rank inequality Mr. Nasab's magazine opposed — so I guess you could say Mr. Rahmani has an Islamic point. Of course, such Islamic "crimes" equal Western virtues. This, it seems, leaves Afghan officials unimpressed.

"The decision made by the lower court on Mohaqeq Nasab will in no way satisfy the public prosecutor's office," Zmarai Amiri told the Institute for War and Peace Reporting. Mr. Amiri ought to know: He's Kabul's chief prosecutor. "Nasab must be punished more severely, up to and including execution." There are sure to be more arrests, Mr. Amiri continued rather Stalinistically, if anyone, including government officials, comes to Mr. Nasab's defense.

So much for post-Taliban — and, come to think of it, post-Operation-Enduring-Freedom — life in Afghanistan. Maybe the more useful exercise here is not to wonder how we became midwife to a theocratic police state, but to see what we can learn from it. One thing is clear: where Islam is protected from so-called blasphemy, freedom of conscience and freedom of speech — let alone women's rights — are not.

This same notion of Islam's "protection" came up when Iran's Ayatollah Khomeini sentenced Salman Rushdie to death in 1989 for his "blasphemous" novel, "The Satanic Verses," pitching the Western world into craven fits of appeasement. As JWR contributor Daniel Pipes has written, the Organization of the Islamic Conference (OIC) not only endorsed Iran's charges of "blasphemy" and Mr. Rushdie's "heresy," it also called for "necessary legislation to insure the protection of the religious beliefs of others." Saliently, the OIC declared that "blasphemy cannot be justified on the basis of freedom of expression and opinion."

Some things never change. As we see in Afghanistan — and, increasingly, elsewhere — this fundamental tenet of Islamic society is one of them. And it is on this point that the West and Islam are struggling to come to terms.

For example, the Islamic furor over a dozen Muhammad cartoons published in a Danish newspaper — and Danish Prime Minister Anders Fogh Rasmussen's refusal to meddle with his country's freedom of speech — continues to rise up the food chain, from death threats and street riots, to ambassadorial protests, to heads-of-state deliberations at the December OIC meeting in Mecca.

Turkish prime minister Recep Erdogan's reaction not only sums up the official Islamic response, but is also highly significant given Turkey's bid to become the European Union bridge between the West and Islam. On a recent trip to Denmark, as recounted in the Internet edition of the Turkish newspaper "Zaman," Mr. Erdogan addressed the Muhammad-cartoon issue, saying, "Freedoms have limits, what is sacred should be respected." As columnist Mustafa Unal put it, Mr. Erdogan "indicated that respect toward what is considered sacred is more important than the freedom of expression."

This is a major point of culture clash — or would be, if the West cared to defend its freedoms. Which is a big "if." Meanwhile, Denmark's "Berlingske Tidende," via the blogger Fjordman (fjordman.blogspot.com), reports that the 56 countries of the OIC have now written the United Nations High Commissioner for Human Rights to "help contain this encroachment on Islam, so the situation won't get out of control."

Let's translate. "Encroachment on Islam" equals criticism of Islam — aka "blasphemy" in Islamic quarters. "The situation" equals freedom of speech. "Out of control" equals criticism of Islam as an exercise of freedom of speech. In response, the U.N. human rights commissioner, Louise Arbour, emphasized her "regret" over "any statement or act that could express a lack of respect for the religion of others." Which sounds like the Danes are in U.N.-trouble. But what about the statements or acts — from censorship to death sentences — of the religion that encroach on the rights of others? That's a question no one dares to ask.

2006 is shaping up to be the 'Year of Speaking Dangerously'

12/30/05

Now that Baby New Year is taking over again from Father Time, the observant celebrant might notice something new. In addition to the traditional top hat and diaper, and besides the 2006 banner across his chest, Baby New Year has something else in his kit: a gag. That's because 2006 is shaping up to be the "Year of Speaking Dangerously."

This isn't to suggest that 2005 was a banner year for freedom of speech. But the reaction, tepid at best, to significantly outrageous cases of speech repression during this past year, from Bangladesh to Paris, indicates only one thing: 2006 will be worse.

Take our old friend (making his third appearance in this column) Ali Mohaqeq Nasab, the Afghan editor sentenced in October to two years hard labor. His crime, you may recall, was "blasphemy" — i.e., publishing articles that criticized Islamic law. The magazine he edited questioned the death penalty for converting from Islam; amputation and whippings for certain crimes; and relegating women to legal inferiority. Given that such viewpoints promised to make Islamic reform a topic of debate in post-Taliban Afghanistan, Mr. Nasab's incarceration should have created one of those international incidents you read about, or at least a journalistic cause celebre.

But no. In virtual global silence — not a healthy atmosphere for free speech — Mr. Nasab was left to the non-tender mercies of a Kabul prosecutor seeking the death penalty for those "un-Islamic" articles. And now? Here's an update from The Washington Post: "After refusing for three months to retract his statements, Nasab told an appeals court this week that he was sorry for printing stories that asserted that women should be given equal status to men in court, questioned the use of physical punishments for crimes and suggested converts from Islam should not face execution."

In other words, he was sorry for calling for equality of the sexes. He was sorry for calling for a more humane concept of punishment. He was sorry for calling for freedom of conscience. I'm sorry he was sorry. But having apologized in a Kabul courtroom, Mr. Nasab is now a free man. Or as free as a man can be "under the watch of the government" — as the senior judge in the case told Reuters — "to make sure he does not repeat what he has written."

That's one way to gag a journalist, not to mention his peers. Already, an Afghan human rights proponent told the Post, journalists are saying they "have to be very, very careful in the way that they talk." Which is probably nothing our troops in Afghanistan thought they were fighting for. But no one in the West seems too broken up about it. Then again, maybe no one really cares whether freedom of expression is an attribute of 21st-century civilization after all. The flip side of the Nasab story — flip side of the globe, anyhow — makes this clear.

The last time we checked in with "Jyllands-Posten," the Danish newspaper that ran 12 rather tame cartoons of Muhammad to prove that an Islamic religious injunction against depicting the Islamic prophet didn't apply in a sovereign Western nation, it was bearing up under Islamic street protests and bomb threats, diplomatic attack, and a likely U.N. human rights commission investigation. And so was Denmark. Danes had been warned away from Pakistan, where bounties were placed on the cartoonists' heads; Kashmir was the scene of anti-Dane rioting; and Prime Minister Anders Fogh Rasmussen was under intense pressure to apologize for, and/or meddle with Denmark's freedom of the press. Amazingly — inspirationally — in this age of the about-face, neither the newspaper nor the prime minister has apologized for upholding free speech.

Now, the cartoons have drawn fire from both the Council of Europe and the European Union. The U.N. human rights commission has actually demanded "an official explanation," directing the Danish government to respond to the question, "Do the caricatures insult or discredit?" (This, frankly, presents Denmark with rather a meager choice.) Also, 22 former Danish diplomats have rapped the prime minister for not meeting Muslim diplomats who demanded to discuss the cartoons. As a spokesman for the prime minister explained, "It doesn't serve any purpose to enter into a dialogue to stop the democratic process."

Well said, Denmark, and thanks for keeping the light of liberty burning. What's needed is dialogue to jumpstart the democratic process, particularly when it comes to, well, dialogue. Ideas. Analysis. Even cartoons. The question is, who, in 2006, will speak up for free speech?

Nonsense and sensibility

2/20/06

Maybe there's some rarified irony about the fact that in a society increasingly dependent on imagery, not words, to convey information, it is imagery that the media have denied us in conveying the story of a Danish newspaper's Muhammad cartoons. But with a Gallup Poll reporting that 61 percent of U.S. respondents believe that Europeans who printed the caricatures of Muhammad acted irresponsibly, it's nothing to shrug off.

The rationale goes something like this: "Not all self-censorship is a bad thing."

"Even if all the world had the right of free speech, I still believe there are things that should not be said."

"It's some weird presumption of modernity that says because something can be done it must be done."

The above statements came out of my e-mailbag after last week's column — my cartoon rage 2006, or, as I like to call it, How a Proud Press Bowed Its Head and Submitted to an Islamic Law against Depictions of Muhammad. These letter-writers, representing a small but noticeable contingent, rejected the submission argument as a point of pride, reading into their own contentment to "see no evil" — that is, see no Muhammad cartoons — an elevated sensibility: good manners, good taste and self-restraint. This may be highly commendable — the good manners, taste and self-restraint part — but it is entirely beside the point.

Which is what draws me back to this freak show of a story one more time before its narrative-memory is set, and before the beginning of the end of press freedom is permanently attributed to kindly, responsible behavior, not incipient dhimmitude. In another context, I wouldn't disagree with the readers' comments I quoted above. Indeed, I've been known to make similar arguments against all manner of fetid cultural excess, from lurid children's fiction to the notorious Sensation Exhibition at the Brooklyn Museum in which Dung Virgin first came to fame in 1999. (Or was that infamy? It's easy to get them confused.)

The topic of Dung Virgin, not to mention its companion piece in shock value, Piss Christ, strikes the Good-Mannerists as an important marker in their personal guides to press etiquette. Not grooving to such "artistic" attacks on Christianity, the Good-Mannerists say they can understand the consternation of the Cartoon Ragers — at least to some point shy of death threats, arson and murder — and see media self-censorship as a matter of common decency.

Is the comparison valid? And is the politeness deserved? Absolutely not, and here's one big reason why: Christianity and Islam are not interchangeable belief systems inspired by a generic divinity. One relevant distinction is the way they operate in relation to their societies. Christianity abides by the separation of church and state; Islam knows no separation whatsoever. As a result, the theological teachings of Islam as revealed by Muhammad, which form the basis of the Islamic law (sharia) that drives Islamic societies, necessarily belong to the political sphere in a way that Christianity does not.

This is not to say that Christianity should be, or has been, off the table. Indeed, all the ink (not blood) spilled over assorted Excrement Icons only enhanced their value, not to mention the reputations of their artists (using the word loosely). But the all-encompassing nature of Islam underscores a special need for open, critical examination of the Koran and Muhammad as political, and politically violent, forces that roil our times.

Let's take what are considered the most inflammatory of the Danish Dozen: Bomb-head Muhammad; and Muhammad in the clouds, telling arriving suicide bombers that Islamic paradise is plumb out of virgins. What Denmark's cartoonists did in these caricatures is something few writers have dared to do in words: They made visual reference to the copious, historical and contemporary theological underpinnings of holy war (jihad) and suicide bombings. What is offensive here, then, is not the extremely mild caricature, but rather those theological underpinnings of holy war and suicide bombings. When the widely influential Sheik Yusef al-Qaradawi can praise Muhammad as "an epitome for religious warriors (mujahideen)," Muhammad, a jihad model, shouldn't be a taboo subject in the West, either in caricature or commentary, and certainly shouldn't be super-sacralized, in effect, by a fearfully polite censorship. The subject should be laid out for all to see.

The valiant Dutch parliamentarian and ex-Muslim Ayaan Hirsi Ali put it this way: "You cannot liberalize Islam without criticizing the Prophet and the Koran. ... You cannot redecorate a house without entering inside." And especially when you're not allowed to see what it looks like.

Speak no evil: The new EU lexicon on terrorism

4/21/06

How wunderbar, merveilleux and perfectly ripping that the European Union is creating a new "lexicon" to discuss Islam and terrorism so as never to conflate the two. The Telegraph tells us that EU officials — having double-checked that George Orwell and his satirical pen are dead and gone — are putting together a "non-emotive lexicon for discussing radicalization."

Islamic "radicalization," that is. When it comes to dealing with

Europe's Muslim populations, the old "Sticks and stones ..." proverb is out, particularly the "words can never hurt me" part. These days, the update goes: "Say words that hurt me and I'll blow up a train." As an EU official explained non-emotively, "The basic idea is to avoid the use of improper words that could cause frustration among Muslims and increase the risk of radicalization."

As they say over there: What rot. Only hothouse EU officials could believe that words such as "Islamic terrorism" cause radicalization.

Fanatical bloodlust (not to mention 72-virgin-lust) inspires acts labeled "Islamic terrorism," not the other way around. But not in EU-land. "These words (Islamic terrorism) cannot sit side by side," Omar Faruk, a Muslim barrister and "adviser" to the British government, told Reuters. The phrase "just creates a culture where terrorism actually is identified with Islam," he continued. "That causes me a lot of stress."

And the EU certainly wouldn't want that. Stress leads to frustration, and frustration leads to radicalization, and radicalization leads to — and here's where the new lexicon comes in — to "terrorists who abusively invoke Islam." Take Flight 93: The Sept. 11 hijackers might have invoked Allah 24 times in its final minutes (also causing what Mr. Faruk might recognize as "stress"), but the new lexicon would probably tell us that wasn't "Islamic terrorism," it was an Attack of the Terrorists Abusively Invoking Islam, not to mention Allah. Not only did the hijackers hijack a passenger jet, they hijacked their religion.

This, of course, remains President Bush's general position. "I believe that the terrorists have hijacked a peaceful religion in order to justify their behavior," President Bush said yet again this month.

Problem is — to stick with the idiotic metaphor — the "hijackers" have been piloting the plane for centuries, and the "passengers" have yet to take the controls. They go along for the ride, happy with or resigned to the anti-infidel destination because the jihadist itinerary comes straight from the Koran and other signal Islamic texts.

The grand Western strategy? Not to notice. The Guardian recently reported on a Tehran "recruitment fair" for Islamic suicide bombers.

The sponsoring group asked several hundred volunteers to complete forms specifying whether they wanted to murder Israelis, Americans, Brits or, specifically, British author Salman Rushdie. As a spokesman said, "Britain and other European countries have a lot of disaffected Muslims who are ready. We understand the suspicion with which ... Western countries regard their Muslim populations. We don't condemn them for this because we believe every Muslim has the potential to turn into a bomb against the West."

The phrase "Muslim bomb potential" will surely give Mr. Faruk palpitations, but the Free World remains in denial. "Western diplomats played down the significance of the group's threat," the Guardian reported, "saying it was primarily a campaign to gather signatures of protest against Israel rather than recruit bombers."

Is this some kind of a joke? Much of the news these days ends in such harsh quasi-punch lines. Fatah terrorists demand an apology of Palestinian Authority (PA) Chairman Mahmoud Abbas for his "offense" — condemning this week's Palestinian suicide bombing. Nuke-seeking Iran has an appointment with the U.N. Disarmament Conference — as co-chairman. And then there was the story about the two Al Qaeda fathers discussing their suicide-bomber sons — namely, how kids today blow up so fast.

Hang on a sec. That last one was a real joke, as told by John Vine, a senior Scottish policeman, at a gala dinner for the Perth Bar Association. It actually roused that small corner of the Western world to genuine outrage — and not because everyone already had heard it. It was an "amazing gaffe," said the journalistic consensus. A "deeply offensive comment," commented a politician. Mr. Vine apologized ("profusely"), and the Muslim Council of Britain (MCB) "welcomed the apology" (naturally).

I have to wonder on behalf of whom the MCB accepted the apology — the Suicide-Bomber Dads of Al Qaeda support group? But never mind. Just wait until the non-emotive lexicon is in place. That'll quiet everything.

Just shut up

9/25/06

Shut up.

When all is said and done — when protesters junk their placards, when burning churches cool, when a murdered nun's grave grows grass — "shut up" is the underlying message of Pope Rage, the latest fulmination to come from Islam, this time over Pope Benedict's recent lecture on faith and reason. When the pope argued, quoting a Byzantine source on Mohammed, that the practice of forced conversion — key to Islamic expansion over the centuries — is inimical to both faith and reason, the reaction of anger and violence was instantaneous. Just shut up, the umma exclaimed.

Or, to put it more elegantly, as did Daniel Pipes: "The Muslim uproar has a goal — to prohibit criticism of Islam by Christians and thereby impose Shariah norms in the West. Should Westerners accept this central tenet of Islamic law, others will surely follow. Retaining free speech about Islam, therefore, represents a critical defense against the imposition of an Islamic order."

The question is, Will we retain our free speech about Islam? Speaking at the United Nations this week, Pakistan's Pervez Musharraf asked the international community to ban the "defamation of Islam" — a rendition of "shut up" that's a constant refrain at the UN — but it looks like mum's already the word. Just read through George W. Bush's address to the world body. "Islamic fascists" are out. "Extremists who use terror as a weapon to create fear" are in.

We probably have presidential pal and roving ambassador Karen Hughes to thank for Mr. Bush's discreet-to-the-point-of-incomprehensible talk. "Diplomats say that Muslims hear [the phrase "Islamic fascists"] as an attack on their religion, thereby validating the extremists' false charge that the United States is at war with Islam," writes Morton Kondracke, explaining Mrs. Hughes' semantic sentiments, which he says have put the kibosh on administration straight talk. But maybe there's more (less) to it. Earlier this month, Mrs. Hughes wrote: "As I have traveled the world, I have met those who try to justify the violence based on policy differences, long-held grievances or a perceived threat from the West."

Differences, grievances, threat: Isn't she missing some little old jihad thing? Not that she's alone. Take Hughes mentor Edward Djerejian. Veteran diplomat to assorted Middle Eastern countries — warm to Arabs, cool to Israel (just like his close associate James Baker, who now co-chairs the vaunted Iraq Study Group) — Mr. Djerejian is another happy warrior of ambiguity. The "seminal challenge" of our age, as Mr. Djerejian describes it, is "the struggle for ideas between the forces of moderation and extremism, whether it be secular extremism or religious extremism of no matter what religion, no matter what culture."

This is a challenge, all right — a challenge to know what he's talking about. But such obfuscation is more than just the antithesis of reasoned critique. It also happens to comply with what Mr. Pipes calls "Shariah norms" in the West.

Islam prohibits "blasphemy," which includes criticism of its prophet Mohammed. The Shariah penalty is death. But if it is "extremists" who carry the penalty out — as in the ritual murders of Theo van Gogh in Amsterdam (2004) and Mohammed Taha in Sudan (2006) — what Pope Rage reveals is how shockingly little separates "moderates" from "extremists" when it comes to the blasphemy-taboo in the first place.

"Even the most moderate and Westernized Muslim will not tolerate insults to the Prophet Mohammed," writes Tulin Daloglu, commenting on Pope Rage from the moderate side of Islam in The Washington Times. "Each offense unites Muslims against Western prejudices and rejection — and the extremists gain more credibility."

So shut up.

Blogging online, columnist Mona Charen reported on another moderate, George Washington University's Seyyed Hossein Nasr. In an interview with NPR host Diane Rehm, Mr. Nasr contested the notion that Pope Rage violence against Christians was not unprovoked. As Mrs. Charen wrote, "Diane Rehm equably restated his position (I paraphrase): 'So you think words are violence.' He confirmed."

So shut up.

Meanwhile, listen to the voice of bona fide "extremism," Great Britain's own Anjem Choudary, as reported in the Evening Standard: "The Muslims take their religion very seriously and non-Muslims must appreciate that and must also understand that there may be serious consequences if you insult Islam and the prophet."

He continued: "Whoever insults the message of Mohammed is going to be subject to capital punishment."

"Shut up," say the moderates, "or else," say the extremists. Frankly, this sounds an awful lot as if the "moderates" are as non-reasonable as the "extremists." This may be shocking-but it's nothing to be left speechless over.

Hogans, heroes

11/17/06

Whatever comes of gridlock on Iraq and everything else, here's a rule of thumb: When the flak flies, don't jump into a foxhole with a Republican. Quite simply, Republicans are a menace, at least to other Republicans.

Take Mel Martinez, the Republican senator from Florida President Bush tapped to become Republican National Committee chairman. Best known for cheering on amnesty for illegals by the millions (i.e, for supporting President Bush's "comprehensive" immigration plan), Martinez marked his RNC nomination by baiting some large number of Republicans who would like to see the government secure the nation's borders instead. Equating what he called "border security only" with "harshness only," Martinez referred to Republican electoral losses and said: "It's not about bashing people; it's about presenting a hopeful face." Too bad it's not about presenting a "hopeful face" to all those Republicans Martinez was bashing.

Where can bashed Republicans go? The modern GOP is about as politically correct and prey to special interest groups as the Democratic Party. I say this following a shameful party purge in Florida. There, the state Republican Party, up to and including Gov. Jeb Bush, came down ton-of-bricks-like on two Hernando County Republicans who publicly decried Islam as a "hateful and frightening religion."

Actually, it was Mary Ann Hogan who used the language in a blistering, pre-election letter to Hernando Today complaining about county employees being used to ferry children's games to a mosque celebrating the end of Ramadan (a holiday, she noted, that "Muslims in Iraq" marked by killing more American soldiers than we had lost in a long time). When asked to apologize, her husband, County Commissioner Tom Hogan Sr., steadfastly echoed his wife's opinion: "Overall, worldwide, it certainly is," said Hogan, a founder of the county GOP. "Don't you read your own paper?"

Faster than you can say "Stalinist show trial," the Council on American-Islamic Relations (CAIR) called on Gov. Bush to fire Hogan, whose term, as it happened, expired this week. I wish I could report that Gov. Bush, outraged, sent CAIR — the Hamas-linked group, several of whose associates have been convicted or deported on terrorism-related charges — packing. But he didn't. He condemned the couple, triggering a chain of condemnations from the state GOP chairman, the Republican gubernatorial candidate (now Gov.-elect Charlie Crist), and, of course, in the local media. The Democratic gubernatorial candidate condemned them, too, and Crist dropped Mrs. Hogan from his campaign organization, Women for Crist. When CAIR calls, the GOP jumps.

Bucking this trend of capitulation, Rep. Ginny Brown-Waite (Florida Republican) responded with a vigorous defense of the Hogans' freedom of speech — a freedom, she wrote, Jeb Bush and Co. were quick to forget — advising CAIR that its "area of concern should not be focused on the statements of the Hogans, but rather upon the actions of many in your community who created these beliefs." This bold congresswoman (thankfully re-elected) was the GOP exception. The party line demanded the Hogans recant.

The couple refused to apologize for calling Islam "hateful and frightening." I can only say, bravo, Hogans.

Why? Having written thousands of words on Islam, I haven't used precisely the Hogans' language. I have used many other words to refute the comforting but untrue consensus that Islam has nothing to do with the generic "terrorism" that has reduced our liberties, and, by introducing fear into American life, diminished us as a people. I have used many other words to describe the appalling process of Islamization, whereby Europe, via Muslim immigration, is being transformed into an Islamic continent increasingly subject to sharia, the Islamic legal system antithetical to Western-style freedom of conscience and equality before the law, and to urge the United States to amend its immigration laws to prevent the same transformation from occurring here.

Is such analysis "bashing people," as Mel Martinez might say, or something to apologize for, as Jeb Bush might demand? Does ostracizing the Hogans render jihad and sharia, the signal points of contact between Islam and the West, not "frightening" and not "hateful"? Of course not. When the GOP renounced the gutsy Hogans for voicing their apprehensions about Islam it also renounced key teachings on freedom of speech (not to mention logic), and that's frightening and hateful in itself.

To be sure, if the Hogans and Ginny Brown-Waite had agreed to mouth the mantra "Islam is peace," it would have made them good Republicans. But it would also have made them lousy in a foxhole.

The Year of Shutting Up

12/29/06

Taking a whack at prognostication at the end of 2005, it wasn't hard to imagine, as I did, that 2006 would be a rotten year for freedom of speech. Both inside the Islamic world and, more alarmingly, outside the Islamic world, Shariah laws prohibiting criticism of Islam were already working smoothly. When in 2005 we watched the death-penalty-seeking prosecution of editor Ali Mohaqeq Nasab for "blasphemy" in U.S.-liberated Afghanistan, we could see we were dealing with a Shariah state. When in 2005 we watched the early stages of what later became known as "Cartoon Rage" in Denmark, we could see we were dealing with a Shariah state of mind. It wasn't exactly going out on a limb to predict things would only get worse.

And, of course, in 2006, they did. Just ask Abdul Rahman if you can find him. The "apostate" fled Afghanistan for his life last spring. Or Robert Redeker, if you can find him. The teacher who published a critique of Islam in September still lives in hiding in France. Or maybe Salah Uddin Shoaib Choudhury. The Bangladeshi journalist faces the death penalty when he goes on trial in January for "blasphemy" and treason for writing favorably about Israel and unfavorably about Islamic terrorism. Of course, such censorship is "Over There" and beyond, not in the United States of America, right? And it can't, as they say, happen here. Right? Please, right?

I called 2006 "The Year of Speaking Dangerously," and that was before anyone likely imagined seeing "Behead Those Who Insult Islam" placards on jihadist display outside the Danish Embassy in London. What kind of year will 2007 be? What I fear most is that it will turn out to be "The Year of Shutting Up." As in: Why speak dangerously when you can simply not speak at all?

In fact, the Year of Shutting Up probably began back in September when Pope Benedict famously argued that the practice of forced conversion — key to Islamic expansion over the centuries — is inimical to both faith and reason. The eruption of anger among Muslims at such criticism was instantaneous and severe. Just shut up, the umma exclaimed. Basically, the pope did exactly that.

At the time, Daniel Pipes explained why placating such anger with silence was dangerous for the West: "The Muslim uproar has a goal — to prohibit criticism of Islam by Christians and thereby impose Shariah norms in the West. Should Westerners accept this central tenet of Islamic law, others will surely follow. Retaining free speech about Islam, therefore, represents a critical defense against the imposition of an Islamic order."

Mr. Pipes' language — "shariah norms in the West," "the imposition of an Islamic order" — evokes a potential transformation of our culture that is nothing short of revolutionary. Our elites seem not to have the slightest clue how devastating such a change, which comes under the rubric of Islamization, would be to our Judeo-Christian-rooted civilization. Indeed, it is increasingly clear that they don't know the difference between "an Islamic order" and Judeo-Christian-rooted civilization — or even that there is a difference.

There are exceptions. In November, there was Rep. Ginny Brown-Waite, Florida Republican, who stood up for constituents' free speech under CAIR pressure. Now Rep. Virgil Goode, Virginia Republican, has become both the lone standard-bearer of free speech about Islam and the favorite whipping boy of the PC elites. In a letter to constituents about the decision of Rep.-elect Keith Ellison, Minnesota Democrat, to use a Koran at his swearing-in ceremony, Mr. Goode expressed what I take to be his recognition that the laws of Islam — which prohibit religious freedom, freedom of speech and conscience, equality before the law and women's rights — do not augment but rather contravene the founding principles of the United States.

He also wrote: "I fear that in the next century we will have many more Muslims in the United States if we do not adopt the strict immigration policies that I believe are necessary to preserve the values and beliefs traditional to the United States of America." It's difficult to argue with Mr. Goode's logic. Indeed, the test case of the age — Europe — demonstrates that Islamic immigration brings Islamic law, which is demonstrably at odds with American values and beliefs. Forgoing debate, however, Mr. Goode's critics have resorted to name-calling and platitudes about "tolerance," failing utterly to notice the gross intolerance of the Islamic tradition. Worst of all, their tactics seem designed to shut up Mr. Goode, and anyone else who might follow his bold example. Will they?

It's the question of 2007.

The education of the deputy assistant secretary of defense for captured jihadists

1/19/07

Imagine waiting for that other shoe to drop only to realize it has kicked you in the pants. That's how I imagine the current state of mind of Cully Stimson, the deputy assistant secretary of defense for detainee affairs, i.e. jihad terrorists captured by the U.S. on the global battlefield and incarcerated in Guantanamo Bay, Cuba.

How did Mr. Stimson go from practically smug to very sore? Last week, the Pentagon official declared in a radio interview that it was "shocking" the extent to which the nation's top law firms, whether pro bono or paid, represent terrorists in Gitmo. Ticking off a roster of so-called white-shoe firms that make up what's known as the Guantanamo Bar, Mr. Stimson predicted that when these same firms' corporate clients discover they share legal counsel with terrorists — "the very terrorists who hit their bottom line back in 2001," he added — they would "make those law firms choose between representing terrorists and representing reputable firms."

I, for one — and probably the only one — was impressed. Here was a Pentagon official who seemed to believe that not only was there a dividing line between representing terrorists and representing businesses, but there was also a connection between helping those terrorists and hurting those businesses. Quaint thought. In our advanced state of political correctness, such a line is crossed so often and so enthusiastically by our legal elites and others that it has disappeared altogether. Indeed, we live in a day when one man's wanted terrorist is another man's prized pro bono client. But Mr. Stimson seemed not to have noticed. He actually thought that if Big Business knew Big Law was rushing to defend enemy combatants committed to the destruction of this country (not to mention Big Business and Big Law), CEOs would pressure legal elites to withdraw from the Guantanamo Bar. After all, what's good for Guantanamo is not good for the country. Time to win one for the Babbitt.

hat was then. I don't think Mr. Stimson even saw what was coming next: An avalanche of moral outrage and high dudgeon that flattened him for suggesting that anything but moral kudos and undying gratitude are due fat cat lawyers who see to it that Al Qaeda terrorists — sorry, people in legal trouble — have due process under U.S. law. So what if they want to blow up U.S. law? Our best and brightest have determined they are owed due process first. What makes us succeed as a country isn't keeping soldiers of jihad away from our people (how crass) but rather providing them with the legal mumbo jumbo to get out of jail (how enlightened).

And woe to anyone whose heart doesn't swell at the sight. The notion, as imagined by Mr. Stimson, that a non-terrorist client might actually disapprove of this enthusiastically offered legal largesse was depicted as downright un-American. For that matter, o was Mr. Stimson. Not even his colleagues at the Pentagon supported him for suggesting that the veritable stampede of white shoes to Gitmo was the least bit unseemly.

Then, quite suddenly, Cully Stimson changed his mind. In a letter to the Washington Post, he recanted all. "During a radio interview last week, I brought up the topic of pro bono work and habeas corpus representation of detainees in Guantanamo Bay, Cuba. Regrettably, my comments left the impression that I questioned the integrity of those engaged in the zealous defense of detainees in Guantanamo. I do not ... I apologize for what I said to those lawyers who are representing clients at Guantanamo. I hope that my record of public service makes clear that those comments do no reflect my core beliefs."

I guess that's what they call an about-face. What's more interesting than the dust kicked up, though, is the naive notion that got Cully Stimson into trouble in the first place. This would be his apparent belief that in 21st-century America there still exists what we think of as an establishment that automatically identifies American interests with victories against terrorists. The fact is, a victory for Gitmo due process isn't the same as a victory in the "war on terror." What probably eluded Mr. Stimson is that along with the very nature of the establishment, the definition of victory has also changed. Even more confusing is that so, too, has the definition of the enemy.

Promoting jihad, targeting free speech

8/13/07

Remember when we heard that if only our leaders had known how to "connect the dots," the September 11 attacks could have been prevented? After nearly six years without a similar attack, the government has learned much about detecting the outlines of jihadist terror plots before they take shape. As a result, and after all the aggravations and humiliations of what I still hope are temporary safety procedures, our security has remained essentially intact. But can we say the same thing about our freedoms?

At this point, I must interrupt this column to apologize to all leftists settling in for a juicy tirade against the Patriot Act, wiretaps for terrorists, or the sufferings of sensitive poets in residence at Guantanamo Bay. It is not the Bush administration's efforts to protect us from "terror" (more maturely known as jihad) that compromise our freedoms, it is jihad itself. And the basic freedom to discuss, analyze, debate, imagine, and, therefore, resist jihad is now under unprecedented assault.

Consider the following events.

• On or about July 30, Cambridge University Press surrendered to a libel suit brought in British court by Khalid bin Mahfouz over the 2006 book, "Alms for Jihad," which identifies the Saudi billionaire as a supporter of al Qaeda. The publisher apologized for allegations documented by the authors, paid damages and promised to destroy all unsold copies of the book, and to request libraries and universities, even in the United States, to destroy their copies.

• On Aug. 1, Chauncey Bailey, editor of the Oakland Press, was murdered. Mr. Bailey had been investigating what sounds like a black Muslim crime family operating out of Your Black Muslim Bakery, and its connections to crime in the Oakland area, where, not incidentally, Muslims associated with the bakery have used violence against liquor stores, a la Taliban, to enforce aspects of Islamic law. A 19-year-old Muslim bakery employee has confessed to the crime.

• Also on Aug. 1, the Web site, Radar, recounted a familiar tale of Hollywood woe — a screenplay project terminated by a producer before completion. But this one had a post-September 11 twist. The screenwriter, Jason Ressler, maintains that his screenplay, "Dove Hunting," a thriller with a Saudi prince for a villain, was terminated after the producer he was working with, Mark "March of the Penguins" Gill, received a massive infusion of cash from backers including, well, a Saudi prince: Sheikh Walid al-Ibrahim, an owner of al-Arabiya network and a brother-in-law of the late King Fahd. Mr. Gill denies politics affected his decision.

• On Aug. 2, the Young America's Foundation was threatened with legal action by lawyers for the Hamas-linked Council on American-Islamic Relations (CAIR) if the conservative student group didn't cancel a scheduled talk on CAIR by best-selling author and Islamic expert Robert Spencer. To be sure, neither the redoubtable Mr. Spencer nor the student group buckled under CAIR's bullying, and, to date, CAIR's threats have not materialized. Indeed, both Mr. Spencer's resolve and Young America's Foundation response — "CAIR can go to hell and take their 72 virgins with them" — are an inspiration.

• There's even a bright spot in the Cambridge disgrace. The two American authors of "Alms for Jihad," J. Millard Burr and Robert O. Collins, were not sued; just the British publisher. For this protection, we can probably thank courageous Rachel Ehrenfeld, terror expert and author of the 2003 book, "Funding Evil." When Miss Ehrenfeld was sued in 2004 by the same litigious Saudi billionaire in British court (he has brought or threatened suit 36 times on similar grounds), she refused to accept the premise that a British court should have jurisdiction over an American writer's American-published book. She took legal action in

U.S. courts, where, to date, her case is finding protection for American writers from British law.

We can take heart from such victories. But these individual acts of courage will only amount to gallant sacrifices if they aren't upheld as victories over a jihadist effort to shut the rest of us up to curb everybody's freedom to name the Muslim billionaires behind global jihad, to investigate the thuggery of an Islamic city gang, to create thrillers about Saudi terror-princes, to speak out about CAIR's jihadist links and more.

In other words, these are the new dots that urgently need connecting. And what connects them all, from street violence to legal intimidation, is the chilling effect they each bring to bear on the free and unfettered investigation, analysis and assessment of Islam and jihad.

Frank talk about Islamic law? Blasphemy!

1/18/08

Mazar-i-Sharif. Ring a bell? In 2001, a 32-year-old Marine captain and CIA officer named John Michael Spann was killed there in a prison riot, thus becoming the first American combat death in Afghanistan. Not incidentally, Spann, before violence broke out, had interrogated an uncooperative John Walker Lindh, the American Taliban. This all took place before the U.S. military completely toppled Afghanistan's Taliban oppressors.

Nearly seven years later, American-liberated Mazar-i-Sharif has again made headlines — well, one or two — as the site of the prison where a 23-year-old Afghan journalist has been detained for three months (and counting) on blasphemy charges.

These charges derive, Reuters reports, from Sayed Perwiz Kambakhsh "distributing an article which said Prophet Mohammad had ignored the rights of women." As President Bush might say ... well, what might President Bush say: Let freedom reign? Then there's Halabja.

Remember Halabja? The name is notorious for being the town where in 1988, 15 years before Operation Iraqi Freedom, Saddam Hussein gassed thousands of Kurdish civilians to death. This month, American-liberated Halabja made headlines as the site of the court that sentenced a Kurdish author in absentia to six months in prison for blasphemy: namely, for writing in a book that Mohammed had 19 wives, married a 9-year-old when he was 54, and took part in murder and rape. (These points, Robert Spencer notes at jihadwatch.com, "can be readily established from early texts written by pious Muslims.")

The author, Mariwan Halabjaee, who has asylum in Norway, says there's also a fatwa calling for his death unless he asks forgiveness.

Think about it. Where Americans have died, not just to de-fang jihadist threats but to "democratize" Islamic populations, freedom of speech is against the law. And not the law according to "militants" or "extremists," but the law as enforced by democratically elected governments that we, as a nation, support with everything we've got. What would Bush say to that?

I doubt he'd know what to say. Neither, for that matter, would anyone in his Cabinet, starting with Condoleezza Rice. Nor, I doubt, would the chairman of the Joint Chiefs, Adm. Mike Mullen. Nor — to open things up — would the presidential candidates, the Fox News All-Stars or Simon Cowell. The fact is, to discuss blasphemy laws in Afghanistan and Iraq (Kurdistan, even) is to discuss Islam — specifically, its laws and doctrines. And we, as a politically correct people, don't know how to do that. Instead, we act as though they don't exist.

And not just blasphemy laws. Jihad doctrine; Sharia (Islamic law); designs for a global caliphate through jihad (terrorism) and the spread of Sharia (Islamization): We pretend they are not factors in the Free World's experience with Islam. We certainly don't discuss their implications for the freeness of the world. Look at what passes for "debate" among our presidential candidates: Republicans argue over who supported "the surge" first; Democrats argue over who will withdraw troops first.

Such resolute blindness on Islam probably explains the institutional apathy — including (with few exceptions) conservative apathy — on the termination of Pentagon analyst Stephen Coughlin, which I recently wrote about. The military's primary expert on Islamic law, Coughlin was reportedly fired at the behest of a highly placed Pentagon aide named Hesham Islam whom Steven Emerson has since thumb-nailed as "an Islamist with a pro-Muslim Brotherhood bent." Thankfully, Rep. Sue Myrick of the bipartisan House Anti-Terrorism Caucus is considering action, but there is little public sense that this outrage of a story is happening to us as a nation.

But it's something that should deeply concern Americans, particularly as a nation with soldiers under arms. Coughlin's meticulously researched legal brief not only links Islamic law to Islamic terrorism, but also demonstrates the professional negligence involved in ignoring Islamic law when devising strategies against Islamic terrorism.

Of course, that right there may explain the silence, particularly among many conservatives. The kind of negligence Coughlin is talking about, deriving from a PC ignorance of Islamic law, is quite evident in the strategies and tactics of the so-called war on terror that conservatives have widely championed — up to and including "the surge" in Iraq, which, for example, presupposes that American-won security will trigger a set of cultural behaviors and aspirations in Iraqi society best described as non-Islamic.

In other words, we seem to have arrived at a strange junction where neither jihadist apologists nor surge enthusiasts want to hear the facts about Islamic law. You might say it's become the new blasphemy.

Some questions for the next leader of the free world

1/25/08

News flash from U.S.-liberated Afghanistan.

Remember the 23-year-old Afghan journalist I recently mentioned, the one detained in a Mazar-i-sharif jail for three months on "blasphemy" charges? Well, his limbo is over, his cased resolved.

For "insulting" Islam, the Afghan court has sentenced Sayed Parwez Kaambakhsh to death.

According to the law of that land, which, not incidentally, is supported and protected by U.S. troops, only Afghan president Hamid Karzai — only U.S.-supported, Afghan president Hamid Karzai, that is — can do anything on the young man's behalf. Will he? That's the first question that comes to mind. But there are others, including two for all presidential candidates currently perusing this column: Should the United States force Karzai into leniency? Also, given post-Taliban Afghanistan's dependency on U.S. troops for survival, would the implementation of this Sharia (Islamic law) death sentence against Kaambakhsh make us a party to a Sharia crime against universal human rights?

This last question takes us to a topic I wish someone in power would consider — particularly those Americans now vying to lead this country for the next four years. (I regret to say the current administration is hopeless on this vital matter.) Does our "war on terror," which currently includes stabilizing U.S.-fostered governments that enshrine Sharia in Afghanistan and Iraq, in effect place the United States in the role of making the world safe ... for Sharia? That's one debate question I'd certainly like to see asked. And: Given Islamic terror groups' shared predilection for spreading Sharia, does this current U.S. strategy best serve what we like to think of as the cause of liberty?

Consider the Afghan blasphemy case. Calling on Karzai to intercede "before it's too late," Reporters Without Borders issued a statement saying, "We are deeply shocked by this trial, carried out in haste and without any concern for the law or for free expression, which is protected by the (Afghan) constitution."

Just to make sure all presidential candidates still reading this column are paying attention: Is the journalist rights group correct? Is it true that free expression is protected by the U.S.-midwifed Afghan constitution?

The answer is no. (And aren't you candidates lucky this isn't a nationally televised debate?) Sure, the Afghan constitution dubs freedom of expression "inviolable," but, like the U.S.-fostered constitution of Iraq, it makes Sharia supreme. "No law can be contrary to the beliefs and provisions of the sacred religion of Islam," says the Afghan constitution.

Goodbye, freedom of expression.

Of course, Islamic reasoning says otherwise. The deputy attorney general of Balkh Province, Hafizullah Khaliqyar, defended the Kaambakhsh blasphemy trial for being "very Islamic." In a most instructive interview with Radio Free Afghanistan, he made it clear that he considered blasphemy to be in a separate category from "inviolable" journalistic freedoms. "This was not a violation of human rights or press freedom, not a violation of rights of a journalist," he said. The defendant "violated the values of Islam," Khaliqyar continued. "He did not make a journalistic mistake; he insulted our religion.

He misinterpreted the verses of the Koran and distributed this paper to others. All ulama (clerics) have condemned his act."

Off with his head, naturally.

More questions for presidential candidates, beginning with: Well? What do you say to that? After all, this wasn't some wild-eyed Taliban mullah shooting off his gun over perceived insults to Islam, but a deputy attorney general employed by the Afghan government that is supported by the United States. In other words, candidates, what is your opinion of the current policy which forges anti-jihadist alliances ultimately designed to thwart the spread of Sharia with countries that are, no matter how we want to cut it, themselves based in Sharia?

In order for the Westerner to grasp the Islamic line of thinking, as expressed by Khaliqyar, he must appreciate the difference between the Western understanding of freedom, which is rooted in the workings of the individual conscience and naturally gives rise to such institutions as a free press, and the Islamic understanding of freedom, which describes a state of divine enthrallment, even slavery, to Allah, and finds expression in the dictates of Sharia.

Heavy stuff? Not really. If the candidates could just drop the schoolyard sniping, they might have time to bone up on it before the next debate — certainly before one of them moves into the Oval Office. Or is that too much to ask the next leader of the free world?

Free speech jilted by Muhammad romance novel 'warpath'

8/12/08

Reading about the late Aleksandr Solzhenitsyn, we are reminded of his epic force of will — despite the threat to life and limb posed by the Soviet police state — to bear witness, to document, to record everything he could about totalitarianism in the USSR. Then, reading about Random House Publishing Group, which called off the publication of a romance novel about Muhammad "for fear of a possible terrorist threat from extremist Muslims," we should be reminded of something else: How apt was Solzhenitsyn's much-maligned critique of the West, which he excoriated for, among other things, a decline in "civil courage" that was "particularly noticeable among the ruling groups and the intellectual elites."

In the week after Solzhenitsyn's death, accounts of his determination and toil filled the news. When he had a typewriter, he typed single-spaced on both sides of a sheet; when he had pen and paper, he wrote in miniscule print. When he had neither — as at a remote penal colony in Kazahkstan — he devised a memorization technique involving a rosary made of bread in which each "bead" came to represent a passage of work that he committed to memory. He would later write that he memorized 12,000 lines this way.

By 1973, microfilms of The Gulag Archipelago, the writer's massive history of the Soviet prison camps, had been smuggled out of the USSR to publishers in New York and Paris. Solzhenitsyn asked them to delay publication, however, hoping to see the work come out first in the Soviet Union. But then he changed his mind.

Why? Solzhenitsyn had learned that the KGB, after interrogating his typist Elizaveta Voronyanskaya, had found a buried copy of the book. She hanged herself soon afterward. The author quickly approved the immediate publication of his 300,000-word indictment of the communist system.

This is the most serious stuff of history, epoch-changing events on which the wheel actually turned. What happened with a romance novel at Random House this summer isn't going to change any epochs — but it may tell us something about how much our times have already changed.

As the Wall Street Journal reported, author Sherry Jones also "toiled," writing weekends since 2002 to tell a "tale of lust, love and intrigue in the prophet's harem" through a fictionalized story of Aisha, Muhammad's 9-year-old bride. All was well enough until Random House sent out galleys of the book to seek endorsements from writers and scholars. Among them was Denise Spellberg, an associate professor of Islamic history at the University of Texas at Austin. According to the Journal, Spellberg read the novel and became "frantic," explaining, "You can't play with a sacred history and turn it into soft-core pornography."

You can't? Says who in our free-speech world?

Says Islam in our formerly free-speech world. (That's what I mean about how much our times have changed.) Whether Spellberg is herself a Muslim isn't clear, but she certainly went on the warpath (jihadpath?) over this bodice-ripper (burqa-ripper?), activating a chain of Muslim bloggers and Web sites that spread the word, as one Islamic Web site put it, about a "new attempt to slander the Prophet of Islam." Soon, there was a "seven-point strategy" online to ensure "the writer withdraws this book" and apologizes to "Muslims across the world."

But that turned out to be unnecessary. Spellberg also e-mailed her editor at Random House — did I mention Spellberg has a contract with another Random House imprint to write a book called "Thomas Jefferson's Qur'an"? — labeling the Jones novel nothing less than "a declaration of war," "a national security issue," and "far more controversial" than either "The Satanic Verses" or the Danish cartoons. She said the book should be withdrawn "ASAP."

And so it was after Random House consulted "security experts and Islam scholars" — possibly the same ones who urged the U.S. government never again to use the words "Islamic" or "jihad," but I digress. Thomas Perry, deputy publisher at Random House Publishing Group, said the company received "cautionary advice not only that the publication of this book might be offensive to some of the Muslim community, but also that it could incite acts of violence by a small, radical segment."

So, Perry, by all means, just give in to this thuggish blackmail. In fact, why not just stop publishing altogether?

It's too late to ask Solzhenitsyn for his opinion of this capitulation by our elites. But then again he already offered it long ago.

"Should one point out," he asked, "that from ancient times a decline in courage has been considered the beginning of the end"?

Yale Economics 101: Crush cartoons, get Sharia-backed gold

8/20/09

The official story is that fear of Muslim violence drove Yale University Press (YUP) to censor the Danish Muhammad Cartoons and other imagery of Muhammad from an upcoming book about, well, the Danish Muhammad Cartoons. That's what Yale, its administration and press, says publicly, matter-of-factly, and, it seems, without shame.

But it is a shameful thing. Yale's decision to censor pictures of Muhammad from an academic text about them is one of those watershed moments that history will record as institutional capitulation to Sharia (Islamic law) at one of the storied centers of Western learning, American branch. It also happens to be my alma mater.

Yale is hardly unique in academia in bending to Islamic law. Harvard, for instance, is a cheerleader for Sharia-compliant finance, operates a gym on Islamic rules separating the sexes, and permits a Harvard chaplain to condone the Islamic penalty of death for leaving Islam without sanction. Such deference to Islam is the embodiment of what historian Bat Ye'or calls "dhimmitude," the stunted cultural existence of non-Muslims living in thrall to Sharia. If Yale is not unique in this, censoring its press according to Islamic restrictions on Muhammad imagery makes Yale a leading contender for All-Ivy dhimmi.

But is fear of violence alone driving Yale's dhimmitude? I don't think so, and not just because the book in question, "The Cartoons that Shook the World" by Jytte Klausen, promises a pro-Muslim essence ("I am not Geert Wilders," Klausen recently told a Dutch newspaper). The university was muscularly involved in this Sharia-affirming publishing decision. For example, Yale Vice President and Secretary Linda Lorimer helped YUP break the censorship news to author Klausen. The university is also muscularly involved in pursuing Sharia-affirming donors. If Yale suddenly feared the contents of a book—turned in three years ago and due out in three months—I think the fear was not over violence that might break out, but over money that might dry up—Islamic money. Or that such money might never come Yale's way.

Linda Lorimer figures prominently in Yale's "Middle East outreach," which so far hasn't much paid off. Sure, Lorimer in April declared herself and Yale to be "inspired" by the work of the Mohammed bin Rashid Al Maktoum Foundation after this new United Arab Emirates fund announced a preliminary agreement with several business schools including Yale's. But before Lorimer further rhapsodizes about "partnering with the foundation for years to come," I suggest she examine the Al Maktoum family's history of supporting jihad causes, including the Taliban, Hamas-linked CAIR and Muslim Brotherhood spiritual leader Yusuf al-Qaradawi. I suggest concerned alumni do the same.

Still, Yale—whose endowment, like those of other institutions, is off this year (30 percent) -- has yet to receive a massive infusion of cash from the typical Muslim sources. Georgetown and Harvard, for example, both accepted $20 million apiece in 2005 from Saudi Prince Al-Waleed bin Talal, who has likewise reportedly contributed millions to families of Palestinian "martyrs," and whose part-owned Iqra TV incites jihad.

That's the same Saudi prince, by the way, to whom then-New York Mayor Rudy Giuliani defiantly returned $10 million after Talal blamed U.S. Middle East policy for 9/11.

Yale has also failed to "partner" with the new, multi-billion-dollar King Abdullah University of Science and Technology (KAUST), whose founding trustees include Princeton President Shirley Tilghman and Cornell President Emeritus Frank H.T. Rhodes. According to a publication of the National Center for Public Policy and Higher Education, KAUST largesse includes $36 million to UC Berkeley, $60 million to Stanford, and miscellaneous millions ($8 million to $25 million) to other institutions. Nothing, as far as I can tell, directly to Yale. To date, the Middle East looks like just one big dry well for Old Eli: Yale's long-term negotiations with Abu Dhabi to franchise a Yale arts institute ended in failure last year.

Imagine the frustration. What's Yale gotta do for its share of Sharia bucks? Censor those Sharia-defying Danish Muhammad Cartoons?

Hmm. Not a bad idea.

And here's more "outreach" for you: As one of its 2009 "world fellows," Yale selected Muna Abu Sulayman, general secretary of the charitable foundation of — what a coincidence — Prince Al-Waleed bin Talal.

Pita bread on Gulf waters, Yale may think. But how does that old line go? "... God ha' mercy on such as we, Baa! Yah! Bah!"

Sharia trumps Yale's free speech

10/9/09

Last week's column was about something that doesn't exist — a multi-level strategy to combat the advance of sharia (Islamic law) across the West.

The strategy doesn't exist because there's little understanding that the entrenchment of sharia in the Western zone poses a threat to liberty in the Western zone.

This understanding doesn't exist because the critique of sharia (a legal system best described as sacralized totalitarianism) required to devise a defensive anti-sharia strategy, is not considered possible. Why not? The main obstacle is, well, the advance of sharia across the West. In other words, we cannot criticize the spread of sharia simply because sharia, or its influence, has spread. Thus, from Norway to New Haven, from BBC to Fox News, the reflex reaction to critical commentary — even a newspaper page of political cartoons — is to follow Islamic law and stop it (or try), or just shut up.

That's certainly what Yale University has done, as events beginning in August demonstrate. That's when news broke that Yale and Yale University Press were omitting the Danish Mohammed cartoons (and other Mohammed imagery) from a forthcoming book expressly about the Danish Mohammed cartoons. This sudden act of censorship, Yale said, was due to fear of Muslim outrage over the Mohammed cartoons again turning into Muslim violence. (Roger Kimball, Stanley Kramer and I have laid out evidence that Yale's censorship was also due to fear of alienating Muslim donors.) This violence, along with general Muslim outrage, has its roots in Islamic legal prohibitions of life imagery, criticism of Mohammed and sarcasm about Islamic law — all outlawed by the standard Al Ahzar University-approved sharia manual, Reliance of the Traveller, and all tools for the political cartoonist moved to comment on the connection between Mohammed and jihad violence. And why not? Indeed, Sheikh Yusuf al-Qaradawi, arguably the most influential Islamic cleric in the world, calls Mohammed "an epitome for religious warriors."

The publication of the Danish cartoons forced the question: What is more important to the West — freedom of speech, or Islamic law masquerading as something Orwellianly known as community harmony?

With its censorship of the Mohammed imagery, Yale chose sharia. But that wasn't all. Wearing my hat as vice president of the International Free Press Society (IFPS), I asked Yale's Steven Smith, master of Branford College, one of Yale's 12 residential colleges, if he would be interested in hosting Kurt Westergaard, the most famous of the Danish cartoonists, at a "master's tea" for students. The IFPS was then finalizing Westergaard's U.S. tour long-planned to coincide with the fourth anniversary of the publication of the cartoons on Sept. 30. Smith agreed and held the event on Oct. 1. And Yale, it seems, will never be the same.

Of course, Yale was already "never the same," something the Westergaard visit further confirmed. If the Western reaction to the Danish Mohammed cartoons exposed the humiliating bargain the West had already made with Islam, trading away freedom of the press in exchange for "community harmony," the Yale reaction to Westergaard's visit following its censorship of the Mohammed cartoons exposed the rotten fruit at the core of American academia: namely, the politically correct drive to censor material "offensive" to multiculturalism mated to the sharia-correct drive to censor material "offensive" to Islam.

Even now, institutional consternation at Yale over Westergaard continues. In the pages of the Yale Daily News, ire is directed at Westergaard's Yale host, Steven Smith, simply for having issued the invitation, as attested by letters from University Chaplain Sharon Kugler and "coordinator of Muslim Life for the University" Omer Bajwa, and even Smith's fellow Yale masters, Davenport College's Richard

Schottenfeld and Tanina Rostain. At a panel this week sponsored by the Chaplain's Office and the Yale Muslim Student Association, several Yale professors discussed "what made the cartoons offensive ... and how the West's response heightened tension." (Given the West's near-universal capitulation, I'd like to have heard that last bit.)

The lesson here? Free speech about Islam at Yale is a liability: something to censor, oppose, even remove physically, as symbolized by the administration's decision to bus students to the edge of campus to attend Westergaard's talk. Campus security — bomb-sniffing dogs, two SWAT teams — was so extreme it stood as a reproach to critics of Islam, and perhaps as justification for Yale's decision to censor the cartoons in the first place.

Having shrouded free speech in the Islamic veil, Yale stands exposed.

Will Islam conquer The Netherlands?

10/15/10

All eyes are on the war on free speech, the one that Dutch powers-that-be are waging inside an Amsterdam courtroom. That's where Geert Wilders is standing trial for his increasingly popular political platform, based on his analysis of the anti-Western laws and principles of Islam, that rejects the Islamization of the Netherlands.

But don't stop there. There's much more to see in the trial of Wilders, whose Partij voor de Vrijheid (Party for Freedom) is the silent partner in the Netherlands' brand new center-right coalition government. That camel in the courtroom is the tip off.

You haven't noticed it? I've been watching it since last year, when sometime after Dutch prosecutors announced in January 2009 that Wilders would go to trial for "insulting" Muslims and "inciting" hatred against them, Stephen Coughlin, famous in national security circles in Washington for his airtight and exhaustive briefs on jihad, clued me in to his analysis of the Wilders trial to date.

What we know now we knew then: that this trial presented a watershed moment. Wilders, leader of a growing democratic movement to save his Western nation from Islamization, risks one year in prison for speaking out about the facts and consequences of Islamization. Such speech is prohibited not by the Western tradition of free speech Wilders upholds, but rather by the Islamic laws against free speech that he rejects.

Wilders' plight demonstrates the extent to which the West has already been Islamized.

"It is irrelevant whether Wilder's witnesses might prove Wilders' observations to be correct," the public prosecutor stated back at the beginning. "What's relevant is that his observations are illegal." Since when are observations "illegal"? Under communist dictatorships is one answer. Under Sharia is another.

Writing in Wilders' defense in the Wall Street Journal, Ayaan Hirsi Ali, herself a former Dutch parliamentarian, reported that Dutch multiculturalist parliamentarians, "spooked" by Wilders rising political star, modified the Dutch penal code in the fall of 2009 to fit Wilders' alleged crimes. They crafted what Hirsi Ali went on to call "the national version of what OIC diplomats peddle at the U.N. and E.U." when trying to criminalize defamation (criticism) of religion (Islam).

This is a crucial point to understand, and one that takes me back to what Stephen Coughlin posited last year. Everywhere the OIC (Organization of the Islamic Conference) goes, it peddles Islamic law. In effect, then, to build on Hirsi Ali's point, the Dutch modified their laws to conform with Islam's. This gibes precisely with how Coughlin saw the trial from the start: as an attempt to apply Islamic law, as advanced by the OIC, in the Netherlands.

The OIC is an international body guided by policy set by the kings and heads of state of 57 Islamic countries in accordance with Islamic law. Such law permeates OIC activities, which are shaped by the Sharia-based Cairo Declaration of Human Rights in Islam. The OIC relies on the Cairo Declaration as its "frame of reference and the basis ... regarding issues related to human rights." (These include free speech rights as restricted by Sharia.) The organization's 57 foreign ministers meet annually, as the OIC's website explains, to "consider the means for the implementation" of OIC policy. As Coughlin puts it, these are "real state actors using real state power to further real state objectives."

Sharia objectives.

Topping the OIC wish list is its effort to criminalize criticism of Islam in the non-Muslim world. And this is what makes the Wilders case is so significant. It's one thing if Islamic street thugs mount assassination attempts in Western nations against violators of Islamic law (i.e., elderly Danish cartoonists), or Muslim ambassadors to Western nations lobby them to punish such violations (the free press), or OIC representatives introduce similar Sharia resolutions at the United Nations. It would be something else again if a Western government were itself to convict a democratically elected leader for violating the Sharia ban on criticizing Islam. That's not war anymore; that's conquest.

In this context, Wilders' trial was never a straight judicial process; it was a political battle from the start, a proving ground for Sharia in the West, dovetailing with the OIC's "10 year Plan," which includes a global campaign against so-called Islamophobia. It remains a test of the tolerance of Dutch elites—tolerance for the truth—and their openness to the intolerance of Sharia.

When did free speech become illegal?

6/1/12

Back in 2001, Britain's political parties signed a fantastic pledge. They agreed to say nothing to "stir up racial or religious hatred, or lead to prejudice on grounds of race, nationality or religion."

This gag order did more than keep the parties polite. Vital issues — from massive immigration and multiculturalism to their eradicating effects on British civilization — were officially banned. Thus, such concerns became impermissible thoughts. Not that such issues weren't already thoughtcrime, as George Orwell would have put it. But this unprecedented pledge turned "violators" into political lepers.

I thought of that elite code of cowardice this week when a London judge sentenced a 42-year-old British secretary named Jacqueline Woodhouse to 21 weeks in jail. Her crime? An expletive-laden rant about immigration, multiculturalism and the disappearance of British civilization. Not in so many words. But that was the unmistakable gist of Woodhouse's commentary one January night on the London Underground.

This same week, another London judge ordered two black girls, 18 and 19, to perform community service after a savage physical attack on two white legal secretaries. "I am satisfied what you both did, you did that night because you were fueled by alcohol," Judge Stephen Kramer said, as though tut-tutting a child's unknowing apple theft.

A few months ago, another London judge freed four Somali Muslim women who set upon a white couple, yelling, "Kill the white slag," and other anti-white slurs. The gang beat the woman to the ground and ripped out a patch of her hair. Judge Robert Brown was lenient because, he ruled, as Muslims, the women were not used to being drunk.

Jacqueline Woodhouse was drunk, too, but that was no mitigating factor in her case. She harmed no one, but that was no mitigating factor, either. Judge Michael Snow invoked the "deep sense of shame" Woodhouse's display elicited, because "our citizens ... may, as a consequence, believe that it secretly represents the views of other white people."

"Thoughtcrime is death," as Orwell wrote in "1984."

And, thanks to YouTube, it becomes continuous spectacle. Woodhouse's court-deemed "victim," Galbant Singh Juttla, recorded and uploaded her display. After the six-minute clip went viral, Woodhouse turned herself in to police.

But what might she have confessed to?

I did it, mates. I said: "I used to live in England. Now I live in the United Nations."

That'll be 21 weeks in the clink?

Woodhouse said a lot of other things as she surveyed her fellow passengers, her squawky voice weirdly reminiscent of an Eliza Doolittle grown old without having met her Henry Higgins. "All bleeping foreign bleeping bleeps," she says. "Where do you come from? Where do you come from? Where do you come from?" She estimated that 30 percent of the train's passengers were in the country illegally.

Off with her head.

Expletives fly regarding England ("this bleeping country is a bleeping joke"), Pakistanis, illegals, pigs.

"I wouldn't mind if you loved our country," she said, lucid, to a Pakistani beside her.

"Long live Pakistan," he said twice in Urdu, later leading a chorus of the Pakistani national anthem.

Woodhouse then notices her "victim" recording her. "Oh, look, he's filming," she says. "Hello, government." She leans into the camera.

"Why don't you tell us your name, as well?" Juttla the "victim" says.

"Why don't you tell me where you're from?" she says.

"I'm British, I'm British, yeah? I'm British," he tells her.

"Right. OK," she says.

"So, what's your problem?" he says.

"Oh, what's your problem?" she says.

"Yeah, you should watch what you say."

"Watch what I say?"

"Yeah."

"I used to live in England. Now I live in the United Nations."

"So keep your mouth shut then."

"Why should I?"

Twenty-one weeks in jail, folks.

Why, Woodhouse quite rationally asks, "am I not allowed to express my opinions?"

"We don't want to hear your opinions," Juttla replies.

This tears it. "Why is it all right for you but not all right for me?" She's shrieking now, her voice cutting the air like a ragged-edged razor.

There is background laughter, but nothing is funny. For a few, farcical minutes, a nation's tragedy, its unmarked passing, has taken the spotlight, the lead role played by a drunken secretary because there is no one else.

"Just keep your mouth shut," Juttla says for the umpteenth time.

"Why should you open your gob and I can't open mine?"

"Because you questioned me first," he says, which isn't true. Juttla questioned Woodhouse first, asking for her name. Surely, Big Brother would want to know.

"I'm sorry," she says. "Not one rule for you and one rule for me."

Oh, yes, Jacqueline. One rule for indigenous islanders.

One rule for everyone else.

Free speech at risk as U.S. synchronizes with Islam

9/21/12

What's wrong with the following Associated Press headline? "Charlie Hebdo cartoon spurs French gov't to order embassies, schools to close."

Cartoons of Muhammad in the satirical French weekly Charlie Hebdo didn't send France into lockdown. Their publication this week was a simple exercise in free speech on Islam, which Muslims in France and everywhere else in the world oppose as a violation of Islamic law (Shariah). It is Islamic rage over the fact that Islamic law is not dominant everywhere, all the time—Muslims' signal weapon against a timid West—that drove French authorities to take security precautions, not the publication of cartoons.

What's wrong with the following headline? "Cinemaniac: Feds question loon who set Muslim world on fire." Again, this headline in the New York Post leaves the actual pyromaniacs out of the picture, instead demonizing an individual who made a film about Muhammad—his lawful right. Muslims set "the world" (American embassies) on fire in one more fit of jihad to punish a violation of Islamic law. Like other cycles of Islamic rage before it—whether the pretext is a Miss World pageant in Nigeria or cartoons in a Danish newspaper—this one, too, will temporarily abate, ready to flare up next time the point must be driven home: Criticism of Islam and its prophet is verboten.

This is no media flap. This is war. Islam is attempting to dominate the West by attacking the basis of the West—freedom of speech. Our leaders won't tell us that because too many of them have already surrendered. They deplore the violence against our people and our sovereign territory, yes, but their priority is not to defend free speech but to see that Islamic speech codes are enforced. They have already decided to discard liberty for Shariah. The U.S. government and the Islamic bloc known as the Organisation of Islamic Cooperation (OIC) couldn't be more in sync on this vital issue.

How to get around the First Amendment? Through "some old-fashioned techniques of peer pressure and shaming," Secretary of State Hillary Clinton said last year. She was speaking about the so-called Istanbul Process, the international effort she and the OIC are spearheading to see Islamic anti-"blasphemy" laws enforced around the world.

Since last week, the Obama administration has made not one but two attempts to persuade YouTube to remove "Innocence of Muslims," the Islamic riot-button du jour. The administration has denounced and practically jumped up and down on the video clip as "the cause" of Islamic rampaging. (To its credit, YouTube owner Google so far has refused.)

Amid the rioting, President Obama called on Turkish Prime Minister Recep Erdogan for political support. Erdogan obliged by condemning violence against U.S. personnel in Libya, but he identified the video as "provocation" — indeed, all the more reason for blasphemy laws. When free speech "is in the form of a provocation," Erdogan said, "there should be international legal regulations against attacks ... on religion." There should be domestic laws, too, he said, continuing: "Freedom of thought and belief ends where the freedom of thought and belief of others starts."

That's not how it works in the West. But such Shariah norms are what all of Islam — not just a "tiny band of extremists" — is pressing on us. A survey of the week's news in the Islamic world reveals that whether terror kingpins (Hassan Nasrallah of Hezbollah and Indonesia's convicted Abu Bakar Bashir) or Islamic scholar (Grand Imam of Al-Azhar Ahmed el-Tayeb), whether smashing U.S. Embassy windows in Yemen or meeting in the offices of the Arab League, whether Pakistani lawyers or Hamas fighters, whether under U.S. sanctions (Iran's Ayatollah Ali Khamenei) or an Obama ally (Turkey's Erdogan), the Islamic world is speaking in one voice. Criticism of Islam must be outlawed, and violators punished.

And more audaciously than ever. Just this week, an Iranian group increased the bounty on Salman Rushdie's fatwa'ed head to 2.5 million euros for "insulting" Islam 23 years ago in his novel "The Satanic Verses." The influential Union of Islamic Scholars, headed by Muslim Brotherhood spiritual adviser Yusuf al-Qaradawi, demanded that Pope Benedict XVI apologize for his 2006 address in Regensburg, Germany, linking Islam and violence. Egyptian cleric Ahmad Fouad Ashoush issued a fatwa (death sentence) against the cast and crew of "Innocence of Muslims." The Pakistani government declared a national holiday for anti-U.S. protests. And the Egyptian government, still begging for U.S. cash, not only sentenced an Egyptian Christian to six years in jail this week for "insulting the prophet" (and Egypt's president and a lawyer), it also issued arrest warrants for six U.S.-based Egyptians who made the "offending" film and pastor Terry Jones for promoting it.

This is what a world without the First Amendment looks like. In the eyes of the Obama White House, however, the First Amendment is just an obstacle to synchronicity with the Islamic world. They are right, of course. That makes it our lifeline to liberty.

'Slander' and free speech are one and the same

9/28/12

Who said the following: "The future must not belong to those who slander the prophet of Islam."

Iran's Ahmadinejad? Egypt's Morsi? Some little-known, fatwa-flinging cleric increasing the bounty on Salman Rushdie's head?

None of the above. The words are President Obama's, and he spoke them this week to the U.N. General Assembly.

No Big Media outlet reported this stunning pronouncement. It's as if Ronald Reagan addressed the National Association of Evangelicals in 1983 and the media failed to report that he used the phrase "evil empire." To make the comparison more direct, imagine if a Republican president declared that "the future must not belong to those who slander the messiah of Christianity" — or, for that matter, the prophet of Latter-day Saints. We would have heard all about it, and for the rest of our lives.

Of course, the Islam-Christianity comparison isn't a perfect match, given the peculiar definition of "slander" under Islamic law (Shariah). According to such authoritative sources as "Reliance of the Traveller," a standard Sunni law book approved by Cairo's Al-Azhar University, "slander" in Islam includes anything that Muslims perceive to reflect badly on Islam and its prophet, including the truth. In other words, any negative fact about Islam and Muhammad is, under Islamic law, deemed "slander."

Does the president, son of a Muslim father and raised for four years as a Muslim by his stepfather in Indonesia, understand this? Shouldn't someone in the White House press corps bother to ask?

Whether the president is ignorant or knowing, the Organization of Islamic Cooperation (OIC), the Islamic bloc of 56 nations and the Palestinian Authority, certainly understood the Islamic meaning as its representatives sat in the General Assembly. They heard the U.S. president declare that the future "must not belong" to those who analytically or critically approach Muhammad and, by natural extension, Muhammad's totalitarian religious/legal system of governance. According to this understanding, We the People who prize the First Amendment are out. Those who enforce and follow Shariah are in. I can't think of another instance in which an American president has publicly uttered such a rank betrayal of American principles. And the media censored it!

But, but, but ... the president also said the future "must not belong" to those who "target Coptic Christians in Egypt" (no word on Christians "targeted" in other Islamic countries) and "bully women."

First of all, "target" and "bully" are wan verbs to describe the terror, bloodletting and systemic abuse that Christian populations and women suffer at the hands of Islam. More important, though, the violence inherent to religious cleansing and female oppression is in no way comparable to the most critical words or pictures on a page or screen. Such an equivalence is immoral. The president should be ashamed.

But we should be afraid. As Secretary of State Hillary Clinton said last December, the Obama administration has been working with the OIC to "move to implementation" of U.N. Human Rights Council Resolution 16/18, an international law that would criminalize criticism of Islam. Obama's "slander" speech just greases the skids.

But, but, but ... the president also said: "The strongest weapon against hateful speech is not repression; it is more speech—the voices of tolerance that rally against bigotry and blasphemy, and lift up the values of understanding and mutual respect."

Let's crack that code. "More speech" as a weapon sounds perfectly fine until the president defines it. What does he mean by "voices of tolerance" rallying against "blasphemy"? (Since when does a supposedly secular politician decry "blasphemy"?) Obama's "voices of tolerance" sound like the public pressure-cooker Hillary Clinton described when proposing to enforce the U.N. blasphemy resolution through "some old-fashioned techniques of peer pressure and shaming, so that people don't feel that they have the support to do what we abhor."

Excuse me, but who's "we"? The Obama administration and the Islamic bloc? Are these the progenitors of what President Obama calls "the values of understanding and mutual respect" that must triumph over "hateful speech"?

Clearly, this president is not protecting free speech as our founders guaranteed it, and, in fact, he gravely endangers it. Meanwhile, if I choose to write against child rape as condoned under Islamic law with roots in Muhammad's consummation of a marriage with a 9-year-old—Islamic "slander," for sure—in what way is the "mutual respect" President Obama calls for even conceivable as an antidote?

Here's the secret that blasphemy laws are written to smother: Regarding the fundamentals of freedom of conscience, the autonomy of the individual, protection of children and equality of women, Islamic and Western doctrines have nothing in common and are, in fact, at irreconcilable, dagger's-point odds. Silence—Shariah blasphemy laws—is the Obama-Clinton-OIC Islamic answer. Indeed, in the Shariah-compliant end, silence will replace the questions, too.

But we're already used to it. Don't believe me? Afshin Ellian, an Iranian-born Dutch law professor, poet and columnist, puts it this way: "If you cannot say that Islam is a backward religion and that Muhammad is a criminal, then you are living in an Islamic country, my friend, because there you also cannot say such things. I may say Christ was a homosexual and Mary was a prostitute, but apparently I should stay off of Muhammad."

Another attempt to silence critics of Islam

2/8/13

I may be the only American who has seen both the "panic room" where Danish cartoonist Kurt Westergaard fled in 2010 as a Somali Muslim man hacked at the door with an ax, and the apartment house where this week Danish journalist Lars Hedegaard, 70, was almost killed by an "Arab"- or "Pakistani"-looking man posing as a postman. Since our vast media don't consider these items news, I will tell you about them.

First, Westergaard's panic room. It is a bathroom off the front hall of a modest, modern-style home in the small Danish city of Aarhus. The tiny room is equipped with a buzzer that rings through to the local police station, and it has a steel door. While the Somali was breaking through the front door of his home, Westergaard, then 74, who walks with a cane, made his way into the secure room, hoping the police would reach him in time. As he listened to each strike of the ax on his door, the assailant screamed, "Blood! Revenge!"

Blood and revenge for what? Four years earlier, Westergaard had drawn a cartoon of Muhammad. It was one of 12 such cartoons commissioned by his newspaper, Jyllands-Posten, to demonstrate that Denmark's media do not follow Islamic laws against depicting Muhammad. You haven't seen Westergaard's cartoon in American media? That's because American media do follow this Islamic prohibition—only they call it being "sensitive" or "inclusive" or something. (Google "Westergaard" and "cartoon" to see if the image makes you want to pick up an ax.)

No matter what our media chiefs say, however, there is nothing "sensitive" or "inclusive" about capitulating to what is, in reality, fear of Islamic violence, thus allowing an elderly Danish artist to face this jihad alone.

The other front-line outpost of jihad manned by Danish senior citizens with pens that I can claim to have seen for myself is Lars Hedegaard's apartment building. Just a few stories high, it stands on a quiet street in Frederiksberg, a municipality adjoining Copenhagen that is known for the city zoo and nearby park and gardens. On Tuesday, Lars got a call from the front door telling him he had a package. He opened a window and looked down on the postman—or, rather, on a man wearing the distinctive red jacket of the Danish postal service. Lars said he'd be right down, since the buzzer to let visitors into the building didn't work.

Lars opened the front door, and the man, whom Lars judged to be about 30, handed him a package. As Lars took it, the man pulled out a gun and fired at Lars' head. Lars sensed the bullet passing over his right ear. After Lars threw a punch at the man's face, the man dropped the gun and the two men scuffled, Lars trying to shut the front door against his assailant. The man inserted his foot inside the door, got hold of his gun again and fired at Lars once (click—the gun jammed), then twice (click—jammed again). Then the gunman fled the scene. Not one but two men wearing ski masks were soon seen hopping over the wall into the zoo, near where the hippopotamuses live. Police arrived. Lars disappeared, enveloped by state security.

Why did someone try to kill Lars Hedegaard? I take the question personally, because Lars is a dear friend and a colleague. In 2009, I joined him and others to form the International Free Press Society as a sister group to the very successful Danish Free Press Society, which he founded in 2004. The goal was to support free speech, long imperiled by the application of the Marxist-derived speech codes we know as "political correctness," and more recently constrained by the influence of Islamic law in Western society. Lars' most recent venture is the new weekly newspaper called Dispatch International, which he co-edits with Swedish journalist Ingrid Carlqvist. I am Washington correspondent.

Police do not yet have a suspect in custody, but European media instantly seized on the veteran journalist's unflinching reporting and editorializing about the impact of Islam on Europe as being the possible motive for attack. This is logical given the suspect's description, which indicates he is likely Muslim, and the frequency with which Muslims resort to violence in Europe and elsewhere to silence those who oppose the erosion of Western culture under the increasing application, officially and informally, of Islamic law in Europe and the wider West.

Still, that's nothing new for Lars. So why the attempt to kill him now? The feeling at both Dispatch International and the Danish Free Press Society is that the trigger was the advent of the new newspaper, which last month began regular publication and, in its Swedish edition, delivery. (It is available online in Danish and Swedish, and in English here: www.d-intl.com/?lang=en.) Covering all manner of issues that mainstream media ignore—much of it (not all) regarding the effects of Islamic law and immigration on indigenous European peoples—the newspaper clearly hit multiple nerves, even coming under a sustained cyberattack in December, which police are still investigating.

This is why it is equal parts laughable and shameful to read the widely published Associated Press report of the incident—the primary source in the U.S. for news of the attack. Noting the attempted killing of Hedegaard, whom it describes as "a Danish writer and prominent critic of Islam," the AP goes on to say: "Hedegaard heads the International Free Press Society, a group that claims press freedom is under threat from Islam."

What does it take to prove it—a more effective assassin?

Turning Points on the Road to Jihad

This war is more than Afghanistan

10/24/01

HOW did he do it? How did State Department spokesman Phillip Reeker keep from bursting into undiplomatic laughter when making the preposterous case for there being no parallel between what happened on the West Bank on Sunday morning, and what's going on day and night in Afghanistan?

Here are the facts. With America's high techno-bombers still straining to draw a bead on Saudi terrorist Osama bin Laden, Israel hit a bull's-eye in its own unending war on terrorism by killing Abed Rahman Hamad, the Hamas mastermind behind the June 1 Tel Aviv disco massacre that left more than a score of teen-agers dead and dozens wounded. The operation took no more than an undisclosed number of Israeli sharpshooters, two bullets, and zero so-called "collateral damage." But far from hearing congratulations from its great friend and patron, Israel drew a public rebuke.

"We oppose the policy of targeted killings," said Reeker, who, with any luck, will one day stand behind the same lectern to discuss the "targeted killing" of the man President Bush likes to call "the evil one." "I really can't draw a parallel between the two," Reeker added as he tried to scotch the obvious comparison between the American and Israeli efforts — plainly and simply two related fronts of the same, general war against Islamic terror networks. If they aren't, of course, then you have to wonder why, according to press reports, the American military has been briefed on Israeli "liquidation" techniques for possible use against Osama bin Laden and his men in Afghanistan.

So what makes the government hedge? For starters, coalition politics. Not only do our coalition "partners" in the Muslim world — and also Great Britain—balk at taking the war on Islamic terrorism beyond Afghanistan to, say, Iraq, but these same Muslim nations also balk at the notion they could ever have common cause with the state of Israel. Know what? They don't. States who support, sponsor or even, let's say, enable terrorism (Syria and Saudi Arabia, for example), don't have common cause with Israel or any other state that vows to end, or, as Middle East Forum Director Daniel Pipes more realistically suggests, contain terrorism. And that, of course, includes us.

Pretending otherwise smacks of gamesmanship, of treating the battlefield as the chessboard it used to be and not the city streets and office buildings it has unbelievably become. The point of this struggle, frankly, is not to build a coalition, but to win a war. A real war. Last month, unimaginable carnage in the air and on the ground; this month, among other horrors, a puff of highly refined, weapons-grade anthrax actually closed a branch of the federal government. Coalition-building is no longer a priority. Post-Sept. 11, our priority is stopping terrorism before it strikes again. That's why Pentagon planners would like to make Iraq our next military destination, a journey not too many Muslim countries are likely to join us on, coalition or no coalition.

Early one June morning a little more than 20 years ago, the state of Israel sent 16 American jets on a vital mission: to destroy Iraq's nearly operational facilities for making weapons-grade plutonium. A nuclear bomb in the hands of Saddam Hussein, as then-Israeli Prime Minister Menachem Begin would later say, was a nightmare Israel had been living with for two years. By 1981, this nightmare was about to become reality. Fooling Saudi and Jordanian air traffic controllers by speaking Arabic en route, two waves of specially trained Israeli pilots flew to Iraq's French-built Osirak nuclear reactor outside Baghdad, where they neatly and completely destroyed the reactor core before it had been developed to the point of being "hot."

Fabulous, right? The world, including practically the entire U.S. government (with the notable exception of the late Sen. Alan Cranston and also Jerry Falwell) thought otherwise. Or, at least, it said otherwise. Israel was universally and vigorously condemned—literally in the United Nations, where the United States worked closely with Iraq in crafting the resolution denouncing the raid. Arab nations, naturally, railed against "Israeli terrorism," while France, naturally, expressed its bitterness over Israel's "obvious lack of regard for the difficulties ... created for France." But there was another view.

As then-Sen. Rudy Boschwitz put it, "Very frankly, [the Israelis] probably did the world a favor." It was a favor we should have thanked them for even 10 years later when the troops of Desert Storm faced an Iraq that still had no nuclear arsenal.

Menachem Begin would later justify the raid as an act of "supreme national self-defense." It was. And the world was a safer place. It is now time for the United States to act in "supreme national self-defense." It may be the only way the world will ever be a safer place again.

Holy sanctuary or terrorist shield?

4/17/02

A visit to Jerusalem's Temple Mount in the fall of 2000 by Ariel Sharon was enough to kick off this second Palestinian war of terror on Israel known as the Intifada. Or so the legend goes.

In fact, as even Palestinian Authority spokesman Imad Al-Faluji has stated on more than one occasion, Palestinian military action against the Jewish state was planned long before Sharon's "provocative visit" to Judaism's most holy site, which adjoins a site revered by Muslims as Haram-as-Sharif.

But imagine: If a mere day trip by Sharon into the vicinity of an Islamic holy site—which, frankly, as Islamic sites go, ranks way below your Meccas and your Medinas—could be considered reason enough to go to war, what about the armed Palestinian occupation, now into its second week, of one of Christianity's most sacred sites, the Church of the Nativity?

Needless to say, the seizure of the 1,677-year-old church by 250 guerrillas affiliated with Islamic terror factions has hardly roused the armies of Christendom. Crusades, Christian-soldiering and all that went out in the last millennium. Still, it's a shock to realize that this desecration of the ancient church built over what's believed to be the birthplace of the Christian savior has brought down neither Christian wrath nor international pressure on the desecrators to lay down their arms and leave. The closest thing to a meaningful call for action out of Rome, for instance, comes from Father David Jaeger, a Catholic spokesman, who said this week, "We appeal to the world to condemn this act and stop this behavior from continuing."

Father Jaeger's statement would be a good start—only he was referring to the Israeli troops who have encircled the church, not the terrorists who have occupied it. Church officials, meanwhile, insist on styling the latter "refuge" seekers, but you could say only heaven knows why. They also insist that the Franciscan friars and nuns inside the church are not, emphatically not (perhaps too emphatically not), hostages. This line is starting to wear thin as contradictory stories leak out of Bethlehem, including a Thursday report by UPI of a cell phone call made to German journalists from "a German" inside the church who said, "The Palestinians use us like human shields."

Occupier or guest, this band of sanctuary-seekers doesn't exactly call to mind a hunted herd of panting Bambis. According to the Israeli government, among those inside the church are notorious killers from Yasser Arafat's Fatah, Tanzim and Hamas rosters. They include Ibrahim Musa Salem Abayat and Ismail Musa Muhammad Hamdan, two leading Tanzim operatives responsible for — among multiple terrorist attacks — the kidnapping and murder on Jan. 15 of Avi Boaz, a 72-year-old American citizen. Also inside are Nidal Ahmad Isa Abu Gali'if and Muhammad Sa'id Attallah Salem, a pair of henchmen thought to be in on the March 29 suicide bombing at an Israeli supermarket that killed, among others, a 17-year-old girl out shopping for a Passover meal. There's a Fatah general secretary named Kamel Hassan Hamid, who reports to the Palestinian Authority's Marwan Barghouti, and is said to be responsible for distributing funds to terrorist agents. Hamas is also represented by such operatives as Ibrahim Muhammad Salem Abyat, a chief organizer of the faction's terror operations.

In other words, Sunday school it ain't. No wonder Israeli Prime Minister Ariel Sharon told the Israeli parliament he would "expect the international community to demand that they (the terrorists) lay down their arms and leave the holy place." But no. A strange hush hangs over the world, including the still-mainly Christian West. From the European Union to the Holy See, from the resolution-happy United Nations to the newly "involved" United States of America, no official of church or state has demanded that Yasser Arafat order the Palestinians holed up over Christ's birthplace to drop their arms and leave the church ASAP.

Very politely, Israel this week rejected the Vatican's idea of a solution, one that would have guaranteed all 250 terrorists safe passage to Gaza Strip, where they would only rearm and regroup — and re-attack. As Israeli President Moshe Katsav wrote the Pope, "Under the circumstances, I regret with all respect and consideration we have for Christian Holy Places, we have no alternative but to prevent armed Palestinian terrorists, who have murdered innocent Jews, from escaping and continuing their acts of bloodshed." Katsav might have also mentioned that the Vatican's solution would have turned sacred religious sites into sure-fire escape hatches, all but guaranteeing future seizures.

And so the standoff continues, with surrender being the only solution to avoid a pitched battle. Whose surrender will it be — terrorism's or civilization's? You would think — you would hope — that the world wouldn't want to stay quiet on this one.

Springtime for Hamas

4/22/05

More shocking than the White House seal of approval for Hamas "business professionals" is an emerging consensus that the murder "wing" of the outfit isn't so heinous after all

There's something in the air — and it's not the prattle of baby birds. It's chatter. Some people listen to the sound, hear dialogue and say it's swell. I think it sounds like a new language of capitulation.

It surfaced in a Beirut hotel, and spread to a castle in Luxembourg; it whipped through a convention in Qatar, and last week popped up in the White House. There, Scott McLellan — spokesman for the president who told the world that when it comes to fighting terrorism, you're either with us or you're with the terrorists — lapsed into this new lingo. He shut his eyes to reality and opened his mouth to sophistry to say that the Hamas ticket in the Palestinian Authority was A-OK; just a bunch of "businesspeople." He continued: "While they might have been members of Hamas, they were business professionals" interested in "improving the quality of life for the Palestinian people," he said. "Not terrorists."

Since when? Maybe since the Bush administration realized that democratic yearnings in the Palestinian Authority might actually find fulfillment in these same "business professionals" — whose charter, not incidentally, draws inspiration from the Quran and cites the fraudulent "Protocols of the Elders of Zion" in its calls for the total destruction of Israel.

As Andrew C. McCarthy noted at National Review Online, the old "improving people's lives" routine is a hallmark of every terror organization from the Nazis to Al Qaeda. And as Islamic history professor Raphael Israeli has explained, "The so-called military wing (of Hamas) cannot exist without the financial backing of the so-called social welfare wing." This suggests both so-called "wings" find the words of the Hamas charter equally thrilling: "Israel will rise and remain erect until Islam eliminates it as it had eliminated all its predecessors."

More shocking than the White House seal of approval for Hamas "business professionals" is an emerging consensus that the murder "wing" of the outfit isn't so heinous after all. Last week, Reuters reported that E.U. foreign ministers gathered at a Luxembourg castle to consider "the previously taboo idea of dialogue with Islamic opposition groups" — namely, Hamas and Hezbollah. The question before them, posed by E.U. foreign minister Javier Solana, was: "Has the time come for the E.U. to become more engaged with Islamic 'faith-based' civil societies?"

Silly them. The European Union has been engaged in multifarious ways with such "faith-based" societies since lo, about, 1973, according to Bat Ye'or's new book, "Eurabia" (Farleigh Dickinson University Press).

Still, the bloc could always become more openly engaged. No more skulking around, as revealed by a recently released transcript of a secret 2002 meeting between Alistair Crooke, then a high-ranking E.U. official, and Hamas leader Sheikh Ahmed Yassin, subsequently assassinated by Israel in 2004. In the 2002 meeting, according to World Net Daily, Crooke blamed terrorism on "Israeli occupation," referred to Hamas terrorists as "freedom fighters," and let stand a Hamas claim that Israel was behind the Sept. 11 attacks.

Crooke remains "faith-based" busy, having launched Conflicts Forum, a think tank devoted to finding common ground between jihadists and Westerners (gag). Last month in Beirut, Crooke hosted policy-interested Yanks and Brits and terrorists from Hamas, Hezbollah, the Muslim Brotherhood and Pakistan's Jamaa Islamiyya. Said Crooke to the Lebanese newspaper, The Daily Star: "The issues of use of violence and accusations of terrorism must be addressed, of course" — of course — "but frontloading the process by demanding that groups be disarmed before anything else can happen is likely to fail." I wonder if he asked any of his guests to check their suicide-belts at the door.

Such spring feverishness seems contagious. Last week, the Brookings Institution and Qatar assembled 150 international notables, including a former White House adviser (Rand Beers), Euro-Islamist Tariq Ramadan, Judea Pearl (Daniel Pearl's father) and a deputy assistant secretary of state, to discuss, among other things, as the Daily Star put it, "whether and how" to include jihadist groups in democracies. Even broaching the subject has got to be encouraging to terrorists, rewarding murder and intimidation with the increasingly tawdry trappings of self-rule and international recognition. By conference's end, Islam Online, reliably or not, was trumpeting "the U.S. is ready to 'accept' the involvement of Islamist groups ... should they understand 'the rules of the game.'"

But they already do. Also this spring, at yet another convention, Hamas's Khaled Mashal declared, according to a MEMRI translation, that "tahdiah," or calm, in the Palestinian Authority was only a trick and that "resistance" would continue as long as the "occupation" (read: Israel) exists.

Some trick. Some rules. Maybe the real problem is that the West doesn't realize it's all a deadly game.

Teatime for the terrorists

7/5/05

When asked to verify a British account of meetings at a summer villa north of Baghdad between American officials and "some members of the insurgency," as NBC's Tim Russert fashionably put it, Donald Rumsfeld disputed only one assertion: the number of meetings said to have taken place. The Times of London counted two, but "there have probably been many more than that," the secretary of Defense replied, launching into a secretarial defense of "reaching out to the people who are not supporting the (Iraqi) government."

Can we take a roll call of these "people" who are "not supporting" the Iraqi government? According to the Times report — which, again, Rumsfeld let stand, correcting only that one small detail — it seems that an American delegation, including senior military and intelligence officers, a congressional staffer and an employee of the U.S. embassy in Baghdad, has met probably multiple times with non-supportive people, including representatives of Ansar al-Sunna, the Islamic Army in Iraq, the Iraqi Liberation Army, Jaish Mohammed, Thawarat al-Ishreen, the Shoura Council of Mujahideen and "other smaller factions." In other words, some number of U.S. officials have sat down to tea with some number of Islamic terrorists — or, as they are now officially known, "people who are not supporting the government."

There are two absolutely mind-boggling aspects to this story. The first is that such meetings even took place. Aren't we the people who don't negotiate with terrorists? The ones who voted George W. "You're-Either-with-Us-or-Against-Us" Bush back into office?

Apparently not. Or, if we are, something has changed to the point that such lines in the sand don't matter anymore. Additionally mind-boggling is the fact that practically no one in the world has noticed the change, or considered its disastrous ramifications.

After all, who are these groups we apparently had in for tea? They may not exactly register with the Chamber of Commerce, but Ansar al-Sunna, for example, is known to be either an offshoot of or an alias for Ansar al-Islam, a post-9/11 jihadist group believed to have ties with Iran and Al-Qaeda. Moreover, Ansar al-Sunna, which officially opened shop in 2003, is said to be linked to the Zarqawi network. Among the many bestial acts it is believed to have committed in the name of Allah are last year's murders of 12 Nepalese laborers — one beheaded with a knife and 11 shot in the back of the head, with their point of death on perpetual Internet display — as well as 22 American servicemen, Iraqi soldiers and civilian contractors, suicide-bombed to death as they sat down to lunch in a Mosul mess tent a few days before Christmas.

Islamic Army in Iraq has achieved its own measure of bloody infamy: the murder last August of Italian journalist Enzo Baldoni. It also claims the shoot-down of a civilian helicopter that killed 11 passengers earlier this year, including six Americans. The lone survivor, a Bulgarian pilot, emerged from the videotaped crash injured but alive before being shot dead to cries of "Allahu akbar" (Allah is great).

If "Jaish Mohammed" is the same as "Jaish-e-Mohammed," U.S. officials sat down with still another gang of thugs — this one Pakistani-based — with ties to the Taliban and Osama bin Laden. As for the Shoura Council of Mujahideen, which the Times described as "lesser known," a Google search turned up a possible clue at ArabicNews.com. The Web site reported that the "Iraqi Mujahideen Shoura Council" was the group responsible for kidnapping Douglas Wood, the Australian engineer recently rescued by American and Iraqi forces. If these slightly different names stand for the same group, it could well be that while these mujahideen were holding an Australian captive, they were also dunking crumpets with American brass.

In other words, that was some tea party the United States of America threw. If this guest list is legit, it represents a ghastly capitulation to terrorists and a strategic victory for terrorism — living proof that it's possible to kill and behead and hack and dismember and terrify your way to a peace parlay with the U.S.A.

This suggests that we may now be seeking an accommodation with Islamic terror networks rather than their obliteration or even containment. And that suggests a sea change in strategy, vision and soul.

But maybe, after almost four years into this brutal war, that sea change is already behind us. For what is also remarkable about these no-longer-secret talks is how unremarkable their revelation has been. Talking with terrorists is no longer taboo. Come Hamas, come Hezbollah, come Ansar al-Sunna: America is pouring tea.

A 'listening tour' turns to capitulation

9/30/05

Karen Hughes, stay home.

The president's confidante has been on a "listening tour" to "start a conversation with the rest of the world" — namely, the Muslim world, beginning with Egypt, Saudi Arabia and Turkey — but there were too many times when she just didn't know what to say.

A Washington Post anecdote from day one captures the disconnect. Asked in Egypt whether she was going to meet with the Muslim Brotherhood, the opposition party banned by Egyptian president Hosni Mubarak with deep roots in terrorism and a catchy motto ("Allah is our objective. The Prophet is our leader. The Qur'an is our law. Jihad is our way. Dying in the way of Allah is our highest hope"), Hughes "turned to an aide and indicated she was not sure of the answer. The aide whispered back, and Hughes replied, 'We are respectful of Egypt's laws.'"

I guess that means no, but the non-denial denial is open to interpretation. Maybe she wanted to meet with the Muslim Brotherhood, but couldn't. Or maybe she didn't want to say something as harshly non-conversational as "no" because the popular MB might be elected one of these days. Or maybe she just didn't know.

But worse than not knowing what to say is saying too much. Or saying the wrong thing. Or even saying anything at all. Hughes committed all of the above, a faux-pas trifecta, after meeting with Sheikh Muhammad Sayyed Tantawi, the Grand Imam of Al-Azhar University, the academic center of Sunni Islam. It was a "wonderful meeting," she explained, because the two of them were able to talk "about the common language of the heart."

Oh, brother. Is this an Under Secretary of State or a sorority sister? Hughes burbled on about the leadership of Al-Azhar "in speaking out against extremism, against terrorism, (which) is not in keeping with the tenets of Islam" — natch. The sheikh "made the point that all divine religions are built on a spirit of love," she said, "and (that) it is important that all of us work together to fight extremism, to fight terrorism."

What a guy. Hearing Hughes talk about Sheikh Tantawi, you could almost forget what he said in 2002, as translated from a report by the Middle East Media Research Institute (MEMRI), when he called on Palestinian Muslims to "intensify the martyrdom operations against the Zionist enemy" — men, women and children — and described the barbarous slaughter as "the highest form of Jihad operations" and "a legitimate act according to (Islamic) law." Maybe that's the "spirit of love" Hughes was gushing about.

Then there was what Sheikh Tantawi said in 2003, also reported by MEMRI, when he called for jihad against U.S. forces in Iraq. "Jihad is an obligation for every Muslim when Muslim countries are subject to aggression," he explained. "The gates of Jihad are open until the Day of Judgment, and he who denies this is an infidel or one who abandons his religion." This he said during a sermon at — where else? — Al-Azhar.

I juxtapose Hughes' hearts-and-flowers assessment with the hate-and-fanaticism reality for a reason. Obviously, the resources available to me — the invaluable MEMRI Web site — are available to the State Department. I find it difficult to believe that Hughes or her advisors were unaware of the jihadist incitement Sheikh Tantawi is prone to, even though he's also on record with contradictory statements. Why did the Bush administration determine that this meeting was in the best interests of our nation? If the war on terror — always a PC punch-pulling moniker — is turning into the accommodation of terror, maybe it makes sense to make nice. There is, actually, a long tradition of such accommodation between the non-Muslim world and the Muslim world, and it is contained within the blighted history of "dhimmitude." This is the term coined by historian Bat Ye'or to describe the institutionalized inferiority of non-Muslims (dhimmi) under Muslim rule. Hughes' paying tribute to the likes of Sheikh Tantawi is dhimmi behavior. As is, frankly, the whole "listening tour" — an ill-conceived campaign to improve Uncle Sam's "image" with a Muslim world whose opposition to a viable Israel and a free Iraq is hardly skin deep.

Personally, I'd like to see a "like it or lump it tour." But that, of course, would mean keeping up the fight.

Jimmy Carter makes me sick

4/18/08

In mustering arguments against Jimmy Carter's head-to-head, if not heart-to-heart, get-togethers with the arch-murderers of Hamas — the Iranian-supported, Muslim Brotherhood-linked terror organization openly dedicated to the annihilation of the state of Israel — it becomes clear that these disastrous meetings aren't a question of misunderstood or overlooked facts, or a matter of persuasion based on such facts. They come down to a stark choice between evil and good: to meet with Hamas, or not to meet with Hamas; to lend legitimacy to a terror group, or to shun it; to degrade the office of the presidency, or to honor it. Jimmy Carter has made all the wrong choices.

The horror of it all comes from the fact that Carter, as a former president of the United States, doesn't choose in the anonymity of a private person. With lifelong recognition for his permanent, if dubious, place in American history, he makes his immoral choice as a venerable representative of the presidency, indeed, as an enduring symbol of the nation.

It was as such a symbol that the former president hugged a former Hamas official at a reception in Ramallah on Tuesday. Unfortunately, Carter didn't arrive in time for last Friday's sermon, delivered by a Hamas cleric and MP, and translated by MEMRI. It called for Islamic conquest, first of Rome — "the Crusader capital, which has declared its hostility to Islam, and planted the brothers of apes and pigs in Palestine (Koranic motifs describing Jews) in order to prevent the reawakening of Islam," and then "Europe in its entirety ... the two Americas and even Eastern Europe."

He could have hugged that Hamas official, too.

And it was as such a symbol that the former president, along with wife, Rosalynn, the former first lady, visited the grave of Yasser Arafat, the founding father of global terrorism, who, in his time on Earth, watered it with the blood of innocents, including that of two American diplomats he ordered assassinated in 1973 in Sudan. Did the thought of all this blood temper Mr. Carter's enthusiasm? Hailing Arafat's "historic role," the 39th president of the United States laid a wreath of red — red — roses on the terrorist's grave, calling him a "dear friend."

Too bad a column can't come with a sick bag.

This laying of the wreath seems to have particularly thrilled Abdel Rahim, a top aide to Palestinian Authority Holocaust denier — I mean, Palestinian Authority President Mahmoud Abbas (Arafat's longtime associate and successor). The Jerusalem Post reminded readers that this presidential salute was a first, given that "U.S. President George W. Bush and other top administration officials had refused to honor Arafat during their visits to Ramallah." Rahim was positively brimming with enthusiasm, burbling on to Carter about the day Arafat's tomb would be moved to Jerusalem, "the capital of the Palestinian state."

And these — Abbas & Co. (Fatah) — are the "moderates." More such moderation came out in recent news reports that Abbas had to be convinced by Israel not to carry out plans to bestow official honors next week on two female accessories to Israeli murder, including the driver of the bomber of the infamous 2001 Sbarro pizzeria massacre.

Maybe Carter can arrange recognition for these women. Having honored the PLO murderer Arafat, Carter would surely like to honor others from his terrorist camp. Oh, I forgot. The former president is already doing just that in meetings with Hamas murderers even as they continue to kill.

This would seem to register high on the outrage meter, but, for the most part, what is audible from the White House, the State Department and the Congress, is so much tepid background noise to the effect of, "We wouldn't do that if we were you, sir." Not much else. At least not until Rep. Sue Myrick, North Carolina Republican, got involved.

Because Carter's meetings with the Hamas leadership run counter to international agreements to isolate Hamas, and to U.S. policy and international policy regarding this terrorist group, Myrick has publicly called on Secretary of State Condoleezza Rice to revoke Jimmy Carter's passport.

Hallelujah. With this request, an American leader has actually taken a stand for American security interests, for victims of terrorism, for the principle of not bargaining with terrorists, for an important ally, and, perhaps most important, for a grown-up, restorative moral order. Jimmy Carter should certainly lose his passport for his shameful and degrading and harmful Hamas overtures.

And preferably before he flies back home.

Forget bonus outrage, what about 'ShariAIG'?

3/20/09

Congratulations, American taxpayer. Finally, something has roused you from the stupor, the torpor, the catatonia of lingering Obamania.

It was those bonuses. Those AIG bonuses of $165 million. Because that's your money, your millions of dollars paid out to the same incompetents who got us into this mess, right? Sure. But you're on the case now.

You're on top of it. Gave your representatives in Washington a piece of your mind, too. Nobody fools the American taxpayer like that and gets away with it, right?

Sigh. Dear American Taxpayer: If only you knew how easily you have been gulled, played like a greenhorn, a rube, a Madoff mark. This $165 million scandal may have unleashed the first genuine feeding frenzy of the Obama administration, but it is a distraction, a sideshow, a smokescreen over what is really going on: namely, the Bush-initiated, Obama-Pelosi-Reid-led incursion into the private sector designed to nationalize the workings of the economy in order to take over, capture and enslave enough of the free market to transform the fundamental character of this nation.

Remember what our 44th president said back in 1995: "In America," he told the Chicago Reader, "we have this strong bias toward individual action. You know, we idolize the John Wayne hero who comes in to correct things with both guns blazing. But individual actions, individual dreams are not sufficient. We must unite in collective action, build collective institutions and organizations."

That is exactly what's going on behind the $165 million smokescreen — truly, a masterpiece of misdirection. I have no reason to believe it was planned, although I am open to suggestion. After all, it is notable that the nearly $4 billion in Merill Lynch bonuses, doled out just before the dying firm's Jan. 1 takeover by Bank of America (which received bailout funds partly due to the takeover), failed to churn the same national waters.

But I digress.

Up in arms about the AIG bonuses, the body politic remains calm, cool, practically collected about the trillions of taxpayer dollars Obama & Co. are drawing on to buy out the economy, expanding the population's dependency on Biggest Government in the process. There are simply too few of us seeing red, for example, over the surprise Federal Reserve decision (announced this week at the height of Bonus Rage) to pump another $1 trillion into the economy, money the International Herald Tribune said the Fed "will create out of thin air."

Still, there is good in Bonus Rage. It's a sign of life. As the president said this week, "I don't want to quell anger. People are right to be angry. I'm angry. What I want us to do is channel our anger in a constructive way." My sentiments exactly (this must be a first), although I'm sure we differ when it comes to what constitutes a "constructive way."

For starters, Bonus Rage should finally drive Democratic Sen. Christopher Dodd from office when he runs for re-election in 2010 —

unless he peels off the blindfold and sees the error of his ways sometime sooner. Dodd, after all, is the largest recipient of AIG largesse, "most of it," as John Batchelor reports, "from a dozen AIG executives whose bonuses are protected under the legislation Dodd now admits he wrote."

Ouch. For several days this week, the influential Senate Banking chairman — he who never met a sweetheart deal he didn't find irresistible — lied about his role in writing legislation that protects AIG's bonuses. Repeatedly, Dodd insisted that he had had nothing to do with the bonus-protection language in the, ahem, Dodd Amendment until, mirabile dictu, he remembered that he had. As he finally told CNN on Wednesday evening, he actually wrote the provision himself with, he added, input from the administration.

Did I mention President Obama was the No. 2 recipient of AIG largesse? Dodd received $103,100. Obama received $101,332. Now Dodd, after being scorched by these disclosures, says he'll give his AIG money back. Will Obama? Does it matter? The proof is already in the pudding, even if the burnt offerings go back to the kitchen.

Fume, baby, fume. But there's more. The nationalization of AIG is not just bankrupting the country by throwing billions of our dollars at AIG's toxic assets. The nationalization of AIG is forcing the American taxpayer to support a very different kind of toxic asset. I refer to AIG's promotion of Sharia (Islamic law) in its Takaful division, the Sharia-compliant insurance sector of AIG. Since we the people own 80 percent of AIG, we the people now promote Sharia, too.

Don't believe me? Takaful insurance, our very own AIG Takaful Web site explains, "avoids prohibited elements in accordance with the Sharia law," adding: "We do not invest in anything that is haram (prohibited under Sharia). We do not borrow, lend or enter into any financial transaction that is unIslamic."

At the very least — aside from promoting from the law of the Koran, Osama bin Laden, the Taliban, the mullahs of Iran, the clerics of Saudi Arabia (not to mention Afghanistan, whose Sharia-supreme "justice" system recently upheld a journalist's 20-year prison sentence for "blasphemy") — taxpayer support for AIG is by definition sectarian and therefore in violation of the Establishment Clause of the Constitution.

It is on these grounds — that the American taxpayer is now directly funding sectarian Islamic religious activities — that a lawsuit, conducted by the Thomas More Law Center, has been filed against the government. Recently, the Justice Department, another U.S. taxpayer-funded entity last time I checked, entered the case to defend the AIG bailout, filing a motion to dismiss, the Thomas More Law Center notes, based on this being a time of "crisis."

You better believe this is a time of crisis — but not the crisis envisioned by Justice officials charged with safeguarding gross government fecklessness. Only two of our elected officials — Reps. Sue Myrick, R-N.C., and Frank Wolf, R-Va., and bless them for it — have publicly decried the government's AIG Sharia-bailout; that's a crisis. Chump change bonuses arouse the wrath of the nation — not the nefarious movement to nationalize the marketplace; that's a crisis, too. The American people are angry, good. But we need to understand there are far more important things to be angry about.

Making sense of crazy reality

8/15/12

It would be nice to go fishing.

It would be nice to worry about John Roberts.

It would be really nice to think Karl Rove was worth worrying about.

But something wholly distracting is going on. Must be that war on whatever it is, and its very real casualties.

Barbecues smoke, kids come home from summer camp and ballplayers get busted for steroids. Life goes on.

But does it really? I wondered this recently, as my laptop was profiled (or not) in an examination at an airport security checkpoint. Watching the guard wave a practically magic wand over every angle and face of the thing, it struck me that here we are, Americans in high summer, at the dawnish of the 21st century. We may be citizens of a nation conceived in liberty and dedicated to the proposition that all men are created equal, but our liberty has shrunk under measures we take to ward off Islamic terror attacks, and our dedication to equality looks tatty as we go about making the world safe for ... sharia.

It sounds crazy, but this is reality. Today promises to be a great day for *sharia*, or Islamic law. It marks the end of the constitutional wrangling in Iraq and the beginning of the Israeli withdrawal from Gaza and parts of the West Bank. Both events — fought for, facilitated, even micromanaged by the U.S. of A. — should expand the domain of Islamic law, which codifies female inferiority and religious inequality. I don't know a better way to quantify the two events. By day's end, Iraq, if it settles as expected on a draft constitution based in sharia, and Gaza, as a new sector of the already sharia-vested Palestinian Authority, will have joined the community of nations at odds with the Free World.

That sounds crazy, too. But no more so than the thought of American troops fighting off Iranian-supported death squads to shore up a government led by a possible Iranian agent — Ibrahim Jaafari, the Iraqi prime minister and leader of the Tehran-allied Dawa faction.

It sounds fantastic, but the notion comes from the serious-minded

JWR columnist Caroline Glick of The Jerusalem Post, who recently wrote: "Both U.S. and Iraqi officials — Shi'ite and Sunni — have since the inauguration of the Iraqi Governing Council in the summer of 2003 stated repeatedly and matter-of-factly that he (Mr. Jaafari) is an Iranian agent." Mr. Jaafari spent years under Iranian protection during Saddam's regime; he also just concluded a three-day visit to Tehran where he sealed oil, military and tourism deals. I don't recall hearing any word on ending Iran's recognized sponsorship of terror and unrest in Iraq.

More craziness: The spectacle of an American Secretary of State, Condoleeza Rice, propping up the Holocaust-denying Palestinian Authority leader, Mahmoud Abbas, in the strategic dismemberment of Israel wrought by the mystifying old general Ariel Sharon. The Israeli move includes not only the destruction or dismantling of 25 Israeli settlements and the relocation of 9,000 Israelis, but also the disinterment and reburial of 48 Israeli graves. Horrific, yes, but not crazy. The threat of Muslim desecration of Jewish graves in the Gush Katif Cemetery is too real for Israel to allow the dead to remain where they rest. In 1948, Muslim armies captured the Mount of Olives cemetery in Jerusalem and turned tens of thousands of Jewish tombstones into construction material for roads, buildings, even latrines.

Six of the 48 Gush Katif graves belong to residents murdered by Muslim terrorists. Five of them may well belong to members of the Hatuel family — a mother and four daughters — who were shot to death last May at close range by Palestinian terrorists. They had been driving to a rally against the withdrawal, their car bumper sticker reading "Uprooting the Settlements, Victory for Terror."

Certainly, the terrorists see the withdrawal as victory — although not ultimate victory. Jamal Abu Samhadaneh, commander of the Popular Resistance Committees, a Palestinian terror network behind (among other things) the 2003 attack in Gaza on a U.S. diplomatic convoy that killed three Americans, is already planning Intifada 3. "We will transfer all our fighting methods and capabilities to the West Bank," he told The Jerusalem Post. "The withdrawal will not be complete without the West Bank and Jerusalem, which is even more precious to us than the West Bank."

Not surprisingly, Abu Samhadaneh is wanted by Israel. But he's also wanted by the Palestinian Authority, he says — to become a senior official in its Military Intelligence Force.

There may be a peculiarly Middle Eastern logic to all this, but it's not one we seem able to understand.

What have we paid for with 'Palestinian' handouts?

9/16/05

Has America financed holy war (jihad)? Have we supported a "peace partner"? Or have we just helped create a terrorist state?

Maybe it was that last $50 million that George W. Bush forked over to the Palestinian Authority in May that made the Gaza transfer between Israel and the PA this week so ... What was Condoleezza Rice's word for the lawless Palestinian stampede of looting and desecration that erupted after the Israeli withdrawal?

"Successful."

That is, something must have sweetened the deal to make Israeli-Palestinian coordination on this territorial handover so very ... How did Ms. Rice describe the dynamic that led to the flags of jihad terrorism being hoisted into a sky darkened by burning synagogues?

"Effective."

Successful and effective? Not everyone's first reaction, but maybe it all depends on what Ms. Rice was hoping for. The fact that burning synagogues failed even to singe the Secretary of State's assessment of diplomatic success and effective statecraft is nothing less than chilling. But maybe it reflects our arrival at a cold, new reality that calls into question administration attitudes toward longstanding American motives and goals in the Middle East.

Since the Oslo "peace process" began in 1993, Palestinians have received more than $1.5 billion from the United States — more aid, as the San Francisco Chronicle pointed out in August, than from any other single country. Not that other countries, mainly European ones, haven't been generous. The Atlantic Monthly's David Samuels tallied up post-Oslo P aid at $7 billion, estimating that as much as half of that money was siphoned off by Yasir Arafat and his cronies.

Still the bucks flow. This year alone, the Chronicle reported, the United States will double last year's $275 million PA aid package, paying out $550 million (not including the $50 million handed out in May, as near as I can tell). In July, even as jihadis struck the London Underground, the Group of Eight countries couldn't pile up money for the PA fast enough, agreeing by 2008 to present its government — which by then could very well include landslide-elected terrorists from Hamas, Islamic Jihad, Al Qaeda, whatever — with $9 billion.

(According to the Chronicle article, Arab financial support is, alas, rather skimpy, amounting to some Egyptian materiel — ammunition, trucks and whatnot. Palestinian Authority President Mahmoud Abbas, the paper reports, "will seek to rally Arab financial support" in the fall.

Maybe the price of Arab oil is too low for Arab aid to flow.)

They say you get what you pay for. But what exactly have we paid for? As recently as Sept. 2, according to Palestinian Media Watch, the PA's "Voice of Palestine" was sermonizing against "heretical" America, exhorting the Muslim faithful to attack Americans in Iraq — just the latest instance of anti-U.S. propaganda carried on PA-run radio. A few weeks ago, the PA's so-called Ministry of Culture released its "Book of the Month," a collection of poetry honoring murder-bomber Hanadi Jaradat. This "Rose of Palestine" killed 29 Israeli Jews and Arabs at a crowded Haifa eatery in October 2003, back when such carnage was still shocking. Palestinian Media Watch also noted a PA government newspaper report about female Hamas terrorists — photographed holding American-made automatic rifles.

All of which should make us wonder: Have we paid for a "peace process," or have we financed holy war (jihad)? Have we supported a "peace partner"? Or have we just helped create a terrorist state?

Time, maybe a very short time, will tell what already seems clear — except to our secretary of state. Or so I wish. That is, I wish it were myopia alone that had brought us to this not-so-pretty pass. It could be, however, that with the rise of Condoleezza Rice, the current Bush administration now reflects the re-ascendance of the old Bush-Baker-Scowcroft school of foreign policy Arabism.

That would explain the distressing symbolism in the State Department's apparent snub of Israeli offers of aid in the early aftermath of Hurricane Katrina, as reported by the news Web site World Tribune. com. Certainly, State Department spokesmen have quite remarkably omitted Israel's name when ticking off countries participating in the relief effort. By now, the United States has received offers of assistance from Israel as well as Arab countries, the latter diplomatically elevated by silence on the former. In the strange, subtle (and not-so-subtle) world of diplomacy, the American cold shoulder "alarmed" Israeli diplomats "concerned that their country was being marginalized," World Tribune. com reported.

But why? Citing unnamed sources, the Web site wrote that "the administration was concerned that (Israeli aid) would deter Arab and Islamic countries from offering assistance." Frankly, if Israeli participation is considered a deal-breaker, then nuts to Arab and Islamic assistance. If we tolerate such bigotry — like burning synagogues — our future, I am afraid, does not look very bright.

Hamastan dreaming

2/6/06

There comes a point, sometimes, when logic is denied, reason is abandoned, and that vital connection to reality is severed. Once upon a time, we called this a nervous breakdown and prescribed a rest cure. Now, we call it a press conference and take notes.

The fact is, with the Hamas victory — the democratic election by Palestinian Arabs of a Nazi-like terrorist organization dedicated to annihilating Israel and replacing it with a Sharia state — something in the common culture of world elites has snapped. From the White House to the European Union, the Hamas victory, with its disastrous implications for peace and democracy, is more than any one powerful person seems able to accept. So they don't. They are, as the therapeutic community might say, in denial.

Take President Bush's analysis of the PA election results. "The people are demanding honest government," he said. "The people want services. They want to be able to raise their children in an environment in which they can get a decent education and they can find health care."

Honest government? Services? Hamas is "honest," all right, when it comes to its blood-lust for Jews, and maybe it can deliver to its constituents "services" related to Israel's destruction, but I doubt that's what the president had in mind. But neither did he have in mind anything connected to the reality that Palestinians have voted for terror with no "peace process" (Hamas), not a "peace process" with terror (Fatah). Not much actually separates Hamas from Fatah, but it's enough to send the global-erati over the edge.

Such as the United Nation's Kofi Annan. He said: "I think most of them" — "them" being Palestinian voters, who, kind of like "Mr. Smith Goes to Washington," sent Umm Nidal, proud "Martyr Mom" of three suicide bombers, to parliament — "were voting for peace, they were voting for better conditions, they were voting for an honest government." Funny how he didn't mention they were voting for terrorists.

The EU's Javier Solana also looked the other way. "It's my guess that a good number of people who voted for Hamas didn't vote for the Hamas platform. They voted for a group of people they believed were less corrupt... I don't think that the majority of the people that voted for Hamas voted to be an Islamic Palestine."

A polite term for this is wishful thinking. It's okay when you're a kid trying to extend the myth of Ho-ho-ho for just one more Christmas; it's not okay when you are a world leader trying to rationalize millions in aid to a maniacal killing machine. And therein lies the rub. Between Europe and the United States, the PA receives about $850 million a year, and the election of Hamas brought the Western moneybags to a moment of truth.

But only briefly. There was talk in Europe of withholding money from Hamastan until the terror-gang exchanged its covenant of mass murder for the Boy Scout pledge, but that went on just long enough to find a new rationale to fund the PA, at least for the time being. Eureka: "Of course Hamas is a terrorist organization," a European diplomat said, no doubt exhausted after several hours of standing on principle. "But cutting off aid to the Palestinian Authority would play straight into the hands of the extremists among them."

Funny, I didn't know there were non-extremists among them. "If their leadership [Hamas] can find a way to live up to the obligations that have been undertaken, to peace, to the existence of Israel, to renouncing violence, I think there's a very good way forward," said Secretary of State Condoleezza Rice.

If? Once, there was realpolitik; now, we are deeply into dreampolitik, where policy is based on an irrational wish of what might be. Miss Rice seems particularly afflicted, lately given to raving that Palestinians have "long been known for their tolerance." Tolerance of what — Hamas?

Harvard psychiatry instructor Kenneth Levin has written an illuminating new study of such political denial called "The Oslo Syndrome: Delusions of a People under Siege." In this book, Dr. Levin applies the lessons of psychopathology to explain self-destructive patterns of delusion and appeasement that have characterized the Israeli experience in recent years. It looks like this dangerous syndrome is proving contagious to the rest of the world in an era when there's no time for a rest cure.

No 'mas: When are we getting tough with the PA?

5/15/06

If democracy makes leaders accountable to the people who elect them, it works the other way as well: People are also accountable for their elected leaders. Which is why the United States, in agreeing to provide a $10 million care package to the Palestinian Authority (PA), is so dangerously wrong in failing to hold the people of the PA accountable for the democratically elected terror chieftains of Hamas.

Here's what Secretary of State Condoleezza Rice said this week when she announced the United States would provide medical and other supplies to the PA, which, after two months of no American or European Union aid, has run desperately low on such necessities: "The Hamas-run Palestinian Authority government bears sole responsibility for the hardships facing the Palestinian people and the international isolation that the PA is now experiencing due to its refusal to recognize Israel, renounce terrorism, and abide by previous agreements and obligations."

That's a lot of refusal, but never mind. The real here question is, Why does the Hamas-run government bear "sole" responsibility? What about its supporters, i.e. the Palestinian voters who gave that Hamas-run government a landslide victory? In the world according to the Bush administration, they remain voiceless victims even after exercising their political will at the ballot box, voting into power an outlaw organization whose charter unfolds under a statement by Muslim Brotherhood founder Hassan al-Banna: "Israel will exist and will continue to exist until Islam will obliterate it, just as it obliterated others before it." Regardless of whether this heinous call to jihad leaves any peace for the so-called "Quartet" to process, Rice continued: "Hamas' policies and actions should not deprive the Palestinian people of their legitimate humanitarian needs."

Why ever not? Why shouldn't Hamas' "policies and actions," driven by a Hitlerian plan to "obliterate" Israel, deprive Hamas constituents of their "needs," humanitarian or otherwise — and particularly when it comes to support from civilized nation-states spilling blood and treasure to fend off Islamic jihad in the so-called "war on terror"?

There is a strategic and moral senselessness to the administration's willful disconnect. After all, the United States and the European Union cut off aid to the PA two months ago in order to extract concessions — like, for instance, on Israel's right to exist. Hamas' response? No concessions. The United States and European Union are now cranking aid back up — sure, in humanitarian dribs and drabs, but this is probably just the beginning — and still no concessions. This doesn't sound like successful statecraft.

On the other hand, it seems that statecraft is no longer the craft of our state. After predictions of cash and gas shortages, and a couple of stories about sick Palestinian babies made the papers — youngsters languishing "because funds have been withheld from the West" (oil-rich Islam is never to blame) — the United States blinked. Or, rather, we teared up. Acting like an emotional individual rather than the leader of the Free World, the United States traded its goals and principles (pressuring Hamas, not supporting terrorists) for a big wet hanky. But notice Hamas didn't get weepy over its own young and decide to "save the children" by simply recognizing Israel's right to exist. Nor did any of Hamas' oil-rich Muslim brethren feel moved to come to the rescue, either. No. Hamas remained true to its creed (Kill the Jews), the Arab-Muslim world sat tight, and the United States gave in on its anti-terrorist stance and agreed to airlift necessities — which is a disgrace.

Of course, the administration would probably emphasize that it's "only" $10 million worth of Band-Aids and such; and it's not going to Hamas officials, it's going to Hamas constituents — or maybe even Fatah constituents, whose outlook on life and Israel is so different from Hamas that they support the Al Aqsa Martyr Brigades. (Yes, I'm being sarcastic.) But there is more to this incident than $10 million, Band-Aids or Hamas. What we are witnessing is the stumbling behavior of a superpower that doesn't know how to act either super or powerful.

Maybe waging a nebulous "war on terror" has hopelessly confused us. Maybe finding ourselves in the costly business of making the world safe for sharia has muddled our objectives. But if we cannot retrieve the simple, precious principle that took us into war — you're either with us or you're against us — not only will we never achieve victory, we won't even know what it looks like.

The big blur: Who's us? Who's them?

4/16/07

If anyone still paid attention to the mythical Bush doctrine — the part about our enemy being terrorist networks and the governments that support them — it would be time to add another government to the enemy watch list: our own.

How else to react to Congress' rubberstamp on a White House request for tens of millions of dollars for the Palestinian Authority's Hamas-Fatah coalition government? And so what if the money is earmarked for terrorist Fatah, not terrorist Hamas? "You're either with us or you're against us" was the way it was supposed to go, and Fatah is no more "with us" than Hamas in any struggle against jihad terror. By rights, our support for the P.A. should put us on our own worst enemies list.

It doesn't work that way, of course, because the United States, along with Israel, has decided to pretend that Fatah is "moderate." This makes our support for Fatah, and, by extension, its coalition partner Hamas, practically kosher.

To borrow from the late Sen. Daniel Patrick Moynihan, this semantic con may be thought of as "defining terrorism down," lowering the bar on what constitutes civilized statecraft to a point where Fatah can stay involved in suicide-bombing attacks through its Al Aqsa Martyrs Brigades, and keep its hands clean enough to shake those of Quartet players.

Defining terrorism down allows Fatah, — whose constitution declares as its first goal the "eradication of Zionist economic, political, military and cultural existence" and its "opposition to any political ...

alternative to demolishing the Zionist occupation in Palestine," — to be seen as "moderate," at least in the eyes of its willfully degraded "peace process" partners. Defining terrorism down also eliminates a crucial line between "Us" and "Them."

Let the U.S. tax dollars flow. Instead of the dividing lines the first Bush term was known for, we now abide by something more like a big blur. Its amorphousness gives cover not just to parleys with Palestinian terror groups, but to negotiations with Iraqi terrorists (a major flopola), and even meet-and-greets with assorted terror-masters (think House Speaker Nancy Pelosi and Syria's Assad, and House Majority Leader Steny Hoyer and the Muslim Brotherhood). Without traditional guidelines, we lose our bearings. Without words that mean what they say, we fail to realize we have done so.

Meanwhile, new guidelines, even new words, come into practice. For example, the European Union has now compiled a handbook full of "non-offensive" phrases to use when discussing Islamic terrorism. "Islamic terrorism" is out (the phrase, not the practice), replaced by "terrorists who abusively invoke Islam" — or so it is reported.

We don't know for sure because this handbook of sweet non-offensivenesses is actually classified. According to the Daily Telegraph, other terms banned by this "common lexicon" likely include "jihad," "Islamic" and "fundamentalist." This could pose a problem if anyone wants to discuss a fundamentalist on an Islamic jihad. Then again, thanks to the secret codebook, nobody ever will, right?

Sounds like a plan to define jihad terror down and out — which is not at all the same thing as getting rid of jihad terror. Instead, it eliminates the means by which jihad terror is named, categorized, and understood. Fatah is "moderate." "Jihad" is verboten. "Islamic terrorism" is unmentionable, which, as far as EU-crats are concerned, is like saying it doesn't exist. Meanwhile, more or less nonviolent "Islamization" isn't even on the charts.

Such Orwellian movements also eliminate the very concept of an "enemy," an "other side," and certainly an "other side" defined by its Islamic precepts of jihad and dhimmitude. Sure, we still have the Al Qaedists to kick around, that tiny-band-of-"extremists" we always hear about from political leaders. This same little band was invoked just this week by Sen. John McCain as "a tiny percentage of hundreds of millions of peaceful Muslims ... the vast majority of (whom) are trying to modernize their societies ... to build the same elements of a good life that all of us want."

Hmmm. If the vast majority of hundreds of millions of Muslims are trying to build "the good life," what's the problem? The problem is with the rhetoric. Any rational assessment of, say, the rapid entrenchment of Sharia across Europe — by no stretch the "good life" we "all" want —

turns it into sloppy goop. But rational assessments are out.

Blur is in. It's the post-Bush Doctrine way to define away that vexing problem of Us and Them.

Us, anyway.

Ramadan revisionism

10/8/07

I wasn't going to write about Ramadan in official Washington this fall season not again. But I just can't resist.

First, there are all the holiday trappings of this by-now annual column such seasonal staples as my all-time favorite "war on terror" quotation from Abu Qatada, the al Qaeda-linked cleric. I just love to trot it out around Ramadan after President Bush has said something utterly ignorant about Islam meaning peace, or, addressing the Muslim pooh-bahs he always has in to the White House for a fast-breaking Iftar dinner, about how the jihadists have "twisted" Islam.

"I am astonished by President Bush when he claims there is nothing in the Koran that justifies jihad violence in the name of Islam," Abu Qatada said about six years ago. "Is he some kind of Islamic scholar? Has he ever actually read the Koran?" Ah, me. Good stuff.

Then there's the holiday excitement of combing through the White House Iftar dinner guest list looking for unindicted co-conspirators. Since I had to put this column together before White House Iftar 2007, I turned to White House Ramadans past, reading through the president's old speeches-2001 through 2006 to see if I'd missed anybody he'd singled out for a mention.

And I had. White House Ramadan is so much better than bingo. In 2003 and 2004, Mr. Bush asked Faizul Khan, who is affiliated with the Saudi-funded Islamic Center of Washington and serves on the board of directors of the Islamic Society of North America, to give the blessing. This year, the Justice Department officially labeled Islamic Society as a U.S. branch of the Muslim Brotherhood, the movement aiming to establish a global Islamic empire, and also as an unindicted co-conspirator in the Hamas fund-raising Holy Land Foundation trial still awaiting a verdict in Dallas.

Then again, maybe the Islamic Society score doesn't count in this holiday game since the official co-conspiratorialness of the group is practically brand new. Still, as Steven Emerson has pointed out, the Islamic Society has "never condemned terror groups like Hamas and Hezbollah by name," which really should have come under White House consideration, if, that is, anyone at the White House ever considered anything. Heaven knows it's hard enough finding good moderates these days. Look too closely and they might find a Shariah supporter. Shariah, of course, is Islamic law — wholly antithetical to Western-style liberty.

Take Talal Eid. In 2006, Mr. Eid gave the blessing at the White House Ramadan dinner, and this year Mr. Bush appointed him to the U.S. Commission on International Religious Freedom. As Robert Spencer has reported, Mr. Eid is a Wahhabi-trained imam certified by the anti-American Muslim World League who has actually called for the establishment of Shariah courts in the United States to regulate the family affairs of American Muslims.

Is a proponent of Shariah in the United States someone the leader of the Western world should be honoring? Hmmm. Let's ask Ayaan Hirsi Ali, the courageous former Muslim opponent of Shariah from the Netherlands whose collaborator, Theo van Gogh, was assassinated in 2004 for their film critique of the Islamic repression of women under Shariah.

Oops. I forgot. This very Ramadan week, Ms. Ali had to leave Washington and return to the Netherlands for security reasons. Too bad Mr. Bush "forgot" to invite her to the White House before she left — not to mention all the other brave critics of Islamic repression, including Bat Ye'or, Brigitte Gabriel, Nonie Darwish and Wafa Sultan.

But in these post-September 11 days, only supporters of Shariah get those coveted holiday invites. Take the ambassadors from the countries of the Organization of the Islamic Conference (OIC). The organization not only coddles terrorists and lobbies against freedom of speech at the highest diplomatic levels, but it also supports a code of human rights derived from Shariah, which, of course, denies human rights to women and non-Muslims.

These are the people who sup with the president every Ramadan, and, I imagine, chuckle discreetly through Mr. Bush's remarks, as in 2006, about Islam's "commitment to tolerance and religious freedom." How do you say "we sure pulled the camel wool over his eyes" in Arabic? Under Shariah, of course, there is no religious freedom.

But who's checking? No one at this White House. What about the next administration? I hereby pledge to vote for the presidential candidate who promises to stop submitting to Shariah suppers at Ramadan — even though that means I'll have to think of something else to write about.

Stop letting them treat us like a turkey

11/30/07

What could the USS Kitty Hawk and Citigroup possibly have in common?

I'll start with the aircraft carrier because I'm still stewing over what happened when the People's Republic of China abruptly denied the USS Kitty Hawk and its accompanying ships and submarines their routine, scheduled Thanksgiving berth in Hong Kong, where hundreds of crew members' families had gathered (at considerable expense) to celebrate the holiday with their loved ones.

First, there was the nasty act itself. News accounts speculated about the "reason" — was it President Bush's recent meeting with the Dalai Lama? Our latest arms agreement with Taiwan? -- but there's no rationale worth gleaning beyond the fact the Chinese wished to snub us very publicly on a quintessential American holiday. And so they did.

Then there was our reaction, best described as muted. Indeed, "perplexed" was one of the stronger words used to describe the U.S. attitude, which was also quick to assert that future military exchanges and whatnot with the Communist Chinese wouldn't suffer.

Well, couldn't they suffer just a little bit? There's got to be a better U.S. response — somewhere between imitating a doormat and lobbing a nuclear warhead — to abusive Chinese gamesmanship. The Pentagon has now issued a formal protest of the incident, which includes a second even more egregious instance in which China denied access to two U.S. minesweepers seeking shelter in Hong Kong from a storm. But overall, as a nation, we slap a relentlessly happy face on things.

And that goes for all of us, certainly as consumers. The day after the Hong Kong Affront, millions of us set out on pilgrimages all across America to malls where we scooped up all manner of goods "made in China" without a second thought for the Kitty Hawk sailors chugging back to home port in Japan without seeing their families in Hong Kong. We weren't thinking of much besides that giant plasma TV at 40 percent off. We certainly weren't wondering whether it was (dare I say it?) patriotic to buy Chinese. And not simply because of this recent cat-and-mousing around. China is using the dollars we pay for heaps of stuff we don't need to bulk up as our military and political rival.

As consumers in a global economy where brand loyalty usually trumps national consciousness, we don't think of it that way. Partly that's because our leaders don't think of it that way, either. They certainly don't talk about it that way. "Money makes the world go around" sums up the conventional wisdom. Which is probably as good a point as any to bring in the Abu Dhabi Investment Authority's recent infusion of $7.5 billion into Citigroup.

In exchange, Abu Dhabi will receive a guaranteed, whopping 11 percent return on its investment, which analysts flag as an indicator of Citigroup's desperation. But there's something else about the deal, something few consider: The deal necessarily accelerates the Islamization of Western finance. The Abu Dhabi government is now Citigroup's largest stockholder. The second-largest stockholder is a Saudi prince — Prince Alwaleed bin Talal, the one whose millions then-Mayor of New York Rudy Giuliani turned down, Harvard and Georgetown snapped up, and who also owns 5.5 percent of Fox News.

Is this a great thing for America? Or is the Islamization of American banking a concern? All Western financial institutions are increasingly accommodating Islamic finance, with its adherence to Sharia (Islamic law) and the collection of zakat (charitable tax), which analysts such as Rachel Ehrenfeld and Jeffrey Imm tell us help finance jihadist indoctrination and terror groups. Do the financial mechanisms to support these anti-Western practices belong at the center of American finance?

Stunningly, the question doesn't seem to occur to the powers that be — including Congress, where hearings on Sharia finance would well serve the nation. In a paper called "Islamic Finance or Financing Islamism?" Alex Alexiev of the Center for Security Policy outlines the threat this way: "To put it simply, any Western institution that endorses Shariah-compliant products, ipso facto endorses the hateful Islamic ideology behind it, whether they know it or not. Shariah is an integral doctrine and there is no such thing as selecting just a few convenient Shariah tenets and rejecting the rest. By endorsing Shariah, Western banks end up becoming what Lenin called useful idiots or worse to the Islamists. And it is a very thin line between that and outright complicity in the Islamist agenda."

Something else for our leaders to become, er, perplexed about.

The Pentagon mantra: PC trumps security?

1/11/08

The year is 1942. The place, the Pentagon. A Berlin-born aide to the U.S. deputy secretary of Defense has learned that a military intelligence officer has not only read Hitler's "Mein Kampf," but is lecturing senior officers about Hitler's heretofore unexamined goals of world domination.

This schweinhund must go. At least, that's what the German-born staffer thinks. Did I mention he's fluent in German? That's partly why the deputy secretary of Defense relies so heavily on his aide's judgment on all things German, particularly when it comes to the War on Nazism's German outreach program. This program brings Nazi apologists into the inner sanctum of the American war machine ...

Sound crazy?

Travel forward to 1973. The deputy secretary of Defense's Soviet-born, Russian-speaking aide is gunning for the one intelligence officer who has boned up on Marx, Engels and Soviet military doctrine. Why? Because the officer refuses to "soften" his brief on communist ideology, and is presenting it to the military leadership — now hearing it for the first time since the Cold War began. If communist plans for global domination become common knowledge, the aide realizes, gazing thoughtfully at a blown-up photo of Soviet mouthpiece Vladimir Posner on his office wall, the Pentagon will surely change strategy and halt the USSR outreach program, which gives commie symps Pentagon access ...

Totally outlandish, right?

Once upon a time, yes. But this month, the Washington Times' Bill Gertz reported on a not entirely dissimilar real-life version of such fictions, the termination of Maj. Stephen Coughlin (USAR). Coughlin, a lawyer and reserve military intelligence officer, has been the Pentagon's sole specialist on Islamic law charged with lecturing senior officers on jihad doctrine — military leaders who have been fighting the so-called war on terror for years without an inkling of Islamic ideology. His contract with the Joint Staff will end in March, Gertz wrote, because Coughlin "had run afoul of a key aide" to the Deputy Secretary of Defense Gordon England.

That "key aide" is Cmdr. Hesham Islam (USN ret.), an Egyptian-born, Arabic-speaking Muslim whom Gordon England describes as "my interlocutor" and "personal, close confidante." According to Gertz, England's interlocutor and confidante confronted Stephen Coughlin seeking "to have Mr. Coughlin soften his views of Islamist extremism."

Note the irony in this choice of words. "Islamist" and "extremism," like "Islamofascism" and other euphemisms, are words that draw a PC curtain over mainstream Islam. They effectively shield the religion and its tenets from the scrutiny necessary to assess the ideology driving our jihadist enemies. Of course, lifting that PC curtain on Islam and its jihadist tenets is precisely the affect of Stephen Coughlin's Pentagon brief. It goes against what political correctness tells us; it also goes against what Islamic advocacy groups tell us.

For example, Ingrid Mattson, president of the Islamic Society of North America (ISNA), is someone who advocates decoupling the word "Islamic" from the word "terrorism" for discussions of, well, Islamic terrorism. Why do I mention this? ISNA is a group that has been strenuously "outreached" by Gordon England's Pentagon even as the Justice Department has officially labeled it a branch of the Muslim Brotherhood. Wonder if England ever thought much about the large picture of Mattson — head of what Justice has said is an MB front organization — hanging amid the photos on Hesham Islam's office wall.

What Hesham Islam wanted from Stephen Coughlin was a softer interpretation of Islamic law and jihad, and, as Gertz reported, in the process he slurred Coughlin as "a Christian zealot or extremist 'with a pen.' " Now Coughlin is out.

This high-level effort, in effect, to deny the connection between Islamic law and what the military calls the "enemy threat doctrine" should ring bells, not just in the military, but in Congress, which obviously has Pentagon oversight responsibilities. And what about the FBI? When a citizen is denounced as a "Christian zealot or extremist" shortly before his government contract is dropped, has a civil rights violation occurred?

More questions. Why is the deputy secretary of Defense engaged in Muslim "outreach" in the first place? And how good (safe) is his "outreach" advice if, to name a couple of examples, it brings ISNA into a bizarro relationship with the Pentagon, and sends a longtime apologist for assorted terrorists, Muslim Public Affairs Council's Salam Al-Marayati, on a Pentagon-sponsored trip to Guantanamo Bay? When such advice brings the military's woefully belated education on jihad to a halt, it becomes shockingly clear that the Pentagon is more concerned with political correctness than protecting the nation.

Obama bows to no one ... unless you're a Saudi king

4/13/09

Chances are good you haven't heard this one: that, while in Buckingham Palace last week, milling about with G-20 leaders, the current president of the United States bowed deeply at the waist, one knee bent, on meeting the current King, so-called, of Saudi Arabia, who did not bow back. Chances are even better you haven't seen the video.

That's because Big Media, from viewer-deprived networks to newspapers considering bailouts, have neither aired the video of the incident nor reported on it. ("The O'Reilly Factor" doesn't count.) Washington Post reporter Michael A. Fletcher's breezy dismissal of a reader's online query exemplifies media disinterest: "I'm not sure what the etiquette is for such greetings, but I'm sure the president was only trying to convey respect ... Remember some years ago when President Bush touched cheeks with and held the hand of a Saudi monarch during a visit to his Texas ranch? Another sign of respect. I would not make too much of it."

Well, I would.

The assorted supplications George W. Bush engaged in, from holding hands with and kissing Abdullah, to joining in a Saudi "sword dance" while trying to beg down the price of oil, made me sick then, and Barack Obama's obeisance to the protector of Mecca and Medina (widely available online if not in the "news") makes me sick now. But just as disturbing is the American reaction.

This includes, first, the unconscionable failure of media organizations to spare a few inches of column or seconds of airtime from Michelle Obama's campy cardigans for this deferential display by the United States toward Saudi Arabia. But much of the mainly conservative blog commentary on the incident, while welcome as bona fide signs of life out there, has come off as strangely beside the point.

Or, rather, as largely limited to one point: etiquette. It's true that Americans don't bow to royalty, period — a point made repeatedly in blogs expressing frosty outrage over the incident as though the Obama-Abdullah bow were no more than a generic breach of protocol. A Washington Times editorial hammered home this same abstraction.

But an American bow to Saudi Arabia is more than "unbecoming," as Clarice Feldman wrote at The American Thinker, more than "a simple but costly breakdown in basic command of protocol," as Camille Paglia wrote at Slate, more than "baseness," as Richard Brookhiser wrote at The Corner, and more than "the kind of rookie mistake you get from a president who was a state senator five years ago," as Michael Goldfarb wrote at the Weekly Standard blog. It was calumny on a historic level.

King Abdullah, after all, is the head of a state that is the very caricature of modern-day evil, a Sharia dictatorship that fosters religious repression, de facto slavery, subjugation of women, and, not least, the international export of jihad and Sharia through "charities," mosques, madrassas, textbooks, university endowments, Sharia finance and, of course, terrorists, some 15 of whom attacked the United States in 2001. Just last month, Abdullah elevated the delusionally hard-line interior minister Prince Nayef, who long promoted the crackpot theory that Saudis were not involved in 9/11 (it was the Jews, he said), to a direct line of succession to the Saudi throne. Abdullah himself has donated at least $1.35 million to Saudi telethons that raised $174 million for the families of Palestinian suicide bombers from Hamas and the al-Aqsa Martyrs Brigades. In 2007, Abdullah explicitly denounced the U.S. presence in Iraq as "illegitimate," thus encouraging attacks on Americans in Iraq, where, not incidentally, Saudis are thought to have carried out more suicide bombings than any other nationality.

That's just for starters. In other words, this is not a personage an American president can ever, ever show deference to without besmirching the memories and lives of the American dead and maimed.

But that's just what President Obama did (despite lame claims from the White House that Obama was just shaking hands), making this incident more than a simple gaffe.

But it's not much different from anything George W. Bush did. It's time to acknowledge the similarities between Presidents Obama and

Bush regarding Islam. Barack Obama hits the word "respect" repeatedly in regard to Islam, whose Sharia law, putting it mildly, disrespects non-Muslims and women; well, so did George W. Bush. Obama insists the United States is not at war with Islam; so did Bush. Who can forget the Bush mantra of "Islam is love" that began on 9/12? Maybe these Bush echoes account for the conservative block on really zapping the Obama bow here. Or maybe this is the consensus they want to live with.

Meanwhile, Obama's Bush-like approach is depicted as something new under the Arabian sun. Akbar Ahmed, visiting chairman of Islamic Studies at the U.S. Naval Academy, calls Obama "the first president to talk about respect for the Muslim world." Ridiculous.

What's not ridiculous is Ahmed's statement calling Obama "uniquely qualified ... to really reach out and change the mood of the relationship between America and the Islamic world."

Uniquely qualified indeed. Obama is the first Muslim-born U.S. president. Could that have something to do with the deepness of the bow?

Team O turns left on sanity with 'right-wing extremists'

4/17/09

I've got it.

After reading and rereading the surreal Department of Homeland Security intel report on "right-wing extremism" that clearly designates conservative political dissent as part of the threat, I finally figured out why it all seems so familiar.

First, there's the report's leading villain, the "military veteran" returning from war in Iraq and Afghanistan — the "potential lone wolf" terrorist with the lethal capabilities. That could raise goose bumps in anyone, right?

Then there are the "white supremacists" well known for their "longstanding exploitation of social issues such as abortion, interracial crime and same-sex marriage."

(I don't get the connection either.)

According to the government, we just might see a growing movement of similarly pro-life, pro-law-and-order, pro-marriage ... "white supremacists." Enough to make anyone hyperventilate, of course.

And what about the "right-wing extremist" who "adopts the immigration issue as a call to action"? Or the "many right-wing extremists" who "are antagonistic toward the new presidential administration and its perceived" — perceived? — "stance on a range of issues" including immigration, expanding government programs and gun control?

According to the report, such "right-wing extremists are increasingly galvanized by these concerns and leverage them as drivers for recruitment." Sounds like a GOP voter drive to me. Cue up "Psycho"-strains of shrieking violins.

The fact is, we've seen this cast of characters before — many times before — in all of the schlock Hollywood movies that year after year harvest a diseased crop of villains from the American heartland, endlessly returning them to the screen as the "crazed veteran," the "religious zealot" and the anti-immigration "Nazi." These are the stock villains — all racist, naturally — who are now similarly demonized in the government's report.

This fantastic worldview that sees the country imperiled by military heroes, traditional values and even border security meshes perfectly with the also-official flip side to such paranoid liberal fantasy: namely, the harmlessness of the Islamic brand of "extremism," which Homeland Security Secretary Janet Napolitano recently renamed, and with a straight face, "man-caused disasters." Hollywood, of course, doesn't touch such "extremism" either, sticking with right-wingers-gone-wild to the very last reel.

But Hollywood-fantasy-turned -Washington-reality isn't simply crummy entertainment. It presents a grave menace to political discourse in this country. "We want to move away from the politics of fear," Napolitano declared last month to explain her new secretary-caused euphemism for Islamic terrorism.

But not too far. That is, Napolitano, who supports the DHS report, is plenty content to deal in the politics of fear — just not fear of Islam. Fear of conservatism, however, is OK by her.

How to make it stick? The DHS report repeatedly reaches back for inspiration to the 1995 Oklahoma City bombing of a federal building, citing "military veteran" and domestic terrorist Timothy McVeigh, one of 42 million veterans who, not incidentally, have not blown up a federal building, as American Legion chief David Rehbein noted in an outraged letter to Napolitano. But while the DHS report is thin on specifics and devoid of sources, it nonetheless quite helpfully exposes the federal government's outrageous strategy to portray conservatism as "right-wing extremism."

The report defines the term this way: "Right-wing extremism in the United States can be broadly divided into those groups, movements, and adherents that are primarily hate-oriented (based on hatred of particular religious, racial or ethnic groups), and those that are mainly antigovernment, rejecting federal authority in favor of state or local authority, or rejecting government authority entirely. It may include groups and individuals that are dedicated to a single issue, such as opposition to abortion or immigration."

Presto — the federal government has just taken key conservative positions, from opposition to Islamic law to support for security along our Mexican border, and cast them as primitive, "primarily hate-oriented" pathologies that are therefore beyond civilized political discourse. So, too, is opposition to overweening federal powers and "single-issue" opposition to abortion. What we are seeing, in other words, is the most extraordinary governmental attempt in history to limit the spectrum of debate by demonizing a range of positions as "right-wing extremism." This attempt is surely not only unconstitutional but also un-American.

But not in the Obama era. This is a time when the following statement would surely set off a red alert with all federal, state, local and tribal law enforcement authorities who received Homeland's report:

"What we have to do is bring back the recognition that the people of this country can solve its problems. I still believe the answer to any problem lies with the people. I believe in state's rights and I believe in people doing as much as they can for themselves at the community level and at the private level. I believe we have distorted the balance of our government today by giving powers that were never intended to be given in the Constitution to that federal establishment."

In the language of Homeland Security, which "right-wing extremist" preparing for "right-wing radicalization and recruitment" said that?

Ronald Reagan.

A sudden turn against Israel

3/26/10

It's mind-boggling how quickly the Jerusalem housing project realigned the stars over Israel to shine down on a new, official vision of the Jewish state as a drag on our interests in the world — endangering the lives of our troops.

That was the message Vice President Biden delivered in Israel this month: "What you're doing here undermines the security of our troops ..." according to Israeli media. The White House denied it.

That was the feeling the president conveyed in treating visiting Israeli president Benjamin Netanyahu like an international leper this week (no pictures, no press, no statements, no nothing).

And very sensationally, that was the narrative CENTCOM Commander Gen. David Petraeus put in writing to the U.S. Senate (sending hero-worshipping conservatives into denial) as noted in last week's column.

Disregarding the impetus of 14 centuries of Muslims' doctrinally driven aggression on non-Muslims, Petraeus advanced a line that echoed the Arab League's: namely, that "Arab anger over the Palestinian question" drives violence throughout the CENTCOM region, which includes Iraq and Afghanistan, and enhances the powers of Iran and al-Qaida. One prominent conservative commentator who strongly supported the Bush-Petraeus policy in Iraq expressed his shock to me in an e-mail: "I would think that Jewish leaders would be appalled by Petraeus' statement ('The Jews are protecting their property with the blood from the bodies of our dead young men!!!') It is about 95 percent the way to the 'blood libel' that, I hate to admit, Christians used in the Middle Ages against the Jewish people."

And it energized the Israel bashers, from Stephen Walt, who quoted Petraeus in a Washington Post op-ed, to Robert Malley, erstwhile Middle East adviser to candidate Obama — let go for his contact with Hamas, who bluntly underscored the same line at a conference: "Israeli actions are threatening U.S. actions and military presence in Iraq and Afghanistan."

Meanwhile, Palestinians in Gaza launched about a dozen terror rockets into Israel, drawing zero international comment. Next, Great Britain took the extreme measure of expelling an Israeli diplomat over British passport forgeries used in the alleged Mossad assassination of a Hamas terrorist. Is the international noose around Israel drawing tighter or is the "peace process" just intensifying? When executing terrorists and building apartment houses violates "peace," and launching rockets is part of the "process," it's impossible to tell the difference.

Obviously, there is more to this than apartment houses. In his book "The Legacy of Islamic Antisemitism," Andrew Bostom explains the doctrinal basis not just of Islamic antisemitism — an eternal driver of the jihad on Israel — but also of the concept that there exists a kind of eternal right of return of Muslims to any former Muslim conquest. "All of historical Palestine," he writes, "whose pre-Islamic inhabitants, Jews, Samaritans and Christians were conquered by jihad in the fourth decade of the seventh century, is considered 'fay territory.'" In other words, having once been conquered by Islam, such land is considered by Muslims to be "a permanent part of the Dar al Islam, where Islamic law must forever prevail." According to this thinking, Israel, governed by "usurper" infidel Jews who are no longer a subjugated dhimmi people, "must be destroyed in a collective jihad by the entire Muslim community."

Hard to ignore such a potent source of aggrieved aggression. But we do, and to the point of denying its very existence. And then what? Oskar Freysinger of the Swiss People's Party, famous for leading the campaign to ban minaret construction in Switzerland, when explaining why his party, known for its anti-Islamization policies, had always supported Israel, once told me: "We are well aware that if Israel disappears, we lose a vanguard. They (the Israelis) are fighting our fight, in fact. As long as the Muslims are concentrated on Israel, it's not so hard for us. But as soon as Israel will have disappeared, they will come to get the other part" — namely, Europe.

What Freysinger sees better than most (including Israelis) is the apocalyptic dimension to global jihad, regardless of the "peace process" and other camouflage. Not only are we witnessing what could be the final stages of jihad on Israel; the United States is now openly supporting the wrong side.

How is Israel the guilty party?

6/18/10

We may not live in an Islamic world — yet — but we do live with an Islamic worldview. Witness the uniformly Islamicized consensus that met Israel's successful if costly defense of its Gaza blockade.

The blockade, by the way, is a defensive measure that Israel devised after Hamas terrorists were elected to govern Israel-ceded Gaza in 2005 and — no surprise to any student of jihad — decided to continue their charter-commanded war on Israel, raining down nearly 10,000 rockets onto Israeli civilians.

The rocketing, of course, was OK with the Islamicized consensus. What wasn't OK happened on the night of May 31 when Israeli commandos, lightly armed with paintball guns and emergency sidearms, unexpectedly battled aboard the Mavi Marmara against trained fighters with ties to the Turkish government, specifically to the ruling AKP party of Prime Minister Tayyip Erdogan, to maintain Israel's lawful blockade.

These hostile forces were organized by the Turkish terror-linked organization known as IHH (which purchased the boat from an AKP entity). They were armed with knives, axes, clubs, Molotov cocktails and more, and they formed a militant cadre barely camouflaged by the "humanitarian cargo" (including night vision goggles, bulletproof vests and nearly a million euros) and other "peace activists," among whom were Muslim Brothers, Hamas partisans (at least one Hamas operative was later arrested), and members of the Turkish supremacist group BBP. At least five "passengers" publicly expressed their wish to become "shahids," or Islamic martyrs. Three got their wish in the fighting that ensued after the ship refused to yield to the Israeli Navy. Some of the Israeli blockade-defenders were wounded, a few seriously; nine jihadist blockade-runners were killed.

An Islamicized world wrath came down on Israel. And with such force as to obliterate what remnants of the Western system — logic, morality, history - somehow still existed. Simultaneous to the instant apotheosis of blockade-running jihadis into ocean-going pacifists came an avalanche of rage so violent as to reverse the gravitational pull of global politics entirely. Or so it seems.

Thus, Islamicized international pressure weighs on Israel's Netanyahu to justify, to apologize — and not Turkey's Erdogan, who supports the jihadist outlaws. Outrage boils over at the defense of a lawful blockade to protect civilians from terrorist attack, and not at the Hamas attackers, or at the Turks and others who aid them — and, again, with the Turkish head of state's support. While Israelis have reason to re-examine the efficiency of their strategy to maintain the blockade, the only so-called "impartial" international investigation required is not, as demanded, into Israel's line of defense, but rather into Turkey's destabilizing culpability in the aggression.

Pure and simple, this was an act of jihadist provocation, even an act of war. If the Western system were still functional, it would be Turkey called to account in the international arena, not Israel; it would be Turkey pressured to unmask itself as a fomenter of global jihad — not Israel for defending itself against it.

If.

But the Western system no longer functions; it takes its lead from "peace activists." And so --- and this is the tragedy of Western collapse - it is Turkey that the West appeases. There is no logic to this; there is fear. There's no morality here; only dhimmitude.

History, meanwhile, is ignored. We hide from the gravity of resurgent jihad in the Ottoman land of the last caliphate, deaf to the declarations of cultural and religious war that Erdogan, for one, has always made, from the 1970s, when he engaged in anti-Semitic agitprop with a play he wrote, directed and acted in known as "Mas-kom-Ya," an acronym for Mason, komunist (communist), and Yahudi (Jew); to the 1990s, when he invoked jihad with the lines, "the mosques are our barracks, the domes our helmets, the minarets our bayonets and the faithful our soldiers"; to today, as he exhorts Turks in Europe to cultural conquest, declaring, "Assimilation is a crime against humanity."

Sounds like the call of the marauder to me. But the United States, pondering "Who lost Turkey?" plugs its ears and scapegoats Israel, or, just as fantastic, blames Europe for a vestigial self-preservation instinct that prevents it from committing demographic suicide by admitting 78 million Muslims into the union.

Anything for "peace."

Uncle Sucker, world's rent-a-cop?

3/25/11

I'll admit there is an argument — a thin, riddled, web of an argument — that it was U.S. interests that drove military interventions gone wrong in Iraq and Afghanistan. I don't buy the argument: It morphed into a nation-building fantasy, it became disastrously, tragically and recklessly mistaken. But I can see at least that tarnished glimmer of national interest flash in the sludge before sinking from sight.

Nothing like this is to be found in the sands of Libya. This is why the weirdo-bizarre assault on Gaddafi's forces led, but supposedly not really, by the United States under order of the U.N. Security Council (motley crew) and the Arab League (rogue's gallery), crossed a fat red line. The president of the United States sent the U.S. military, already stretched and worn by darn near a decade of wars, into harm's way for no compelling American reason. And I mean none. The sudden whim to rid the planet of Gaddafi, while never a bad notion, is, if anything, oddly anticlimactic after his Bush-era debut as a newly minted ally in the "war on terror." Funny thing: "ally" sounds like a ghastly stretch, but WikiLeaks tells us Gaddafi was in fact most cooperative in providing anti-jihad intelligence — which may or may not have been credible. Still, he should know. It was Libyans, according to a 2007 West Point study, who made the strongest showing, per capita, of foreign insurgents in Iraq. It's hard not to believe that some who didn't end up dead or in Gitmo are now "rebels" receiving U.S. air and sea support.

Ain't it ironic? Or something. It helps explain why Sunni Islam's leading cleric Yusuf al-Qaradawi — proponent of jihad, Shariah, the caliphate, the Muslim Brotherhood, suicide-bombing all Israelis and U.S. soldiers — is supporting the rebels. According to the Global Muslim Brotherhood Daily Report, the umbrella group for anti-Gaddafi forces prominently features Qaradawi's endorsement on its website.

There's more. Abu Yahya al-Libi, the al-Qaida star-honcho who escaped from American clutches in Afghanistan, posted a rah-rah video on jihadist websites urging the Libyan "rebels" to keep fighting Gaddafi, predicting dire consequences from defeat.

Just think: Those are "our" rebs, too. I can't imagine the crew of the USS Kearsarge, now in the Mediterranean, would like that very much. Or the pilots flying F-15s over Libya, either. But what about our Congress? Flatlining. As for President Obama, if it isn't impeachable to fight on behalf of America's enemies, what is?

The fact is, when it comes to American interest, Obama couldn't care less. He demonstrated that by seeking and taking America's marching orders solely from the United Nations and the Arab League, without even saying howdy-do to Congress (whose answering chorus of silence is a disgrace), later kicking soccer balls around Rio instead of addressing the American people as to why he was ordering another U.S. military intervention — this one with al-Qaida support.

It's as if Obama considers the interest he serves as being above all that Congress-American-people-stuff. "Humanitarians" are like that, and what we're seeing is so-called humanitarian military intervention, the doctrine is promulgated by Obama's human rights adviser Samantha Power. Known as a genocide expert, Power has gone so far as to argue for the insertion of a "mammoth" American "protection" force into Israeli-Palestinian environs to prevent "human rights abuses" — code for neutralizing Israeli self-defense.

Writing at National Review Online, Stanley Kurtz explains: "Obama dithered when it was simply a matter of replacing Gaddafi, yet quickly acted when slaughter in Benghazi became the issue. What Samantha Power and her supporters want is to solidify the principle of " responsibility to protect" in international law. That requires a "pure" case of intervention on humanitarian grounds. Power's agenda would explain why Obama acted when he acted, and why the public rationale for action has not included regime change." Kurtz continues: "Yet Obama has so far been reluctant to fully explain any of this to either Congress or the American public, perhaps because he realizes that the ideological basis of his actions would not be popular if openly admitted."

Nor would the non-nationalist basis of his actions. If this continues, don't be surprised to find Uncle Sucker "promoted" to World's Permanent Rent-a-Cop, setting up the next no-fly-zone over Israel to intervene for the "humanitarian" cause of Hamas in Gaza.

What's the 'flicker' Uncle Sucker's helping?

4/1/11

This week, the commander of NATO, U.S. Adm. James Stavridis, let the jihad out of the bag. He told the U.S. Senate that among the Libyan rebels—you know, our guys, the ones on whose behalf we've fired off about $1 billion worth of ordinance at Libya—"we have seen flickers in the intelligence of potential al-Qaida, Hezbollah."

That means the U.S. military is fighting on behalf of the flickers that took down the World Trade Center in 2001 and the Marine Barracks in Beirut in 1983.

Does anyone care?

Next question: Wouldn't we all salute if Stavridis had next told the Senate that, as a result of this heinous policy, which orders U.S. forces to participate in a mission to advance the cause of global jihad, he would be stepping down from his command in protest?

Sigh. Instead, Stavridis reassured the Senate, "We are examining very closely the content, composition, the personalities, who are the leaders of these opposition forces," he said.

Next question: Do I feel better?

The Daily Mail picked up the story, noting: "The comments have sparked an embarrassing diplomatic spat between NATO and the U.S. ambassador to the United Nations Susan Rice, who disagreed that al-Qaida was involved in the rebel movement. 'I would like to think I'm reading much of the same stuff and no,' Ms. Rice told Fox News when asked whether she had seen any evidence to support Stavridis' assessment."

No evidence. Not even a shimmer, according to Ms. Rice. That's funny. I've been reading, not intelligence reports, but regular news stories about the predilection for jihad among the people of eastern Libya, which is the seat of the rebellion, and which, according to a 2007 West Point study, sent more jihadis per capita to Iraq to fight American forces than any other region in the world. One of their military leaders, Abdel Hakim al-Hasidi, is reported to have fought for years in Afghanistan—and, to be precise, that would have been against us and for bin Laden—or so he used to brag, back a week or so ago when it wasn't politically risky.

Now the rebs are practically media-savvy, as the Independent discovered: "'We are not al-Qaida,' were the first words of Khalid Arshad Ali as he dusted the triggering mechanism of an anti-aircraft artillery gun. 'We are Mujahedin. We are here to fight for Libya and no one else. We are Muslims in this country and we are all Sunnis. We know that Gaddafi is getting paid by the Jews. We know that Israel is supplying him with special guns. He is not a proper Muslim and it is our duty to fight him.' "

Now, I did say "practically." But hey—what's wrong with Uncle Sucker given a helping hand to a few self-described "Mujahedin" who can't keep their poison for Jews from spraying all over themselves? Certainly, no one in Congress seems to mind. Maybe our representatives got the good word from U.S. ambassador to Libya Gene Cretz, whom the Wall Street Journal recently described as "point man for U.S. contacts with the rebels." Cretz tells us the rebs are totally on top of it, that they actually caught "maybe three or four" members of an al-Qaida affiliate trying to infiltrate.

Phew. That was close. Wish we could thank them—"heckuva job, rebels"—only we don't know who the rebels are. Asked about those "flickers" of al-Qaida and Hezbollah among rebel forces, Secretary of State Hillary Clinton said: "We do not have any specific information about specific individuals from any organization who are part of this, but of course, we're still getting to know those who are leading the

Transitional National Council. And that will be a process that continues."

Not to worry; the president doesn't. "So far, they're saying the right things," President Barack Obama said Tuesday on "CBS Evening News" when asked about Libyan opposition leaders.

And how. They even issued a "vision statement," which, according to the Guardian uses all the right words: "transparent," "empowerment," "tolerance," "green" ...

Green?

No "flickers" of jihad, but plenty of concern for the environment. Uh-huh.

Any flickers of intelligence in the minds of our leaders?

U.S. and Pakistan allied forever? Really?

5/6/11

Stirrings of life on Capitol Hill: Rep. Ted Poe, R-Texas, has introduced a bill to stop distribution of $3 billion in aid that Congress appropriated for Pakistan this year until the State Department certifies that Pakistan was not harboring Osama bin Laden Unless it were to serve as a rubber stamp, such a bill could be a step toward long overdue accountability on Pakistan.

It at least offers a way to call out the pathological inertia that drives the U.S.-Pakistani relationship not forward, but in circles, causing dizzy policy-making. Even after Pakistan appears to have been caught in flagrante delicto with Public Enemy No. 1, House Speaker John Boehner, for example, was still prattling on about Pakistan being "critical to breaking the back of al-Qaida." Like the battered spouse who can't see what's wrong with another shiner, Boehner insisted: "This is not a time to back away from Pakistan. We need more engagement, not less." He also said: "We both benefit from having a strong bilateral relationship."

He's half right. With $20 billion in U.S. aid filling Pakistani coffers since 9/11, I see how Pakistan benefits. But I don't see how the U.S. benefits — unless "partnering" with Pakistan while it supports four militant jihad networks in and around Afghanistan, or paying Pakistan billions while it more than doubles its nuclear arsenal, are things that count as benefits. If they do, the attacks on 9/11 were a brilliant stroke of luck. This week, I heard an expert panel hosted by The National Interest magazine discuss aspects of the U.S.-Pakistan relationship, so far the sleeper topic in this post-bin-Laden era. I got the same sense of inertia, that U.S.-Pakistani relations are our permanent ball and chain, coming from speakers and some audience members alike. You can't just turn your back on Pakistan's 200 million people and 100 nuclear weapons, a war college professor told me, just as though the USA were a mouse locked in a death-gaze with a boa constrictor. Why not? We certainly turned on a dime when it came to breaking with Egypt and Libya, both of which yielded jihad intelligence, peace with Israel in Egypt's case, and a cache of nuclear weaponry from Libya now in Oak Ridge, Tenn.—greater benefits than anything coming out of Pakistan.

But like hostages self-handcuffed to Pakistan's nukes, we remain locked in a dysfunctional relationship. There is a great irony in this given that Pakistan remaining nuclear-free was once the criterion for U.S. aid in the first place. This was the crux of the 1985 Pressler Amendment (named for Sen. Larry Pressler, R-S.D.) that required the president to certify annually that Pakistan did not have an explosive nuclear device as a condition of .U.S aid, and which halted the flow of U.S. government aid to Pakistan from 1990 to 1994.

This law should have regulated all related nuclear anti-proliferation policy, but it was not to be. Both the Bush (the father) and the Clinton administrations chafed at it, seeking ways around it, undermining the carrot-stick order the law set until finally the Clinton administration was able to end sanctions on Pakistan in 1995. As the New York Times noted at the time, the Clinton White House "argued that it is more important to improve relations with a country that it calls a large, moderate Islamic democracy in a troubled region than to punish Pakistan for building a weapons arsenal that it is not about to dismantle."

In other words, thanks largely to the first Bush and Clinton White Houses, the United States lost this battle of wills and set out to "improve relations" by paying tribute to the victor. This, of course, didn't translate into leverage, either. After-the-nuclear-fact sanctions went back into effect in 1998 when India and Pakistan both tested nuclear bombs, but after 9/11, George W. Bush had the bright idea that Pakistan, despite ties to the Taliban organization then sheltering al-Qaida, was the perfect ally for the "war on terror."

Billions of dollars later, we know how that story came out, but is it written in stone? That's the question Rep. Poe's Pakistan Accountability Act at least gives us pause to consider, whether we really have to remain in (and pay for) a sham alliance with a failed nuclear state on the Other Side—forever.

Libyan rebels are a rogues' gallery

8/26/11

Here are three things Americans need to know about the Libyan "rebels" that the U.S. government isn't telling us.

One: The inspiration of the Libyan war is as much anti-Western as it is anti-Gadhafi.

The "Day of Rage" that kick-started the Libyan war on Feb. 17 marked the fifth anniversary of violent protests in Benghazi, which included an assault on the Italian consulate during which at least 11 were killed. The 2006 mayhem, as John Rosenthal has reported, during which consulate staff was evacuated after 1,000 to several thousand men tried to storm and burn the building, may be linked to the Italian TV appearance two days earlier of Italian minister Roberto Calderoli. It was then that Calderoli, in defiance of worldwide Islamic rioting against cartoons of Muhammad in a tiny Danish newspaper, revealed he was wearing an undershirt decorated with such a cartoon. In remarks widely reported in Arab media, Calderoli explained that "the gesture was a matter of a 'battle for freedom.'" The minister said: "When they (the cartoon rioters) recognize our rights, I'll take off the shirt."

Unfortunately—and not just for the Italian minister—Calderoli's boss, Italian Prime Minister Silvio Berlusconi, didn't recognize those rights. One day after the Benghazi rioting ("We feared for our lives," the consul general's wife told the Italian newspaper Corriere della Sera), Calderoli resigned, a political collapse indicative of Western tendencies to renounce rights that conflict with Islamic law (Shariah).

Two: The anti-Gadhafi, anti-Western forces that NATO power has brought to apparent victory through an air war and not-so-secret deployment of special forces (so far costing U.S. taxpayers $1 billion) include jihadist forces the U.S. and NATO allies have been fighting for the past decade in Iraq and Afghanistan.

Captured al-Qaida documents analyzed at West Point reveal that not only did Libya send far more recruits per capita to fight with al-Qaida in Iraq than any other nation (including Saudi Arabia), but also that the "rebel" stronghold of Darnah sent more recruits per capita than any other city. Bonus info: 85 percent of Libyan recruits in Iraq listed their "work" as "suicide bombers."

This Libyan surge, the report explains, may have been due to the "increasingly cooperative relationship" with al-Qaida of the Libyan Islamic Fighting Group (LIFG). What is the LIFG? Designated a terrorist organization by the United States in 2004, the LIFG is a prominent faction among anti-Gadhafi forces today. Little wonder the Los Angeles Times discovered there are "at least 20 former Islamic militant leaders in battlefield roles" in Libya (while what the paper called "hundreds of Islamists" are either "participating or watching from the sidelines").

These include LIFG leader Abdelhakim Belhaj, described in recent days as the rebel commander in Tripoli. Another rebel leader and LIFG member, Abu Sufian Ibrahim Ahmed Hamuda bin Qumu, is also an ex-Gitmo detainee, as The New York Times has pointed out. And another rebel leader, Abdul Hakim al-Hasadi, as John Rosenthal has reported, admitted to Italian media earlier this year not only to "fighting against

U.S. troops in Afghanistan, but also to recruiting Libyans to fight against American forces in Iraq." Some of those same recruits "have come back and today are on the front at Ajdabiya," al-Hasadi explained, referring to a northeastern Libyan town. "They are patriots and good Muslims, not terrorists. The members of al-Qaida are also good Muslims and are fighting against the invader," al-Hasadi added.

Three: The draft constitution of the anti-Gadhafi forces cites "Shariah" as the "principal source of legislation."

Shariah is Islamic law, the basis of conquest or control of non-Muslims, conscience, speech and other Western-style liberties. Not too surprisingly, rebel spokesman Mustafa Abdul Jalil, former Libyan justice minister, sports a "zabibah," the forehead bruise of fanatical adherence to Islamic law. He also has animus toward Israel on the brain. WikiLeaks tells us, as Andrew Bostom has reported: "In the course of the discussion of the Criminal Code (with U.S. Ambassador Gene A. Cretz in 2010), Abdul Jalil abruptly changed the subject from freedom of speech to the 'Libyan people's concern about the U.S. government's support for Israel.'" In 1998, Abdul Jalil grotesquely sentenced six Bulgarian nurses to death in a notorious show trial.

Such is the man touted as one of the powers-to-be in post-Gadhafi Libya, which U.S. government officials, such as Assistant Secretary of State Jeffrey Feltman, promise will be "moderate," "modern" and "secular." But don't laugh too hard. The joke is on us.

Israel Is On Its Own In War Against Terrorism

7/13/12

The *Washington Free Beacon* reported this week on the continuing omission of Israel from a U.S.-sponsored organization called the Global Counterterrorism Forum (GCTF). At a recent forum meeting in Spain, Maria Otero, U.S. undersecretary of state for civilian security, democracy and human rights, delivered a speech titled "Victims of Terrorism," but, in her roll call of victims, she didn't mention Israel. The conference at which she spoke was described as a "high-level conference on the victims of terrorism," but Israel wasn't a participant.

It bears repeating because it is so fantastic: At an international conference devoted to victims of terrorism, the world's leading victim or, better, leading target of terrorism — Israel — was nowhere in sight, or mind.

Welcome to the GCTF — U.S. counterterrorism's new "normal." This 30-member organization got its official start last September as a "major initiative" of the Obama administration when Secretary of State Hillary Clinton announced its launch in New York.

It was quite an occasion; Hillary curled her hair. Seated next to her Turkish co-chairman, ensconced amid ministers from Algeria, Egypt, Indonesia, Jordan, Morocco, Pakistan, Qatar, Saudi Arabia, the United Arab Emirates and 18 other miscellaneous member-states plus the European Union, she then said the magic words: "From London to Lahore, from Madrid to Mumbai, from Kabul to Kampala, it's innocent civilians who have been targeted ..."

Jerusalem, Tel Aviv, Ashkelon? Poof, gone. And that's the point: This new counterterrorism organization, with its related counterterrorism center coming soon to Abu Dhabi, is Judenfrei. Not coincidentally, it is also heavily Islamic. Eleven member-states — slightly more than one-third of the organization's membership — also belong to the Organization of Islamic Cooperation (OIC), a bloc of 56 Islamic countries working to impose Islamic law (Shariah) on the world. Six of those 11 members additionally belong to the Arab League. Both groups have defined "terrorism" to exclude Israeli victims (sometimes U.S. soldiers), and "terrorists" to exclude groups dedicated to the destruction of Israel, such as Hamas and Hezbollah. It is no wonder the Arab-Islamic members would now unite in "counterterrorism" without Israel.

What is both shocking and shameful, however, is that the U.S. would, too. It shows that the U.S. has implicitly but clearly accepted the Arab League/OIC definitions of terrorism and terrorists.

As in Libya, where the U.S. supported the jihad-linked side, as in Egypt (same), as in Syria (same), this side-switching sparks scant comment. Oh, sure, there was some media yapping last month when Hillary jetted to Istanbul to pronounce another Israel-free incantation about efforts to "defeat extremist ideology." Two — count 'em, two — U.S. senators (independent Joe Lieberman of Connecticut and Republican Mark Kirk of Illinois) wrote her letters. But such complaints are nothing next to the smiles and cooperation coming our way from the Islamic core of the GCTF. And it was so easy! Why didn't we think of this before? All we have to do is see things the way the Islamic world does; pretend things like Israel don't exist (just as maps in Arab countries already indicate); and insist that Islam is a boon to mankind — not the animating doctrine of global jihad against Israel and the wider West.

I would like to say this is all something President Barack Obama initiated, but such appeasement goes back a long way. If we look to the Gulf War in 1990-1991, we see this same denial of Israel's existence take shape in the makeup of President George H.W. Bush's "international coalition" — sans Israel. The same is true in 2003 with the formation of President George W. Bush's "coalition of the willing" in Iraq (also Afghanistan) -- sans Israel.

These omissions were in no way due to Israel's unwillingness to join the "war on terror." They were due to the same Islamic pressure in force today. Both Bushes bowed to it, accepting a state of dhimmitude (inferiority of non-Muslims under Islam) for the high privilege of spilling American blood and treasure into the ungrateful desert. Israel, both Bushes agreed with their Islamic "allies," just wasn't fit to fight on Islamic sand. Thus, Israel was excluded from these wartime alliances.

Such dhimmitude only intensifies, as the latest developments show. Under the Bushes, after all, while Israel was not permitted to fight alongside coalition forces, at least it was still recognized for withstanding more than 60 years of Islamic terrorist attacks. Today, under the auspices of the Obama administration, Israel no longer rates mention even as a victim. "Big Satan" has thrown "Little Satan" to the sharks. Which says two things about Big Satan. Our institutions now see the world from the Islamic perspective, and, as far as the sharks go, we're next.

Why are we handing Muslim extremists the house keys?

8/3/12

Two weeks ago, I wrote about the handful of House Republicans, led by Rep. Michele Bachmann of Minnesota, who sent letters in June to inspectors general at five government departments, asking them to investigate evidence of Muslim Brotherhood influence on U.S. government policymaking. The Muslim Brotherhood is a global Islamic movement engaged, according to the group's own internal document, on a "grand jihad" in North America to destroy "Western civilization from within." To date, the inspectors general haven't responded.

Nonetheless, Bachmann and her colleagues — Trent Franks of Arizona, Louie Gohmert of Texas, Tom Rooney of Florida and Lynn Westmoreland of Georgia — have focused attention on the disastrous policy of bringing members of known Muslim Brotherhood fronts and their associates into Uncle Sam's policymaking chain. The representatives' letters went to inspectors general at State, Justice, Defense, Homeland Security and the Office of the National Intelligence Director. These government nerve centers are increasingly advancing policies American leaders once would have excoriated for supporting the enemies of this country.

Is it by chance, for example, that director of national intelligence James Clapper, reading from prepared notes, absurdly described the Muslim Brotherhood to the House Intelligence Committee last year as a "largely secular" organization? Is it an accident that in June the State

Department issued a visa to Hani Nour Eldin of Egypt to meet with senior White House officials? Eldin is a member of Gama'a al-Islamiyya, a terrorist organization once led by Omar Abdel Rahman, "the blind sheikh" convicted of the first attack on the World Trade Center. In the person of Rahman's successor, Refai Ahmed Taha, the group is one of the five signatories of Osama bin Laden's February 1998 "World Islamic Front Statement Urging Jihad Against Jews and Crusaders." Isn't it imperative to review the policy mechanism that permitted a member of bin Laden's jihad front into the White House?

According to our elected officials, the answer is no. Not one House member, Democrat, Republican or tea party, has come out in solidarity with the National Security Five. Typically, the mainstream media have reacted not by digging up facts themselves (what are they, journalists?), but rather by throwing mud on Michele Bachmann. "Stop 'witch-hunting' Huma Abedin, top aide to Hillary Clinton," is the war cry from CNN to USA Today. Many conservative outlets, such as Fox and The Washington Examiner, are strangely silent.

To be sure, one of the Bachmann letters notes the case of Huma Abedin — a confidante of the secretary of state whose family has dense ties to Muslim Brotherhood organizations. She has become the human face used to distract from the overarching national security issue. Honest answers to the wide array of questions the House members have asked would expose high elected officials in both parties as dupes of our enemies, at best. The American people would find out how Uncle Sam came to support al-Qaida in Libya; Muslim Brothers in Egypt; and, now, al-Qaida and Muslim Brothers in Syria. An honest investigation would spotlight the internal process that led Uncle Sam to sponsor a new international counterterrorism organization without Israel. The shameful fact is, our power-elites don't want these questions answered because the answers would threaten their hold on power.

Bachmann & Co. haven't alleged wrongdoing on Abedin's part. Rather, their question turns on the process that permitted a person with close family ties to an array of world Islamic movements and figures hostile to the United States to gain the security clearance Abedin requires to serve alongside the secretary of state.

I looked over the lengthy Form 86 that federal employees fill out to apply for national security positions. One portion is devoted to an applicant's relatives, with a question about relatives' affiliations with any "foreign movement." If Abedin answered fully — and there are stiff penalties for failing to do so — she would have noted, for starters, that her mother, Saleha Abedin, belongs to the Muslim Sisterhood (the Brotherhood's auxiliary, primarily for relatives of prominent Brothers) and serves on the board of the International Islamic Council for Dawah and Relief, a group banned in Israel for supporting Hamas. Saleha

Abedin has been a representative of the Muslim World League, whose affiliates have been charged by the U.S. government with funding terrorism. Any ensuing investigation would turn up Saleha's work with the Institute of Muslim Minority Affairs, where she edits the journal that Huma, too, worked on for a dozen years. That same institute was founded by Huma's father in Saudi Arabia with the assistance and long-term involvement of Abdullah Omar Naseef. Naseef was secretary-general of the Muslim World League and also founded the Rabita Trust, a U.S.-designated international terrorist organization with ties to al-Qaida.

There's more, but just imagine the light dawning on the background-checker: So, Ms. Abedin, let me get this straight: Your folks, and you, too, worked with a guy who founded a terrorist organization linked to al-Qaida, your mom's on the board of a group banned in Israel for supporting Hamas, and you want top-secret clearance to work for the secretary of state.

Then what happened?

What is Terrorism, Anyway?

Whose definition of terrorism?

10/16/01

Early last month, about a million years ago, the United States and Israel turned their backs on the international community and walked out on a United Nations conference on racism in Durban. Remember why? As Secretary of State Colin Powell crisply explained at the time, "You do not combat racism [with a conference] ... that singles out only one country in the world, Israel, for censure and abuse."

Those, of course, were the good old days, back before our nation had to acknowledge how much 6,000 people, two hundred stories, five rings and four airplanes meant to its peace and well-being. In retrospect, washing our hands of Durban's rising bile came naturally enough, an expression of high principle rather than high emotion. In other words, it was pretty easy back then to behave well. As far the United States was concerned, it was still a war of words, not deeds. No more. Now, as our government tries to stitch together a wide-ranging, international coalition against terrorism, we find ourselves seeking common ground — some ground, any ground — with many of the same states that only weeks ago we left in our diplomatic dust. And it turns out, those same states, largely members of the Arab and Muslim world, are slandering Israel again, this time not regarding such old saws as "racism" or "colonialism," but on the dire topic of terrorism.

It sounds fantastic. But having left the international coalition wide open to any country "committed" to ending terrorism, the United States has left something else wide open: the definition of terrorism itself. As a result, Arab and Muslim leaders have cranked up a massive disinformation campaign to depict Israel — war-weary, terror-targeted Israel — as a fountainhead of "terrorism" second only, perhaps, to Osama bin Laden.

First, there is the name-calling. From Mecca's Grand Mosque in Saudi Arabia, Islam's most sacred mosque, Sheik Saleh bin Hamid declared his support for an international coalition to fight terrorism—citing Israel as "a living example of terrorism in practice." Yasser Arafat, one of the great charlatans of modern times, briefly displaced his suicide-bombing countrymen in the news this week to "demand" that the nations of the world stop Israeli "terrorism." Meanwhile, in mostly Muslim Malaysia, Prime Minister Mahathir Mohamad offered to support the international coalition if only the United States and Britain would pick their terrorist-targets better: "I would support them," he said, "if they wanted to take action against Israel." Acting on the counsel of Messrs. bin Hamid, Arafat and Mohamad might not do much to end the threat of terrorism as we know it, but it would obviously do wonders for keeping that "international coalition" together.

Second, there is the "debate" about the "meaning" of terrorism. At a recent summit in Qatar, the Organization of the Islamic Conference (OIC), the world's largest Muslim body, came up with an utterly baseless distinction between blowing up American civilians and blowing up Israeli civilians by condemning the former as "terrorism" and hailing the latter as "national resistance." Enlarging on this same theme, Syria, a state-sponsor of terrorism if ever there was one, joined with "moderate" Jordan to condemn "terrorism in all its forms"—except, of course, pizza-parlor bombings in Tel Aviv and other examples of "the resistance of the Palestinian people." The Jerusalem Post picked up on this working definition of terrorism from the state-run Syria Times: "Terrorists are those [forces] of evil that violate human rights and kill innocent people." Sounds reasonable, right? Just wait: "They are not only the terrorists of New York and Washington," the Syrian newspaper editorial continued, "they are also the Israeli occupation troops that kill defenseless Palestinians in the West Bank and Gaza. Bring them all to justice." Good thing Syria just won a seat on the U.N. Security Council.

The fact is, Osama bin Laden, Al Qaeda, and the Taliban won't be—at least, shouldn't be—our sole objective forever. The global terrorists that threaten the democracies are a far larger and more complex enemy. By our government policy, though, we have chosen to avert our eyes from crucial links in the Islamist terror network including Hezbollah, Hamas, and Islamic Jihad—those vaunted "resistance" fighters of the Arab and Muslim world who still aren't on the list of groups whose assets we have frozen. Could it be that we have accepted a morally and expressively deficient definition of "terrorism" in order to fight terrorism? The stakes are higher now than they were in Durban, but the principle is the same. And what principle—what purpose—is served if it turns out that our objective—defeating terrorism—has been rendered literally meaningless?

This war is more than Afghanistan

10/24/01

How did he do it? How did State Department spokesman Phillip Reeker keep from bursting into undiplomatic laughter when making the preposterous case for there being no parallel between what happened on the West Bank on Sunday morning, and what's going on day and night in Afghanistan?

Here are the facts. With America's high techno-bombers still straining to draw a bead on Saudi terrorist Osama bin Laden, Israel hit a bull's-eye in its own unending war on terrorism by killing Abed Rahman Hamad, the Hamas mastermind behind the June 1 Tel Aviv disco massacre that left more than a score of teen-agers dead and dozens wounded. The operation took no more than an undisclosed number of Israeli sharpshooters, two bullets, and zero so-called "collateral damage." But far from hearing congratulations from its great friend and patron, Israel drew a public rebuke.

"We oppose the policy of targeted killings," said Reeker, who, with any luck, will one day stand behind the same lectern to discuss the "targeted killing" of the man President Bush likes to call "the evil one." "I really can't draw a parallel between the two," Reeker added as he tried to scotch the obvious comparison between the American and Israeli efforts—plainly and simply two related fronts of the same, general war against Islamist terror networks. If they aren't, of course, then you have to wonder why, according to press reports, the American military has been briefed on Israeli "liquidation" techniques for possible use against Osama bin Laden and his men in Afghanistan.

So what makes the government hedge? For starters, coalition politics. Not only do our coalition "partners" in the Muslim world—and also Great Britain—balk at taking the war on Islamist terrorism beyond Afghanistan to, say, Iraq, but these same Muslim nations also balk at the notion they could ever have common cause with the state of Israel. Know what? They don't. States who support, sponsor or even, let's say, enable terrorism (Syria and Saudi Arabia, for example), don't have common cause with Israel or any other state that vows to end, or, as Middle East Forum Director Daniel Pipes more realistically suggests, contain terrorism. And that, of course, includes us.

Pretending otherwise smacks of gamesmanship, of treating the battlefield as the chessboard it used to be and not the city streets and office buildings it has unbelievably become. The point of this struggle, frankly, is not to build a coalition, but to win a war. A real war. Last month, unimaginable carnage in the air and on the ground; this month, among other horrors, a puff of highly refined, weapons-grade anthrax actually closed a branch of the federal government. Coalition-building is no longer a priority. Post-Sept. 11, our priority is stopping terrorism before it strikes again. That's why Pentagon planners would like to make Iraq our next military destination, a journey not too many Muslim countries are likely to join us on, coalition or no coalition.

Early one June morning a little more than 20 years ago, the state of Israel sent 16 American jets on a vital mission: to destroy Iraq's nearly operational facilities for making weapons-grade plutonium. A nuclear bomb in the hands of Saddam Hussein, as then-Israeli Prime Minister Menachem Begin would later say, was a nightmare Israel had been living with for two years. By 1981, this nightmare was about to become reality. Fooling Saudi and Jordanian air traffic controllers by speaking Arabic en route, two waves of specially trained Israeli pilots flew to Iraq's French-built Osirak nuclear reactor outside Baghdad, where they neatly and completely destroyed the reactor core before it had been developed to the point of being "hot."

Fabulous, right? The world, including practically the entire U.S. government (with the notable exception of the late Sen. Alan Cranston and also Jerry Falwell) thought otherwise. Or, at least, it said otherwise. Israel was universally and vigorously condemned—literally in the United Nations, where the United States worked closely with Iraq in crafting the resolution denouncing the raid. Arab nations, naturally, railed against "Israeli terrorism," while France, naturally, expressed its bitterness over Israel's "obvious lack of regard for the difficulties ... created for France." But there was another view.

As then-Sen. Rudy Boschwitz put it, "Very frankly, [the Israelis] probably did the world a favor." It was a favor we should have thanked them for even 10 years later when the troops of Desert Storm faced an Iraq that still had no nuclear arsenal.

Menachem Begin would later justify the raid as an act of "supreme national self-defense." It was. And the world was a safer place. It is now time for the United States to act in "supreme national self-defense." It may be the only way the world will ever be a safer place again.

The ties that bind (and gag)

10/26/01

That international coalition of ours has problems—and not just politically speaking. It's one thing to have to buck up a bunch of what used to be known as "weak sisters" with a shot of political courage now and then. It's another situation entirely when it becomes clear—hopelessly clear—that not only is there, among coalition members, no common grasp of political reality, but there is also no common grasp of reality, period.

Let's begin with Saudi Arabia. Sure, it's a headache that this allegedly close ally has barred American warplanes from Saudi bases — and particularly from the bases we actually built. And it doesn't bode too well for the ties that bind when the Saudi interior minister, Prince Nayef, goes around telling the press that if the United States takes its war on Islamist terrorism beyond Afghanistan to any Arab country, "we will side with our Arab brethren."

But such political differences pale next to the mind-bending conundrum of dealing with a government in denial over the simple fact that between eight and 12 of the 19 suicide hijackers on Sept. 11 were Saudi Arabian. As Prince Nayef told reporters in Riyadh as recently as last week, he doubts whether the hijackers were even Arabs in the first place. "There were more than 600 passengers on the four hijacked planes," Prince Nayef explained, according to the London Telegraph. "We are still wondering why they [the Americans] have singled out Arabs, especially Saudis."

We aren't. Nor is anyone else familiar with the facts and, more important, the desire to assess them truthfully. Truth, however, doesn't serve the ends of every country with an invitation to join the coalition. Take Syria, the newly minted member of the U.N. Security Council. Last week, Syrian defense minister Mustafa Tlass gave voice to a particularly heinous lie that has been surfacing with feverish frequency in the Arab and Muslim media when he told a delegation from a British military college that Israel is responsible for the Sept. 11 massacre. Not only that, the Syrian official continued, but the Mossad, Israel's intelligence agency, warned thousands of Jews employed in the World Trade Center not to go to work on the day of the attack. As the Jerusalem Post noted, comments like these indicate this grotesque slander "has been commuted to fact among senior Arab officialdom."

Such eye-popping reports, often limited to Arabic, rarely seep into the Western media. Westerners, in fact, will sometimes get another story entirely. Consider the bilingual example of Sheikh Dr. Mohammad Gemeaha, Imam of New York City's Islamic Cultural Center and U.S. representative of Al-Azhar University, the Cairo Islamic center constitutionally associated with the Egyptian government. Incidentally, it is Al-Azhar, The New York Times reported, where "clerics ... have cast themselves again and again as the guides to a gentle Islam." (More on that below.)

Gemeaha sounded gentle enough in New York City where he sermonized about being "hurt and saddened" after Sept. 11 by "this act against all humanity." He was anything but gentle, however, in an Arabic interview with an unofficial Web site of Al-Azhar University a few weeks later.

In extended remarks translated by the Middle East Media Research

Institute Web site (http://www.memri.org), Gemeaha venomously elaborated on the same libel repeated by the Syrian defense minister — that Israel perpetrated the Sept. 11 attacks — and added that "we, the Arabs, were innocent." Americans knew this to be true, he continued, but were afraid to admit it. He dubbed the American campaign in Afghanistan "terrorism," predicted "this war will be the end of America," and said, "if the Americans knew that the Jews carried out the Sept. 11 attacks they would do to them what Hitler did." Just for good measure, he added that since Sept. 11, "sick Muslim children" in America have been murdered by "Jewish doctors."

And the man was just warming up. Eventually he would hit all the high notes in the anti-Semitic repertoire about "Zionist control" of the world, which now, apparently, extends to "decision-making in the airports." Guide to "gentle Islam" that he is, Gemeaha also quoted from the Koran: "The Jewish element is as Allah described it when he said, 'They disseminate corruption in the land.'" This corruption, he ranted on, includes heresy, homosexuality, alcoholism, drugs and strip clubs.

So much for Egypt's mainstream clerics. Meanwhile, Egyptian president Hosni Mubarak hasn't exactly followed President Bush's lead to repudiate hate speech from the government mosque. In a slightly more perfect world, this sort of talk, now circulating throughout the Arab and Muslim world, would get you tossed out on your ear. But these days, of course, it doesn't even get you tossed out of the coalition.

Tough talk at the United Nations

11/20/01

Were the members of the U.N. General Assembly listening when George W. Bush gave them a lesson in the new way of the world? Bush's U.N. address last Saturday, delivered with the unadorned grace of plainspoken English, may have marked the first time diplomats accustomed to well-padded euphemism ever heard anything like it.

After expressing America's gratitude for condolences received since Sept. 11, Bush made a simple but spine-straightening point: "The time for sympathy has now passed. The time for action has now arrived." Such action, Bush informed the world body, includes freezing and confiscating terrorist assets, coordinating law enforcement and denying sanctuary or transit to terrorists.

"Every known terrorist camp must be shut down, its operators apprehended and evidence of their arrest presented to the United Nations," he said, adding, "These obligations are urgent, and they are binding on every nation with a place in this chamber."

Urgent? Binding? On every nation? With language like this, pointed enough to pierce the buffers of diplomatic doublespeak, Bush made it clear that just another U.N. resolution won't satisfy his resolve. "In this world there are good causes and bad causes," he continued, "and we may disagree on where the line is drawn. Yet there is no such thing as a good terrorist. No national aspiration, no remembered wrong can ever justify the deliberate murder of the innocent. Any government that rejects this principle, trying to pick and choose its terrorist friends, will know the consequences."

To nations still mourning the deliberate murder of the innocent, such moral clarity is an inspiration. To nations still resisting the pull of the coalition, it is a warning. The response? The General Assembly gave the American president one measly round of applause—prompted less by Bush's call to arms, no doubt, than by his invocation of "a day when two states, Israel and Palestine, live peacefully together." That single burst of applause was probably muted by the president's assertion that Israeli-Palestinian peace is possible only "when all have sworn off, forever, incitement, violence and terror."

If fulfilled, of course, such an oath would likely leave Palestinian leader Yasser Arafat out of a job. Meanwhile, even as Secretary of State Colin Powell continues to meet with Arafat, Bush shuns him for not rooting terrorists out of his own domain—a failing, it should be noted, that doesn't exactly give the General Assembly pause. A day after Bush's U.N. appearance, delegates warmly greeted the Palestinian Authority chairman with applause, interrupting his familiar tirade against the state of Israel—which he fantastically accused of practicing "ethnic cleansing" and "state terror against the Palestinian people"—with "frequent and loud applause," according to one news account.

What's going on here?

While anti-Israeli and anti-American speechifying have always been rallying cries at the United Nations, now isn't the time to ignore them. Bush may talk tough, but he's facing a formidable communication gap—chasm, really—which seems to defy the reach of cross-cultural understanding. The international community seems willing enough to fight against terrorism so long as it is defined by Al Qaeda gang—and, implausibly, not to mention immorally, by the democratic state of Israel. This is not only absurd, it is anathema, potentially aligning members of the anti-terrorist coalition with such terrorist organizations as Hamas and Hezbollah. As National Security Adviser Condoleeza Rice put it last week, however, "You cannot help us with Al Qaeda and hug Hezbollah." That, of course, is precisely what too many nations wish to do.

Bush has argued eloquently for action, but that doesn't mean there isn't more to be said to address this urgent dispute. It not only keeps Bush from meeting with Yasser Arafat, it also knocks the international coalition perpetually off-kilter. That is a fact, as unsettling as it is officially unmentionable, and there can be no solid foundation to the war on terrorism until it is well understood.

Speaking of terror

6-16-03

If you (still) read The New York Times, pretty much all you know about the bedside interview of Abdel Aziz Rantisi, the Hamas arch terrorist and pediatrician who escaped an Israeli missile assault this week with a minor leg injury, is that he "vowed revenge from his hospital bed."

However, this Dumas-like description doesn't quite fit Rantisi's hospital-room rant as reported elsewhere. Knowing what the Hamas leader actually said makes Palestinian government insistence on all "dialogue" and no action regarding Hamas (or, in the words of Prime Minister Mahmoud Abbas, "the brothers of Hamas") seem even more like the dangerous sham that it is.

Here are some of the Hamas leader's choicer words: "I swear we will not leave a single Jew in Palestine"—which, in terror-speak, means "not a single Jew in Israel." This statement appeared in the Washington Times. "I am telling Sharon and all the Israeli murderers, you don't have any security unless you leave the country" (i.e., leave Israel), the Washington Post reported.

Such statements strike me more as conversation-enders than dialogue-openers. These sentiments don't promise "revenge" as much as they reaffirm the same old strategy of annihilation by terrorism that imperils Israel in the modern age—now to a calamitous degree. Indeed, Internet news service IslamOnline.net characterized Rantisi's words as having "reaffirmed" the strategy of "resistance and rifle"—terror-speak, it seems, for donning Orthodox garb and self-detonating a bus filled with office-bound commuters. That's exactly what a Hamas terrorist did the day after Rantisi spoke. Sixteen Israelis were killed during the afternoon rush hour on Wednesday, leaving scores maimed and wounded on a sunny Jerusalem thoroughfare.

"You have no option but Jihad and martyrdom," Rantisi told IslamOnline.net. "By Allah Almighty, we will pursue Jihad until we bring back all Palestinian refugees to their homeland and restore every inch of our usurped land"—terror-speak, of course, for every inch of Israel. This wasn't Rantisi's first rant (and, regrettably, won't be his last). A few months back, Rantisi justified the loss of the space shuttle Columbia as "part of the divine punishment of America and, together with it, Zionism." Before that, the good doctor was calling for "thousands of squads of martyrs" to be equipped with "thousands of sophisticated explosives belts" to kill themselves, along with as many

Americans and British troops as possible, for the greater glory of Saddam Hussein.

"In order to defend the homeland from the terrorist Crusader attack," he wrote, according to MEMRI's online translation, "there is a need for people who yearn for Paradise, and the shortest way to Paradise is death for (the sake of) Allah."

Suicide killers haven't materialized in Iraq by the thousands, but a scattered few have murdered American soldiers. And, according to the grim tally of the Zionist Organization of America, 29 of the 39 Americans killed by Palestinian Arab terrorists since 1993 were murdered by Hamas. Such statistics make all the more distressing the fact that George W. Bush, a big-game terrorist-hunter himself, would be "deeply troubled" because the Israelis took aim at a big-game terrorist following post-summit terror attacks that left five Israeli soldiers dead.

Almost worse than the hypocrisy, however, is the illogic behind the president's stated reason: Mr. Bush was concerned, he said, that the Israeli action would impede official Palestinian efforts to fight terrorism. How it could be that drying up a poisonous source of terrorism could be a drain on any legitimate fight against terrorism is an argument for the mentally double-jointed. Without engaging in dangerous gymnastics, it's still easy to see that such thinking, taken seriously, would require the United States to cease all efforts to target Osama bin Laden.

Prime Minister Abbas has declared himself unable or unwilling to act against Palestinian terror groups; Israel, attacked again, must defend itself. In so doing, it is helping defend every other country threatened by Islamist terror. The accelerated road map to a Palestinian state comes not as a hopeful result of any Palestinian reform; it comes as a weary concession to Palestinian terror. This is a dangerous precedent for the entire Western world. Even worse would be an Israeli concession on the right to self-defense.

Look again to the maniacal words of Rantisi: "The enemies of Allah ... are cowards. They crave life, while Muslims crave martyrdom. The martyrdom operations (suicide murders) that shock can ensure that horror is sowed in the (enemies') hearts, and horror is one of the causes of defeat."

Life vs. martyrdom: an easy choice in the West. But in choosing life, we must defend it everywhere—the only triumph there can be over Dr. Rantisi's horror.

'Terrorism' disconnect

12/5/05

Two international conferences last month wrangled over definitions of terrorism. The conference in Europe, the Barcelona Euro-Mediterranean Summit, promised to fight terrorism, but couldn't agree on what "terrorism" was. This somehow added up to "an unprecedented feat," according to summit organizer and Spanish prime minister Jose Zapatero, who fatuously ballyhooed the "unmitigated, energetic," but literally meaningless condemnation of terrorism offered by European and Middle Eastern nations.

Hooey is right.

The other conference was in the Middle East. The Iraqi reconciliation talks, sponsored by the Arab League in Cairo, agreed on a definition of terrorism, all right, but it was one that seemed to legitimize the blowing up of American soldiers, even as they fight terrorism.

For starters, this Iraqi communiqué — hammered out by some 200 Shiite, Sunni and Kurdish leaders — called "resistance" a "legitimate right." You know, "resistance": the killers who blast soldiers on patrol, or kids getting candy, or worshippers inside rival mosques to bits. This line was already a poisonous sop to Sunni proponents of "resistance" (read: death squads).

The communiqué went on to note that "terrorism does not represent resistance," which sounded a little more promising. Then it said: "Therefore, we condemn terrorism and acts of violence, killing and kidnapping targeting Iraqi citizens and humanitarian, civil, government institutions, national resources and houses of worship." Notice who and what is missing from the Iraqi convention's protection list: our own fantastic soldiers of the U.S. military.

What did Secretary of State Condoleezza Rice have to say about this unacceptable omission? "I think what they were trying to do was to get a sense of political inclusion while recognizing that violence and terrorism should not be part of resistance," she told CNN.

Trying to get a sense of "political inclusion" — by signaling open "resistance" season on U.S. soldiers? This is happy, Oprah spin, the doctrine of Feelpolitik — not superpower strategy. She continued: "After all, do Iraqis really want to — any Iraqi, sitting around that table, want to suggest that killing an innocent Iraqi child standing at a bus stop is legitimate? Or that killing Iraqi soldiers who are lining up at recruitment centers is legitimate? Or even that multinational forces" (that's us) — "who are, by the way, there under a U.N. mandate" (I feel better?) — "are somehow legitimate targets?"

Well, no and yes, Madame Secretary. It's no good to appeal reflexively to a Western framework of fair play without considering what the Iraqi document actually says. Yes, the document specifically protects the Iraqi child standing at the bus stop, and maybe even the Iraqi recruits. It's the Americans risking their lives 24-7 to protect that child and those recruits who seem to have become "legitimate" targets, according to this declaration by leaders across the Iraqi political spectrum. Shouldn't that set off, not soothing psychobabble, but angry sirens in Washington?

Funny how some stories never build a head of steam. Running smack into Thanksgiving weekend didn't help, but no holiday hiatus should have put this one on ice. It feels as if it hasn't played out at home, although I wonder if it registered overseas. Days later, at the Barcelona conference, the attempt to reach a Euro-Arab consensus on terrorism practically blew up the conference — metaphorically speaking, of course. That's because European Union (EU) leaders refused to sign onto an Arab-Muslim definition of terrorism similar to the one in the Iraqi communiqué, one that would have legitimized the Arab-Muslim notion of "resistance" to "occupation" — as in "resistance" (suicide bombing) to "occupation" (Israeli buses and supermarkets, not to mention coalition troops in Iraq). Perhaps having lately suffered enough "resistance" in their own backyards, the EU countries — miracle of miracles — felt spinally enhanced enough to stick to their stated conviction that terrorism is never justified. Conversely, this was a moral statement the Arab-Muslim countries refused to endorse.

But it was the Europeans who were characteristically apologetic about the failure to reach a Euro-Arab consensus. "It's been difficult to find that perfect word to explain that concept which is shared by everybody," said EU foreign policy chief Javier Solana in one news account, sounding a little absurd. "We all know what we mean by terrorism," he said in another, sounding a little desperate. "In reality, there is total cooperation between the countries north and south of the Mediterranean against terrorism."

Come on. One place there is not total cooperation is in reality. More than a language barrier separates the Western and Islamic definitions of terrorism, and no amount of happy talk about "inclusion" or conferences about "cooperation" changes that.

What We Learned From 9/11

How we learned to revere the 'holy' Koran, protect 'the Prophet Mohammed' and never spit toward Mecca

What's being desecrated here?

6/13/05

Thank you, Michael Isikoff. Because of Newsweek's commode Quran story — the one that went down the drain in a retraction — a previously undisclosed threat to our very existence has been revealed. It may be too late to avert, but before admitting defeat, I just wish every American would take a good long moment to reflect, not on the hysterical headlines trumpeting "Quran abuse," but rather on the U.S. Army's Quranic Code of Conduct in place at Guantanamo Bay.

The orders aren't called that, of course, but that's as apt a title as any for the relevant sections of the officially titled "Detention Operations Group Standard Operating Procedures" that go for Gitmo. And, it bears repeating, every American should take a good long moment to reflect on what they mean.

Since all of Guantanamo's inmates happen to be members of the same famed band of Muslim extremists, the Army has seen fit to distribute Qurans.

So far, so good, I guess. But the Army doesn't just distribute its Qurans like any other religious book. That is, the Bible may get passed around, riffled through, dropped, tossed and stuffed into hotel room drawers. But not the Quran. According to United States Army policy, the standard operating procedure is: "Handle the Quran as if it were a fragile piece of delicate art."

What's going on here? By official order, a whole lot of "respecting the dignity of the Quran." According to Section 6-5-c(3), should a

Quran need to be removed from a detainee's cell — you know, carried somewhere — and the detainee is personally unable to move it (best option), and the Muslim chaplain, librarian and interpreter are also unable to move it (second-best option), then the U.S. Army guard, as a very last resort, may take action.

Then the insanity really begins. The guard is directed to don "clean gloves ... in full view of the detainees prior to handling." He must use "two hands ... at all times when handling the Quran in manner signaling respect and reverence." Why "respect" alone isn't abundantly sufficient isn't mentioned. While signaling two-handed respect and reverence, however, the guard must be mindful that "care should be used so that the right hand is the primary one used to manipulate any part of the Quran due to the cultural association with the left hand."

It goes on. There's more "reverent manner," more instructions for conveying the book inside a "clean, dry detainee towel." The cockeyed picture is clear. But it doesn't explain what's going on.

At first glance, this scene may seem to exemplify a bizarre excess of good manners, an absurdly obsequious respect for a largely foreign faith. Since when does the United States specifically direct its soldiers to show two-handed "reverence" in the handling of any religious book? But it seems to me that there's more behind this charade. The "clean gloves" and "detainee" towels are the tip-off. The fact is, under Islamic law, non-Muslims are deemed unfit to touch the Quran. That much is generally known. What is not usually considered is the reason:

According to the Islamic law, we are unclean.

The term is "najis." On the multilingual Web site of the Grand Ayatollah Ali al-Husseini al-Sistani, the leading Iraqi Shi'ite cleric, there is a catalogue of Islamic laws (www.sistani.org). This includes a list of "najis things." There are 10, beginning with an assortment of excretions and body fluids — obvious stuff that really shouldn't need special mention. On the "najis" list with urine, feces, etc., are the pig, the dog and the "kafir." That means the Christian, the Jew, the unbeliever in Islam — and, chances are, the Gitmo guard.

In effect, then, with its official policy of clean cloves and detainee towels, the United States military is promoting, enabling and accepting the Islamic concept of najis — the unclean infidel — a barbarous notion that has helped fuel the bloodlust of jihad and the non-Muslim subjugation of dhimmitude. Our soldiers are many things: self-sacrificing, bold, loyal and true. They are not unclean.

Is this political correctness run amok? Not exactly. It's something else again, a new threat from within that needs vigilant redress. P.C. is about victimology, the elevation of perceived victim groups to the canonical pantheon. The Gitmo rules are more blatantly about surrender, a voluntary self-extinguishment, a spreading condition of denial of what is right and worth standing for. Not what you expect from the United States Southern Command.

Sniper shooting Koran hardly 'criminal behavior'

5/27/08

It is late August 1939. American columnist Augusta "Gusto" Nash, played by the incomparable Claudette Colbert in the 1940 movie "Arise, My Love," is sitting in a French railway car taking her from Paris (and love interest Ray Milland) to her next assignment: Adolph Hitler's Berlin. Not surprisingly, she is boning up for her new post in the Nazi capital by reading "Mein Kampf." Turning the pages, she looks increasingly disgusted, finally becoming incensed to the point where she slams the book shut and tosses it out the window.

The audience doesn't learn precisely what that final straw was, but given the book's notorious anti-Semitism, racism and militaristic plans for world domination, it's not hard to imagine. Which makes me wonder: What if, in a 21st-century update of the movie, a columnist were filmed en route to Riyadh reading the Koran? Given the book's notorious anti-Semitism (not to mention anti-Christianism), Islamic supremacism and jihadist exhortations for world domination, what if a postmodern-day Western-reared correspondent were depicted becoming agitated to the point of throwing the Koran out the window?

Not very easy to imagine this scenario coming to a multiplex near you. At least not without bomb threats, bombast and boycotts from the world of Islam (not to mention assorted yelps and cries from the stateside sensitivity police).

But it's a setup worth considering — quietly, privately, in that shrinking mental domain still free from speech controls (for now, anyway) — if only as a bit of a culture check on a real-live news story that came out of Iraq this week when a U.S. sniper was discovered to have used a Koran for target practice in the former insurgent stronghold of Radwaniyah.

And what is the point of comparison here between movie fiction and recent fact?

Namely, the contrasting reactions to these two manifestations of contempt for anti-liberty ideologies. Americans in 1940 widely shared Gusto Nash's loathing for Hitler's totalitarian message. In 2008, the superiors of the soldier in question, right on up the chain of command to commander-in-chief George W. Bush, only express their respect for, and, in a very frightening way, submission to the Koran despite its totalitarian message — and even at the expense of the soldier's Constitutional rights.

The fact is, assuming this Koran belonged to the soldier, there is nothing illegal about shooting it or throwing it away. Impolitic, perhaps; but snipers — trained rather specifically in this conflict to kill jihadists, who are, above all, inspired by the violent exhortations contained within the Koran — are not diplomats.

But neither are generals. Missing a teachable moment — "Turn the other cheek?"

"Nuts!" "The soldier fired on an inanimate object that urges jihad; he didn't self-detonate in a teeming marketplace to advance jihad" — Maj. Gen. Jeffrey Hammond chose to abase himself before the local Sunni tribe. "In a most humble manner, I look into your eyes today and I say 'Please forgive me and my soldiers,'" he said. Then he called his sniper's actions "nothing more than criminal behavior."

The general was dead wrong — unless, that is, he was talking about criminal behavior under Sharia, or Islamic law, which isn't, or certainly shouldn't be, the guiding light of the U.S. military. But, alas, this is what increasingly appears to be the case. For example, in presenting a new Koran to this gathering of local Sunnis who were very likely insurgents not so long ago, another American officer kissed the Islamic book. Last time I looked, kissing Korans wasn't a Yankee custom — unless dhimmitude now counts as one.

Let's play around some more with the story. Imagine if, during the Allied occupation of post-Nazi Germany, a GI had been discovered using "Mein Kampf" for target practice. Would Gen. George S. Patton have kissed a new copy of the Nazi bible as he presented it to a cadre of former Nazis? In the words of Ol' Blood and Guts — oh, wait; this is a family newspaper. Let's just put it this way: Not likely. Difference is, of course, the anti-Semitism and imperialistic supremacism contained within "Mein Kampf" were recognized and treated as an existential threat to the rest of the Western world. In the so-called war on terror, however, our primary strategy is directed at masking or ignoring the overall anti-infidelism and imperialistic supremacism contained within the Koran.

And — in spite of the actions of the occasional "criminal" soldier — that's one front where we're certainly winning.

Blind defense of Koran abrogates reality

5/30/08

What interested me most about the official reaction to this month's Koran Sniper story — apologies galore, a kissed Koran for probable former insurgents, a punished soldier — was what it made vivid about our society: American deference to Islam, from the sacralization of Islam's book to the ideology of anti-infidelism, supremacism and totalitarian conquest within it. After all, Maj. Gen. Jeffrey Hammond called the sniper's action "criminal behavior," but the only law broken was Islamic law.

Contrast that, I wrote last week, with the repudiation Americans once displayed toward a similarly anti-Semitic, supremacist and warlike ideology as codified in "Mein Kampf" — the treatise Winston Churchill dubbed "the new Koran of faith and war, turgid, verbose, but pregnant with its message." Had a mid-century GI used "Mein Kampf" for target practice, I noted, Gen. George S. Patton would hardly have kissed one to appease a band of former Nazis.

Suffice to say, I've received considerable comment, both positive and negative about this analogy. One letter compared the post-Hitler, U.S. policy of de-Nazification in Germany with the post-Saddam, U.S.-fostered enshrinement of Sharia in new constitutions in both Iraq and Afghanistan. Naturally, "Mein Kampf" would be vilified in the former, and the Koran protected in the latter. We have approved the religious rules to do so.

But other responses made clear the extent to which we also protect the Koran here. I don't mean from target practice, or other acts of desecration — permitted, not incidentally, for the symbols of other religions, not to mention those of the nation itself.

I was particularly struck by this on reading Contentions, the blog of Commentary magazine. In a post about my recent column, Contentions blogger Abe Greenwald wrote: "This won't do, Diana. While the Qu'ran is sacred to our enemies in Iraq, it is also sacred to our allies."

Amazing that this fact is seen as a rationale for silence, not as a cause for concern. It is also never, ever contemplated in our debates about "democratizing" the Islamic world. Apparently, "enemies" and "allies" alike being inspired by the same Koranic message doesn't call into question the nature or potential of the "allies." It only seems to inspire reticence about the nature or potential of the message.

While I hardly claim originality in comparing central tenets of the Koran and "Mein Kampf" (see Winnie's comment above), Greenwald didn't care for that, either. "Yes," he wrote, "there are many nasty injunctions in the Qur'an. Yes, there are calls to anti-Semitism and supremacy. But ... there are nasty parts in the foundational works of other major religions. Second, there are Qur'anic passages promoting humanity and understanding. ... If you're going to wage wholesale war on an entire religion, you'll need more than a tabulation showing that the religion's core text is, on balance, nastier than the next."

How can it be, nearly seven years after 9/11, such thin gruel is still being served as an argument? Without citing sura and verse, the first point fizzles in the absence of Jewish and Christian terrorists justifying acts of violence with references to their scriptures. As for the second point, I hereby introduce the Commentary blog to the Koranic doctrine of "abrogation," according to which Koranic passages are abrogated (canceled) by subsequently "revealed" verses that, as Ibn Warraq writes in his book "What the Koran Really Says," convey a "different or contrary meaning."

Warraq continues: "This was supposedly taught by Muhammad at Sura II.105: 'Whatever verses we (i.e., G-d) cancel or cause you to forget, we bring a better or its like.'" While resolving the abundant contradictions to be found in the Koran, abrogation, he writes, "does pose problems for apologists of Islam, since all the passages preaching tolerance are found in Meccan (i.e., early) suras, and all the passages recommending killing, decapitating and maiming, the so-called Sword Verses, are Medinan (i.e., later)." His conclusion: "'Tolerance' has been abrogated by 'intolerance.' For example, the famous Sword verse ... at Sura IX.5, 'Slay the idolators wherever you find them,' is said to have canceled 124 verses that enjoin toleration and patience." So much for Greenwald's "passages promoting humanity and understanding."

More perplexing, however, is Greenwald's assumption that a frank appraisal of the Koran is akin to waging "war on an entire religion." On the contrary, such an appraisal is simply the basis of any rational defense against the war Islam is waging on the West.

Marines warned: Don't spit toward Mecca

11/4/11

Uncle Sam is getting a little weird. Make that a lot weird. Having dumped hundreds of billions of dollars into a sinkhole called Afghanistan—populated by misogynistic, pederastic, tribalistic and religiously supremacist primitives—to no avail, he has hit on a new plan for winning those ever-elusive Afghan "hearts and minds."

Uncle Sam has decided that the answer lies in the latrine with the U.S. Marine Corps. No kidding. When nature calls, Uncle Sam has decided he wants every U.S. Marine equipped with a map and compass, or some other way of knowing direction. This is to ensure that no U.S. Marine in Afghanistan urinates in the direction of Mecca ever again.

Now, there's a winning strategy.

It's still OK, of course, to spread baksheesh (payola) indiscriminately, chase jihadis into twisting mountain gorges, clear any road laced with improvised explosives - blow up, even, and bleed all over the place. Just make sure your sense of direction is sharp when it really counts.

Take spitting. According to an article in the North County Times, the word is: Ix-nay on itting-spay toward ecca-May, guys. If there's a pinch between teeth and gum while you're hiding out in a cold valley, figure out where Mecca is (2,000 miles away) before letting anything out of your mouth. Oh, and when it's time to catch some shut-eye "when sharing a base with Afghan army troops" - if you can sleep, given the frightening odds an Afghan National Army soldier might turn his gun on you - don't, whatever you do, let your combat boots point toward you-know-where.

That would be "culturally insensitive" and, therefore, it seems, worse than anything Afghani (or Pakistani) jihadist butchers might do (beheadings, rape) because they, as Muslims, are automatically "culturally sensitive." Apparently to compensate, senior Pentagon brass created something called the USMC Center for Advanced Operational Culture Learning to teach Marines to exist in the Islamically approved fashion.

When Marines learn not to excrete in the direction of Mecca - home of the black cube known as the Kaaba - and not to sleep with their boots toward Mecca, what are they really learning? They are learning to become intensely sensitized to the whereabouts of Mecca; how to be guided by that magnetic north for Muslims as a matter of the most personal habits and hygiene, all in accordance with Shariah (Islamic law). They are learning to act like Muslims.

If you can't beat 'em, join 'em?

Such "culture learning" blends seamlessly with an International Security Assistance Force (ISAF) guidance to all troops in Afghanistan to revere the Quran and its teachings. That's the unmistakable message of COIN Advisory #20100924-001, which I found on the ISAF website.

"Never talk badly about the Quran or its contents," says the guidance, a no-nonsense formulation of Islamic prohibitions against any criticism of Islam. Touching it is out, too. "It is considered culturally insensitive for any non-Muslim to touch a copy of the Quran," ISAF explains. Why that is indeed the Islamic case, ISAF doesn't explain. Presumably, it might upset troops to learn that this injunction exists because Muslims consider non-Muslim "najis," or unclean, and thus unfit to touch their religious book. Before searching people, ISAF advises, "ask them if they have a Quran or religious item present. If so, ask them to remove it or put it in a suitable place before conducting the search."

Think the Navy SEALs who zapped Osama bin Laden asked him to put his Quran in a "suitable place" first? We can only hope.

Of course, there's more: "Additionally," ISAF continues, "verbal disrespect for Islam and/or the Quran is considered as inappropriate as physical desecration of the Quran. Insulting the Quran is an act of blasphemy."

The way Islam treats women stinks = verbal disrespect for Islam.

The verses of the Quran that call for jihad against infidels are heinous = insulting the Quran. But ISAF, veritable mouthpiece of the coming caliphate, deems such talk "inappropriate" and outright "blasphemy." This might win the generals an extra cushion at the foot of the caliph's throne, but, as the Marines are learning in their Culture Learning classes, they'll have to drink all their chai and finish their goat, first.

Latrine directive another step on path to Islamification

12/2/11

Having written countless columns and blog posts arguing that the see-no-Islam counterinsurgency strategy (COIN) has led to failure in two wars in the umma (Muslim world) and the dhimmification of the U.S. military, it's almost funny to see the debate more or less officially joined over my recent column on what appears to be simply the gross-out, PG-13 movie topic of peeing toward Mecca. Or, rather, not peeing toward Mecca.

Scatological or not, what we are talking about here is an untenable invasion of privacy of American citizens in uniform via religious dictate as taught by the U.S. Marine Corps.

The Nov. 28 print edition of Marine Corps Times carries both an article and a lead editorial on what the paper is politely calling "excretory etiquette" regarding Marines and Mecca — which, incidentally, is about 2,000 miles from Afghanistan. But this isn't just about etiquette. Given its Islamic religious derivation, the Marines' excretory instruction strikes me as a violation of religious freedom. Who is the U.S. Marine Corps to instruct American citizens to bring their personal hygiene practices into accord with Islamic law? The Corps in this case is acting as a vehicle of Islamic law, which comprehensively rules on all manner of personal habits, as well as on civil and legal affairs.

Needless to say, the Marine Corps doesn't see it that way. Its spokesmen have contended narrowly that this lesson taught by a contractor (hired by the Corps) isn't "formal Marine Corps doctrine," as the Marine Corps Times editorial puts it. Formal or not, the editors also don't think this Marine Shariah (Islamic law) is a bad idea. Headlined "Respect differences," the editorial states: "Thing is, there's value to this sort of insight." Perhaps in the name of respecting "differences"?

Heavens, no. This is all about respecting Islam, not "differences." After all, if it were about "differences," the respect in question would extend to the non-Islamic belief that not all bodily functions taking place on planet Earth must key off the location of a town in Saudi Arabia. To each his own.

That's not the editorial's subject. The value, it says, comes "in light of the tense conditions under which both groups must coexist."

Tense conditions—as in border firefights? Roadside bombs? No, again. The editorial refers to tensions between Muslims and infidels *inside the wire*. "Consider that in the last four years," the editorial continues, "nearly 60 coalition troops have been killed by their Afghan counterparts."

So "respecting differences" here means pee straight or die. That's the lesson the military wants to teach young Americans heading into the war zone—again, inside the wire. The only way it knows to increase their safety while on their own bases or when "partnering" with Afghans is to school them in the practice of Islamic law. In effect, then, collaboration with the Islamic Republic of Afghanistan requires the United States of America to Islamify its infidel forces, just a little, just to keep those religious crazies in the Afghan ranks from popping off.

More guidelines for U.S. forces: "If you must pass a man praying, pass at a respectful distance. Do not walk between a man praying and Mecca—always walk behind him. ... Do not touch Qurans or prayer rugs." To be fair to the Marines, those rules come from the Center for Army Lessons Learned. But it's all of a Pentagon piece. And guess where such "safety" education—the dhimmi rules of Shariah—will be taught next?

I bet it would surprise the brass at the Pentagon to learn that Islam means "submission," and that the age-old choice Islam has offered infidels is to submit or die. Still, they seem to have learned, as the editorial puts it, that "certain behavior that wouldn't get a second look stateside could lead to problems at a patrol base in Helmand province."

"Problems." What a way to invoke shootings of our people by Afghan forces—the spurting, flaring jihad none dares name. "Counseling Marines to aim east ultimately may head off trouble," the editorial concludes. Submission always does.

Why is the U.S. apologizing for scorched Korans?

2/24/12

I've got it.

We've come a long way since the days of the Global War on Terror. Frankly, the GWOT—whatever that was supposed to mean (how do you fight against a tactic?) -- is so 10 years ago. "Terror," meanwhile, has morphed into "extremism," but that's only made things more unclear.

We still don't know what it's all supposed to be about.

Until today.

Mr. and Mrs. America, boys and girls, welcome to the Global War on Quran-Burning, as led by the United States Masochists To Make the World Safe for Shariah (Islamic law).

If a column could have special effects, this is where piercing beams of sunlight would dispel clouds of confusion as pink bunnies jump up and down, squeaking, "That's it, that's it!" And a sigh of relief would spread across the happy valley ...

Or would it? If my title for the war our country has engaged us in is apt, have I described a cause most Americans support? I don't think so, but, of course, I don't claim to know the answer. That's partly because I see no upset in the land over the latest and greatest display of American dhimmitude—the subservient state of Jews and Christians in thrall to Islamic law—that we have witnessed in Afghanistan all week. Afghan Muslims have convulsed in rioting and killing (among other fatalities, two U.S. military personnel have been murdered by an Afghan army member) on word that Qurans and other religious materials were disposed of on a U.S. military base after authorities discovered the books were being used at Parwan prison in what the BBC said may have been "a secret Taliban message system."

You didn't hear about that last part? I'm not surprised. This crucial piece of the story—the logical reason for the books' destruction—is treated by the media, and also by the U.S. government, as secondary material. At least one unnamed "U.S. official" imparted this part of the story to the press (Reuters and AFP); unnamed "Afghan officials" have told the BBC the same thing. Judging by the gingerly way this news is being handled, it almost seems as if the perfectly logical rationale for the disposal of these materials is regarded as an embarrassment.

Not so the outrageous, primitive response of rioting Muslims. In our state of abject apology, we have, in effect, condoned this murderous behavior according to the Islamic rules governing treatment of the Quran. This isn't just political correctness run amok; it's open submission to Islamic law. After all, the Quran is an inanimate object, a thing, cheaply printed and distributed by the gazillion, often by Saudi Arabia. We—if by "we" I may still refer to the Judeo-Christian-humanist world—do not rampage and shoot people when an inanimate object, a thing, even a Bible, is torn, written on or thrown away. In fact, we have constitutional rights to do all of those things as a matter of free speech.

Nonetheless, we as a nation—spilling blood for the "noble people of Afghanistan," as top commander Marine Gen. John R. Allen says in his prostration video--have deemed it vital to accommodate, apologize, slurp and scrape to those who do. Equally as tragic, in the frenzy to apologize, the logic behind throwing the stuff away has been sacrificed.

Reason itself has been discarded in a shameful and irrational act of fealty. This isn't just dysfunctional behavior. This is full-blown dhimmitude.

Sorry to disappoint the pink bunnies.

Islamic rages aimed at enslaving the West

3/2/12

Six U.S. military men have been murdered by Afghan security forces seized by what may be labeled Quran-Burning Rage.

Quran-Burning Rage follows Pastor Jones Rage, which, after a Florida pastor burned a Quran in 2011, seized Afghan Muslims and inspired rioting. Some rioters overran a United Nations outpost and murdered seven U.N. personnel.

Pastor Jones Rage followed "Fitna" Rage, which seized Muslims worldwide even before the release of Dutch parliamentarian Geert Wilders' short 2008 film "Fitna." That film sparked rioting, arson, boycotts, death threats and, as a bonus, charges that led to the protracted trial in the Netherlands of Wilders for "insulting Muslims." (He was acquitted in 2011.)

"Fitna" Rage followed Teddy Bear Rage, which, in 2007, seized Muslims in Sudan after a British teacher, whose class named a teddy bear "Muhammad," was sentenced to 15 days for "insulting religion." Ten thousand Sudanese turned out to call for the teacher's head instead.

Teddy Bear Rage followed Pope Rage, which seized Muslims after a 2006 address in which Pope Benedict XVI noted a historic reference to Islam's propensity to spread by violence. Muslim rioting, arson (including church burnings) and the murder of a 65-year-old Italian nun in Somalia ensued.

All of these rages followed or coincided with the most sustained rage of all, Danish Muhammad Cartoon Rage, which, since the 2005 publication of a dozen Muhammad cartoons in a Danish newspaper, has seized countless Muslims in recurring waves of rioting, boycotts and arson. More than 100 deaths have resulted.

I could continue, but I think the pattern is clear. Critical discussion or representation of Islam — including stated facts; satirical, political or religious commentary; or acts deemed by Islam to be "blasphemy" or "desecration" — spur Muslims to violence. This violence spurs Westerners to apology. But apology is always an act of dhimmitude: submitting to Islamic definitions of crime or grievance that only under Islamic law require contrition.

Today, the pattern intensifies. Muslim violence is more brazen with the murders of American troops, and Western apologies are more exaggerated. The United States hasn't even quashed Afghan demands for a trial of those who last month disposed of several Qurans.

Meanwhile, the chorus for punishment grows. "After the first step of a profound apology, there must be a second step ... of disciplinary action," Jan Kubis, the United Nations representative in Afghanistan, said this week. "Only after this, after such a disciplinary action, can the international forces say, 'Yes, we're sincere in our apology.'"

Or, rather, yes, we're sincere in our dhimmitude.

Demonstrating his own "sincerity," Kubis continued: "We deeply, deeply, profoundly respect Islam. ... We were very hurt that the international military allowed the desecration of the Quran. We rejected and condemned this act; it doesn't matter that it was a mistake."

Kubis' example is most instructive. Speaking for the United Nations, he mimics the aggrievement of Islam. Indeed, Islam's aggrievement becomes the United Nations' own as it draws power from the demonstrably more kinetic Islamic position.

The fact is, this whole affair, like those that preceded it, is a power play. Feigned victimhood becomes a trap for the "perpetrator" — in this case, the U.S. military. Falling for the trap means submitting to violent Islamic dictates for exactly the same reason a co-dependent family member submits to dictates of a mentally ill relative — to stop the outburst, to make it all "better," even if "better" is only a lull before the next power play.

Just as such actions bring a co-dependent family member more closely into the behavioral orbit of the sick family member, they bring the United States more closely into the behavioral orbit regulated by Islamic law. They force the "perpetrator" into accepting the sacredness of an inanimate object; they force the "perpetrator" into accepting the Islamic position that a Christian or Jew is unfit (unclean) to dispose of the sacred thing without desecrating it. They force the "perpetrator" to accept the Islamic belief that such "desecration" constitutes a crime of literally capital proportions.

They force the "perpetrator" to act Islamic. This is the pattern of dhimmitude, and we must break it.

Made in the USA
Middletown, DE
18 January 2015